THE
ANNUAL REGISTER
Vol. 256

THE
ANNUAL REGISTER

World Events 2014

Edited by
D.S. LEWIS
and
WENDY SLATER

FIRST EDITED IN 1758
BY EDMUND BURKE

Colophon from 1758 volume.

The 2015 Annual Register: WORLD EVENTS, 256th Ed.
Published by ProQuest

789 E. Eisenhower Parkway,
P.O. Box 1346 Ann Arbor, MI 48106-1346, USA

The Quorum,
Barnwell Road, Cambridge, CB5 8SW, UK

www.proquest.com

Phone: +1-734-761-4700 Toll-free +1-800-521-0600
Fax: +1-800-864-0019
Email: info@proquest.com

ISBN: 978-1-61540-480-3 / ISSN: 0266-6170

British Library Cataloguing in Publication Data:
The Annual Register—2015
1. History—Periodicals
909.82'8'05 D410

Library of Congress Catalog Card Number:
4-17979

Set in Times Roman by
NEW AGE GRAPHICS, Silver Spring, MD, USA

Printed in the USA by
THE SHERIDAN BOOKS, Chelsea, MI, USA

Jacket Design: JOHN C. MOSS

Printed on permanent recycled paper, acid-free.

CONTENTS

IV   THE AMERICAS AND THE CARIBBEAN

V   MIDDLE EAST AND NORTH AFRICA

VI   EQUATORIAL AFRICA

VII   CENTRAL AND SOUTHERN AFRICA

VIII   SOUTH ASIA AND INDIAN OCEAN

IX   SOUTH-EAST AND EAST ASIA

X   AUSTRALASIA AND THE PACIFIC

XI   INTERNATIONAL ORGANISATIONS

CONTRIBUTORS

Shirin Akiner, PhD, Lecturer in Central Asian Studies, School of Oriental & African Studies, University of London

KAZAKHSTAN, TURKMENISTAN, UZBEKISTAN, KYRGYZSTAN, TAJIKISTAN, EURASIAN ORGANISATIONS

R.W. Baldock, PhD, Managing Director, Yale University Press; writer on African affairs

ZIMBABWE

Richard Barltrop, DPhil, writer and consultant specialising in Sudanese and Middle Eastern affairs

SUDAN & SOUTH SUDAN

Lewis Baston, BA, Senior Research Fellow at Democratic Audit

UNITED KINGDOM

Kerry Brown, MA, PhD, Professor of Chinese politics and Director of the China Studies Centre, University of Sydney

CHINA, HONG KONG, TAIWAN

David Butter, MA, Chief Energy Analyst, Economist Intelligence Unit; Editor *Business Middle East*; Editor ViewsWire Middle East

ISRAEL, PALESTINE, EGYPT, JORDAN, SYRIA, LEBANON, IRAQ, ARAB ORGANISATIONS

Mark Chapman, PhD, Vice Principal, Ripon College Cuddesdon, Oxford

RELIGION: CHRISTIANITY

James Chiriyankandath, PhD, Senior Research Fellow, Institute of Commonwealth Studies, School of Advanced Study, University of London

INDIA, PAKISTAN, SRI LANKA, BANGLADESH, NEPAL, BHUTAN

William Chislett, former correspondent of *The Times*, Spain, and the *Financial Times*, Mexico

SPAIN, GIBRALTAR

Clive H. Church, BA, PhD, Emeritus Professor of European Studies, University of Kent

SWITZERLAND

Peter Clegg, MSc, PhD, Senior Lecturer in Politics, University of the West of England

MEXICO, CENTRAL AMERICA, THE CARIBBEAN, URUGUAY, PARAGUAY, AMERICAN & CARIBBEAN ORGANISATIONS

Giles Constantine, BA, MSc, Writer for Pulsamerica

CHILE, COLOMBIA

Paul Cornish, PhD, Research Group Director, Defence, Security & Infrastructure, RAND Europe

NATO

Terence Corrigan, BA Hons, Research Director, the Small Business Project, Johannesburg

BOTSWANA, LESOTHO, NAMIBIA, SWAZILAND, SOUTH AFRICA

John Crabtree, PhD, Research Associate, Latin American Centre, University of Oxford

PERU, BOLIVIA, ECUADOR

Colin Darch, PhD, Senior Information Specialist, African Studies Library, University of Cape Town

HORN OF AFRICA, DEMOCRATIC REPUBLIC OF CONGO, BURUNDI, RWANDA, MOZAMBIQUE

David de Bruijn, PhD candidate, Teaching Fellow, Department of Philosophy, University of Pittsburgh

RELIGION: JUDAISM

Daniel Dombey, BA, MA, *Financial Times* Turkey correspondent

TURKEY

Mark Donovan, PhD, Senior Lecturer in Politics, Cardiff University; Editor, *Modern Italy*

ITALY

Martin Eaton, PhD, FRGS/IBG, Reader in
Human Geography, University of Ulster at Coleraine
PORTUGAL

Bronwen Everill, PhD, Leverhulme Early
Career Fellow, King's College London
GHANA, SIERRA LEONE,
THE GAMBIA, LIBERIA

Farideh Farhi, PhD, Researcher;
affiliate of University of Hawaii-Manoa
IRAN

Dominic Fenech, DPhil, Professor of History,
University of Malta
MALTA

Sharon Fisher, PhD, Analyst in East European political
& economic affairs, IHS Economics & Country Risk
CZECH REPUBLIC, SLOVAKIA

Liz Fuller, BA, Writer on developments in the Caucasus
GEORGIA, ARMENIA, AZERBAIJAN

Alan Greer, PhD, Associate Professor in Politics &
Public Policy, University of the West of England, Bristol
NORTHERN IRELAND,
REPUBLIC OF IRELAND

Martin Harrison, Emeritus Professor, Keele University
FRANCE, BENELUX, EUROPEAN
MINI-STATES, OSCE, COUNCIL OF EUROPE

Adam Higazi, DPhil, Research Fellow in
African Studies, King's College, Cambridge
NIGERIA

J.E. Hoare, PhD, Consultant on East Asia;
former chargé d'affaires in Pyongyang
NORTH & SOUTH KOREA

Tom Holbrook, BA (Hons), Dip Arch RIBA,
Founding Director of 5th Studio, a spatial design agency
ARCHITECTURE

N. March Hunnings, LLM, PhD, Editor, *Encyclopaedia
of European Union Law: Constitutional Texts*
EU LAW

Daniel Izsak, MA, PhD candidate and teaching assistant,
Central European University
HUNGARY

Gwyn Jenkins, MA, Director of Collection Services,
The National Library of Wales, Aberystwyth
WALES

Jane Kinninmont, MSc, Deputy Head and Senior
Research Fellow, Middle East & North Africa
Programme, Chatham House
SAUDI ARABIA, BAHRAIN, KUWAIT, OMAN,
QATAR UAE, YEMEN

Genc Lamani, MA, Journalist, BBC World Service
News & Current Affairs
BULGARIA, ALBANIA

Stephen Levine, PhD, ONZM, Professor and Head of
School of History, Philosophy, Political Science &
International Relations, Victoria University of Wellington
BURMA, THAILAND, MALAYSIA, BRUNEI,
SINGAPORE, VIETNAM, CAMBODIA, LAOS,
NEW ZEALAND, PACIFIC ISLAND STATES,
ASIA-PACIFIC ORGANISATIONS

D.S. Lewis, PhD, Editor of *The Annual Register*;
former Editor of *Keesing's Record of World Events*
EDITOR; PREFACE, AFGHANISTAN,
JAPAN, OBITUARY

Richard Luther, Professor of Comparative Politics,
Keele University; visiting professor
Tongji University, Shanghai
AUSTRIA

Gabrielle Lynch, DPhil, Associate Professor of
Comparative Politics, University of Warwick
KENYA, TANZANIA, UGANDA

Charlotte Lythe, MA, Honorary Research Fellow in
Economic Studies, University of Dundee
SCOTLAND

Gabrielle Maas, DPhil, former Scouloudi Fellow,
Institute of Historical Research, London
LIBYA, TUNISIA, ALGERIA, MOROCCO,
WESTERN SAHARA

Norrie MacQueen, MSc, DPhil, formerly
University of Dundee
INDONESIA, PHILIPPINES,
TIMOR LESTE, PAPUA NEW GUINEA

Derek Malcolm, Cinema critic, *The Guardian*
CINEMA

J. Nathan Matias, MA, Research Assistant,
MIT Media Lab
INFORMATION TECHNOLOGY

Michael McCarthy, former Environment Editor
of *The Independent*
THE ENVIRONMENT

Robert McDonald, Writer and broadcaster on Cyprus,
Greece and Turkey
CYPRUS

Andrew Mellor, Freelance music critic and
cultural commentator
OPERA, CLASSICAL MUSIC

Paul Melly, BA, Journalist, Associate Fellow,
Africa Programme, Chatham House
FRANCOPHONE WEST AFRICA

David Milne, PhD, Senior Lecturer in Political History,
University of East Anglia
THE USA

Malyn Newitt, PhD, Emeritus Professor of History,
King's College London
INDIAN OCEAN STATES

Paul Newman, Tennis correspondent for *The Independent*
SPORT

Alastair Niven, LVO, OBE, Fellow,
Harris Manchester College, University of Oxford
LITERATURE

Graeme Orr, PhD, Professor, School of Law,
University of Queensland
AUSTRALIA

Gabriel Partos, MA, Balkan Affairs Analyst and Editor,
Economist Intelligence Unit
ROMANIA

Anthony Pereira, MA, PhD, Professor, King's College
London and Director of King's Brazil Institute
BRAZIL

Jane Pritchard, Curator of Dance, the Victoria &
Albert Museum of Performing Arts, London
BALLET & DANCE

Paul Rayment, MA, former Director of the Economic
Analysis Division of the UN Economic Commission
for Europe, Geneva
ECONOMIC ORGANISATIONS,
THE INTERNATIONAL ECONOMY

Daniel Rey, Writer at Pulsamerica
VENEZUELA

David Reynolds, FBA, Professor of International
History, University of Cambridge
EXTRACTS FROM PAST VOLUMES

Christian E. Rieck, MSc, Senior Analyst,
Global Governance Institute, Brussels
ARGENTINA

Paul Rogers, PhD, Professor of Peace Studies,
Bradford University; Global Security Consultant
to Oxford Research Group
2014: THE YEAR IN REVIEW

George Sanford, MPhil, PhD, Professor Emeritus of
East European Politics, University of Bristol
POLAND

Christopher Saunders, DPhil, Professor,
Department of Historical Studies,
University of Cape Town
GUINEA BISSAU, CABO VERDE,
SÃO TOMÉ & PRÍNCIPE, ANGOLA,
ZAMBIA, MALAWI,
AFRICAN ORGANISATIONS

Diane Shugart, Editor *Odyssey: The World of Greece*
GREECE

Allan Sikk, PhD, Lecturer in Baltic Politics, ESTONIA, LATVIA, LITHUANIA
University College London
David Sinclair, Pop music critic of *The Times*, London ROCK & POP MUSIC
Toby Skeggs, MA, arts editor and correspondent VISUAL ARTS
for *The Art Newspaper*
Wendy Slater, MA, PhD, Editor of EDITOR; RUSSIA, UKRAINE, BELARUS,
The Annual Register; writer on Russia MOLDOVA, MONGOLIA, CHRONICLE OF 2014
Raymond Snoddy, Freelance journalist specialising TV & RADIO
in media issues, writing for *The Independent*
Robert J. Spjut, ID, LLD, Member of the State Bars LAW IN THE USA
of California and Florida
Will Stos, MA, Editor of the *Canadian* CANADA
Parliamentary Review
Johan Strang, PhD, Post-doctoral researcher, DENMARK, ICELAND, NORWAY,
Centre for Nordic studies, Helsinki University SWEDEN, FINLAND
Marcus Tanner, MA, Editor, *Balkan Insight*; author MACEDONIA, KOSOVO, SERBIA,
MONTENEGRO, BOSNIA & HERZEGOVINA,
CROATIA, SLOVENIA
David Travers, former lecturer in Politics & THE UNITED NATIONS
International Relations, University of Lancaste
Ed Turner, PhD, Lecturer in Politics & International GERMANY
Relations, Aston University
Guglielmo Verdirame, LLM, PhD, Professor of INTERNATIONAL LAW
International Law, King's College London
Sir Stephen Wall, BA, GCMG, LVO, THE EUROPEAN UNION
Official Government Historian of Britain and the EU
Neil Weir, FRCS, Consultant otolaryngologist MEDICAL RESEARCH
Peter Willetts, PhD, Emeritus Professor of NON-ALIGNED MOVEMENT & G-77
Global Politics, City University, London
Frederick Wilmot-Smith, MA, BCL, MPhil, LAW IN THE UK
Examination Fellow, All Souls Oxford
Lorelly Wilson, FRSC, Honorary Teaching Fellow, SCIENTIFIC RESEARCH
University of Manchester
Timothy Winter, MA, Sheikh Zayed Lecturer in RELIGION: ISLAM
Islamic Studies, University of Cambridge
Matt Wolf, London theatre critic of THEATRE: NEW YORK AND LONDON
The International New York Times
Noam Zamir, PhD, Cleary Gottlieb Steen & INTERNATIONAL LAW
Hamilton LLP

ABBREVIATIONS AND ACRONYMS

AC	Arctic Council
ACS	Association of Caribbean States
ADB	Asian Development Bank
ALBA	Bolivarian Alliance for the Peoples of Our Americas
ANZUS	Australia-New Zealand-US Security Treaty
APEC	Asia-Pacific Economic Co-operation
ASEAN	Association of South-East Asian Nations
AU	African Union
Benelux	Belgium-Netherlands-Luxembourg Economic Union
BSEC	Black Sea Economic Co-operation
CAN/Ancom	Andean Community of Nations
CARICOM	Caribbean Community and Common Market
CBSS	Council of the Baltic Sea States
CCTS	Co-operation Council of Turkic-Speaking States
CE	Council of Europe
CEEAC	Economic Community of Central African States
CEFTA	Central European Free Trade Agreement
CEI	Central European Initiative
CELAC	Community of Latin American and Caribbean States
CENSAD	Community of Sahel-Saharan States
CEO	chief executive officer
CIA	US Central Intelligence Agency
CIS	Commonwealth of Independent States
COMESA	Common Market of Eastern and Southern Africa
CPLP	Community of Portuguese-Speaking Countries
CSTO	Collective Security Treaty Organisation
DRC	Democratic Republic of Congo
EAC	East African Community
EBRD	European Bank for Reconstruction and Development
ECB	European Central Bank
ECOWAS	Economic Community of West African States
ECtHR	European Court of Human Rights
EEA	European Economic Area
EFTA	European Free Trade Association
EMEs	emerging market economies
ESM	European Stability Mechanism
EU	European Union
EurAsEC	Eurasian Economic Community
G-8	Group of Eight
G-7	Group of Seven
G-20	Group of Twenty
G-77	Group of 77
GCC	Gulf Co-operation Council
GDP	gross domestic product
GNI	gross national income
GCHQ	UK General Communications Headquarters
HIPC	Heavily Indebted Poor Countries

HIV/AIDS	Human Immunodeficiency Virus/Acquired Immune Deficiency Syndrome
IBRD	International Bank for Reconstruction and Development
IAEA	International Atomic Energy Agency
IDA	International Development Association
IEA	International Energy Agency
IGAD	Inter-Governmental Authority on Development
IGO	inter-governmental organisation
IMF	International Monetary Fund
IPCC	UN Intergovernmental Panel on Climate Change
IOC	Indian Ocean Commission
ISP	Internet service provider
ISIS	Islamic State in Iraq and Syria, also known as ISIL (Islamic State in Syria and the Levant), and as Islamic State
LDCs	least developed countries
MERCOSUR	Southern Cone Common Market
NAFTA	North American Free Trade Agreement
NAM	Non-Aligned Movement
NASA	the US National Aeronautics and Space Administration
NATO	North Atlantic Treaty Organisation
NEPAD	New Partnership for Africa's Development
NGO	non-governmental organisation
NSA	US National Security Agency
OAS	Organisation of American States
OECD	Organisation for Economic Co-operation and Development
OECS	Organisation of Eastern Caribbean States
OIC	Organisation of Islamic Co-operation
OIF	International Organisation of Francophonie
OPEC	Organisation of the Petroleum Exporting Countries
OSCE	Organisation for Security and Co-operation in Europe
PACE	Parliamentary Assembly of the Council of Europe
PC	Pacific Community
PFP	Partnership for Peace
PIF	Pacific Islands Forum
PPP	purchasing power parity
PRGF	Poverty Reduction and Growth Facility
SAARC	South Asian Association for Regional Co-operation
SADC	Southern African Development Community
SCO	Shanghai Co-operation Organisation
SDR	special drawing rights
SELA	Latin American Economic System
UAE	United Arab Emirates
UEMOA	West African Economic and Monetary Union
UNASUR	Union of South American Nations
UNCTAD	United Nations Conference on Trade and Development
UNESCO	United Nations Educational, Scientific and Cultural Organisation
UNHRC	United Nations Human Rights Council
WHO	World Health Organisation
WMO	UN World Meteorological Organisation
WTO	World Trade Organisation

EDITORS' NOTES

THE editors gratefully acknowledge their debt to the principal sources for the national and IGO data sections (showing the situation at end 2014 unless otherwise stated), namely the World Bank Group's *World Development Indicators 2014*, and *World Development Report 2015*; the United Nations; the IMF; the *Financial Times* (London); the Foreign and Commonwealth Office; the Economist Intelligence Unit's *Democracy Index 2013: Democracy in limbo*; Transparency International's *Corruption Perceptions Index 2014*; and *Keesing's Record of World Events* (Keesing's Worldwide). Whilst every effort is made to ensure accuracy, the Board and the bodies which nominate its members, the editors, and the publisher disclaim responsibility for any opinions expressed or the accuracy of facts recorded in this volume.

POPULATION: figures are mid-year estimates, produced by the World Bank unless otherwise indicated, based on the de facto definition of population, which counts all residents regardless of legal status or citizenship (except for refugees not permanently settled in the country of asylum who are generally considered part of the population of their country of origin).

GNI PER CAPITA US$: is the gross national income, converted to US dollars using the World Bank Atlas method, divided by the mid-year population. GNI is the sum of value added by all resident producers, plus any product taxes (less subsidies) not included in the valuation of output, plus net receipts of primary income (compensation of employees and property income) from abroad. Data from the World Bank Group's *World Development Indicators*, unless otherwise indicated.

GNI PER CAPITA Intl$ at PPP: is a measure of GNI that allows a standard comparison of real price levels between countries by using purchasing power parity (PPP) rates. An international dollar has the same purchasing power over domestic GNI as a US dollar has in the United States.

DEMOCRACY INDEX: rates the state of democracy, at the end of 2013, based on five categories: electoral process and pluralism, civil liberties, the functioning of government, political participation, and political culture. Scored on a scale of 1-10 (the higher the score, the more "democratic"); ranked out of 167 (165 independent states and two territories). Derived from Economist Intelligence Unit (see above).

CORRUPTION INDEX: rates the perceived levels of public-sector corruption. Scored on a scale of 0-100 (the higher the score, the "cleaner" the country); ranked out of 177 countries. Derived from Transparency International (see above).

THE EDITORS wish to record with regret the deaths of three long-standing contributors to *The Annual Register*. A.J.A. Mango, since 1962 (Turkey); Darren Sagar, since 1989 (Middle East); Kaye Whiteman, since 1968 (Francophone Africa).

WORLD EVENTS FROM THE ANNUAL REGISTER 1758-2014

Selected by Philip M.H. Bell, Advisory Board of The Annual Register, 2002-2011.

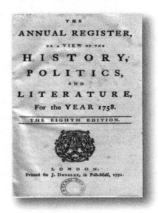

1758 Halley's Comet returns, as calculated by Edmond Halley in 1705

1759 British conquer Quebec from the French; death of Montcalm and Wolfe

1760 Britain: accession of George III, the first British Hanoverian monarch

1761 Transit of Venus on 6 June helps understanding of the movement of planets

1762 Russia: assassination of Tsar Peter III; accession of Catherine the Great

1763 Peace of Paris ends Seven Years' War; British control in Canada and India

1764 Stanislaus Poniatowski elected King of Poland

1765 British Parliament passes Stamp Act, to tax American colonies

1766 Repeal of Stamp Act in face of American opposition

1767 Expulsion of the Jesuits from all Spanish dominions

1768 France purchases Corsica from Genoa; conquest of island

1769 Britain imposes Tea Duties on American colonies

1770 The "Boston Massacre": casualty list 4 dead, 7 wounded

1771 Dispute between Britain and Spain over Falkland Islands

1772 First Partition of Poland by Russia, Prussia and Austria

1773 "Boston Tea Party" staged as protest against Tea Duty

1774 Continental Congress in Philadelphia draws together the American colonies

1775 American victories over British forces at battles of Lexington and Concord

1776 American Declaration of Independence, 4 July

1777 Publication of *A Voyage towards the South Pole and round the World* by James Cook

1778 Death of Voltaire, 30 May

1779 Spanish and French forces begin siege of Gibraltar

1780 Gordon Riots in London: "No Popery!"

1781 Cornwallis surrenders at Yorktown; decisive defeat for British in America

1782 Admiral Rodney's victory over the French at the Saints; British naval recovery

1783 Treaty of Versailles: Britain recognises American independence

1784 Pitt the Younger becomes British prime minister at age 24

1785 Flight of Blanchard and Jeffries by balloon from Dover to Calais

1786 Death of Frederick the Great, the creator of the new Kingdom of Prussia

1787 France: Louis XVI convenes Assembly of Notables; dissolved without result

1788 Russo-Turkish war: Potemkin besieges Ochakov

1789 Revolution in France; storming of the Bastille, 14 July

1790 Death of Benjamin Franklin, statesman and polymath

1791 France: Feast of the National Confederation to acclaim the Revolution

1792 Battle of Valmy, 20 September; victory of French revolutionary army

1793 Execution of Louis XVI of France

1794 Erasmus Darwin publishes *Zoonomia*, foreshadowing the idea of evolution

1795 Third and final partition of Poland; Poland disappears from the map

1796 Napoleon's victory at Lodi marks his emergence as a dominant figure

1797 First bank-notes issued in Britain; paper currency replaces specie

1798 Napoleon's expedition to Egypt results in conquest and scientific exploration

1799 Pitt introduces income tax in Britain

1800 Act of Union between Britain and Ireland passed; takes effect, 1 January 1801

1801 Thomas Jefferson becomes president of the USA

1802 Peace of Amiens brings war between Britain and France to temporary end

1803 Louisiana Purchase: USA buys Louisiana territories from France

1804 Napoleon crowns himself Emperor of the French

1805 Battle of Trafalgar establishes British naval dominance for a century

1806 Humphry Davy presents paper on electro-chemistry to Royal Society

1807 Abolition of slave trade in British Empire

1808 Napoleon imposes Joseph Bonaparte as King of Spain; Spanish revolt

1809 Napoleon defeats Austrians at Wagram, and imposes severe peace terms

1810 Venezuela revolts against Spain; rebellion spreads to other colonies

1811 Birth of a son to Napoleon and Marie Louise, thereby starting a dynasty

1812 Napoleon captures Moscow, but is forced into disastrous winter retreat

1813 Napoleon decisively defeated at Leipzig in the Battle of the Nations

1814 Napoleon abdicates and is exiled to Elba

1815 Napoleon returns for the "Hundred Days", is defeated at Waterloo and exiled to St Helena

1816 Declaration of Argentinian independence at Buenos Aires

1817 Discontent and disorder in Britain; Habeas Corpus suspended

1818 France: abolition of slave trade in all French territories

1819 Britain: parliamentary reform rally in Manchester ends in "Peterloo" massacre

1820 Spain ratifies treaty for purchase of Florida by USA

1821 Mexican independence declared, under Iturbide as generalissimo

1822 Declaration of Greek independence; Turkish massacre of Greeks at Chios

1823 Monroe Doctrine: American continent declared closed to European colonisation

1824 Death of Byron at Missolonghi marks the creation of a Romantic legend

1825 Russia: Decembrist rising crushed in St Petersburg

1826 Opening of Telford's suspension bridge across Menai Straits, the first of its kind

1827 Battle of Navarino: Turkish defeat assists Greek struggle for independence

1828 Frontier treaty between Brazil and Argentina; establishment of Uruguay

1829 Catholic Emancipation in Britain; extension of franchise to Catholics

1830 French expedition captures Algiers; beginning of French Algeria

1831 Five-power treaty on Belgian independence declares it to be perpetually neutral

1832 Great Reform Act in Britain provides limited but significant extension of franchise

1833 General Santanna elected President of Mexico; Texas declares independence

1834 Introduction of new Poor Law in Britain creates Poor Law Boards and houses

1835 Prussia establishes Zollverein, bringing all German states into a customs union

1836 Civil war in Spain involves intervention by British warships and volunteers

1837 Accession of Queen Victoria to British throne

1838 Insurrection in Canada; Lord Durham's enquiry into its causes

1839 Chartist movement in Britain; National Petition and People's Charter

1840 British expedition to Canton to force Chinese government to accept opium trade

1841 Union of the two Canadas (Upper and Lower) comes into effect

1842 Destruction of British army in Afghanistan

1843 South Africa: Britain annexes Natal

1844 New Zealand: Maori War

1845 USA: annexation of Texas approved by Congress

1846 Ireland: failure of potato crop; resulting famine leads to large-scale emigration

1847 Vatican: first year of Pius IX's papacy shows him to be a liberal pope

1848 Year of Revolutions in Europe; Marx and Engels issue Communist Manifesto

1849 Mazzini proclaims Roman Republic; crushed by French army

1850 USA: California admitted as a state of the Union

1851 Britain: Jews allowed to sit in Parliament

1852 France: Louis Napoleon is proclaimed Emperor Napoleon III

1853 Japan: US expedition under Commodore Perry forcibly opens Japan to US trade

1854 Crimean War begins: British and French troops lay siege to Sevastopol

1855 Henry Bessemer takes out patents, which transform steel production

1856 Treaty of Paris ends Crimean War

1857 Indian Mutiny: widespread uprising against British rule in India

1858 British Crown takes over government of India from East India Company

1859 War in Italy: Sardinia and France against Austria; Battle of Magenta

1860 Election of Lincoln, an opponent of the extension of slavery, as US president

1861 American Civil War begins after secession of Confederate States

1862 Lincoln signs Emancipation Proclamation, which frees slaves in Confederate territory

1863 Battles of Vicksburg and Gettysburg mark turning-points in Civil War

1864 Prussia and Austria defeat Denmark over Schleswig-Holstein

1865 Defeat of Confederacy marks end of American Civil War; assassination of Lincoln

1866 Prussian victory over Austria at Sadowa; Prussian predominance in Germany

1867 Dual Monarchy established in Austria-Hungary

1868 British expedition to Abyssinia; capture of Magdala, and withdrawal

1869 Opening of Suez Canal, a channel for world commerce

1870 Franco-Prussian War: crushing French defeat at Sedan leads to fall of Napoleon III

1871 Darwin's *The Descent of Man* published, amid sharp debate

1872 Britain: Ballot Act introduces voting in elections by secret ballot

1873 Russian advance into Central Asia; occupation of Khiva

1874 Britain: defeat of Gladstone; Disraeli forms Conservative government

1875 Disraeli purchases Khedive's shares in Suez Canal Company for Britain

1876 Bulgarian revolt suppressed by Turks; Gladstone denounces Bulgarian massacres

1877 Invention of "talking phonograph", a recording machine, by Thomas Edison

1878 Congress of Berlin: independence of Balkan states from Turkey

1879 Zulu War: defeat of British army at Isandlwana; defence of Rorke's Drift

1880 Ireland: ostracism of Captain Boycott by the Land League creates new word

1881 International Medical Congress: Pasteur's account of vaccination experiments

1882 Egypt: British bombard Alexandria and occupy Egypt

1883 French occupation of Madagascar and expedition to Tonkin (Indo-China)

1884 Congo Conference in Berlin on partition of Africa

1885 Death of General Gordon at Khartoum

1886 Gladstone's first Home Rule Bill for Ireland; Liberal split and defeat

1887 Indian National Congress meets at Calcutta; demands representative institutions

1888 Accession of William II as Emperor of Germany

1889 Austria-Hungary: death of Crown Prince Rudolph at Mayerling

1890 USA: McKinley Tariff to protect US industry

1891 First rail of Trans-Siberian Railway laid by the future Tsar Nicholas II

1892 Britain: Gladstone forms his fourth administration after Liberals win election

1893 Arctic exploration: Nansen sails in *Fram;* Peary sets out for North Pole

1894 France: Captain Dreyfus convicted of treason; start of Dreyfus Affair

1895 Treaty of Shimonosiki ends First Sino-Japanese War; Japan annexes Formosa

1896 Ethiopia: Battle of Adowa; defeat of Italian army by Ethiopians

1897 German Navy Bill initiates naval expansion and maritime rivalry with Britain

1898 Spanish-American War; US annexation of Hawaii, Puerto Rico and Philippines

1899 Boer War begins between Britain and Boer Republics

1900 Australian Commonwealth Act: Commonwealth of Australia established

1901 Marconi sends first trans-Atlantic wireless communication

1902 Treaty of Vereeniging ends Boer War

1903 Independence of Panama from Colombia; USA begins Panama Canal

1904 Signing of Entente Cordiale between Britain and France

1905 Russo-Japanese War: Russian fleet destroyed at Tsushima

1906 Huge earthquake destroys San Francisco

1907 Finland becomes first European country to grant female suffrage

1908 Orville Wright makes flight of 1 hour and 10 minutes

1909 Britain: House of Lords rejects Finance Bill, leading to constitutional crisis

1910 China asserts suzerainty in Tibet: expedition to Lhasa, flight of Dalai Lama

1911 Moroccan crisis: French expedition to Fez, German gunboat to Agadir

1912 *Titanic* sunk by collision with iceberg, 15-16 April

1913 Niels Bohr introduces new quantum theory of atomic structure

1914 Assassination of Archduke Franz Ferdinand leads to outbreak of World War I

1915 Dardanelles campaign; ANZAC troops in action

1916 Battles of Verdun and the Somme epitomise attritional war on Western Front

1917 USA enters war; Bolshevik Revolution in Russia

1918 Treaty of Brest-Litovsk, March; armistice in France, 11 November

1919 Paris Peace Conference and Treaty of Versailles redraw world map. Einstein's new theory of the principle of relativity changes views of the universe

1920 Britain accepts mandate for Palestine, to establish a "National Home" for the Jews

1921 Washington Conference on naval disarmament and the Pacific

1922 Mussolini assumes dictatorial power in Italy; creation of fascist regime

1923 French occupation of the Ruhr; hyper-inflation in Germany

1924 Death of Lenin; struggle for succession begins

1925 Treaties of Locarno normalise relations between Germany and former Allied Powers

1926 Britain: General Strike brings country almost to a standstill

1927 Lindbergh's journey from New York to Le Bourget marks first trans-Atlantic flight

1928 China denounces all unequal treaties imposed by outside powers

1929 The Wall Street Crash: symbol of the Great Depression

1930 India: Gandhi's salt march, to protest against tax on salt manufacture

1931 Mukden Incident: Japanese occupation of Manchuria

1932 Election of Franklin D. Roosevelt as president of the USA

1933 Hitler becomes chancellor of Germany, 30 January, with conservative support

1934 Discovery of induced radio-activity by the Joliot-Curies, Paris

1935 Italian invasion of Ethiopia; enactment of Nuremberg Laws in Germany

1936 Civil War in Spain: Franco attacks Madrid; arrival of International Brigades

1937 USA: Neutrality Act forbids export of arms to belligerent states

1938 Munich Conference marks high point of appeasement of Nazi Germany

1939 German attack on Poland initiates World War II

1940 Fall of France and creation of Vichy government; German defeat in Battle of Britain

1941 German invasion of Soviet Union; Japanese attack on Pearl Harbour

1942 Decisive defeats of German army at Stalingrad and of Japanese navy at Midway

1943 Teheran Conference cements British-US-Soviet alliance; overthrow of Mussolini

1944 Normandy Landings lead to liberation of France

1945 Surrender of Germany and discovery of Nazi death camps; surrender of Japan after atomic bombs dropped on Hiroshima and Nagasaki

1946 First Session of General Assembly of the United Nations, involving 51 member states

1947 End of British rule in India; partition between India and Pakistan

1948 Palestine: establishment of Israel; conflict with Arab states

1949 Communist victory in Chinese civil war leads to establishment of Mao's regime

1950 Communist North Korea invades South; intervention by US-led UN forces

1951 Soviet Union detonates its first atomic bomb

1952 Britain: death of George VI and accession of Queen Elizabeth II

1953 Death of Stalin

1954 Defeat of French garrison at Dien Bien Phu marks end of French rule in Indo-China

1955 Asian-African Conference at Bandung (Indonesia); emergence of "Third World"

1956 Suez Crisis: Nasser nationalises Canal, prompting British-French-Israeli attack

1957 Treaties of Rome, founding the European Economic Community. Launch of Sputnik, the first man-made earth satellite, by Soviet Union

1958 France: end of 4th Republic; de Gaulle becomes president of new 5th Republic

1959 China: disastrous consequences of "Great Leap Forward", begun in 1958

1960 CERN cyclotron in Geneva produces crucial results in particle acceleration

1961 Soviet Union puts first man into space; Yury Gagarin orbits the earth

1962 Cuban Missile Crisis brings USA and Soviet Union to the brink of nuclear war

1963 USA: assassination of President Kennedy, 22 November

1964 South Africa: Nelson Mandela is sentenced to life imprisonment

1965 Britain: death and state funeral of Winston Churchill

1966 China: Cultural Revolution, led by Red Guards

1967 Six-Day War: Israel attacks and defeats Egypt, Syria and Jordan

1968 France: establishment shaken by student revolt. Soviet invasion of Czechoslovakia

1969 USA lands first men on the moon

1970 Introduction of Boeing 747 airliner marks start of mass air travel

1971 War between India and Pakistan; independence of Bangladesh

1972 Germany: success of Brandt's Ostpolitik; treaty between West and East Germany

1973 Ceasefire agreement in Vietnam War; Arab attack on Israel starts Yom Kippur war

1974 "Oil Shock" ends many years of economic growth

1975 North Vietnam conquers South. Death of General Franco in Spain

1976 China: deaths of Chou En-lai and Mao Tse-tung lead to power struggle

1977 Czechoslovakia: publication of Charter 77, against violations of human rights

1978 Election of Karol Wojtyla as Pope John Paul II, a Polish pope

1979 Islamic revolution in Iran overthrows the Shah; Ayatollah Khomeini takes power

1980 Soviet army struggles to subdue guerrillas in Afghanistan

1981 Poland: conflict between government and Solidarity trade union; martial law imposed

1982 Falklands War: Falkland Islands invaded by Argentina and recovered by Britain

1983 Missile crisis in Europe; deployment of US Pershing and Soviet SS-20 missiles

1984 India: storming of Sikh Golden Temple; Indira Gandhi assassinated by Sikhs

1985 Mikhail Gorbachev becomes Soviet leader and embarks on reform programme

1986 Explosion at Chernobyl nuclear reactor: fallout affects much of Europe

1987 Reagan-Gorbachev summit: abolition of medium and short range missiles

1988 Geneva agreement on phased withdrawal of Soviet troops from Afghanistan

1989 Fall of Berlin Wall, symbolising collapse of communism in Eastern Europe

1990 Russia declares sovereignty, heralding the demise of the Soviet Union in 1991

1991 USA and allied powers defeat Iraq after its invasion of Kuwait in 1990

1992 Former Yugoslavia: civil war in Bosnia; Croatia declares independence

1993 South Africa: new, non-racial constitution adopted

1994 Rwanda: massacre of Tutsis by Hutu militants leaves up to 500,000 dead

1995 World Health Organisation estimates number of AIDS sufferers at over one million

1996 Comprehensive Nuclear Test Ban Treaty adopted by UN General Assembly

1997 Cloning of Dolly the sheep by researchers in Edinburgh

1998 Nuclear tests conducted by India and Pakistan

1999 Russia: resignation of Boris Yeltsin; Vladimir Putin becomes acting president

2000 Completion of mapping of the human genome, the human genetic blueprint

2001 Terrorist attacks on 11 September against World Trade Centre and Pentagon

2002 European Union: introduction of single currency (the euro) by 11 member states

2003 US-led invasion of Iraq

2004 Indian Ocean earthquake unleashes tsunami, which kills several hundred thousand

2005 Kyoto Protocol on Climate Change comes into effect

2006 Israeli offensive against Hezbullah in Lebanon

2007 USA implements troop "surge" in attempt to achieve success in Iraq conflict

2008 Election of Barack Obama as US president

2009 Worst world economic crisis since 1930s—unemployment, banking crises, government debts

2010 Craig Venter creates the first living organism with a fully synthetic genome— a bacterium

2011 The "Arab Spring". Earthquake, tsunami and nuclear disaster in Japan.

2012 Re-election of President Barack Obama

2013 Revelation of mass surveillance programmes by Western states

2014 Proclamation of "caliphate" by jihadist movement, ISIS

EXTRACTS FROM PAST VOLUMES

Selected by Professor David Reynolds, FBA

250 years ago

1764.   Preface. We have endeavoured to procure as many and as various materials as was consistent with our desire of keeping our collection chaste, and of preserving the order and method, which the public indulgence had formerly approved. If the materials for the foreign history have, through the felicity of the times, been less abundant than in former years, our domestic dissentions have supplied the place of those foreign events, and displayed a scene almost as animated, but much less hurtful to humanity. These jars, such is the excellent temperament of our constitution, have done and will, probably, do very little mischief. Without materially checking the necessary operations of government, they prevent the minds of men from stagnating in a state so full of prosperity as our present; and keep alive the spirit of liberty at a time when the real and undisturbed enjoyment of that invaluable blessing might, perhaps, without this spur, abate something of that jealous zeal for its preservation, which, once extinguished, is not so easily kindled. There are times when the spirit of liberty must owe something to the spirit of faction.

225 years ago

1789.   The next day, which was the famous Tuesday the 14th of July, will long be remembered in the history of mankind. On that morning the newly formed army completed their means for offensive and defensive operations . . . Thus provided, the idea of attacking the Bastile was instantly adopted, and De Launay, the governor, summoned to lay down his arms and surrender the fortress . . . [T]he enthusiasm and fury of the people was so great that, to the astonishment of all military men (who did not yet know the weakness of its garrison) the Bastile, the citadel of Paris, with its seemingly impassable ditches, and its inaccessible towers and ramparts, covered with a powerful artillery, was, after an attack of two hours, carried by storm. De Launay was immediately dragged to the Place de Greve, and miserably murdered. M. de Losme, the major of the Bastile, met with an equal fate and equal cruelty; although it has since been generally acknowledged, even by democratic writers, that he was a man of great humanity . . .

On this day it was that that the savage custom of insulting and mutilating the remains of the dead, and of exhibiting their heads to public view upon pikes, which had so long been the opprobrium of the governments and people in Constantinople, Fez and Morocco, was first introduced into the polished city of Paris; and, like other evil habits, has since taken so deep a root, that it may seem a question whether it can ever be eradicated, except by some convulsion similar in violence to that from which it derived its origin.

200 years ago

1814.   The state of affairs at the close of the year 1813 was such as afforded an almost certain prospect of a speedy termination of the mighty contest which had so long been subsisting between the French empire and the powers coalesced to limit its exorbitant aggrandisement, and curb the unbridled ambition of its ruler. The presence of four great armies on the proper territory of France, acting in concert and tending to a common centre, could not fail of producing events which in some mode or other must prove decisive of the objects for which the war was undertaken. Public expectation throughout Europe was raised to the highest pitch, and it was not disappointed. After a short but vigorous struggle, in which France, deprived of the greater part of those veteran troops which had carried its conquering arms through so many other countries, saw itself at length incompetent to its own defence: a concluding battle placed the capital at the mercy of the confederates, and effected the immediate overthrow of that despotism under which the French had at the same time been triumphant and enslaved, with the restoration of the ancient monarchy and a general peace as the result. The treaty of Paris, signed within its walls by sovereigns whose capitals had not long before been in the possession of French troops, will ever rank among the most memorable events in modern history.

175 years ago

1839.   The two great parties which divide opinion in England - whether we call them whig or tory, conservatives or reformers - have maintained nearly the same relations, both of position and force: the whigs just strong enough to remain in power; and their opponents uniformly precluding their making any use of it. To statesmen who look in office to something beyond the mere emolument of salary and patronage, such a situation might be supposed anything but desirable. We do not assume that such is the only inducement for the adherence of the present government to their places, but really it is not easy to see what other consolation they can have in the possession of them, unless it be, as we formerly hinted - the satisfaction of keeping their adversaries out.

150 years ago

1864.   America. Although Atlanta had fallen into the possession of the Federals they were not able to hold it long. General Hood in strong force occupied General Sherman's line of communications, and it was impossible to subsist in Atlanta without supplies. Sherman therefore had one of two courses to adopt. Either he must attack Hood and defeat him, or endeavour to force his way to the sea and so make his escape. He resolved upon the latter plan . . . The distance from Atlanta to Savannah is ninety-three miles, and General Sherman accomplished the march in twenty-three days . . . General Sherman then entered Savannah, and took possession of it, together with 150 cannon, a large quantity of ammunition, and 25,000 bales of cotton. The joy throughout the North was jubilant and excessive; and beyond all doubt it was a heavy blow to the Confederate cause - not only as affording the enemy a new base of operations in connexion with the sea on the South, but also on account of the loss of prestige which the Confederate commanders sustained by the mode in which General Sherman had been able to out-manoeuvre and baffle them. But we do not, for a moment, believe that the capture of Savannah will have any serious effect on the issue of the war, - even if the Federals are able to keep their prize.

125 years ago

1889.　　　　The Mikado of Japan in 1881 announced his purpose to introduce a system of representative government in his dominions, and to establish a parliament, and fixed upon the year 1889 as the date of this change. He proposed to give up the pure despotism which had existed from the earliest times in Japan, and to present to his people as a free and gracious gift a portion of the unlimited power which has been held by the Mikados for so many centuries, stipulating, however, himself in what manner this power should be employed . . . In framing the new constitution, that of Prussia was the model most closely adopted . . . The public promulgation of the constitution took place in the splendid new palace, in the presence of a great assemblage representing the power, wealth, intellect and high lineage of the country, as well as all classes of the people, and with the pomp and solemnity befitting the occasion. Public rejoicings and festivities followed, the parks and gardens were illuminated, and the people universally showed their appreciation of the great boon which the Emperor had conferred upon them.

100 years ago

1914.　　　　On Christmas Day another German aeroplane was sighted over Sheerness at 12.35 mid-day; aided by fog it went up the Thames as far as Erith, probably to drop bombs on Woolwich Arsenal; but it was chased by three British aeroplanes . . . Earlier on that day a British raid of considerable significance had been made on Cuxhaven and the German warships lying off that port . . . But these exciting episodes had no direct bearing on the fortunes of the war. Its ultimate outcome was likely to depend partly on the cohesive and combative power of the British Empire, partly on the attitude of the greater neutral nations, partly on the economic pressure exercised on Germany by the British Navy, and partly on the ability of Great Britain to adjust her trade to the new conditions imposed by the loss of her best customer and of the sources of supply of the components of many of her manufactured goods. On all these the outlook as the year closed was encouraging . . . [T]he British nation felt itself entitled to look forward to the issue of the struggle with quiet confidence, and to possess its soul in patience until a vigorous offensive should be possible in the spring.

75 years ago

1939.　　　　England. The first batch of militiamen, from the ages of 20 to 21, had been called to the colours in the middle of July, and at the end of that month

12,000 naval reservists were called up, ostensibly to take part in the great Fleet exercises which were to be held in the second week in August. Plans for the evacuation of children from danger zones had been perfected, additional stocks of wheat and petrol had been laid in, and arrangements had been made for controlling the supply of coal, petrol, and foodstuffs if war should break out . . . The spirit of the nation had also by now become thoroughly attuned to the prospect of war . . . The hysterical peace clamour which had broken out after the Munich meeting had almost completely died down, and the spirit of determination and self-sacrifice which even then had been noticeable among the more democratic elements of the population had now spread to those other elements which at that time had so pitiably given way to pusillanimity and self-deception.

50 years ago

1964.   China. In the field of science and technology the most outstanding event of the year was the successful test of China's first atomic bomb . . . The Chinese official statement simply said that the test had taken place in West China at 15.00 hours on 16 October. It described it as a major achievement of the Chinese people in their struggle to increase national defence capability and to oppose United States imperialist policies of nuclear blackmail and nuclear threats . . . It denounced the 1963 partial nuclear test ban treaty of Moscow as a big fraud and an attempt to perpetuate the nuclear monopoly of the USA, the Soviet Union and the United Kingdom. The Chinese success in breaking this nuclear monopoly would, the statement declared, diminish and not increase the menace of a nuclear conflict. This was because China still held to Mr Mao Tse-tung's view that the atom bomb was a paper tiger and that it was the people who decided the outcome of any war and not the use of any weapon . . . The explosion was greeted with great pride in the Chinese press because it had been accomplished without foreign assistance and made China the first Asian country to enter the ranks of the nuclear Powers. It thus enhanced its prestige and its claim to Great Power status.

25 years ago

1989.   As we look back on 1989, the bicentenary celebrations of the French Revolution in July seem like a historical overture to the actual drama of events in Eastern Europe, from October onwards, which by their range and speed gained a revolutionary label . . . Public and political concern, both East and West, focused on the potential reunification of Germany, with its implicit threat of re-born pan-German ambition in a region of ethnic German minorities and memories of past empires. But that was not the only cause of anxiety, shading the pleasure at the end of the Cold War and the opportunities for deep cuts in armed forces. Ever since 1945, Soviet hegemony had frozen many an old dispute over territory, population and culture. There was no assurance that, relieved of enmity towards the West, the nations of Eastern and Central Europe would enjoy amity among themselves and with their other neighbours . . . Nationalism has its very seamy side: ancient grudges, territorial irredentism, backing for linguistic and cultural minorities in other countries. If what was once called 'the Balkan problem' is not to haunt the statesmen of the major powers and even threaten a European war, as some whose memories go back beyond 1914 may fear, the lesson of history is that the greater nations must keep their hands off such quarrels. Non-intervention, and reliance on international means of persuasion and settlement, are the cardinal rule for all powers, in every continent, if peace is to be assured in these turbulent times.

It is idle to try to guess the future. A stable settlement of the political map of Europe up to the Urals may take a long time to achieve. Who could have seen the lineaments of 1815 in the flushed visage of 1989?

PREFACE

THE most dramatic development of 2014 was the spectacular advance of the Sunni jihadist group, ISIS. Its fast-moving and ferocious fighters poured out of Syria and north-west Iraq in the middle of the year and swept south, routing the corrupt and poorly trained Iraqi army units that stood in their way. They overran a vast swath of territory, for a time threatening to take Baghdad, and their success catapulted the movement onto the world stage.

ISIS displayed breathtaking levels of savagery, with the routine slaughter of enemy prisoners, the enslavement and sexual exploitation of captured women and children, and the highly public decapitation of Western hostages, including men who had been seized whilst engaged in humanitarian aid work in the region. More sophisticated in its use of propaganda than earlier jihadist movements—including even al-Qaida, from which it had evolved but which had publicly broken with it—ISIS skilfully exploited social media to promote its aims and recruit fresh adherents from across the globe. It also used the Internet to flaunt an image of implacable opposition to the West. The movement wantonly destroyed, or sold, looted ancient artefacts which it deemed idolatrous. Such acts, undertaken without any recognition that the objects of destruction belonged to humanity at large, were condemned by UNESCO as a form of "cultural cleansing". But it was the movement's slickly produced execution videos that provided the most disturbing image of the year, as shackled hostages—wearing a parody of the orange overalls used in the US prison camp at Guantanamo Bay—were made to kneel before a black-clad executioner. The masked killer issued a stream of anti-Western taunts and invective (in a native British accent) before hacking off the victim's head with a knife.

Notwithstanding this barbarity, what differentiated ISIS most completely from its predecessors was its proclamation in June of a "caliphate": an Islamic state governed by religious authorities and presided over by a caliph—supreme leader—in the tradition of the Prophet Muhammad. This concept of the caliphate—a single state for all Muslims—had been central to Islam since the religion's foundation in the seventh century. Although the caliphate had undergone various incarnations, including competing entities, as an institution it had survived until 1924 when the Ottoman caliphate was formally abolished by the new, secular, Turkish state. ISIS's re-establishment of a caliphate—at which point the movement rebranded itself officially as Islamic State (IS)—made it significantly different from those jihadists who sought to establish sharia law within existing state boundaries, or even from al-Qaida which had been fighting towards the long-term goal of establishing a caliphate.

ISIS claimed to have traced the lineage of its leader, and newly proclaimed caliph, Abu Bakr al-Baghdadi, back to the Prophet Muhammad. Certainly the new caliphate demanded the allegiance of all devout Muslims. Their duty was defined as expanding the entity, through a process of conquest that included a march on "Rome" (i.e. the West). The ultimate aim was the creation of a global political order in which all humanity would live under Islamic rule, either as adherents or subject peoples. As such, it offered no prospect of an accommodation with other states or ideologies. Indeed, in proclaiming the caliphate, ISIS made clear that "The legality of all emirates, sudden insecurity issues in 2014, that element will get the main attention, but this does not in any way suggest that longer term problems relating to constrained environmental and economic limitations are not of enduring importance.

ISLAMIC STATE. Although Western security thinking was much affected by the crisis with Russia over Crimea and eastern Ukraine, a much more dominant issue was the rapid rise of Islamic State, an extreme and often brutal Islamist movement in Syria and Iraq, that had its origins in an al-Qaida affiliate in Iraq in the mid-2000s.

At the end of 2013 after nearly three years of bitter civil war in Syria, the regime of President Bashar al-Assad remained in control, its dominance aided by a diverse and divided opposition. During 2014, 76,000 people died, including nearly 18,000 civilians, of whom 3,500 were children. Over 10 million Syrians were displaced by the conflict, with 3.2 million refugees in neighbouring countries. Within the opposition to the regime two radical Islamist paramilitary movements—al-Nusra Front and the Islamic State of Iraq and Syria (or the Levant) (ISIS), were to the fore. The former was an affiliate of the al-Qaida movement and the latter more independent and even more brutal in its methods. In the first few months of 2014, ISIS made rapid and unexpected territorial gains in north-west Iraq.

Iraq had already been in a position of considerable internal violence, with radical Sunni paramilitaries, mostly from ISIS, active against government security forces and Shia communities. By the end of 2013 the violence was beginning to approach the appalling levels of the height of the Iraq War in 2004-07, and in 2014 over 17,000 civilians died. The Sunni jihadist insurgents were not without support from the wider Sunni community that was aggrieved by the failure of the government of Nouri al-Maliki to allow consensus politics to emerge. Maliki, though, held power through the electoral support of the Shia majority that had been marginalised under the Saddam Hussein regime and was unwilling to embrace the critical need for such governance to develop.

In early 2014 ISIS controlled a number of towns and villages in north-west and central Iraq, including Fallujah, the "city of mosques" close to Baghdad, which had been at the centre of the insurgency against Western occupying forces in 2004. It had also gained control of substantial territory across northern Syria, centred on the city of Raqqa. From its base, and with the tacit support of Sunni clans and former Baathists from the Saddam Hussein era, the movement made rapid gains towards central Iraq, the key event being the taking of Iraq's second most populous city, Mosul, on 10 June.

This was achieved by a few thousand Islamic State paramilitaries against Iraqi army and police units numbering in the tens of thousands, who fled at the approach of ISIS despite their having been in receipt of a massive training and re-equipment programme by the United States. One reason was that Prime Minister Maliki had placed his own supporters in key positions in the army at the expense of more professional officers, and many of these left their posts hurriedly in the face of the ISIS assault, leaving their soldiers to fend for themselves. The capture of Mosul was so rapid that numerous army bases and supply dumps were overrun, allowing ISIS to gain control of many weapons, vehicles and other materiel.

The advance briefly threatened the capital of the Kurdish semi-autonomous region of Iraq, although that was due more to temporary disorganisation and internal rivalries within the Kurdish Peshmerga militia defences than an innate ability of ISIS to take and hold the Kurdish region. In the process, though, non-Sunni communities such as the Yazidi were greatly threatened by the ISIS advance, raising considerable international alarm and pressure on Western states to intervene.

Concern over developments was aided by the evident support that the movement was getting from across the region, as well as a steady flow of young recruits from Western countries. Furthermore, at the end of June, the leader of ISIS, the Jordanian Abu Bakr al-Baghdadi, proclaimed himself as the caliph of what would now be called "the State of the Islamic Caliphate". In the face of the threat to Iraq as a whole, the government in Baghdad called for immediate international military assistance and received swift, if largely unpublicised, support from Iran, with Revolutionary Guard forces quickly involved with the Iraqi army and Shia militias.

In the face of considerable public pressure, US President Barack Obama eventually countenanced air strikes against Islamic State forces in Iraq while using diplomatic pressure on Maliki to be far more inclusive. Air strikes started on 8 August, the stated initial aim being to protect US citizens, Yazidi and other refugees, and Kurdish Iraq. However, this quickly escalated into attacks on ISIS in Syria and the formation of a coalition of states providing air power and, in the case of the UK, armed drones as well. By the end of the year the main states involved were the USA, France, the UK, Denmark, Belgium, Canada and Australia, together with several regional countries including Jordan and Saudi Arabia.

As well as the use of air power, the United States and some coalition partners rapidly deployed military personnel to train and equip the Iraqi Army as it sought to recover from the Mosul debacle. By the year's end there were already 3,000 US troops deployed, back in Iraq in significant numbers for the first time since the withdrawal in 2011. At least a thousand more were likely to deploy early in 2015, with many hundreds of soldiers from states such as the UK also involved, taking the foreign involvement to over 5,000. In addition, and scarcely reported, Special Forces were involved, principally from the United States, and there were credible indications that these were, on occasion, directly engaged in ground combat, in spite of repeated assurances from the Obama administration that combat roles were not envisaged.

By the end of the year Islamic State controlled territory across Syria and Iraq inhabited by well over 4 million people in a land area around the size of Britain. Whilst much of it was arid, it also included the fertile valley of the Euphrates as well as hydroelectric and irrigation dams and a number of small oilfields. ISIS was under some pressure from Western air strikes but there was little evidence of its serious decline, just a more limited capability to make further territorial gains. A substantial programme was under way to re-energise the Iraqi Army but security analysts expected it to take at least two years before Iraqi forces were capable of retaking and then holding ISIS-controlled territory.

There were two other relevant developments. One was that Nouri al-Maliki was finally forced to resign as Iraqi prime minister on 14 August, not least because of pressure from Iran. He was replaced by Haider Abadi, who sought conciliation with the Sunni minority, widely viewed as a positive development though it would take many months to have much impact on domestic Sunni support for ISIS. The other development was that while the civil war continued in Syria, the double-proxy element to that war was eroding. Prior to the rise of Islamic State, UN mediation in the war had been a continual failure, not least because both the rebels and the regime had double-proxy support: the rebels from the Saudis with Western states behind them; the regime from Iran and, at a higher level, from Russia. Islamic State, though, presented a threat not just to the Saudis and Western states but also to Shia Iran and even, indirectly, to Russia with its Islamist separatist movement in the Caucasus.

THE MIDDLE EAST. Elsewhere in the Middle East, five developments among many were of particular note. One was the continuing violence in Libya, with competing militias vying for control of cities, towns and even villages. The militias included some extreme Islamist groups that had been kept in check by the previous autocratic Kadhafi regime, and the overall situation was of an oil-rich state that was close to failing, with even the security of the capital city, Tripoli, being under threat towards the end of the year.

Immediately to the east, the regime of President Abdel-Fattah Sisi had thoroughly consolidated its control in Egypt, following the coup of 2013 against the elected if unpopular Muslim Brotherhood government (see AR 2014, pp. 173-75). During the course of the year, the government continued to detain thousands of Muslim Brotherhood supporters and enacted harsh laws to ensure control, also with the detention of a number of foreign journalists. Though the regime firmly retained power, there were indications of a new wave of Islamist radicalisation developing in response, not least in Sinai.

The Sisi regime also maintained its opposition to the Palestinian Islamic group Hamas in Gaza, with this relating to the third development—a short but very violent 50-day confrontation, in July and August, between the Israeli Defence Forces (IDF) and Hamas. Israel's "Operation Protective Edge" was designed to prevent Hamas and other groups from firing unguided rockets into Israel, but an intensive aerial bombardment failed to do this and IDF troops then mounted a ground offensive against launch sites and a number of penetration tunnels. When an eventual ceasefire took effect, more than 2,000 Palestinians—including 400 children—were dead, and several thousand injured. While the Israeli government presented the operation as a success, its ground forces suffered unexpectedly high losses including 64 soldiers killed and 463 wounded. Thirteen soldiers of the elite Golani Brigade were killed in a single night.

The two other regional developments were more welcome. First, relations between Iran and the United States remained positive through further negotiations on the issue of Iran's nuclear programme. A satisfactory outcome was not achieved but both sides agreed to continue discussions into the New Year. In Tunisia, meanwhile, there was further progress towards parliamentary governance, culminating in the second stage of the presidential election on 21 December which followed earlier parliamentary elections. It should be noted, though, that Tunisia was making this progress while a disproportionately large number of young men were leaving the country to fight with Islamic State. Partly, this exodus stemmed from the economic problems within the country—a stark reminder that the public demonstrations which spread across the region in 2010-11 may have been motivated by opposition to autocracy but that there was also a strong element of perceived marginalisation, often made worse by youth unemployment.

AFGHANISTAN AND NIGERIA. Beyond the Middle East, the main security focus was on Russia and Ukraine, but there were significant developments, too, in Afghanistan and Nigeria. The Afghan president, Hamid Karzai, stood down after a more than a decade as leader—a period marked by maladministration and corruption as well as an insurgency that cost tens of thousands of lives. After a first round of voting in April, the run-off contest in June was strongly contested by two candidates: Ashraf Ghani and Abdullah Abdullah. After a protracted post-election controversy and claims of fraud, Ashfraf Ghani eventually took office with Abdullah Abdullah as chief executive, effectively prime minister.

Ghani's background as a respected technocrat and former senior official at the World Bank was welcomed in Western countries as NATO's International Security Assistance Force (ISAF) finally stood down in December. It was replaced by a NATO-led military presence of around 12,000 (primarily US) troops that was intended to provide a wide range of support and training for Afghan security forces. Although the details were not fully clear, some of these Western troops would continue to conduct counter-terrorist operations in a bid to ensure that al-Qaida and other linked groups did not once again operate from within the country.

From 1 January 2015, the Afghan government would be responsible for internal security, albeit with some Western support, but the Taliban and other armed opposition groups remained highly active and were controlling substantial parts of the south and east of the country. Their activities continued, unusually, into the winter months, with the Afghan National Army suffering further casualties. In 2014 alone Afghan security forces suffered over 7,000 killed or injured. Even with the leadership potential of President Ghani, Afghanistan had formidable problems ahead.

Islamist movements came under some pressure in Somalia and Mali, maintained viability in Yemen, and made considerable progress in Nigeria where the Boko Haram movement had taken control of many towns and villages in the north-east of the country. The kidnapping of hundreds of schoolgirls and the failure of the Nigerian security forces to recover them brought the uprising to international attention. Some military assistance was provided but by the end of the year the Nigerian government had systematically failed to handle the much wider threat from the movement, which was also having an impact in neighbouring Niger and Cameroon. In effect, Boko Haram was in the process of establishing a quasi-caliphate, with considerable brutality evident on both sides.

UKRAINE. The crisis in Ukraine began in February with the overthrow of the elected pro-Russian leader, President Viktor Yanukovych. The change was popular in many quarters but not in Russian-speaking eastern Ukraine and Crimea and certainly not in Russia where President Vladimir Putin saw it as a further sign of Western encroachment into what Russia considered its "near abroad". The interim government in Kiev further angered Russia by deciding to abolish Russian as an official language and to seek closer trade links with the EU, rejecting Russia's efforts to entice Ukraine into the "Eurasian Economic Union". During the course of late February and early March armed men took control of much of the Crimean peninsula, which had been part of Russia until 1954 and still housed a major Russian naval base at Sevastopol. Russian special forces were assumed to be involved and political separatists subsequently organised an independence referendum in March, which was followed by the annexation of Crimea and Sevastopol by Russia. This was not accepted by many states and the Ukraine parliament declared in April that it was Ukraine territory temporarily occupied by Russia.

More significantly, pro-Russian rebel forces in the east of the country then sought to break away from Ukraine, leading to a bitter civil war, much of it centred around the city of Donetsk. When Ukrainian military forces made gains against the rebels in August, the latter were able to utilise equipment and personnel supplied by Russia, and by late in 2014 the situation had approached a stalemate with uneasy ceasefires operating and Russia increasingly subject to sanctions by the United States and the European Union. The situation was complicated by differing attitudes within the EU. Some eastern European states, especially Poland and the Baltic republics, were fearful of Russian expansionism while others, such as Germany, were much more cautious. Overall the emergence of the crisis and the ensuing violence and loss of life raised fears of a new Cold War, and NATO, having largely withdrawn from Afghanistan, refocused its attention much closer to home.

CLIMATE CHANGE. During 2014 evidence continued to mount that the global climate was changing, with particular concerns over the state of the Greenland ice cap and a number of tropical high level glacier systems in the Himalayas, the Karakorams and the Andes. Appropriately enough, the latter included Andean glaciers that were significant in supplying water to the city of Lima, with its population of 9.7 million people and already prone to water shortages. Lima was the location for the COP 20 intergovernmental conference on climate change which was intended to prepare the way for the key meeting, COP 21, in Paris in December 2015. That meeting—the 21st Conference of the Parties to the UN 1992 conference on climate change—would, it was hoped, agree plans for a world-wide agreement on limiting carbon emissions.

The Lima conference was more successful than recent meetings, most notably the COP 15 conference in Copenhagen in 2009 which had signally failed in its modest aims (see AR 2010, pp. 458-61). In Lima the participating governments did agree in principle to a plan which would commit all countries to cutting their carbon emissions, and this was a breakthrough in relation to previous experience. Even so, there were problems in the approach to the Paris meeting that appeared difficult to resolve. Some key governments remained unconvinced of the seriousness of the issue, including Canada and Russia which were both major fossil fuel exporters and also stood to benefit from the early stages of climate warming as parts of the Arctic became available for commercial exploitation. They were backed by fossil fuel interests, which continued to offer financial support to organisations that were sceptical of the scientific evidence. Although a broad agreement was reached at Lima, there remained a degree of criticism of the "old" industrial powers by emerging economies, notably China and India, as they would be required to cap emissions in the future, even though historically high atmospheric carbon dioxide levels were primarily due to the past activities of European and North American states.

Against this, a number of factors pointed the way towards a more positive response to controlling carbon emissions. The most important of these were numerous technical developments relating to the use of renewable energy resources, and also improvements in energy storage and conservation. One of the key anticipated stages would arrive when electricity generated from renewables was as cheap as that generated from fossil fuels. This "grid parity" was already being reached in especially favourable locations for wind and solar power, with the latter benefitting particularly from remarkable decreases in the cost of photovoltaic panels. Development of larger and more efficient wind turbines in the multi-megawatt range was also happening faster than many analysts expected, with the world's largest wind turbine, the 8-megawatt Vestas 164 being launched in January 2014. There was also impressive progress in the large-scale production of high capacity batteries.

Renewable energy systems remained a minor part of energy use, but that was changing. In December 2014, over 40 per cent of the electricity consumed by homes in the UK was generated by wind power, and in Germany 31 per cent of the country's overall electric power came from renewables in the first six months of 2014. In the same period, Denmark's proportion of power from renewable sources peaked at 41 per cent. Though all of these were record figures they illustrated a trend, even though electricity only supplied one-third of the power used by most countries.

With 2014 the hottest year globally since accurate records were first kept, it was likely that 2015 would see even more attention focused on renewable energy systems. One of the key issues that became apparent during 2014 was the question of how emerging economies would develop novel energy policies that would enable them to evolve low-carbon economies which still satisfied consumer demand. While many new technologies were available, such economic evolution would require a combination of substantial development investment (much of it from the more wealthy economies), combined with a degree of governmental economic management that contradicted the trend towards freer markets which was a feature of the past several decades.

THE GLOBAL ECONOMY. During 2014 the world economy continued to grow, albeit still at the slow pace of recent years, though with some major variations. Overall growth was at 3.3 per cent, with the IMF predicting an increase to 3.5 per cent in 2015. The United States experienced higher levels of growth than predicted and much of sub-Saharan Africa witnessed rapid change. Relative stagnation continued in Japan; China's growth continued, but not matching the high levels of the first years of the new century, and its rate of growth was expected to decline in the coming years. Across much of Europe economic stagnation and austerity continued and towards the end of the year Russia experienced formidable problems, stemming partly from Ukraine-related sanctions but also a near-halving of global oil prices.

Whilst the aftermath of the 2007-08 financial crisis appeared to be over, there remained multiple concerns. In many countries living standards had not recovered to the level of the early 2000s, even though interest rates remained low and key central banks were feeding financial liquidity into their economies through mechanisms such as quantitative easing. Thus, there was a risk that any return to growth would lead to inflationary pressure and the higher interest rates that this would bring. Furthermore, public anger at austerity was evident across much of Europe, one effect being to increase support for protest parties of the far-right. In Greece, though, the collapse of the government in mid-December led to the calling of a general election with the prospect that the anti-austerity Syriza Party (Coalition of the Radical Left) would perform very well.

Another concern was that while financial regulation had been improved in a number of northern economies following the toxic loan and other banking crises of 2007-08, this was not the case across the world. Nor was there sufficient transnational coordination of regulation which, given the level of integration of the global economy, was seen as a necessary requirement for responding to further crises.

The one issue that emerged in the second half of 2014, both unexpected and difficult to predict as to its effects, was the sharp decline in oil prices. In the ordinary way this would be welcomed by most consumer economies, but there were concerns even with this apparently positive development. One was that such a major fall would lead to a sudden and substantial decline in investment in new oil reserves, especially as these, apart from some limited fracking deposits, now tended to be very expensive to develop and exploit. The fear was that this would lead to a decrease in production relatively quickly, with sudden and unpredictable price rises increasingly likely. The potential for serious price volatility might therefore be the consequence of the 2014 decrease in oil prices.

If low prices were sustained for more than a few months, one other consequence might be a curtailing of investment in renewable energy resources just at a time when climate disruption and the need to move to low-carbon economies was widely recognised in the approach to COP 21 in Paris in December 2015. One further final issue was that sustained, low oil prices produced a particular effect on weaker economies dependent on their own oil revenues for significant parts of their budgets. Among these were Iran, Algeria, Iraq, Libya and especially Nigeria, the latter three of which faced major internal problems stemming from extreme Islamist movements. Since much of the public protest in the Arab Awakening of recent years stemmed from perceptions and experience of economic marginalisation, further economic pressures could exacerbate the levels of anger and resentment, aiding the further development of extremist movements.

Paul Rogers

II WESTERN AND SOUTHERN EUROPE

UNITED KINGDOM

CAPITAL: London   AREA: 243,610 sq km   POPULATION: 64,097,085 ('13)
OFFICIAL LANGUAGES: English; plus Welsh in Wales, Gaelic in Scotland
HEAD OF STATE: Queen Elizabeth II (since Feb '52)
RULING PARTIES: Conservative-Liberal Democrat coalition (since May '10)
HEAD OF GOVERNMENT: Prime Minister David Cameron (Conservative) (since May '10)
DEMOCRACY INDEX: 8.31; 14th of 167   CORRUPTION PERCEPTIONS INDEX: 76; 14th of 175
CURRENCY: Pound Sterling (Dec '14 US$1=GBP 0.64)
GNI PER CAPITA: US$39,140, Intl$35,760 at PPP ('13)

IT is not every year that a country, particularly an established democracy like the United Kingdom, goes through what can accurately be called an existential crisis. But it seemed possible, even for a while probable, that 2014 would start the formal process of the dissolution of the United Kingdom. The referendum in Scotland that took place on 18 September on whether to become independent or remain part of the UK was of historic dimensions, even if the choice of the Scottish electorate— by a margin of 11 percentage points—was to stay. The constitution and political landscape of Scotland, and therefore the UK, were changed profoundly by the referendum campaign and result; as "No" campaigners argued, it was not a vote for no-change, but for change of a different sort. But while the "No" campaign won the day on 18 September, this was widely perceived by the end of the year as something of a pyrrhic victory, as the Scottish National Party (SNP) went from strength to strength in the polls and in its dominance of the Scottish political landscape. It was starting to seem that the referendum vote marked a way-station on the road to independence, rather than the closing off of that road. While ostensibly the question of Scottish independence had been resolved, in practice the referendum seemed to have solved remarkably little by the end of the year.

Though Scotland was the only truly existential challenge to the UK, there were other signs in 2014 of the system's fragility. The populist, anti-Europe and anti-immigration United Kingdom Independence Party (UKIP) made much of the political running in England. Its leader Nigel Farage, who was hardly ever to be pictured without a pint of traditional English beer in his hand—except on the many occasions when he was invited onto the broadcast media (he was the most frequent panellist on the BBC's *Question Time*)—was dubbed "Briton of the Year" by the *Times* newspaper. UKIP won the most votes in the European Parliament elections on 22 May, the first time a party other than Conservative or Labour had come first in a national election for more than a century.

THE UK AFTER THE SCOTTISH REFERENDUM. While the referendum is primarily a story to be told elsewhere in this volume (see the article on Scotland), it had strong effects on the rest of the UK. The British government had proclaimed that it had not done contingency planning for the possibility of Scotland's voting for independence, but in the last two weeks of the campaign this outcome seemed to become a strong possibility. On 10 September the three main party leaders (David

Cameron as prime minister and Conservative leader, Ed Miliband for Labour and Nick Clegg for the Liberal Democrats) abandoned their intended business and headed to Scotland to argue the case for maintaining the Union. The leaders also agreed on promises to devolve further powers to the Scottish Parliament and government, to preserve the Scottish National Health Service, and maintain the Barnett formula distributing central tax revenues among the constituent parts of the UK (whose author Joel Barnett, the chief secretary to the Treasury in 1979, died in 2014). These policies, known as "the vow", and a rapid timetable for implementation, had been brokered by the former prime minister, Gordon Brown, who played an active role in campaigning and behind the scenes during the referendum.

On the morning after the referendum, Cameron made two policy announcements. One was the establishment of the Smith Commission, under Lord Smith of Kelvin, to consider further devolution for Scotland and which reported on 27 November. While Smith was a consensus matter, Cameron also launched a non-consensus initiative on the thorny question of "English votes for English laws" (EVEL). This was one of the messy points of asymmetrical devolution and the intertwined fiscal arrangements of the UK, and one that involved a considerable amount of complexity and partisan interests: it would create the possibility of a right-of-centre majority on English domestic policy run by the UK government, concurrent with a left-of-centre majority on non-devolved issues like the Budget and foreign affairs. A previous study of the issue, the Mackay Commission, had reported in 2013 but the government wished to return to the problem. As with legislation to implement the recommendations of the Smith Report, EVEL and its perplexities were left for the parliament to be elected in May 2015.

Though the "Yes" campaign lost the referendum, the SNP emerged from the process in remarkably good spirits, with its claimed membership boosted from 25,000 at the start of the year to 100,000 in October and a series of post-referendum opinion polls giving it a huge lead in voting intention for the forthcoming Westminster (2015) and Scottish (2016) general elections. The party changed its leader, with Alex Salmond stepping down and Nicola Sturgeon taking over as SNP leader and first minister of Scotland. Rather less smoothly, Labour's leader in Scotland, Johann Lamont, resigned on 24 October, strongly criticising the national party leadership. The new leader, Jim Murphy, was elected on 13 December, with a considerable task before him.

ELECTIONS. The Scottish referendum was of genuinely historic dimensions, but there were other important elections in the United Kingdom during 2014 that produced significant results.

There were five parliamentary by-elections for seats in the House of Commons. The first was on 13 February at Wythenshawe and Sale East, in Greater Manchester, where Labour candidate Mike Kane held the constituency vacated by the death of Labour MP Paul Goggins with a comfortable majority, although in a foretaste of what was to come later in the year UKIP came second.

The European Parliament elections took place on 22 May 2014, alongside the annual round of elections for local authorities. By the time the votes were counted, few were surprised that UKIP had won its first national election. It was also the first time the Conservatives had ever come third nationally. The result was a fairly close three-way spread between UKIP (27.5 per cent), Labour (25.4 per cent) and Conservative (23.9 per cent), with the Liberal Democrats languishing in fifth place (6.9 per cent) behind the Greens (7.9 per cent). The regional list proportional representation electoral system ensured a result (for the UK) more or less in line with the votes cast, UKIP returning 24 MEPs, Labour 20, the Conservatives 19, the Greens three, the SNP two, and the Liberal Democrats but one, alongside one each for Plaid Cymru (in Wales), and Sinn Féin, the Democratic Unionists and Ulster Unionists (in Northern Ireland).

The local government elections were broadly successful for Labour, which made a net gain of 324 seats, and bad for the Liberal Democrats in particular with a net loss of 310 seats. Labour's strength was most apparent in London, where the party gained control of five more borough councils (including, for the first time, the traditionally Tory borough of Redbridge). Outside London the picture was patchier, with UKIP polling well, particularly in eastern England and along the east coast, depriving Labour of control of Great Yarmouth for instance. Labour also lost ground in many white working class areas outside the big cities, particularly in Rotherham in South Yorkshire. Overall, UKIP made 161 net gains.

There were four House of Commons by-elections in the remainder of the year. In Newark, the Conservative candidate, Robert Jenrick, held the seat on 5 June, after the resignation of incumbent MP Patrick Mercer following a finding against him by the House of Commons committee on standards. The most dramatic was triggered on 28 August when the Conservative MP for Clacton, Douglas Carswell, announced that he was leaving the Conservatives to join UKIP and had decided to resign his seat to seek the consent of his electors. Carswell won the resulting by-election with a huge majority on 9 October, making him the first MP to be elected under UKIP's colours. On the same day, UKIP polled strongly in a by-election for the Labour seat of Heywood and Middleton, falling just 617 votes short of the successful Labour candidate Liz McInnes. UKIP rounded out the year by holding the seat of another ex-Conservative MP and defector to the party, Mark Reckless, in a by-election on 20 November in Rochester and Strood.

There were some elections for other authorities, including for Northern Ireland local government, and Labour successfully defended the Scottish Parliament seat of Cowdenbeath in January. There were two by-elections for the newly created positions of police and crime commissioner (PCC), Labour holding both vacancies (West Midlands and South Yorkshire) on the low turnouts that had already become customary in PCC elections.

THE ECONOMY. The UK economy had a relatively good year as the recovery apparent during 2013 was consolidated, and in the third quarter of the year the economy had grown by 2.6 per cent compared to its position at the equivalent point in 2013. Output finally passed its pre-recession peak (measured at the start of 2008) in June, although on a per capita basis it was still significantly below the peak. Inflation remained low, with the government's preferred measure, the Consumer Price

Index (CPI), rising 1 per cent. Recorded unemployment continued to fall through-out the year, although much of the growth appeared to be in casual and part-time work and sole trader self-employment, and some because of an increasingly restrictive system of "sanctioning" those claiming benefits for alleged failure to observe the rules. Concern was expressed by Labour and the trade unions over the growing use of zero-hours contracts, the most restrictive of which meant that employees were effectively on-call to their employers.

However, productivity remained poor and living standards were stagnant for the majority of the population. The additional tax revenues usually generated by eco-nomic recovery were weak, with the consequence that the public sector deficit, apparently the lodestar of UK government policy, remained stubbornly high.

In the Budget on 19 March Chancellor George Osborne raised the income tax-free personal allowance to £10,500, completing the implementation of a flagship policy from the 2010 coalition agreement. He also expanded the size of tax-free savings schemes, and made a major change to pension policy by announcing that it would no longer be obligatory for pensioners to buy an annuity with their lump sum of savings. The 3 December autumn statement, which had in effect become a second Budget over the previous couple of decades (as well as drifting chrono-logically into being a winter statement) made changes to stamp duty—the tax on property purchases that formed an increasingly important source of revenue. The statement was an important political document as it set out the Conservatives' intentions in the medium term, and opponents argued that it proposed extremely harsh cuts in public spending which had not been spelled out in any detail.

LEGISLATION. Parliament passed 30 Acts of public legislation (and one locally spe-cific Act) during 2014, a fairly average level of output by recent standards. Several of these were contentious, particularly the cumbersomely and somewhat mislead-ingly titled Transparency of Lobbying, Non-Party Campaigning and Trade Union Administration Act, which did relatively little about what might normally be con-sidered lobbying but did impose various requirements on charities and campaign-ing bodies before they were permitted to speak on anything politically sensitive during election campaigns. Another contentious piece of legislation was the Immi-gration Act, which streamlined the process by which the Home Office could deport foreign citizens, enabled the Home Office to remove individuals pending immi-gration appeals, and replaced rights of appeal with "administrative review". Other significant Acts included the Children and Families Act, which made a number of significant changes to family law, including a more integrated approach between education, health and social services in helping vulnerable children and more use of mediation before embarking upon formal court proceedings. Also, while much attention was paid to Scotland's status, a Wales Act provided for some further devolution for Wales including, subject to a future referendum, limited taxation powers (see the article on Wales in this volume).

FOREIGN POLICY. Europe remained a divisive issue in British politics, particularly with the threat presented by UKIP to the main political parties that was so apparent at the European Parliament election and in by-elections. David Cameron was in a particularly difficult position, since the competing pressures of his increasingly eurosceptic or outright anti-EU backbenchers and the perhaps limited patience of other European Union member states for British special pleading placed a satisfactory outcome at the outer limits of politics-as-the-art-of-the-possible. The project to renegotiate the terms of UK membership of the EU, and then submit the result to a referendum in 2017, had not progressed very far in political terms by the end of the year, although some solid work on detail had been done at the Foreign and Commonwealth Office in the "balance of competences review" assessing exactly what was done at EU and national government level, which concluded in December. This review drew heavy criticism from anti-EU MPs and commentators, who claimed that it was unduly pro-European, although its defenders insisted that it was entirely factual.

Relations with fellow EU leaders were strained by Cameron's objection to the nomination of Jean-Claude Juncker, the former prime minister of Luxembourg, as president of the European Commission. The objection was raised both on procedural grounds, because the UK Conservatives disapproved of the role of the European Parliament and its election campaign in determining the nomination, and because of Juncker's political positions. But only Hungary joined the UK in voting against Juncker at the European Council on 27 June.

Another difficult moment followed on 24 October, when the UK's GDP figures—higher than expected not only because of higher growth than in most of the eurozone but also because of statistical revisions, including the assessment of output from the informal economy such as drugs and sex work—triggered a bill for £1.7 billion in contributions to EU funds. Despite being the result of a treaty to which the UK was already party, the bill was received with outrage in the press and by the government, and was certainly regarded as helpful to the UKIP campaign in the by-election in Rochester and Strood. An agreement on 7 November gave the UK and the Netherlands more time to pay their contributions, pushing the issue to the other side of the 2015 general election, and the amount was adjusted with reference to the UK's long-standing EU rebate.

In other foreign policy matters, the government's unwillingness to criticise the Israeli Defence Force's bombardment of Gaza during the summer's conflict led to the first resignation from the coalition on an issue of principle. Minister for Faiths and Communities Baroness (Sayeeda) Warsi resigned on 5 August. "My view has been," she wrote in her resignation letter, "that our policy in relation to the Middle East peace process generally but more recently our approach and language during the current crisis in Gaza is morally indefensible, is not in Britain's national interest and will have a long term detrimental impact on our reputation internationally and domestically."

The UK hosted the NATO summit in Wales in March and a special Global Summit to End Sexual Violence in Conflict, in London in June. The issue of sexual violence in war had been a particular concern of the foreign secretary, William Hague, and the summit was organised in conjunction with the UN special envoy on the subject, the actor Angelina Jolie. Hague remarked at the conference that "the fact that we have never given this issue the prominence it deserves owes much to societal attitudes and failings: our failure never decisively to reject and condemn the denial or stifling of the full expression of women's rights over a very long time." Some of those societal attitudes were on display, with press criticism of Hague for allegedly being "starstruck" at meeting Jolie.

The new government in India was the object of some determined diplomacy, with Foreign Secretary Hague visiting in July and Deputy Prime Minister Clegg in August. The closer relationship that had been developing with China was consolidated with the visit to London of Chinese Premier Li Keqiang. Cameron also made visits to several countries, including Israel and Turkey.

One of the main foreign policy concerns of 2014 for the UK, and for governments around the world, was the rise of the so-called Islamic State of Iraq and Syria (or the Levant) (ISIS, also known as ISIL). On 26 September David Cameron stated: "ISIL is a terrorist organisation unlike those we have dealt with before. The brutality is staggering, but it is not just the brutality; it is backed by billions of dollars and has captured an arsenal of the most modern weapons." The brutality of the organisation was amply demonstrated by the filmed beheadings of two British aid workers, David Haines and Alan Henning, who had been held hostage by ISIS. The murderer appeared to have been of British origin, and he acquired the distasteful tabloid nickname of "Jihadi John". During September in particular the UK initiated or was involved in a number of diplomatic moves against Islamic State at an intergovernmental and United Nations level, including humanitarian aid for refugees, and support and training for Iraqi and Kurdish forces opposing ISIS militants. Concern was expressed about the risks of British citizens travelling to the conflict zone to fight and returning violently radicalised, with a national police campaign against this phenomenon and a large increase in the number of arrests in the UK for terrorist offences committed abroad (69 people in the first half of 2014). In December a 15-year old girl believed to be travelling to join the conflict in Syria was stopped at Heathrow Airport in London.

DEFENCE. The notable development in defence matters during 2014 was the withdrawal of the last British combat troops from Afghanistan, with the Task Force command in Helmand province disbanded on 1 April and the last troops redeployed in November. A small military contingent remained in Afghanistan, whose work was to train the Afghan army and national police force. Six members of UK forces died in this last year of the deployment, five of them in a helicopter crash on 26 April. Two British aid workers also died in a suicide bombing in Kabul on 18 January.

On 26 September the House of Commons voted overwhelmingly in favour of assisting US-led operations against Islamic State, and British forces subsequently participated in air operations over Iraq against ISIS targets. British forces were also deployed overseas in a wide range of non-combat capacities, including, from 5 November, the operation of a special hospital in Sierra Leone to assist in the treatment of those suffering from the Ebola virus.

DOMESTIC POLITICS AND CULTURE. The political year was dominated by UKIP and Scotland. Away from these challenges, there was growing evidence of pressure on public services, with heavy delays early in the year for the issue of UK passports, and lengthening waiting times at hospital accident and emergency departments in the autumn and winter. There were severe storms in many areas early in the year, particularly in Wales and the south-west, where the main railway line was washed away at Dawlish on 5 February. Rainfall in southern England in January was its highest for at least a century. There was further flooding in some areas during the summer, and warm, wet and stormy weather was widely anticipated to increase with global climate change.

There were two sets of Cabinet-level changes during the year. The first was on 9 April when, in a reverberation of the scandal over MPs' expenses that broke in 2009 (see AR 2010, pp. 9-10), the secretary of state for culture, media and sport, Maria Miller, resigned after having been ordered to repay some expenses that she had claimed; she had been further criticised for the brevity and alleged gracelessness of her formal apology in the House of Commons. Her replacement was Sajid Javid, who became the first member of the 2010 intake of MPs to reach the Cabinet. Miller's responsibilities as minister for women were transferred to Nicky Morgan.

A more thorough reshuffle took place on 14-15 July. The most significant change was that William Hague stood down as foreign secretary after four years, to become Leader of the House of Commons, and was replaced by Philip Hammond, previously secretary of state for defence. Another noteworthy change was the departure of Michael Gove, secretary of state for education, to become government chief whip. Gove's years at education, with experiments such as "free schools" and an apparently contemptuous attitude to the education policy establishment, which he dubbed "the blob", had been highly controversial among the teaching profession in particular. His replacement was the rapidly rising Nicky Morgan.

The political party conference season was largely a matter of routine and, strangely, its most notable moment was something that a politician did not say. Ed Miliband had previously made very successful conference appearances without speaking from notes, but in 2014 the limitations of the technique were showing; it was a poorly organised speech and Miliband forgot to use the section on the budget deficit—an omission his political opponents seized upon. While David Cameron's speech was better received on the day, its promise of (unfunded) tax cuts of £7 billion was incongruous given the government's general emphasis on austerity.

The result of the Rochester and Strood by-election featured rather less in the media than an incident during polling day, in which the shadow attorney general, Emily Thornberry, posted a picture on the Twitter social media site that featured a house in Rochester displaying an enormous England flag and with a white van in the driveway (and some mock Georgian pillars outside, too), and which she captioned "Image from #Rochester". Thornberry instantly became the target for vicious and often personal online hostility; it was widely assumed that she was being snobbish about the resident of the house, and by extension, the white working class English. Sensitive to the dangers of Labour being perceived as looking down on the white working class (and, therefore, losing support to UKIP and others), Miliband was reportedly furious and accepted Thornberry's resignation with alacrity. On calmer reflection, it was possibly Thornberry who was the victim of prejudice in that, as a well-spoken MP from Islington, she was assumed to be a metropolitan snob. The resident of the house was snapped up by the tabloid press, and "White Van Dan" had a personal manifesto published in the *Sun*, which consisted of populist right wing clichés, right down to making-the-trains-run-on-time. The incident was fodder for much semiotic and sociological analysis.

There were a number of developments in the legal and criminal justice systems. The scale of the cuts to legal aid and the courts aroused criticism from representatives of the legal profession and, unusually, a collective objection from the senior judiciary through the Judicial Executive Board. The Lord Chancellor and minister of justice, Chris Grayling—the first non-lawyer to hold the office for perhaps 440 years—was involved in other controversies including, on 5 December, the reversal in the courts of his policy of banning prisoners from receiving books. A former minister, Andrew Mitchell, who had resigned from the government in 2012 following allegations that he had sworn at police officers and called them "plebs" in Downing Street, lost a libel action against News Group Newspapers for their publishing the allegations in the *Sun* newspaper. This probably marked the end to the "pleb-gate" affair that began in 2012 (see AR 2013 p. 12; AR 2014, p. 10). An even longer-running saga, the attempts by the *Guardian* newspaper to gain access through freedom of information legislation to correspondence sent by Prince Charles to government ministers in 2004-05, reached a Supreme Court hearing on 24-25 November. The government had resisted publication on the intriguing grounds that it would be seriously damaging to the neutrality of the monarchy if these "black spider memos" showed the heir to the throne disagreeing with government policy.

The post-Savile scandal climate of concern over past sexual abuse of children (see AR 2013, p. 16) was reflected in the successful prosecution of the entertainer, Rolf Harris, and the announcement by Home Secretary Theresa May on 7 July that the government would set up an inquiry into the alleged failure of the Home Office to take action on allegations made in the 1980s and the wider failure of institutions to protect children. However, the inquiry's workings were troubled and it lost two successive panel chairs, Dame Elizabeth Butler-Sloss and Fiona Woolf.

On 24 June former Downing Street director of communications Andy Coulson was found guilty of conspiracy to commit "phone hacking" (the unauthorised interception of mobile phone voicemail) and was sentenced to 18 months in prison, of which he served five. The offence was committed during his period as editor of the *News of the World* in 2003-07 (see AR 2012, p. 10).

While in 2013 the British Right lost its most revered leader, Margaret Thatcher (see AR 2014, pp. 9; 525-26), in 2014 the British Left lost—if not a leader—at the very least, a favourite uncle, with the death of Tony Benn on 14 March (see Obituary). Benn's democratic socialist political vision may have seemed outdated to many commentators, but he was one of only a handful of political figures who could attract mass audiences to speaking events and bridge the growing gap between professional politics and the electorate. Though no successor to Benn, the actor Russell Brand emerged as a figurehead of populist left-wing anti-politics with the publication of his book *Revolution* in October. His support for non-voting was unpopular with many other activists, the veteran Sex Pistol John Lydon (Johnny Rotten) saying "if you don't vote, you don't count" and making an anatomical reference to people who argued against voting. Brand's political statements were ridiculed by many commentators, but he was able to talk to people who had long been alienated by normal politics. Other, perhaps more widely-regarded books, such as *The Establishment* by Owen Jones and *Capital in the Twenty-First Century* by Thomas Piketty, plus the idealistic ferment of the Scottish referendum, meant that it was not a bad year for left-of-centre polemics.

In broader public opinion, there was no sharp change. Labour's lead in the polls narrowed throughout the year, with the two main parties locked in a virtual dead heat by December. But one-third of the electors were supporting other parties, principally UKIP, with the SNP and the Green Party adding support towards the end of the year.

Culturally, there were few new, pronounced trends. Probably the most mocked phenomenon in British culture was "the hipster", a term to describe young, urban people who were obsessive followers of fashion, the more obscure and inexplicable the fashion the better, and reputed to be found in greatest number in east London.

Four of the top-10 best-selling books were about a computer game, *Minecraft*, which had been growing in popularity exponentially since 2009 and had been dubbed "the best game to play at work"—perhaps explaining some of Britain's poor productivity, although, ironically, gaming itself was a small but strong growth-sector in the UK economy, expanding by 7 per cent over the year. After 2013's "selfie", 2014 was the year of the "selfie stick", which probably represented progress as it introduced a little more perspective and proportion to a somewhat narcissistic phenomenon. It was a strange and lamentable development that British retailers seemed to have succeeded in their bid to introduce "Black Friday" to the UK on 28 November—a key date in the retail calendar in the United States, being the day after Thanksgiving (a festival which did not—yet—exist in the UK) when the Christmas shopping bonanza was deemed to begin. The retail sector was under pressure throughout the year, facing long term changes as shopping moved increasingly online. A more short term problem struck the once-dominant supermarket chain, Tesco, which had to admit that its profits had been severely overstated; internal inquiries followed and a criminal fraud investigation started.

The year saw several steps towards a more equal society in Britain. On 29 March the first same-sex weddings took place in England following legislation adopted in 2013 (see AR 2014, pp. 10-11). The neighbouring London boroughs of Camden and Islington both held weddings shortly after midnight. The Scottish Parliament passed its own legislation and the first Scottish same-sex weddings took place on Hogmanay (31 December). The Church of England was not reconciled to same-sex marriage but did take an historic step in another direction, approving legislation to allow women to become bishops. The announcement that Libby Lane would be ordained bishop of Stockport early in the New Year was made on 17 December.

CONCLUSION. The shadow of a more sombre age fell over the year. There were numerous events across Britain to commemorate the start of the Great War in 1914, which, in general, took place in a spirit of mourning and remembrance of the human losses of the war, rather than nationalistic celebration. Nevertheless, there was a sharp dispute on this point in January between the then education secretary, Michael Gove, and prominent historians. The memorial installation *Blood Swept Lands and Seas of Red*, by artists Paul Cummins and Tom Piper, at the Tower of London was instantly iconic: a single ceramic poppy for every British military fatality in 1914-18 was gradually added to the moat until all 888,246 emblems formed a sea of red around the Tower. Perhaps, just as the London Olympics of 2012 had demonstrated that the British could still organise a good public event, the 1914 commemorations showed that Britain could still be dignified, and did good public art. And the Scottish referendum of 2014 showed that Britain was even capable, occasionally, of political debates that aroused mass public enthusiasm.

Lewis Baston

SCOTLAND

CAPITAL: Edinburgh   AREA: 78,313 sq km   POPULATION: 5,327,700 ('13) (National Records of
    Scotland)
OFFICIAL LANGUAGES: English and Gaelic
HEAD OF STATE: Queen Elizabeth II (since Feb '52)
RULING PARTY: Scottish National Party
HEAD OF GOVERNMENT: First Minister Nicola Sturgeon (SNP) (since Nov '14)

THE referendum on Scottish independence, held on 18 September, was the major event of 2014. The outcome—"No" to an independent Scotland—whilst reasonably decisive, did not end the debate on the powers to be wielded by the Scottish government, and also opened a wider discussion about devolution in the rest of the UK.

In the months before the referendum, both the "Yes" campaign (arguing for complete Scottish independence) and the "No" campaign (advocating some version of the status quo) made great efforts to encourage those not on the electoral roll to register to vote and to maximise turnout. The "Yes" campaign was particularly successful in persuading people in the poorer, inner-city areas that supporting their side in the referendum was the best method of saving Scotland from the impact of the unpopular social policies being pursued by the UK government at Westminster. Grass-roots community groups sprang up in areas of multiple deprivation to argue the case for "Yes" and, since UK Labour party policy was increasingly led to accept that continued "austerity" was required to eliminate the budget deficit, the Scottish National Party (SNP) could position itself as the only significant socialist party in Scotland.

During most of the year opinion polls showed a steady majority of around 50 per cent for "No" and 35 per cent for "Yes", with the remainder undecided, but in late August and early September, as increasing numbers of undecided voters backed "Yes", the margin became narrower, and a poll on 5 September put "Yes" ahead. This belatedly galvanised the UK government and opposition, neither of which wanted Scotland to become independent, into urgent visits to Scotland, with the Conservative, Labour and Liberal Democrat leaders all arriving on 10 September bearing rather vague promises of significantly more devolution. An important late intervention by Gordon Brown, the former Labour prime minister and still an MP for a Scottish constituency, asserted that there was nothing unpatriotic for a Scot to vote "No". He set out a timetable for greater devolution, with a committee to be established urgently to report by St Andrew's Day (30 November) and draft legislation to be prepared by Burns Night (25 January) in 2015, to be put to the vote in the new UK parliament after the 2015 general election (in May). The three UK party leaders responded by agreeing a "vow" of further devolution, to Brown's timetable, in a joint newspaper article published on 16 September.

The outcome of the referendum was a clear majority for "No": 55.3 per cent to 44.7 per cent for "Yes". The turnout was very high, averaging 84.6 per cent across the country; in no area was it less than 75 per cent. There was little relationship between the voting pattern and pre-existing support for the SNP, but the "Yes" vote was highest in some traditional Labour heartlands. The only areas where there was a "Yes" majority were Glasgow city (53 per cent "Yes"), and also in the greater Glasgow area—North Lanarkshire (51 per cent) and West Dunbartonshire (54 per cent); most strikingly, there was a 57 per cent "Yes" majority in Dundee, the only SNP stronghold with significant urban deprivation.

The defeat of the "Yes" campaign caused great distress among its supporters, some of whom flocked to join the SNP. The resurgence of the SNP was perhaps also helped by the decision of its leader, First Minister Alex Salmond, to resign immediately after the vote. Salmond had been a somewhat divisive figure and was succeeded unopposed by his deputy, Nicola Sturgeon, who duly became first minister. Salmond subsequently announced his intention to stand for election to the Westminster Parliament in 2015. The leader of the Scottish Labour Party, Johann Lamont, also resigned, protesting that the UK Labour Party was interfering too much in Scottish Labour's affairs; after an election she was succeeded by MP Jim Murphy, who had risen to prominence as one of the more effective "No" campaigners.

To honour "the vow", Lord Smith of Kelvin was appointed to chair a commission of politicians and independent experts to produce a report to the timetable set out by Gordon Brown. The Smith Commission managed to meet the tight timetable and reported on 27 November. Its main recommendations were that the Scottish Parliament should have full power over income tax rates and bands in Scotland, that it should receive a share of Scottish VAT receipts, that it should have increased borrowing powers, that it should control some benefit payment rates, that it should set air passenger duty at Scottish airports, that it should determine the franchise for Scottish Parliament elections, and that the Barnett formula, driving financial transfers from the UK Treasury to Scotland, should be retained. All the members of the commission endorsed the report, although the SNP members later made clear that they wished it could have gone further and that it fell short of the "devo-max" they felt "the vow" had promised. Political reaction in the rest of the UK, however, was that the report was far too favourable to Scotland and that the power of Scottish MPs to vote on matters relevant only to England should be severely curbed. Within Scotland, the Smith Commission report helped a little to heal the divisions created by the fervour of the "Yes" and "No" campaigns.

In contrast to the excitement of the referendum, the elections in May to the European Parliament were relatively low-key, even though they could be regarded as a dummy run to identify the relative strength of the pro- and anti-independence parties. Scotland was a single constituency, with 6 MEPs since 2009. The 2009 elections had returned two SNP, two Scottish Labour, one Scottish Conservative and one Scottish Liberal Democrat members. It was generally expected that the Liberal Democrat seat would be lost, and most prior comment speculated about whether a third SNP or second Conservative candidate would be successful, the UK Independence Party (UKIP) being regarded as a predominantly "English" party and the accepted wisdom being that Scotland was much more favourably disposed than England towards the European Union. Voter turnout was 33.5 per cent (an improvement on the 28.5 per cent seen in 2009), and the sixth candidate elected, with 10.5 per cent of the vote, was UKIP's David Coburn.

Outside politics, Scotland was prominent in the sporting world, hosting the Commonwealth Games in Glasgow in July-August and the Ryder Cup at Gleneagles in September. Both events, whilst causing local disruption, were well received, and Scotland came fourth in the Commonwealth Games medals table. Departing from its historical tradition, the Royal and Ancient Golf Club of St Andrews voted in September to admit women members, thus putting pressure on the remaining men-only clubs to follow suit.

At the end of the year, Scotland experienced its first case of Ebola virus. Pauline Cafferkey, an NHS nurse from South Lanarkshire who had been working as a volunteer with Save the Children in Sierra Leone, was diagnosed after returning to Glasgow via Casablanca (Morocco) and London Heathrow, raising questions about screening at airports. She was admitted to Glasgow's Gartnavel Hospital, which was equipped to handle such cases; subsequently she was transferred for more specialist care to the Royal Free Hospital in London.

Charlotte Lythe

WALES

CAPITAL: Cardiff   AREA: 20,755 sq km   POPULATION: 3,0082,400 ('13) (Office for National Statistics)
OFFICIAL LANGUAGES: Welsh & English
HEAD OF STATE: Queen Elizabeth II (since Feb '52)
RULING PARTY: Labour
HEAD OF GOVERNMENT: First Minister Carwyn Jones (Labour) (since Dec '09)

THE first week of January 2014 saw the west coast of Wales battered by massive tidal surges, which caused damage to properties and infrastructure. Most badly hit was the attractive promenade at Aberystwyth, as huge waves caused flooding and structural damage leading to the evacuation of residents. Whereas much of the damage in coastal areas had been repaired by the end of the year, it was reported that some parts of the coast could not be protected in the long term from rising sea levels and erosion.

Also eroding was the support for the mainstream political parties—including the Labour Party, for so long the dominant political force in Wales—notably by the United Kingdom Independence Party (UKIP). UKIP's strong showing in the European Parliament elections in May ensured that Labour failed to reach its target of increasing its number of MEPs from Wales. It retained its one member, with UKIP, the Conservatives and Plaid Cymru each returning one member. Opinion polls throughout the year suggested that UKIP's appeal to disaffected voters might damage Labour's hopes of victory in the 2015 UK general election and would probably lead to the election of several UKIP members to the Welsh National Assembly in 2016.

Relations between the Labour-led Welsh government and the UK government improved in July, following the sacking of Secretary of State for Wales David Jones and the appointment of the young MP for Preseli Pembrokeshire, Stephen Crabb. The new minister's more positive approach swiftly soothed the atmosphere of mistrust and bitterness which had developed in recent years between Westminster and Cardiff.

Also in July the Welsh government announced that a new £1 billion relief road for the M4 motorway was to be built near Newport. This, the largest capital investment programme ever announced by the Welsh government, was criticised because alternative cheaper routes had not been properly considered and because the enormous cost of the project meant that other much-needed road schemes elsewhere in Wales could no longer be funded. Later in the year it was announced that the UK government would fund the electrification of the Swansea-London railway by 2018 and pay almost half the estimated £500 million cost of electrifying the Welsh Valley lines.

In September the 2014 NATO summit was held at the Celtic Manor, Newport. The event brought together more than 60 national leaders and 4,000 delegates amid tight security. Barack Obama became the first serving president of the United States to visit Wales, praising the country's "extraordinary beauty, wonderful people and great hospitality". First Minister Carwyn Jones hailed the Welsh government's £3 million budget for the event as money well spent, but some traders claimed that security barriers in Cardiff city centre drove away customers.

meeting in mid-December ended in failure, although UK Prime Minister David Cameron stated that progress had been made and that he had offered the Northern Ireland Executive "financial fire-power" estimated at some £2 billion as an incentive. In a rare show of unity, all parties criticised the government, with Sinn Féin complaining that no "new money" had been offered to allow the Executive to protect essential public services.

After further negotiations, the Stormont House Agreement was concluded, subject to endorsement by the parties. Welfare reform was accepted but the impact would be cushioned by local funding and fines imposed by the Treasury would be reduced if the reforms were accelerated; a Treasury loan was to fund infrastructure projects, the development of shared and integrated education, and a programme of redundancies in the Civil Service. The demand of the Executive for the devolution of corporation tax was met, but at the price of a cut in the block grant. The number of government departments would be reduced from 12 to nine, Assembly seats cut from 108 to 90 by 2021, and parties would be able to opt out of government to form an official opposition. However, no agreement was reached on the difficult issues of flags and parades which essentially were "parked", and only minor progress was made on dealing with the legacy of the past.

The end of a long chapter in the history of Northern Ireland came in October with the death, aged 88, of former first minister and DUP leader, Ian Paisley (see Obituary). More than 800 people attended a memorial service in Belfast's Ulster Hall, including former political enemies of Paisley, Martin McGuinness and former Taoiseach Bertie Ahern; notable absentees were one-time DUP colleagues, regarded by Paisleyites as complicit in forcing his resignation as DUP leader.

Alan Greer

REPUBLIC OF IRELAND

CAPITAL: Dublin   AREA: 70,270 sq km   POPULATION: 4,595,281 ('13)
OFFICIAL LANGUAGES: Irish & English
HEAD OF STATE: President Michael D. Higgins (since Nov '11)
RULING PARTIES: Fine Gael-led coalition
HEAD OF GOVERNMENT: Prime Minister/Taoiseach Enda Kenny (since March '11)
DEMOCRACY INDEX: 8.68; 12th of 167   CORRUPTION PERCEPTIONS INDEX: 74; =17th of 175
CURRENCY: Euro (Dec '14 £1.00=EUR 1.275, US$1.00=EUR 0.821)
GNI PER CAPITA: US$39,110, Intl$35,090 at PPP ('12)

DISSATISFACTION with the performance of the governing parties—Fine Gael and Labour—was highlighted during 2014 by election results and high profile controversies in justice and health. In February, the Dáil (the lower chamber of the legislature) debated a motion of no confidence in Minister for Justice Alan Shatter, amid criticisms of the government's handling of allegations made by Sgt Maurice McCabe of malpractice within the Garda (Irish police). Garda Commissioner Martin Callinan was forced to resign in March, and with new revelations emerging about the tapping of phone calls, the government announced an independent enquiry. The strongly critical report by barrister Seán Guerin, published in May, found that the justice department had failed properly to investigate the matter and led to the resignation of the minister; Shatter was replaced by Frances Fitzgerald. The Cabinet announced an independent review of the department of justice, the creation of a new Independent Garda Authority and legislation to strengthen the Garda ombudsman.

Elections to the European Parliament and local councils took place on 23 May and highlighted the unpopularity of the government. In the poll for the 11 European seats, Fianna Fáil emerged as the largest party with 22 per cent of the first preferences but won just one seat; Fine Gael also polled just over 22 per cent but won four seats. Both Sinn Féin and the Independents won three seats and polled over 19 per cent of the vote. The brunt of popular discontent was borne by the Labour Party, which polled just over 5 per cent and lost all its three seats.

Following restructuring that reduced the number of authorities from 114 to 31, the governing parties fared badly in the local elections for 949 councillors. Fine Gael won 24 per cent of the vote and Labour around 7 per cent (down 11 per cent and 7 per cent respectively on 2009). Fianna Fáil gained most votes (25 per cent), and Sinn Féin became the third largest party by winning 15 per cent and 159 seats (an increase of 7 per cent and 105 councillors). Independents won nearly one-quarter of the votes and smaller anti-austerity parties and the Greens also gained seats. In Dáil by-elections, Gabrielle McFadden of Fine Gael retained the seat in Longford-Westmeath following the death of her sister, TD (Member of the Dáil) Nicky McFadden; in Dublin West, following the resignation of independent TD Patrick Nulty, Sinn Féin topped the poll with 21 per cent, fewer than 100 votes ahead of the successful Socialist Party candidate, Ruth Coppinger.

A high profile issue that energised politics was opposition to the introduction of water charges, which produced large protests across the country in the autumn. The political impact of the issue was demonstrated in by-elections in October needed because the incumbents (Fine Gael's Brian Hayes and Independent Luke "Ming" Flanagan) had won seats in the European elections. Independent Michael Fitzmaurice won in Roscommon-South Leitrim but the big surprise came in Dublin South West, where Paul Murphy of the Anti-Austerity Alliance overcame the hotly favoured Sinn Féin candidate. In a by-election for the Seanad (upper house), independent Gerard Craughwell defeated the Fine Gael candidate John McNulty, who had been embroiled in controversy following his appointment to the board of the Irish Museum of Modern Art, a state quango.

In the wake of the Labour Party's poor performance, Tánaiste (deputy prime minister) Eamon Gilmore resigned as party leader and was replaced in early July by Joan Burton, who defeated Alex White in the leadership election. In the extensive Cabinet reshuffle that followed, White took the post of minister for communications; Alan Kelly, victor in the four-way contest for Labour deputy leader, became minister of the environment replacing Phil Hogan, who had resigned on his appointment as Ireland's new EU commissioner. In other changes, Charles Flanagan replaced Gilmore as minister for foreign affairs; Leo Varadkar moved to the health ministry; and Heather Humphries became minister for arts, heritage and the Gaeltacht.

Claims by Maíria Cahill that, aged 16, she had been raped by a senior member of the IRA in 1997, "interrogated" during an investigation of the claims by the IRA, and had then raised the matter at meetings with Sinn Féin president Gerry Adams, led to heated exchanges in the Dáil in October. Taoiseach Enda Kenny and Fianna Fáil leader Micheál Martin met Cahill to discuss the case but Sinn Féin denied claims that it had covered-up cases of child abuse, although Adams did admit that victims had been failed by the "not appropriate" IRA policy of shooting alleged sex offenders.

Alan Greer

GERMANY

CAPITAL: Berlin   AREA: 357,050 sq km   POPULATION: 80,621,788 ('13)
OFFICIAL LANGUAGE: German
HEAD OF STATE: President Joachim Gauck (since March '12)
RULING PARTIES: Christian Democratic Union/Christian Social Union (CDU/CSU)-led coalition
HEAD OF GOVERNMENT: Federal Chancellor Angela Merkel (CDU) (since Oct '05)
DEMOCRACY INDEX: 8.31; 15th of 167   CORRUPTION PERCEPTIONS INDEX: 79; =12th of 175
CURRENCY: Euro (Dec '14 £1.00=EUR 1.275, US$1.00=EUR 0.821)
GNI PER CAPITA: US$46,100, Intl$44,540 at PPP ('13)

ALTHOUGH it was the year of Chancellor Angela Merkel's 60th birthday, and also the 25th anniversary of the fall of the Berlin Wall (behind which she grew up), 2014 began rather inauspiciously for her with a fractured pelvis in a ski accident. However, she was soon back on her feet and her birthday, in July, was marked by a gathering at her Christian Democratic Union (CDU) party headquarters and a lengthy lecture by the historian Jürgen Osterhammel, as well as congratulations from elsewhere on the political spectrum. Meanwhile, the anniversary of the fall of the Berlin Wall, in November, was commemorated by Merkel and guests from around the world, and by the staging of a large pop concert near the Brandenburg Gate. At the CDU's annual conference in December, Merkel was re-elected with 96.7 per cent of delegates' votes, highlighting her pre-eminent role in Germany's political scene.

Chancellor Merkel continued to confront turbulent times in Europe. Although for most of the year the common currency appeared more stable, events in Ukraine provided drama. Popular protests in February led to the toppling of President Viktor Yanukovych, and then Russia's annexation of Crimea and its fostering of instability in parts of the east of the country. Merkel and her Social Democratic foreign minister, Frank-Walter Steinmeier, backed EU sanctions against Russia and Steinmeier reacted with fury at a rally in Berlin, when a small number of activists campaigning against Germany's stance on Russia accused him of being a "warmonger". Not all German political figures were as critical of Russia, however: in April, former chancellor Gerhard Schröder celebrated his birthday with Russia's President Vladimir Putin in St Petersburg, and Philipp Missfelder, a senior CDU member of the Bundestag and the CDU's foreign affairs spokesperson, also went along. Missfelder was strongly criticised for this, especially since the event coincided with the incarceration, by pro-Russian rebels in eastern Ukraine, of a group of military observers from the OSCE, including four Germans.

In 2014, Germany saw a substantial increase in the number of new asylum claims (some 155,000 by the end of November, compared with 110,000 in 2013, and 65,000 in 2012). The largest share of these claims came from Syria, and in addition Germany agreed to take 20,000 Syrian refugees. Indeed, Germany's ministers argued that other EU member states should accept a greater responsibility for taking in Syrian refugees.

Whether as a result of increasing pressure on Germany's asylum system, of Chancellor Merkel's "grand coalition" with the main opposition party, the Social Democrats (SPD), or because of Germany's perceived role as the "paymaster of Europe", forces on the right of the political spectrum gained in strength in 2014. A eurosceptic party, the Alliance for Germany (AfD), won 7.1 per cent in the elections to the European Parliament, as well as achieving 9.7 per cent of the vote in state elections in Saxony, 10.6 per cent in Thuringia, and 12.2 per cent in Brandenburg. The party campaigned on issues such as a return to national currencies and holding a referendum about future financial contributions to the eurozone, as well as tightening the rules on benefits for migrants. Notwithstanding the AfD's election victories in 2014, however, there were signs of the internal fragmentation that had beset all previous attempts to form a serious challenger to the right of the CDU. The leading figure in the party, the economist Bernd Lucke, appeared dissatisfied with having to share the formal role as leader with two others, Frauke Petry and Konrad Adam, and pressed for the introduction of a single leader, attracting significant criticism from those who would be marginalised by such a move.

Attention was also drawn by a more radical branch of right-wing politics, the so-called "Pegida" movement ("Patriotic Europeans against the Islamisation of the Occident"). This held a first demonstration in the east German city of Dresden in October 2014, attracting 350 protestors, but by the end of the year tens of thousands were drawn to demonstrate there, although attempts to hold similar marches in other German cities, such as Bonn and Munich, attracted less of a following. The group included familiar faces from the far Right, but also seemed to attract discontented citizens who had not been involved in such activity hitherto. Germany's established politicians were unable to respond with one clear voice. The Social Democrat justice minister called the demonstrations a "disgrace for Germany", while the Christian Social Union (the CDU's sister party in Bavaria) expressed "understanding" for "peacefully demonstrating citizens". Chancellor Merkel herself was sharply critical of those behind the demonstrations in her speech at the end of the year, pointing to "prejudice, cold, and even hatred in their hearts".

Not for the first time, German politics was shaken by the Federal Constitutional Court which ruled in February that no "hurdle" should apply in the elections to the European Parliament. Previously, in order to gain representation, a party had needed to win at least 3 per cent of the vote, meaning that the smallest parties remained excluded. As a result of the Court's decision, however, at the European elections in May parties managed to win a seat with just 0.6 per cent of the vote, among them groups such as the Animal Welfare Party and a satirical organisation,

"The Party". Each won one of Germany's 96 allotted seats in the Parliament. Amongst the major parties, Merkel's Christian Democrats were comfortably in front with 35.3 per cent of the vote (34 seats), albeit slightly down on their 2009 result; the Social Democrats were in second place with 27.3 per cent (27 seats), up 6.5 per cent on a poor 2009 result, buoyed by their member Martin Schulz being the lead candidate of Social Democrats across Europe. The Greens (10.7 per cent, down 1.4 per cent) and Left Party (7.4 per cent, down 0.1 per cent) saw little change, while the liberal FDP (Free Democratic Party) achieved a truly dreadful result, winning just 3.4 per cent (down 7.6 per cent). This demonstrated with abundant clarity that the youthful FDP leader, Christian Lindner, would need to fight hard to see the party survive, after it had lost all its seats in the Bundestag the previous year (see AR 2014, pp. 24-25). The 7.1 per cent won by the newly-launched AfD no doubt contributed to the FDP's weakness, and Chancellor Merkel was irritated when the AfD joined forces with the British Conservative Party in the European Parliament.

There were three state elections, all in eastern Germany. In Saxony on 31 August the CDU was clear winner in a region in which, since reunification, it had never failed to top the poll, but the party needed a coalition partner and found one in the Social Democrats after its previous coalition partner, the FDP, failed to win any seats. The CDU's minister president of Saxony, Stanislaw Tillich, a member of the Slavic Sorb minority, comfortably won re-election to office. On 14 September, Brandenburg held its state election and the Social Democrats topped the poll, as they had in every election since reunification. It was notable that, while the SPD's score of 31.9 per cent was only slightly down on its 2009 result, the Left Party, the SPD's coalition partner in the previous parliament, fell 8.6 per cent to 18.6 per cent. Nonetheless, the Left Party once again agreed to enter a coalition with the Social Democrats and Dietmar Woidke (SPD) was re-elected minister president.

The state election in Thuringia, also on 14 September, proved to have the most significant consequences. Before the election, the state was governed by a coalition between the CDU and SPD under the CDU's Christine Lieberknecht. Although the CDU held its ground and became the largest party (with 33.5 per cent, slightly up on the previous election), the SPD lost a lot of support, its share of the vote falling from 18.5 to just 12.4 per cent. The Left Party, traditionally strong in Thuringia, won 28.2 per cent. Both Lieberknecht and the leader of the Left Party in Thuringia, Bodo Ramelow, expressed a wish to become minister president: Lieberknecht in a coalition with the SPD, Ramelow in a coalition with the SPD and the Greens. The SPD held a referendum amongst its members, who voted by a substantial majority for an alliance with Ramelow and the Greens. This gave rise to considerable public criticism (including from Federal President Joachim Gauck), but Ramelow was elected in December as the Left Party's first minister president. Ramelow, a former trade union official from West Germany, was a moderate Left Party politician and drew some criticism from within his own party for the statement in the coalition agreement that the German Democratic Republic was an "unjust state".

Another important change in German state politics was the departure of Klaus Wowereit, mayor of Berlin since 2001. A high profile SPD politician, Wowereit was one of the first openly gay figures in German political life, and was credited with having done much to give the capital its vibrancy, lively cultural scene and attraction as a tourist destination. However, recent years had been less kind to "Wowi", with the fiasco of Berlin's new airport—still unfinished and massively over-budget—a particular focus of criticism. Michael Müller, a former senator (minister) in Berlin, was elected to replace him.

The SPD suffered other internal blows during 2014. In February, Sebastian Edathy, a member of the Bundestag who had some prominence as chairman of the committee investigating crimes of the far-right NSU organisation, resigned and it emerged that he was being investigated for possession of child pornography. The affair also cost CSU politician Hans-Peter Friedrich his job. Friedrich admitted to having informed the SPD leader, Sigmar Gabriel, of the investigation into Edathy in 2013 when he (Friedrich) was Germany's interior minister, and had to resign his new post of agriculture minister when legal proceedings began against him (although these were subsequently halted). In July the SPD's spokesperson for internal affairs in the Bundestag, Michael Hartmann, had to resign after he admitted using the drug crystal meth. He was also investigated for his role in the Edathy affair after Edathy stated that Hartmann had tipped him off about the investigation into his activities.

On a happier note, the former federal president, Christian Wulff, was finally cleared of all the corruption charges he had faced, although he was bitter than prosecutors had forced him from office in 2012 (see AR 2013, p. 26)

Politicians were not the only high profile Germans to be affected by scandal in 2014. Uli Hoeness, president of the leading club, Bayern Munich FC, was sentenced in March to three-and-a-half years in prison for tax evasion. Thomas Middelhoff, the former head of media company Bertellsmann and subsequently of Arcandor, a retail group (and owner of the department store chain, Karstadt) which went bankrupt in 2009, was arrested on charges of tax evasion and embezzlement, and was sentenced in November to three years in prison.

As many European countries discussed how to tackle their budget deficits, Germany's finance minister, Wolfgang Schäuble, was able to propose a balanced budget for 2015 onwards (Germany's first since 1969); this was approved by the Federal Parliament in November. The budget was criticised by the opposition Left Party for insufficient investment in infrastructure, and by the Green Party for raiding social insurance funds in order to create the impression of balance. Germany's economic growth in 2014 was modest, with 1.2 per cent projected by the government for 2014, but unemployment towards the end of the year was 6.3 per cent, down by 1 per cent since the start of 2014, and tax revenues continued to climb. Germany's economy thus continued its reputation for robustness.

Germans had further reason to celebrate in 2014: the football World Cup in Brazil. In July, captain Philipp Lahm lifted the trophy for the fourth time in the country's history after a 1-0 victory against Argentina, with Mario Götze scoring the winning goal. Chancellor Merkel and President Gauck were photographed celebrating with the team in the changing rooms in Rio after the final whistle.

Another aspect of Germany's reputation—for efficient public transport—was substantially damaged, however. The train drivers' trade union, GDL, held a three-day strike in November, the longest in recent history, bringing trains to a standstill across the country.

Ed Turner

FRANCE

CAPITAL: Paris   AREA: 551,500 sq km   POPULATION: 66,028,467 ('13)
OFFICIAL LANGUAGE: French
HEAD OF STATE: President François Hollande (PS) (since May '12)
RULING PARTY: Socialist Party (PS)
HEAD OF GOVERNMENT: Prime Minister Manuel Valls (PS) (since April '14)
DEMOCRACY INDEX: 7.92; =27th of 167   CORRUPTION PERCEPTIONS INDEX: 69; =26th of 175
CURRENCY: Euro (Dec '14 £1.00=EUR 1.275, US$1.00=EUR 0.821)
GNI PER CAPITA: US$42,250, Intl$37,580 at PPP ('13)

IT was a year that many in France would gladly forget. The economy was stagnant throughout 2014 and unemployment stayed stubbornly over 10 per cent. Morose in January, the public mood was just as glum at Christmas. The president, François Hollande, was deeply unpopular; opening the year with a dismal 20 per cent giving him a "favourable" rating in the polls, which slid still further to a record low of 13 per cent by the end.

In a brief New Year address, Hollande admitted to having underestimated the depth of the recession and acknowledged that taxation had become too heavy (see AR 2014, p. 29). He warned that there would have to be cuts in public expenditure but also announced a €1 billion reduction in company taxation to encourage job creation. His business-friendly tone irked many on the Socialist party's left, to whom any social-democratic tendency was a form of heresy. He also called on ministers to quicken the pace of reform. This was easier said than done. A proposed "ecotax" on heavy road transport had to be abandoned in the face of violent demonstrations centred on Brittany, leaving the government with a bill for €839 million to compensate firms that had bought into the scheme. In February, many thousands of opponents of same-sex marriage—legalised in 2013—took to the streets to voice their continuing opposition to it, to homosexuals gaining access to IVF and adoption and to the teaching of gender theory in schools. A promised family law Bill, much of it uncontroversial, was quickly "postponed" until 2015. In September a strike by Air France pilots put paid to proposals for a new low-cost airline. Subsequently, pharmacists, doctors, taxi drivers, members of paralegal professions, opponents of relaxing the Sunday trading laws or of easing restrictions on inter-city coach services all resisted proposals to deregulate their sector of activity or encourage competition.

Opponents were not always successful. The government faced down a costly and disruptive strike by railway workers fearful that a proposed merger would adversely affect their working conditions. It also scored a notable success against rearguard opposition with a long overdue reduction in the number of administrative regions in metropolitan France, from 22 to 15 super-regions. Successful or not, though, all these issues took their political toll, not least in causing subsequent proposals for reform to be unduly timid.

The year also opened with an unforeseen and unwanted distraction with the revelation by a celebrity magazine of the president's liaison with an actress, complete with a pictorial spread of him arriving at a rendezvous on his scooter. His distraught companion, Valérie Trierweiler, was admitted to hospital. The breakdown in the relationship played out as soap opera before a fascinated public, shattering a longstanding convention that public figures were entitled to a private life. Hollande unceremoniously dumped both women. There was little moral condemnation of his behaviour but neither did the French relish their president becoming an object of derision. A vengeful kiss-and-tell memoir by Trierweiler gave the story a fresh airing in the autumn.

Collectively, these diverse strands contributed to a sense of incompetence, indecision and drift in high places. It was the government's misfortune that the electoral calendar offered disenchanted voters the means to punish it. In municipal elections in March, on a low turnout of 63 per cent, the Left suffered a sweeping defeat, losing 155 towns with populations of 9,000 or more (including 68 with over 30,000), mainly to the centre-right Union for a Popular Majority (UMP), though the Socialists did hold Paris, which elected its first female mayor in Anne Hidalgo. The far-right National Front (FN) won few towns but greatly increased its vote and laid the basis for its first entry into the indirectly elected upper House, the Senate, in the autumn.

Hollande acknowledged that the voters had sent a clear message: "not enough change and too much slowness; not enough jobs and too much unemployment; not enough social justice and too many taxes". In keeping with Fifth Republic practice the prime minister promptly paid for the president's failure: Jean-Marc Ayrault resigned. Hollande replaced him with the minister of the interior, Manuel Valls—energetic, tough, ambitious and popular with the general public, though too much of a social democrat for the socialist Left or for the Greens, who refused to serve under him. The new government, slimmed down from 38 ministers to 16, won a confidence vote in the National Assembly (the lower house) by 306 votes to 29. The voters were less supportive. The European Parliament elections in May were always expected to go badly for the government but they turned out to be disastrous for all the established parties. The anti-Europe, anti-immigrant, National Front, so long a pariah, headed the poll with 24.85 per cent of votes, winning 24 seats—a gain of 21. The centre-right opposition UMP took 20 seats with 20.8 per cent of votes—a loss of seven seats. The Socialists lost only one seat but trailed a miserable third with 13.98 per cent of votes, taking 13 seats. Modern Democracy (MoDem) with 9.94 per cent of votes took seven seats, gaining one. The Greens were the other big losers; they received 8.95 per cent of the votes, holding six seats and losing nine; Left Front with 6.61 per cent of votes held four seats and lost one. Turnout at 42.43 per cent was almost the same as in 2009.

The National Front clearly benefitted from the factors that brought a surge in protest votes across much of the EU, while also drawing on specifically French discontents. Its victory now posed an existential challenge to all the traditional parties. Their response had yet to emerge, not least because of their internal divisions. On the Left there were deep rifts, mainly along ideological lines, while on the Right they largely centred upon personalities, although here, too, there were tensions between europhiles and eurosceptics. The UMP had long been distracted by the rivalry between the secretary-general, Jean-François Copé, and the former prime minister, François Fillon, both with an eye on the 2017 presidential election. However, in March, accusations about Copé's links with a company that had supplied services to the UMP in the 2012 elections led to his resignation. Control of the party passed to a triumvirate of former prime ministers until its autumn congress. When Nicolas Sarkozy announced his withdrawal from politics after losing the presidency in 2012 few believed they had indeed seen the last of him. His return had been rumoured for months. He now declared his candidacy for the vacant UMP presidency and won it with a substantial, though not compelling, 65 per cent of party members voting. He was now well-placed to bid to be the UMP's candidate in the 2017 national presidential election, for which all parties were already laying their plans. He set about his task with characteristic energy and the immediate aim of binding the party's wounds. However, one obstacle of uncertain substance still hampered his putative candidacy: hanging over him was the possibility of charges of influence peddling and infringing laws on election expenditure. In July he was placed under formal examination and briefly held in custody—but not charged. He denied all allegations of wrongdoing, alleging that he was the victim of dirty politics.

Meanwhile, the government wrestled with the economy and the public finances. Prime Minister Valls ordered cuts of €50 billion over the next three years: local government would have €11 billion less to spend and central departments would see their budgets cut by 15 per cent. Many public sector jobs would go. Only education, policing and justice would be spared. A range of social benefits would be frozen, though there would be a modest easement for very low incomes. Companies would receive reductions in payroll taxes and corporation taxes in the hope they would create more jobs. This change of emphasis to a more business-friendly approach had a mixed reception. Business was naturally gratified but tension was increasing in the Socialist ranks. In August, the minister for the economy, Arnaud Montebourg, who had taken the job only a few weeks earlier, assailed government economic policy, denouncing the "absurd" insistence on austerity, which was throttling recovery, aggravating the deficit and would result in deflation. He called for a fresh concentration on growth. He and two other ministers immediately left the government. With symbolic resonance he was replaced by a former investment banker, Emmanuel Macron. Rallying the party, Valls denied pursuing austerity, assuring it that the traditional French welfare state and the cherished 35-hour working week were not in danger. The Cabinet was now more cohesive; Valls even felt secure enough to tell a conference of employers, "I love business" and win their applause—unthinkable when the Socialists first came to office. Nevertheless, he still had to contend with a substantial bunch of left-wing dissidents on the back-benches. In September he challenged them with a confidence vote in the National Assembly, which he won by 269 votes to 244.

By now, though, it was clear that, far from moving towards the EU target of 3 per cent, the public deficit would actually increase in 2015, and an early resumption of significant growth remained problematic. In December, EU finance ministers ruled that the draft budget breached the EU's Stability and Growth Pact. France would again have to approach her increasingly sceptical partners for a delay in meeting her commitments. Action was deferred until March and France was told that further structural reforms were needed. The cruel reality was that, for all the year's speeches, programmes and resolutions, none had as yet produced substantial results.

France's accumulation of economic and political woes and the strained political and personal relationship between Hollande and Germany's Chancellor Angela Merkel weakened French influence within the EU. France was also felt not to have been a team player, notably by persisting for months with the intention to deliver two *Mistral* class amphibious assault ships to Russia, despite the western embargo over Russian action in Ukraine. Outside Europe, the picture was rather different. Hollande, so indecisive at home, was markedly more assured in dealing with crises in the Middle East, where he was a willing ally of the United States, in contrast to the prickliness and suspicion of a recent past. He was hawkish over Syria from an early stage and France was the first western country to dispatch planes against ISIS targets as well as supplying arms to the Kurdish region of Iraq. The National Assembly approved 339-246 a (non-binding) resolution recognising a separate Palestinian state and French support at the UN Security Council for a Jordanian resolution on recognition drew Israel's ire. In Africa, a French force countered the terrorist threat in the Sahel, working closely with the USA. A key factor in the French approach was apprehension about the possible radicalisation among the 5 million-strong Muslim population at home, particularly from returning jihadists.

Martin Harrison

ITALY

CAPITAL: Rome   AREA: 301,340 sq km   POPULATION: 59,831,093 ('13)
OFFICIAL LANGUAGE: Italian
HEAD OF STATE: President Giorgio Napolitano (since May '06)
RULING PARTIES: Democratic Party (PD)-led Coalition
HEAD OF GOVERNMENT: Prime Minister Matteo Renzi (PD) (since Feb '14)
DEMOCRACY INDEX: 7.85; 31st of 167   CORRUPTION PERCEPTIONS INDEX: 43; =69th of 175
CURRENCY: Euro (Dec '14 £1.00=EUR 1.275, US$1.00=EUR 0.821)
GNI PER CAPITA: US$34,400, Intl$34,100 at PPP ('13)

IN many respects 2014 began in Italy on 22 February, when the new government of Matteo Renzi was sworn in. At 39, Renzi became the country's youngest ever prime minister, having led a campaign within the Democratic Party (PD) to "scrap" its older leaders. This had climaxed in his overthrowing the PD party secretary, Pier Luigi Bersani, in December 2013, following the party's poor performance in the February 2013 general election (see AR 2014, pp. 32-33). Two months later, then, he defenestrated the prime minister, his colleague, Enrico Letta. Catapulted into national office from Florence, where he had become mayor in 2009, Renzi promised to rejuvenate Italy. The change was symbolised in his informal dress style, flashy repartee and ostentatious use of Twitter. His new Cabinet comprised the PD and a clutch of centrist parties and party fragments, most notably the New Centre Right (NCD). This had split from Forza Italia (FI) in November 2013 when three-time prime minister Silvio Berlusconi, on the eve of his expulsion from Parliament, had withdrawn his party's support from the Letta government. More innovative than the government coalition formula was the gender balance, at least at the ministerial level, where half of the 16 ministers were female. Of the 58 members of the government, however, 41 were male.

The new government gained a good deal of popular support, though well-informed observers were sceptical of whether its ability to mobilise such enthusiasm would suffice to overcome the many vetoes that tended to block policy innovation. Nominally, the new government proposed to boost the economy by cutting payroll taxes through reducing the costs of the public administration by 15 per cent; providing kindergartens for 40 per cent of children, thus boosting the female employment rate whilst creating nearly half-a-million jobs; and promoting foreign direct investment by taking stronger action against tax evasion and corruption. Liberal measures such as civil partnerships for same-sex couples were also promised; as well as environmental ones, such as ending the reinstatement of nuclear power undertaken by the Berlusconi governments; and populist ones, such as abolishing public funding to parties (from 2017). Renzi also promised bold constitutional proposals to end the country's equal bicameralism by turning the Senate into a chamber of the regions and local authorities whilst also effecting electoral reform. To achieve these aims on a consensual footing, thus avoiding an opposition veto and referendum, Renzi shocked his supporters by co-opting Berlusconi, still FI's de facto leader, albeit now a convicted criminal (for tax evasion) doing community service, and banned from seeking public office for six years.

In the European Parliament elections held on 25 May, Renzi's PD performed spectacularly well. It gained 41 per cent of the vote, more than the once predominant Christian Democrats had ever obtained, becoming the leading party in 107 of Italy's 110 provinces. Essentially, Renzi won the votes of those who, in 2013, had voted for Mario Monti's Civic Choice (SC). Forza Italia fared badly, becoming the third party, with just 17 per cent of the vote, 4 per cent less than the insurgent, anti-establishment, Five Star Movement (5SM). This latter continued to hold up in opinion polls throughout 2014, though it haemorrhaged MPs unhappy with the despotic, extra-parliamentary leadership of Beppe Grillo and Roberto Casaleggio. Two other parties gained seats in the European elections. The NCD's joint list with the tiny Centre Union (UDC), the historical heir of the Christian Democratic centre-right, just surmounted the 4 per cent threshold, electing three MEPs. The alliance was more significant than this result suggested, however. In the Italian Senate, where the PD (and government) was weak, the joint parliamentary group, established in December 2014, had 11 per cent of the seats.

More electorally successful was the Northern League (LN). Now under the leadership of Matteo Salvini, the party gained 6 per cent of the vote, demonstrating its ability to survive the resignation of its historic leader, Umberto Bossi. The League's success was partly due to its becoming Italy's anti-EU, anti-immigrant party. It thus tended to becoming a nationwide party, having originated as a regional movement. Indeed, in early December Salvini launched a new movement, "We're with Salvini", a personal party intended to spearhead the League's expansion in central and southern Italy. By the end of 2014, the League's support in the polls had doubled. Some predicted growth to rival FI and the 5SM. Indeed, in the November regional election in Emilia Romagna, the League provided the regional presidential candidate for the centre-right alliance, gaining 19 per cent of the vote to just 8 per cent for FI. Salvini, another youngster at 41, was the other major reason for the party's success. By the end of the year he was trusted by over one-third of the electorate, well ahead of Berlusconi and Grillo (at around 20 per cent each), and second only to Renzi.

Renzi's support in the opinion polls peaked at 74 per cent in June in the wake of the PD's European election triumph. The new prime minister now gained recognition as a major European figure on the eve of Italy's chairing of the Council of the European Union, from July to December. As leader of the largest social democratic grouping in the European Parliament, Renzi became, to some extent, the leader of the opposition to the "austerity politics" championed by Germany's Chancellor Angela Merkel. Insofar as Renzi intended to remain loyal to the EU's economic management criteria, however, he remained part of the dominant centrist coalition, against which Europe's new wave of anti-establishment parties made significant advances. The shift in the balance of power in Europe was thus subtle, even minimal, with the president of the European Central Bank, Mario Draghi, remaining a key figure.

In autumn negotiations with the European Commission, Italy's economics minister, Pier Carlo Padoan, urged the need for Italy to avoid a fourth year of recession whilst Renzi adopted a more confrontational bargaining strategy. In the end, agreement was reached that Italy's deficit be cut by 0.3 per cent in 2015, rather than the 0.1 per cent which Italy initially proposed, or the 0.7 per cent apparently sought by the Commission. This necessitated €18 billion in tax cuts. Already a 1 million-strong trade union rally had taken place against austerity politics on 26 October, followed by a general strike on 12 December.

Whilst these protests caused Renzi to adopt a less hostile stance to the union confederations, the bigger picture was one of declining union influence and a changing relationship between PD voters and the unions. In the previous five years, public support for the main, socialist union confederation (the CGIL) had fallen from 35 to 22 per cent, whilst that for the Catholic (CISL) and reformist (UIL) confederations had fallen to 16 per cent. Support for the CGIL in the changing PD electorate had fallen from 53 per cent in 2012 to half that. Concomitantly, support for the PD from entrepreneurs and the self-employed grew from 13 per cent in 2013 to double that in the European Parliament vote and higher still in subsequent polls. Under Renzi's leadership, the PD was becoming a catch-all party. By the end of 2014 it had won four regions from the centre-right (giving it control of 15 of the 18 ethnically Italian regions); and increased its share of provincial capitals and large towns to some two-thirds of those contested. The protests of the party's Left were muted, though a split was debated—and would be consistent with the party's history. The main response of disillusioned voters, visible especially in the November regional elections in Calabria and Emilia Romagna, was abstention. The Left, Freedom and Ecology party (SEL) remained weak (under 5 per cent), whilst the 5SM vote stalled.

The scale of the problems that Renzi faced was underlined by continuing economic stagnation, major local government scandals and increasing immigration. In June, 35 people, including the mayor of Venice (of the PD), were arrested over corruption related to the flood defence system. On 22 July Parliament voted to allow the arrest of the former regional president, 1995-2010 (of FI). In mid-July, meanwhile, the Lombard regional president, Roberto Maroni (LN), and his head of secretariat were placed under investigation for corruption. In early December, the "Mafia capital" scandal saw 37 people arrested in Rome, accused of skimming millions of euros from public contracts with the connivance of politicians of Left and Right. Assets worth €250 million were seized. Some believed these developments jeopardised Italy's bid for the 2024 Olympic Games.

Migration to Italy across the Mediterranean increased to some 170,000 during 2014. The Italian navy's humanitarian operation, Mare Nostrum, saved thousands of lives but provoked internal opposition, not least from the LN. Formally, the operation ended on 1 November when, following the government's attempt to broaden the operation to other European countries, the EU border agency, Frontex, began collaboration with the Italian navy in Operation Triton. For the first time, the onset of winter did not bring a reduction in the rate of attempted crossings, confirming the structural nature of the migration phenomenon. In practice, the role of the Italian navy seemed to change little, if at all.

The government's main economic initiative, the so-called Jobs Act, was approved by Parliament in May and the first two decrees implementing specific measures were passed in December. The new legislation made hiring and firing easier whilst extending universal unemployment benefits, but most commentators were sceptical that the decrees would have a major impact on job creation.

In late December, President Giorgio Napolitano confirmed that, given his advancing years, he would resign his unprecedented second mandate in mid-January. The new year (2015) would thus see Parliament grappling with the election of a new president as well as, at least in intention, electoral reform.

Mark Donovan

BELGIUM, THE NETHERLANDS, AND LUXEMBOURG

Belgium

CAPITAL: Brussels   AREA: 30,530 sq km   POPULATION: 11,195,138 ('13)
OFFICIAL LANGUAGES: French, Flemish & German
HEAD OF STATE: King Philippe (since July '13)
RULING PARTIES: Four-party coalition
HEAD OF GOVERNMENT: Prime Minister Charles Michel (Reformist Movement) (since Oct '14)
DEMOCRACY INDEX: 8.05; 23rd of 167   CORRUPTION PERCEPTIONS INDEX: 76; =15th of 175
CURRENCY: Euro (Dec '14 £1.00=EUR 1.275, US$1.00=EUR 0.821)
GNI PER CAPITA: US$45,210, Intl$40,280 at PPP ('13)

The Netherlands

CAPITAL: Amsterdam   AREA: 41,530 sq km   POPULATION: 16,804,224 ('13)
OFFICIAL LANGUAGE: Dutch
HEAD OF STATE: King Willem-Alexander (since April '13)
RULING PARTIES: People's Party for Freedom and Democracy (VVD) and Labour Party (PvdA)
HEAD OF GOVERNMENT: Prime Minister Mark Rutte (VVD) (since Oct '10)
DEMOCRACY INDEX: 8.84; 11th of 167   CORRUPTION PERCEPTIONS INDEX: 83; 8th of 175
CURRENCY: Euro (Dec '14 £1.00=EUR 1.275, US$1.00=EUR 0.821)
GNI PER CAPITA: US$47,440, Intl$43,220 at PPP ('13)

Luxembourg

CAPITAL: Luxembourg   AREA: 2,590 sq km   POPULATION: 543,202 ('13)
OFFICIAL LANGUAGE: Letzeburgish
HEAD OF STATE: Grand Duke Henri (since Oct '00)
RULING PARTIES: Democratic Party (DP)-led coalition
HEAD OF GOVERNMENT: Prime Minister Xavier Bettel (DP) (since Dec '13)
DEMOCRACY INDEX: 8.88; 10th of 167   CORRUPTION PERCEPTIONS INDEX: 82; 9th of 175
CURRENCY: Euro (Dec '14 £1.00=EUR 1.275, US$1.00=EUR 0.821)
GNI PER CAPITA: US$71,810, Intl$59,750 at PPP ('12)

ON 25 May Belgians went to the polls in three elections: to the federal Chamber of Representatives, regional assemblies and the European Parliament. (There were no elections to the upper house, the Senate, which was no longer directly elected under reforms approved under the old Parliament.) Since voting was formally compulsory in **Belgium** the turnout was a shade under 90 per cent. After a campaign that mostly centred on the economy and pensions reform, the outcome at the federal level was that the separatist New Flemish Alliance (N-VA) gained substantial ground, winning 33 of the 150 seats, a gain of six. The Socialists lost ground with 23 seats (down three), while the liberal-conservative Reformist Movement (MR) won 20 seats (up two) and Christian Democrats and Flemish (CD&V) with 18 (down one), followed by the Open Flemish Liberals (Open Vld) with 14 seats (up one) and the Socialist Party-Differently (SP-D) with 13 seats (unchanged). The big losers were the far-right separatist Flemish Interest, which lost nine of its 12 seats. Other parties winning seats were the Greens with six (down one), Humanists with nine (unchanged), Workers Party three (up two), Francophone Democrats and Federalists two (a gain of two), Ecologists six (up two) and the People's Party with a single seat (up one), bringing the tally of parties in the new Chamber to 13.

Following customary practice King Philippe invited Bart De Wever, the N-VA leader, as head of the largest party, to explore the possibilities for a new coalition. Bargaining over federal and regional ministerial posts ensued until, after two changes of "explorer", and amid mounting concern about the eurozone economy and with the deadline for submitting Belgium's expenditure plans to the EU rapidly approaching, a deal including the 2015 budget was finally struck on 7 October. The new government comprised three Flemish and one Walloon party but the new prime minister, Charles Michel, from MR, was French speaking (and also the youngest Belgian to hold the office). The Socialists were left out of power for the first time in 25 years.

The government introduced a range of measures designed to make the economy more competitive, including an increase in the state pensionable age, curbing indexation of wages, streamlining the civil service, tax reforms to cut labour costs and tighter rules on immigration and asylum. The unions gave the changes a hostile reception; scattered strikes ensued, culminating in a one-day national strike that paralysed the country in December.

In February, after fierce debate, and by 86 votes to 44, with 12 abstentions, the Chamber of Representatives voted to allow euthanasia for terminally ill children. There was also a growing preoccupation with terrorism. On the eve of the elections four people were shot dead at the Jewish museum in Brussels, allegedly by a French Muslim. In September the trial opened of 46 alleged members of Sharia4Belgium, officially classed as a terrorist group. Later, concerns deepened over young Belgians going to fight as jihadis in Syria or Iraq and the possible dangers when they returned.

In **Luxembourg**, that most europhile of EU member states, elections to the European Parliament passed quietly. The turnout was 90 per cent. No seats changed hands; the Christian Social Party held its three seats with a gain of 6.29 per cent in its share of the vote, while the Liberal Party (DP), the Greens and the Socialist Workers Party (LSAP) each held their single seat but with a drop in their share of the poll. Three smaller parties were unrepresented.

Long famed for its banking secrecy laws, Luxembourg finally bowed to international pressure to observe international norms on financial transparency. In the event this caused little pain, but worse followed thanks to the publication by the WikiLeaks website of material provided via the International Consortium of Investigative Journalists. It demonstrated in detail the scale and ingenuity of tax avoidance by international companies channelling their profits through low-tax Luxembourg. Anger grew with the revelation that these schemes had been facilitated by Jean-Claude Juncker, until recently Luxembourg's prime minister and long-serving chairman of the EU's finance ministers, now freshly minted president of the European Commission. Juncker was unrepentant.

There were further developments in the long-running Bommeleeër affair—a series of bomb attacks in the mid-1980s for which nobody had been convicted, though complicity in high places was sensationally rumoured. The trial of two former police officers who were allegedly implicated was abruptly interrupted in May when six former gendarmes were formally investigated. A few days later, with no official explanation but dark hints, three very senior policemen were removed from their posts.

Prosperous Luxembourg may be, but it was not immune to the crisis in the euro-zone: the government put forward 258 measures to enhance transparency and efficiency and bring the public debt down from 25 per cent of GDP to 21.8 per cent by 2018. The chief elements in the package were an increase of 2 per cent in VAT rates and a curbing of pension indexation.

In **the Netherlands**, 17 July would long be remembered as the day when 298 people, two-thirds of them Dutch, died when Malaysian Airlines Flight MH17, from Amsterdam to Kuala Lumpur, was shot down over eastern Ukraine. Nobody claimed responsibility for the attack and, at least until the official investigation under the Dutch Safety Board had made its final report, there would be no conclusive proof of guilt, though Ukrainian pro-Russian separatist militia were the most frequently canvassed culprits. Meanwhile, the task of retrieving the remains of the victims and the aircraft wreckage from a war zone proved desperately slow and was frequently interrupted; large silently respectful crowds lined the route of the funeral cortèges as the remains were brought home.

As in neighbouring countries, there was mounting concern at the numbers of young Muslims going to fight in Syria, and the threat they might pose on their return. The Netherlands' official involvement in the Middle East conflict took the form of a flight of F-16s joining coalition action there against the forces of ISIS. For the first time in several years, the Netherlands' budget included increases in defence and security expenditure. Meanwhile, drawing a line under an inglorious episode from the recent past, a Dutch civil court ruled that the state must compensate the families of over 5,000 Bosniaks (Bosnian Muslims) whom Dutch UN peacekeepers had failed to protect from Bosnian Serb troops at Srebrenica in eastern Bosnia in 1995 (see AR 1996, p. 121)

Economically, the country stayed on course to meet its targets for public expenditure and debt reduction and the IMF and the European Commission concurred that it was emerging from recession—though growth remained fragile. With unemployment persistently high, a low-key "prudent" budget encouraged innovation and job creation, with measures to reduce labour costs, while the jobless would lose benefits after two years rather than three and would have to accept lower-grade jobs after being unemployed for more than six months. There was strong adverse reaction to the government's decision to abolish student grants.

Municipal elections in March were marked by the success of the liberal-democratic D66, in Amsterdam and a string of other cities, at the expense of the Labour Party (PvdA) and the right-wing Party for Freedom and Democracy (VVD). In the European Parliament elections in May D66 again prospered, gaining a seat and increasing its share of the vote by 4 per cent. The Christian Democrats (CDA) were losers, along with the Party for Freedom (PVV), whose leader, Geert Wilders, had scandalised some voters with offensive references to Moroccans.

Martin Harrison

DENMARK, ICELAND, NORWAY, SWEDEN AND FINLAND

Denmark

CAPITAL: Copenhagen   AREA: 43,090 sq km   POPULATION: 5,613,706 ('13)
OFFICIAL LANGUAGE: Danish
HEAD OF STATE: Queen Margrethe II (since Jan '72)
RULING PARTIES: Social Democrat (SD)-led minority coalition
HEAD OF GOVERNMENT: Prime Minister Helle Thorning-Schmidt (SD) (since Oct '11)
DEMOCRACY INDEX: 9.38; 4th of 167   CORRUPTION PERCEPTIONS INDEX: 92; 1st of 175
CURRENCY: Danish Krone (Dec '14   £1.00=DKK 9.49, US$1.00=DKK 6.12)
GNI PER CAPITA: US$61,160, Intl$44,460 at PPP ('13)

Iceland

CAPITAL: Reykjavík   AREA: 103,000 sq km   POPULATION: 323,002 ('13)
OFFICIAL LANGUAGE: Icelandic
HEAD OF STATE: President Ólafur Ragnar Grímsson (since Aug '96)
RULING PARTIES: Progressive Party-Independence Party coalition
HEAD OF GOVERNMENT: Prime Minister Sigmundur David Gunnlaugsson (Progressive Party) (since May '13)
DEMOCRACY INDEX: 9.65; 3rd of 167   CORRUPTION PERCEPTIONS INDEX: 79; =12th of 175
CURRENCY: Icelandic Krona (Dec '14 £1.00=ISK 197.1, US$1.00=ISK 126.9)
GNI PER CAPITA: US$43,930, Intl$38,870 at PPP ('13)

Norway

CAPITAL: Oslo   AREA: 323,800 sq km   POPULATION: 5,084,190 ('13)
OFFICIAL LANGUAGE: Norwegian
HEAD OF STATE: King Harald V (since Jan '91)
RULING PARTIES: Conservative Party (H)-led coalition
HEAD OF GOVERNMENT: Prime Minister Erna Solberg (H) (since Oct '13)
DEMOCRACY INDEX: 9.93; 1st of 167   CORRUPTION PERCEPTIONS INDEX: 86; =5th of 175
CURRENCY: Norwegian Krone (Dec '14 £1.00=NOK 11.57, US$1.00=NOK 7.45)
GNI PER CAPITA: US$102,610, Intl$66,520 at PPP ('13)

Sweden

CAPITAL: Stockholm   AREA: 450,290 sq km   POPULATION: 9,592,552 ('13)
OFFICIAL LANGUAGE: Swedish
HEAD OF STATE: King Carl XVI Gustav (since Sept '73)
RULING PARTIES: Social Democratic Party (SAP)-Green Party (MP) coalition
HEAD OF GOVERNMENT: Prime Minister Stefan Löfven (SAP) (since Oct '14)
DEMOCRACY INDEX: 9.73; 2nd of 167   CORRUPTION PERCEPTIONS INDEX: 87; 4th of 175
CURRENCY: Swedish Krona (Dec '14 £1.00=SEK 12.15, US$1.00=SEK 7.83)
GNI PER CAPITA: US$59,240, Intl$44,760 at PPP ('13)

Finland

CAPITAL: Helsinki   AREA: 338,150 sq km   POPULATION: 5,439,407 ('13)
OFFICIAL LANGUAGES: Finnish & Swedish
HEAD OF STATE: President Sauli Niinisto (KOK) (since March '12)
RULING PARTIES: National Coalition Party (KOK)-led coalition
HEAD OF GOVERNMENT: Prime Minister Alexander Stubb (KOK) (since June '14)
DEMOCRACY INDEX: 9.03; 9th of 167   CORRUPTION PERCEPTIONS INDEX: 89; 3rd of 175
CURRENCY: Euro (Dec '14 £1.00=EUR 1.275, US$1.00=EUR 0.821)
GNI PER CAPITA: US$47,110, Intl$38,480 at PPP ('13)

THE year 2014 was a turbulent one for Nordic politics, marked by unstable governments and many Cabinet changes. In **Sweden**, Fredrik Reinfeldt resigned as prime minister and chair of the conservative Moderate Party (M) as a result of the parliamentary elections on 14 September. With Reinfeldt's own party particularly struggling (down 6.7 per cent since the 2010 elections to take 23.3 per cent), his electoral coalition ended up with 38.4 per cent of the votes, whereas the rival block in the race for government received 43.6 per cent: the Social Democrats (SAP) rose 0.4 of a percentage point to 31 per cent, the Left Party (V) up 0.1 to 5.7 per cent and the Greens (MP) down 0.5 to 6.7 per cent.

The main winner of the elections was, however, the populist Sweden Democrats (SD), which, with 12.9 per cent (a rise of 7.2 per cent), became the third largest party. Polls suggested that SD—being the only party with an explicitly anti-immigration profile—had stolen votes particularly from the Moderates. Some analysts argued that Reinfeldt had made a crucial mistake in urging his voters to "open their hearts" to increased immigration only four weeks before the elections. SD remained stigmatised in the campaign, with all the other parties promising to cede them no influence whatsoever. But the results gave SD a pivotal role in the parliament, since neither of the rival coalitions had a majority.

The Social Democratic Party (SAP) leader, Stefan Löfven, formed a minority coalition government consisting only of the Social Democrats and the Greens. Representing merely 138 of the 349 seats in the parliament, Löfven's government was weak from the outset and rested on support from not only the Left Party but also from the conservative block. But the first major hurdle proved fatal. On 3 December, the conservative block presented its own budget proposal for which it gained a majority in parliament with the support of SD. Thus Löfven found himself in the precarious situation of having to govern with the budget of the opposition. Refusing to resign, Löfven saw no other solution than to threaten fresh elections. However, on 27 December, he reached an agreement with the conservative block that rendered this unnecessary. According to this "December Agreement", the two major blocks would not vote against the government's budget if this looked likely to be rejected. The agreement was widely welcomed as a harbinger of stability and a way to minimise the influence of SD, though some commentators suggested it violated basic principles of parliamentary democracy.

The year saw major reshuffles in **Finland's** government. On 5 April Jyrki Katainen announced his retirement as prime minister and as chairman of the conservative National Coalition Party (KOK), in order to take up a post as vice-president of the new European Commission. At the KOK convention on 14 July, the former foreign minister and minister of foreign trade, Alexander Stubb, was chosen as Katainen's successor. A popular figure on social media and particularly among the liberal urban elite, Stubb was unable to appeal to a wider audience and in December KOK had lost 4.5 percentage points in the opinion polls, falling to 17.3 per cent. The other major party in the governing coalition, the Social Democrats (SDP), also changed their leader in 2014 as Antti Rinne defeated Jutta Urpilainen at the party convention on 9 May. Rinne's trade union background appealed to members who believed that Urpilainen had compromised party principles in her collaboration with KOK. On 6 June, Rinne also replaced Urpilainen as minister of finance.

The Finnish government was also destabilised by the departure of two parties. On 25 March, the Left Alliance (VAS) resigned following disagreement over a package of spending cuts in the social sector. Later, on 9 September, the Greens (VIHR) followed suit as a result of the government decision to proceed with plans to build Finland's fifth nuclear power plant. Although it had been expected, the decision was controversial, since the power consortium that had been awarded the contract, Fennovoima, had commissioned the Russian state-owned company, Rosatom, to build the plant. Given the EU sanctions against Russia, there were accusations of a return to the politics of "finlandisation".

In **Denmark**, the revolving door of Prime Minister Helle Thorning-Schmidt's Social Democrat-led government continued to turn as Annette Vilhelmsen's Socialist People's Party (SF) left the coalition on 30 January, following the decision to sell 19 per cent of the state-owned energy company, DONG, to the US investment banking firm, Goldman Sachs, for 8 billion krone. Polls suggested that 68 per cent of Danes were opposed to the deal. Some claimed that the price was too low, but for the Socialists, Goldman Sachs was a particularly unpopular suitor because of its alleged tax evasion strategies. Facing uproar from within her party, Vilhelmsen chose to withdraw SF from government and to resign as party chairman. On 2 February, Thorning-Schmidt announced a new minority coalition government, comprising only the Social Democrats (SD) and the Social Liberal Party (RV).

The major opposition party in Denmark, the liberal Left (V), was unable to capitalise on the government's difficulties as it remained beset by scandals involving its chairman, Lars Lokke Rasmussen. The storm that had ensued from the GGGI affair in 2013, when Rasmussen had spent over 1 million krone on extravagant travel arrangements as chairman of the Global Green Growth Institute (see AR 2013, pp. 42), had barely calmed down before it was revealed, on 12 May, that Rasmussen had used party funds to buy clothing costing in total 152,000 krone. This, in combination with an appalling result in the European Parliament elections, made Rasmussen the target of heavy criticism but, following a seven-hour long meeting on 3 June, the party board agreed that he would continue as chairman.

As elsewhere in Europe, elections in Nordic EU member-states to the European Parliament (EP) on 25 May saw established parties struggling and smaller parties, often with populist agendas, thrive. In Denmark, the Danish People's Party (DF) took first place in a national election for the first time, with a landslide 26.6 per cent of the vote (up by 11.3 per cent since the previous EP elections in 2009). The DF's success was undoubtedly facilitated by the struggles of both the government—the Social Democrats declined 2.4 per cent to 19.1—and Lokke Rasmussen's crisis-stricken Left (V) (down 3.5 per cent to 16.7). In Finland, the True

Finns ended in third place (up 3.1 per cent to 12.9), below KOK (22.6 per cent, down 0.6) and the Centre Party (19.7 per cent, up 0.6). In Sweden, SD received 9.7 per cent (up 6.4), but it was two parties to the left of SD that were the main surprises. The Greens (MP) at 15.4 per cent (up 4.4) became the second largest party, behind the Social Democrats on 24.2 (down 0.2), whilst Feminist Initiative (FI) received 5.5 per cent of the votes, making Soraya Post Europe's first ever MEP from an exclusively feminist party.

In the Nordic countries that were not part of the European Union, **Iceland's** capital, Reykjavik, got a new mayor as a result of municipal elections on 31 May which saw Dagur B. Eggertsson's Social Democratic Alliance secure 31.9 per cent of the votes (up 12.8 points since 2010). The former mayor, comedian Jón Gnarr, had announced his retirement in advance and the Bright Future party, the successor to Gnarr's Best Party, was unable to repeat its success of 2010, falling 19.1 per cent to 15.6 per cent. The elections saw the Independence Party prevail in all municipalities outside Reykjavik, but the main talking point was the derogatory remarks of the Progressive Party's Sveinbjorg Birna Sveinbjornsdottir about plans to construct a mosque in Iceland.

Immigration was also central to the so-called "leak-affair", which ultimately saw Hanna Birna Kristjansdottir of the Independence Party step down as interior minister on 21 November after her assistant had been convicted for having leaked confidential information regarding an asylum seeker in order to dampen planned protests against his eviction.

By comparison with the struggles of her Nordic colleagues, the life of Erna Solberg's Conservative party (H) coalition in **Norway** was surprisingly calm, despite the fact that towards the end of 2014 the record low global oil price put an unusual dent in Norwegian economic forecasts. In May the government did, however, receive criticism for snubbing the Dalai Lama when he visited Oslo at the invitation of the Nobel committee to mark the 25th anniversary of the award of his Nobel Peace Prize (see AR 1989, p. 430). The government wanted to avoid adding further damage to relations with China, strained since 2010 when the Peace Prize had been awarded to the Chinese dissident, Liu Xiabo.

On 28 March it was announced that the former Norwegian prime minister, Jens Stoltenberg, would take over from the Dane, Anders Fogh Rasmussen, as general secretary of NATO. Thus Stoltenberg resigned as chairman of the Norwegian Labour Party (AP), with the former foreign minister Jonas Gahr Store being elected to succeed him.

Norwegian summer holidays were interrupted on 24 July when the police security service announced that it had information that individuals affiliated with an extremist Islamist group in Syria were planning a terrorist attack in Norway. Security measures were put in place at strategic locations and, with the 2011 Utoya massacre still a vivid memory (see AR 2012, p. 45), parents were afraid of sending their children to summer camps. However, nothing transpired and the alert was called off within a week.

Defence and security were matters of concern in the Nordic countries in 2014, following Russia's annexation of Crimea, the situation in east Ukraine in general, and the repeated violations of Nordic airspace by Russian military aircraft in particular. In October there was even talk about a return of the Cold War, as the Swedish navy conducted a large-scale operation provoked by unidentified underwater activity in the archipelago of Stockholm. In the media, links were drawn to the submarine hunts of the 1980s. Though the underwater vessel remained unidentified, the incident fuelled the debate about whether Sweden (and Finland) might one day join NATO. Relations with NATO were already close; in February, Finland and Sweden joined a NATO-led exercise—the Iceland Air Meet 2014—at the former US airbase at Keflavik.

On 30 October Sweden became the eighth EU member state to recognise the state of Palestine. Foreign Minister Margot Wallstrom argued that peace negotiations would benefit from the participation of two, more equal, parties. Among the Nordic countries, Iceland recognised Palestine in 2011.

In Uppsala, Antje Jackelén was installed as the first ever female archbishop of the Church of Sweden on 15 June. Meanwhile, in Finland, Parliament approved a citizens' initiative for a gender-neutral marriage law on 28 November, thus joining the rest of the Nordic countries in accepting gay marriage.

The Copenhagen Zoo came under fire in February following the decision to put down the two-year old giraffe, Marius. The director of the Zoo received death threats but was later elected Copenhagener of the year for his handling of the international media storm.

Nature showed its might again in 2014. After weeks of anticipation on Iceland, the Holuhraun volcanic eruption started on 31 August and showed no signs of diminishing by the end of the year. With a lava field covering an area larger than 80 sq km, the eruption was said to be the largest (by volume) in 232 years.

Dry weather and stormy winds proved destructive as 42 houses were burned down in the fire that ravaged the historically significant Laerdal village in western Norway on 18 January. No lives were lost. The exceptionally warm summer was a contributing factor to the largest wildfire in Sweden in 40 years, which stretched over 150 sq km of the Vastmanland region in the beginning of August. One life was lost in the fire. There was good news in the autumn for the Baltic Sea, widely considered one of the most polluted on the planet, when a new "saline pulse"—a natural phenomenon, last seen in 2003—pushed a large influx of much needed salt water through the Danish sounds.

Johan Strang

AUSTRIA

CAPITAL: Vienna   AREA: 83,870 sq km   POPULATION: 8,473,786 ('13)
OFFICIAL LANGUAGE: German
HEAD OF STATE: Federal President Heinz Fischer (since July '04)
RULING PARTIES: "Grand Coalition" of Social Democratic Party (SPÖ) and Austrian People's Party
    (ÖVP)
HEAD OF GOVERNMENT: Chancellor Werner Faymann (SPÖ) Federal (since Dec '08)
DEMOCRACY INDEX: 8.48; 13th of 167   CORRUPTION PERCEPTIONS INDEX: 72; 23rd of 175
CURRENCY: Euro (Dec '14 £1.00=EUR 1.275, US$1.00=EUR 0.821)
GNI PER CAPITA: US$48,610, Intl$43,840 at PPP ('13)

AUSTRIA'S reconstituted Social Democrat (SPÖ) and People's Party (ÖVP) government had achieved a wafer-thin plurality of votes (51 per cent) and seats (54 per cent) in the general election of September 2013. Despite promises to the contrary, the coalition proved to be as inharmonious and incapable of delivering reform as had its predecessor. Its aversion to political risk was enhanced by the parties' poor opinion poll ratings. By January, their combined strength had plummeted to the low 40s and only restabilised at just over 50 per cent from late October. Until then, most polls had been led by the right-wing radical Freedom Party (FPÖ), typically by up to 3 points over Chancellor Werner Faymann's SPÖ. Meanwhile, Vice-Chancellor Michael Spindelegger's ÖVP seemed rooted in third place, occasionally 9 or 10 points adrift and often under 20 per cent.

Weak poll ratings exacerbated conflict within and between the governing parties. Weeks after May's coalition budget agreement, the SPÖ succumbed to pressure from its trade union allies and demanded a growth package featuring a wealth tax and early tax reductions on labour. There were even threats to trigger new elections, though in reality, both parties knew these would favour the FPÖ and perhaps end Austria's tradition of grand coalition government. Branding the unions' proposals "irresponsible", Finance Minister Spindelegger argued for expenditure cuts, but was openly criticised within a traditionally highly decentralised ÖVP that was increasingly nervous about its poll rating. He was further damaged by the coalition's controversial decision in June to void Carinthia's deficiency guarantees for the nationalised Hypo Alpe-Adria bank, to which Moodys responded by downgrading Austrian banks' credit rating. On 26 August 2014, Spindelegger unexpectedly resigned from all political offices, criticising those in the ÖVP who had "jumped on the populist bandwagon". He was immediately replaced by Economics Minister Reinhold Mitterlehner, who was endorsed by over 99 per cent of delegates at November's party congress, and by the end of 2014 the ÖVP had achieved a modest poll lead. Meanwhile, Faymann's union critics had been joined inter alia by left-wingers incensed by high levels of youth unemployment and the SPÖ women's section, which attacked his recruitment practices. At the 28 November party conference Faymann was re-elected by a mere 83.9 per cent of votes, an outcome that SPÖ left-wingers dismissed as "pseudo unity".

2014 saw significant change for Austria's newest parliamentary parties. With its founder withdrawing from politics, Team Stronach became increasingly irrelevant. By contrast, although the liberal NEOS' political honeymoon proved ephemeral, by the end of 2014, their poll rating had settled at around 8 per cent, the figure they had achieved in May's European Parliament election when their market-liberal and markedly pro-EU stance had contributed to a below-expectation result.

That the ÖVP came first in the European Parliament election masked its 3-point decline (to 27 per cent) on the 2009 result, and provided Spindelegger temporary relief from intra-party criticism. Meanwhile, the SPÖ's meagre increase (up 0.4 per cent to 24.1 per cent) failed to distract from the poor performance of Faymann's choice for leading candidate. The FPÖ made the largest overall gains (up 7 per cent to 19.7 per cent). Its result might have been higher, but for the furore surrounding its short-lived lead candidate, who described the EU as a "conglomerate of negroes" and a dictatorship, compared to which the Third Reich was probably unstructured. In September, the FPÖ won 23.5 per cent (up 6.5 per cent) of the vote in the Vorarlberg provincial elections. The erstwhile hegemonic Vorarlberg ÖVP had the worst result in its history, obtaining merely 42 per cent (down 9 points), whilst the traditionally weak SPO also turned in an historic low (9 per cent).

Commentary on Austrian politics has tended to focus on the success of the FPÖ and neglect the Greens' sustained political progress. During 2014, their poll ratings remained remarkably steady at around 12 to 14 per cent and they increased their European Parliament vote by 4.6 points to 14.5 per cent, their highest-ever national result. Before 2003, they had had no government experience but, following their success at the 2014 Vorarlberg elections (up 7 points to 17 per cent), they formed a coalition with the ÖVP, thereby putting them in government in six of Austria's nine provinces.

Austria's economy slowed during 2014 and in the last quarter, there were distinct signs of weakness. In December, the Austrian National Bank (the central bank) noted reported unemployment at 5 per cent and youth unemployment at 9.6 per cent and downgraded its August economic growth forecast for 2014 from 0.9 per cent to 0.4 per cent. Given concerns around political developments in Greece and a possible renewed threat to the euro, as well as eurozone deflation, year-end economic forecasts for 2015 envisaged only modest growth (0.7 per cent) and a further increase in unemployment, possibly to 5.3 per cent. Compared to most eurozone countries, these figures were relatively healthy, but domestically there was considerable concern, especially regarding unemployment.

A further concern related to the Hypo Alpe-Adria, which continued to cast a shadow over Austria's political decision-makers and financial institutions. At the end of 2014, an official government commission identified failures by the bank, by Austria's financial authorities and by provincial and federal politicians. It also challenged the government's persistent assertion that there had been no alternative to the 2009 nationalisation. With Parliament preparing to launch a committee of enquiry that had the potential to revive a number of questions of financial and political probity, 2015 was likely to be politically challenging. Moreover, elections were due in four provinces, including Vienna, and observers expected many of these contests would see significant losses for the SPÖ and ÖVP. Whether their shared fear of a loss of power would cause them to maintain their mutual embrace remained to be seen, as did whether they could deliver the numerous structural reforms widely regarded as long overdue.

Kurt Richard Luther

SWITZERLAND

CAPITAL: Berne   AREA: 41,280 sq km   POPULATION: 8,081,482 ('13)
OFFICIAL LANGUAGES: German, French, Italian & Rhaeto-Romanic
HEAD OF STATE: Seven-member Federal Council
RULING PARTIES: Swiss People's Party (SVP)-led coalition
HEAD OF GOVERNMENT: Chairman of Federal Council for 2014 Didier Burkhalter
DEMOCRACY INDEX: 9.09; 7th of 167   CORRUPTION PERCEPTIONS INDEX: 86; =5th of 175
CURRENCY: Swiss Franc (Dec '14 £1.00=CHF 1.53 US$1.00=CHF 0.99)
GNI PER CAPITA: US$86,600, Intl$56,580 at PPP ('13)

THE year 2014 was dominated by the linked questions of Europe and immigration. This was because of the success of the Swiss People's Party (SVP) initiative "Against Mass Migration", which passed by 50.3 per cent on a 56.7 per cent
turnout in the referendum on 9 February. Because it required renegotiation of
any treaties that conflicted with the principle of national control of migration, it
posed a direct threat to Switzerland's bilateral accords with the EU. This was
probably the real target of the initiative. A frontal attack on bilateralism would
have failed but using the emotive issue of immigration enabled it to sneak
through. This caused uproar and, while the SVP claimed it pushed EU entry off
to the Greek calends, it encouraged the Social Democrats to take up the idea and
then produced a Pro Libero support movement, opposed to Christoph Blocher's
new "EU-No" organisation. There was also much talk of a new initiative which
would enshrine the bilateral approach and quash the 9 February decisions, something which eventually pushed the SVP to consider a new initiative on cancelling
the bilaterals and ensuring the full implementation of the 9 February text.

In the event, the EU reacted in a low key way, leaving it to the Swiss to resolve
the problem they had created while compromises were found to allow Croats
(newly members of the EU) free movement and Swiss universities to take part
in EU student exchange projects such as ERASMUS Plus and Horizon 2020.
Progress on finding a long term solution was slow. An Expert Group was created
to advise the government, although without SVP participation. Out of this came
a request in July for negotiations on the principle of free movement. This was
politely declined by the EU. Nonetheless in October the government produced a
draft mandate for negotiation, while failing to produce an implementing bill by
the year's end. Things were complicated by the November anti-immigration initiative proposed by the group Ecopop (Ecology and Population), which, had it
passed, would have meant a further break with free movement. In fact it was
heavily defeated. Before this, perhaps surprisingly, the EU agreed to start negotiations on an institutional framework agreement to rationalise relations with
Switzerland. Talks began in May but subsequently stalled.

All this affected party politics. Because of its 9 February victory the SVP
came under increasing attack for the way its extremism threatened to isolate
Switzerland, leading to a humiliating defeat of its proposals for national gold
reserves, declining opinion poll standings and the potential threat of an initiative
to cancel the 9 February constitutional article. The party was also defending a
controversial initiative demanding the subordination of international law to that
of Switzerland, leading the SVP minister in the Federal Council to try and per-

suade the government to resile from the European Convention on Human Rights. The party continued unbowed, despite having problems with unruly members and seeing Blocher, its de facto leader, step down from the National Council (legislature) to concentrate on extra parliamentary politics. Hence it attacked schooling, the wearing of Islamic veils and over-generous welfare payments. The party was also considering a further initiative to whittle down asylum to virtual vanishing point. This reflected the fact that the numbers of requests, primarily from Eritrea, shot up in the second half of the year, forcing the cantons to open new reception centres. Using disused barracks was much resented by asylum seekers.

Other parties had to respond to this. The Radical leadership refused to distance itself from the SVP, though its grassroots baulked at alliances. It also cut links with pro-European movements. Centrist parties did well in the polls but talk of closer liaisons between the Christian Democrats and the Conservative Democrats came to nothing. The way that all the parties began positioning themselves ahead of the 2015 elections made collaboration difficult. The Social Democrats were one of the few parties not to launch an initiative to publicise themselves.

The 9 February vote also had an impact on the Swiss economy, damping down expectations of growth to 1.8 per cent. And, after falling for six consecutive months, unemployment began to edge up again from September. The property boom also began to subside while Swiss bank UBS continued to suffer problems. Despite this, share prices remained high and the state budget remained in surplus. At the end of the year, the National Bank imposed a negative interest rate so as to prevent the franc from rising too far.

The country experienced other outside pressures. Laws adopted by the EU and the United States forced the government to distance itself from banking secrecy, which would disappear in 2017. Taxation also remained a problem in European relations. However, on 30 November, a Socialist initiative to end special tax arrangements for foreigners was defeated. The country also had to steer a difficult course as president of the OSCE between seeking peace in the eastern Ukraine and sanctioning Russia. At home an attempt to expand the canton of Jura to French-speaking areas of Berne failed, while the teaching of French was challenged in many German-speaking cantons. The fact that several Swiss went to serve as jihadis with Islamic State also caused concern

Clive H. Church

EUROPEAN MINI-STATES

Andorra

CAPITAL: Andorra la Vella   AREA: 470 sq km   POPULATION: 79,218 ('13)
OFFICIAL LANGUAGE: Catalan
HEADS OF STATE: President François Hollande of France & Bishop Joan Enric Vives of Urgel (co-princes)
RULING PARTY: Democrats for Andorra (DA)
HEAD OF GOVERNMENT: Antoni Marti Petit (DA) (since May '11)
CURRENCY: Euro (Dec '14 £1.00=EUR 1.275, US$1.00=EUR 0.821)
GNI PER CAPITA: US$41,517 ('11) (UN data)

Vatican City State

CAPITAL: Vatican City   AREA: 0.44 sq km   POPULATION: 1,000 ('13) (UN data)
OFFICIAL LANGUAGES: Italian & Latin
HEAD OF STATE: Pope Francis (since March '13)
HEAD OF GOVERNMENT: President of the Governorate Guiseppe Bertello (since Oct '11)
CURRENCY: Euro (Dec '14 £1.00=EUR 1.275, US$1.00=EUR 0.821)

Liechtenstein

CAPITAL: Vaduz   AREA: 160 sq km   POPULATION: 36,925 ('13)
OFFICIAL LANGUAGE: German
HEAD OF STATE: Prince Hans Adam II (since Nov '89)
RULING PARTY: Progressive Citizens' Party (FBP)
HEAD OF GOVERNMENT: Prime Minister Adrian Hasler (FBP) (since March '13)
CURRENCY: Swiss Franc (Dec '14 £1.00=CHF 1.53, US$1.00=CHF 0.99)
GNI PER CAPITA: US$136,770 ('09)

Monaco

CAPITAL: Monaco-Ville   AREA: 2 sq km   POPULATION: 37,831 ('13)
OFFICIAL LANGUAGE: French
HEAD OF STATE: Prince Albert II (since April '05)
RULING PARTIES: Union for Monaco (UNAM) alliance
HEAD OF GOVERNMENT: Minister of State Michel Roger (since March '10)
CURRENCY: Euro (Dec '14 £1.00=EUR 1.275, US$1.00=EUR 0.821)
GNI PER CAPITA: US$167,021 ('11) (UN data)

San Marino

CAPITAL: San Marino   AREA: 60 sq km   POPULATION: 31,448 ('13)
OFFICIAL LANGUAGE: Italian
HEADS OF STATE: Captains-Regent Gianfranco Terenzi and Guerrino Zammoti (since Oct '14, for six months)
RULING PARTIES: Pact for San Marino (PSM) coalition
CURRENCY: Euro (Dec '14 £1.00=EUR 1.275, US$1.00=EUR 0.821)
GNI PER CAPITA: US$56,364 ('11) (UN data)

HAVING brought VAT, corporation tax and non-resident income tax to **Andorra** the government continued its fiscal reforms with the introduction in 2015 of a flat tax of 10 per cent on incomes exceeding €40,000. (The Socialist opposition had pressed for a more progressive system.) The year also brought reforms of prisons and company law, and measures to tackle money laundering and corruption. Controversial proposals were brought forward for civil service reform.

Efforts to diversify the economy continued and unemployment fell, but the relationship with the EU remained uncertain. The European Commission favoured a multilateral agreement covering Andorra, Liechtenstein, Monaco and San Marino. Meanwhile, the introduction of euro coinage specific to Andorra, pencilled in for January, had still not been achieved by the year's end.

In January, spokesmen for the **Holy See** received a rare grilling from the UN committee on the rights of the child. A damning report on the Roman Catholic Church's handling of sex abuse duly followed. The Vatican responded robustly but Pope Francis showed on a number of occasions that he was well aware of the Church's failings. He sharply rebuked church leaders who had failed to grasp the problem adequately and called for reparation. He also rebuked lax, venal or extravagant clerics. In April, in an unprecedented ceremony attended by large crowds, he canonised two 20th-century popes—John XXIII and John-Paul II—in the presence of his predecessor, Pope Benedict XVI

In October a special Synod, summoned by the pope and attended by 180 bishops and cardinals from around the world, discussed issues relating to the modern family, including remarriage, communion for divorcees and gay relationships. Although no changes in doctrine emerged, and there were powerful assertions of traditional views, the tone softened. The pope oversaw a major overhaul in the administration of the Vatican (the Curia), describing it as threatened with "fossilisation" and "spiritual Alzheimer's". He appointed a new cardinal secretary of state and ordered reforms to the dysfunctional "Vatican Bank". He also played an instrumental role in the reopening of diplomatic relations between the USA and Cuba, announced in December.

In December the European Council agreed to open negotiations in 2015 with four European microstates including **Liechtenstein** and **Monaco** on a collective form of association. Within Monaco the issue was became increasingly contentious.

With the ratification of a taxation agreement in February, after years of negotiations, **San Marino** finally exited from the Italian government's black list of tax havens. Modest progress was made with tackling the country's economic problems: after five difficult years in which GDP fell cumulatively by 30 per cent, remedial measures limited further losses to just 1 per cent. However, the annual IMF report described the remaining challenges as "daunting". It identified a need for a reduction in public sector wages, further budget cuts amounting to 1 per cent of GDP and savings on pensions. Additional reforms would be needed in the banking system but there was also a need to diversify from finance in ways that would require a wider range of skills.

Martin Harrison

SPAIN

CAPITAL: Madrid   AREA: 505,370 sq km   POPULATION: 46,647,421 ('13)
OFFICIAL LANGUAGE: Spanish
HEAD OF STATE: King Felipe VI (since June '14)
RULING PARTY: People's Party (PP)
HEAD OF GOVERNMENT: Prime Minister Mariano Rajoy Brey (PP) (since Dec '11)
DEMOCRACY INDEX: 8.02; 25th of 167   CORRUPTION PERCEPTIONS INDEX: 60; =37th of 175
CURRENCY: Euro (Dec '14 £1.00=EUR 1.275, US$1.00=EUR 0.821)
GNI PER CAPITA: US$29,180, Intl$31,850 at PPP ('13)

SPAIN came out of a long recession in 2014,with growth of around 1.4 per cent, but the official unemployment rate was still more than 23 per cent and two-thirds of the 5.4 million jobless had been without work for more than two years. The ailing banking sector was also restored to health: the government exited the €41.3 billion bailout programme with its eurozone partners and all banks sailed through the health check conducted by the European Central Bank and the European Banking Authority, signalling they did not need any more capital.

The deep crisis, with three years of austerity measures that had increased income inequality and child poverty, coupled with a spate of corruption scandals, led to the spectacular rise of the radical anti-establishment party Podemos ("We can"). It was created out of the 2011 grass roots movement of "los indignados" ("the indignant ones") (see AR 2012, p. 56) and stunned the political class by winning five seats in May's European Parliament elections and 1.2 million votes. Podemos, according to voting intention polls, looked set to be the second or third largest party in the general election due to be held by December 2015, thereby ending Spain's two-party system.

As a result of the many corruption scandals involving the ruling conservative Popular Party (PP) of Mariano Rajoy Brey and the opposition Socialists, and rising public anger, Spain finally fell into line with the rest of the European Union when its first ever transparency law came into effect on 10 December. The new law—almost 40 years after the end of the dictatorship of Francisco Franco Bahamonde—only operated at the state level (from December 2015, it would be extended to municipal and regional levels, where most corruption occurred). More than 800 town halls (10 per cent of the total) were under investigation and several thousand people had been accused in corruption cases. A government website began to publish the salaries of senior officials, details of public sector contracts, state subsidies and other information of public interest. Citizens could request information that was not on the website and should receive a reply within 30 days, though information could be denied for 12 reasons. The Spanish chapter of the Berlin-based Transparency International organisation criticised the law for being too restrictive and said that the limits on providing information were "excessively ambiguous". If they were interpreted narrowly, access to information would be reduced to a minimum. Spain improved slightly in the 2014 Transparency International corruption perceptions index, which measured perceived levels of corruption in the public sector. It was ranked the (joint) 37th least corrupt country out of 175 nations, up from 4th in 2013.

The push for independence in Catalonia, Spain's most economically dynamic region, came to a head on 9 November when Artur Mas i Gavarró, the region's centre-right president, defied the central government and went ahead with a pseudo referendum for a separate state. Volunteers manned polling booths. The mock poll was called after the Constitutional Court had ruled the non-binding referendum scheduled for the same day illegal. Of the 2.3 million votes cast, more than 80 per cent were in favour of independence (29 per cent of the total possible votes of 6.3 million). The majority of anti-independence voters stayed at home. Supporters of independence hailed the turnout of 37 per cent as a victory and opponents said it was a failure. Voter turnout in the 2012 election in Catalonia was 69.6 per cent and 49.4 per cent in the 2006 referendum on a new statute of autonomy. Eduardo Torres-Dulce Lifante, the attorney general, charged Mas with disobedience, perverting the course of justice, misuse of public funds and abuse of power. Rajoy continued to resist reforming the 1978 constitution, partly out of fear of stimulating a rash of competing demands from other regions.

Crown Prince Felipe was proclaimed king after his father, Juan Carlos, aged 76, abdicated on 18 June. Widely credited with Spain's successful transition to democracy, Juan Carlos was in poor health, and had lost support, not least because the institution of the monarchy was tarnished by the probe into his son-in-law Iñaki Urdangarín y Liebaert for alleged fraud, embezzlement and falsifying documents. Urdangarín faced up to 18 years in jail when he eventually came to trial. His wife, Princess Cristina Federica Victoria Antonia de la Santísima Trinidad de Borbón y Grecia (Cristina de Borbón), also faced charges related to her husband's business practices. Support for the restoration of a republic (abolished after Franco won the three-year Civil War in 1939) increased.

In the social sphere, the government withdrew its controversial and restrictive abortion bill that had provoked widespread criticism including from within the PP. Alberto Ruíz Gallardon, the justice minister and architect of the bill, resigned. The new law would have rolled back parts of the 2010 abortion reform that brought Spain broadly into line with the rest of Europe. That law, passed by the previous Socialist government, allowed women to opt for abortion in the first 14 weeks of pregnancy, and up to 22 weeks if the foetus was seriously deformed or if the birth posed a serious health risk to the mother. The scrapped bill would have restricted abortion to only cases of rape or serious health risks.

The overall population continued to fall; by July it was provisionally estimated at 46.5 million, 50,000 lower than at the start of the year, mainly because of emigration by foreigners fleeing the economic crisis. Of the 206,492 people who emigrated in the first half of 2014, 42,685 were Spaniards. The population had not stopped falling since 2012 when it stood at 47.3 million. The foreign population dropped by 138,556 to 4.7 million (9.7 per cent of the total compared to a peak of 12.2 per cent in 2010). The largest drop was in the number of Ecuadorians, 27,000 of whom left in the first half of the year.

In a move to make amends with the past, a new law allowed descendants of Jews forced to leave Spain in 1492 to apply for Spanish nationality. Up to 300,000 Jews lived in Spain before the Catholic monarchs Isabella and Ferdinand ordered Jews and Muslims to convert to the Roman Catholic faith or leave the country. Applicants had to prove their Sephardic background through a certificate from the federation of the Jewish community in Spain or from the head of the Jewish community in which they resided.

The main foreign policy achievement was Spain's election to the UN Security Council for the period 2015-17, but only by beating Turkey in the third round of run-off voting for the second of the two Western European group seats.

In the corporate world, the red tape for setting up a company was reduced. The number of days needed to create a business in Spain dropped from 23 to 13, as a result of which the country rose in the World Bank's 2015 Doing Business ranking—an index closely watched by international investors—from 115th place to 74th out of 189 countries. Spain led the world market for transport infrastructure, with six companies in the top 12 transportation developers, according to the US publication, *Public Works Finance*. Repsol, the oil and gas group, agreed to acquire Canada's Talisman Energy for €6.64 billion, making it one of the world's 15 largest energy companies.

William Chislett

GIBRALTAR

CAPITAL: Gibraltar   AREA: 6.5 sq km   POPULATION: 29,000 ('13) (UN data)
OFFICIAL LANGUAGE: English
HEAD OF STATE: Queen Elizabeth II (since Feb '52)
GOVERNOR-GENERAL: Sir James Dutton (since Dec '13)
RULING PARTY: Gibraltar Socialist Labour Party
HEAD OF GOVERNMENT: Chief Minister Fabian Picardo (GSLP) (since Dec '11)
CURRENCY: Gibraltar Pound (Dec '14 £1.00=GIP 1.00,   US$1.00=GIP 0.64)
GNI PER CAPITA: US$50,000 ('10) (Gibraltar gvt est.)

THERE was no easing of the tensions between the Spanish and UK governments over Gibraltar. The stringent border controls introduced in July 2013 after Gibraltar enraged Spain by tossing 70 concrete blocks into contested waters off its coast, in order to encourage sea-life to flourish, continued to cause lengthy queues of cars and pedestrians.

As well as the border controls—which were ostensibly a crackdown on tobacco smuggling, as prices were much lower in Gibraltar—the Spanish government did its utmost to make life difficult in other areas. The territorial dispute threatened the inclusion of the Rock's airport in the Single European Sky (SES) initiative, launched in 2004 to merge flight corridors into transnational "blocks". More direct flight paths would cut costs and reduce carbon dioxide emissions. In December, the Italian presidency of the European Council allowed Spain to exclude Gibraltar from the SES. Ana Pastor Julián, Spain's minister of public works and transport, described the airport on the narrow strip of land linking Gibraltar to Spain as "an area that is being illegally occupied by the United Kingdom".

As a result, the European airspace reforms could not be implemented until the wrangle was resolved. Philip Hammond, the UK's foreign secretary, accused Spain of using the EU to further its claims over Gibraltar, which was ceded to Britain under the 1713 Treaty of Utrecht. Earlier in the year, Spain tried to use the dispute to block the UK opting back into a series of EU police and criminal justice agreements, but then yielded.

Spain had withdrawn from the Trilateral Forum for Dialogue (the UK, Spain and Gibraltar) at the end of 2011, after the Popular Party won the general election. Consequently, there was no active mechanism for discussing common issues other than sovereignty—which the UK was adamant was not on the table—and little more than megaphone diplomacy. Efforts to start ad hoc talks did not come to fruition. The Spanish government wanted a return to the 1984 Brussels Declaration, which envisaged bilateral talks on issues including sovereignty.

William Chislett

PORTUGAL

CAPITAL: Lisbon   AREA: 92,120 sq km   POPULATION: 10,459,806 ('13)
OFFICIAL LANGUAGE: Portuguese
HEAD OF STATE: President Anibal Cavaco Silva (PSD) (since March '06)
RULING PARTIES: Social Democratic Party (PSD)-led coalition
HEAD OF GOVERNMENT: Prime Minister Pedro Passos Coelho (PSD) (since June '11)
DEMOCRACY INDEX: 7.65; =34th of 167   CORRUPTION PERCEPTIONS INDEX: 63; =31st of 175
CURRENCY: Euro (Dec '14 £1.00=EUR 1.275, US$1.00=EUR 0.821)
GNI PER CAPITA: US$20,670, Intl$25,360 at PPP ('13)

AMIDST several green shoots of economic recovery, Portugal spent 2014 embroiled in a series of corruption scandals, a catastrophic banking failure and an embarrassing debacle involving school-teachers. The year began, however, with three days of national mourning after the death from heart failure on 5 January of Eusébio da Silva Ferreira. Born in Mozambique and nicknamed the "Black Pearl", the 71-year old was renowned as one of Portugal's finest soccer players (see Obituary). Later in the month, football superstar Cristiano Ronaldo dos Santos Aveiro was made a Grand Officer of the Order of Prince Henry, a national award that recognised his outstanding sporting achievements.

Celebrations of the 40th anniversary of the April 1974 Carnation Revolution preceded an official announcement, on 17 May, that the country would exit its three-year, €78 billion bail-out programme (see AR 2012, pp. 59-60). Buoyed by falling bond yields, a surge in energy exports, a rise in tourist revenue and a significant decline in the unemployment rate, Portugal left the loan deal without the safety net of a precautionary credit line in place. This success did not, however, prevent the opposition Socialist Party (PS) from collecting 31.5 per cent of the vote in the European Parliament elections on 25 May, translating into eight of Portugal's 21 MEPs. It was not a resounding victory because the centre-right Portugal Alliance (PSD-PCD) coalition gained 27.7 per cent and seven MEPs but the most telling feature was a record abstention rate of 66 per cent. The low turnout was partly explained by the continued emigration of young adults in search of work, many of them to the UK. The Portuguese public had also grown apathetic on a diet of punitive austerity measures, a course which continued with a fresh onslaught from the tax inspector. A clampdown was announced in April on undeclared incomes from rental accommodation in coastal resorts and close to universities. At the end of August new legislation was announced meaning that anyone buying a car costing in excess of €35,000, or a motorcycle costing more than €7,500, would be tagged with a "manifestation of wealth". This would automatically transform them into a potential tax-evader worthy of closer scrutiny. One fiscal reprieve emerged, however, on 1 October when the national minimum wage rose to €505 a month, a level of remuneration that had been frozen since 2011.

In the first six months of the year, Portugal's second largest private financial institution, Banco Espírito Santo SA (BES), lost the equivalent of almost €3.6 billion. Coupled with an 89 per cent fall in the value of its shares, serious concerns were raised as to the bank's health and stability. The shaky nature of BES could be traced to a number of dubious loans that had been made to prop up other businesses that were controlled by the bank's parent company. On 4 August BES was split into two banks: Novo Banco, which kept its healthy operations, and the existing "bad" bank, which kept its toxic assets and debts. The New Bank received an injection of €4.9 billion from the Bank of Portugal's Resolution Fund, thus safeguarding the bank's deposits, branches and 9,860 employees. BES shareholders and some of the banks' creditors were, however, expected to lose most of their money as a consequence of the bail-out plan.

Chaos ensued at the start of the new school year in September as teachers who had accepted placements began receiving additional demands for their services. Thousands were offered more than one job, often in different parts of the country. The shambolic distribution meant that many state schools did not have a full staff complement until the end of November. The minister of education and science, Nuno Paulo de Sousa Arrobas Crato, had his offer of resignation rejected by Prime Minister Pedro Passos Coelho but the secretary of state for primary and secondary education, João Grancho, was not so fortunate.

In a foretaste of what was to come, former executive chairman of BES, Ricardo Espírito Santo Salgado, was detained on 25 July on suspicion of tax evasion and money laundering. Then, on 21 November, in an unprecedented move , the former prime minster, José Sócrates Carvalho Pinto de Sousa (PS), was arrested on charges of alleged tax fraud, money laundering and corruption. Earlier in the month Manuel Jarmela Palos, head of the country's (SEF) immigration service, was detained as part of an investigation into corruption linked to the issuing of "golden visas" to wealthy foreign investors. The scandals were unrelenting and, with a general election due in May 2015, left many Portuguese in a state of shock and anger. The opinion polls suggested that the newly elected PS leader, António Luís Santos da Costa, was the frontrunner to defeat Passos Coelho. However, because of Costa's association with Sócrates, the year ended with that prospect shrouded in uncertainty.

Martin Eaton

MALTA

CAPITAL: Valletta   AREA: 320 sq km   POPULATION: 423,282 ('13)
OFFICIAL LANGUAGES: Maltese & English
HEAD OF STATE: President Marie Louise Coleiro (since April '14)
RULING PARTY: Labour Party (LP)
HEAD OF GOVERNMENT: Prime Minister Joseph Muscat (LP) (since March '13)
DEMOCRACY INDEX: 8.28; 16th of 167   CORRUPTION PERCEPTIONS INDEX: 55; =43rd of 175
CURRENCY: Euro (Dec '14 £1.00=EUR 1.275, US$1.00=EUR 0.821)
GNI PER CAPITA: US$20,980, Intl$28,030 at PPP ('13)

HAVING been met with disfavour in the European Parliament in January, Malta's much-debated Individual Investment Programme, a scheme that awarded citizenship against investment in Malta, was cleared by the European Commission as containing nothing fundamentally objectionable. When the European parliamentary elections were held in May, the opposition Nationalist Party (PN), whose MEPs had actively supported the Parliament's January resolution, hoped to recover some of the vast ground lost in the 2013 general election. In the event, Labour (LP) retained its lead over the PN undiminished. In EU matters the government was further comforted by the considerable portfolio—environment, maritime affairs and fisheries—allocated to the new Maltese commissioner, in contraposition to recurring criticism in European environmental circles of Maltese bird-hunting practices. Locally, meanwhile, environmental groups collected signatures to petition for a referendum to ban the traditional spring shoot of migrating birds. The hunting lobby responded with a counter-petition challenging the use of the referendum to deny minority rights. The matter was referred to the Constitutional Court.

Politically the high point was the legislation giving gay partners in civil unions equal rights with married couples. The bill's enactment had to await the expiry of the presidential term, as incumbent George Abela had reservations of conscience about signing. His successor was Marie-Louise Coleiro, formerly the minister for social solidarity. Her portfolio was then offered to the minister of health, but he declined and resigned. More newsworthy was the departure later of the minister of the interior, after he had implicitly covered for his policeman-driver, who had given chase and shot at another car that had scraped the minister's car without stopping.

One unprecedented resignation was that of Archbishop Paul Cremona in October, ostensibly for health reasons but weighted with criticism from certain priests of his leadership of the Roman Catholic Church in Malta. Once all-powerful, the Church was contending with declining public participation, secularisation and, more topically, the legalisation of divorce and gay civil unions.

Economic performance remained stable, with an estimated growth of 3 per cent, again outperforming the EU average. With the deficit slightly down to 2.5 per cent, Malta expected to exit the EU's excessive deficit procedure in 2015. The budget for 2015 envisaged financial consolidation through higher growth while focusing on job creation and reduction of welfare dependency. In December the way was opened for the introduction of cheaper gas-powered electricity production with Chinese investment when Shanghai Electric Power bought a 33 per cent holding in the energy monopoly, Enemalta.

In foreign affairs, apart from the habitual engagement with the EU over shared responsibility for stranded Europe-bound migrants, Malta's main concern was the troubles of neighbouring Libya. Malta followed UN and EU guidelines in recognising the elected government in Tobruk, but otherwise would not be drawn into Libya's internal affairs. It allowed the Tobruk government use of the Maltese consular offices, without requiring Tripoli's rival "salvation government" to relinquish the old embassy. At the end of the year the rival representatives were vying with each other over the right to issue visas to Maltese businessmen and workers with long-standing Libyan connections.

Dominic Fenech

GREECE

CAPITAL: Athens   AREA: 131,960 sq km   POPULATION: 11,032,328 ('13)
OFFICIAL LANGUAGE: Greek
HEAD OF STATE: President Karolos Papoulias (since March '05)
RULING PARTIES: New Democracy (ND)-led coalition
HEAD OF GOVERNMENT: Prime Minister Antonis Samaras (ND) (since June '12)
DEMOCRACY INDEX: 7.65; =34th of 167   CORRUPTION PERCEPTIONS INDEX: 43; =69th of 175
CURRENCY: Euro (Dec '14 £1.00=EUR 1.275, US$1.00=EUR 0.821)
GNI PER CAPITA: US$22,530, Intl$25,630 at PPP ('13)

FOR Greece, 2014 ended on a cliff-hanger: Parliament's failure to elect a president on the third-round ballot on 29 December forced Prime Minister Antonis Samaras to call early elections, set for 25 January 2015. Greek voters were faced with an ultimatum rather than a choice, as the two main contenders—the conservative New Democracy and the Coalition of the Radical Left (Syriza)—pushed them to decide, respectively, between fear and anger. New Democracy, which had governed at the head of an uneasy coalition since winning the June 2012 elections, foretold the gloom-and-doom of a Greek exit from the eurozone; Syriza rode Greeks' resentment of austerity to come from the political margins in 2009 (the last election before the imposition of austerity) to achieve opinion poll figures nudging 30 per cent.

Syriza had tilled the political soil throughout the year, with an eye to elections in 2015 after the president's term expired in March of that year. At home, the party's charismatic young leader, Alexis Tsipras, turned up the populist rhetoric, alternately mocking the government's "success story" claims when its privatisation plans floundered, and censuring it as unemployment rose to 28 per cent. Abroad, Tsipras tweaked his image slightly. He cultivated the European Left, positioning Greece, and Syriza, as the vanguard of a continent-wide rebellion against austerity. At the same time, he sought to assuage EU leaders and financial markets with assurances that a Syriza government would not take unilateral action against either its creditors or the euro. Analysts spent hours trying to decipher these contradictions; Greeks took them in their stride. Tsipras's railing against the bailout troika—the EU, European Central Bank, and IMF—resonated with Greeks but only enough to push Syriza ahead of New Democracy in opinion polls, albeit without a commanding lead. Even in the European Parliament elections in May, Syriza only managed 26.5 per cent to New Democracy's 22.7 per cent.

For its part, the New Democracy government spent the year trying to persuade Greeks and its creditors alike that Greece was on track. In April, the European Commission confirmed that Greece had overshot its targets for 2013 by recording a primary surplus of €1.5 billion. Then, in July, the Centre of Planning and Economic Research (KEPE) reported that the Greek economy had returned to growth in the second quarter of 2014 after 20 successive quarters of contraction. Despite a shortfall in first-quarter tax revenues, finance ministry officials remained confident that 2014 would also close with a primary surplus. Still, it was deemed necessary by both sides to extend the bailout program for two months into 2015.

The Greek success also fell short on structural reforms—most notably, trimming the public sector—and privatisation. Indeed, critics noted that the government's much-ballyhooed "success" came from a combination of a new property tax and a repayment scheme of up to 100 instalments for owed taxes, rather than reforms. Greece also continued to rank high in corruption, despite promises to combat this evil by tightening procedures for arms and other procurements.

In February, an investigation was launched into the sale of the state gambling monopoly, Opap, several months earlier. Key state assets like the ports, highways, utilities, former Olympic venues, and other choice real estate were offered but foreign investors were wary, forcing the government to once again downwardly revise its target to less than half the €3.56 billion originally set for 2014. New Democracy lay the blame on Syriza's threats of future nationalisations but whiffs of scandal, such as that surrounding the sale of the former Athens airport at Hellenikon, and successive resignations from the privatisation agency also had a hand. The government was also forced to retreat from plans to privatise the long Greek coastline and beaches by a spontaneous grassroots movement that took even opposition parties by surprise.

Samaras also had to deal with problems within the government coalition. Without the thin veil of political legitimacy provided by the shrinking Democratic Left (which had withdrawn support from the government in June 2013), New Democracy and its coalition partner, the Panhellenic Socialist Movement (Pasok), found themselves in the sights of both left and right opposition parties. Supplanted by Syriza in the political battle of good and evil, Pasok saw its support erode. Beyond its perception as a pro-bailout party, Pasok's association with New Democracy cost it further support when the neo-Nazi Golden Dawn published tapes in April of secret meetings between a Golden Dawn spokesman and the Cabinet secretary, a senior Samaras aide.

Political polarisation between the two leading parties squeezed the smaller opposition parties on the Right, with the breakaway Independent Greeks struggling to keep their support above the 3 per cent threshold for entering Parliament. Out of nowhere, a new party emerged to claim the centre—To Potami, or The River, led by a prominent magazine and television commentator, Stavros Theodorakis. Launched in March, Potami won 6.6 per cent in the European Parliament elections. It subsequently maintained that percentage, vying with Golden Dawn for third place in the polls. Although there was no ideological overlap between the politically nebulous Potami and the fascist Golden Dawn, the new party strangely acted as a counterweight—although Golden Dawn's presence was less strongly felt since several prominent members, including MPs, were remanded in custody pending trial on an array of criminal charges.

With Greece poised to return to the markets as its bailout programme ended, 2014 appeared to have closed the circle opened four years previously when Prime Minister George Papandreou dramatically informed Greeks, in a televised address from Europe's most remote border, that their country was effectively bankrupt. But, with a strong sense of déjà vu, Greece ended the year once again in the head-lines. With Syriza poised to win the January 2015 elections, there was once again talk of a "Grexit", or Greek exit from the eurozone, and Papandreou had returned to the political scene, having split from the Pasok founded by his father to create a new vision of *allaghi*, or change. Which in Greece, as the campaign exchanges between New Democracy and Syriza amply illustrated, usually meant as little as possible.

Diane Shugart

CYPRUS

CAPITAL: Nicosia   AREA: 9,250 sq km (3,355 sq km in the Turkish Republic of Northern Cyprus, TRNC)   POPULATION: 1,141,166 ('13); Greek Cypriot 886,201; Turkish Cypriots and Turks 286,257 ('14, extrapolation from Eurostat data)
HEAD OF STATE AND GOVERNMENT: President Nicos Anastasiades (DISY) (since Feb '13); in the TRNC: President Dervis Eroglu (since April '10)
RULING PARTIES: Democratic Rally (DISY); in the TRNC: coalition of Republican Turkish Party (CTP)-Democratic Party (DP)
DEMOCRACY INDEX: 7.29; 42nd of 167   CORRUPTION PERCEPTIONS INDEX: 63; =31st of 175
CURRENCY: Euro (Dec '14 £1.00=EUR 1.275, US$1.00=EUR 0.821)
GNI PER CAPITA: US$28,830, Intl$25,210 at PPP ('13); in the TRNC: US$15,038 ('12, State Planning Organisation)

THE year 2014 marked the 40th anniversary of the division of Cyprus in July 1974 following the Greek junta-sponsored coup against President Archbishop Makarios and the Turkish invasion and occupation of the northern third of the island (see AR 1974, pp. 194-99). Yet another round of UN-brokered negotiations to reunite the two territories as a federated state trundled on between February and October but finally collapsed after the Greek Cypriot side withdrew in protest at Turkish off-shore hydrocarbon exploration in waters claimed by the government of Cyprus.

UN initiatives in 2013 had led to the collation of elements of convergence and to a commitment by the Greek and Turkish Cypriot leaderships to move towards a comprehensive settlement. Fresh talks were launched on 11 February at a high-level meeting under UN auspices between the Greek Cypriot president Nicos Anastasiades and the Turkish Cypriot leader Dervis Eroglu. They issued a joint declaration reiterating the notion of a federation consisting of two equal commu-nities but having a single sovereignty and international personality.

This promising start was followed by high-level meetings at roughly monthly intervals, interspersed with regular meetings of the negotiators who hammered out agendas and details. The meetings were not easy, with Eroglu accusing the Greek Cypriots of trying to re-open the agreed Convergence text and Anastasiades blaming the Turkish Cypriots for "inconsistency in their proposals". The 24 July meeting ended prematurely when Anastasiades stormed out in frustration at Eroglu's negotiating tactics.

Special envoys from the European Commission, the United Nations and the US state department streamed through the island to offer advice and support and US Vice President Joe Biden spent two days in May canvassing a settlement with specific emphasis on the thorny issue of property.

A new UN secretary general's special advisor for Cyprus—Norway's former foreign minister, Espen Barth Eide—arrived on the island in time to chair the September high-level meeting. He was to present a package of bridging proposals to the next session, scheduled for 8-9 October, but the talks were broken off by the Greek Cypriots on 7 October in protest at the activities of Turkey in conducting hydrocarbon exploration in waters claimed by the Greek Cypriots as part of the island's exclusive economic zone (EEZ).

The government of Cyprus had exercised its rights under the UN Convention on the Law of the Sea (UNCLOS) to declare a 200-mile EEZ in waters to the south and east of the island and had negotiated boundaries with Israel, Lebanon and Egypt. It had not managed to delineate waters to the north with Turkey, which was not a signatory to UNCLOS and refused to recognise the government of Cyprus. Turkey insisted that the EEZ claimed by Cyprus overlapped its continental shelf. The Greek Cypriots nevertheless granted an exploration concession in Block 9 to an Italian-Korean consortium, ENI-KOGAS. Turkey responded by sending the Turkish Petroleum seismic survey vessel, *Barbaros*, to explore the same block, accompanied by the guided-missile frigate, *Gelibolou*. By year's end there had been no confrontations but tensions were high.

In the south, on 26 February, the Democratic Party (DIKO) withdrew its four ministers from the government led by Democratic Rally (DISY) because it disagreed with the approach to the renewed settlement negotiations. Anastasiades replaced them with four technocrats. DISY, which held only 20 of the 56 seats in the House of Representatives (the unicameral legislature) still relied on DIKO's eight votes and those of minority parties to secure passage of legislation through the House. It was bitterly opposed by the Communist Party (AKEL), which commanded 19 of the seats, and by the Movement for Social Democracy (EDEK), which held five. In the 25 May European Parliament elections, however, DISY considerably increased its polling lead over AKEL (37.8 per cent to 27 per cent) although, because of the method of seat distribution, each took two of the country's six places.

In the Turkish Republic of Northern Cyprus municipal elections on 29 June saw the Republican Turkish Party (CTP) lose control of the three main cities— Nicosia, Famagusta and Kyrenia—but still secure 14 of the 28 posts of mayor with 38 per cent of the vote, well ahead of an opposition coalition of the Social

Democratic Party (TDP) and the United Cyprus Party (BKP), which polled 29.5 per cent.

Four candidates declared for the 2015 presidential election: the incumbent Dervis Eroglu, former head of the right-wing National Unity Party (UBP); Kudret Ozersay, the Turkish Cypriot negotiator; Mustafa Acinci, a social democratic politician currently with the Communal Democracy Party but standing as an independent; and Sibel Siber, the sole female candidate, representing the CTP. The Eroglu administration dismissed Ozersay as TRNC negotiator after he declared his candidacy and replaced him with Ergun Olgun, a former negotiator. Ozersay, an associate professor of international relations at the East Mediterranean University in Famagusta, had been an accommodating negotiator whereas Olgun, a former undersecretary of the TRNC presidency and a close associate of the late Turkish Cypriot leader, Rauf Denktash, was noted for his intransigence.

Robert McDonald

TURKEY

CAPITAL: Ankara   AREA: 783,560 sq km   POPULATION: 74,932,641 ('13)
OFFICIAL LANGUAGE: Turkish
HEAD OF STATE: President Recep Tayyip Erdogan (since Aug '14)
RULING PARTY: Justice and Development Party (AKP)
HEAD OF GOVERNMENT: Prime Minister Ahmet Davutoglu (AKP) (since Aug '14)
DEMOCRACY INDEX: 5.63; 93rd of 167   CORRUPTION PERCEPTIONS INDEX: 45; =64th of 175
CURRENCY: New Lira (Dec '14 £1.00=TRY 3.60, US$1.00=TRY 2.32)
GNI PER CAPITA: US$10,950, Intl$18,760 at PPP ('13)

THE year 2014 was a tumultuous and historic one for Turkey: 12 months marked by an epic political fight, a new jihadi menace, momentous elections and an international fall from grace.

If one image loomed over the drama, it was that of Recep Tayyip Erdogan's new $600 million presidential palace, a complex with four times the floor space of Louis XIV's Versailles. To his supporters, its size was commensurate with the country's ambitions on the world stage and with Erdogan's unbroken string of political victories, which in 2014 saw him defeat Islamic allies-turned-enemies and become Turkey's first directly elected president. To critics, the sprawling palace incarnated excess and autocracy in a country that was discarding or undermining many of its institutions and heading towards one-man rule.

Beyond such differences, however, the building's symbolism was inescapable: it was Erdogan's dominance of the Turkish political landscape taken concrete form. At times, particularly at the start of the year, that dominance seemed open to doubt. At the very end of 2013, simmering tensions with the movement of Fethullah Gulen, an exiled Islamic preacher with thousands of followers in Turkish institutions, had boiled over (see AR 2014, pp. 60-61). Erdogan's Justice and Development Party (AKP) and the Gulenists had formed an alliance of convenience when the common enemy was Turkey's old, military-backed order. But, after those self-styled secularists were beaten back, Erdogan sought to rein in the influence of the Gulenists, which sometimes seemed an Islamic admixture of characteristics of Opus Dei and the Jesuits—a network whose emphasis on education both served as an engine of recruitment and helped funnel adepts into positions of power.

Erdogan blamed the Gulenists for launching corruption cases in December 2013 against his inner circle—including his son, Bilal—in apparent retaliation for his own drive to close down Gulenist cramming schools. His response was to rain down blow after blow on the movement in 2014, even as he described the corruption investigation, which brought to light large scale cash transfers to ministers, as a coup against his government. Thousands of supposedly Gulenist police officers, prosecutors and judges were shifted from their positions. Purges took place throughout the state bureaucracy. Imprisoned corruption suspects were released and the cases eventually dropped.

When presumed Gulenists responded to the stalling of the corruption investigation by leaking ostensibly incriminating recordings—including of Erdogan himself—onto the Internet via Twitter, the prime minister had access to the microblogging network shut down. Another leak, this time of an illegally recorded government meeting on Syria, led the government to ban YouTube. (Both decisions were subsequently reversed by the Constitutional Court which emerged in 2014 as the biggest check on Erdogan's power.)

Despite it all, Erdogan triumphed, in March municipal elections that became a referendum on his rule and in the August vote that transformed him from longserving prime minister to head of state. Psephological analyses of both contests showed some attrition in the AKP vote, but Erdogan's assertive leadership and his record for both empathising with and providing for the country's once-neglected pious masses remained formidable. Turkey's opposition remained hapless.

After the elections, Erdogan moved towards his long-held goal of an executive presidency. Turkey was formally a parliamentary system—and a constitutional change might be difficult to achieve—but the new president made clear his view that his election would give him a greater role than his predecessors. He both chose Ahmet Davutoglu, his replacement as prime minister and AKP leader, and outlined the new government's chief tasks, including fighting the Gulenists and continuing efforts to end the country's 30-year-old Kurdish conflict.

If 2014 was a year of domestic political victories, it was also a year when Turkey's international reputation received a battering. The United States and the European Union expressed deep concern about the rule of law. Erdogan attracted more bad headlines by angrily confronting mourners after 301 coal miners died in May—the country's worst industrial accident—and one of his aides was photographed kicking a bereaved man pinioned to the floor.

The Turkish economy, largely sustained by debt and relatively short term international financing, suffered along with other emerging markets amid expectations that US interest rates would rise, increasing the cost of borrowing. The lira fell 9 per cent against the dollar, following an even greater tumble in 2013, although the famously volatile stock market rose more than 26 per cent in lira terms. Growth slumped to 1.7 per cent for the third quarter, although economists expected a subsequent pickup. More generally, institutions such as the IMF warned that without structural reform Turkey would both grow below long term trends and remain painfully vulnerable to economic shocks. The head of the World Bank's Turkey office added that problems such as corruption had deterred new investment.

Yet the country's strategic importance was undeniable, a fact hammered home by the spread of the jihadis of the Islamic State of Iraq and the Levant (or ISIS) in neighbouring Iraq and Syria. Leaders such as UK Prime Minister David Cameron put a premium on co-operating with Turkey against the threat of "foreign fighters"—radicalised Muslims returning home after fighting for ISIS—over any concerns about governance within Turkey itself. Meanwhile, the USA lobbied a reluctant Turkey to give direct aid for attacks on ISIS, without clear success. In contrast to most other world leaders, Erdogan depicted both the Syrian government and outlawed Kurdish militants as at least as bad as the jihadi group. Turkish tanks stood by on the other side of the border at the height of the ISIS attack on the Syrian Kurdish town of Kobani in October—a sight that helped inflame violence in Turkey's own Kurdish south-east, in which some 40 people died. The riots highlighted the high stakes and precariousness of the country's opaque Kurdish peace talks.

At times during the year, Erdogan's statements appeared utterly inimical to the Western values that Turkey had (at least outwardly) endorsed for decades. He announced that sexual equality was unnatural, that outsiders (for which read the West) wanted to see Muslims and their children die, denounced the US and its allies' interest in the Middle East as purely oil-focused and claimed that Muslims had travelled to the Americas before Columbus.

Amid the heightened alarm about authoritarianism, some substantial developments went relatively unnoticed. The split between the government and the Gulenists had a direct impact on highly politicised legal cases that the Gulenists had championed but which had been increasingly denounced as show trials. The Constitutional Court effectively ordered the retrial of one such case, known as "Sledgehammer"—an alleged military conspiracy to overthrow the government—because of doubts about due process and fabricated evidence. Over 200 past and present military officers went free, while suspects in another, similar, case, known as "Ergenekon", were also released pending trial.

The year ended as it began: with the furious battle against the Gulenists. In December, the editor of *Zaman*, the Gulenist newspaper that branded itself Turkey's biggest, and the chief executive of a Gulenist television network were both detained on terrorist charges. A Turkish court issued an arrest warrant for Gulen himself, resident since 1999 in Pennsylvania.

Meanwhile, Erdogan let it be known that he would start chairing Cabinet meetings in January 2015, thus further consolidating his leadership of the country. Naturally, the venue would be the palace.

Daniel Dombey

III CENTRAL AND EASTERN EUROPE

POLAND

CAPITAL: Warsaw   AREA:: 312,690 sq km   POPULATION: 38,530,725 ('13)
OFFICIAL LANGUAGE: Polish
HEAD OF STATE: President Bronislaw Komorowski (PO) (since Aug '10)
RULING PARTIES: Civic Platform (PO) coalition with Polish Peasant Party (PSL)
HEAD OF GOVERNMENT: Prime Minister Ewa Kopacz (PO) (since Oct '14)
DEMOCRACY INDEX: 7.12; =44th of 167   CORRUPTION PERCEPTIONS INDEX: 61; =35th of 175
CURRENCY: Zloty (Dec '14 £1.00=PLN 5.49, US$1.00=PLN 3.53)
GNI PER CAPITA: US$12,960, Intl$22,300 at PPP ('13)

POLAND'S political life in 2014 was marked by unexpected twists and turns. The main one was that Donald Tusk, who had dominated Polish politics since 2007 as prime minister and leader of the ruling Civic Platform (PO), left for Brussels at the end of the year to become president of the EU Council. Tusk had proved himself to be a highly capable and conciliatory politician but as he had a somewhat challenged knowledge of foreign languages, he declared that his immediate task was "to polish his English!"

The replacement for Tusk as PO leader and prime minister in September was Ewa Kopacz, formerly minister of education and Sejm-marshal (speaker of the legislature). This transformed the run-up to decisive presidential and parliamentary elections due in 2015. The PO also managed to rein back what had seemed to be a firm 5 to 10 per cent public opinion lead by the main opposition Law and Justice (PiS) party by holding its own in the European and local elections of 2014.

The worsening Ukrainian crisis from February onwards allowed the PO to highlight Tusk's role as an international statesman, safeguarding Poland's security through EU collaboration. The PO thus overcame its unpopularity on domestic bread-and-butter issues, narrowly defeating PiS by 32.1 to 31.8 per cent of the vote (though both gaining 19 MEPs apiece) in the European Parliament election in May. The government was also strengthened by the success of its junior coalition partner. The Polish Peasant Party (PSL) gained 6.8 per cent of the vote and retained its four MEPs, a result that consolidated the position of its much criticised leader, Janusz Piechocinski. Hopes of a revival for the Left were also rebuffed. The vote for the Democratic Left Alliance (SLD) fell to 9.4 per cent, compared with 12.3 per cent in 2009, reducing their MEPs from nine to seven. A more significant failure for the possible restructuring of the party system was that the Palikot Movement (RP), which had been part of a wider Europa Plus Movement formally led by ex President of the Republic Aleksander Kwasniewski, fizzled out, only receiving 3.6 per cent and gaining no seats.

Suppressed discontent was reflected in the 22.7 per cent turnout at the European elections, the second-lowest ever. It also showed itself in the 7.2 per cent vote (four MEPs) for an extreme right, populist "flash party", the Congress of the New Right (KPN). Led by the veteran anti-establishment, habitually politically incorrect but, apparently, extremely virile, Janusz Korwin-Mikke (born October 1942), who was reported as having recently fathered two illegitimate children, the KPN channelled the frustrations of extremist, anti-state, populist-nationalist youth. It seemed that Green, feminist and other progressive rivals might have to wait a while longer before having their day in Poland.

The new prime minister, Ewa Kopacz (Poland's second female premier), had relatively little political standing initially. She started shakily in September, with an unconvincing government reshuffle designed to neutralise rivals within the PO. Grzegorz Schetyna, a major figure in the PO and opponent of Tusk, replaced Radoslaw Sikorski as foreign minister. Sikorski became Sejm-marshal: his position was undermined further by an expenses scandal and by rumours that he had dismissed the US alliance as "worthless" and that Russia's President Vladimir Putin had discussed a possible partition of Ukraine with him in 2008. Another potential rival, the very impressive regional minister, Elzbieta Bienkowska, also left Warsaw to become Poland's EU commissioner. Kopacz took some time to assert herself as a decisive personality with clear policies distinct from those of her predecessor. She also had to distance herself from yet another typically Polish scandal, which had erupted in June. The influential weekly journal *Wprost* published illicit tape recordings of private conversations between prominent government figures, notably the interior minister exhorting the chairman of the National Bank to support the government with its financial measures.

Buoyed by the "tapes affair" and a 10 per cent public opinion lead, Jaroslaw Kaczynski, the PiS leader, attempted to overcome centre-right disunity. He made deals with prominent ex PiS and PO politicians, notably Jaroslaw Gowin (Poland Together (PR)) and Zbigniew Ziobro (United Poland (SP)), ahead of the November three-tier local government elections, involving 47,000 councillors and 2,500 mayors. PiS hopes were, however, marred by the "Madrid scandal", which led to the expulsion of three PiS deputies for fiddling their travel expenses. Although PiS narrowly defeated PO by 26.7 to 26.4 per cent in the regional elections, they only gained 171 seats to the PO's 179. As the PSL had an astounding score with 23.7 per cent of the vote, the overall result left PiS with control of a single region while PO and its allies controlled the remaining 15. But there had been delays, wide variations from exit poll predictions and an unprecedented 17.9 per cent of the regional vote had been declared invalid, so there were strong grounds for believing that the election had not been run efficiently. As usual, Kaczynski and PiS spoilt their case by claiming "falsification" at wild protest meetings. The withering of credible alternatives to the dominant centre-right tandem also continued with the decline of the SLD's regional vote from 15.2 to 8.8 per cent.

Tusk outmanoeuvred Kaczynski during 2014 by stressing that his foreign policy was building "a strong Poland in a secure Europe". Common EU policies supporting Ukraine in its conflict with Russia anchored Poland firmly in the European mainstream. This transformed Tusk into a major EU figure, prefiguring his election as president of the EU Council. PiS was stridently anti-Russian, nationalist and eurosceptic but its promotion of Poland as a regional leader handling Russia directly seemed archaic and unconvincing. However, Poland was vulnerable to Russia's retaliation against EU economic sanctions—a ban on the import of EU foodstuffs, which affected Poland's fruit and vegetable exports. The minister of agriculture also mismanaged his patriotic appeal to Poles to eat more of their own apples.

Nevertheless, the Polish model of steady economic growth (GDP rose 3.4 per cent during 2014), coupled with financial discipline, continued, as did the construction boom. Poland thus increased its GDP per capita to 68 per cent of the EU average. The social costs of a 13.4 per cent unemployment rate and massive labour emigration were offset by the £1.79 billion in annual remittances from Poles working in the UK.

By the end of 2014 Prime Minister Kopacz had asserted herself politically and strengthened the government's position. Kaczynski, therefore, ducked out of contesting the presidential election of summer 2015. PiS nominated an amiable, but relatively little known MEP, Andrzej Duda, to challenge the popular PO incumbent, Bronislaw Komorowski. Given PiS's lack of potential allies, its prospects of gaining a single-party majority in the subsequent parliamentary election seemed slim.

George Sanford

ESTONIA, LATVIA, AND LITHUANIA

Estonia

CAPITAL: Tallinn   AREA:: 45,230 sq km   POPULATION: 1,324,612 ('13)
OFFICIAL LANGUAGE: Estonian
HEAD OF STATE: President Toomas Hendrik Ilves (since Sept '06)
RULING PARTIES: Reform Party (ER) in coalition with Social Democratic Party (SDE) (since March '14)
HEAD OF GOVERNMENT: Prime Minister Taavi Roivas (ER) (since March '14)
DEMOCRACY INDEX: 7.61; 36th of 167   CORRUPTION PERCEPTIONS INDEX: 69; =26th of 175
CURRENCY: Euro (Dec '14 £1.00=EUR 1.275, US$1.00=EUR 0.821)
GNI PER CAPITA: US$17,370, Intl$24,230 at PPP ('13)

Latvia

CAPITAL: Riga   AREA:: 64,590 sq km   POPULATION: 2,013,385 ('13)
OFFICIAL LANGUAGE: Latvian
HEAD OF STATE: President Andris Berzins (since July '11)
RULING PARTIES: Unity (V)-led coalition
HEAD OF GOVERNMENT: Prime Minister Laimdota Straujuma (V) (since Jan '14)
DEMOCRACY INDEX: 7.05; 47th of 167   CORRUPTION PERCEPTIONS INDEX: 55; =43rd of 175
CURRENCY: Euro (Dec '14 £1.00=EUR 1.275, US$1.00=EUR 0.821)
GNI PER CAPITA: US$15,280, Intl$22,970 at PPP ('13)

Lithuania

CAPITAL: Vilnius   AREA: 65,300 sq km   POPULATION: 2,956,121 ('13)
OFFICIAL LANGUAGE: Lithuanian
HEAD OF STATE: President Dalia Grybauskaite (since July '09)
RULING PARTIES: Social Democratic Party of Lithuania (LSDP)-led coalition
HEAD OF GOVERNMENT: Algirdas Butkevicius (LSDP) Prime Minister (since Dec '12)
DEMOCRACY INDEX: 754; 38th of 167   CORRUPTION PERCEPTIONS INDEX: 58; =39th of 175
CURRENCY: Litas (Dec '14 £1.00=LTL 4.40, US$1.00=LTL 2.83)
GNI PER CAPITA: US$14,900, Intl$24,500 at PPP ('13)

WHILE economic growth remained anaemic in the EU, Lithuania, Latvia and Estonia slightly bucked the trend. In the third quarter of 2014, all the Baltic states recorded above average growth rates, year-on-year (all around 2.5 per cent, compared to 1.3 per cent across the EU). Unemployment decreased to levels close to the EU average in Latvia and Lithuania and remained below that in Estonia (10.7, 9.9 and 6.9 per cent respectively, in October). In line with the rest of the EU, annual inflation was minimal and all three maintained very low budget deficits: negligible in the case of Estonia, and low in Latvia and Lithuania (0.4, 1.4 and 1.2 per cent of GDP, respectively). A balanced budget was particularly important for Lithuania, as the country was preparing to introduce the euro on 1 January 2015. Despite the enthusiasm amongst most of the political elite, popular opinion on joining the eurozone was highly divided and rather sceptical about its consequences—as had already been the case in Estonia and Latvia.

Tensions between Russia and the Baltic states escalated in the wake of the crisis in Ukraine. In February, shortly before the annexation of Crimea, Estonia and Russia signed a border treaty, breaking a long stalemate. Yet at the year's end, the treaty remained to be ratified by the parliaments. In September, Estonia accused Russia of abducting an internal security service officer over the border. Russia accused the officer of spying, argued that he had been on the Russian side of the border, and kept him in custody.

At the request of Baltic governments, NATO bolstered its military presence in the Baltic states. That included increased air defence patrols (the countries had no fighter jets and their airspace was policed in rotation by other NATO member states), partly in response to more frequent violations of airspace by Russian aircraft. Also, the ground forces of other NATO member states—most notably, those of the USA—were deployed at Baltic military bases on a rotational basis. In September, US President Barack Obama visited Estonia to reassure the Baltic states of NATO's commitment to security guarantees.

Stakes were also high in the information war for the hearts and minds of the Baltic Russian minorities (most sizable in Latvia and Estonia). In April, Lithuania suspended the re-broadcasts of Russia's NTV-Mir television channel, accusing it of propaganda. To counter the misinformation by Russian channels that remained popular amongst the Russophone communities, the establishment of a Baltic or even pan-European Russian-language television channel was discussed. In a parallel development, in November, Russia announced the establishment of Sputnik, an expansive foreign-language media service also planned to be delivered in Estonian and Latvian.

In May, the Baltic states held elections to the European Parliament, for the third time. The outcomes were not particularly surprising, with the governing and other main parties generally doing well in Latvia and Estonia. In Lithuania, the Social Democratic Party of Lithuania (LSDP) of Prime Minster Butkevicius lost one of its two MEPs, despite projections that it would gain seats. As in earlier ballots, there was little popular enthusiasm about European elections, reflected in a turnout that was below the EU average in Latvia and Estonia. In Lithuania, however, turnout was more than double that of 2009, largely because the European poll was held concurrently with the second round of presidential elections.

In **Lithuania**, the presidential election in May was won by the incumbent Dalia Grybauskaite, who became the first Lithuanian president to win two consecutive terms in office. She ran as an independent candidate and beat Zigmantas Balcytis, the candidate of the LSDP, in the second round of voting comfortably (59 to 41 per cent). In her victory, Grybauskaite was aided by her highly critical stance on Russia that became particularly relevant as international events unfolded during the campaign.

In June, a referendum was held after 300,000 signatures were collected on a motion to extend the ban on the sale of land to foreigners after the expiry of a transitional period granted by the EU in 2004 when Lithuania joined the union. A large majority—73 per cent—of those who voted supported the controversial ban, but the turnout stood at only 15 per cent, far short of the constitutional 50 per cent requirement. A related initiative to hold a referendum on the adoption of the euro was blocked on constitutional grounds before the gathering of signatures began.

On 1 January 2014, **Latvia** became the newest member of the eurozone. Enthusiasm for the euro had not been universal: all opposition MPs had voted against the euro adoption in 2013, and the popular support was lukewarm. However, support amongst citizens increased considerably in only a matter of weeks after the changeover.

In January, Laimdota Straujuma became the country's first female prime minister, heading an expanded governing coalition as the Union of Greens and Farmers (ZZS), the former party of President Andris Berzins, was added as a partner. The crumbling Reform Party (of former president Valdis Zatlers) and the nationalist right-wing National Alliance (NA) continued as members of the coalition, which was led by the Unity (V) party. Over just a couple of months, NA lost two of its ministers. The environment minister was sacked after ignoring the prime minister's call not to attend a controversial ceremony honouring Latvian soldiers who had fought with the Nazis in World War II; then Justice Minister Baiba Broka resigned as she was not granted access to classified information.

In June, the parliament voted in favour of adding a preamble to the Latvian constitution. The opponents (principally the Social Democratic Party "Harmony" (SDPS)) argued that references to protecting the existence of the Latvian nation and Latvian language would divide a society, in which 38 per cent of people belonged to ethnic minorities.

The composition of the government remained unchanged after October parliamentary elections that were dominated by concerns about Russia. The largely Russophone SDPS once again became the biggest parliamentary party, remaining slightly ahead of V despite a small drop in popularity (23 and 22 per cent of votes, respectively). SDPS remained excluded from the government, reflecting increased reluctance to grant ethnic Russians executive positions. This reluctance only intensified after a friendly visit to Moscow shortly before the election by Nils Usakovs, the leader of SDPS and mayor of Riga. He met Russia's Prime Minister Dmitry Medvedev and the Russian Orthodox Patriarch Kirill, amongst others.

In **Estonia** in March a new government entered office, with Taavi Roivas of Reform Party (ER) as the prime minister. His predecessor, Andrus Ansip—the longest serving prime minister in the EU at the time—had resigned in order to prepare for the European Parliament elections and a possible post in the European Commission. Initially, ER nominated Siim Kallas—a sitting European commissioner and former prime minister—to form a government. However, he came under media pressure over letters of guarantee worth an unaccounted-for $100 million, which had been signed when he was the head of the central bank in the 1990s. After some soul-searching, ER unexpectedly nominated the 34-year old Roivas, the minister of social affairs, as formateur, and he swiftly concluded the coalition negotiations, replacing the Pro Patria and Res Publica Union (IRL) with the Social Democrats (SDE) as the coalition partner.

In November Jürgen Ligi, a long-serving minister of finance for ER, was forced to resign following a careless comment on Facebook, the social media website, about the ethnic background of Jevgeni Ossinovski (SDE), the ethnic Russian minister of education and science. Ligi was replaced by Maris Lauri, a former economic advisor to the prime minister, whose appointment brought the share of female cabinet ministers to the highest-ever in Estonia (43 per cent). In October, the Estonian parliament legalised same-sex partnerships, the first of the countries of the former Soviet Union to do so and in stark contrast to increasing restrictions on gay rights in Russia and other former Soviet states.

Allan Sikk

CZECH REPUBLIC AND SLOVAKIA

Czech Republic

CAPITAL: Prague   AREA: 78,870 sq km   POPULATION: 10,521,468 ('13)
OFFICIAL LANGUAGE: Czech
HEAD OF STATE: President Milos Zeman (since March '13)
RULING PARTIES: Social Democratic Party (CSSD)-led coalition
HEAD OF GOVERNMENT: Prime Minister Bohuslav Sobotka (CSSD) (since Jan '14)
DEMOCRACY INDEX: 8.06; =21st of 167   CORRUPTION PERCEPTIONS INDEX: 51; 53rd of 175
CURRENCY: Czech Koruna (Dec '14 £1.00=CZK 35.32, US$1.00=CZK 22.75)
GNI PER CAPITA: US$18,060, Intl$25,530 at PPP ('13)

Slovakia

CAPITAL: Bratislava   AREA: 49,030 sq km   POPULATION: 5,414,095 ('13)
OFFICIAL LANGUAGE: Slovak
HEAD OF STATE: President Andrej Kiska (since June '14)
RULING PARTY: Direction-Social Democracy (S-SD)
HEAD OF GOVERNMENT: Prime Minister Robert Fico (S-SD) (since April '12)
DEMOCRACY INDEX: 7.35; 41st of 167   CORRUPTION PERCEPTIONS INDEX: 50; 54th of 175
CURRENCY: Euro (Dec '14 £1.00=EUR 1.275, US$1.00=EUR 0.821)
GNI PER CAPITA: US$17,390, Intl$25,500 at PPP ('13)

AFTER a long-running recession and months of political uncertainty, the year 2014 brought stabilisation to the **Czech Republic**. A new centre-left government finally emerged in January with Social Democratic Party (CSSD) chairman Bohuslav Sobotka as prime minister, replacing an interim Cabinet headed by Jiri Rusnok. Rusnok had been appointed by President Milos Zeman in June 2013 after the previous centre-right Cabinet collapsed in a corruption scandal. Early elections were held in October 2013, but the process of forming a government was slow.

The CSSD finally reached agreement in early January with two parties: the Action of Dissatisfied Citizens (ANO) and the Christian Democratic Union (KDU-CSL). While Sobotka was selected as prime minister, ANO leader Andrej Babis became finance minister and KDU-CSL chairman Pavel Belobradek was named minister without portfolio for science, research and innovation. The CSSD and KDU-CSL were established parties, but the ANO was new, drawing concerns about its predictability as a coalition partner. Beyond being anti-establishment, ANO lacked a clear political programme, and its strong electoral results were based largely on perceptions that Babis's wealth would make him less corrupt than other politicians. Babis, who owned a vast empire of agricultural and chemicals firms as well as prominent media groups under the Agrofert umbrella, was listed by *Forbes* magazine as the Czech Republic's second-richest person.

Initially, Zeman threatened to block the government's formation due to objections to several ministerial nominations, citing lack of experience for the role. Other ministers faced concerns about potential conflicts of interests, particularly in the case of Babis. In compliance with Czech law, Babis relinquished his business responsibilities upon joining the Cabinet; however, he refused to sell Agrofert. Babis also faced allegations of collaboration with the Communist-era secret police. Despite reservations, President Zeman appointed the government on 29 January, and Sobotka won a parliamentary vote of confidence on 18 February.

The coalition parties controlled 111 seats in the 200-member lower house of parliament, while the parliamentary opposition comprised four parties. In a sign of public confidence, the ruling parties gained 11 out of 21 seats in the May elections to the European Parliament, and ANO performed especially well. ANO also prevailed in October's local elections. In the election to the Czech Senate (the upper house) that same month, the three ruling parties combined won 19 out of 27 contested seats, meaning that they controlled 46 out of 81 Senate seats. Nevertheless, the total number of CSSD seats declined.

Under Sobotka's government, the Czech Republic's stance toward the European Union warmed, in contrast to the euroscepticism of its centre-right predecessor. In March, the Cabinet backed the country's accession to the EU fiscal pact, committing the Czech Republic to maintaining a balanced budget upon entering the eurozone. Still, Sobotka's Cabinet did not put forward a target date for adopting the common currency. In October, ANO's Vera Jourova became the Czech Republic's representative on the European Commission, taking the justice portfolio.

Both Zeman and Sobotka criticised the EU's sanctions against Russia, imposed following the annexation of Crimea. Zeman's warmth towards Russia went a step further, and his statesmanship was called into question after he used vulgar language in a live radio interview in November. That same month, the Czech Republic celebrated the 25th anniversary of the Velvet Revolution that had brought the end of the communist regime, and many Czechs used the occasion as a protest against Zeman.

On the economic front, the Czech Republic exited the EU's excessive deficit procedure in 2014, as the previous year's government deficit fell below 3 per cent of GDP. After four straight years of fiscal austerity aimed at bringing public finances back under control, public spending was loosened modestly in 2014. While the state budget deficit was below the projected figures in 2014, the government planned for more fiscal loosening in 2015, attracting criticism from the opposition. The government refused to guarantee future electricity prices, leading the CEZ utility company to cancel a tender for the construction of two new reactors at the Temelin nuclear power plant in April.

The end to fiscal austerity contributed to a moderate recovery of domestic demand in 2014, which benefited from low inflation and interest rates, falling unemployment rates, and a recovery of real wage growth after declines in 2012-13. The Czech National Bank (CNB) kept interest rates unchanged at 0.05 per cent throughout the year. The CNB also maintained its policy, introduced in November 2013, aimed at keeping the koruna weak, at approximately 27 to the euro. The depreciating koruna helped the Czech Republic to avoid deflation, and average annual inflation reached 0.4 per cent in 2014. Meanwhile, retail sales and exports grew at healthy rates, despite the impact of the Ukraine crisis. Indeed, Czech car output hit a record 1.25 million units, an increase of 10.5 per cent over the 2013 level.

The year 2014 brought some political surprises for **Slovakia**, while its economy improved. Although the government's position remained solid, Prime Minister Robert Fico experienced a major upset in the March presidential election, losing to independent Andrej Kiska. The presidency was a largely ceremonial role, but many Slovaks feared that a victory for Fico would have concentrated too much power in the hands of his party, Smer-SD (Direction-Social Democracy), which already led a one-party government and had held a majority of parliamentary seats since the 2012 election.

Kiska, who was virtually unknown upon entering the presidential race, unexpectedly defeated Fico in the second round run-off. A businessman and philanthropist, Kiska gained name recognition thanks to an extensive billboard campaign and was the first president to be elected without political party support. Kiska was inaugurated in June as the independent Slovakia's fourth president. His three predecessors had been former Communists, and many Slovaks welcomed the fact that Kiska had never joined any political party.

After taking office, Kiska presented himself as a non-partisan president. Although relations with the government were mostly cordial, Kiska clashed with Smer leaders over the judiciary, rejecting a number of the parliament's appointees and vetoing key legislation. Another point of contention related to foreign policy. Fico publicly questioned the effectiveness of EU sanctions against Russia following the annexation of Crimea, and he repeatedly criticised neighbouring Ukraine. Kiska, in contrast, took steps to reassure Slovakia's partners about the country's commitments as a member of NATO and the EU.

Slovakia assisted Ukraine by opening a reverse-flow pipeline, leading to retaliatory cuts in natural gas supplies from Russia. In October, Slovak EU commissioner Maros Sefkovic was appointed as vice president for the Energy Union.

Fico's failed presidential run led to the dismissal of two ministers (education and economy) and a number of state secretaries. In November, further personnel changes took place following a scandal linking Smer representative Pavol Paska to the alleged purchase of overpriced medical equipment for hospitals. Amid public protests, Paska resigned as speaker of the parliament, and the health minister also lost her post.

In other polls held during the year, Smer won just four out of 13 seats allocated to Slovakia in the European Parliament elections in May, amid record low turnout. In November's local elections, independent candidates were the big winners, gaining 38 per cent of all mayoral seats. Nevertheless, Smer won more mayoral posts than it had four years previously, whilst the centre-right opposition parties performed poorly. Following the presidential polls, the local election confirmed voters' frustration with traditional political parties.

Slovakia's economy improved in 2014, as domestic demand strengthened at the fastest rate since 2008. Consumers benefited from declining unemployment rates, rising real wages, low interest rates, and falling prices, with average annual inflation dropping to 0.1 per cent. External demand was strained in 2014, due to the impact of the conflict in eastern Ukraine, as well as preparations for the launch of new models in the automotive sector. Slovak exports struggled in the second half of 2014, and industrial output growth weakened. Still, the direct impact of the retaliatory sanctions imposed by Russia was limited, and car output was higher than anticipated in 2014 as producers found alternative markets.

Slovakia also recorded fiscal success in 2014 and the country was able to exit the EU's excessive deficit procedure, since the 2013 general government budget deficit fell below the 3 per cent-of-GDP Maastricht limit for the first time in five years. The state budget deficit stood below target in 2014, but inflows of EU cohesion funds fell sharply, signalling a missed opportunity to upgrade Slovakia's infrastructure and labour force.

Debates on family values and media freedom gained prominence. In June, the conservative opposition Christian Democratic Movement joined forces with Smer to push through a constitutional amendment defining marriage as a unique bond between a man and a woman. The Alliance for Family group subsequently initiated a referendum on family values, and the Constitutional Court in October approved three out of four proposed referendum questions. A referendum on the "protection of the family" was set for February 2015. On the media front, the Penta investment group acquired shares in several prominent media organisations in 2014, triggering large-scale resignations at the country's most popular non-tabloid daily newspaper, *Sme*. *Sme* had a history of independent journalism and the staff were concerned that the publication would be misused to promote Penta's business interests.

Sharon Fisher

HUNGARY

CAPITAL: Budapest   AREA: 93,030 sq km   POPULATION: 9,897,247 ('13)
OFFICIAL LANGUAGE: Hungarian
HEAD OF STATE: President Janos Ader (since May '12)
RULING PARTY: Fidesz-Hungarian Civic Alliance (Fidesz-MPSz)
HEAD OF GOVERNMENT: Prime Minister Viktor Orban (Fidesz-MPSz) (since May '10)
DEMOCRACY INDEX: 6.96; 49th of 167   CORRUPTION PERCEPTIONS INDEX: 54; =47th of 175
CURRENCY: Forint (Dec '14 £1.00=HUF 401.6, US$1.00=HUF 258.6)
GNI PER CAPITA: US$12,450, Intl$21,000 at PPP ('12)

THE year 2014 brought triple electoral victory to Prime Minister Viktor Orban and his Fidesz-Hungarian Civic Alliance (Fidesz-MPSz) at general, European and local elections. Yet by the autumn cracks had started to appear in his political edifice for the first time since his return to power in 2010 (see AR 2010, pp. 85-87). Challenges arose from within Orban's party, from the street and from the United States, which resorted to measures hitherto unseen against a fellow member-state of NATO and that sent a shiver of the Cold War through the 25th anniversary celebrations of Hungary's dismantling of the Iron Curtain.

On 6 April though, Orban still had a spring in his step. Fidesz, together with its Christian Democratic (KDNP) allies, won another landslide at a general election that was called free, but unfair, by the observers from the Organisation for Security and Co-operation in Europe (OSCE). In its final report, it said that Fidesz had enjoyed an "undue advantage" and that the "separation between the ruling political party and the state" had been blurred. A unilaterally altered election law helped Fidesz-KDNP win 133 seats in the reduced, 199-seat, National Assembly; thus, Orban continued to command a two-thirds majority, enough to change the constitution. Nevertheless, his best campaign asset was the divided left-liberal opposition, which remained unattractive to voters. Their uneasy electoral alliance, led by the Hungarian Socialist Party (MSzP), gained 38 seats. The green Politics Can Be Different (LMP) party won five seats. The far-right Jobbik secured 23 seats with 20 per cent of the vote. On 25 May, Fidesz-KDNP also comfortably won the elections to the European Parliament: it got 12 of the 22 seats allocated to Hungary. Jobbik came in second place with three seats. Four left-wing and liberal parties won seven seats between them. On 12 October, local elections brought similar results.

Emboldened by his victories, Orban picked new fights at home and abroad. On 11 June, a new tax on advertising revenue was passed. Media firms said it would bankrupt them; the Council of Europe saw it as a threat to media pluralism. Half of the income from the levy was to come from the German-owned RTL Klub, the biggest commercial television channel. In retaliation, its previously tabloid-heavy news programme began pursuing stories about government corruption. It soon became the most popular newscast in the country. The levy also set a pro-government media empire on a collision course with Orban. Previously veiled tensions and conflicts inside Fidesz suddenly became visible, and occasionally it appeared as if governing was mainly about managing oligarchic groups. In fact, according to Transparency International, a corruption watchdog, cronyism and corruption had become so rampant that Hungary "resembled an eastern autocracy". The government said that its priority was supporting domestic businesses and ownership.

Non-governmental organisations (NGOs) that were critical of the government became the next target for Orban. On 2 June, riot police accompanied by pro-government reporters raided NGOs managing the "Norway Fund", which supported civil society in Hungary. Orban said that the NGOs were "paid political activists" advancing "foreign interests", and accused Norway of trying to "influence" Hungarian politics. On 28 July, in a speech in Baile Tusnad, Romania, Orban appeared to admit the goal that his critics had accused him of pursuing for years: that he wanted to abandon liberal democracy and build an "illiberal state", citing Russia as an example. On 1 August, the government signed a €10 billion credit agreement with Russia to finance the expansion of Hungary's nuclear power station by Russia's state-owned Rosatom. Many saw this as cosying up to Russia in the midst of the crisis in eastern Ukraine.

Whilst the EU remained silent, pressure from the USA reached levels unseen since the Cold War. On 18 September, former President Bill Clinton said on a television show that Orban liked "authoritarian capitalism" and wanted to stay in power indefinitely. On 23 September current President Barack Obama said in a keynote speech that in Hungary "overt intimidation" against civil society was increasing. In October six Hungarian government officials, including the head of the tax authority, Ildiko Vida, were banned from entering the United States on suspicion of corruption. The unprecedented step was interpreted as a warning to Orban to reverse policies that undermined democratic values. He called it a "CIA plot" and pressured Vida to sue the US chargé d'affaires for libel. On 2 December, with little penchant for diplomatic finesse, former Republican presidential candidate John McCain called Orban a "neo-fascist dictator" in the US Senate.

The year ended with anti-government demonstrations. On 28 October, up to 100,000 people protested against a planned tax on Internet usage—which forced the government to retreat from a policy for the first time—and against what they saw as the government's incessant conflicts, corruption and incompetence. Whilst one-third of the population lived below the poverty line despite strong GDP growth of 3.9 per cent, a mainly young, pro-Western, middle-class crowd took to the streets—the kind of people Fidesz used to attract. The unnecessary battles that Orban provoked took their toll: Fidesz, while remaining the most popular party, lost up to a million voters in a month, the largest opinion poll fall ever recorded in Hungary.

Daniel Izsak

ROMANIA

CAPITAL: Bucharest   AREA: 238,390 sq km   POPULATION: 19,963,581 ('13)
OFFICIAL LANGUAGE: Romanian
HEAD OF STATE: President Klaus Iohannis (since Dec '14)
RULING PARTIES: Social Democratic Party (PSD)-led coalition
HEAD OF GOVERNMENT: Prime Minister Victor Ponta (PSD) (since May '12)
DEMOCRACY INDEX: 6.54; =60th of 167   CORRUPTION PERCEPTIONS INDEX: 43; =69th of 175
CURRENCY: New Leu (Dec '14 £1.00=RON 5.70, US$1.00=RON 3.67)
GNI PER CAPITA: US$9,060, Intl$18,060 at PPP ('13)

A TURBULENT year in politics began with the collapse of the broad-based governing coalition and ended with the inauguration of a new head of state, Klaus
Iohannes, following his unexpected victory in the presidential election in November. In between these two events there was a great deal of political manoeuvring,
which included the brief return of the ethnic Hungarian party to the government
and the unification of the two main centre-right parties. Relations with Russia
were strained by its annexation of Crimea, but the reciprocal trade sanctions
between the EU and Russia had relatively little impact on the Romanian economy,
which performed reasonably well.

At the start of the year the two main partners in the governing Social Liberal
Union (USL)—the Social Democratic Party (PSD) and the National Liberal Party
(PNL)—attempted to paper over the many cracks in their shaky coalition by
directing their fire at President Traian Basescu, whose interventionist approach
had angered both parties. However, the coalition partners' pledge to maintain their
alliance until the next parliamentary elections, due at the end of 2016, barely lasted
a month, and the government collapsed in late February after the PSD refused to
accept the PNL's nominees in a proposed reshuffle.

Prime Minister Victor Ponta, the leader of the PSD, formed a new government
in early March, which included the PSD's two junior partners in the outgoing
coalition: the National Union for the Progress of Romania (UNPR) and the Conservative Party (PC). To give the government a comfortable majority, the Democratic Union of Hungarians in Romania (UDMR) was invited to join the coalition.
Political stability seemed assured when the PSD, in alliance with the UNPR and
the PC, came first with 37.6 per cent of the vote in the European Parliament elections on 25 May. The UDMR, running on a separate ticket, won 6.3 per cent.
Among the opposition parties, the PNL gained 15 per cent of the vote, ahead of
the Democratic Liberal Party (PDL) with 12.2 per cent, whilst Mircea Diaconu, a
former PNL senator, running as an independent, won 6.8 per cent.

The election results highlighted the need for the centre-right parties to join
forces in order to mount a serious challenge to the PSD at the presidential contest
in November. Crin Antonescu, the leader of the PNL, resigned after the European
elections and was replaced by Klaus Iohannes, the long-serving mayor of the Tran-
sylvanian city of Sibiu. Iohannes, who came from an ethnic German and Protestant background in a country with a largely Romanian and Orthodox Christian
population, also became the joint presidential candidate of the PNL and the PDL.
The two parties, which intensified their negotiations aimed at a merger, were
hoping to exploit their presidential candidate's success in bringing foreign investment and prosperity to Sibiu.

Despite his undoubted popularity, Iohannes, with 30.4 per cent of the vote in the first round held on 2 November, trailed Ponta by exactly 10 percentage points. However, Iohannes nearly doubled his vote in the second round, on 16 November, to win the contest by 54.4 per cent to Ponta's 45.6 per cent. Apart from the complacency displayed by Ponta after his first-round success, the main factor behind the shock result was the galvanising effect of media reports showing Romanian expatriates—usually supporters of the centre-right—forming lengthy queues outside their country's foreign missions to cast their ballots and frequently being unable to do so, owing to poor organisation. The anger this created resulted in a huge increase in the turnout, which reached 64.1 per cent in the second round, compared with 36.7 per cent in the first.

Ponta's unexpected defeat weakened his government's position. The UDMR withdrew from the government in early December, with the party's leadership arguing that it had to respect its electorate, which had voted overwhelmingly for Iohannes. The PNL and the PDL announced their merger after the presidential ballot, inaugurating a united opposition, which adopted the PNL's name. The government came under further pressure when the new president pledged to do his utmost to root out corruption in the administration. Iohannes's promise was an acknowledgement of the lack of progress made since January, when the European Commission's annual report on Romania had expressed concern about politically-motivated attacks on the judiciary and a reluctance to combat high-level corruption.

In foreign affairs there were few differences between the government and the opposition, both of which condemned Russia's annexation of Crimea from Ukraine in March and Russian support for the separatist forces in Ukraine's eastern regions. Romania was a strong supporter of EU sanctions against Russia. It was able to adopt a firm position, partly because it was less dependent on Russian energy supplies than most other countries in the region, and partly because Romanian exports to Russia amounted to only 3 per cent of total foreign sales. In terms of economic output, Romania outperformed most of its neighbours, but real GDP growth, at 3 per cent, remained unspectacular.

Gabriel Partos

BULGARIA

CAPITAL: Sofia   AREA: 111,000 sq km   POPULATION: 7,265,115 ('13)
OFFICIAL LANGUAGE: Bulgarian
HEAD OF STATE: President Rosen Plevneliev (since Jan '12)
RULING PARTIES: GERB-led coalition
HEAD OF GOVERNMENT: Prime Minister Boiko Borisov (GERB) (since Nov '14)
DEMOCRACY INDEX: 6.83; 53rd of 167   CORRUPTION PERCEPTIONS INDEX: 43; =69th of 175
CURRENCY: Lev (Dec '14 £1.00=BGN 2.49, US$1.00=BGN 1.61)
GNI PER CAPITA: US$7,030, Intl$15,200 at PPP ('13)

THE volatile political situation that prevailed for most of the year precipitated a snap election in October—the second in as many years—which returned to power Boiko Borisov of the centre-right Citizens for European Development of Bulgaria

(GERB). His predecessor, Plamen Oresharski, at the head of a fragile Bulgarian Socialist Party (BSP)-led government, had remained under sustained pressure to turn around the economy and appease protesters, unhappy with widespread corruption and the growing cost of living.

Criticism also came from the European Commission through the so-called "cooperation and verification mechanism", which was established when Bulgaria joined the EU in 2007 to monitor the reform of its judicial system. The Commission's report in January concluded that, despite efforts to tackle corruption and organised crime, overall progress was very limited.

There was more pressure in June, when the EU temporarily froze tens of millions of euro in regional development funds for Bulgaria. It also asked Bulgaria to suspend work on the proposed South Stream gas pipeline. This was to have run from Russia to Europe through Bulgaria, thus bypassing Ukraine. The Commission argued that the awarding of the construction permit, without a public tender, to a Russian consortium was in breach of EU competition rules. But there was also a broader issue regarding the attempt to reduce many EU countries' excessive reliance on Russian gas supplies. The move sparked controversy, especially in the ranks of the BSP, with some concerned about the loss of economic benefits as well as the alienation of their traditional Russian ally. It also prompted the pro-Russian nationalist Ataka party to withdraw its tacit support from the fragile governing coalition.

Since taking office in May 2013, the BSP-led government had faced no fewer than four opposition no-confidence motions, which it survived thanks to support from its junior coalition partner, the Movement for Rights and Freedoms (DPS), and the tacit support from Ataka. But the BSP's credibility was seriously shaken by the result of the European Parliament elections in May, in which it received just under 20 per cent of the vote. The BSP's disappointing performance prompted GERB, which was the biggest winner with 30.4 per cent of the vote, to lead opposition calls for the government to step down, which it finally did in July when it lost the support of the DPS.

The election on 5 October resulted in a highly fragmented parliament, with eight parties represented in the National Assembly, compared with four in the previous parliament. The BSP suffered a humiliating defeat, winning just 39 seats in the 240-seat National Assembly. Its new leader, Mikhail Mikov, said he would rebuild the party and lead the opposition along with its former coalition ally, the DPS, which did rather well in the poll, winning 38 seats. The mandate to form a government went to GERB's Boiko Borisov, whose party won 84 seats, well short of an overall majority. He formed a minority coalition government with the fractious Reformist Block, which won 23 seats. For a parliamentary majority, the GERB-led coalition relied on the 19 seats of the nationalist Patriotic Front and the 11 won by the centre-left Alternative for Bulgarian Revival, which had split from the BSP in early 2014.

The new government faced a number of serious challenges, including reviving the country's sluggish economy. It had to improve the business environment, which made it difficult for companies to access credit, especially after the banking crisis. Business activity was also adversely affected by the freeze on EU development funds. The new governing coalition adopted a number of measures, including raising the debt ceiling to reduce the budget deficit and bring down the public debt, which had ballooned due to unchecked pre-election spending and a shortfall in revenue collection.

Genc Lamani

ALBANIA

CAPITAL: Tirana   AREA: 28,750 sq km   POPULATION: 2,773,620 ('13)
OFFICIAL LANGUAGE: Albanian
HEAD OF STATE: President Bujar Nishani (since July '12)
RULING PARTIES: Democratic Party of Albania (PDSh)-led coalition
HEAD OF GOVERNMENT: Prime Minister Edi Rama (Socialist Party) (since Sept '13)
DEMOCRACY INDEX: 5.67; 92nd of 167   CORRUPTION PERCEPTIONS INDEX: 33; =110th of 175
CURRENCY: Lek (Dec '14 £1.00=ALL 178.32, US$1.00=ALL 114.83)
GNI PER CAPITA: US$4,700, Intl$10,520 at PPP ('13)

THE centre-left governing coalition led by Edi Rama tried to show that it was not to be distracted from the path of reform and was determined to accelerate Albania's EU integration process.

It defended its reform of the police service, including key changes in the force's leadership. Responding to opposition claims that many of the new appointments, including the police chief, had a shady past, the government agreed to an opposition-led parliamentary inquiry on the issue. It also pressed ahead with a controversial administrative territorial reform, prompted by major demographic changes since the collapse of communism. The new administrative map adopted in July drastically reduced the number of urban municipalities to 61 from the previous 350, but was challenged in the Constitutional Court by the opposition Democratic Party (PDSh). The Court did not accept the PDSh contention that the new administrative map was designed for political gain.

To demonstrate their commitment to fighting organised crime, the authorities raided, in June, the southern village of Lazarat, known as the country's "cannabis capital", which had been outside police control for 20 years. Some 800 officers were engaged in heavy gun battles with gangs who had turned the village into Europe's largest marijuana producer, with an annual output worth almost half of Albania's GDP. A similar operation followed in cannabis-growing areas in northern Albania. Days later (on 24 June) EU foreign ministers granted Albania EU candidate status more than five years after it had applied to join the 28-member block. But in its annual progress report in October the European Commission reiterated the need for Albania to meet a number of conditions in full before accession talks could begin.

The Bank of Albania (BoA), the central bank, was shaken by revelations in July that one of its employees had stolen about $7 million (713 million lek) from the bank's cash vault. The crisis worsened in September with the arrest of the BoA governor, Ardian Fullani, on charges of dereliction of duty, which he denied. His arrest brought the number of BoA staff detained in the case to 19.

The government embarked upon a campaign against electricity theft, and Rama dismissed a number of senior officials, including a deputy minister, for not paying their electricity bills. According to the World Bank almost 30 per cent of electricity that entered the grid in 2013 was stolen.

Albanian public opinion was stunned by the fallout from an incident during a European Championship football match between Serbia and Albania, in Belgrade, the Serbian capital, in October. The match, from which away-supporters had been banned, was abandoned after a drone flew an Albanian nationalist flag over the stadium. The resulting violence involving players and Serb fans led to the postponement of Rama's visit to Belgrade, the first by an Albanian leader in 68 years. The fixture had been identified as high-risk because of lingering tensions over the mainly Albanian former Serbian province of Kosovo. The political tension peaked during Rama's rearranged visit to Belgrade, in November, when his host, Serbia's Prime Minister Aleksandar Vucic, accused Rama of "a provocation", after the latter stated that "independent Kosovo was an undeniable regional and European reality, which must be respected".

Genc Lamani

MACEDONIA

CAPITAL: Skopje   AREA: 25,710 sq km   POPULATION: 2,107,158 ('13)
OFFICIAL LANGUAGE: Macedonian
HEAD OF STATE: President Gjorgje Ivanov (VMRO-DPMNE) (since May '09)
RULING PARTY: Internal Macedonian Revolutionary Organisation - Democratic Party for
    Macedonian National Unity (VMRO-DPMNE)-led coalition
HEAD OF GOVERNMENT: Prime Minister Nikola Gruevski (VMRO-DPMNE) (since Aug '06)
DEMOCRACY INDEX: 6.16; 74th of 167   CORRUPTION PERCEPTIONS INDEX: 45; =64th of 175
CURRENCY: Denar (Dec '14 £1.00=MKD 78.33, US$1.00=MKD 50.45)
GNI PER CAPITA: US$4,800, Intl$11,520 at PPP ('13)

ELECTIONS consumed the energies of the political class in Macedonia in 2014. Both the presidency and seats in the Assembly of the Republic (the parliament) were contested. Government parties triumphed in both polls, after which the Social Democrat-led opposition walked out of parliament, claiming it had been cheated of victory by fraud.

In the presidential election, the main candidates were the incumbent, Gjorgje Ivanov, supported by the main governing VMRO-DPMNE party, and Stevo Pendarovski, candidate of the opposition Social Democratic Party (SDSM). Neither won outright in the first round on 13 March. After the other candidates withdrew, Ivanov won the second round on 27 March by a comfortable margin, winning 55.28 per cent to 41.14 per cent cast for Pendarovski.

In the general election, brought forward to coincide with the second round of the presidential election, VMRO-DPMNE increased its share of the vote, winning 42.98 per cent and taking 61 of the 123 seats in parliament—an increase of five on its result in the last general election in 2011. The SDSM won 25.34 per cent and 34 seats, a loss of eight. VMRO's partner party in the ethnic Albanian community, the Democratic Union for Integration (DUI), also polled well, winning 13.71 per cent and 19 seats, an increase of four. The rival Democratic Party of Albanians (DPA), won seven seats, a loss of one.

The SDSM, led by Zoran Zaev, cried foul, refused to take up its seats and said it would not return to the chamber until VMRO-DPMNE agreed to the formation of a caretaker government that would oversee new elections. Government parties dismissed the idea. Indeed, the boycott had little effect on day-to-day business in parliament as VMRO-DPMNE and the DUI between them held almost two-thirds of the seats. The DPA had also declined to join the boycott, so its seven MPs were still in the chamber. The new Assembly took office on 10 May.

On 4 July, police clashed with several thousand ethnic Albanians who took to the streets of Skopje to condemn court verdicts in the so-called "Monster" trial. The protest started after a court had imposed life-sentences on six ethnic Albanians for the murders in 2012 of five Macedonian fishermen at a lake near Skopje (see AR 2013, p. 79). The street clashes stirred memories of the large-scale ethnic violence that had rocked the country in 2001. In the event, the protests subsided, although relations between the authorities and ethnic Albanians, who comprised about one-quarter of the population, remained tense, aggravated by the exceptionally high rate of unemployment in the community and by a perception that VMRO-DPMNE was trying to render them invisible, partly by erecting a mass of new monuments representing Orthodox Christian saints and ethnic Macedonian heroes.

In November, parliament began the process of stripping the 31 absent opposition MPs of their mandates. It was unclear whether fresh elections would be held for the seats in question, or whether they would be offered to the runners-up of the March general election.

Marcus Tanner

KOSOVO

CAPITAL: Pristina   AREA: 10,887 sq km   POPULATION: 1,824,000 ('13)
OFFICIAL LANGUAGE: Albanian, Serbian
HEAD OF STATE: President Atifete Jahjaga (since April '11)
RULING PARTIES: Democratic Party of Kosovo (PDK) in coalition with Democratic League of
    Kosovo (LDK)
HEAD OF GOVERNMENT: Prime Minister Isa Mustafa (PDK) (since Dec '14)
CORRUPTION PERCEPTIONS INDEX: 33; =110th of 175
CURRENCY: Euro (not formal member of the Eurozone) (Dec '14 £1.00=EUR 1.275, US$1.00=EUR
    0.821); Serbian Dinar (Dec '14 £1.00=RSD 154.4, US$1.00=RSD 99.4)
GNI PER CAPITA: US$3,890, Intl$8,940 at PPP ('13)

KOSOVO spent most of the year in political deadlock after general elections were called on 7 May. Polling day was set for 8 June but the results failed to clarify matters. The governing Democratic Party of Kosovo (PDK), led by Prime Minister Hashim Thaci, won more votes than any other party—just over 30 per cent—taking 37 of the 120 seats in the Assembly, an increase of three on the December

2010 result. Its main rival, the Democratic League of Kosovo (LDK), came second with 25 per cent, taking 30 seats, also three up on the last election. Neither party was close to commanding a majority.

The LDK then formed a coalition with two other parties—the Alliance for the Future of Kosovo (AAK) and the Initiative for Kosovo (NISMA)—which the nationalist Vetevendosje (Self-determination) movement promised to support in parliament. The opposition coalition succeeded in having the LDK leader, Isa Mustafa, elected speaker (president of the Assembly) on 17 July. However, the PDK insisted that the opposition coalition was politically illegitimate, as it had been formed after the election, not before, and it took the matter of the speaker's election before the Constitutional Court. Late in August the Court ruled in favour of the PDK, maintaining that the right to elect the speaker belonged exclusively to the party that won most seats in the election. Mustafa had to stand down but the PDK was still unable to get its own candidate elected. Without a speaker, none of the other institutions of government could be formed.

Day-to-day government remained in the hands of the outgoing administration, which took few initiatives. As a result, progress on other fronts, such as the EU-led talks with Serbia on the normalisation of relations, was limited (see AR 2013, pp. 80; 82). An NGO report in November concluded that only one-quarter of the agreements reached under EU auspices in Brussels between Serbia and Kosovo had been implemented, blaming the delays on elections cycles in both Kosovo and Serbia. However, in July, Kosovo completed negotiations with the EU on a Stabilisation and Association Agreement, a milestone on the path toward eventual EU membership.

Towards the end of October, the EU rule of law mission, EULEX Kosovo, appointed to investigate organised crime in the country, was rocked by bribery allegations. The row began after the newspaper *Koha Ditore* published internal EULEX files, containing information that a British prosecutor attached to the mission had accused an Italian judge and one other official of shutting down cases for money. The scandal deepened after the alleged whistleblower, Maria Bamieh, was suspended, after which she gave several interviews to the local media declaring EULEX a corrupt waste of money.

As the year ended, six months of political stalemate came to an end. In November, the LDK suddenly detached itself from the opposition coalition and said it was ready to form a government with the PDK after all. On 9 December the terms of a coalition deal were agreed, under which Mustafa would become prime minister whilst Thaci would swap the post of prime minister for that of first deputy prime minister and foreign minister, with the right to succeed Atifete Jahjaga as president of Kosovo in 2016.

Marcus Tanner

SERBIA

CAPITAL: Belgrade   AREA: 88,361 sq km   POPULATION: 7,163,976 ('13)
OFFICIAL LANGUAGE: Serbo-Croat
HEAD OF STATE: President Tomislav Nikolic (SNS) (since June '12)
RULING PARTIES: Serbian Progressive Party (SNS)-led coalition
HEAD OF GOVERNMENT: Aleksandar Vucic (SNS) (since April '14)
DEMOCRACY INDEX: 6.67; 57th of 167   CORRUPTION PERCEPTIONS INDEX: 41; 78th of 175
CURRENCY: Serbian Dinar (Dec '14 £1.00=RSD 154.4, US$1.00=RSD 99.4)
GNI PER CAPITA: US$5,730, Intl$12,020 at PPP ('13)

THE governing Serbian Progressive Party (SNS) consolidated its political dominance in early general elections called on 16 March. The SNS won 48.35 per cent
of votes and 158 seats in the National Assembly, more than double the 73 seats it
had won in the last general elections in 2012. Its former partner, the Socialist Party
of Serbia (SPS), came second with 13.49 per cent, winning 44 seats. The Democratic Party (DS), the dominant party in government from 2008 until 2012, barely
passed the 5 per cent threshold needed to enter parliament with a meagre 6.03 per
cent of the votes and 19 seats. Part of its vote went to a new party led by the former
DS leader and former president of Serbia, Boris Tadic, which won 5.7 per cent of
the vote and 18 seats. Ethnic minority parties (which did not need to cross the 5
per cent barrier) took another 11 seats.

Although the Progressives now had an absolute majority in the 250-seat Assembly, Prime Minister-designate Aleksandar Vucic invited the Socialists to rejoin the
government and also offered posts to an ethnic minority party, the Alliance of
Vojvodina Hungarians. The new Cabinet of 19 ministers was inaugurated on 27
April. Vucic said that its priorities would be reform of the economy, cutting the
deficit and accelerating progress towards EU membership. The EU accession
process did move forward. At the first intergovernmental conference, in January, it
was agreed that Chapters 23, 24 and 35 of the acquis communautaire—on the judiciary, rule of law and relations with Kosovo—would be opened first, probably
early in 2015.

A natural disaster, meanwhile, struck on 19 May when the heaviest rainfall in
memory hit Serbia, Bosnia and parts of Croatia. Some 30,000 people were forced
from their homes in Serbia. The town of Obrenovac, south of Belgrade, was almost
completely submerged. On 20 May, the government proclaimed three days of
mourning for an estimated 33 casualties: the precise death toll was unclear. Serbia
put the cost of repairing the damage at €1.5 billion. At the international donors'
conference, held on 16 July in Brussels, Serbia received pledges of €995.2 million
in aid, mostly in loans.

A football match with Albania on 14 October ended in violence and derailed the
first visit to Serbia in decades by an Albanian prime minister. The Euro 2016 qualifying match at the Partizan stadium in Belgrade descended into chaos some 40
minutes into the game when a small drone carrying the flag of "Greater Albania"
flew over the pitch, sparking a brawl amongst the players. Serbian fans (Albania's
fans having been banned from attending by UEFA) then invaded the pitch. The
Serbian authorities accused the brother of Albania's Prime Minister Edi Rama of
guiding the drone from the VIP stands, calling the stunt "a provocation". Rama

delayed his visit to allow tempers to cool but the trip went ahead on 10 November. It was not a success. President Tomislav Nikolic refused to meet him and after Rama told a joint press conference held with Prime Minister Vucic that it was time for Serbia to recognise the independence of its former province of Kosovo, Vucic accused him of trying to "humiliate" Serbia. Foreign Minister Ivica Dacic later said an attempt to "turn the page of history" had failed, but also blamed Rama for the debacle.

While relations with Albania remained dire, ties with Russia were as cordial as ever. Serbia flatly refused to join EU and Western sanctions on Russia, imposed in connection to its role in the Ukraine crisis, saying it would never turn its back on its traditional ally. On 16 October, Russia's President Vladimir Putin received a hero's welcome in Belgrade as guest of honour at a military parade marking the 70th anniversary of the liberation of Belgrade from Nazi occupation. Patriarch Kirill of Moscow and All Rus paid his own high-profile visit to Serbia shortly afterwards, in November. There was bitter disappointment in Serbia when President Putin announced early in December that Russia was abandoning plans for its South Stream gas pipeline to western Europe, which was to have run through Serbia. The authorities had talked up the potential gains to be made from transit fees and from other investment arising from construction of the pipeline.

The ultra-nationalist leader of the Serbian Radical Party, Vojislav Seselj, returned from The Hague on 12 November after the International Criminal Tribunal for the former Yugoslavia, the ICTY, ordered his temporary release for health reasons. Seselj was suffering from cancer, and the verdict in his marathon trial for war crimes was not expected until late in 2015 (the trial had opened in 2006, see AR 2007, p. 103). Making it clear that neither years nor illness had mellowed him, he immediately announced his intention of toppling the president and prime minister.

Marcus Tanner

MONTENEGRO

CAPITAL: Podgorica   AREA: 14,026 sq km   POPULATION: 621,383 ('13)
OFFICIAL LANGUAGE: Montenegrin
HEAD OF STATE: President Filip Vujanovic (since May '03, in union with Serbia)
RULING PARTIES: Democratic Party of Socialists (DPS)-led coalition
HEAD OF GOVERNMENT: Prime Minister Milo Djukanovic (DPS) (since Dec '12)
DEMOCRACY INDEX: 5.94; 79th of 167   CORRUPTION PERCEPTIONS INDEX: 42; =76th of 175
CURRENCY: Euro [not formal member of eurozone]   (Dec '14 £1.00=EUR 1.275, US$1.00=EUR 0.821)
GNI PER CAPITA: US$7,260, Intl$14,600 at PPP ('13)

THE EU accession process preoccupied the country for the first part of the year. In May Montenegro completed the so-called screening process in its EU membership negotiations. By September, 12 chapters in the acquis communautaire had been opened and two closed.

Local elections held on 25 May, meanwhile, saw the ruling Democratic Party of Socialists (DPS) continuing to perform strongly. Opposition parties did better than in the last elections in 2010, but the DPS still came first in 11 of the 12 municipalities, although it only won outright in three. The result in the capital, Podgorica, was confusing. The DPS won 29 of the 59 seats in the city assembly to 25 for the main opposition parties. The Social Democrats (SDP) with whom the DPS was in coalition nationally—but not locally in Podgorica—won five. It took months of wrangling before the SDP and DPS finally agreed in September that a DPS candidate, the education minister, Slavoljub Stijepovic, would become the city's next mayor.

There was much disappointment at NATO's failure to invite Montenegro to join the Alliance at the summit held in Wales early in September. With an eye on the forthcoming summit, the government had demonstrated its pro-Western credentials by supporting the imposition of sanctions on Russia in connection with the crisis in Ukraine in March, and again in April when the package of Western sanctions was increased. However, while the Alliance in its summit conclusions welcomed Montenegro's "constructive role in the western Balkan region", it put off reaching a final decision on a membership bid until 2015. In the meantime, NATO urged the government to work harder on security matters and on the rule of law. The low level of public support in Montenegro for joining NATO was one issue, as were perceived security problems in its intelligence agency, the National Security Agency (ANB), which, according to some reports, had been heavily penetrated by Russian agents. The ANB director, Boro Vucinic, unexpectedly resigned in December.

The capital's second-ever "Gay Pride" march went off more or less peacefully on 2 November when about 200 gays, lesbians and supporters marched through Podgorica, their route secured by a larger force of several hundred riot police. The head of the Serbian Orthodox Church in Montenegro was declared "homophobe of the year" at the event. Metropolitan Amfilohije had earlier likened the gay rights march to "a parade of death and self-destruction".

Marcus Tanner

BOSNIA & HERZEGOVINA

CONSTITUENT REPUBLICS: Federation of Bosnia & Herzegovina (FBiH, Muslim-Croat Federation); and Republika Srpska (RS, Serb Republic)
CAPITAL: Sarajevo   AREA: 51,210 sq km   POPULATION: 3,829,307 ('13)
OFFICIAL LANGUAGES: Bosnian, Croatian, Serbian
HEAD OF STATE: Tripartite presidency: Mladen Ivanic (SDS) (Serb); Bakir Izetbegovic (SDA), Bosniak; Dragan Covic (HDZ BiH) (Croat) (since Nov '14)
PRESIDENTS OF REPUBLICS: FBiH: Zivko Budimir (HSP BiH) (since March '11); RS: Milorad Dodic (SNSD) (since Oct '10)
HEAD OF GOVERNMENT: Chairman of Council of Ministers Vjekoslav Bevanda (HDZ) (since Jan '12)
DEMOCRACY INDEX: 5.02; 99th of 167   CORRUPTION PERCEPTIONS INDEX: 39; =80th of 175
CURRENCY: Marka (Dec '14   £1.00=BAM 2.49, US$1.00=BAM 1.61)
GNI PER CAPITA: US$4,740, Intl$9,820 at PPP ('13)

THE year 2014 saw the worst social unrest since the 1992-95 war, followed by the worst natural disaster in memory. Weeks of street protests began in the northern town of Tuzla on 4 February when unemployed workers from privatised companies demonstrated outside the headquarters of the cantonal government against mismanagement of the privatisation process, corruption and poverty in general.

Within days the protests had spread across much of Bosnia, culminating on 7 February when rioters in the capital, Sarajevo, set fire to the state presidency and the building of the state archives. Police used rubber bullets and tear gas to disperse the crowds and 130 people were reported injured. Elsewhere, government buildings in Zenica and Mostar came under attack. By the end of the week, so-called "citizens plenums" had established themselves as alternative sources of authority in several towns and it initially seemed that these self-appointed bodies might displace the elected authorities in all or most of the 10 cantons inside the Federation of Bosnia and Herzegovina (FBiH), the larger of Bosnia's two autonomous entities.

However, the protest movement and the plenums lost momentum, partly because the protesters lacked clear economic and political objectives and partly because the Bosnian Serbs held themselves aloof. Political leaders in the predominantly Serbian entity, Republika Srpska (RS), accused the protest movement of concealing a Bosniak (Muslim) agenda. The violent scenes in Sarajevo also forced the movement onto the defensive. After indicating that he might quit, the FBiH prime minister, Nermin Niksic, soon changed his mind and said he would not resign after all.

Bosnia's worst natural disaster in recorded history then intervened. On 13 May, three days of extraordinarily heavy rain began. On 15 May—by which time parts of Bosnia were virtually submerged—the government declared a national state of emergency. Within a week, over 90,000 people had been forced from their homes and dozens of flood-related deaths recorded. Mini-landslides destroyed houses, schools, bridges, roads and other items of infrastructure. The government estimated that it would cost €2 billion to repair the damage. On 16 July, the European Union hosted an international donors' conference in Brussels at which 60 participating countries pledged €809.2 million in relief for Bosnia, with similar sums promised to Serbia and Croatia, which had also suffered in the disaster. Most of the money was not offered as a gift but in loan form. The process of distributing foreign aid was marked by predictable rows between Bosnia's two entities, the Bosniak- and Croat-dominated Federation and the mainly Serbian RS.

Similar quarrels marred attempts to mark the centenary of the assassination of the Archduke Franz Ferdinand in Sarajevo in June 1914 (see AR 1914, pp. 328-29), the proximate cause of the First World War. As a result, the two entities held separate commemorations and Bosnian Serb leaders boycotted the main event in Sarajevo, a performance by the Vienna Philharmonic.

In September campaigning began for elections to the 10 cantonal assemblies in the Federation entity, the parliaments of the two entities, the state Parliamentary Assembly and the tripartite state presidency. The elections, which took place on 12 October, were a triumph for Bosnia's three main ethnic parties: the (Serbian) Alliance of Independent Social Democrats (SNSD), the (Bosniak) Party of Democratic Action (SDA), and the Croatian Democratic Union of Bosnia and Herzegovina (HDZ BiH).

The results were a disaster for the non-ethnic Social Democratic Party (SDP), which had been the dominant force in the previous state and Federation entity governments. The SDA and HDZ BiH between them won in all 10 Federation cantons, the SDA coming first in six and HDZ BiH in four. In elections to the Federation parliament, the SDA won 274,000 votes, far more than the nearest runner-up, the Democratic Front, which won 150,000. The SDP polled a disappointing 92,000 votes.

In elections to the state presidency, the SDA and HDZ BiH candidates won the two seats reserved for Bosniaks and Croats, Bakir Izetbegovic of the SDA regaining his seat after winning 247,235 votes and Dragan Covic of the HDZ BiH winning his seat with 128,053 votes. The failure of the SNSD to get its candidate elected to the Serbian seat was a surprise. By a narrow margin, the post went to Mladen Ivanic, candidate of a rival Serbian bloc gathered round the Serbian Democratic Party (SDS), who won with 317,799 votes.

While SNSD had lost its foothold on the state presidency, it still formed the next government in Republika Srpska, after winning 249,000 votes in the entity to 211,000 cast for the SDS and its allies. The SDA and HDZ BiH pledged to work together in the Federation entity and at state level. However, no one expected torturous negotiations between the various parties on forming a state government to conclude before the spring of 2015.

Marcus Tanner

CROATIA

CAPITAL: Zagreb   AREA: 56,540 sq km   POPULATION: 4,252,700 ('13)
OFFICIAL LANGUAGE: Croatian
HEAD OF STATE: President Ivo Josipovic (since Feb '10)
PRESIDENT ELECT: Kolinda Grabar-Kitarovic
RULING PARTIES: Social Democratic Party (SDP)-led coalition
HEAD OF GOVERNMENT: Prime Minister Zoran Milanovic (SDP) (since Dec '11)
DEMOCRACY INDEX: 6.93; 50th of 167   CORRUPTION PERCEPTIONS INDEX: 48; =61st of 175
CURRENCY: Kuna (Dec '14 £1.00=HRK 9.76, US$1.00=HRK 6.29)
GNI PER CAPITA: US$13,330, Intl$20,370 at PPP ('13)

ELECTIONS to the European Parliament on 25 May were a setback for the centre-left government, led by the Social Democrats (SDP). The centre-right opposition Croatian Democratic Union (HDZ) won 41.4 per cent of the votes, well ahead of the SDP and its allies, who won 29.9 per cent. A new Green alliance won 9.4 per cent. The HDZ took six of the 11 European Parliament seats allocated to Croatia, the SDP four and the Greens, one. The relative success of the scandal-hit HDZ, whose former leader, Ivo Sanader, had been jailed in 2012 for corruption, was interpreted as a sign of declining confidence in the SDP's ability to manage the economy.

In August, the Constitutional Court struck down plans by right-wing campaigners to force the government to agree to a referendum on the public use of the Serbian Cyrillic script. By law, ethnic minorities were entitled to the official use of their languages and scripts in areas where they comprised at least one-third of the population. The campaigners for a referendum, mainly veterans of the independence war of the early 1990s, in particular objected to a campaign to enforce the display of Serbian Cyrillic street signs in the eastern town of Vukovar, to which Serbian paramilitary and Yugoslav Army forces had laid waste before overrunning it in November 1991. Ethnic Serbs by 2014 comprised just over one-third of the population of the town and were thus entitled to signs in Cyrillic. However, each time the authorities erected such signs, hostile elements tended to tear them down or deface them.

The campaigners hoped to replicate the success of an earlier referendum, held in December 2013 against the wishes of the government, which obliged the authorities to redefine marriage in Croatia's constitution in strictly heterosexual terms (see AR 2014, p. 88). The "Headquarters for the Defence of Croatian Vukovar", as the campaigners styled themselves, duly gathered over 650,000 signatures and sent them to parliament, which after much delay referred the question to the Constitutional Court. The Court, however, pronounced the terms of the question incompatible with Croatia's constitution and its international legal commitments in terms of equality and human rights.

On 19 October, police arrested the mayor of Zagreb, Milan Bandic, and several accomplices, on suspicion of corruption and abuse of office. He was later released on bail. Bandic, mayor of the capital since 2000, had formerly been a member of the SDP, which he quit in 2009 to run as an independent in the presidential elections.

Vukovar returned to the news again, following the temporary release of the Serbian ultra-nationalist, Vojislav Seselj, by the International Criminal Tribunal for the former Yugoslavia (ICTY). The Hague court allowed the leader of the Serbian Radical Party, who was on trial for war crimes committed in Croatia, Bosnia and Serbia in the 1990s, to go home for cancer treatment and because no verdict in his protracted case was expected for months (see article on Serbia). He returned to Belgrade on 12 November and soon made a number of inflammatory statements, one of which mocked the annual Croatian commemoration of the fall of Vukovar to the Yugoslav Army and Serbian paramilitaries on 18 November. The message, describing the fall of town as an act of "liberation", angered politicians on all sides of the political divide in Croatia. President Ivo Josipovic wrote to the president of the ICTY, Theodor Meron, describing the decision to release Seselj from custody as a "defeat for justice and international law". A particularly large crowd of around 100,000 converged on Vukovar for the 2014 commemoration, including the Croatian president and most politicians. On the initiative of a Croatian MEP, Andrej Plenkovic, on 27 November the European Parliament passed a resolution condemning Seselj's "warmongering" rhetoric.

On 19 November the government announced that presidential elections would go ahead on 28 December. Although the SDP-led government was unpopular, Josipovic, who was backed by the SDP, was still expected to beat Kolinda Grabar-Kitarovic, candidate of the HDZ and its allies. However, with no outright winner in December, a second round was held on 11 January, 2015, in which Grabar-Kitarovic defeated the incumbent by the slimmest of margins.

Marcus Tanner

SLOVENIA

CAPITAL: Ljubljana   AREA: 20,270 sq km   POPULATION: 2,060,484 ('13)
OFFICIAL LANGUAGE: Slovene
HEAD OF STATE: President Borut Pahor (since Dec '12)
RULING PARTIES: Party of Miro Cerar (SMC)-led coalition
HEAD OF GOVERNMENT: Prime Minister Miro Cerar (SMC) (since Sept '14)
DEMOCRACY INDEX: 7.88; 30th of 167   CORRUPTION PERCEPTIONS INDEX: 58; =39th of 175
CURRENCY: Euro (Dec '14 £1.00=EUR 1.275, US$1.00=EUR 0.821)
GNI PER CAPITA: US$22,750, Intl$28,130 at PPP ('13)

SLOVENIA'S first woman prime minister, Alenka Bratusek, lost her job after only 13 months in May following an internal coup inside her Positive Slovenia party. After a party congress ousted her as leader and restored the previous leader, Zoran Jankovic, Bratusek stepped down as prime minister and urged parliament to call fresh elections. At the end of May, she formed her own party, the Alliance of Alenka Bratusek. Chaos within the ranks of Positive Slovenia contributed to its poor showing in the European Parliament elections on 25 May, when it won only 6.6 per cent of the vote. In spite of the fact that its leader, Janez Jansa, had been jailed for corruption, the opposition centre-right Slovenian Democratic Party (SDS) did best, winning 24.9 per cent of the vote and taking three of the eight Slovenian seats in the European Parliament.

On 1 June, President Borut Pahor announced that a general election would take place on 13 July. In the election, voters took their revenge on Positive Slovenia: the party failed to win a single seat. Bratusek's new formation, on the other hand, won four seats. However, the winner by far was another political novice, Miro Cerar, whose own new formation, the Party of Miro Cerar (SMC), won an astonishing 38.4 per cent of the vote, giving it 36 of the 90 seats in parliament. The SDS came second with 20.6 per cent and 21 seats, followed by the Pensioners' Party, DeSus, with 10.2 per cent of the vote and 10 seats, and the Social Democrats (SD) who came fourth with 5.98 per cent of the vote and took six seats.

The vote was seen as a powerful demonstration of voters' almost complete distrust of the established parties. Cerar had only formed his party six weeks before the elections and was best known for being the son of a once-popular Olympic gymnast. In September, he formed a new government with the DeSus and the Social Democrats. In the febrile political atmosphere, the popularity of the new government—unsurprisingly—sank rapidly. A poll conducted by the Vox populi agency late in November found that only 18 per cent of respondents approved of the new government's policies.

One of Cerar's first acts was to select a Slovene to serve on the new European Commission. His choice for the transport portfolio was an unconventional businesswoman, Violeta Bulc, whose listed interests included shamanism and firewalking. At the end of her hearing before European parliamentarians, Bulc remarked, "You learned I walk on fire", adding, "There were some moments when I thought I would get burnt, but that did not happen." Indeed it did not; she got the job.

Marcus Tanner

RUSSIA

CAPITAL: Moscow   AREA: 17,098,240 sq km   POPULATION: 143,499,861 ('13)
OFFICIAL LANGUAGE: Russian
HEAD OF STATE: President Vladimir Putin (since May '12)
RULING PARTY: United Russia party
HEAD OF GOVERNMENT: Prime Minister Dmitry Medvedev (since May '12)
DEMOCRACY INDEX: 3.59; 125th of 167   CORRUPTION PERCEPTIONS INDEX: 27; =136th of 175
CURRENCY: Rouble (Dec '14 £1.00=RUB 88.79, US$1.00=RUB 57.18)
GNI PER CAPITA: US$13,860, Intl$23,200 at PPP ('13)

RUSSIA ended 2014 in a far weaker position than it had been at the beginning of the year. The triumphant staging of the Winter Olympic Games in Sochi in February was followed in March by the swift (re)absorption of Ukraine's Crimean peninsula into the Russian Federation. Riding high on these successes, President Vladimir Putin's popularity ratings soared. But by December the Russian currency had collapsed in value, the economy was suffering from Western sanctions, and Russia's ill-advised venture into the Donbas area of eastern Ukraine had severely tarnished the country's international reputation. Speculation began to be raised about a Russia after Putin.

The reasons given for Russia's intervening in Ukraine, loudly proclaimed in Putin's speeches and in the state-controlled media, were to protect its Russophone population from the newly-installed "fascist" government in Kiev, which had come to power on the wave of popular outrage against the authoritarian and deeply corrupt government of President Viktor Yanukovych (see the article on Ukraine). In a speech to both chambers of the Federal Assembly (the Russian legislature) on 18 March—the day that Crimea officially became part of Russia—Putin summoned a greater Russia, blaming the demise of the Soviet Union for leaving many Russians as ethnic minorities in former Soviet republics and turning the Russian people into "one of the biggest, if not the biggest, divided nation in the world". But there were also important security preoccupations behind Russia's actions in Ukraine. The new Ukrainian government, less amenable to Russia than Yanukovych, was believed to represent a threat to Russia's security because it was more likely to seek membership of the West's alliances, both economic and military. The annexation of Crimea secured Russia's control over its Black Sea naval base at Sevastopol (leased by Russia from Ukraine); the conflict in the Donbas, in which Russia supported proxy irredentist forces opposed to the new government in Kiev, weakened and destabilised Ukraine. Rather than taking Ukrainian territory per se, Putin's aimed to control the Ukrainian government's choices, fundamentally, to veto its membership of NATO. The new Ukrainian government was also seen as illegitimate, having come to power as a result of a sustained popular revolt that the Russian presidency believed had been instigated and backed by the West, and which raised alarming memories of a similar kind of urban opposition movement in Russia that had seemed briefly to threaten Putin's own authority in the winter of 2011-12.

The amendments to Russia's 2010 military doctrine, adopted in December 2014, made these preoccupations plain. The new doctrine identified as a key external threat the increasing military potential of NATO, and NATO countries' military infrastructure coming closer to Russia's borders, "including through further expansion of the bloc". The new doctrine expanded the list of military risks to Russia to include the use of information and communications technology, and the overthrow of legitimate governments and imposition of regimes hostile to Russian interests (a reference to the Ukrainian revolution). Related to this was the identification in the doctrine of the key domestic military threat: violent attempts to change the constitutional system—a clear reference to the events of 2011-12.

CRIMEA. The annexation of Crimea was greeted with much fanfare in Russia. After Russian special forces—masquerading as local "self-defence" volunteers—took control of the peninsula, and a referendum on union with Russia was hastily organised, a treaty was signed on 18 March between Putin and three Crimean officials, who favoured union with Russia and whose appointments had been engineered just prior to the referendum. The treaty officially declared the "republic of Crimea" and the city of Sevastopol to be the 84th and 85th constituent regions of the Russian Federation. They now comprised the newly-created "Crimean Federal District" of Russia, which brought the number of federal districts (or "super-regions") to nine. Oleg Belaventsev, a vice-admiral close to Russian Defence Minister Sergei Shoigu, was appointed plenipotentiary representative, or presidential envoy, to the new federal district.

Administrative changes were made that detached Crimea and Sevastopol from Ukraine and brought them into line with Russia. These included the adoption of Moscow time (two hours ahead of Kiev), the introduction of the Russian rouble, and the issuing of Russian passports and driving licences. Russia also promised to raise state salaries and social benefits for the population of Crimea and fund its budget shortfall, allocating 55.5 billion roubles for this in May (44.8 billion to Crimea and 10.6 billion to Sevastopol). But the potential drain on the Russian budget from annexing Crimea was huge. Russia stood to benefit from the acquisition of property and natural resources in Crimea, and from declaring invalid the agreement under which it had supplied Ukraine with cheaper gas in return for the lease on the Sevastopol naval base. However, the Crimean peninsula had no land connection with Russia, which would have to invest heavily to reduce the region's dependence upon Ukraine for supplies of food, water and power. As the war in eastern Ukraine intensified towards the end of the year, Ukraine made good on threats to cut power and transport links with Crimea.

Nevertheless, the annexation of Crimea was generally accepted in Russia as righting an historical wrong. There was an emotional attachment to Crimea, which had only been administratively a part of Ukraine since 1954, when it had been transferred from Russia in "an act of noble generosity" marking the tercentenary of their union (see AR 1954, p. 191). Two-thirds of respondents in a poll conducted by the Levada Centre, just before the annexation, stated their belief that Crimea, and eastern Ukraine, were "essentially" Russian lands. "Crimea", said Putin in his speech to the Federal Assembly on 18 March, "has always been and remains an inseparable part of Russia", and he compared its annexation by Russia with the reunification of Germany. In a rally on Red Square on the same day, Putin told the crowd: "Crimea and Sevastopol are returning to their home shores, to their home port, to Russia!" The president's popularity ratings soared to about 70 per cent following the annexation.

SANCTIONS AND THE ECONOMY. Russia's policy in the east of Ukraine was not aimed at annexation: this was both a more diverse region, and would represent an even greater drain on Russia's budget were it to be incorporated into the Russian Federation. The intention in supporting the pro-Russian separatist movement was rather to destabilise the government in Kiev. And Russia clearly had less control over the paramilitary separatist movements in eastern Ukraine than it had in Crimea, as was manifested tragically in the shooting down of the Malaysian Airlines passenger jet in July (see article on Ukraine for detail of developments).

The West's diplomatic measures in response to the annexation of Crimea were largely ineffective. Russia vetoed a US-sponsored UN Security Council resolution on 15 March declaring the Crimean referendum on joining Russia to be illegal; China abstained; the other 13 Council members supported it. On 24 March Russia was suspended from the G-8, which it had joined in 1998; Canada, France, Germany, Italy, Japan, the UK and the USA would meet as the G-7 "until Russia changes course". And a non-binding—and largely symbolic—resolution adopted at the UN General Assembly on 27 March declared the Crimean referendum invalid. In April Russia was deprived of voting rights, for 2014, in the Parliamentary Assembly of the Council of Europe; NATO also suspended military co-operation with Russia, although the NATO-Russia Council would continue to meet.

Stronger opposition took the form of sanctions against Russia. The EU and the USA, and a number of other countries including Japan, Norway and Canada, took measures against individuals, on an ever-expanding list, named for their involvement in the Ukraine crisis, as well as against certain associated companies. Five rounds of sanctions were issued by the USA over the course of the year and eight rounds by the EU. Measures initially included visa bans for certain Russian government officials, members of the Crimean government, and businessmen, and the freezing of their assets abroad. Among them were people known to be close allies and, allegedly, business partners, of President Putin, including Igor Sechin, the chief executive of oil company Rosneft, Gennady Timchenko, founder of the commodity trading group Gunvor, and Vyacheslav Volodin, first deputy presidential chief of staff. Later in the year, in response to the escalating war and, particularly, the shooting down of Malaysian Airlines flight MH17 on 17 July, the EU and the USA adopted economic, or "sectoral" sanctions, which targeted banks, energy and arms companies. A number of major state-owned Russian banks, energy companies and defence companies would no longer be able to raise capital on Western markets; in addition, an arms embargo was introduced, and exports of Western technology for the Russian oil industry were interdicted, though the gas industry escaped EU sanctions because of Europe's reliance upon Russia's gas.

Sectoral sanctions had a significant impact, as indicated by the request from Rosneft in August for a government bailout to repay 1,100 billion roubles of its 1,500 billion rouble (around $45 billion) debt. According to the newspaper *Vedomosti*,

Rosneft's chief executive Sechin had asked the government to use the national wealth fund—which was earmarked for pensions—to buy Rosneft bonds.

In retaliation, Russia imposed an import ban on Western food products. Putin had instructed officials to draw up retaliatory sanctions "very carefully, in order to support domestic producers but not hurt consumers". In detail, government proposals announced on 7 August barred the import of fresh and some processed forms of meat, fish, seafood, vegetables, fruit, milk and dairy products from the USA, the EU, Australia, Canada and Norway for one year. The authorities immediately began to promote the virtues of Russian self-sufficiency and healthy, fresh Russian food products, but given the poorly developed agricultural sector and the fact that more than 40 per cent of Russian food was imported, it was unlikely that Russian food production could be ramped up swiftly enough to compensate for the excluded products.

The sanctions hit an economy that had already attracted warnings from the IMF about the need for structural reform. An IMF report issued on 30 April blamed "geopolitical tension coming on top of existing serious structural bottlenecks" for a sharp slowdown in GDP growth. The economy showed its first contraction in five years, when figures for November indicated a 0.5 per cent fall compared with the same month of 2013. With oil and gas revenues providing more than half of state budget revenue, the Russian economy also suffered from the falling global oil price. The initial version of the 2015 budget, which had predicted an oil price of $100 per barrel, required major revision as the global price fell to around half that. On 27 December, the finance ministry predicted that the Russian economy would shrink by 4 per cent in 2015.

Western sanctions and the sharp fall in the price of oil contributed to a currency crisis, which began developing in October. Heavy intervention by the Russian Central Bank before the New Year and Orthodox Christmas holidays avoided a bank run—though the Bank had to rescue Trust Bank, a consumer lender, injecting 99 billion roubles to save it from bankruptcy. Over the course of 2014 the Russian rouble lost more than half of its value against the US dollar, dropping at one point on "black Tuesday"—16 December—to 80 roubles to the dollar before rallying to close the year at around 58 to the dollar. The Central Bank had raised interest rates to 17 per cent overnight on 15-16 December in an attempt to halt the rouble's decline, having already attempted a sharp interest rate rise in October. Overall the Bank spent around $80 billion—around one-fifth of its foreign currency reserves—to support the rouble in 2014.

The respected former finance minister, Aleksei Kudrin, made the danger to Russia's economic situation explicit when he warned on 22 December that Russia had entered "a full blown economic crisis" that it would "feel in full force" in 2015, when there would be series of defaults by medium sized and large companies, a "painful" fall in living standards and, as a result, "protest activity will increase".

NORTH CAUCASUS. The security situation in Russia's North Caucasus republics remained unstable, as Islamist groups there continued to stage attacks, though nothing matched the impact of the Volgograd bombings of late December 2013. The perpetrators of that attack were identified in January as members of a group from Dagestan.

Nevertheless, the Caucasus Emirate, the main Islamist group in the region, failed to carry out its threat to stage attacks on the Sochi Winter Olympics, which passed off without incident, albeit under conditions of extreme security. In Chechnya—where the anti-Russian insurgency had started in the 1990s but which had been brought to heel by the brutal regime of its president, Ramzan Kadyrov—militants staged a bold attack in central Grozny, the capital, in December, one day before Putin's annual speech to the Federal Assembly. Despite this embarrassing breach, Kadyrov demonstrated his usefulness to the Russian president in 2014 by despatching his security forces to assist the separatist forces in Ukraine, although it was claimed that any Chechens fighting there were "volunteers".

The leader of the Caucasus Emirate, Doku Umarov, was reported to have died in March, possibly of natural causes. Umarov had claimed responsibility for the Volgograd bombings and the Domodedovo airport bombing of 2011.

DOMESTIC POLITICS. Domestic politics took place in separate spheres. For the opposition, it consisted of fighting court cases brought on largely spurious grounds to harass and silence its most prominent leaders. Meanwhile, elections took place under the system of "managed democracy" where candidates were pre-approved by the authorities and the opposition excluded.

A "single day of voting" on 14 September saw elections held across Russia for the post of governor (or president) in 30 out of the 85 regions and republics of the Russian Federation, and 14 regional legislatures, as well as for numerous lower-level bodies.

In every gubernatorial election, the incumbent was re-elected, usually with a large majority. All bar two of the re-elected governors were members of United Russia, the ruling party. Elections to these powerful positions had been reinstated only in 2012, having been abolished in 2004 for a system of presidential appointments. A significant number of the governors re-elected on 14 September had come to office as presidential appointees but they had resigned early from their posts during 2014, thereby forcing elections. Upon resigning, they were all reappointed by the president in an acting capacity, and thus went into the elections with the significant advantage of incumbency. With economic difficulties looming, this gave the president the security of extended terms of office for loyal governors, whom he had originally appointed.

Recent amendments to electoral legislation complicated the opposition's attempts to stage a challenge through the polls. Candidates for gubernatorial elections were required to receive the endorsement of a proportion of members of the regional legislature (the "municipal filter"), making it difficult for opposition figures to compete. And in elections for regional legislatures, independent candidates (those without party backing) were required to collect thousands of signatures before they could be registered. Thus, in Moscow, where the opposition was strongest, a number of independent candidates were unable to compete for seats on the Moscow City Duma (council). In 2013, the mayoral elections in Moscow had seen opposition leader Aleksei Navalny come a relatively close second to the incumbent. But allies of Navalny who planned to compete for the City Duma in September found themselves the target of fraud investigations and were placed under house arrest in June. The turnout for the Moscow Duma election was only 21 per cent (average turnout across the country on the "single day of voting" was 46 per cent), and there was no opposition figure among the 45 Duma members elected.

Elections were also staged for the regional legislatures in Russia's new constituent regions of Crimea and Sevastopol, which United Russia won overwhelmingly. Turnout in Crimea was 54 per cent, and in Sevastopol, 49 per cent.

Unable to make much impact at the polls, the opposition was also relatively muted on the street, although there were some demonstrations against Russian action in Ukraine, with one of the largest rallies seen since the anti-Putin demonstrations of 2011-12 held in Moscow on 15 March. This protest, against the annexation of Crimea, attracted 30,000 participants according to its organisers; a rally in support of Crimea's union with Russia was held at the same time. And on 21 September, a "march for peace" was attended by around 26,000 people in Moscow, according to independent monitors.

Meanwhile, the courts pursued those arrested after the May 2012 anti-Putin protests on Moscow's Bolotnaya Square, which had become violent. Among them were two of the most prominent organisers of the 2011-12 anti-Putin demonstrations—Sergei Udaltsov, a leader of the Left Front group and a vocal critic of the authorities, and Leonid Razvozzhayev, political aide to lone Duma opposition member Ilya Ponomaryov. Both were found guilty of "organising mass disorder" in connection with the Bolotnaya protest in July and sentenced to four-and-a-half years in prison. Earlier, in February, seven out of eight defendants charged with public order offences in relation to the Bolotnaya protest also received prison terms (the eighth, the only woman amongst the defendants, received a suspended sentence).

The most prominent leader of the opposition movement, Aleksei Navalny, spent the year fighting various court cases on embezzlement charges. Navalny was already serving a five-year suspended sentence but on 31 March he was sentenced to house arrest in connection with the investigation of an embezzlement case brought against him and his brother, Oleg. The terms of his house arrest, crucially, banned him from using the Internet or talking to the media. At the very end of the year, the case against the Navalny brothers came to trial. Both were found guilty of defrauding the Russian branch of Yves Rocher, a French cosmetics company, which issued a statement to the effect that it had no complaint against them. On 30 December they were sentenced: Aleksei to another suspended sentence, but Oleg Navalny to three-and-a-half years in prison. The court session that sentenced the brothers had been scheduled for 15 January 2015, but was advanced after more than 30,000 people pledged, via social media, to attend a rally in the brothers' support on that day. Only a few hundred came to the hastily organised demonstration on 30 December—among them, in breach of his house arrest, Aleksei Navalny.

Several pieces of legislation adopted in 2014 attempted to curtail Internet use: social media remained one of the most powerful opposition weapons against the authorities, and several opposition websites had been blocked in March for promoting "unlawful actions and participation in mass events", after they promoted the opposition rally against the annexation of Crimea. The "bloggers' law" came into force on 1 August. This measure required Internet diarists (bloggers) who had more than 3,000 readers to register with Roskomnadzor, the media oversight agency, and not to remain anonymous in their online postings. Organisations providing the platform for bloggers were required to keep computer records, within Russia, of postings on their websites. Other regulations adopted in August required people using wireless Internet connections (Wi-Fi) in public places to identify themselves through some form of official documentation.

Another bill, signed in July, imposed criminal penalties for the dissemination of online of material that was deemed extremist, whilst legislation was also drafted that required Internet service providers that stored personal data on Russian citizens to locate their servers inside Russia. The legislation, which would come into force in 2016 if passed, would mean that companies which stored their user-data on servers outside Russia would be required to open offices inside the country. According to opposition Duma deputy Ilya Ponomaryov, the new regulations would "be used as a bargaining point with Google and Facebook".

One of the most prominent young Internet entrepreneurs in Russia, Pavel Durov, the founder and chief executive of social network VKontakte, left the company—and the country—in April, saying that he was no longer able to uphold the guiding principles of the social network. Durov had sold his stake in VKontakte in January, after the company's ownership structure had changed in favour of investment funds connected with associates of Putin. Durov had come under pressure to pass on the identities of people who had expressed support on VKontakte for the anti-Putin protests of 2011-12, and for the protests in Kiev in 2014.

Another young Internet specialist, who was being hounded by a different government, chose to stay in Russia. US citizen Edward Snowden, wanted for espionage in the USA for having revealed in 2013 the extent of governments' surveillance of people's private communications, was granted a three-year residency permit for Russia after his 12-month asylum expired in August. According to his Russia lawyer, Snowden was working as an IT specialist, travelling and learning Russian.

There was one piece of good news: from October, Russia abandoned the policy of year-round summertime that had been introduced in March 2011 by then President Dmitry Medvedev. More light on winter mornings might improve the population's mood. By the end of the year, it seemed this would be necessary.

Wendy Slater

UKRAINE

CAPITAL: Kyiv (Kiev)   AREA: 603,550 sq km   POPULATION: 45,489,600 ('13)
OFFICIAL LANGUAGE: Ukrainian
HEAD OF STATE: President Petro Poroshenko (since June '14)
RULING PARTIES: "European Ukraine" five-party coalition
HEAD OF GOVERNMENT: Prime Minister Arseny Yatsenyuk (Popular Front) (since Feb '14)
DEMOCRACY INDEX: 5.84; =85th of 167   CORRUPTION PERCEPTIONS INDEX: 26; =142nd of 175
CURRENCY: Hryvna (Dec '14 £1.00=UAH 24.57, US$1.00=UAH 15.82)
GNI PER CAPITA: US$3,960, Intl$8,960 at PPP ('13)

IT was a year of violence in Ukraine. The popular protests that began in November 2013 succeeded in overthrowing the government of President Viktor Yanukovych in February, at the cost of the lives of over 100 protesters. Then, at the end of February, pro-Russian activists in Crimea seized power, with the covert support of Russian special forces, and the following month the region became part of the Russian Federation. In the east of Ukraine, too, pro-Russian activists, with covert Russian military support, began attempts to seize power. The Ukrainian army resisted and localised conflicts began which, by the end of the year, had caused maybe as many as 11,500 deaths and left over 610,000 people displaced.

After a lull during the New Year and Orthodox Christmas holidays, the large-scale protests in Kiev that had been prompted by President Yanukovych's abrupt rejection of an EU Association Agreement in favour of aid from Russia resumed (see AR 2014, pp. 99-101). An estimated 100,000 people massed on Kiev's Maidan Nezalezhnosti (Independence Square) on 19 January—the eighth consecutive Sunday demonstration in the "Euromaidan" movement—angered by new laws that aimed to criminalise the peaceful protest methods used hitherto. Violent clashes between police and protesters saw the first fatalities of the uprising on 22 January, and protests spread to other cities, where anti-government forces gained control of local administration buildings. The resignation of the prime minister on 28 January and the partial repeal of the anti-protest laws failed to satisfy the protest leaders, whose demands now extended to constitutional change and the resignation of Yanukovych.

On 18 February riot police tried to regain control of Maidan and used live ammunition for the first time. As the violence in Kiev escalated, and the opposition's command centre at the Trade Union building was torched, snipers stationed on the roofs of buildings surrounding Maidan opened fire against demonstrators on 20 February, bringing the death toll to over 100 people.

Thereafter, events moved swiftly: support in the Verkhovna Rada, the unicameral legislature, drained away from the president and his party, Regions of Ukraine. Opposition deputies in the Rada, who had attempted to reach a deal with Yanukovych, were forced to accept the more radical demands of the protest leaders. On 22 February, Rada deputies re-enacted the 2004 constitution that limited the powers of the presidency, voted to remove Yanukovych from power with immediate effect, and ordered the release from prison of the ex-prime minister Yuliya Tymoshenko, leader of the opposition Fatherland party, who went immediately to Maidan and made an emotional speech to protesters from her wheelchair.

With Oleksandr Turchynov, a leader of Fatherland in the Rada, as interim Ukrainian president pending elections called for 25 May, a new, interim government was appointed under Arseny Yatsenyuk, also from Fatherland. The members of the new Cabinet were presented before the crowd on Maidan on 26 February for their "approval". Ministers who had risen to prominence as leaders of the Euromaidan movement met wild applause. The deposed Yanukovych fled Kiev, reappearing several days later in Rostov-on-Don in southern Russia, still insisting that he remained Ukraine's legitimate president and urging Russia to use "all means at its disposal" against the new government in Kiev.

The overthrow of an elected, but unpopular and corrupt, regime as a result of pressure from the street alarmed the Russian authorities, which had faced down a series of similar demonstrations at the end of 2011 (see AR 2012, pp. 102-04). Moreover, the new Ukrainian government, as well as being determinedly pro-EU, was less well-disposed towards Russia than the Yanukovych regime. One of its first actions was, provocatively, to rescind a law that gave the Russian language official status in Russophone areas of the country, prompting Russia to claim that the rights of Russians and other minorities in Ukraine were being infringed. Crimea was the only region where ethnic Russians constituted a majority, with a heavy contingent of Russian military personnel from Russia's Black Sea naval base at Sevastopol; it had, until 1954, been part of the RSFSR (the Soviet Russian Federation). Here, there were pro-Russian demonstrations and activists advocating union with Russia seized control of the local government, but not without assistance, for armed men in unmarked uniforms began to seize control of strategic points on the peninsula at the end of February, forcing Ukrainian troops stationed there to disarm. Though Russia said they were local "self-defence" troops, it was widely believed that the "green men" were Russian special forces. On 1 March, Russia's President Vladimir Putin received formal authorisation from the Russian legislature to use Russia's armed forces on Ukrainian territory, because of the "threat" that had arisen there to the lives of Russian citizens and military personnel in Crimea.

The annexation of Crimea was completed with a referendum on 16 March, in which 96.8 per cent were said to have endorsed the proposal to become part of the Russian Federation. On 18 March, Crimea and the city of Sevastopol officially became the 84th and 85th constituent regions of the Russian Federation.

Meanwhile, in the eastern regions of Ukraine, pro-Russian activists who opposed the new authorities in Kiev also started to occupy government buildings. Support for Yanukovych was strongest in the Donbas region, and despite the appointment of loyal oligarchs as governors of Dnepropetrovsk, Donetsk and Kharkov oblasts (regions) the new Kiev government rapidly lost control of the east. Several weeks of minor clashes between pro-Russian demonstrators and supporters of the new government escalated on 6 April when protesters occupied regional administration buildings in Donetsk, Kharkov and Lugansk; an apparently co-ordinated operation saw around a dozen smaller towns, situated on strategically important roads and railways, also come under rebel control. Russia denied having any role in the operation, but it was widely believed that its special forces were at least directing, if not participating in, the capture of strategic sites. On 15 April, Ukrainian forces launched operations to retake Slavyansk and Kramatorsk, which Russia described as an escalation. Meanwhile, large scale troop movements were repeatedly observed on the Russian side of the border.

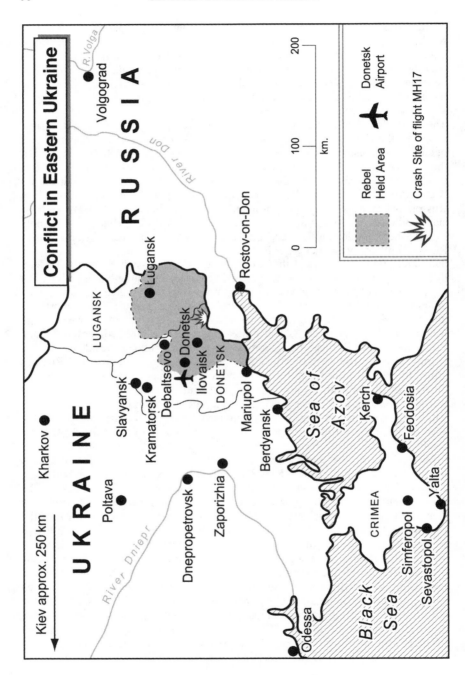

An international conference in Geneva on 17 April agreed measures to "de-escalate" the situation, but rapidly broke down, as separatist forces' efforts to take control of Donetsk and Lugansk intensified and the Ukrainian side responded with countermeasures. The localised violence continued, with efforts to retake Slavyansk a particular focus. Ukraine's prosecutor general accused Yanukovych and his associates of funding the separatists with the alleged $32 billion that he had corruptly acquired during his time as president.

On 11 May the separatists organised a referendum on self-rule in the Donetsk and Lugansk regions. Organisers claimed overwhelming support and a turnout of above 70 per cent; the Ukrainian interior ministry suggested turnout was only about 25 per cent. Russia, which had called on the separatists to postpone the referendums, said only that it would "respect", rather than recognise, the apparent endorsement for independence—which suggested that Russia was not intending to annex eastern Ukraine outright, unlike Crimea.

A more focused campaign against the eastern rebels began, after the Ukrainian presidential elections on 25 May had produced a decisive victory for Petro Poroshenko. Taking 54.7 per cent of the vote, Poroshenko comprehensively defeated Yuliya Tymoshenko, who came second with just under 13 per cent, underlining the voters' suspicion of all previous governments. Poroshenko was described by some as a "reformist oligarch". Known as the "chocolate king", he had established control over a number of businesses during the collapse of the Soviet Union (among them the confectionary business), and had held several ministerial portfolios since 2004. During the Euromaidan events he had been prominent in support of the demonstrators, regularly appearing on Maidan with protest leaders. A deal with prominent opposition leader Vitali Klitschko of the new UDAR opposition party (and a former heavyweight boxer) had cleared the way for Poroshenko's victory, when Klitschko agreed to forgo the presidential contest in order to fight (and win) Kiev's mayoral elections, also held on 25 May.

In his first speech as president, on 7 June, Poroshenko proposed a number of concessions to the eastern regions, including a decentralisation of government, the use of the Russian language, and an amnesty for rebels. A 14-point plan to end the conflict incorporated these measures with a ceasefire and followed several days of heavy fighting near the border with Russia. Putin apparently endorsed the plan and, in a largely symbolic move, asked the Russian legislature to rescind the mandate it had given him in March to use Russian military forces in Ukraine. However, at the same time as proposals to de-escalate the conflict, Ukraine accused Russia on 12 June of allowing tanks and heavy artillery to cross the border into Ukraine.

A more focused Ukrainian campaign against the rebels began in July, after the largely ignored ceasefire expired on 30 June. A new defence minister was appointed, Col.-Gen. Valery Geletey, who had been feted for successfully leading a Ukrainian military attack on a strategic position near the rebel-held city of Slavyansk. Poroshenko also instigated a campaign to rid the Ukrainian military of "thieves and grafters": some units were so poorly equipped that volunteer groups were organising supplies of food and clothing. Meanwhile, the civilian population of eastern Ukraine began to suffer severely from the bombardment of urban centres as Ukrainian forces moved to recapture rebel-held towns and rebel forces were supplied with increasing amounts of heavy weaponry by Russia, according to US and NATO briefings, though Russia continued to deny this.

The level of Russia's control over the rebel forces came into sharp focus, however, on 17 July when a passenger jet—Malaysian Airlines flight MH17—crashed in eastern Ukraine, near Grabovo, 40 km from the border with Russia. All 298 people on board were killed. The airliner had been flying over Ukraine, having taken off from Amsterdam's Schiphol airport bound for Kuala Lumpur. Ukraine accused rebel forces of shooting down the aircraft, with a *Buk* surface-to-air missile supplied by Russia, and which had been seen recently in the region. Russia denied this, and blamed Ukraine. It seemed, from intercepts, that the rebels believed they had targeted a Ukrainian military aircraft, several of which they had already successfully shot down during the conflict.

Ukrainian forces pressed their advantage in July and early August, surrounding Donetsk and Lugansk. On 5 August Poroshenko praised their "heroic" efforts to liberate three-quarters of Donetsk and Lugansk oblasts from rebel control. Shelling intensified, with large numbers of civilians fleeing the cities—up to half of the 400,000-strong population of Lugansk, where water, power and telephones were cut off, was thought to have left. By mid-August, Ukrainian forces were close to recapturing the cities. However, rebel forces then embarked upon a counter-offensive, with considerably increased Russian assistance. A Ukrainian defence ministry official warned on 27 August that, "We are increasingly facing genuine Russian soldiers in addition to mercenaries armed by Russia."

By the end of August, the rebels had regained the ground lost in July and had opened a new front in the south of Ukraine with the capture of the town of Novoazovsk, which was close to the strategically important port of Mariupol, used as a logistics base by the Ukrainian army. It was feared that this was a prelude to the capture of territory that would open a direct land corridor, under Russian control, between the Russian border and the Crimean peninsula. On 30 August, Ukrainian forces were also forced to abandon the town of Ilovaisk, east of Donetsk, which had been encircled by rebel troops. The defeat at Ilovaisk illustrated the inability of the Ukrainian Army to regain control of the Donbas, if Russia were determined to resist. (It also led, in October, to the resignation of Defence Minister Geletey.)

Following the retreat from Ilovaisk, Poroshenko announced a halt to the "anti-terrorist operation" against the rebels and talks were arranged in Minsk that produced, on 5 September, a 12-point protocol for a ceasefire agreement. The talks were held between representatives of the rebel "Donetsk People's Republic" and the "Lugansk People's Republic" (the DNR and LNR) and the "trilateral contact group on Ukraine", which consisted of Russian, Ukrainian and OSCE representatives. The 12-point Minsk Protocol largely resembled Poroshenko's June peace plan. A follow-up memorandum to this, drawn up on 19 September, clarified some of the measures to achieve a ceasefire, among them, the creation of a 30 km buffer zone either side of the frontline between rebel and Ukrainian forces in the Donetsk and Lugansk regions. Aside from the military measures, the Minsk Protocol stipulated a level of self-government for the separatist-held areas. The Ukrainian legislature adopted a "law on special status" for certain areas of the Donetsk and Lugansk regions on 16 September. Effective for three years, the new law would permit self-rule, within Ukrainian sovereignty, and also guaranteed Russian-language rights, with elections scheduled for 7 December to the leadership of the self-governing areas.

The provisions of the Minsk Protocol were widely disregarded. The September ceasefire was repeatedly broken, by both sides, with Donetsk airport a focus of heavy fighting as rebels launched an offensive at the end of September to recapture the strategically-important site from a unit of the Ukrainian army. Human Rights Watch, the New York based monitoring group, accused both the Ukrainian military and the rebels of using cluster bombs—weapons banned by international treaty—having documented 12 such incidents during a week-long monitoring exercise in eastern Ukraine. The UN said that, on average, 13 people had been killed every day since the ceasefire until the end of 2014.

Meanwhile, the DNR and LNR leaders, predictably, rejected the "special status" arrangements, which fell short of their demands for autonomy, and went ahead with organising their own elections on 2 November, in which the incumbent DNR and LNR leaders were returned to power as "presidents". The Ukrainian government retaliated by proposing to rescind the "law on special status" and, significantly, by suspending payment of social security and state salaries to the rebel-held regions. "So long as those territories are controlled by those who appointed themselves," said Prime Minister Yatsenyuk, "the government will not provide subsidies."

The newly-elected "presidents" of the DNR and LNR—Aleksandr Zakharchenko in Donetsk, Ihor Plotnitsky in Lugansk—had been appointed in August as prime ministers of these self-proclaimed "republics", in which posts they had replaced Russian citizens allegedly linked with the Russian security services, who had come to power at the head of the rebel forces. The replacement of Russian-trained rebel leaders by locals indicated the crystallisation of the rebel ideology around the idea of "Novorossiya" (New Russia)—a tsarist-era name for the eastern and southern areas of current Ukraine and Russia. This ideology, such as it was, highlighted the Russian Orthodox cultural traditions and social conservatism that were features of the Russian presidency; it also echoed Russian propaganda in denouncing the Kiev government as "fascist", pro-Western, and seeking to exploit the eastern Ukrainian region for the benefit of its foreign masters.

As well as the failure of the Minsk Protocol's political arrangements, its provision for a demilitarised buffer zone separating rebel-held areas from the rest of Ukraine was also disregarded. The zone was reinforced by the rebels, thereby becoming a virtual border between rebel-held areas and the rest of Ukraine. Meanwhile, the internationally recognised border between Russia and (eastern) Ukraine had become "completely porous" to weapons and troops, in the view of NATO's supreme commander in Europe, General Philip Breedlove. NATO foreign ministers issued a statement on 2 December denouncing Russia's "continued and deliberate destabilisation of eastern Ukraine in breach of international law, including the provision of tanks, advanced air defence systems and other heavy weapon to the separatists".

At the end of the year, a new round of peace talks in Minsk was abandoned. With Ukraine having deployed more troops in November to guard the cities of Kharkov and Dnepropetrovsk in the east and Mariupol and Berdyansk in the south from possible rebel attack, the main fear was that Russia might now be aiming to secure a land corridor across southern Ukraine to facilitate supplying Crimea, which Russia could currently access only by sea.

Accurate figures for the human cost of the conflict were hard to ascertain. According to Ukraine's State Emergency Service, there were over 610,000 internally-displaced persons by the end of the year; the UN's regular report on the situation, for December, assessed deaths at 4,707 and at least 10,322 wounded, though it noted that the actual number was likely to be higher. However, a Ukrainian online newspaper, *Euromaidan Press*, assessed total deaths—including military on both sides as well as civilian fatalities—at around 11,500.

The pro-EU trend in Ukrainian public opinion manifested by the Euromaidan revolution was borne out in the results of the legislative elections, held on 26 October, in which the pro-Europe coalitions led by Prime Minister Yatsenyuk (Popular Front) and President Poroshenko (the Petro Poroshenko Bloc) together won 214 of the 423 seats filled. (No elections were held in Crimea, or the LNR or DNR, leaving 27 seats vacant.) The strong performance of a new formation, Samopomich (Self-Reliance), which came third with 33 seats, also highlighted the popular desire for change and for measures against corruption. Ukrainian nationalist parties were unsuccessful, further undermining Russian claims that the Ukrainian revolution had been led by "fascists" seeking to deny rights to Russian-speakers. Also indicative of the desire for change was the poor performance of the Opposition Bloc, which comprised members of ex-president Yanukovych's Party of Regions—this had its strongest support in the eastern regions—and the dismal result achieved by the Communist Party of Ukraine, the rump of the former ruling class, which won no seats at all.

A five-party coalition, "European Ukraine", with 303 deputies, was formed in November, but it took another month before a Cabinet was named, with Yatsenyuk again at its head. There were three non-Ukrainians in the Cabinet, appointed for their expertise in areas where reform was urgently needed: Natalia Yaresko (a US citizen), at the finance ministry; Aivaras Abromavicius from Lithuania in economy and trade, and the former Georgian health minister, Alexander Kvitashvili, at the health ministry.

The new government immediately sought the passage of legislation to repeal Ukraine's non-aligned status and require it to "deepen co-operation with NATO" with a view to achieving membership. This was condemned by Russia, which had always seen NATO membership for Ukraine as an infringement upon its own security.

A more immediate concern, however, was the Ukrainian economy, which had suffered from the destruction of the war in the east, where the bulk of Ukraine's heavy industry was based, and the disruption in relations with Russia, a major trading partner and creditor, as well as gas supplier. The Ukrainian currency, the hryvna, lost half of its value in 2014. Supporting the hryvna, making gas payments to Russia which had suspended supplies in June, and the cost of the war ($10 million per day, according to the president) left the Ukrainian government with only $7.5 billion in foreign reserves (enough for five weeks' import cover) by December. GDP was down 7 per cent; in 2015, Ukraine was scheduled to pay $11 billion in debt repayments; and a $17 billion stand-by arrangement with the IMF had been agreed in April, but by December the Fund was warning that Ukraine would need an additional $15 billion in financing if it were not to default.

The threat that Russia would cut all gas supplies had been temporarily averted by an EU-brokered "winter package" on 31 October. Nevertheless, Russia remained in a position to choke off Ukraine's economy through demands for early loan repayments, and the EU appeared hesitant about offering finance to support the Ukrainian government and allow it time to root out the deeply entrenched bureaucratic and oligarchic corruption that had flourished under Yanukovych. This position was illustrated in September when the Ukrainian Verkhovna Rada and the European Parliament ratified, simultaneously, the EU Association Agreement that had triggered the popular revolt against Yanukovych back in 2013. At Russia's insistence, however, full implementation of the trade aspects of the Agreement were suspended until the end of 2015 at least, and, in a letter to then European Commission president, José Manuel Barroso, Putin demanded "systematic adjustments of the association agreement" in order to maintain Russian-Ukrainian economic relations. It was a clear statement of Putin's conviction that Ukraine belonged naturally with Russia.

Wendy Slater

BELARUS

CAPITAL: Minsk   AREA: 207,600 sq km   POPULATION: 9,466,000 ('13)
OFFICIAL LANGUAGES: Belarusian & Russian
HEAD OF STATE: President Alyaksandr Lukashenka (since July '94)
RULING PARTY: Non-party supporters of President Lukashenka
HEAD OF GOVERNMENT: Prime Minister Andrei Kobyakov (since Dec '14)
DEMOCRACY INDEX: 3.04; 142nd of 167   CORRUPTION PERCEPTIONS INDEX: 31; =119th of 175
CURRENCY: Belarusian Rouble 1 (Dec '14 £1.00=BYR 17,082, US$1.00=BYR 11,000)
GNI PER CAPITA: US$6,720, Intl$16,940 at PPP ('13)

BELARUS extracted some benefit from the crisis in Ukraine. Celebrating 20 years in power in 2014—and facing re-election in 2015—Belarus's President Alyaksandr Lukashenka saw an improvement in his opinion poll ratings as the chaos in Ukraine contrasted with his insistence upon stability. Meanwhile, Belarusian exporters profited from the Russian embargo on imports of Western food products.

Relations with the West also improved slightly after Minsk hosted peace talks for the Ukraine conflict. However, towards the end of 2014 the collapse in the value of the Russian rouble threatened to infect the Belarusian economy, and a major government reshuffle ensued.

In February Lukashenka pronounced himself "disgusted and repelled" by the popular removal of Ukraine's equally authoritarian president, Viktor Yanukovych. However, with a significant ethnic Russian minority (about 11 per cent of the population) and Russian universally spoken, Belarus was potentially vulnerable to the Russian justification for intervening in Ukraine on the grounds of protecting the rights of ethnic Russians and Russian speakers. Thus, Lukashenka reacted without enthusiasm to Russia's annexation of Crimea. Speaking to reporters on 23 March, he acknowledged that Crimea was "today a part of Russia", de facto if not de jure; reiterated Belarus's choice to "always be with the Russian Federation"; and blamed the new Ukrainian authorities for provoking Russia by putting pressure on Russian-speakers in the country. But Lukashenka also spoke of the importance of "maintaining Ukraine's territorial integrity" and in June he attended the inauguration of Ukraine's new president, Petro Poroshenko.

Political repression remained tight. In May, Minsk hosted the first major international sporting event ever to be held in Belarus: the ice-hockey world championships, which was a personal triumph for Lukashenka, a fan of the sport. Some opposition activists were jailed pre-emptively before the championships opened. In June, Ales Belyatsky of the Vesna human rights group, who was internationally recognised as a prisoner of conscience, was released one year early from a four-and-a-half-year prison sentence. He urged the immediate release of seven other activists, regarded as political prisoners.

The main consequence of the Ukraine crisis was economic. Russia's imposition in August of retaliatory sanctions on the West, banning food imports for one year, was described as "a Klondike for Belarus" by the deputy agriculture minister. EU foodstuffs now processed in Belarus, and crudely re-labelled as products from the EU, made their way to Russia, where some restaurateurs found themselves importing "Parmigiano Belarussiano" or even seafood from landlocked Belarus. However, as Western sanctions and the falling oil price damaged the Russian economy, Belarus took steps to protect itself from the effects of the collapse in the value of the Russian rouble. More than half of Belarus's total exports went to Russia, over 90 per cent of the trade paid for in Russian roubles. On 19 December, Lukashenka ordered trade with Russia to be denominated in euro or US dollars, and also took measures to prevent a run on the Belarusian rouble, including a 30 per cent fee to purchase foreign currency.

A major government reshuffle announced on 27 December was presented as a strengthening of the economic team. The prime minister, Mikhail Myasnikovich (appointed in December 2010), was replaced by the presidential chief of staff, Andrei Kobyakov. The reshuffle also saw the promotion of deputy National Bank governor Pavel Kalavur to replace his boss, Nadzeya Yermakova. In total, 24 senior officials were replaced, though most were moved sideways to other bodies, and the new ministers and officials were advocates of the state-managed economic model in the same mould as their predecessors. Government figures released in November revised down the GDP growth forecast for 2015 from 2 per cent to 0.2-0.7 per cent. Inflation for 2014 was expected to hit 16-17 per cent. In a meeting with his new prime minister on 30 December, Lukashenka said that the country's goals for 2015 must be to diversify exports and reduce economic dependence upon Russia. It was not clear how this was to be achieved.

Wendy Slater

MOLDOVA

CAPITAL: Chisinau (Kishinev)   AREA: 33,840 sq km   POPULATION: 3,559,000 ('13)
OFFICIAL LANGUAGE: Moldovan
HEAD OF STATE: President Nicolae Timofti (since March '12)
RULING PARTIES: Alliance for European Integration-coalition
HEAD OF GOVERNMENT: acting Prime Minister Iurie Leanca (Liberal Democratic Party) (since May '13)
DEMOCRACY INDEX: 6.32; 69th of 167   CORRUPTION PERCEPTIONS INDEX: 35; =103rd of 175
CURRENCY: Leu (Dec '14 £1.00=MDL 24.26, US$1.00=MDL 15.63)
GNI PER CAPITA: US$2,460, Intl$5,190 at PPP ('13)

THE results of parliamentary elections on 30 November reflected the deep division in the Moldovan electorate between those who favoured closer ties with the EU, building on the 2013 EU-Moldova Association Agreement, and those leaning towards Russia. Three pro-European parties—the Liberal Democratic Party (PLDM), the Democratic Party (PDM), and the Liberal Party (PL)—together won just under 46 per cent of the vote, which gave them jointly 55 seats in the 101-seat Parliament (the PLDM had 23 seats; the PDM had 19; and the PL 13 seats). These parties, in varying combinations, had formed the governing Alliance for European Integration (AIE) since the 2009 elections that saw the defeat of the Communist Party of Moldova (PCM) (see AR 2010, p. 116). However, as of year's end no new coalition agreement had been formed.

The largest single share of the vote, however, went to the openly pro-Russian Party of Socialists (PSRM), which won 20.51 per cent of the vote (25 seats) to 20.16 per cent for the PLDM. Socialist leader Igor Dodon said that he did not rule out forming an opposition coalition with the PCM, which had come third in the poll with 17.48 per cent (21 seats).

Dodon and the Socialists benefitted from the exclusion from the ballot of another pro-Russia party: Patria was the creation of Renato Usatii, a Russian businessman of Moldovan extraction and a strong opponent of the EU Association Agreement. Patria had been barred from the elections as late as 27 November on the grounds that it had received campaign financing from abroad. The OSCE's election monitors were highly critical of the timing of the decision to exclude Patria, although overall their assessment of the elections was positive.

The relatively low turnout of 55.85 per cent and the broadly even split in the vote revealed the level of popular dissatisfaction with the pro-European government. Though the AIE coalition had achieved notable successes in negotiating the Association Agreement with the EU (ratified by the Moldovan and European parliaments in November 2014) and in concluding a visa-free travel regime with the EU's Schengen area, there remained a sense of popular disillusion and a suspicion of widespread and unaddressed corruption.

The conclusion of the EU Association Agreement had foiled Russia's ambitions to draw Moldova into its Eurasian Economic Union (EEU). In 2013, Russia had responded with an embargo on Moldovan wine and spirits. In July 2014, Russia did the same for Moldovan apples, plums, peaches and canned fruit, which was a major blow to Moldovan producers, since in 2012 over 90 per cent of Moldova's exported fruit had been consumed in Russia. Russia also hinted at the possible expulsion of Moldovan migrant workers (remittances from Moldovans working in Russia reached $1.5 billion in 2013, according to a German expert assessment). For the time being, Moldova also remained heavily dependent upon Russian gas for its energy needs, although in August the Iasi-Ungheni pipeline, which would eventually bring gas into the country from Romania, was inaugurated as a step towards diversifying Moldova's energy supplies.

The Ukrainian crisis raised fears that Russia might also intervene in Moldova, seeking to annexe the separatist, Russian-speaking Transdniester Republic as it had annexed Crimea. Future European Commission president Jean-Claude Juncker said in March that Moldova could "become the next victim of Russian aggression". On 16 April the Transdniester parliament issued an appeal to the Russian president and legislature to recognise Transdniester's independence: under the Crimea scenario, this was the first step towards integration into Russia. However, the Russian response was lukewarm: presidential press secretary Dmitry Peskov said on 21 April that each request to be admitted to the Russian Federation "must be assessed extremely carefully". A more likely outcome was that Transdniester would maintain its status as a "frozen conflict" and a de facto state, in which Russia's influence was paramount. Thus, rather than a Crimea, Transdniester perhaps represented the model for the eastern regions of Ukraine.

Wendy Slater

ARMENIA—GEORGIA—AZERBAIJAN

Armenia
CAPITAL: Yerevan   AREA: 29,800 sq km   POPULATION: 2,976,566 ('13)
OFFICIAL LANGUAGE: Armenian
HEAD OF STATE: President Serzh Sarkisian (HHK) (since April '08)
RULING PARTIES: Republican Party of Armenia (HHK)-led coalition
HEAD OF GOVERNMENT: Prime Minister Hovik Abrahamian (HHK) (since April '14)
DEMOCRACY INDEX: 4.02; 116th of 167   CORRUPTION PERCEPTIONS INDEX: 37; =94th of 175
CURRENCY: Armenian Dram (Dec '14 £1.00=AMD 725.22, US$1.00=AMD 467.00)
GNI PER CAPITA: US$3,790, Intl$8,140 at PPP ('13)

Georgia

CAPITAL: Tbilisi   AREA: 69,700 sq km   POPULATION: 4,476,900 ('13)
OFFICIAL LANGUAGE: Georgian
HEAD OF STATE: President Giorgi Margvelashvili (GD-DG) (since Nov '13)
RULING PARTIES: Georgian Dream alliance (GD-DG)
HEAD OF GOVERNMENT: Prime Minister Irakli Gharibashvili (GD-DG) (since Nov '13)
DEMOCRACY INDEX: 5.95; 78th of 167   CORRUPTION PERCEPTIONS INDEX: 52; =50th of 175
CURRENCY: Lari (Dec '14 £1.00=GEL 2.87, US$1.00=GEL 1.84)
GNI PER CAPITA: US$3,570, Intl$7,040 at PPP ('13)

Azerbaijan

CAPITAL: Baku   AREA: 86,600 sq km   POPULATION: 9,416,598 ('13)
OFFICIAL LANGUAGE: Azeri
HEAD OF STATE: President Ilham Aliyev (YAP) (since Oct '03)
RULING PARTY: New Azerbaijan Party (YAP)
HEAD OF GOVERNMENT: Prime Minister Artur Rasizade (YAP) (since July '96)
DEMOCRACY INDEX: 3.06; =140th of 167   CORRUPTION PERCEPTIONS INDEX: 29; =126th of 175
CURRENCY: New Manat (Dec '14 £1=AZN 1.22, US$1=AZN 0.78)
GNI PER CAPITA: US$7,350, Intl$16,180 at PPP ('13)

IN all three South Caucasus states, policies or trends from the previous year gained momentum in 2014.

Mass protests planned by **Armenia's** parliamentary opposition to demand the resignation of Prime Minister Tigran Sarkisian, and a vote of no-confidence in the Cabinet, were averted when Sarkisian resigned on 3 April. Sarkisian was subsequently named Armenia's ambassador to the USA. Parliament speaker Hovik Abrahamian (also of the ruling Republican Party of Armenia, HHK) took over as premier, while Galust Sahakian became parliament speaker.

Four opposition parties—Prosperous Armenia (BH), the Armenian Pan-National Movement (HHSh), Zharangutiun (Heritage) and the Armenian Revolutionary Federation-Dashnaktsutiun—issued in June a list of 12 demands to President Serzh Sarkisian's HHK, including suspension of the controversial pension reform that had triggered mass protests in 2013 (see AR 2014, p. 104). The HHK failed to meet any of those demands by the 30 September deadline, whereupon the opposition convened protest demonstrations on 24 October and 10 December to push for regime change. National Security Service head Gorik Hakobian warned on 20 December against further attempts to bring down the government, while the commander of Interior Ministry forces, General Levon Yeranosian, vowed to "cut off the ears" of anyone who criticised the president.

On 17 October, a Yerevan district court sentenced opposition figure Shant Harutiunian to six years' imprisonment for leading a protest in Yerevan 11 months earlier that had turned violent.

Meanwhile, a state commission set up by President Sarkisian in 2013 unveiled proposals in October for constitutional amendments that would transform the country into a parliamentary republic with a strong prime minister.

Georgia held municipal elections on 15 June, in which the ruling Georgian Dream coalition trounced the United National Movement (ENM) of former President Mikheil Saakashvili, against whom the prosecutor general subsequently brought criminal charges of exceeding his authority and misuse of budget funds. Saakashvili's close associate, former ENM chairman Vano Merabishvili, was jailed for five years in February on corruption charges, while the former defence and interior minister, Bacho Akhalaia, was sentenced to seven-and-a-half years for torture and abuse of power.

Prime Minister Irakli Gharibashvili reshuffled the Cabinet in late July, dismissing five ministers and transferring two more to different posts. Then in November, he fired popular Defence Minister Irakli Alasania after the latter publicly protested against the dismissal of several ministry officials without his prior knowledge over the handling of a tender. Foreign Minister Maya Pandjikidze and Minister for European Integration Aleksi Petriashvili, both members of Alasania's Our Georgia party, resigned in solidarity. The party also pulled out of the Georgian Dream coalition, which managed to retain its parliamentary majority only thanks to defections from other parliament factions. Tensions also emerged between Gharibashvili and President Giorgi Margvelashvili over which of them should represent the country internationally.

Eduard Shevardnadze, the former Soviet foreign minister and Georgian president, died in July, aged 86 (see Obituary).

In the breakaway Republic of Abkhazia, the opposition Coordinating Council finally forced the resignation on 1 June of de facto President Aleksandr Ankvab. Long-time oppositionist Raul Khadjimba was elected on 24 August to succeed him, defeating three rival candidates, and proceeded to negotiate, despite widespread public disquiet, a new strategic treaty on friendship and union relations with Russia. The Georgian Parliament formally condemned that treaty on 17 October as an attempt by Russia to annex Abkhazia, but voted down on 28 November a resolution drafted by the ENM that called for suspending the ongoing talks with Russia in retaliation.

The 8 June parliamentary election in the similarly unrecognised Republic of South Ossetia was won by the One Ossetia party of former Cabinet minister Anatolii Bibilov, who had called in January for a referendum on whether the region should join the Russian Federation.

Though it held the chairmanship of the Council of Europe's Council of Ministers between May and October, **Azerbaijan** nevertheless intensified in 2014 the relentless crackdown on dissent begun after the October 2013 presidential ballot, in which incumbent Ilham Aliyev had been elected for a third term. Those arrested on dubious charges included human rights campaigners Arif Yunusov and Leyla Yunusova; Human Rights Club chairman Rasul Djafarov; Legal Education Society head Intigam Aliyev (no relation to the president); opposition Musavat Party activist Orkhan Eyub-zase; and journalists Rauf Mirkadyrov and Khadija Ismailova.

In March, a court in Sheki jailed Ilgar Mamedov, the leader of the opposition party Republican Alternative, for seven years for his imputed involvement in mass unrest in the provincial town of Ismailly in January 2013 (see AR 2014, p. 105). On 15 May, journalist and human rights activist Parviz Gashimly was sentenced to eight years' imprisonment for allegedly organising the sale of weapons to Iran. Ten days later, the head of the Centre for Monitoring Elections, Anar Mamedli, was sentenced to five-and-a-half years in prison on charges of tax evasion and illegal business activity.

Azerbaijani officials rejected as misplaced criticism by the USA and human rights organisations of those arrests and sentences. President Aliyev nonetheless included 10 prisoners of conscience amongst persons he pardoned in December.

Predictably, the ruling New Azerbaijan Party (YAP) won 60 per cent of the seats in municipal elections on 23 December, in which many opposition candidates were denied registration and just 39 per cent of the electorate voted. Only a few hundred people attended an opposition demonstration on 14 December, for which the Baku City Council granted permission.

The conflict between Armenia and Azerbaijan over Nagorno-Karabakh remained deadlocked. At least 22 servicemen were killed in July and August in the worst upsurge of fighting since the 1994 ceasefire. A summit in Sochi on 9 August between Russian President Vladimir Putin and his Armenian and Azerbaijani counterparts resulted in a temporary lull in hostilities; further meetings between Presidents Sarkisian and Aliyev took place on the sidelines of the September NATO summit in Wales and in late October in Paris, mediated by US Secretary of State John Kerry and French President François Hollande, respectively. Then on 12 November, during large-scale Armenian military manoeuvres, Azerbaijan shot down an Armenian Mi-24 combat helicopter, killing the three crew members, whose remains were retrieved only 10 days later as Azerbaijan refuse to allow access to the crash site.

Two Azerbaijanis were sentenced on 29 December in Stepanakert, the unrecognised enclave's capital, to 22 years' and life imprisonment for the murder in July of an Armenian youth who had inadvertently strayed onto Azerbaijani territory.

In line with President Sarkisian's decision of September 2013 (see AR 2014, p. 105), Armenian diplomacy focused in 2014 on negotiating the terms for Armenia's accession to the Eurasian Economic Union, comprising Russia, Belarus and Kazakhstan. After several unexplained postponements, the four countries' presidents signed the relevant treaty in Minsk on 10 October. At the same time, Armenian officials consistently stressed the desire for closer co-operation and economic relations with the European Union, which in December disbursed €10 million in aid.

Addressing the UN General Assembly in September, President Sarkisian threatened to recall from parliament the agreements signed in 2009 on normalising Armenia's relations with Turkey. Turkey had pegged their ratification to a solution of the Karabakh conflict that was acceptable to Azerbaijan.

Georgia made some progress towards its goal of European integration, signing an Association Agreement with the European Union on 27 June, but the government was warned in November at the first session of the EU-Georgia Association Council, which had the task of implementing the Agreement, of the need to avoid "political retribution, confrontation and polarisation".

At the NATO summit in early September, Georgia was offered substantial military aid but not the long-hoped-for Membership Action Plan. Georgian forces' four-year deployment to Afghanistan as part of the ISAF mission ended in July.

The slowdown in the Russian economy, the precipitous decline in the value of the rouble, and the ensuing slump in remittances sent home by Armenians working in Russia contributed to Armenia's failure to meet its target of 4 per cent GDP growth, which had already been revised downward in May from 5 per cent. The Armenian dram depreciated sharply in value in mid-December but subsequently recovered.

Azerbaijan registered 2.8 per cent economic growth, despite falling oil prices. Inflation was at its lowest rate for a decade, at 1.5 per cent. The first section of the South Caucasus pipeline from Azerbaijan that was to export gas from Azerbaijan's Shah Deniz Caspian field via the Trans-Anatolia (TANAP) gas pipeline to southern Europe was laid in Baku in September.

The Georgian lari lost 11 per cent of its value in early December, but Georgia registered the strongest economic growth in the region, though at 4.7 per cent GDP growth fell just short of the government's target figure of 5 per cent.

Liz Fuller

IV THE AMERICAS AND THE CARIBBEAN

THE UNITED STATES OF AMERICA

CAPITAL: Washington, DC   AREA: 9,632,030 sq km   POPULATION: 316,128,839 ('13)
OFFICIAL LANGUAGE: English (de facto); Spanish widely used
HEAD OF STATE AND GOVERNMENT: Barack Obama (Democrat) (since Jan '09)
RULING PARTIES: Democrats control presidency; Republicans control Congress
DEMOCRACY INDEX: 8.11; 19th of 167   CORRUPTION PERCEPTIONS INDEX: 74; =17th of 175
CURRENCY: US Dollar (Dec '14 £1.00=USD 1.55)
GNI PER CAPITA: US$53,670, Intl$53,960 at PPP ('13)

ACCORDING to the numbers, 2014 was a good year for the United States but a bad one for President Barack Obama. On 23 December, GDP growth for the third quarter was revised upwards to a heady 5 per cent—the fastest rate since 2003. Economic growth over the year ran at 2.7 per cent, and was predicted to rise to an annualised rate of 3 per cent in 2015. The Dow Jones Industrial Average cleared 18,000 just before Christmas: when Obama took office in January 2009 the index had languished at just under 8,000 points. Unemployment fell to 5.8 per cent, job growth accelerated sharply at year's end, and real income for the median household increased by 1.2 per cent for the first 11 months of the year, following a steep drop of 8 per cent from 2008 to 2011 and stagnancy thereafter. When, at the end of January 2013, Obama had claimed that "2014 can be a breakthrough year," critics had dismissed the president's misplaced optimism. But it turned out that Obama's assessment was largely correct in respect to the economy. As *The Economist* reported at year's end, "Growth is likely to be robust in 2015—and will start to benefit ordinary families."

Not that this strong performance did the Democratic Party much good at the polls. In the mid-term elections of 2014, Republicans secured control of the Senate, winning 24 of the 36 seats contested, and gained 13 seats in the House of Representatives. The GOP's 247 seats, compared with the Democratic Party's 188, gave the party its largest congressional majority since 1928—the year that Herbert Hoover crushed Al Smith with over 58 per cent of the popular vote. If the Democrats had performed solidly in gubernatorial elections, then the party might have been able to draw solace from its broader-based appeal, which augured well for the general election. But Republican candidates won elections in Massachusetts, Maryland and Arkansas—following the retirement of Democrats—and defeated an incumbent, Pat Quinn, in Illinois. No single issue dominated the mid-terms, but pollsters identified "Obamacare", immigration and income inequality as the three issues that particularly concentrated voters' minds. That the first two favoured Republican candidates was no surprise; that inequality did so ran more counter to intuition. At the end of 2014, President Obama's approval rating stood at 46 per cent, up slightly from a low point of 40 per cent in the aftermath of the elections, but low enough to suggest that Democrats who politely declined Obama's support on the campaign trail in 2014 were wise to do so.

There was no doubt that Obama had some wretched moments in 2014. Russian President Vladimir Putin's aggression in Ukraine made the USA appear a weak and irresolute ally; the rise of the Islamic State of Iraq and Syria (ISIS, also known as ISIL and IS) appeared to catch the administration off-guard and the subsequent beheadings of US hostages made for grotesque theatre; critics made great hay of Obama's supposedly complacent response to the horrendous Ebola outbreak in West Africa; and "Obamacare" remained an epithet that was virtually guaranteed to wound. Yet the president's response to this comprehensive electoral defeat ran unhappily counter to what Republicans had anticipated. By executive order, on 20 November, Obama enacted sweeping immigration reform, which would allow approximately 45 per cent of all illegal immigrants to remain and work legally in the United States. In December, he announced that the US had embarked on the process of normalising relations with Cuba, rejecting the policy of economic embargo and ostracisation that had been pursued since Fidel Castro's rise to power. "I wish he had accepted the results of the election and decided it was time maybe to go in a different direction," lamented Senator John Thune (R-SD), clearly nonplussed that defeat appeared to have emboldened rather than humbled the president, "I don't know that he got that message." When asked if he would rate Obama's 2014 as better than his 2013, Senator Richard Blumenthal (D-Conn) answered, "You know, my experience in life is every year is better than the last."

DOMESTIC AFFAIRS. In his State of the Union speech at the end of January, President Obama issued a list of promises, of which some were more familiar than others. He pledged to push hard for immigration reform, raise the minimum wage for federal government employees, redouble efforts to close Guantánamo Bay, and veto any attempts made by Congress to constrain his freedom of action in negotiating an agreement with Iran over its nuclear programme. While he declared his usual preference for working productively with Congress, he also indicated his willingness to ignore the legislature where necessary: "Wherever and whenever I can take steps without legislation to expand opportunity for more American families, that's what I'm going to do." It was quite a change of emphasis from Obama's first term, a period in which he signed the fewest number of executive actions since the 1930s. The president gave fair warning that—irrespective of what transpired in the mid-terms—2014 was going to be "a year of action".

There was an understandable hesitation on the part of Democrats and Republicans to take Obama at his word. After all, Obama had earlier pledged to move ahead on gun control "with or without Congress", and had not got very far. It had not taken long for the president to figure, through rudimentary cost-benefit analysis, that this was not an issue on which to spend significant political capital—the obstacles were too great and his opponents too well-funded. Republicans suspected that history would repeat itself and the president would eschew bold action. In an official televised response, which largely ignored Obama's threats to proceed via executive action, Representative Cathy McMorris Rodgers (R-WA) observed, "The president talks a lot about income inequality. But the real gap we face today is one of opportunity equality." The economic arguments that informed campaigning in the mid-terms later in the year were becoming apparent: Democrats would decry income inequality; Republicans would bemoan a rise in statism and a decline in social mobility.

One previously divisive issue that became increasingly normalised over the course of the year was same-sex marriage. On 13 February a federal judge in Virginia struck down the state's ban on such unions. "Our constitution declared that 'all men' are created equal," observed Arenda Wright Allen, "Surely this means all of us." The decision in Virginia had followed similar rulings in previous months that had overturned the ban in Utah and Oklahoma. By the end of the year, same-sex marriage was legal in 36 states. It was a swift and remarkable turnaround—Obama had been extremely reluctant to take a clear stance on same-sex marriage during his first term—during a year in which many aspects of social policy followed a liberal rather than conservative direction of travel.

This trend was certainly evident in respect to the decriminalisation of cannabis. At year's end, the use of medicinal and recreational marijuana was legal in Colorado, Washington, Alaska and Oregon, and the drug was legal for medical use in 23 states. A state senator in Oklahoma quoted Genesis 1:29 in campaigning to legalise the drug: "God said, 'Behold, I have given you every herb-bearing seed ... upon the face of all the earth'." Where this momentum would lead was difficult to foresee. But an academic based at the University of California, Los Angeles, Mark Kleiman, made a bold prediction: "I see [legalisation] as a second-term [Hillary] Clinton thing."

In the national conversation over the appropriate size of government, however, conservatives continued to set the terms of the debate. GOP strategists and political candidates attacked "Obamacare" throughout the year, judging that this was a likely vote-winner in the mid-term elections of November. The Obama administration was actually able to announce some positive healthcare news on 1 May. At that point, 8 million Americans had signed up for coverage through insurance exchanges (on a website that had overcome significant teething problems). The Urban Institute think-tank reported that enrolments were 15 per cent higher than expected, and that the most significant demographic that had signed up for coverage were those on a low income—85 per cent of healthcare.gov enrollers were eligible for subsidies. This broadly positive headline figure hid some significant variations, however. While 85 per cent of those eligible for an Affordable Care Act-sanctioned healthcare plan had signed up for one in Vermont, only 11 per cent had done so in South Dakota. The young were generally less inclined to sign up than the elderly. The process through which the United States edged toward expanding healthcare coverage—it remained the only rich nation without universal healthcare coverage—remained painful and precarious.

This reality was doubly reinforced in June, when the Supreme Court made a ruling that could have a significant impact on the comprehensiveness of healthcare provision. In *Burwell v Hobby Lobby*, the Court decided by a margin of 5-4 that employers with religious objections did not have pay for contraceptives for their staff, thereby contravening the stipulations of the Affordable Care Act. Responding to Justice Ruth Bader Ginsburg's strong objections, Justice Samuel Alito reassured that the ruling would not create a "flood of religious objections" to established federal law. Ginsburg was not mollified; and nor were the ruling's many other critics. It was another setback for Obama's signature achievement in domestic politics, one that his political opponents were pleased to keep centre stage.

While "Obamacare" remained a potent weapon for Republicans to deploy against Democrats, the party's most radical wing—the so-called "Tea Party" movement—did not fare so well in 2014. In North Carolina, for example, Greg Brannon had hoped to secure his party's nomination to run for the Senate. Brannon had lambasted the Federal Reserve for "piracy" and "treason", and described income taxes as "unacceptable". He further fretted that chipping away at the sacrosanct "right to life" would ultimately lead to the government euthanising the unproductive elderly: "That's Plato's Republic, not the American republic," he thundered, fancifully. Yet in spite of considerable Tea Party enthusiasm, and a ringing endorsement from Senator Rand Paul (R-KY), Brannon was beaten to the nomination by the centrist (by the standards of the modern-day GOP) Thom Tillis, the speaker of North Carolina's state assembly. Tillis then went on to defeat the Democratic incumbent, Kay Hagan, in the November election, providing his party with a crucial gain in the Senate. In microcosm, this race suggested that the GOP had learned its lesson from previous election years, when beatable Democrats had held on largely due to the extremism of their Tea Party-backed opponents, such as Todd Akin in Missouri, Christine O'Donnell in Delaware, and Richard Mourdock in Indiana. When the Senate minority leader, Mitch McConnell, defeated the insurgent Tea Party-backed candidate Matt Bevin whom Mark Levin and Glenn Beck had endorsed—it appeared that the logic of Anthony Downs's "Median Voter Theorem"—that securing the allegiance of the median voter is crucial to electoral success—was renascent in the GOP. The defeat of Eric Cantor, the House majority leader, by a Tea Party-supported candidate in Virginia was very much the exception rather than the rule.

A harsh light was cast on race relations and draconian policing practices on 9 August, when a white policeman, Darren Wilson, shot dead an unarmed African-American teenager named Michael Brown in Ferguson, Missouri, a suburb of St Louis. The police maintained that the 18-year old had attacked the officer and tried to grab his gun. A friend who was with Brown said that he had his arms in the air at the time he was shot. The population of Ferguson was around 21,000, of which two-thirds were black. Yet the police force had only three black officers in its employ. These statistics become more pertinent as protests flared up in the aftermath of the shooting, leading to rioting, looting, and the use of tear gas and flash grenades to disperse protestors. Remarking on the shooting of Brown and the violence that followed, the Democratic governor of Missouri, Jay Nixon, remarked that it "felt like an open wound torn fresh." In September, Eric Holder, the US attorney general, announced he was launching a federal investigation into the Missouri police force to establish whether its officers engaged in systemic racial profiling and excessive use of force. On 1 December, President Obama announced that $75 million would be spent on body cameras for law enforcement officials— an innovation that Brown's parents had called for.

The fatal shooting in Ferguson happened not long after another unarmed black man, Eric Garner, had been killed by a white police officer—in this case by a chokehold—following a confrontation about his illegally selling single cigarettes. Videotaped footage of the incident, viewed by tens of millions on YouTube and other social media, showed Brown repeating the words "I can't breathe" 11 times before he died. On 4 December, a Grand Jury in New York opted not to indict Daniel Pantaleo, who had executed the chokehold. There were widespread national protests against police brutality and racism—300 were arrested at the New York protest alone. Shock and discontent at the Grand Jury's decision was widespread. Former President George W. Bush described the ruling as "hard to understand" and "very sad". At his end-of-year press conference, Obama discussed Ferguson and the Garner case, and expressed dismay, noting "a growing awareness in the broader population of what I think many communities of colour have understood for some time, and that is that there are specific instances at least where law enforcement doesn't feel as if it's being applied in a colour-blind fashion." In 2014, policing in the United States became a civil rights issue.

A serious outbreak of Ebola in West Africa worsened through the course of 2014, killing upwards of 8,000 people. Prominent Republicans criticised the Obama administration for regarding so complacently the threat posed by the disease to the United States. Senator Rand Paul observed that the administration's reassurances that the disease was difficult to catch were shaded by "political correctness", and that Ebola was in fact "incredibly transmissible". Governor Bobby Jindal observed that incoming flights from affected areas had to be grounded "to protect our people". In the run-up to the mid-term elections, Republican candidates creatively fused Ebola with immigration to conjure nightmare scenarios. In a debate with his opponent, Senator Kay Hagan, Thom Tillis remarked, "Ladies and gentlemen, we've got an Ebola outbreak. We have bad actors that can come across the border. We need to seal the border." Democrats also found it difficult to resist the temptation to politicise Ebola. Senator Mark Udall of Colorado suggested that the administration's response would have been better coordinated had Republicans not insisted on slashing the budgets of the National Institutes of Health and the Centres for Disease Control and Prevention.

Thanks in large part to the attention accorded it by cable television news outlets, Ebola—a disease that claimed the life of one US citizen in 2014—was a genuinely significant issue as polling day approached. But it was not the only issue to be distorted and deployed as a political weapon. As *The Economist* observed on 1 November, "The Republicans, if you believe Democratic attack ads, oppose equal pay for women, want to ban contraception and just love it when big corporations ship American jobs overseas. The Democrats, according to Republicans, have stood idly by as Islamic State terrorists—possibly carrying Ebola—prepare to cross the southern border. And they, too, are delighted to see American jobs shipped overseas." As the mudslinging intensified, most signs suggested that the Democrats were poised to lose control of the Senate. Indeed, the popularity or otherwise of the incumbent president might not have made a huge difference. Ronald Reagan's approval ratings stood at 60 per cent in 1986, but the GOP still lost control of the Senate, because the match-ups that year were unfavourable. The same was largely true in 2014, where those Democrats who had won unexpected victories in the Senate thanks to Obama's resounding victory in 2008, faced the formidable task of trying to repeat the feat in a less forgiving political climate.

According to the exit polls, two-thirds of voters stated that the country was heading in the wrong direction, a scenario blamed on President Obama *and* a dysfunctional Congress. The GOP strategy, by and large, was to establish bonds of affection between all Democratic candidates (regardless of their position on their party's political spectrum) and the unpopular Obama (and "Obamacare"). It worked very well indeed. The Republican Party won control of the Senate,

---

Final results of mid-term US elections 2014

Senate (36 out of 100 seats contested)

Party	Seats in 114th Congress	(Seats at dissolution of 113th Congress)
Republican	54	(45)
Democratic	44	(53)
*Independent	2	(2)
Total	100	(100)

*Both independents were aligned with the Democratic Party.

House of Representatives (all 435 seats contested)

Party	Seats in 114th Congress	% of vote	(Seats won in 2012 election)
Republican	247	51.0	(234)
Democratic	188	45.2	(201)
Total	435		(435)

Governorships (36 of the 50 state governorships were contested)

Party	Governorships held after election	(Governorships held before election)
Republican	31	(29)
Democratic	18	(21)
Independent	1	(0)
Total	50	(50)

improved its majority in the House, and won a series of governorships in Democrat-leaning states such as Maryland and Massachusetts.

The new Senate majority leader, Mitch McConnell, declined to gloat, instead striking a note (albeit fairly muted) of bipartisanship: "I don't expect the president to wake up tomorrow and view the world any differently than he did when he woke up this morning. He knows I won't either. But look, we have an obligation to work together on issues where we can agree." The other senator from Kentucky was less emollient. "We will send the president bill after bill until he wearies of it," warned Rand Paul, and this would include working tirelessly to repeal every "vestige" of the Affordable Care Act.

While conservative candidates did well at the polls, liberal issues fared well on ballot initiatives. Voters in Alaska, Arkansas, Nebraska and South Dakota all voted to raise the minimum wage, while at the same time electing Republican candidates to the Senate who were uniformly opposed or equivocal about raising the threshold. In California, Proposition 47 reclassified most "non-serious and non-violent property and drug crimes" from a felony to a misdemeanour—a move almost certain to decrease the size of the state's bulging prison population. In Washington state, to the dismay of the National Rifle Association, a measure passed that would require a background check for all gun sales, including private sales and those at gun shows. But these small victories at the state level were all the Democrats had to cheer on a dismal night for the party.

Reflecting on the results, Barack Obama observed, "Both parties are going to have to come together and compromise to get something done here." But the president was in no mood for self-flagellation. On 20 November he unveiled a major executive action on immigration policy. First, the president offered a legal reprieve to undocumented parents of US citizens or permanent residents who had lived in the country for more than five years. Secondly, the executive action expanded the 2012 Deferred Action for Childhood Arrivals programme that permitted immigrants aged 30 years and younger, who had arrived in the USA as children, to apply for a deportation deferral, leading to legal residency. It amended the programme's remit to include more recent arrivals, and those over the age of 30. The Migration Policy Institute estimated that approximately 4 million undocumented workers were directly affected by the president's bold move. Republicans were incensed, and a little surprised. It was not the response they had expected from the leader of a party that had just been humbled at the polls.

Obama's immigration gambit certainly made the debate about the annual budget particularly rancorous, though one might argue that it could scarcely have been worse than in previous years. The government's funding was set to run out on 11 December, and Washington witnessed the usual brinkmanship regarding the deadline and what grim scenarios might follow. Democrats had a significant weapon in their armoury, however, in the form of a shrinking deficit. In 2009, the deficit peaked at $1.4 trillion, which amounted to 9.8 per cent of the nation's GDP. Yet the deficit as a proportion of GDP had dropped to 2.8 per cent in September—not a number from which nightmares could be plausibly conjured. Polls in early 2013 showed that one-quarter of Americans viewed the deficit as the nation's most significant problem; by the end of 2014 this figure had dropped to 10 per cent. It was a remarkable turnaround which testified to the Obama administration's effective stewardship of the economy.

The budget was passed on time, although many Democrats were incensed by riders added by Republicans at the eleventh hour which, they argued, contravened the Dodd-Frank Wall Street Reform and Consumer Protection Act of 2010. On her Facebook page, Senator Elizabeth Warren wrote, "The House is about to vote on a closed-door budget deal that slips in a provision—literally written by Citigroup lobbyists—to let Wall Street derivatives traders once again gamble with our economy. We all need to fight back immediately against this giveaway to the most powerful banks in the country." Warren's rallying cry was made to no avail. Democrats girded themselves for further reversals in 2015, when the Senate filibuster and presidential veto would remain the only defensive manoeuvres available.

At the end of the year, President Obama might have been forgiven for revelling in a series of highly positive economic indicators. The economist Paul Krugman had earlier criticised some of the administration's decisions, particularly those pertaining to the "stress test" devised by Timothy Geithner when he was treasury secretary. But reviewing Geithner's memoir in the *New York Review of Books* in July, Krugman admitted he had been mistaken: "A principal part of Geithner's argument against nationalisation was the belief that a 'stress test' of banks would show them to be in fairly decent shape, and that publishing the results of such a test would, in conjunction with promises to shore up banks when necessary, end the crisis. And so it proved. He was right; I was wrong; and the triumph of the stress test gave him the title for his book."

Yet Obama's Republican critics did not join Krugman in conceding that the administration had actually made an occasional sound economic decision. Writing in *The New York Times* on 28 December, Krugman rounded on the narrative of strangulating statism that the GOP had so effectively developed: "You know the spiel: that the US economy is ailing because 'Obamacare' is a job killer and the president is a redistributionist, that Mr. Obama's anti-business speeches (he hasn't actually made any, but never mind) have hurt entrepreneurs' feelings, inducing them to take their marbles and go home." Krugman wondered how this line had proven so successful, given that it diverged so sharply from reality. "The truth is that the private sector has done surprisingly well under Mr. Obama, adding 6.7 million jobs since he took office, compared with just 3.1 million at this point under George W. Bush. Corporate profits have soared, as have stock prices. What held us back was unprecedented public sector austerity. At this point in the Bush years, government unemployment was up by 1.2 million, but under Mr. Obama it's down by 600,000. Sure enough, now that this de facto austerity is easing, the economy is perking up."

Krugman's partisanship on the issue of austerity was never in doubt. But at the close of 2014 he was in a position to marshal some strong evidence to support his case. Thus, lambasting Obama and the Democratic Party for feckless economic management was largely taken away from the GOP as a line of attack. Most signs suggested that the presidential primaries and the 2016 elections would play out against a backdrop of healthy growth, rising employment, and low inflation. This would not necessarily make Hillary Clinton a shoo-in, even if she secured her party's nomination, for economic conditions were benign in 2000 when Al Gore lost the presidential election to George W. Bush. However, a strong economy would not harm the prospects of the next Democratic candidate for president.

FOREIGN POLICY. In a long profile published in the *New Yorker* in January 2014, David Remnick asked President Obama if he was "haunted" by his decision not to intervene in Syria. "I am not haunted by my decision not to engage in another Middle Eastern war," replied Obama. "It is very difficult to imagine a scenario in which our involvement in Syria would have led to a better outcome, short of us being willing to undertake an effort in size and scope similar to what we did in Iraq." Another Iraq-style military intervention was, of course, a simply fantastical prospect to Obama, and—if the opinion polls were correct—to the public he served. But Obama also provided Remnick with a revealing description of his policymaking method: "I have strengths and I have weaknesses, like every President, like every person. I do think one of my strengths is temperament. I am comfortable with complexity, and I think I'm pretty good at keeping my moral compass while recognising that I am a product of original sin. And every morning and every night I'm taking measure of my actions against the options and possibilities available to me, understanding that there are going to be mistakes that I make and my team makes and that America makes; understanding that there are going to be limits to the good we can do and the bad that we can prevent, and that there's going to be tragedy out there and, by occupying this office, I am part of that tragedy occasionally, but that if I am doing my very best and basing my decisions on the core values and ideals that I was brought up with and that I think are pretty consistent with those of most Americans, that at the end of the day things will be better rather than worse."

These words, on the limits of what was realistically achievable, could have been authored by one of the president's inspirations, the Protestant theologian and foreign policy thinker, Reinhold Niebuhr. But they were not to everyone's taste. Throughout the year, critics would continue to lambast the Obama administration for failing to enunciate a grand strategy—an "Obama Doctrine"—in the manner of its predecessors.

Not long after the publication of the *New Yorker* profile, former Defence Secretary Robert Gates (2006-11) published a memoir, *Duty*, which would have made uncomfortable reading for Obama (and indeed for his predecessor, George W. Bush). Though admiring and respectful in the main, Gates directed ire at the president's inner-circle of advisers, who in his opinion had engaged in the most damaging levels of micromanagement "since Richard Nixon and Henry Kissinger ruled the roost". He also directed a barb at an old antagonist, Vice President Joe Biden, with whom he had clashed throughout his career. Gates observed brutally that while he liked Biden personally, the vice president had been "wrong on nearly every major foreign policy and national security issue over the past four decades". The former defence secretary and the vice president had sharply disagreed over policy toward Afghanistan—the former favouring an ongoing military commit-ment; the latter a swift withdrawal—and he expressed dismay that the president, after agreeing to launch a troop "surge" in 2009, had ultimately sided with Biden in heading so quickly thereafter for the exits. Observing a 2011 meeting between Obama and General David Petraeus, who at that point was the military com-mander in Afghanistan, Gates recalled thinking, "The president doesn't trust his commander, can't stand [Afghan President] Karzai, doesn't believe his own strat-egy, and doesn't consider the war to be his. For him, it's all about getting out." Sen-ator Lindsey Graham latched upon these revelations to decry Obama's tendency to overrule the military on how to proceed in theatres like Iraq and Syria. Yet what appeared ill-advised to Graham was restrained and clear-headed to others.

Obama's preference for diplomatic solutions where possible was placed front and centre on 20 January when an interim deal with Iran came into effect, which eased international sanctions on Iran in exchange for slowing down its nuclear pro-gramme. Throughout the year, efforts were expended on transforming the interim deal—agreed in November 2013—into something more permanent, but harder line elements in both Iran and the United States constrained US Secretary of State John Kerry and Iranian Foreign Minister Mohammad Javad Zarif. After talks in Vienna broke down in November, Zarif observed that he believed that the two positions could be bridged, but that the "major problem is a compounded mis-trust". Zarif concluded by rejecting any Cold War parallels, when the Soviet Union and the United States engaged in negotiating brinkmanship: "If you are looking for a zero-sum game in nuclear negotiations, you are doomed to failure," he cau-tioned. Reflecting on the situation in December, and the significantly altered Con-gressional calculus following the mid-term elections, President Obama vowed to veto any GOP attempts to reintroduce sanctions and stated his belief that a com-prehensive deal was "possible" which would allow Iran to transition from pariah to "a very successful regional power". Negotiations remained highly precarious, and it was highly likely that Obama would have to deploy that veto power at some point in 2015.

On 24 February, the secretary of defence, Chuck Hagel, unveiled a $496 billion defence budget which stirred disquiet among Republican critics. The budget necessitated a cut in the size of the army from 522,000 to 440,000 troops, the lowest level since the Second World War—and 50,000 fewer than the proposal announced in 2011. Former Vice President Dick Cheney intemperately observed that this decision showed that President Obama "would rather spend money on Food Stamps" than on keeping the nation strong. Senator John McCain denounced the proposed reduction as a "serious mistake". But like most political disputes in Washington, this contretemps was blighted by histrionics. The United States still possessed 11 aircraft carrier groups—whereas Russia and China had just one each, fitted with significantly poorer technology. The United States still spent more on defence than the next 10 countries combined; its total military expenditure in 2015 constituted approximately 35 per cent of the global total. According to *The Econ-omist*, "Chinese commanders talk about not being able to match American hard power until 2050 at the earliest." Yet decreasing the US military to a size comparable to 1940 clearly struck a nerve, providing Obama's political opponents with more ammunition to attack his alleged weakness and irresolution.

In March 2014, Russian President Vladimir Putin ordered Russian special forces to take control of military and government installations in Crimea, the southerly region of Ukraine hosting Sevastopol—and Russia's Black Sea Fleet—and a large ethnic Russian majority. Putin explained that his hand was forced by the ousting of the pro-Russian Ukrainian President Viktor Yanukovych, following a series of demonstrations against him, and by the odious pro-European government that replaced him. Putin claimed that the opposition groups that had compelled Yanukovych to flee Kiev for Rostov-on-Don on 21 February had far-right or fascistic tendencies and that he had intervened in Crimea to protect ethnic Russians from reprisals. Russia set up a referendum on 16 March in which 97 per cent of Crimeans supported incorporation into Russia (the pro-Ukrainian Tatar minority declined to take part). That Wilsonian self-determination had been deployed to serve cynical purposes was made clear by the speaker of Russia's upper house of parliament, Valentina Matviyenko: "Deciding to hold [a] referendum is a sovereign right of Crimea's legitimately elected parliament ... the right of people to self-determination." Clearly, the Obama administration possessed no realistic military options to discourage Putin. But this did not stop his critics from suggesting that Obama's irresolution had invited Russia's move, and that his response to this flagrant Russian aggression was weak on substance and tepid in presentation.

America's foreign policy commentariat weighed in with a series of editorials, and most were entirely predictable. Zbigniew Brzezinski suggested that the West should privately convey to Russia "that the Ukrainian army can count on immediate and direct Western aid so as it enhance its defensive capabilities" and recommended that "NATO's forces, consistent with the organisation's planning, should be put on high alert". Charles Krauthammer endorsed Brzezinski's approach 10 days later, but also suggested sending "the chairman of the Joint Chiefs to the Baltics to arrange joint manoeuvres", and proposed that Obama should "order the energy department" to expedite the export of more gas to Europe to render crippling sanctions against Russia more palatable to the UK, France and Germany. On the Left, Stephen Cohen, a professor of Russian history at New York University, criticised the United States for failing to comprehend Putin's strategic perspective and for needlessly inflaming the situation.

Aged 90, and liberated from his usual default position of pursuing or advising power—which had led to an embarrassing tête-à-tête with Sarah Palin in 2008—Henry Kissinger drafted one of the most nuanced analyses of the crisis. Writing in the *Washington Post* on 5 March, Kissinger faulted Russia for failing to comprehend that forcing Ukraine into accepting satellite status "would doom Moscow to repeat its history of self-fulfilling cycles of reciprocal pressures with Europe and the United States". But he also chided many in "the West" for failing to comprehend that "to Russia, Ukraine can never be just a foreign country. Russian history began in what was called Kievan-Rus. The Russian religion spread from there. Ukraine has been part of Russia for centuries, and their histories were intertwined before then." Historically literate, elegantly crafted, and eminently sensible,

Kissinger's analysis offered a penetrating account of the misconceptions, and lack of empathy, blighting both sides. "The United States needs to avoid treating Russia as an aberrant to be patiently taught rules of conduct established by Washington. Putin is a serious strategist—on the premises of Russian history. Understanding US values and psychology are not his strong suits. Nor has understanding Russian history and psychology been a strong point of US policymakers. Leaders of all sides should return to examining outcomes, not compete in posturing."

For Kissinger, Obama's response to the Ukrainian crisis had little connection to credibility, which was only ever at stake in genuinely contested areas. Crimea fell within the Russian sphere of influence, and this had to be recognised. Managing the crisis was about understanding Putin's perspective, clearly communicating how damaging the annexation of Crimea would be to Russia's world position, and not needlessly inflaming the situation through reckless promises: Kissinger echoed George Kennan in warning that Ukrainian membership of NATO was not an option.

President Obama appeared to side with Kissinger over the best way to deal with Putin's aggression. On 19 February Obama had described Ukraine as a "client state of Russia" and cautioned that the region should not be seen as "some Cold War chessboard in which we are in competition with Russia". On 25 March, in response to a question on the magnitude of the threat posed by Moscow, Obama observed cuttingly, "Russia is a regional power that is threatening some of its immediate neighbours—not out of strength but out of weakness." The president's implication was even if left largely alone, history suggested that Russia would suffer in the long run for its belligerence and the sham referendum. A grave financial crisis that afflicted Russia at the end of the year caused by plummeting oil prices and the imposition of Western sanctions and which led to a 40 per cent drop in the value of the rouble over three weeks in December appeared to vindicate the president's assessment. "I think it would be dishonest to suggest that there's a simple solution to resolving what has already taken place in Crimea," Obama observed, "Although history has a funny way of moving in twists and turns and not just in a straight line." A hawkish John McCain was not persuaded by Obama's assessment, describing the crisis as the "ultimate result of a feckless foreign policy where nobody believes in America's strength anymore". Without quite specifying how, Dick Cheney declared that "Russian aggression must not go unanswered."

On 28 April, responding to a question during a tour of Asia regarding his country's supposed "weakness", Obama replied tartly: "Why is it that everybody is so eager to use military force?" A Pew survey a few months before had shown that 52 per cent of Americans wanted their country "to mind its own business internationally", which amounted to the highest percentage response to that question in half a century. Through the spring and summer of 2014 President Obama confronted multiple crises: Putin's land grab in Ukraine; a brutal civil war in Syria; increased Chinese bellicosity in the South China Sea; deadlock in locating a diplomatic resolution to the Israel-Palestine dispute and the descent into asymmetrical military exchanges. Yet on the first two issues, Obama was clear that there were no good options, and that it was foolish to implement bad ones for the sake of appearances: "Very rarely have I seen the exercise of military power providing a definitive answer," the president told an audience in Seoul.

On 8 May the House of Representatives voted to launch another congressional investigation into the 2012 attack on the US embassy in Benghazi, Libya, during which Ambassador Christopher Stevens had been killed. It was the ninth such investigation in total. Led by Trey Gowdy, a theatrical Tea Party-backed Republican congressman from South Carolina, the committee kept Hillary Clinton—who had been secretary of state at the time—in its sights throughout the year, but did not unearth compelling evidence that corroborated any of the various theories cited to explain what had transpired. There were clear risks—appearing obsessed with an issue that had already been thoroughly investigated—but also opportunities—damaging Clinton and her presidential ambitions—for Republicans in doggedly pursuing this line of inquiry. In her memoir, *Hard Choices*, published in August 2014, Clinton accused Republican critics of launching "a political slugfest on the backs of dead Americans". Wherever one stood on the issue, the steady stream of accusations and denials made for an unedifying spectacle.

On 28 May President Obama delivered an important speech at West Point that declined, yet again, to set out an overarching strategic doctrine: "It is absolutely true that in the 21st century American isolationism is not an option. We don't have a choice to ignore what happens beyond our borders ... But to say that we have an interest in pursuing peace and freedom beyond our borders is not to say that every problem has a military solution. Since World War II, some of our most costly mistakes came not from our restraint, but from our willingness to rush into military adventures without thinking through the consequences—without building international support and legitimacy for our action; without levelling with the American people about the sacrifices required."

The usual suspects assailed the speech as weak and unprincipled—"One can only marvel at the smallness of it all," wrote Krauthammer in the *Washington Post*, under the headline "Emptiness at West Point". Krauthammer fairly observed that no one seriously believed that every crisis had a military solution, and in this sense the president was disingenuous in setting up "a sombre parade of straw men", as he wittily phrased it.

During supposedly off-the-record discussion with reporters in the summer of 2014, Obama observed that his core strategic doctrine could be summarised simply as: "Don't do stupid shit." During an on-the-record interview with *The Atlantic*, Hillary Clinton disagreed: "Great nations need organising principles, and 'don't do stupid stuff' is not an organising principle." Yet when the interviewer invited Clinton to spell out her own organising principle, she answered with "Peace, progress, and prosperity": alliterative boilerplate that any American politician since the inception of the Republic could have uttered. Clinton understood all too well the problems with neat organising principles. As she wrote in *Hard Choices*, "[a]lthough some may have yearned for an Obama Doctrine—a grand unified theory that would provide a simple and elegant road map for foreign policy in a new era, like 'containment' did during the Cold War—there was nothing simple or elegant about the problems we faced."

So it was in the Middle East. By the beginning of August, ISIS militants in Iraq had captured the towns of Zumar, Sinjar and Wana, forcing thousands of Yazidis—believers in an ancient monotheistic religion linked to Zoroastianism—to flee to nearby Mount Sinjar. ISIS's goal was to establish a brutal, hard-line Caliphate and during its rapid advance through Iraq and Syria it had captured and executed—often by beheading—those it deemed heretics. Confronted with a potential genocide against the Yazidis, President Obama on 7 August launched a humanitarian mission to supply the them, and launched airstrikes against ISIS positions from an aircraft carrier in the Persian Gulf. In a speech at the UN the following month, Obama observed that "there can be no reasoning—no negotiation—with this brand of evil" and described ISIS as "a network of death". Throughout the year, ISIS beheaded numerous captives, including James Foley, Steven Sotloff, and Peter Kassig (also known by the name he assumed in captivity, Abdul-Rahman Kassig) all of whom were US citizens. "In this effort, we do not act alone," said Obama during his UN speech. "Nor do we intend to send US troops to occupy foreign lands. Instead, we will support Iraqis and Syrians fighting to reclaim their communities. We will use our military might in a campaign of air strikes to roll back ISIL." This effort was likely to take a long time, and the administration made clear that the burden would not fall exclusively on the United States. Soon after the president's UN speech, Secretary of Defence Hagel observed that ISIS represented "a very significant threat to the security of Iraq," but noted that "this is not a US responsibility."

The advance of ISIS in Syria—where throughout the year it had launched brutal attacks against the regime of the secular President Bashar al-Assad—appeared to vindicate Obama's 2013 decision not to launch airstrikes against Syria. It also provided an opportunity for Senator Rand Paul to showcase the wisdom of his retrenchment-inclined worldview, particularly when compared with the recklessness of the woman he was likely to face in the forthcoming presidential election, should he win the Republican nomination. Writing in the *Wall Street Journal* on 27 August, Paul observed: "To interventionists like former Secretary of State Hillary Clinton, we would caution that arming the Islamic rebels in Syria created a haven for the Islamic State. We are lucky Mrs. Clinton didn't get her way and the Obama administration did not bring about regime change in Syria. That new regime might well be ISIS." One suspected the incumbent president would have agreed with much of this analysis. Obama had described as a "fantasy" the notion that the United States could direct military aid to only the "moderate" opposition to Assad in Syria, a constituency which he described as "essentially an opposition made up of former doctors, farmers, pharmacists and so forth". Instead, he struck directly, ordering airstrikes against ISIS units and against an al-Qaida cell, the so-called Khorosan group, which administration officials stated had been threatening to strike directly against the West. A year after the Assad regime had used chemical weapons, and only narrowly avoided US-led airstrikes, Syria and the United States were inadvertently fighting against the same enemy.

An old adversary, the Taliban, remained a resolute enemy in Afghanistan. On 29 September, after a four month stand-off during which accusations of electoral fraud were rife, Ashraf Ghani was inaugurated as the new president of the country, having defeated Abdullah Abdullah at the polls. Under the terms of a US-brokered deal the latter conceded defeat in return for the newly-created post of "chief executive" (effectively prime minister). On 30 September the new government concluded a bilateral security arrangement (BSA) with the United States, and a "status-of-forces" agreement followed soon after. Put together, the agreements established the legal basis under which detachments of Western troops would remain following the scheduled cessation of combat operations at year's end. The BSA agreement should have been signed much earlier, but the previous president, Hamid Karzai, had refused to do so.

Rather than following the advice of his military advisers, who had recommended the despatch of an "enduring force" of some 15,000 troops, Obama ultimately decided that just 9,800 US troops would remain at the beginning of 2015. Half of those would be withdrawn a year later, with the remainder heading home afterwards. As *The Economist* observed on 4 October: "Understandably, Mr. Obama wants to put no more Americans in harm's way and to boast on leaving office that he has brought all the troops home. But this threatens to be a strategic blunder." Republican critics were discomfited at the speed with which Obama envisioned a full withdrawal. John McCain and Lindsey Graham released a joint statement that accused the president of not appreciating the dire consequences of his headlong rush to leave Iraq: "We... cannot afford to make the same mistake in Afghanistan. We urge President Obama to commit to a conditions-based drawdown in Afghanistan and an enduring US presence to further our counter-terrorism mission and continue advising and assisting Afghan security forces. Failure to do so would endanger US national security and risk squandering the hard-earned gains made possible by the sacrifice of so many brave young Americans."

On 11 November China and the United States (the world's two largest emitters of carbon) signed a major agreement—described by the *New York Times* as a "landmark deal"—on combating the threat posed by global climate change. Jointly announced in Beijing's Great Hall of the People by President Obama and President Xi Jinping following two days of intensive and productive negotiations, the deal included new targets for reducing carbon emissions: reductions by the United States and a commitment by China—its first ever—to stop its emissions from growing by 2030. Obama announced that his nation would emit 26-28 per cent less carbon in 2025 than in 2005—twice the level of reduction for the period from 2005 to 2020. "When the US and China are able to work together effectively," Obama observed, "the whole world benefits." Mitch McConnell, set to become the Senate majority leader following his party's midterm victories, said, "This unrealistic plan that the president would dump on his successor would ensure higher utility rates and far fewer jobs." Representative Tom Cole (R-Okla) made his displeasure clearer still, sketching out the likely political battle lines for 2015: "You can issue all the executive orders you want. If you don't have any money to enforce them, they don't go very far ... We're going to be pretty aggressive in using the power of the purse."

Under duress, Secretary of Defence Hagel announced his resignation on 24 November. It was not a huge shock, as relations between the White House and Hagel had been deteriorating for some time. In late October, administration officials had leaked a memorandum, written by Hagel, which had strongly criticised National Security Adviser Susan Rice's handling of the deteriorating situation in Syria. He had also criticised the "sclerosis" that was increasingly evident to him in the structure of foreign policymaking and the unhelpful way in which Obama's inner circle micromanaged processes that should have remained in the hands of the Cabinet secretaries. Obama had undermined Hagel a month prior to his resignation when he had appointed a retired general, John R. Allen, as his envoy charged with assembling a coalition to take the fight to ISIS. "The bottom line is that Chuck Hagel took over at possibly the worst time anyone has seen in the last 20 years," said a former deputy assistant secretary of defence, Vikram Singh, who had served under Hagel. "Given the state of affairs, I think he's done a creditable job ... I think that he chose to be the quiet warrior and some people wanted a cheerleader." Pending Senate confirmation, Obama announced that Ashton Carter, deputy secretary of defence since October 2011—and who had written an op-ed urging the pre-emptive bombing of North Korea's nuclear facilities in 2006— would succeed Hagel in early 2015.

On 9 December the Senate intelligence committee published a report on the enhanced interrogation techniques—which clearly amounted to torture—deployed by the CIA from 11 September 2001 to the end of the Bush presidency. The report took five years to prepare, and painted a grim picture of the brutal way in which CIA interrogators subjected detainees to water boarding, sleep deprivation, "rectal rehydration", beatings and threats of execution. One footnote alleged that one officer forced prisoners to play Russian roulette. The report maintained that useful intelligence had not been gathered from tortured detainees, contrary to the CIA's repeated claims. It also alleged that the agency had concealed its worst abuses and amplified the importance of those to which it had admitted in briefings to Congress, the media, and to the president. The director of the CIA, John Brennan, conceded that the agency "did not always live up to the high standards that we set for ourselves", but suggested that the worst of the misdeeds occurred soon after the 11 September terrorist attacks when fear of subsequent attacks, and the pressure being exerted on the CIA to prevent these, was at its height. John McCain, who had been tortured as a prisoner of war in North Vietnam, observed that the CIA's tactics had "stained our national honour". A more common Republican response was to decry the political motivations undergirding the investigation. Senator Marc Rubio (R-FL) observed that the publication of the report "places American lives in danger". Republican members of the committee drafted a 167-page rebuttal of its findings. They suggested that antagonism toward the Bush administration made for a partial and flawed telling of recent history.

On 17 December Obama made one of the most startling announcements of his presidency: "In the most significant change in our policy in more than 50 years, we will end an outdated approach that, for decades, has failed to advance our interests, and instead we will begin to normalise relations between our two countries.

Through these changes, we intend to create more opportunities for the American and Cuban people, and begin a new chapter among the nations of the Americas." Vowing to "cut loose the shackles of the past", Obama ordered the restoration of full diplomatic relations with Cuba and the opening of a US embassy in Havana. The president's policy-shift stemmed from 18 months of intensive negotiations— involving a complex prisoner exchange—in which Pope Francis had been involved. It was a remarkably bold move for a president contemplating the looming reality of a Republican-controlled House of Representatives *and* Senate from 3 January, 2015.

On cue, Republicans in the House and the Senate announced that they would resist lifting the 54-year old trade embargo. Some denounced the change of policy with real vehemence. "This entire policy shift announced today is based on an illusion, on a lie, the lie and the illusion that more commerce and access to money and goods will translate to political freedom for the Cuban people," declared Senator Rubio. "All this is going to do is give the Castro regime, which controls every aspect of Cuban life, the opportunity to manipulate these changes to perpetuate itself in power." Yet this appraisal was not shared by a majority of US citizens, according to the polls. A CNN/ORC poll taken soon after the historic announcement showed that six out of 10 Americans supported the restoration of full diplomatic relations, and that two-thirds wanted the travel ban overturned. Among Republicans, Rand Paul, who supported the president's decision, was the usual exception to the hawkish rule. In a press briefing on 19 December, Obama said, "I share the concerns of dissidents there and human rights activists that this is still a regime that represses its people." But he also noted that "the whole point of normalising relations is that it gives us greater opportunity to have influence with that government." It remained to be seen whether the president's adversaries in Congress would come round to this line of reasoning. The normalisation of US-Cuban relations was one issue (among many) that seemed likely to provoke sharp disputes in 2015 and 2016—involving vetoes and executive actions, no doubt— between President Obama and a Republican-controlled Congress.

On 19 December, during opening remarks at his end-of-year press conference, Barack Obama said: "In last year's final press conference, I said that 2014 would be a year of action and would be a breakthrough year for America. And it has been." Buoyed by "breakthroughs" in November and December on immigration, climate change policy, the normalisation of relations with Cuba, and by the release of impressive economic numbers and indicators, Obama might be forgiven for saying: "I told you so." The president appeared almost liberated by the knowledge that he would face no further elections. "My presidency is entering the fourth quarter; interesting stuff happens in the fourth quarter," he said. "And I'm looking forward to it."

The president's triumphalism was, of course, misplaced in other respects. The Democratic Party had been comprehensively beaten during the mid-term elections; there were few positives to be drawn from the experience at the congressional or at the gubernatorial level. That the Republican Party held its largest congressional majority since the 71st Congress of 1929-31 could not fail to reflect poorly on Obama's political leadership. It was also suggestive of a failure of communication on the part of a president who had been so effective in conveying hope and bipartisan promise when running for his party's nomination and the presidency in 2007-08.

Yet Obama remained hopeful at the end of 2014 that Republicans and Democrats could bridge their disagreements in Congress and press ahead with "getting things done". The president cited tax reform as one area where lawmakers on both sides of the political divide shared common ground: "[T]here is a way of us potentially doing corporate tax reform, lowering rates, eliminating loopholes so everybody is paying their fair share, and during that transition also providing a mechanism where we can get some infrastructure built. I'd like to see us work on that issue as well. Historically, obviously, infrastructure has not been a Democratic or a Republican issue, and I'd like to see if we can return to that tradition." After Republican victories in the mid-terms, both the speaker of the House and the incoming majority leader in the Senate had expressed their dedication to working with Democrats on issues where progress was possible, as Obama reminded the assembled press: "I think there are real opportunities to get things done in Congress. As I said before, I take Speaker Boehner and Mitch McConnell at their words that they want to get things done."

Yet Obama was also adamant that he would veto any attempts to unpick what he viewed as established law: "If Republicans seek to take healthcare away from people who just got it, they will meet stiff resistance from me. If they try to water down consumer protections that we put in place in the aftermath of the financial crisis, I will say no. And I'm confident that I'll be able to uphold vetoes of those types of provisions." There is little doubt that 2015 would ask some hard strategic questions of Democrats and Republicans. In response to a swiftly improving economic backdrop, and the bedding in of the Affordable Care Act, should Republicans continue to impugn the profligacy and statist tendencies of Democrats? Given the reality of GOP majorities in the House and Senate, should President Obama decline to use executive orders as a cheap way to pursue his domestic agenda? In reflecting upon a series of remarkable ballot initiative victories—which suggested broad social liberalisation across the United States—should Republicans continue to push against same sex marriage and appeal to "values" voters? As she sought to secure her party's nomination for president, to what degree should Hillary Clinton set herself apart from the president she had served, particularly with regard to foreign policy, where disagreements were clear? Or should she follow public opinion on the matter of America's overseas commitments, which seem to hew more closely to that of a potential Republican adversary, Rand Paul?

Journalistic assessments of Barack Obama's 2013 had been uniformly harsh, in spite of the appearance of some promising economic indicators. If 2014 had ended on 5 November—after the mid-terms—rather than on 31 December, that same pattern of condemnation might well have been repeated. But of course, President Obama responded to defeat at the mid-term elections with major policy initiatives on immigration and Cuba, which seemed to alter the narrative of ineptitude and

weakness that had become entrenched in so many television and print media por-
trayals. Yet even without Obama's late purposeful surge, 2014 had been an excellent year for the United States—particularly in the economic realm. The president
reminded the press corps that "as a country, we have every right to be proud of
what we've accomplished—more jobs; more people insured; a growing economy;
shrinking deficits; bustling industry; booming energy. Pick any metric that you
want—America's resurgence is real. We are better off." It seemed likely that with
the benefit of distance and the perspective of time, subsequent generations of historians might form broadly similar conclusions.

David Milne

CANADA

CAPITAL: Ottawa   AREA: 9,984,670 sq km   POPULATION: 35,158,304 ('13)
OFFICIAL LANGUAGES: English & French
HEAD OF STATE: Queen Elizabeth II (since Feb '52)
GOVERNOR-GENERAL: David Johnston (since Oct '10)
RULING PARTY: Conservative Party of Canada (CPC) (since Jan '06)
HEAD OF GOVERNMENT: Prime Minister Stephen Harper (CPC) (since Feb '06)
DEMOCRACY INDEX: 9.08; 8th of 167   CORRUPTION PERCEPTIONS INDEX: 81; 10th of 175
CURRENCY: Canadian Dollar (Dec '14 £1.00=CAD 1.80, US$1.00=CAD 1.16)
GNI PER CAPITA: US$52,200, Intl$42,610 at PPP ('13)

THE country was shaken by two separate attacks in the span of two days, carried out by individuals believed to be inspired by radical interpretations of
Islam. In one case, the gunman penetrated the Canadian Parliament buildings
and fired his weapon before being overpowered by security officers. The
attacks, which were unconnected, intensified the debate over Canada's involvement in the coalition against Islamic State in Iraq and Syria (ISIS) and fears
over the threat posed by radicalised Canadian citizens returning from fighting
with extremist groups abroad.

On 22 October, Michael Zehaf-Bibeau shot and killed a ceremonial honour
guard at Canada's National War Memorial. He then entered Canada's Parliament
buildings and continued shooting in the Hall of Honour, directly beside unlocked
doors to meeting rooms where MPs, including the prime minister, were gathered.
He was eventually shot dead by the House of Commons sergeant-at-arms, Kevin
Vickers (who was welcomed with a prolonged standing ovation by MPs when they
returned to work the following day). Zehaf-Bibeau, a petty offender from Montreal
with possible mental health issues, was a convert to Islam and was planning to
leave Canada for the Middle East.

Just two days previously, on 20 October, Martin Couture-Rouleau drove his
vehicle into two Canadian officers in a parking lot in St.-Jean-sur-Richelieu,
Quebec, killing one and injuring the other, before himself being killed during the
subsequent high-speed police chase. Couture-Rouleau was a convert to radical
Islam and was known to the authorities, who had confiscated his passport over
fears that he was planning to join ISIS fighters in Iraq.

Whilst both Couture-Rouleau and Zehaf-Bibeau were deemed to be "lone wolves", the government indicated that it would look into strengthening anti-terror legislation, as well as increasing security on Parliament Hill.

There was controversy over a Supreme Court appointment. In a 6-1 decision, on 21 March, the Supreme Court of Canada ruled that Prime Minister Stephen Harper's most recent appointee, Justice Marc Nadon of Quebec, was not legally qualified to sit on the Court's bench. The unprecedented ruling cited sections of the Supreme Court Act designed to protect the unique civil law and social traditions of the province of Quebec. Nadon, who was a Federal Court judge and had not been a practising member of Quebec's bar for 20 years, was best known for being a dissenting vote in a federal court order requiring the federal government to repatriate Canadian citizen Omar Khadr from the US prison camp at Guantanamo Bay (see AR 2011, p. 636).

Unanimously opposed by Quebec's National Assembly, Nadon's appointment had surprised legal observers. Justice Minister Peter McKay and the Prime Minister's Office later suggested that Chief Justice of the Supreme Court Beverley McLachlin had unsuccessfully attempted to contact the prime minister to lobby against the appointment. In a statement, McLachlin noted that it was customary for the chief justice to be involved in consultations and that she had identified the potential qualification issue prior to Nadon's nomination. Critics condemned the government for bringing McLachlin's reputation into question. Quebec Court of Appeal judge Clement Gascon was announced as a replacement nominee on 3 June.

Having tabled the 2014-15 budget, with a modest C\$2.9 billion deficit and a projected surplus for 2015, the long-serving finance minister, Jim Flaherty, announced his retirement from politics on 18 March. Only weeks later, on 10 April, he died of a heart attack; a state funeral was held on 16 April. Known as a fiscal conservative, Flaherty demonstrated pragmatism in his response to the global financial crisis of 2008 when he turned to deficit-spending to spur economic growth. He had also recently publicly disagreed with some of his Cabinet colleagues when questioned whether a C\$2.5 billion income-splitting tax break was sound public policy.

In the minor Cabinet reshuffle that followed Flaherty's resignation, the finance ministry passed to Minister of Natural Resources Joe Oliver, whose portfolio was assumed by Minister of State for Science Greg Rickford. The backbench MP Ed Holder was promoted to Rickford's former role.

Three provinces held general elections in 2014. In Quebec, Philippe Couillard's federalist Liberals won a majority to form a government, having taken 41.5 per cent of the vote (70 seats) on 7 April. The Liberals replaced Premier Pauline Marois's separatist Parti Québécois (PQ), which won only 30 seats and achieved its lowest share of the popular vote in more than 40 years. Marois was also personally defeated in her riding. The nationalist Coalition Avenir Québec and the separatist Québec Solidaire increased their representation to 22 seats and three seats, respectively.

Following a tumultuous period of minority government, Ontario's Liberal Premier Kathleen Wynne led her party back to a majority government on 12 June, with 58 seats and almost 39 per cent of the popular vote. The Progressive Conservatives and New Democratic Party took 28 and 21 seats, respectively.

In New Brunswick, Brian Gallant's Liberals defeated Premier David Alward's one-term Progressive Conservative (PC) government on 22 September, winning 27 seats to the PC's 21. Green Party leader David Coon was elected, giving his party its first seat in the legislature.

Newfoundland and Labrador Premier Kathy Dunderdale, Alberta Premier Alison Redford, and Prince Edward Island Premier Robert Ghiz all announced their resignations during the course of 2014. Following the resignation of five of his Cabinet ministers en masse on 3 November, Manitoba's New Democratic Party Premier Greg Selinger announced he would contest a leadership vote at the party's 2015 convention. On 17 December, Danielle Smith, leader of Alberta's official opposition Wildrose Party, astonished political observers by defecting to Premier Jim Prentice's governing Progressive Conservatives, along with eight members of her former party's caucus.

William Stos

MEXICO

CAPITAL: Mexico City   AREA: 1,964,380 sq km   POPULATION: 122,332,399 ('13)
OFFICIAL LANGUAGE: Spanish
HEAD OF STATE AND GOVERNMENT: President Enrique Peña Nieto (PRI) (since Dec '12)
RULING PARTY: Institutional Revolutionary Party (PRI)
DEMOCRACY INDEX: 6.91; 51st of 167   CORRUPTION PERCEPTIONS INDEX: 35; =103rd of 175
CURRENCY: Mexican Peso (Dec '14 £1.00=MXN 22.83, US$1.00=MXN 14.7)
GNI PER CAPITA: US$9,940, Intl$16,110 at PPP ('13)

MEXICO witnessed a period of serious political and social unrest in the latter part of 2014 after 43 students were killed close to the town of Iguala in Guerrero state.

On 26 September students from a teaching training college had travelled to Iguala to protest against alleged discriminatory hiring practices for teachers, which favoured urban students over rural ones. As the students returned, police opened fire on the buses carrying them. Three students were killed and three other people in nearby vehicles also lost their lives. The police then arrested the remaining students and took them to the local police station, before handing them over to a local drug gang called Guerreros Unidos (United Warriors). The captives were killed and their bodies burnt at a nearby rubbish dump. It was alleged that the mayor of Iguala, José Luis Abarca, and his wife Maria de los Angeles Pineda Villa, had given the orders for the students to be taken, and used their drug connections to make the students "disappear". The motive was unclear, but several theories were put forward: that the students were targeted for their political beliefs; that they had angered Guerreros Unidos for refusing to pay extortion money; or that they were taken due to fears that they would disrupt an event being organised by Pineda Villa.

The reaction to this outrage was swift and substantial. A series of large scale and sometimes violent demonstrations took place in Mexico City and across the country, criticising the authorities in Guerrero but also the government of President Enrique Peña Nieto for not doing enough to investigate the murders or to deal with the wider problems of crime and lawlessness in many parts of the country epitomised by this incident. The president's popularity rating dropped to its lowest point since he took office. Some commentators suggested that it was the worst attack on human rights in the country since the October 1968 massacre of university students by federal security forces in Mexico City (see AR 1968, p. 190).

In response several initiatives were taken, including the deployment of federal police to Iguala and surrounding municipalities and a package of measures to reform the police service. Further, the governor of Guerrero state, Angel Aguirre, resigned on 23 October and Abarca and his wife were arrested on 4 November after a period on the run. But these measures failed to assuage public anger, which grew further after allegations of corruption hit the government. The most damaging was the revelation that a $7 million house, in which the president and his family lived, belonged to a businessman who was linked to a $3.8 billion railway construction project. The contract had been awarded without being put out to tender. Just prior to the story breaking Peña cancelled the contract and shortly afterwards the house was sold.

In separate developments, on 14 July President Peña signed into law secondary legislation linked to his government's telecommunications reform. The legislation was approved by the Chamber of Deputies five days before, and concluded the reform process that had begun in 2013 (see AR 2014, pp. 127-28). The reforms attempted to liberalise the sector and provide wider Internet access, more efficient services, lower costs for consumers and increased competition. However, there was some scepticism as to whether the oligopolies would be broken up. Many opposition legislators argued that the legislation offered favourable terms to the main local television broadcaster, Grupo Televisa.

On 6 August more than 40,000 cubic metres of copper sulphate acid spilt into the River Sonora, affecting 22,000 people and thousands of hectares of crops and livestock. The source of the spill was the Buenavista del Cobre, a copper mine in the north-western part of the country managed by Grupo México. Mexico's environment minister, Juan José Guerra Abud, claimed, "This is the worst natural disaster provoked by the mining industry in Mexico's modern history." The minister blamed the company, while Grupo México blamed "atypical" rains for the spill.

On 30 October Mexico's Supreme Court (SCJN) ruled that it was unconstitutional for a requested referendum to be held on the country's energy reform, which ended the 76-year monopoly of the state oil company and paved the way for private funding in the industry. The SCJN ruled that referendums could not be held on issues related to the federal government's revenue or spending. The ruling was a major setback for Mexico's left-wing opposition parties, which had gathered millions of signatures in support of a referendum.

Peter Clegg

GUATEMALA, EL SALVADOR, HONDURAS, NICARAGUA, COSTA RICA, AND PANAMA

Guatemala

CAPITAL: Guatemala City AREA: 108,890 sq km POPULATION: 15,468,203 ('13)
OFFICIAL LANGUAGE: Spanish
HEAD OF STATE AND GOVERNMENT: President Otto Pérez Molina (PP) (since Jan '12)
RULING PARTY: Patriotic Party (PP)
DEMOCRACY INDEX: 5.81; 87th of 167 CORRUPTION PERCEPTIONS INDEX: 32; =115th of 175
CURRENCY: Quetzal (Dec '14 £1.00=GTQ 11.80, US$1.00=GTQ 7.60)
GNI PER CAPITA: US$3,340, Intl$7,130 at PPP ('13)

El Salvador

CAPITAL: San Salvador AREA: 21,040 sq km POPULATION: 6,340,454 ('13)
OFFICIAL LANGUAGE: Spanish
HEAD OF STATE AND GOVERNMENT: President Salvador Sánchez Cerén (FMLN) (since June '14)
RULING PARTY: Farabundo Martí National Liberation Front (FMLN)
DEMOCRACY INDEX: 6.53; 62nd of 167 CORRUPTION PERCEPTIONS INDEX: 39; =80th of 175
CURRENCY: El Salvador Colon (Dec '14 £1.00=SVC 13.58, US$1.00=SVC 8.75)
GNI PER CAPITA: US$3,720, Intl$7,490 at PPP ('13)

Honduras

CAPITAL: Tegucigalpa AREA: 112,090 sq km POPULATION: 8,097,688 ('13)
OFFICIAL LANGUAGE: Spanish
HEAD OF STATE AND GOVERNMENT: President Juan Orlando Hernandez (PNH) (since Jan '14)
RULING PARTY: National Party of Honduras (PNH) (since Jan '10)
DEMOCRACY INDEX: 5.84; =85th of 167 CORRUPTION PERCEPTIONS INDEX: 29; =126th of 175
CURRENCY: Lempira (Dec '14 £1.00=HNL 32.64, US$1.00=HNL 21.02)
GNI PER CAPITA: US$2,180, Intl$4,270 at PPP ('13)

Nicaragua

CAPITAL: Managua AREA: 130,000 sq km POPULATION: 6,080,478 ('13)
OFFICIAL LANGUAGE: Spanish
HEAD OF STATE AND GOVERNMENT: President Daniel Ortega Saavedra (FSLN) (since Jan '07)
RULING PARTY: Sandinista National Liberation Front (FSLN)
DEMOCRACY INDEX: 5.46; 94th of 167 CORRUPTION PERCEPTIONS INDEX: 28; =133rd of 175
CURRENCY: Gold Cordoba (Dec '14 £1.00=NIO 41.29, US$1.00=NIO 26.59)
GNI PER CAPITA: US$1,780, Intl$4,440 at PPP ('13)

Costa Rica

CAPITAL: San José AREA: 51,100 sq km POPULATION: 4,872,166 ('13)
OFFICIAL LANGUAGE: Spanish
HEAD OF STATE AND GOVERNMENT: President Luis Guillermo Solis (PAC) (since May '14)
RULING PARTY: Citizens' Action Party (PAC)
DEMOCRACY INDEX: 8.03; 24th of 167 CORRUPTION PERCEPTIONS INDEX: 54; =47th of 175
CURRENCY: Costa Rican Colon (Dec '14 £1.00=CRC 837.2, US$1.00=CRC 539.1)
GNI PER CAPITA: US$9,550, Intl$13,570 at PPP ('13)

Panama

CAPITAL: Panama City AREA: 75,520 sq km POPULATION: 3,864,170 ('13)
OFFICIAL LANGUAGE: Spanish
HEAD OF STATE AND GOVERNMENT: President Juan Carlos Varela (PPA) (since July '14)
RULING PARTIES: Panamenista Party (PPA)-led coalition
DEMOCRACY INDEX: 7.08; 46th of 167 CORRUPTION PERCEPTIONS INDEX: 37; =94th of 175
CURRENCY: Balboa (Dec '14 £1.00=PAB 1.55, US$1.00=PAB 1.00)
GNI PER CAPITA: US$10,700, Intl$19,290 at PPP ('13)

THREE sets of elections were held in Central America in 2014. **El Salvador** witnessed a very closely fought presidential run-off election on 9 March. Salvador Sánchez Cerén became the first president from the left-wing Farabundo Martí National Liberation Front (FMLN). Sánchez Cerén won by just 6,364 votes out of nearly three million. In **Costa Rica** Luis Guillermo Solís of the left of centre Citizens' Action Party (PAC) won a convincing victory in the presidential election held on 6 April. Thus Solís broke the monopoly on the presidency that had been held by the National Liberation Party (PLN) and the Social Christian Unity Party (PUSC) since 1930. However, the PAC won only 13 of the 57 seats in the Legislative Assembly, less than any ruling party in Costa Rican history. In order to build support in the Assembly, Solís appointed two PUSC politicians to his Cabinet, and signed two separate accords with the PUSC and the left-wing Broad Front (FA). In **Panama** Vice-President Juan Carlos Varela won the presidential election on 4 May. Representing the right-wing Panamenista Party (PPA) he gained 39.1 per cent of the vote. As in Costa Rica the PPA was far short of a majority in the parliament, so a deal was struck between the PPA and the Democratic Revolutionary Party (PRD), which gave the president a slim majority.

The quality of governance and democracy across the region, but particularly in Guatemala and Nicaragua, was a concern during the year.

In **Guatemala** in late September, the election of new Supreme Court justices (CSJ), appellate court magistrates and their alternates was criticised by local civil society groups, the UN-backed International Commission against Impunity in Guatemala (CICIG) and the UN Special Rapporteur on the Independence of Judges and Lawyers. Serious concerns were raised that the two main political parties, the ruling Patriotic Party (PP) and the opposition Renewed Democratic Liberty (Lider), had manipulated the selection process to make sure their preferred candidates were successful. Then in November a new CSJ president, Josué Felipe Baquiax, was sworn in. The national daily, *Prensa Libre*, noted that Baquiax was linked to Sergio López Villatoro, the former son-in-law of ex-dictator Efraín Ríos Montt, who reportedly retained significant influence in the country. Thus Baquiax's focus on judicial reform was met with scepticism.

In **Nicaragua** a number of controversial constitutional changes were enacted. On 29 January the legislature passed a series of amendments to the constitution. The changes included the removal of term limits for presidents; now indefinite re-election was possible. Also, the previous rule whereby candidates needed at least 35 per cent of the vote to be elected president was removed. Both reforms were considered to favour President Daniel Ortega and his desire to continue in power. Further, defecting national legislators were stripped of their seats. This made sure the governing Sandinista National Liberation Front (FSLN) would retain its two-thirds majority in the current parliament. Another group of changes bolstered the role of the military in civilian affairs, including overturning the ban on military officials holding public positions of a "civilian nature". The public largely backed the changes, while civil society groups protested.

In Costa Rica meanwhile, President Solís talked about the challenges that lay ahead in reforming the political system, which he said was "sinking into a spiral of corruption and inefficiency". However, the chances of real change were hindered by the weak position of PAC within the Legislative Assembly.

Nevertheless, there were some efforts to address corruption. In Nicaragua Edgar Camargo, the head of the prison service, was arrested for allegedly being part of an organised crime ring. The arrest was seen as one of the biggest victories for CICIG since its creation in 2007. In Panama President Varela pledged to improve transparency and punish the alleged corruption that took place under the previous government, and some progress was made. A number of investigations were undertaken against several state bodies and former government ministers accused of corruption. On 14 August Varela revoked all 355 presidential pardons issued by his predecessor, Ricardo Martinelli, in the final days of his term. Further, a number of "autonomous agencies" established by the previous government and whose directors had been given long-term appointments were disbanded. In El Salvador former president Francisco Flores (1999-2004) was arrested on charges of embezzlement and illicit enrichment relating to multi-million dollar donations from Taiwan to aid reconstruction following two earthquakes that hit El Salvador in 2001 (see AR 2001, p. 186). It was also alleged that some funds had been used to support the election campaign of another former president, Elías Antonio Saca (2004-09).

The issue of violence and the responses to it were also common themes during the year. There was some good news for **Honduras** in February when the Observatorio de la Violencia de la Universidad Nacional Autónoma de Honduras (UNAH) released its annual murder figures for 2013. While Honduras continued to have the highest murder rate in the world, UNAH reported a 5.8 per cent decline in the number of murders. The government suggested this was due to the increasingly militarised security policy in the country. However, the decline in 2013 was only a small reverse on the large increase in the murder rate that had been seen during the previous few years. Also, UNAH cautioned that there had been an "increase in the number of atrocious crimes, including mutilations and decapitations, which cause terror in the population".

In El Salvador the murder rate picked up following the collapse of a truce between the Mara Salvatrucha (MS-13) gang and rival Barrio 18 in March. A new truce was agreed in late August, but there were doubts over how effective it would be. Meanwhile, in Guatemala a presidential press release on 23 July cited figures from the human rights group, Grupo de Apoyo Mutuo, which showed an 8.7 per cent decline in homicides in the first six months of 2014 compared with the same period in 2013. The authorities claimed that the controversial use of the military to fight crime, and the increase in numbers, training and professionalism of the national police had contributed to the decline.

In Nicaragua on 19 July—the 35th anniversary of the overthrow of the Somoza dictatorship (see AR 1979, p. 87)—serious violence flared with attacks on two buses carrying FSLN supporters which killed five and wounded 19. In response the government sent troops to the northern departments of Matagalpa and Jinotega. A number of arrests were made, but opposition and civil society groups accused the government of excessive and indiscriminate force. The Roman Catholic bishops expressed their "pain and great concern for the situation of persecutions, unjust detentions, and inexplicable disappearance of persons, terror, and death that has been unleashed".

In other developments in the region, Honduras on 24 August witnessed a "Dignity March" in several cities, led by doctors, nurses and other healthcare workers protesting against the worsening public healthcare system. Two days later a congressional report said that healthcare was in a "deplorable state", with poor basic care and limited medical supplies. In mid-October the government signed a new stand-by arrangement with the IMF that allowed Honduras to access up to $220 million in loans. But in return the IMF's deputy head of the Americas stated that the agreement would involve a "strong fiscal adjustment". Finally, in a report entitled *Trends and Patterns in Latin American and Caribbean Migration in 2010 and Challenges for a Regional Agenda*, the UN's Economic Commission for Latin America and the Caribbean (ECLAC) found that Costa Rica had the highest proportion of immigrants in Latin America at 9 per cent.

Peter Clegg

CUBA, JAMAICA, DOMINICAN REPUBLIC AND HAITI

Cuba

CAPITAL: Havana   AREA: 110,860 sq km   POPULATION: 11,265,629 ('13)
OFFICIAL LANGUAGE: Spanish
HEAD OF STATE AND GOVERNMENT: President Raul Castro Ruz (PCC) (since Feb '08)
RULING PARTY: Cuban Communist Party (PCC)
DEMOCRACY INDEX: 3.52; =126th of 167   CORRUPTION PERCEPTIONS INDEX: 46; 63rd of 175
CURRENCY: Cuban Peso (Dec '14 £1.00=CUP 1.55, US$1.00=CUP 1.00)
GNI PER CAPITA: US$5,890; Intl$18,520 at PPP ('11)

Jamaica

CAPITAL: Kingston   AREA: 10,990 sq km   POPULATION: 2,715,000 ('13)
OFFICIAL LANGUAGE: English
HEAD OF STATE: Queen Elizabeth II (since Feb '52)
GOVERNOR-GENERAL: Sir Patrick Allen (since Feb '09)
RULING PARTY: People's National Party (PNP)
HEAD OF GOVERNMENT: Prime Minister Portia Simpson Miller (PNP) (since Jan '12)
DEMOCRACY INDEX: 7.39; 40th of 167   CORRUPTION PERCEPTIONS INDEX: 38; =85th of 175
CURRENCY: Jamaican Dollar (Dec '14 £1.00=JMD 177.4, US$1.00=JMD 114.3)
GNI PER CAPITA: US$5,220, Intl$8,480 at PPP ('13)

Dominican Republic

CAPITAL: Santo Domingo   AREA: 48,730 sq km   POPULATION: 10,403,761 ('13)
OFFICIAL LANGUAGE: Spanish
HEAD OF STATE AND GOVERNMENT: President Danilo Medina (PLD) (since May '12)
RULING PARTY: Dominican Liberation Party (PLD)
DEMOCRACY INDEX: 6.74; 56th of 167   CORRUPTION PERCEPTIONS INDEX: 32; =115th of 175
CURRENCY: Dominican Peso (Dec '14 £1.00=DOP 68.75, US$1.00=DOP 44.27)
GNI PER CAPITA: US$5,620, Intl$11,150 at PPP ('13)

Haiti

CAPITAL: Port-au-Prince   AREA: 27,750 sq km   POPULATION: 10,317,461 ('13)
OFFICIAL LANGUAGE: French
HEAD OF STATE: President Michel Martelly (since May '11)
HEAD OF GOVERNMENT: acting Prime Minister Florence Duperval Guillaume (ind) (since Dec '14)
DEMOCRACY INDEX: 3.94; 117th of 167   CORRUPTION PERCEPTIONS INDEX: 19; =161st of 175
CURRENCY: Gourde (Dec '14 £1.00=HTG 72.59, US$1.00=HTG 46.75)
GNI PER CAPITA: US$810, Intl$1,710 at PPP ('13)

A REAL breakthrough in relations between **Cuba** and the United States occurred on 17 December when US President Barack Obama used his executive powers to enact a number of important changes in US policy towards the island. This was the culmination of 18 months of secret talks involving several interlocutors, among them Pope Francis. A key part in the thawing of relations was the release of Alan Gross, a US government sub-contractor, who had been held in a Cuban prison since December 2009 on charges of acts against the state; an unnamed US intelligence agent was also released. On the US side, three remaining members of the "Cuban Five"—Cuban intelligence agents arrested in Miami in 1998 and convicted of espionage—were released. In addition, Cuba agreed to free 53 prisoners identified as political detainees by the USA.

The changes enacted by President Obama included the restoration of a US embassy in Havana; making travel to Cuba more straightforward for US citizens; allowing US companies to engage in improving the infrastructure linking the USA and Cuba for commercial telecommunications and Internet services; and lifting the level of permitted remittances sent by US citizens to Cuba, from $500 to $2,000 per quarter. Furthermore, the USA would review Cuba's listing as a state sponsor of terrorism. If successful, this would facilitate Cuba's access to sources of external financing. Announcing the changes, President Obama argued, "These 50 years have shown that isolation has not worked. It's time for a new approach." Both Obama and Cuban President Raul Castro Ruz indicated their hope that more normal relations could be established and that matters of mutual concern, such as counter narcotics co-operation and environmental protection, could be discussed more readily. Reaction in the USA and Cuba was generally favourable, although a number of US Republican politicians criticised the change in approach. This opposition was significant, as only Congress could repeal the 1961 trade embargo on Cuba, which in 1996 was codified into US legislation under the Helms-Burton Act.

Political and social instability returned to **Haiti** in the latter part of the year with the prime minister's resignation, a further delay to parliamentary and municipal elections, and growing street protests. On 14 December Laurent Lamothe stepped down as prime minister, in compliance with the recommendation of an advisory commission. The commission, which included representatives from the Church, the private sector, politics and trade unions, had been established in an attempt to break an impasse between the government and opposition that was preventing the approval of legislation needed to facilitate the long overdue elections.

It was uncertain, however, whether the resignation of Lamothe and the other recommendations of the commission would end the political deadlock. In addition, and perhaps most crucially, the report did not offer any solutions to the underlying reason for the social unrest: what would happen when the legislature's term ended on 12 January 2015. Due to the delay in calling elections, the mandates for all 99 lower chamber seats and a further 10 seats in the Senate (one-third of which were already vacant) would expire without a new parliament ready to take over. If this were to happen, President Michel Martelly would rule by decree. Such a possibility was strongly opposed by many in Haiti. However, on 29 December a provisional deal was struck that extended the mandate of the lower chamber until April 2015 and that of the Senate until September 2015.

Haiti's former "president-for-life" Jean-Claude "Baby Doc" Duvalier (1971-86) died of a heart attack, aged 63 (see Obituary). Another ex-president, Jean-Bertrand Aristide (1991; 1994-96; 2001-04), was placed under house arrest in August pending trial over allegations of corruption, money laundering and drug smuggling. Critics suggested that his detention was politically motivated, whilst also diverting attention from an armed attack on the Croix-des-Bouquets prison in Port-au-Prince, which had allowed 329 of the 899 inmates to escape.

The relationship between Haiti and the **Dominican Republic** remained difficult in 2014 due to the repercussions from the decision of the latter's Constitutional Court, which had stripped citizenship from 200,000 Dominicans of Haitian descent (see AR 2014, p. 134). In August, the Inter-American Court of Human Rights (Corte-IDH) ruled that the decision violated "the right to nationality". Further, it ordered the Dominican Republic to provide redress for human rights abuses suffered by Haitians and Dominicans of Haitian origin between 1999 and 2000, including illegal deportations. In response the Dominican government rejected the rulings and announced that it would leave the Corte-IDH. In turn the Corte-IDH said the decision had "no basis whatsoever in international law, and therefore it can have no effect".

A separate development that affected much of the Caribbean, but particularly the Dominican Republic and also **Jamaica**, was the outbreak of the Chikungunya virus, a mosquito-borne disease causing fever and joint pain. The first cases were reported in Saint Martin in December 2013. By the end of 2014 there had been almost 800,000 cases across the Caribbean; 525,000 of which were in the Dominican Republic. There was a feeling that the authorities had not acted decisively enough to deal with the virus. In an editorial, the *Jamaica Gleaner* on 2 October reprimanded the health minister for his "pompous, unnecessarily blame-deflecting, and ultimately failed communication strategy employed in his hapless management of the [...] epidemic, about which he apparently remains in denial". The impact of the ever-growing number of infections was significant. The Private Sector Organisation of Jamaica, a business group, reported that Chikungunya was causing millions of dollars in losses to the economy, whilst the country's manufacturers' association recorded a high level of employee absenteeism. Fortunately, however, the virus did not undermine Jamaica's economic reform efforts. An IMF review in November reported that the reforms "offer a vibrant path to sustained growth and job creation", that the programme was on track, and that "policy implementation remains strong".

Peter Clegg

WINDWARD AND LEEWARD ISLANDS

Antigua & Barbuda

CAPITAL: St John's   AREA: 440 sq km   POPULATION: 89,985 ('13)
OFFICIAL LANGUAGE: English
HEAD OF STATE: Queen Elizabeth II (since Feb '52)
GOVERNOR-GENERAL: Sir Rodney Williams (since Aug '14)
RULING PARTY: Antigua and Barbuda Labour Party (ABLP)
HEAD OF GOVERNMENT: Prime Minister Gaston Browne (ABLP) (since June '14)
CURRENCY: East Caribbean Dollar (Dec '14 £1.00=XCD 4.19, US$1.00=XCD 2.70)
GNI PER CAPITA: US$12,910, Intl$20,070 at PPP ('13)

Dominica

CAPITAL: Roseau   AREA: 750 sq km   POPULATION: 72,003 ('13)
OFFICIAL LANGUAGE: English
HEAD OF STATE: President Charles Savarin (since Oct '13)
RULING PARTY: Dominica Labour Party (DLP)
HEAD OF GOVERNMENT: Prime Minister Roosevelt Skerrit (DLP) (since Jan '04)
CORRUPTION PERCEPTIONS INDEX: 58; =39th of 175
CURRENCY: East Caribbean Dollar (see above)
GNI PER CAPITA: US$6,760, Intl$9,800 at PPP ('13)

St Christopher (Kitts) & Nevis

CAPITAL: Basseterre   AREA: 260 sq km   POPULATION: 54,191 ('13)
OFFICIAL LANGUAGE: English
HEAD OF STATE: Queen Elizabeth II (since Feb '52)
GOVERNOR-GENERAL: Edmund Lawrence (since Jan '13)
RULING PARTY: St Kitts-Nevis Labour Party (SKNLP)
HEAD OF GOVERNMENT: Prime Minister Denzil Douglas (SKNLP) (since July '95)
CURRENCY: East Caribbean Dollar (see above)
GNI PER CAPITA: US$13,460, Intl$20,400 at PPP ('13)

St Lucia

CAPITAL: Castries   AREA: 620 sq km   POPULATION: 182,273 ('13)
OFFICIAL LANGUAGE: English
HEAD OF STATE: Queen Elizabeth II (since Feb '52)
GOVERNOR-GENERAL: Pearlette Louisy (since Sept '97)
RULING PARTY: St Lucia Labour Party (SLLP)
HEAD OF GOVERNMENT: Prime Minister Kenny Anthony (SLLP) (since Nov '11)
CURRENCY: East Caribbean Dollar (see above)
GNI PER CAPITA: US$7,090, Intl$10,350 at PPP ('13)

St Vincent & the Grenadines

CAPITAL: Kingstown   AREA: 390 sq km   POPULATION: 109,373 ('13)
OFFICIAL LANGUAGE: English
HEAD OF STATE: Queen Elizabeth II (since Feb '52)
GOVERNOR-GENERAL: Freddy Ballantyne (since Sept '02)
RULING PARTY: Unity Labour Party (ULP)
HEAD OF GOVERNMENT: Prime Minister Ralph Gonsalves (ULP) (since April '01)
CORRUPTION PERCEPTIONS INDEX: 67; 29th of 175
CURRENCY: East Caribbean Dollar (see above)
GNI PER CAPITA: US$6,580, Intl$10,610 at PPP ('13)

Grenada

CAPITAL: St George's   AREA: 340 sq km   POPULATION: 105,897 ('13)
OFFICIAL LANGUAGE: English
HEAD OF STATE: Queen Elizabeth II (since Feb '52)
GOVERNOR-GENERAL: Dame Cecile La Grenade (since May '13)
RULING PARTY: New National Party (NNP)
HEAD OF GOVERNMENT: Prime Minister Keith Mitchell (NNP) (since Feb '13)
CURRENCY: East Caribbean Dollar (see above)
GNI PER CAPITA: US$7,460, Intl$11,120 at PPP ('13)

GENERAL elections were held in **Antigua & Barbuda** and **Dominica** on 12 June and 8 December, respectively. In Antigua there was a change of government with the Antigua and Barbuda Labour Party (ABLP) winning 56.4 per cent of the vote and 13 seats; the former ruling United Progressive Party won 41.6 per cent of the vote and the remaining three seats in the House of Representatives. Turnout was high at 90.1 per cent. The victory for the ABLP, which had been out of power since 2004, was not a surprise considering the poor state of the economy, which showed anaemic levels of growth and high unemployment. By contrast, in Dominica the governing party retained power. The Dominica Labour Party won 57 per cent of the vote and 15 seats in the House of Assembly; the opposition United Workers' Party slightly improved its position from 2009 by winning 43 per cent of the vote and six seats. Prime Minister Roosevelt Skerrit thus began his fourth term in office.

In **St Kitts & Nevis** elections were scheduled for January 2015. Despite having lost his majority in January 2013 (see AR 2014, p. 136), Prime Minister Denzil Douglas of the St Kitts & Nevis Labour Party (SKNLP) avoided a no-confidence motion and the possibility of early elections. However, this was achieved by the support of appointed senators, even though only elected members were entitled to vote on a no-confidence motion. Thus, this tactic was extremely controversial. The government's reputation was further damaged when Canada imposed visa restrictions on St Kitts & Nevis nationals. The Canadian authorities were concerned that the government's policy of selling passports and citizenship was being abused by people with terrorist links. In the SKNLP's credit column was the economy, which experienced strong growth and a declining debt-to-GDP ratio.

Grenada also reported an improved economic position. Prime Minister Keith Mitchell revealed on 26 November that the economy would grow by 2.6 per cent in 2014, above the 1.5 per cent projected in December 2013; unemployment also fell. The economies of **St Vincent & The Grenadines** and particularly **St Lucia**, however, continued to struggle. The UN's Economic Commission for Latin America and the Caribbean predicted that St Lucia's economy would contract for the third consecutive year, with a GDP growth figure of -1.5 per cent.

Peter Clegg

BARBADOS, TRINIDAD & TOBAGO, AND THE BAHAMAS

Barbados

CAPITAL: Bridgetown   AREA: 430 sq km   POPULATION: 284,644 ('13)
OFFICIAL LANGUAGE: English
HEAD OF STATE: Queen Elizabeth II (since Feb '52)
GOVERNOR-GENERAL: Sir Elliot Belgrave (since June '12)
RULING PARTY: Democratic Labour Party (DLP)
HEAD OF GOVERNMENT: Prime Minister Freundel Stuart (DLP) (since Oct '10)
CORRUPTION PERCEPTIONS INDEX: 74; =17th of 175
CURRENCY: Barbados Dollar (Dec '14 £1.00=BBD 3.11, US$1.00=BBD 2.00)
GNI PER CAPITA: US$15,080, Intl$15,080 at PPP ('12)

Trinidad & Tobago

CAPITAL: Port of Spain   AREA: 5,130 sq km   POPULATION: 1,341,151 ('13)
OFFICIAL LANGUAGE: English
HEAD OF STATE: President Anthony Carmona (since March '13)
RULING PARTY: People's Partnership coalition
HEAD OF GOVERNMENT: Prime Minister Kamla Persad-Bissessar (United National Congress) (since
    May '10)
DEMOCRACY INDEX: 6.99; 48th of 167   CORRUPTION PERCEPTIONS INDEX: 38; =85th of 175
CURRENCY: Trinidad & Tobago Dollar (Dec '14 £1.00=TTD 9.90, US$1.00=TTD 6.38)
GNI PER CAPITA: US$15,760, Intl$26,210 at PPP ('13)

The Bahamas

CAPITAL: Nassau   AREA: 13,880 sq km   POPULATION: 377,374 ('13)
OFFICIAL LANGUAGE: English
HEAD OF STATE: Queen Elizabeth II (since Feb '52)
GOVERNOR-GENERAL: Dame Marguerite Pindling (since July '14)
RULING PARTY: Progressive Liberal Party (PLP)
HEAD OF GOVERNMENT: Prime Minister Perry Christie (PLP) (since May '12)
CORRUPTION PERCEPTIONS INDEX: 71; 24th of 175
CURRENCY: Bahamian Dollar (Dec '14 £1.00=BSD 1.55, US$1.00=BSD 1.00)
GNI PER CAPITA: US$20,600, Intl$21,540 at PPP ('12)

THE economy in **Barbados** was the primary concern during 2014, and there was ongoing debate as to whether an IMF-backed adjustment programme was required. In 2013 the government had put in place its own fiscal programme but doubts were raised that it would be sufficient to revitalise the economy. The UN's Economic Commission for Latin America and the Caribbean predicted that the economy would remain flat during the year, but that some progress would be made in reducing the fiscal deficit from 12.5 per cent of GDP in 2013-14 to 7.1 per cent in 2014-15. However, this meant that Barbados's net public sector debt continued to rise and was close to 80 per cent of GDP by year's end. Speaking in early November, the country's finance minister said that the fiscal programme was working and, "Based on what we are seeing we know growth will return." In response, the opposition spokesman on finance argued, "All the evidence suggests to me that we are on the wrong course [...] We are destined to erode all of the gains that we've had post-independence." Meanwhile, the former prime minister Owen Arthur (1994-2008) was slightly more upbeat, arguing that the economic situation remained manageable and Barbados had, "Strong residual institutional and other resources" upon which to call.

Economic performance in **Trinidad & Tobago** and **the Bahamas** was slightly better, but both countries tried to assuage local unease about the still difficult economic conditions by introducing restrictive immigration policies. In early November, Trinidad's national security minister revealed that approximately 110,000 immigrants had until January to get their documents in order before deportations would begin. Although the minister stated, "I don't want this to be seen as a witch hunt", he argued that illegal immigration was clearly linked to the large increase in violent crime in recent years; no evidence was provided to support the claim.

A similar approach was taken in the Bahamas. On 1 November measures were introduced requiring all non-nationals to prove that they had permission to be in the country and obtain a state-approved permit. Otherwise, they would be deported to their country of origin. This affected about 70,000 people—close to 20 per cent of the population. As soon as the measures were announced, immigration officials conducted a number of raids in Bahamian-Haitian communities, making dozens of arrests.

Several controversial constitutional changes were enacted in Trinidad & Tobago. The most divisive was the introduction of run-off elections in constituencies when the winner did not receive 50 per cent of the vote. Under the previous rules, whichever candidate had the plurality of votes won the seat. The opposition was very critical of the changes believing they would favour the governing People's Partnership and lead to more political uncertainty. The other constitutional changes included a mechanism to recall non-performing MPs; a limit of two terms in office for prime ministers; and the removal of prime ministerial discretion in setting the date of the election.

Peter Clegg

GUYANA, BELIZE, AND SURINAME

Guyana

CAPITAL: Georgetown   AREA: 214,970 sq km   POPULATION: 799,613 ('13)
OFFICIAL LANGUAGE: English
HEAD OF STATE: President Donald Ramotar (since Dec '11)
RULING PARTY: People's Progressive Party-Civic (PPP-C)
HEAD OF GOVERNMENT: Prime Minister Samuel Hinds (PPP-C) (since Dec '97)
DEMOCRACY INDEX: 6.05; 76th of 167   CORRUPTION PERCEPTIONS INDEX: 30; =124th of 175
CURRENCY: Guyana Dollar (Dec '14 £1.00=GYD 315.6, US$1.00=GYD 203.2)
GNI PER CAPITA: US$3,750, Intl$6,550 at PPP ('13)

Belize

CAPITAL: Belmopan   AREA: 22,970 sq km   POPULATION: 331,900 ('13)
OFFICIAL LANGUAGE: English
HEAD OF STATE: Queen Elizabeth II (since Feb '52)
GOVERNOR-GENERAL: Sir Colville Young (since Nov '93)
RULING PARTY: United Democratic Party (UDP)
HEAD OF GOVERNMENT: Prime Minister Dean Barrow (UDP) (since Feb '08)
CURRENCY: Belize Dollar (Dec '14 £1.00=BZD 3.10, US$1=BZD 1.99)
GNI PER CAPITA: US$4,660, Intl$8,160 at PPP ('13)

Suriname

CAPITAL: Paramaribo   AREA: 163,270 sq km   POPULATION: 539,276 ('13)
OFFICIAL LANGUAGE: Dutch
HEAD OF STATE AND GOVERNMENT: President Desire "Desi" Bouterse (NDP) (since Aug '10)
RULING PARTIES: Mega Combination (MC) coalition, led by National Democratic Party (NDP)
DEMOCRACY INDEX: 6.77; 55th of 167   CORRUPTION PERCEPTIONS INDEX: 36; =100th of 175
CURRENCY: Suriname Dollar (Dec '14 £1.00=SRD 5.12, US$1.00=SRD 3.30)
GNI PER CAPITA: US$9,260, Intl$15,860 at PPP ('13)

THE governments in both **Guyana** and **Suriname** were placed under consider-able pressure during the year. The strained relationship between the government and opposition parties in Guyana worsened significantly on 10 November when President Donald Ramotar of the People's Progressive Party-Civic (PPP-C) pro-rogued parliament in order to prevent a no-confidence motion against his gov-ernment. The opposition A Partnership for National Unity (APNU) had called the vote in protest against some US$22.5 million of government spending, undertaken without parliamentary approval, and the failure to hold local elec-tions since 1994. Had the no-confidence motion been held, the government would have lost, due to APNU's one-seat majority in the National Assembly, and an election would have been held within three months. To avoid this, the presi-dent suspended parliament. Under the constitution, suspension could last for up to six months. President Ramotar said the decision was taken to "give democ-racy a better opportunity to breathe. It opens the door for us to talk."

However, no talks were held and on 6 December President Ramotar said that a general election would take place but he declined to name a date. The political impasse also meant that the necessary legislation to deal with gaps in Guyana's regime to stamp out money laundering and the financing of terrorism remained unattended (see AR 2014, p. 139).

In Suriname, the ruling Mega Combination lost the support of the Pertjajah Luhur party, which had six seats in the National Assembly. This left the govern-ment with a one seat majority in the 51-seat Assembly. President Desi Bouterse said that the government would survive and return stronger after the 2015 elec-tion. However, this claim was placed in some doubt after scandal continued to dog the coalition. In August the president's son, Dino Bouterse, pleaded guilty in New York to charges linked to drug trafficking and attempting to help the Lebanese paramilitary group, Hezbullah (see AR 2014, p. 140). Bouterse faced a prison sentence of between 15 years and life. Then, in September Elton Brunswijk, the son of another leading member of the ruling coalition, Ronnie Brunswijk, was arrested for alleged drug trafficking.

In the international arena efforts were made to improve the relationship between **Belize** and Guatemala. In January, they agreed a "Roadmap for Strengthening Bilateral Relations". This set out a range of confidence-building measures to promote peace, security and cooperation. The governments hoped that the agreement would ensure the good management of relations until Guatemala's territorial claim over Belize was resolved. One early consequence of the improved relationship was a deal to prohibit illegal logging and trade in rosewood. More agreements were signed in December that covered the protection of cultural goods, migratory and visa issues, electric energy, student exchanges and sustainable tourism.

Peter Clegg

UK OVERSEAS TERRITORIES

Anguilla

CAPITAL: The Valley   AREA: 96 sq km   POPULATION: 14,000 ('13 UN figure)
OFFICIAL LANGUAGE: English
HEAD OF STATE: Queen Elizabeth II (since Feb '52)
GOVERNOR-GENERAL: Christina Scott (since July '13)
RULING PARTY: Anguilla United Movement (AUM)
HEAD OF GOVERNMENT: Chief Minister Hubert Hughes (AUM) (since Feb '10)
CURRENCY: East Caribbean Dollar (Dec '14 £1.00=XCD 4.19, US$1.00=XCD 2.70)
GNI PER CAPITA: US$18,403 ('11, UN data)

Bermuda

CAPITAL: Hamilton   AREA: 50 sq km   POPULATION: 65,024 ('13)
OFFICIAL LANGUAGE: English
HEAD OF STATE: Queen Elizabeth II (since Feb '52)
GOVERNOR-GENERAL: George Fergusson (since May '12)
RULING PARTY: One Bermuda Alliance (OBA)
HEAD OF GOVERNMENT: Premier Michael Dunkley (OBA) (since May '14)
CURRENCY: Bermudian Dollar (Dec '14 £1.00=BMD 1.55, US$1.00=BMD 1.00)
GNI PER CAPITA: US$104,610; Intl$66,390 at PPP ('12)

British Virgin Islands

CAPITAL: Road Town   AREA: 153 sq km   POPULATION: 28,000 ('13 UN figures)
OFFICIAL LANGUAGE: English
HEAD OF STATE: Queen Elizabeth II (since Feb '52)
GOVERNOR-GENERAL: John Duncan (since Aug '14)
RULING PARTY: Virgin Islands Party (VIP)
HEAD OF GOVERNMENT: Premier Orlando Smith (VIP) (since Nov '11)
CURRENCY: US Dollar (Dec '14 £1.00=US$1.55)
GNI PER CAPITA: US$35,565 ('11, UN data)

Cayman Islands

CAPITAL: George Town, Grand Cayman   AREA: 260 sq km   POPULATION: 58,435 ('13)
OFFICIAL LANGUAGE: English
HEAD OF STATE: Queen Elizabeth II (since Feb '52)
GOVERNOR-GENERAL: Helen Kilpatrick (since Sept '13)
RULING PARTY: United Democratic Party (UDP)
HEAD OF GOVERNMENT: Premier Alden McLaughlin (UDP) (since May '13)
CURRENCY: Cayman Island Dollar (Dec '14 £1.00=KYD 1.27, US$1.00=KYD 0.82)
GNI PER CAPITA: US$52,185 ('11, UN data)

Montserrat

CAPITAL: Plymouth   AREA: 102 sq km   POPULATION: 5,000 ('13, UN figures)
OFFICIAL LANGUAGE: English
HEAD OF STATE: Queen Elizabeth II (since Feb '52)
GOVERNOR-GENERAL: Adrian Davis (since April '11)
RULING PARTY: People's Democratic Movement (PDM)
HEAD OF GOVERNMENT: Chief Minister Donaldson Romeo (PDM) (since Sept '14)
CURRENCY: East Caribbean Dollar (see above)
GNI PER CAPITA: US$9,797 ('11, UN data)

Turks & Caicos Islands

CAPITAL: Cockburn Town   AREA: 430 sq km   POPULATION: 33,098 ('13)
OFFICIAL LANGUAGE: English
HEAD OF STATE: Queen Elizabeth II (since Feb '52)
GOVERNOR-GENERAL: Peter Beckingham (since Oct '13)
RULING PARTY: Progressive National Party (PNP)
HEAD OF GOVERNMENT: Premier Rufus Washington Ewing (PNP) (since Nov '12)
CURRENCY: US Dollar (Dec '14 £1.00=USD 1.55)
GNI PER CAPITA: US$26,658 ('11, UN data)

IN early December the Overseas Territories and the UK government agreed a 15-point Roadmap. It included agreement on shared best practice on economic planning, investment plans for each territory, and initiatives to raise international standards and deepen cooperation to tackle money laundering, tax evasion, organised crime, and corruption. Other points of agreement included the sharing of information on prison management, border and migration management, environmental issues, human rights, public codes of conduct, and the strengthening of democratic systems. However, the Territories resisted pressure to establish public lists of beneficial ownership for all companies and trust funds based in their jurisdictions. Strong objections were particularly forthcoming from **Bermuda**, **British Virgin Islands**, and **Cayman Islands**.

On 9 September a jury found former Cayman Islands premier McKeeva Bush not guilty on all 11 criminal charges against him. The charges were based on his use of a government-issued credit card between 2009 and 2010 (see AR 2012, p. 145). In **Turks & Caicos Islands** another ex-prime minister, Michael Misick, was extradited from Brazil so he could stand trial for corruption (see AR 2009, p. 161). The trial was scheduled for early 2015.

In **Montserrat** a new political party, the People's Democratic Movement, won the general election held on 11 September.

Peter Clegg

THE DUTCH TERRITORIES

Curaçao

CAPITAL: Willemstad   AREA: 444 sq km   POPULATION: 153,500 ('13)
OFFICIAL LANGUAGE: Dutch
HEAD OF STATE: King Willem-Alexander of the Netherlands (since April '13)
GOVERNOR-GENERAL: Lucille Andrea George-Wout (since Nov '13)
RULING PARTIES: Movement for the Future of Curaçao (MFK)-led coalition
HEAD OF GOVERNMENT: Prime Minister Ivar Aspjes (Sovereign People, PS) (since June '13)
CURRENCY: Antillean Guilder (Dec '14 £1.00=ANG 2.78, US$1.00=ANG 1.79)
GNI PER CAPITA: US$20,187 ('11, UN data)

Sint Maarten

CAPITAL: Philipsburg   AREA: 34 sq km   POPULATION: 39,689 ('13)
OFFICIAL LANGUAGE: Dutch
HEAD OF STATE: King Willem-Alexander of the Netherlands (since April '13)
GOVERNOR-GENERAL: Eugene Holiday (since Oct '10)
RULING PARTIES: coalition of United People's Party (UPP) and Democratic Party (DP)
HEAD OF GOVERNMENT: Prime Minister Marcel Gumbs (UPP) (since Dec '14)
CURRENCY: Antillean Guilder (Dec '14 £1.00=ANG 2.78, US$1.00=ANG 1.79
GNI PER CAPITA: US$20,187 ('11, UN data)

Aruba

CAPITAL: Oranjestad   AREA: 180 sq km   POPULATION: 102,911 ('13)
OFFICIAL LANGUAGE: Dutch
HEAD OF STATE: King Willem-Alexander of the Netherlands (since April '13)
GOVERNOR-GENERAL: Fredis Refunjol (since May '04)
RULING PARTY: Aruban People's Party (AVP)
HEAD OF GOVERNMENT: Prime Minister Mike Eman (AVP) (since Sept '09)
CURRENCY: Florin (Dec '14 £1.00=AWG 2.78, US$1.00=AWG 1.79)
GNI PER CAPITA: US$23,265 ('12, UN data)

In **Aruba**, Prime Minister Mike Emam went on hunger strike for several days in July in protest against alleged interference from the Dutch government. The hunger strike began on 11 July after Aruba Governor-General Fredis Rufenjol announced an independent investigation into the sustainability of Aruba's budget. It ended on 18 July when Governor Rufenjol agreed to a less stringent inquiry. The subsequent report highlighted several problems, most particularly an estimated budget deficit of 9.3 per cent of GDP and a national debt of 80.8 per cent of GDP. In response it was agreed that there would be greater oversight of Aruba's budget from the Netherlands.

In **Curaçao** on 15 July two people were killed and six injured in an alleged gang-related shooting outside the arrivals hall of the country's airport. On 30 August Elvis Kuwas, a principal suspect in the 2013 assassination of political leader Helmin Wiels (see AR 2014, p. 143), was sentenced to life imprisonment after being found guilty of the murder. However, the authorities believed that other individuals had been involved.

Peter Clegg

THE US TERRITORIES

Puerto Rico

CAPITAL: San Juan   AREA: 8,950 sq km   POPULATION: 3,615,086 ('13)
OFFICIAL LANGUAGES: Spanish & English
HEAD OF STATE: US President Barack Obama
RULING PARTY: Popular Democratic Party (PDP)
HEAD OF GOVERNMENT: Governor Alejandro Garcia Padilla (PDP) (since Jan '13)
CORRUPTION PERCEPTIONS INDEX: 63; =31st of 175
CURRENCY: US Dollar (Dec '14 £1.00=USD 1.55)
GNI PER CAPITA: US$19,210, Intl$23,830 at PPP ('13)

US Virgin Islands

CAPITAL: Charlotte Amalie   AREA: 350 sq km   POPULATION: 104,737 ('13)
OFFICIAL LANGUAGE: English
HEAD OF STATE: US President Barack Obama
RULING PARTY: Democrats
HEAD OF GOVERNMENT: Governor John de Jongh (Democratic Party) (since Jan '07)
CURRENCY: US Dollar (Dec '14 £1.00=USD 1.55)
GNI PER CAPITA: high income: US$11,906 or more ('08 est.)

THE economic situation once again dominated the year in **Puerto Rico**. In February, three ratings agencies, Standard & Poor's (S&P), Moody's Investors Services, and Fitch Ratings downgraded the country's credit rating to junk bond status. In response to the continuing bleak economic picture, the government announced on 3 February that it would pull forward its 2015 plan to present a balanced budget and get rid of its budget deficit. The new plans, revealed in late April, included more than $1.4 billion in spending cuts, equivalent to an 8 per cent reduction in discretionary spending. The budget was adopted on 1 July. The government also passed a law creating a de facto bankruptcy regime for state-owned enterprises. The law gave companies nine months to negotiate a settlement acceptable to holders of 75 per cent of their debt. If the parties could not agree, local courts would then impose a solution. However, the lack of growth in the economy was a real barrier to successful reform. It was predicted that the economy would shrink by about 0.7 per cent in 2014, and there were signs towards the end of the year that it was slowing even further. On 24 December it was announced that Puerto Rico's economic activity index (EAI) fell by 2.1 per cent in November, which was the second consecutive month when the decline was over 2 per cent. As measured by the EAI, economic activity was at its lowest level in 20 years.

The economic situation in the **US Virgin Islands** also remained difficult. Final figures released in August for economic growth in 2013 recorded a decline of 5.4 per cent. There was more bad news in December when a plan to re-open the idle Hovensa oil refinery under new owners was rejected by the US Virgin Islands legislature.

Peter Clegg

BRAZIL

CAPITAL: Brasília   AREA: 8,514,880 sq km   POPULATION: 200,361,925 ('13)
OFFICIAL LANGUAGE: Portuguese
HEAD OF STATE AND GOVERNMENT: President Dilma Rousseff (PT) (since Jan '11)
RULING PARTIES: Workers' Party (PT)-led coalition
DEMOCRACY INDEX: 7.12; =44th of 167   CORRUPTION PERCEPTIONS INDEX: 43; =69th of 175
CURRENCY: Real (Dec '14 £1.00=BRL 4.17, US$1.00=BRL 2.69)
GNI PER CAPITA: US$11,690, Intl$14,750 at PPP ('13)

IT was a year of economic difficulties, political division, and sporting disaster. The latter came unexpectedly as Brazil hosted the football World Cup from 12 June to 13 July. Despite fears of problems, the organisation of the tournament went smoothly. However, President Dilma Rousseff was abused by parts of the crowd in São Paulo, prior to the first match (Brazil versus Croatia) on 12 June. (A poll released on 3 July revealed that 76 per cent of those surveyed believed that the fans who had chanted abuse of Rousseff had behaved badly.) However, anticipated popular protests against cost over-runs for stadiums and the government's prioritisation of the Cup over other forms of infrastructure (such as schools and hospitals) were relatively small, with the government estimating that 50,000 people protested. This was far fewer than the over 2 million who protested in June-July 2013 (see AR 2014, p.145).

Events on the pitch were far from ideal for home fans. In a semi-final match on 8 July in the Estádio Mineirão, in Belo Horizonte, Germany routed Brazil 7-1. Four of the goals were scored in the space of 6 minutes in the middle of the first half. It was Brazil's biggest ever defeat in World Cup finals, and a huge blow to the much vaunted image of Brazilian footballing prowess. It also ended the dream of winning the World Cup for a sixth time, at home, and thus wiping out the painful memory of Brazil's defeat to Uruguay in the final of the 1950 World Cup, the last time that the tournament had been staged in Brazil. Luiz Felipe Scolari, the Brazilian coach, immediately resigned after the semi-final debacle. Germany proceeded to the final where, on 13 July, they beat Argentina 1-0.

The election campaign, for president, governorships, the national Congress, and state assemblies, started formally on 6 July but only got underway in earnest after the World Cup final. With public approval of incumbent President Dilma Rousseff, of the PT (Partido dos Trabalhadores, or Workers' Party), relatively low, at around 32 per cent in July, many of her opponents were optimistic about the possibility of defeating her at the polls. The main opposition candidates were the former governor of Minas Gerais, Aécio Neves, of the PSDB (Brazil Social Democratic Party), and former governor of Pernambuco, Eduardo Campos, of the PSB (Brazil Socialist Party). Neves led Campos in the polls until 13 August when the latter was killed in an aeroplane accident. This led to his vice-presidential running mate, Marina Silva, assuming the candidacy of the PSB and rapidly rising in the polls in the aftermath of Campos's death. However, in the first round of the presidential election, on 5 October, a late surge by Neves resulted in his qualifying for the second round, along with

Rousseff. The results for the leading candidates were as follows: Rousseff 41.6 per cent of the vote; Neves 33.6 per cent; and Silva 21.3 per cent.

The campaign for the second round run-off was bitterly fought. Neves claimed that the country needed a sharp change of course in a liberal direction with regard to economic policy, and argued that the incumbent government had irresponsibly overspent and intervened chaotically in various sectors. Rousseff countered by warning working people that social assistance would be reduced and jobs and wages threatened if her opponent were to win. The issue was decided on 26 October, with Rousseff securing 51.6 per cent of the vote compared with 48.4 per cent for Neves. It was the fourth consecutive victory of a PT candidate for president. It was also the closest second round presidential election in Brazil since 1989. A key factor in the election was that, despite slow growth under Rousseff (averaging about 1.5 per cent per year in 2011-14), household income grew at over 3 per cent in 2011-13. The electorate was sharply divided along class lines. Voters living in the poorest 40 per cent of households were far more likely to vote for Rousseff than the rest of the electorate, with the middle class divided and anti-Rousseff sentiment more prevalent among voters with higher incomes.

An estimated one billion reals was spent by candidates on the 2014 elections. According to one newspaper, donations by 10 large firms (JBS, Bradesco, Itaú, Vale, Ambev, Oderbrecht, Queiroz Galvâo, Andrade Gutierrez, OAS and UTC Engenharia) helped elect 70 per cent of the representatives in the lower house of the National Congress. Many of these companies were recipients of large government contracts and subsidised credit from state banks. Their ubiquity in the electoral process might have contributed to disillusionment with party politics, especially among the young, and to the fact that 21 per cent of registered voters did not participate in the second round of the presidential election.

The anti-PT and anti- Rousseff feelings expressed in the 2014 elections reached an unprecedented level in Brazil and revealed divisions within the country. These divisions were not just along class lines, but also racial and regional. Voters in the state of São Paulo, for example, voted against Rousseff at a rate of almost 2 to 1, while 70 per cent of the electorate of the north-east region voted for her. Some people in the opposition spoke ominously of a coming PT "dictatorship", even though the 2014 elections were highly competitive and took place within the framework of independent regulatory institutions capable of checking and balancing the executive branch.

The October legislative elections considerably changed the composition of the National Congress. The PT lost 18 seats in the lower house, where it remained the largest party, while the conservative Democratas (DEM) party lost 21 seats. The overall number of parties in Congress increased from 22 to 28. Some right-wing candidates did well. Jair Bolsonaro in Rio de Janeiro, and Luiz Carlos Heinze in Rio Grande do Sul, got the most votes of any federal deputy in their states, while Celso Russomano of São Paulo, also a conservative, won the most votes of any federal deputy in the country. Following the elections, the PT held only 15 per cent of the seats in the Senate, 14 per cent of the seats in the lower house, and five of 27 governorships.

On 10 December, after a two-year investigation into human rights abuses during the period 1946-88 (and especially during the dictatorship of 1964-85), the National Truth Commission (see AR 2013, p.148) issued its report. It named 377 individuals as being responsible for the political murders and disappearances of 434 victims. The report recommended that the surviving perpetrators (about 200 people) should be prosecuted and made it clear that their acts had been in accordance with policy rather than individual aberrations. The Truth Commission also made a number of recommendations in the area of contemporary public security policy, including de-linking the military police from the army and merging them with the civil police; dismantling state military courts, which judged crimes of the military police, sending these instead to the civilian judiciary; and abolishing the 1983 National Security Law.

The issue of corruption was also significant during 2014. On 17 March the federal police initiated an investigation into an alleged illicit multi-billion dollar scheme in Petrobras, the partially state-owned oil company. The police obtained information from a former director of Petrobras, Paulo Roberto Costa, who was arrested and who claimed to have engaged in a process (known as "Operation Car-wash" by the police) to channel 3 per cent of Petrobras contracts to politicians in the ruling coalition. Costa was found to have Swiss bank accounts containing $23 million. On 11 December prosecutors charged 36 people in connection with the scandal. They alleged that executives in construction companies skimmed money from Petrobras contracts and diverted it to politicians. Those arrested were from the country's biggest construction companies, including OAS, Camargo Corrêa, UTC, Mendes Junior, Engevix and Galvão Engenharia. This case promised to be a test of the Anti Corruption Law passed in August of 2013, which had increased sanctions against companies found to be involved in corrupting the public administration.

In the economic sphere it was a difficult year. Prices fell for most of Brazil's commodity exports, such as soybeans and iron ore. Growth slowed and Brazil entered into a technical recession in the middle of the year. Overall growth in 2014 was less than 1 per cent, leading the government to rethink its economic policies. On 21 November, in the aftermath of the elections, President Rousseff announced the appointment of two new ministers to run the economy: Joaquim Levy (Finance) and Nelson Barbosa (Planning). These appointments—especially that of Levy, who came from the private sector—were intended to signal the new government's determination to adhere to more orthodox economic policies: cutting federal spending, avoiding a downgrading of Brazil's credit risk, and stimulating economic growth

The year ended with traditional New Year's Eve celebrations. Probably the most extravagant of these was in Copacabana, where the theme was the 450th anniversary of the city of Rio de Janeiro, which was due to be celebrated in 2015.

Anthony W. Pereira

ARGENTINA

CAPITAL: Buenos Aires   AREA: 2,780,400 sq km   POPULATION: 41,446,246 ('13)
OFFICIAL LANGUAGE: Spanish
HEAD OF STATE AND GOVERNMENT: President Cristina Fernandez de Kirchner (PJ) (since Dec '07)
RULING PARTY: Front for Victory-Justicialist Party (PJ)
DEMOCRACY INDEX: 6.84; 52nd of 167   CORRUPTION PERCEPTIONS INDEX: 34; =107th of 175
CURRENCY: Argentine Peso (Dec '14 £1.00=ARS 13.28, US$1.00=ARS 8.55)
GNI PER CAPITA: US$14,708, Intl$22,362 at PPP ('13, IMF estimate)

PRIDE at its national football team's stellar World Cup performance, frustration with ongoing government corruption, a stagnant economy, and a protracted legal battle with the remaining sovereign debt holders made Argentine passions run high in 2014.

Corruption at the highest echelons of power continued to fester. For the first time, in June, a court case was opened against a serving vice-president, namely Amado Boudou, who was charged with graft and favouritism over the nationalisation and subsequent sale of Ciccone Calcografica, a printing company for paper money. Despite serious health issues, President Cristina Fernández de Kirchner was as fiery as ever and repeatedly defended her former running mate, attacking the courts and the media for mounting a campaign against him—possibly to deflect accusations of illicit enrichment and money laundering levelled against herself.

The economy stagnated, suffering a slight contraction of 0.2 per cent for 2014, according to the UN's Economic Commission for Latin America and the Caribbean (ECLAC). The main reasons were a currency devaluation in January, stagnating export markets for manufactured goods (especially Brazil and cars) and renewed pressure on the currency after being pushed into "technical default" on 30 July. This occurred after a court in New York declared illegal Argentina's practice of paying back only the bondholders of successfully restructured sovereign debt, whilst ignoring the so-called "holdouts" who chose not to accept the deep "haircuts" to debt negotiated after the 2001 default (see AR 2001, p. 206). These bonds (comprising about 7 per cent of the original debt) were now in the hands of activist hedge funds looking to realise the original claim in full. Giving in to the holdouts would open the door for other bondholders to claim the same privilege, effectively annulling the debt restructuring deals of 2005 and 2010, besides creating a precedent that would complicate future defaults worldwide.

The IMF, the G77 and the OAS all supported Argentina in its stance against the vulture funds, which were seen as bringing unnecessary harm to the international financial system. The country fell into "technical" or "selective default" at the end of July when, despite the willingness of the government to continue honouring its commitments, it (as well as all the banks involved) was barred by the US court from making further debt repayments until it paid the "holdout" bondholders in full. When the country tried to evade the sentence by paying its creditors through other jurisdictions (Argentina or France), it was denounced by Judge Thomas Griesa as "disobeying a court order" in September, although it was unclear what kind of sanctions this would imply. Banks around the world complained that they were being forced under US jurisdiction and could lose their business in Argentina. Tellingly, the international credit market did not dry up, showing how little support the vulture funds enjoyed on the capital markets. This significantly reduced financial uncertainty, as did a debt repayment settlement with the Paris Club of sovereign creditors in May, which was important given that more than $10 billion in sovereign debt would fall due in 2015.

The government tried to compensate for the negative impact of the currency devaluation early in the year—and the rise in interest rates and inflation that accompanied it—with an expansive fiscal policy focused on the most vulnerable sectors of society (especially families, youth and the poor), which remained Kirchnerism's main pillar of support. Here, it continued to make use of non-tributary funds to pay for its spending, mostly from the Central Bank and the Sustainability Guarantee Fund (FGS) of the National Social Security Administration (ANSES). The balance of payments worsened, with exports, imports and foreign direct investment all down from 2013. This left the government with a budget deficit of 1.7 per cent of GDP.

According to ECLAC, inflation remained stuck at around 30 per cent, much higher than the regional average. The government's figures, however, showed price increases of slightly over 20 per cent for 2014, despite a newly designed national price index that was supposed to bring the official numbers more into line with private estimates. The government reacted by introducing extensive price controls on some 320 consumer products in January. Pressured by union calls for a 24-hour general strike in April, it also continued to push for large increases in consumer income to counteract the harmful effects of inflation and keep up the spending power of the electorate. Unemployment, however, increased and reached 7.5 per cent in the third quarter of 2014.

Growing insecurity amidst this economic deceleration became a major political topic in March, after a crime wave linked to the drug trade led to a year-long "security emergency" in Buenos Aires province, decreed by Governor Daniel Scioli, which some saw as cynical electioneering. In the city of Rosario, with a homicide rate four times the national average, a large-scale counter narcotics operation was carried out in April as a show of force by federal security agencies. In October, national legislation was proposed that would deport foreigners involved in violent crime—a surprising move for a president usually bent on integrating immigrants. Nevertheless, the UN declared Argentina the second-safest country in the region (after Chile), with a homicide rate of only 5.8 per 100,000 inhabitants.

Despite the economic situation, Argentina's international business posture improved. Spanish oil giant Repsol settled in February for the forced renationalisation of its majority share in YPF, the Argentine national petroleum company, improving relations with Spain. In July, the presidents of both Russia and China came to Buenos Aires, increasing hopes of more Chinese investment into Argentina's hydroelectric infrastructure, oil and transport, and possible agreements with Russia on oil and civilian nuclear issues. Relations with both powers had been improving for some time, culminating in Argentina's abstention on the UN General Assembly's resolution in March on the situation in Crimea (see article on Russia).

After a spectacular football World Cup organised by Argentina's arch-enemy on the pitch, Brazil, the national team reached the final—but lost to Germany. Economic hardship, frustration and political uncertainty seemed no longer important when millions of Argentine fans united in celebrating their players. Not even bouts of street violence after the party, and the president's remark to television audiences that she had not watched a single game, could taint this glorious day.

Christian E. Rieck

PARAGUAY AND URUGUAY

Paraguay

CAPITAL: Asunción   AREA: 406,750 sq km   POPULATION: 6,802,295 ('13)
OFFICIAL LANGUAGE: Spanish
HEAD OF STATE AND GOVERNMENT: President Horacio Cartes (PC) (since Aug '13)
RULING PARTY: Colorado Party (PC)
DEMOCRACY INDEX: 6.26;=70th of 167   CORRUPTION PERCEPTIONS INDEX: 24; =150th of 175
CURRENCY: Guarani (Dec '14 £1.00=PYG 7,184, US$1.00=PYG 4,626)
GNI PER CAPITA: US$4,040, Intl$7,640 at PPP ('13)

Uruguay

CAPITAL: Montevideo   AREA: 176,220 sq km   POPULATION: 3,407,062 ('13)
OFFICIAL LANGUAGE: Spanish
HEAD OF STATE AND GOVERNMENT: President José Mujica (FA) (since March '10)
PRESIDENT ELECT: Tabare Vazquez (Socialist Party)
RULING PARTY: Broad Front (FA)
DEMOCRACY INDEX: 8.17; =17th of 167   CORRUPTION PERCEPTIONS INDEX: 73; =21st of 175
CURRENCY: Peso Uruguay (Dec '14 £1.00=UYU 37.35, US$1.00=UYU 24.05)
GNI PER CAPITA: US$15,180, Intl$18,930 at PPP ('13)

THE authorities in **Paraguay** were stung into action after the high-profile murders of Pablo Medina, a journalist working for the national newspaper *ABC Color*, and his assistant, Antonia Almada. It was believed that they had been killed because of their investigations into links between politicians and gangs involved in the production and trafficking of marijuana. Paraguay was the largest producer of marijuana in South America. Vilmar Acosta, a mayor from the ruling National Republican Association-Colorado Party (ANR-PC), was placed under investigation over the murders. The killings took place on 16 October and two weeks later, on 3 November, representatives from the government, legislature, and judiciary met to discuss their response. The ensuing agreement included a promise to prevent candidates suspected of involvement in the drugs trade from standing in parliamentary elections, and to bring all court rulings on drug trafficking to Asunción, the capital. The attorney general also said he would try to ensure that the proceeds from goods seized during drug-related investigations went directly to the state. Another aspect of the country's difficult security situation was seen in March when 16-year old Arlan Fick, the son of a Brazilian ranch owner, was abducted by the Paraguayan People's Army. After 267 days in captivity he was freed on 26 December. It was the longest kidnapping case in Paraguayan history.

A scandal of a different kind hit the headlines on 25 September when Pope Francis dismissed Bishop Rogelio Ricardo Livieres Plano from the diocese of Ciudad del Este. In a statement the Vatican explained that Livieres had been dismissed in order to maintain the "unity of both the bishops and of the faithful ... under the weight of serious pastoral concerns". These included protecting an Argentinian priest who was accused of sex abuse in the USA, and allegations of misuse by Livieres of funds from the Itaipú hydroelectric dam which were meant for social programmes in the diocese. In response Livieres said he was a victim of "ideological persecution" and that the Pope would be "answerable to God" for his "unfounded and arbitrary" decision.

In economic matters there was some good news for President Horacio Cartes. Paraguay's beef and soybeans industry recorded record levels of production. Paraguay moved to eighth in the world for beef exports and planned to double the number of cattle slaughtered by 2020, according to the country's Rural Association, ARP. The soybean harvest was over 9 million tonnes—a 13 per cent increase on the previous crop.

In August Paraguay sold 1 billion dollars in 30-year bonds. President Cartes said in a statement that the issue's 6.1 per cent yield was unprecedented for the country, and that the proceeds would be used for highway, building and energy infrastructure, and agricultural production. However, this good news was tempered by significant worker unrest over low wages and the government's privatisation plans. On 26 March a general strike was held, the first in 20 years.

Presidential and parliamentary elections in **Uruguay** were held during the year. In the presidential contest two rounds were needed, but in the end former president Tabaré Vázquez (2005-10), of the ruling left-wing Broad Front (FA) coalition, won a clear victory. In the first round, on 26 October, Vázquez won 47.9 per cent of the vote, compared with 31.0 per cent for Luis Alberto Lacalle Pou, of the main opposition National Party. In the second round, on 30 November, Vázquez beat Lacalle Pou by 12.5 per cent (53.6 per cent to 41.1 per cent). This gave the FA a third straight term in the presidency. In congressional elections, also held on 26 October, the FA won 50 of the 99 seats in the lower chamber and 15 of the 30 Senate seats. But, the FA gained a one-seat majority in the Senate after Vázquez's running mate, Raúl Sendic, was elected vice president and, in turn, a senator. A third national vote was held on 26 October—a plebiscite on reducing the age of sentencing from 18 to 16 for crimes such as homicide and rape. It was narrowly defeated.

The challenges for the new president included maintaining economic growth and stability; dealing with the perceived problem of juvenile crime; improving the country's education performance, which had fallen back despite increased spending; and introducing the legal sale of marijuana to registered users through pharmacies—a policy which his predecessor, Jose Mujica, had supported but about which Vázquez had doubts.

The reason that Vázquez was committed to the policy on marijuana was that much of the legal framework had already been put in place. On 2 May the government issued a decree with over one hundred articles regulating its production, distribution and sale. The articles fixed the price; the maximum allowed quantity for consumers to possess; and the way in which consumers were identified. Prices were fixed at between Ur$20 and Ur$22 (between 87 and 95 US cents) per gram. For consumption there were three options: (i) buy a maximum of 40 grams per month from registered pharmacies (state marijuana plantations would service this demand); (ii) cultivate up to six plants per household with annual production limited to 480 grams; and (iii) belong to a 'cannabis club' entitled to grow up to 99 plants per group with a production cap of 480 grams for each member. It was clearly stipulated that only Uruguayan citizens and residents over 18 were allowed to participate and measures were in place to prevent "marijuana tourism". There was a complicated registration and distribution system with fingerprinting, bar-coding of each bag of marijuana, and a radio-frequency identification tag. Under the scheme pharmacies were not forced to sell marijuana but made a 30 per cent profit if they did. Those who grew marijuana were subject to spot checks. The government estimated that production levels of around 20 tonnes a year were needed to supply the country's 150,000 users. Opinion polls suggested that a large majority of Uruguayans opposed the legalisation of marijuana, while there were concerns that the heavy regulation would undermine the state-supported scheme.

Peter Clegg

CHILE

CAPITAL: Santiago   AREA: 756,630 sq km   POPULATION: 17,619,708 ('13)
OFFICIAL LANGUAGE: Spanish
HEAD OF STATE AND GOVERNMENT: President Michelle Bachelet (Socialist Party) (since March '14)
RULING PARTIES: New Majority coalition
DEMOCRACY INDEX: 7.80; 32nd of 167   CORRUPTION PERCEPTIONS INDEX: 73; =21st of 175
CURRENCY: Chilean Peso (Dec '14 £1.00=CLP 941.6, US$1.00=CLP 606.3)
GNI PER CAPITA: US$15,230, Intl$21,030 at PPP ('13)

THIS was a year that had promised to be an exciting one for Chilean politics. Newly re-elected President Michelle Bachelet was to return to La Moneda in March for a second term, having won the December 2013 election on a platform of ambitious reforms in the political, educational, tax, and social spheres. She was to be accompanied by her new centre-left New Majority coalition, which now included parties from the Communists on the far left to the centrist Christian Democrats.

Before that, however, the headlines were dominated by the 27 January ruling on the Chilean-Peruvian maritime border dispute by the International Court of Justice at The Hague. The ruling, which awarded Peru sovereignty over some 22,000 square km of maritime territory at Chile's expense, was accepted by both parties, thereby bringing to an end years of occasionally bitter diplomatic dispute.

With Bachelet back in office from March onwards, her new government set to work implementing its programme of reforms. The first step was to enact a shake-up of the country's tax system, with a gradual increase in corporation tax one of the more eye-catching elements of the proposed legislation. The aim was to raise the government's tax revenue by some $8 billion, in order to fund the central plank of Bachelet's re-election platform: sweeping education reforms that would introduce free university tuition and abolish profit-making in the schools sector, while also improving the quality of education across the board.

However, even the tax reform proved difficult to push through Congress, as tensions not only with the conservative opposition and business community, but also within the New Majority coalition itself, led to a delayed and significantly modified bill being passed only in September, six months into Bachelet's new term. These difficulties, though, were little compared to what was to come with the proposed education reforms themselves. Not only did Bachelet immediately face stiff opposition from her political adversaries, pupil parents' groups, and the private education sector, but she also came increasingly under fire from the country's strident student movement.

Student organisations had played a key role in Bachelet's election at the end of 2013, as highlighted by the election of several former student leaders—most notably Camila Vallejo—who, as Communist Party (PCCh) members, were now a part of the New Majority government. However, it became increasingly apparent over the course of the year that many students had grown wary of the Bachelet administration and doubted its commitment to its election campaign promises on educational reform, and soon student organisations began to claim that they had been left out of the government's plans. These tensions and the political opposition to the reforms meant that by the end of 2014, the bill remained stuck in Congress.

As for the Chilean economy, the year saw a significant slowdown in the country's GDP in comparison with recent years, in line with the general trend seen across much of Latin America since late 2013. Economic growth was expected to be limited to 1.8 per cent, with the low price of copper—Chile's most important export—amid falling global demand for commodities identified as a key factor.

In the social sphere, 2014 was noteworthy for a worrying rise in terror attacks seemingly carried out by anarchist extremists, with a series of explosions taking place throughout the year, mainly in Santiago. One such attack resulted in the death of the perpetrator, the first time such an incident had caused a fatality since the return to democracy in 1990.

It was also an important year in environmental terms. On 1 April, just weeks into Bachelet's new term, a major earthquake struck the north of Chile, killing six and sparking tsunami warnings. At one stage it threatened to be an echo of the devastating 2010 earthquake and tsunami that had overshadowed the final days of Bachelet's first term, but fortunately the worst fears failed to materialise. Ten days later, though, a far worse environmental disaster was to strike, as a wildfire that began in the hills of Valparaíso spread out of control, and went on to ravage vast swathes of the historic city. Thousands of homes were destroyed, with 15 killed and over 10,000 made homeless.

Elsewhere, several controversial environmental projects were finally shelved by the government after years of opposition from environmentalists and social movements. HidroAysén, a planned 2.7GW hydroelectric complex in the heart of Patagonia, in the south of Chile, was officially scrapped in June. It was seen as a landmark triumph for social movements in forcing a government U-turn on the issue, after the project had been given the initial go-ahead during Bachelet's first term, in 2008. However, other controversial projects, such as the Punta Alcalde thermal power plant and the Alto Maipo hydroelectric project, appeared to have cemented their development despite vociferous opposition from local communities and an increasingly eco-aware Chilean civil society.

Giles Constantine

PERU

CAPITAL: Lima   AREA: 1,285,220 sq km   POPULATION: 30,375,603 ('13)
OFFICIAL LANGUAGES: Spanish, Quechua, Aymara
HEAD OF STATE AND GOVERNMENT: President Ollanta Humala (GP) (since July '11)
RULING PARTIES: Peru Wins (GP) alliance
DEMOCRACY INDEX: 6.54; =60th of 167   CORRUPTION PERCEPTIONS INDEX: 38; =85th of 175
CURRENCY: New Sol (Dec '14 £1.00=PEN 4.64, US$1.00=PEN 2.99)
GNI PER CAPITA: US$6,390, Intl$11,360 at PPP ('13)

AT the end of 2014, Peru looked ahead politically to the next general elections (presidential and legislative), scheduled for April 2016, with an almost certain second round, probably in June 2016. A new head of state was to take office to replace President Ollanta Humala Tasso, whose five-year term would expire on 28 July, 2016. A new legislature was to be elected at the same time, assuming its functions on the same date.

It remained very unclear who was most likely to succeed Humala, constitutionally barred from standing for immediate re-election. This had also been the case in other recent presidential contests, since a proliferation of small parties and the two-round ballotage system made for unexpected results. Few, for example, had expected Humala to win in 2011.

The most likely contenders were all well-known political figures: Alan García Pérez, already twice president (1985-90 and 2006-11), was almost certain to stand, as was Keiko Fujimori Higuchi, the daughter of former President Alberto Fujimori Fujimori (1990-2000). Another leading contender was Pedro Pablo Kuczynski Godard, a former minister, prime minister and third-placed candidate in 2011. Another possible candidate was former president Alejandro Toledo (2001-06). Fujimori was leading the polls at the end of 2014, but—if previous election results were any guide—the front-runner at the beginning of a campaign might not turn out the eventual victor.

It was also unclear whom the ruling Peru Wins (GP) coalition would select as its candidate, since Humala could not stand. It had been widely assumed that his charismatic and politically astute wife, Nadine Heredia Alarcón de Humala, would contest the election. However, there was a law that barred members of a president's family from standing, and there was little chance of this law being modified or repealed. Heredia's possible candidacy had also been the subject of unremitting attacks from García over the previous two years. The interior minister, Daniel Urresti Elera, had pushed himself forward as a possible candidate, but he faced hostility from others within Humala's Nationalist Party (PNP).

As presidential electioneering gathered pace, Peru's economic situation was worsening. Having been one of South America's fastest-growing economies for much of the previous decade, with an annual average of over 5 per cent, Peru's growth in 2014 was likely to be less than half that. The economy had been hit by the global decline in demand for minerals, especially gold and copper. Low prices for key minerals had affected exports, down by nearly 15 per cent in 2014 compared to 2013. They had also led to the postponement of investment decisions on the part of major foreign investors, hit also by declining stock values. Peru, like other countries, was suffering too from expectations of a rise in US interest rates. The government confidently was predicting that growth would be back to around 5 per cent in 2015, but that looked over-optimistic. However, Peru was better placed than many emerging markets to weather the crisis by virtue of the high ratio of its international reserves to outstanding debt.

There were elections in October for regional governments as well as mayors and councillors at the local level. Decentralisation, coupled with large revenues from extractive industries, had greatly increased the spending powers of local government, and with them the scale of corruption. By far the most important single election result was the overwhelming victory of Luis Castañeda Lossio in the Lima mayoral contest. Lima accounted for around one-third of Peru's voting public. Castañeda, a centre-right politician with a reputation for corruption, had twice previously been mayor of the city. In 2014, he won with more than 50 per cent of the vote. It was a heavy blow to the centre-left incumbent, Susana Villarán. Elsewhere, the main winners were local parties with little ideological direction who mainly fought on parochial issues. A large number of the victors, too, had reputations for corruption. One even successfully won re-election having conducted his campaign from inside jail.

Problems of citizen insecurity remained a key issue for most voters in 2014, alongside corruption scandals that were grist to a sensationalist media. Citizen insecurity was compounded by the activities of drug-trafficking gangs, with Peru having overtaken Colombia as the world's largest supplier of coca and cocaine. Port cities like Trujillo had become particularly notorious for indiscriminate street violence and gang warfare. Political violence was also a daily reality in parts of the country, like the Apurímac, Ene and Mantaro river valleys (known as the VRAEM), where the once powerful guerrilla insurgency, Shining Path, still held sway.

Internationally, Peru had taken a lead in promoting the so-called Pacific Alliance, alongside Mexico, Colombia and Chile. All were countries which had adopted business-friendly, pro-US policies. 2014 also saw the final resolution of Peru's longstanding maritime border conflict with Chile. The International Court of Justice (ICJ) arbitration award—announced at the end of January—significantly increased Peru's territorial waters at Chile's expense.

John Crabtree

BOLIVIA

CAPITAL: La Paz and Sucre   AREA: 1,098,580 sq km   POPULATION: 10,671,200 ('13)
OFFICIAL LANGUAGES: Spanish, Quechua, Aymara
HEAD OF STATE AND GOVERNMENT: President Evo Morales (MAS) (since Jan '06)
RULING PARTY: Movement Towards Socialism (MAS) (since Dec '05)
DEMOCRACY INDEX: 5.79; 88th of 167   CORRUPTION PERCEPTIONS INDEX: 35; =103rd of 175
CURRENCY: Boliviano (Dec '14 £1.00=BOB 10.73, US$1.00=BOB 6.91)
GNI PER CAPITA: US$2,550, Intl$5,750 at PPP ('13)

WITH President Evo Morales Ayma due to be sworn in for a third term on 22 January 2015, at the end of 2014 his government seemed well placed to weather possible difficulties ahead. Morales had won re-election on 12 October 2014 for a further five-year period of government. Not only did he win with 61 per cent of valid votes, avoiding the need for a second round under the ballotage rules in the 2009 constitution, but his party—the Movement towards Socialism (MAS)—won a two-thirds majority in the Plurinational Legislative Assembly (PLA), the country's two-chamber parliament. At the same time, Bolivia seemed on track to be one of Latin America's fastest-growing economies in 2014, with GDP growing by around 5.3 per cent. In 2013, GDP had expanded by 6.8 per cent.

The opposition, by contrast, found itself at a low ebb. Its representation in parliament was such as not to represent any real obstacle to government legislation, with two opposition parties (the Fearless Movement (MSM) and the Bolivian Green Party (PVB)) failing even to muster the 3 per cent required to maintain their official legal status as political parties. The opposition had gone into the 2014 elections divided and had suffered accordingly. The most successful candidate in the presidential elections, Samuel Doria Medina from the National Unity (UN) party, won just 25 per cent, followed by Jorge Quiroga Ramírez, a former president (2000-01), who ran under the Christian Democrat Party (PDC) banner, winning 9 per cent. The MAS even managed to make serious electoral inroads into opposition bastions, for example winning more than 50 per cent of the vote in the previously conservative-dominated department of Santa Cruz in the eastern lowlands.

The ability of the MAS to reinforce its hegemonic status in Bolivian politics, however, was due to be tested in elections in March 2015 for departmental governorships and local mayors. In previous elections, the MAS had fared less well when Morales was not the candidate and when local issues predominated over national ones. It seemed probable, at least, that the incumbent governor of Santa Cruz department, Rubén Costas Aguilera, would be re-elected. Since 2006, when Morales first became president, Costas had been amongst his most bitter and effective critics. In 2008, at his behest, Santa Cruz came close to declaring independence from La Paz.

The electoral growth of the MAS had seen it move from a small, peasant-based party in the late 1990s by its incorporation of an array of social movements, including urban-based unions and mineworkers, and latterly widening its appeal to the business class. Its ideology was a potent mix of pro-indigenous sentiment with a strong dose of nationalism. The constitution, rewritten in 2009, encompassed these two elements, whilst reaffirming the role of the state in national development. It thus represented a shift from the ideology that prevailed during governments elected prior to the MAS coming to office in 2006. Morales represented the lynchpin in what, at times, proved to be an unwieldy coalition. He retained huge legitimacy as Bolivia's first-ever truly indigenous head of state, and was the decision-maker of last resort when conflict over policy emerged. Whilst Bolivia's system of government had long been presidentialist, this was reinforced under his aegis. The personalisation of political power therefore seemed likely to make for an easy succession, whenever that might occur.

However, as 2014 closed, it was increasingly clear that economic problems might be looming and that government claims that Bolivia was "protected" from global problems were misplaced. With more than half the country's export earnings derived from a single commodity—natural gas—Bolivia was likely to be hit in 2015 by declining prices. Its export contracts to Brazil and Argentina, both of whose economies faced recession, were linked to the world price for crude oil, which tumbled in late 2014. Much of the country's fiscal resources were derived from gas, a sharp decline in prices would lead to cuts in public spending, especially in public investment (key for employment) and in social welfare spending. Minerals prices—Bolivia's other major source of hard currency—were also depressed. Mining was an important source of employment, too, particularly in Morales's power-base in the highland part of the country.

At the same time, the benefits that Bolivia had received since 2006 from a favourable international situation seemed less certain. The death of Venezuela's President Hugo Chávez Frías in March 2013 had removed a potent ally, with his successor, President Nicolás Maduro Moros, suffering major domestic problems (see the article on Venezuela). Similarly, a transition in Cuba could remove a strong ideological source of support. Perhaps more importantly, a change of government in Argentina, would probably work to Bolivia's detriment, whilst a re-elected President Dilma Rousseff in Brazil seemed less likely to be as indulgent towards Bolivia as her predecessor, President Luiz Inacio "Lula" da Silva, or indeed her first administration. A Republican-dominated US Congress, too, seemed unlikely to be predisposed towards improving ties with Morales and the MAS in La Paz.

John Crabtree

ECUADOR

CAPITAL: Quito   AREA: 283,560 sq km   POPULATION: 15,737,878 ('13)
OFFICIAL LANGUAGE: Spanish
HEAD OF STATE AND GOVERNMENT: President Rafael Correa Delgado (AP) (since Jan '07)
RULING PARTY: PAIS Alliance (AP)
DEMOCRACY INDEX: 5.87; =82nd of 167   CORRUPTION PERCEPTIONS INDEX: 33; =110th of 175
CURRENCY: Sucre (Dec '14 £1.00=38,823, US$1.00=25,000)
GNI PER CAPITA: US$5,510, Intl$10,310 at PPP ('13)

ECUADOR finished 2014 with the collapse in global oil prices threatening the country's near-term fiscal stability. At the end of December, a new tax law came into effect. It had previously been rushed through the National Assembly as a matter of urgency, introducing new measures to boost the tax yield and to reduce evasion. The legislation also contained provision to boost investment in non-oil sectors of the economy. The budget for 2015 had been passed by the Assembly in November 2014 and was predicated on an oil price of just under $80 per barrel; at the end of the year, the oil price had fallen below $60 per barrel.

A prolonged reduction in international oil prices therefore threatened to hit the Ecuadorean Treasury hard, and further measures would probably be needed to raise taxes further, cut government spending and to seek to raise other non-tax revenues. As 2014 ended, President Rafael Correa Delgado was about to make a state visit to Beijing, which he would use to secure further Chinese funding and offers of investment in Ecuador. However, if—as seemed likely—Ecuador's public finances underwent further deterioration as 2015 advanced, it would become more difficult—and more expensive—to secure international funding. Ecuador's credit rating, like that of Venezuela, seemed likely to be downgraded.

The year 2014 began with local elections that underlined some fragilities in the political foundations of the Correa administration. The ruling PAIS Alliance (AP) party lost in some key constituencies, following its strong performance in the 2013 general election, which not only saw Correa returned for a third term but AP winning a large majority of seats in the Assembly. In Quito, the capital, AP's candidate, the incumbent mayor Augusto Barrera Guaderas, went down to an embarrassing defeat to Maurico Rodas Espinel, a centrist opposition leader. In Guayaquil, the country's largest city and principal port, the mayoral contest was won by the incumbent Jaime Nebot Saadi. Nebot was a right-winger who had run unsuccessfully for the presidency on several occasions for the Social Christian Party (PSC) and had been a vociferous and assertive critic of Correa. AP was also beaten in Ecuador's third largest city, Cuenca. However, in smaller cities AP fared better, as it did in retaining control over the majority of provincial prefectures.

The reverse in Quito was particularly galling for Correa. Whereas Nebot's victory in Guayaquil was widely foreseen, this was not the case of Rodas. Correa had enthusiastically campaigned for Barrera and Barrera was expected to win. Following their defeat in the 2013 general election, opposition politicians had concentrated their efforts more on winning at the local level where support for AP was more patchy and where Correa's popularity was less of a factor.

The election reverses prompted Correa to promise an overhaul of his party's organisation, and shortly after the results were announced he made some significant changes in his Cabinet. Aware of these potential challenges to his power, Correa also signalled his intention to amend the 2008 constitution so as to enable him to seek a further term of office when his current term expired in 2017. To this end, in June the government submitted a package of constitutional reforms to the Constitutional Court. At the end of October, the Court issued its verdict, approving the move and the method by which the proposed changes would be made. Amendments to the constitution would require two votes by the National Assembly, at least 12 months apart, with two-thirds of the Assembly voting in favour.

While the government's policies towards business and the media were a significant element in the offensive from the Right, it was its policies on extractive industries that had brought differences on the Left. Correa's policies to encourage extractive investment had estranged him from parties on the Left, especially those that favoured the extension of indigenous rights. Emblematic was the president's decision in August 2013 to abort the Yasuni-ITT project, a scheme to attract foreign finance in order for Ecuador not to proceed with an oil exploration scheme in the environmentally-sensitive Yasuni national park in the Amazon jungle. The Ishpingo-Tambococha-Tiputini field, located in the rainforest close to Ecuador's eastern frontier, represented 20 per cent of the country's proven oil reserves. In February 2014, at the height of the local election campaign, it was revealed that the government had held secret discussions with Chinese officials on access to the Yasuni-ITT reserves in exchange for a $1 billion loan.

At the same time, the Correa government had continued to push ahead with attracting investment in developing the country's mining potential. Notwithstanding changes in 2013 to the country's mining legislation designed to attract investment, the response in 2014 proved disappointing. As with the oil industry, interest came mainly from Chinese companies who appeared less sensitive than those from other countries to short-term downward movements in prices for copper and gold. A major reason for investor caution was the fear of disruption from local communities opposed to extractive activities on their land. A particular bone of contention was the use of water supplies. A new water law was passed in June 2014, aiming to put control over water into the hands of central government.

John Crabtree

COLOMBIA

CAPITAL: Santa Fe de Bogotá   AREA: 1,141,750 sq km   POPULATION: 48,321,405 ('13)
OFFICIAL LANGUAGE: Spanish
HEAD OF STATE AND GOVERNMENT: President Juan Manuel Santos (UP) (since Aug '10)
RULING PARTY: Party of the "U" (UP)
DEMOCRACY INDEX: 6.55; 59th of 167   CORRUPTION PERCEPTIONS INDEX: 37; =94th of 175
CURRENCY: Colombian Peso (Dec '14 £1.00=COP 3,698, US$1.00=COP 2,381)
GNI PER CAPITA: US$7,560, Intl$11,890 at PPP ('13)

WHILE the main regional headlines of 2014 may have been the apparent shift in US-Cuba relations, announced in December, an equally significant development coming out of Havana was the ongoing peace talks between the Colombian government and the leftist Revolutionary Armed Forces of Colombia (FARC) rebels. The landmark attempts, initiated in 2012, to bring half-a-century of divisive civil conflict to an end continued to dominate the Colombian political landscape throughout the year, yet on several occasions the entire process appeared to be in mortal peril.

The first significant threat came during the lead up to elections held in May and June. President Juan Manuel Santos, one of the driving forces behind the peace talks, was seeking re-election but was faced with mediocre approval ratings and some outspoken political opposition, most notably from his predecessor and former ally, Álvaro Uribe. The former president, vehemently opposed to the negotiations in Havana and an advocate of defeating FARC militarily, had formed a new political party, Democratic Centre (CD), which he would go on to lead in the Senate, the first time in modern Colombian history that a former president had returned to parliamentary politics.

Uribe's protégé, Óscar Iván Zuluaga, was selected to run as CD's presidential nominee, in a contest that Santos presented as a plebiscite on the ongoing peace process. Combined with the wide range of candidates on offer to the electorate—various opinion polls suggested as many as five were in with a chance of winning at some point during the election campaign—the overhanging question of a peace process supported by barely half the population led to one of the closest and most unpredictable electoral contests in living memory.

Zuluaga won the 25 May first round with 29 per cent, ahead of Santos on 26 per cent, but with no candidate obtaining an overall majority the contest was forced to a second round on 15 June. For a while it seemed that Zuluaga and Uribe's strategy to tap into public wariness of the government's "softer" approach towards FARC would result in an electoral victory, spelling the end of Santos's presidency and, far more importantly, the peace process itself. In the event, however, members and supporters of the more liberal and left-leaning parties agreed to hold their noses and lend Santos their support for the second round, having considered that the need to keep the peace process alive was of greater concern than their opposition to Santos and his record in power. Ultimately, Santos triumphed in the second round with 51 per cent of the vote, six points ahead of Zuluaga.

Santos's win ensured that the negotiations with the FARC rebels could carry on, and the government continued to voice its satisfaction with the progress being made in Havana, even if things did appear to be moving more slowly than had been initially hoped. After two points of agreement between the government and FARC—on agrarian reform and political participation—had been reached during the previous year, 2014 saw just one further provisional deal. In May, the rebels agreed that they would cut ties with the illegal drugs trade, a key factor given the revenue that this industry had historically provided for the guerrillas.

However, in spite of both parties' commitment to the peace process, on the frontline the fighting continued throughout 2014, with numerous killings on both sides and a further 100,000 people added to the ranks of Colombia's internally displaced population. Furthermore, in November the peace process faced perhaps its gravest threat yet, when it emerged that a senior army general, Rubén Darío Alzate, had been captured by FARC soldiers in a remote western Colombian jungle. Santos immediately announced the suspension of the Havana negotiations, but following several weeks of tense mediation, the rebels agreed to release Alzate, thereby allowing the peace talks to resume once again.

In December FARC surprised many by announcing an indefinite, unilateral ceasefire. While the Santos administration declined the rebels' invitation to follow suit and make the ceasefire a bilateral one, it was hoped that FARC's willingness to lay down their weapons would bode well for the future of the peace talks as they headed into the new year.

Elsewhere, the economy remained among the most robust in the Americas, with GDP growth expected to be near 5 per cent and inflation at 3.6 per cent. Looking ahead, the economy was expected to slow slightly through 2015, due in part to the global fall in the price of oil, which accounted for some 6 per cent of Colombia's GDP and 16 per cent of tax receipts.

Vast swathes of the country were blighted by a devastating drought throughout the summer, with hundreds of municipalities hit by severe water shortages, affecting hundreds of thousands of citizens. The effects were most painfully felt in rural areas, where farmers saw their cattle herds decimated as water sources dried up, but the impact in urban areas was significant enough to trigger riots in protest at the authorities' perceived slow response to the crisis.

Yet for many Colombians, 2014 would be remembered as the year in which they lost their national hero. Gabriel García Márquez, the critically acclaimed author of *One Hundred Years of Solitude,* among many other works of literature, died in his adopted home of Mexico City on 17 April, at the age of 87 (see Obituary). His death sparked a wave of mourning both throughout Colombia and across Latin America, and prompted President Santos to declare: "One Hundred Years of Solitude and sadness for the death of the greatest Colombian of all time".

Giles Constantine

VENEZUELA

CAPITAL: Caracas   AREA: 912,050 sq km   POPULATION: 30,405,207 ('13)
OFFICIAL LANGUAGE: Spanish
HEAD OF STATE AND GOVERNMENT: President Nicolas Maduro (PSUV) (since April '13)
RULING PARTY: United Socialist Party of Venezuela (PSUV)
DEMOCRACY INDEX: 5.07; 97th of 167   CORRUPTION PERCEPTIONS INDEX: 19; =161st of 175
CURRENCY: Bolívar Fuerte (Dec '14 £1.00=VEF 18.64, US$1.00=VEF 12.00)
GNI PER CAPITA: US$12,550, Intl$17,890 at PPP ('13)

IT was another difficult year for Venezuela. Nicolás Maduro Moro, hand-picked successor to the late president, Hugo Rafael Chávez Frías, who died in 2013, was unable to command the same popular loyalty. Lacking El Comandante's charisma, stage presence and revolutionary credentials, President Maduro faced severe challenges to his government, most notably during protests that engulfed the country from February to June, in which 43 people died.

The protests began at the start of February in the western states of Mérida and Táchira after students demanded better security measures following the alleged attempted rape of a classmate. Demonstrations in Táchira also called for action against soaring inflation and shortages of daily essentials such as toilet paper and flour. After the arrest of dissenters, other universities demanded their release, and national opposition leaders Leopoldo López Mendoza and María Corina Machado Parisca called on Venezuelans to march for the resignation of President Maduro. López, who was descended from Latin American independence hero Simón Bolívar, was arrested on 18 February for insurrection and remained in custody at the end of the year.

In March, María Machado was stripped of her parliamentary immunity after addressing the Organisation of American States (OAS) on the subject of the protests as a guest of the Panamanian delegation. The same month, three Air Force generals were arrested for plotting uprisings against the government. In December, Venezuela's chief prosecutor Luisa Ortega Díaz announced a formal investigation of Machado on the charge of plotting the assassination of President Maduro. The prosecutors affirmed that an email thread demonstrated Machado's intentions. She claimed that the emails were forgeries and the charges part of the regime's plan to distract Venezuelans from the country's manifold problems.

The first anniversary of the death of Chávez on 5 March was marked with a military parade. The same day, Venezuela broke diplomatic relations with Panama over the Machado incident at the OAS. From April, the possibility that the Vatican might broker negotiations in the political dispute was mooted, but the ruling United Socialist Party of Venezuela (PSUV) did not countenance the proposal. To tackle the issues of crime and insecurity, which undergirded some of the opposition's grievances, President Maduro launched a $47 million plan in September to disarm civilians, and a $39 million package to put soldiers on the streets of the most dangerous areas. In December, the USA announced sanctions against Venezuelan officials responsible for alleged violence or human rights violations towards the anti-government protestors. However, supporters of the PSUV marched in Caracas to denounce the move.

It was a quieter year for one of the men of 2013, the narrowly defeated candidate in the presidential elections, Henrique Capriles Radonski (see AR 2013, pp. 163-64). This was mainly because the opposition became fractured and his star waned compared to that of López. Capriles, formerly the unchallenged leader of the opposition, was unable to reunite the anti-government factions. Whereas many of his former allies decided that Venezuela could not wait for the next presidential election to force change, Capriles reaffirmed that he believed in the democratic process as the foundation for legitimate governance. He clashed publically with López, and refused to support the demonstrations. In an interview with the Al Jazeera television station in August, Capriles claimed the protests had "given Nicolás [Maduro] oxygen" and that the attempt to force his resignation was "a disaster". The next key electoral test of Venezuela's future would come in the 2015 congressional elections.

In October, Venezuela mourned the death of Robert Serra, a talented young orator (aged just 27) and a high-flyer in the PSUV, who was killed in Caracas. President Maduro also maintained that attempts on the life of Diosdado Cabello Rondón, president of the National Assembly, had been foiled. Jesús Torrealba was named the new leader of the opposition coalition, the Table of Democratic Unity (MUD), with a plan to challenge the Chavista stronghold in poor neighbourhoods.

Venezuela was elected in October to a seat on the UN Security Council, but a month later the UN's committee against torture expressed "alarm in the light of reports that describe high levels of violence in penitentiary centres".

The economy suffered from the collapse in the global oil price, and it was reported on the bond market in December that Venezuela was looking to sell to the US investment bank, Goldman Sachs, debts owed to it by the Dominican Republic and Jamaica, in order to prevent a default. Then, on 30 December, President Maduro announced that the economy had been in recession throughout 2014.

Venezuela's culture of classical music continued to thrive. The world-famous El Sistema model of music education had another strong year. Children from Sistema Scotland performed at the Commonwealth Games opening ceremony in Glasgow in July. It was also the year in which El Sistema's best-known graduate, the conductor Gustavo Dudamel, tried his hand at composing, penning the soundtrack for Venezuela's 2015 Academy Award contender, *Libertador*, a biopic of Simón Bolívar.

Daniel Rey

V MIDDLE EAST AND NORTH AFRICA

ISRAEL

CAPITAL: Jerusalem   AREA: 22,070 sq km   POPULATION: 8,059,400 ('13)
OFFICIAL LANGUAGE: Hebrew
HEAD OF STATE: President Reuben Riblin (since July '14)
RULING PARTIES: Likud-led coalition
HEAD OF GOVERNMENT: Binyamin Netanyahu (Likud) (since March '09)
DEMOCRACY INDEX: 7.53; 39th of 167   CORRUPTION PERCEPTIONS INDEX: 60; =37th of 175
CURRENCY: Shekel (Dec '14 £1.00=ILS 6.06, US$1.00=ILS 3.91)
GNI PER CAPITA: US$34,120, Intl$32,140 at PPP ('13)

HAVING largely insulated itself from the effects of the upheavals around the Arab world since 2011, Israel became more directly involved in the regional conflict in 2014, as the collapse of peace talks with the Palestinians was swiftly followed by a renewed military confrontation with Hamas, the Palestinian group in control of the Gaza Strip. This conflict left more than 2,000 Palestinians dead, the majority of them civilians, and 67 Israeli soldiers and six civilians were also killed. Israel faced harsh international criticism for the way it conducted the war, and the erosion of its global support was reflected in a UN Security Council motion at the end of the year that only narrowly failed to enshrine a deadline for the creation of a Palestinian state. The stresses of the war and its aftermath also contributed to the break-up of the governing coalition, triggering an early general election, to be held in March 2015.

For the first four months of 2014 the Israeli prime minister, Binyamin Netanyahu, was preoccupied with the peace negotiations with the Palestine Liberation Organisation (PLO) that had been launched in July 2013 at the initiative of John Kerry, the US secretary of state. The aim was to reach an agreement by the end of April on a framework for negotiations about a comprehensive settlement, including the establishment of a Palestinian state. The talks had been based on a pledge by Israel to release 104 long-term Palestinian prisoners and to limit the construction of new homes in settlements, in return for a pledge by the Palestinians to desist from seeking membership of UN organisations in the name of state of Palestine. The talks triggered a crisis within the Israeli governing coalition in January when Naftali Bennett, leader of The Jewish Home party, accused Netanyahu of being willing to place Jewish lives at risk by suggesting that Jewish settlers could continue to live in the West Bank under the sovereignty of a Palestinian state. The coalition survived after Bennett made a partial apology, in the face of a threat by Netanyahu to drop The Jewish Home and open negotiations with the Labour party.

Over the next three months the talks made some progress on the questions of dealing with Palestinian refugees after a peace settlement and on defining the borders of the Palestinian state, which would be based on the pre-June 1967 lines, with some territorial swaps. However, big gaps remained, and the process reached a crisis point in April after Israel refused to release the final tranche of prisoners, and the Israeli government approved the construction of hundreds of new homes for Israelis in East Jerusalem. Kerry made strenuous, but ultimately vain, efforts to secure agreement on an extension to the talks. For Israel the last straw was the announcement on 23 April that Fatah, the party of the Palestinian president, Mahmoud Abbas, had agreed with Hamas, the Islamist group in control of Gaza (and not party to the peace talks), on the formation of a unified Palestinian government. Netanyahu declared that the peace negotiations could not continue as long as Hamas, defined by Israel as a terrorist organisation, was involved in the government of the Palestinian Authority.

Just six weeks after the breakdown of peace talks, a serious incident in the West Bank sparked off a chain of events leading to the outbreak of a fresh military conflict between Israel and the Palestinians in the Gaza Strip. On 12 June three Israeli teenagers—Naftali Fraenkel, Gilad Shaer and Eyal Yifrah—were kidnapped at a bus stop/hitchhiking station on a road reserved for Israeli settlers at Gush Etzion, south of Bethlehem. Israel blamed Hamas for the abductions, and deployed hundreds of troops to the area between Bethlehem and Hebron to search for the missing teenagers and their abductors. In the course of this operation Israel detained more than 300 people, including dozens of activists who had been released as part of a 2011 deal between Israel and Hamas that secured the release from Gaza of Gilad Shalit, an Israeli soldier captured five years earlier. Five Palestinians were killed during these operations. The corpses of the three teenagers were discovered on 30 June; they had apparently been shot dead shortly after their abduction. Israel identified a cell of three Palestinians with Hamas affiliation as having been responsible for abducting and killing the teenagers. One of the Palestinians was arrested and the other two were killed when confronted by Israeli soldiers in September.

Tensions increased rapidly in early July. In Jerusalem a group of Israelis abducted a 16-year old Palestinian boy and burned him to death, prompting angry protests by Palestinians in the West Bank. In Gaza, Hamas declared that Israel had violated the November 2012 ceasefire through its operations in the West Bank, and several rockets were fired at Israel from the Palestinian territory. Israel responded with air raids, which provoked further rocket fire. On 8 July Israel launched Operation Protective Edge, with the stated aim of stopping rockets being launched from the Gaza Strip. The operation started with sustained heavy bombardments by air, land and sea, and with the deployment of the newly developed Iron Dome systems to intercept and destroy Palestinian rockets in flight.

One week after the conflict started, Egypt submitted a ceasefire proposal to both sides, entailing a temporary truce to be followed by negotiations in Cairo about conditions for a long-term halt to the fighting. The Israeli cabinet approved the plan, but Hamas rejected it, and stated that it would continue to press for a lifting of the blockade on Gaza and the release of the prisoners detained by Israel in the West Bank in June. The conflict resumed on 17 July, and six days later Israel pushed ground forces into the Gaza Strip. At this point in the conflict Netanyahu enjoyed an approval rating of 82 per cent among the Israeli public.

However, during the ground incursion the casualty toll among both Palestinians and Israeli troops mounted rapidly. The Israeli army and intelligence services came under criticism in the domestic media for having apparently underestimated the extent of the tunnel network built by Hamas beneath the Gaza Strip and within neighbouring Israeli territory. By early August, Israel claimed to have found and destroyed 32 tunnels, and started to withdraw its ground forces. On 10 August Egypt presented a modified version of its earlier ceasefire, and on 26 August the fighting stopped. By this time, Netanyahu's approval rating had fallen to 38 per cent, as more than half of Israelis that were canvassed expressed dissatisfaction with his performance. The Israeli public's concerns related mainly to the failure of the armed forces to eliminate Hamas militarily and to the loss of life among Israeli troops. There was heavy criticism of Israel abroad because of the high level of civilian casualties, including more than 400 children killed, and the extent of the damage inflicted on Gaza's infrastructure, with an estimated 100,000 homes destroyed.

The 50-day conflict had a modest impact on the Israeli economy. The number of tourists visiting Israel declined only slightly in the full year, compared with 2013, but that was mainly thanks to an 8 per cent increase in visitors in the first half of the year, with numbers falling off badly in the third quarter. Real GDP growth was 2.5 per cent in 2014, compared with 3.3 per cent the previous year, and the slowdown could partly be ascribed to the Gaza conflict.

The main focus of Israeli politics turned inwards in the latter part of the year. One of the central issues was a proposed bill on the definition of the Israeli nation state. On 19 November the cabinet reached a decision to support the preliminary reading in the Knesset (parliament) of two versions of the bill, which was aimed at resolving questions arising from the absence of a formal written constitution. The proposals attracted controversy as they appeared to elevate the definition of Israel as a Jewish state above that of it being a democracy, thereby undermining the rights of the substantial Arab minorities. The bill also touched on the sensitive area of the relative powers of the legislature and the judiciary, which many politicians argued were tilted too much in favour of the latter. Differences within the government over the bill contributed to the break-up of the coalition. On 2 December Netanyahu announced the dismissal of Tzipi Livni, the justice minister, and Yair Lapid, the finance minister, accusing them of conspiring against him. Livni had made clear that she had differences with the prime minister over the nation state bill, and Lapid had opposed proposals for tax-breaks for first-time home buyers. The departure of the two ministers left the government without a majority in the Knesset, forcing an early election. The coalition had lasted for only 18 months.

Another critical decision at the end of 2014 was a ruling issued on 23 December by the Antitrust Authority reversing its earlier consent to Noble Energy of the US and the local Delek Energy group to control the Leviathan gas field without being defined as a cartel. Noble and Delek were the lead investors in the Tamar gas field off the coast of Haifa, which had started production in 2013, and whose output averaged about 750 million cubic feet per day in 2014, almost sufficient to cover Israel's entire domestic demand. Leviathan was a bigger field lying to the west of Tamar, and which Noble and Delek, the largest shareholders, were aiming to bring on stream in 2017 or 2018. Tamar and Leviathan together had the potential to produce far more gas than could be absorbed in the Israeli market, and the partners had discussed selling the surplus to Jordan and Egypt.

David Butter

PALESTINE

CAPITAL: Ramallah / East Jerusalem   AREA: (West Bank & Gaza) 6,020 sq km   POPULATION:
    4,169,506 ('13)
OFFICIAL LANGUAGE: Arabic
HEAD OF STATE: President of the Palestine National Authority Mahmoud Abbas (Fatah) (since Jan '05)
RULING PARTIES: Hamas (in Gaza); Fatah (in West Bank)
HEAD OF GOVERNMENT: Prime Minister Rami Hamdallah (Fatah) (since June '13)
DEMOCRACY INDEX: 4.80; 103rd of 167
CURRENCY: Jordanian Dinar (Dec '14 £1.00=JOD 1.17, US$1.00=JOD 0.71) and Israeli Shekel
    (Dec '14 £1.00=ILS 6.06, US$1.00=ILS 3.91)
GNI PER CAPITA: US$2,810, Intl$4,900 at PPP ('12)

THE Palestinians underwent an eventful and traumatic year, with the breakdown of US-mediated peace negotiations with Israel, the formation of a unity government and a devastating, month-long, conflict in Gaza that left more than 2,000 people dead, the majority of them Palestinian civilians. Growing international support for Palestinian aspirations was manifested in the increase in the number of countries formally recognising Palestine as a state.

At the start of 2014 the Palestine Liberation Organisation (PLO) and the Israeli government were deeply engaged in peace talks that had been launched the previous July by US Secretary of State John Kerry. The talks were supposed to culminate at the end of April in an agreement on a framework for negotiations about a comprehensive settlement. The main issues for discussion were: the borders of a Palestinian state, to be based on the lines before the 1967 war, with mutually agreed territorial swaps; security arrangements, including limitations on the military capabilities of the Palestinian state; the sharing of Jerusalem between the Israeli and Palestinian states; and setting limits on the right of Palestinian refugees to return to their families' former homes in what was now Israel. The talks were underpinned by assurances from Israel that it would release 104 long-term Palestinian prisoners and that it would limit the construction of new homes in settlements, and from the Palestinians that they would not seek further membership in UN agencies.

By the start of 2014 it had become clear that the negotiators were struggling to make progress. US proposals on security arrangements in the West Bank had been received positively by both negotiating teams, and the Israeli prime minister, Binyamin Netanyahu, had accepted them as a basis for further discussion. However, Netanyahu faced stiff opposition from hardline members of his cabinet, including the defence minister, Moshe Yaalon, who was quoted as making scathing remarks about Kerry. Another hardline critic was Naftali Bennett, the leader of The Jewish Home party and the minister of the economy, who attacked an implicit suggestion by Netanyahu that Jewish settlers could live under Palestinian rule in a West Bank state.

The Palestinian president, Mahmoud Abbas, and his negotiating team, led by Saeb Erakat, complained that the US had devoted too much effort to accommodating Netanyahu's concerns, and that on issue after issue, the Palestinians were being pushed to make compromises without anything of substance in return. The process reached breaking point during March when Israel stalled on the release of the final batch of 26 prisoners, and on 1 April Abbas announced that Palestine (recognised as an observer state by the UN General Assembly in 2012) would be submitting applications to join 15 UN organisations and conventions. Over the next three weeks the US made strenuous efforts to get agreement from the Israelis and Palestinians on a nine-month extension to the negotiations. However, at the same time Abbas had been engaged in talks with Hamas, the Islamist movement that controlled the Gaza Strip, on setting up a unity government. An agreement to start formal talks on the formation of this government between Abbas's Fatah movement and Hamas was announced on 23 April, which prompted Netanyahu to declare the peace negotiations over, on the grounds that Israel classified Hamas to be a terrorist organisation.

Abbas maintained that the reconciliation with Hamas was not sufficient grounds for abandoning peace negotiations, since it was an internal Palestinian affair and the talks were being conducted by the PLO in its guise as a sovereign Palestinian representative. Moreover, the government, whose formation was announced on 2 June, did not include any Hamas members, and declared its adherence to the three criteria set for the provision of Western aid: non-violence; commitment to upholding previous peace agreements; and recognition of Israel. The government was headed by Rami Hamdallah, a Fatah member who had been prime minister of the previous Palestinian Authority (PA) government in the West Bank. The government was mandated to serve for six months, and to oversee the election of a new parliament that would form the basis of a permanent government.

The main interest of Hamas in giving its blessing to the unity government was that it would provide an opportunity to secure more resources from the PA and international donors for the Gaza Strip. Since being expelled from Gaza in 2007, the PA had continued to pay about 65,000 civil servants who remained in the territory, whether they went to work or not. Hamas had engaged about 40,000 people on its own payroll to run its administration in Gaza, and had financed these operations through its own regional and international funding networks and through taxing the extensive trade through tunnels into northern Sinai in Egypt. The army's removal of Mohammed Morsi as president of Egypt in July 2013 had been a severe blow to Hamas, which had enjoyed warm relations with the Muslim Brotherhood-led administration. The new regime in Egypt closed down much of the tunnel trade, which in turn inhibited flows of funds and weapons from Hamas's regional allies. Hamas had pinned hopes on the unity government being able to take over responsibility for paying the 40,000 civil servants that Hamas had hired, but was no longer able to pay itself. However, it quickly became clear that the new government was unwilling to approve such payments through its systems, as it would expose it to sanctions based on the US and EU designation of Hamas as a terrorist organisation.

Within weeks of the breakdown of the peace negotiations and the formation of the new government, the Palestinians and the Israelis had become embroiled in another bloody military confrontation. The first major violent incident was the kidnapping and subsequent murder of three Israeli teenage hitchhikers in the Hebron area of the West Bank on 12 June. Israel blamed the incident on Hamas, and sent hundreds of troops into the area to search for the missing teenagers and hunt down the perpetrators. Hundreds of Palestinians were arrested, and troops destroyed the homes of the Palestinians who Israel claimed to have carried out the kidnapping. Five Palestinians were killed during the army-led operation. Hamas denied the Israeli accusations that it was behind the abduction. In early August Israel said that it had arrested Hussam Qawasmeh, a Hamas member, who had confessed to organising the kidnapping. The funds for the operation were purportedly raised in Gaza by his brother, Marwan Qawasmeh, but Israel did not furnish conclusive evidence that the Hamas leadership in Gaza or outside the Palestinian territories had been involved in the incident. Khaled Meshaal, the Qatar-based head of the Hamas political bureau, said in an interview with *Vanity Fair* magazine in September that it had emerged that the kidnapping was carried out by a "Hamas field group in the West Bank", but he insisted that they had not been following any specific instructions. The dead bodies of the three teenagers were discovered on 30 June.

Hamas deemed the Israeli military operations in the Hebron area to be a violation of the previous Gaza ceasefire agreement that had been reached in November 2012. A number of rockets were fired from Gaza into Israel, to which Israel responded with air strikes. Tensions were further inflamed on 2 July when Mohammed Khudair, a 16-year old Palestinian was abducted by a group of Israelis from east Jerusalem and burned to death.

On 8 July Israel declared that it had launched Operation Protective Edge with the aim of stopping rocket fire from the Gaza Strip. The previous day Hamas had fired about 40 rockets into Israel after seven of its members were killed in an explosion in a tunnel in Khan Younis, which the Palestinian group blamed on an Israeli air strike. Hamas had previously sought to reinstate the November 2012 ceasefire, on condition that Israel release those detained during the sweep through the Hebron area. After one week of heavy Israeli bombardments of the Gaza Strip, and Hamas rocket fire from the territory, Egypt on 14 July announced a plan to halt the hostilities. The proposal would entail a temporary truce, to be followed by negotiations in Cairo between Israel and all Palestinian factions about a long-term ceasefire. By this stage in the conflict about 200 Palestinians and one Israeli has been killed. The Israeli cabinet approved the plan, and Netanyahu ordered a pause in his forces' operations. Hamas stated that the plan was unacceptable as it did not meet its demand for a lifting of the Israel and Egyptian blockades on Gaza and for the release of the recently detained West Bank prisoners. The conflict resumed, and on 17 July Israel pushed ground forces into Gaza for the first time since the end-2008 conflict.

The ground incursion led to an intensification of the violence as Israel targeted districts that it claimed to contain the entrances to a network of tunnels built by Hamas to protect its military forces. Several of these concrete-lined tunnels stretched into Israeli territory and were used by Hamas to conduct raids behind the Israeli front lines. The Israeli assaults on areas such as Shujaiya, in the eastern part of Gaza City, caused massive destruction and led to tens of thousands of people being displaced. The UN Relief and Works Agency (UNRWA), which provided humanitarian aid and services to the 1.2 million registered refugees in Gaza, said that by the end of the conflict it was housing almost 300,000 people in its schools around Gaza.

The conflict continued at an intense level for the next two weeks, punctuated by a few brief UN-proposed ceasefires to allow humanitarian aid into Gaza. By early August, Israel claimed to have identified and destroyed 32 Hamas tunnels, and it started to pull its grounds forces out of Gaza. Egypt submitted a new version of its ceasefire proposal on 10 August, and after a number of false starts, a truce went into effect on 26 August.

The UN said that the conflict had resulted in the deaths of more than 2,110 Palestinians in Gaza, including almost 1,500 civilians, of whom almost one-third were children. More than 100,000 homes were destroyed or severely damaged. In the course of the conflict Hamas fired an estimated 4,000 missiles into Israel. A large number of these were intercepted by the newly deployed Iron Dome defence systems. Six Israeli civilians were killed during the conflict. Israeli military casualties were considerably higher than in previous engagements with Hamas and its allies in Gaza: 67 Israeli soldiers were killed.

The conflict yielded few advantages to either side. Engaging in another destructive round of fighting with Israel had been one of the options for Hamas to tackle the crisis that it faced as a result of the hardening of Egypt's position towards it, but the group's political leaders had appeared to favour the route of reconciliation with Abbas, even if that meant, in effect, acquiescing to the PLO-led peace negotiations with Israel and allowing the return of some Palestinian Authority security personnel to Gaza. The escalation triggered by the West Bank kidnapping of the three Israelis pushed Hamas back to the war option. The group insisted that any new ceasefire must include a lifting of the blockade, and the establishment of a new airport and sea port in Gaza. These demands were not met. The open-ended ceasefire merely allowed for the entry into Gaza of humanitarian aid and construction materials—the latter subject to restrictions supposed to prevent the rebuilding of tunnels—and an extension of the fishing zone off Gaza to six miles. The way was also cleared for payments to reach civil servants appointed by the Hamas government, but this was a one-off deal financed by Qatar, and the employees were not formally integrated in the PA payroll. In military terms, Hamas showed that it was capable of inflicting heavier costs on Israel than in previous rounds of fighting, both through the extended range of its rockets, some of which reached as far as the outskirts of Haifa, and through the relatively high casualty toll suffered by the Israeli army. Netanyahu enjoyed soaring approval ratings in the early stages of the conflict, but these tailed off as it became clear that Israel was not going to eliminate the Hamas military theat. The army and the government were also criticised for their failure to recognise the extent of the Hamas tunnel infrastructure.

The Palestinian unity government continued to exist in a formal sense until the end of 2014, although it made little progress in its stated aim of organising elections, and it faced mounting criticism from Hamas for its inability to ease the blockade on Gaza. Abbas focused his efforts on international diplomacy, seeking to make use of the growing number of countries recognising Palestine as a state in order to put pressure on Israel to make concessions. Sweden in October became the first European Union member state to recognise Palestine as a state, taking the total number of countries which had taken this step to 135.

On 29 December, Jordan presented to the UN Security Council, on behalf of the PLO, a resolution calling for a peace agreement with Israel within one year, an end to the Israeli occupation of Palestinian territories by 2017, and the establishment of a Palestinian state within three years. The resolution failed to receive the minimum of nine votes required for its adoption, although eight countries, including France, Russia and China voted in favour. The USA and Australia voted against the resolution, and the remaining five members abstained.

Abbas reacted to the failure of the resolution by proceeding to sign 18 international treaties and conventions in the name of the State of Palestine, the most controversial of which was the Rome Statute of the International Criminal Court, which could lead to the pursuit of war crimes suits against Israeli officials. The Palestinian president's action set the scene for intense future battles with Israel over the applicability of international law to the political conflict between the two sides.

David Butter

EGYPT

CAPITAL: Cairo   AREA: 1,001,450 sq km   POPULATION: 82,056,378 ('13)
OFFICIAL LANGUAGE: Arabic
HEAD OF STATE: Abdel Fattah el-Sisi (since June '14)
HEAD OF GOVERNMENT: Ibraham Mahlab (ind) (since March '14)
DEMOCRACY INDEX: 3.27; 135th of 167   CORRUPTION PERCEPTIONS INDEX: 37; =94th of 175
CURRENCY: Egyptian Pound (Dec '14 £1.00=EGP 11.10, US$1.00=EGP 7.15)
GNI PER CAPITA: US$3,160, Intl$10,850 at PPP ('13)

EGYPT's security institutions consolidated their dominance of the state during 2014, in pursuit of the objectives of restoring stability and establishing the basis for economic recovery, as laid out in the aftermath of the army's removal of Mohammed Morsi as president the previous July. The main political event of the year was the election of the former army commander, Abdel-Fattah Sisi, as the new president; the parliamentary election that had been supposed to take place was delayed for procedural reasons relating to redrawing of constituency boundaries. The police and the army harshly repressed most forms of dissent, whether expressed through violence by radical Islamists based in Sinai, or manifested in peaceful forms of protest by supporters of the Muslim Brotherhood, or by activists involved in the movement that had forced Hosni Mubarak out of power in February 2011. The judiciary played an important part in supporting this suppression, as judges delivered harsh sentences against purported opponents of the state, while Mubarak and a number of businessmen accused of corruption won reprieves.

The first significant political measure taken after the passage of a revised constitution at the end of 2013 was a decree issued by the interim president, Adly Mansour, on 26 January stating that the presidential election would take place before the election of a new parliament. The plan for political transition announced by Sisi in July 2013 had implied that the parliamentary election would come first. This was confirmed in early drafts of the constitution, but the final text stated that the interim president would have discretion over the sequence. The elected president would have power to legislate by decree; all these measures would have to be reviewed by the new legislature, but within 15 days of its being inaugurated.

Before the date for the presidential election was set, there was a change of government, amid growing signs of popular discontent with the Cabinet formed after the army's removal of Morsi. At the end of January, Ziad Bahaa el-Din resigned as deputy prime minister for economic affairs, stating that he had decided to focus on political activities—he was a founding member of the Egyptian Social Democratic Party, and the new constitution did not allow members of parliament to serve in the executive. Bahaa el-Din had also voiced his deep reservations about a law passed in November 2013 that had set strict limits on protests. The government also came under fire over its minimum wage policy, when it emerged that the increase from £E700 (about $100) to £E1,200 per month would only apply to direct employees of the state, and did not embrace workers for state-owned entities such as the post office and public transport companies. Hazem Beblawi resigned as prime minister on 24 February, and was replaced by Ibrahim Mahlab, the housing minister in the outgoing Cabinet. The new Cabinet, formed on 2 March, included Hany Kadri Dimian as finance minister, marking the reinstatement of part of a technocratic elite going back to the Mubarak period. Dimian had served as deputy finance minister between 2007 and early 2013, when he had resigned amid increasing Muslim Brotherhood intrusion into the ministry's affairs.

The Presidential Election Commission, made up of senior judicial figures, on 30 March announced the schedule and rules for the presidential contest. The first round was to take place on 26-27 May, and candidates were required to secure 25,000 endorsements from at least 15 governorates. Sisi had previously confirmed his intention to run by giving up his posts of defence minister and army commander on 26 March. He was replaced by Sedky Sobhi, who had been chief of staff of the armed forces. Given the near certainty that Sisi would win, potential rival candidates were thin on the ground, and his sole opponent was Hamdeen Sabahi, a Nasserist politician who had come fourth in the first round of the 2012 election, which was eventually won by Morsi. The Sisi campaign made clear that it wanted a big turnout to affirm the legitimacy of the process. Polling stations were only sparsely attended on the first two days of voting, and the electoral commission decided to extend the election by 24 hours. The result, announced on 3 June, showed that 25.6 million had taken part in the election, giving a turnout of 47.5 per cent. Sisi's share of the vote was 97 per cent, and he was sworn in as president on 8 June.

Sisi reappointed Mahlab as prime minister, whose few changes to the Cabinet included the restoration of the post of investment minister (Ashraf Salman, a former investment banker), and the selection of Sameh Shukri as foreign minister. One of the final acts of the outgoing interim president had been to approve a law for the election of the single-chamber parliament. This specified that 80 per cent of the 540 elected seats would be decided on a single constituency basis, and the remaining 20 per cent would come from party lists on a proportional basis. This law was insufficient for the election to take place, as the constitution required reorganisation of electoral districts in order to ensure fair representations. The electoral districts law was finally approved at the end of 2014, and the Higher Electoral Commission announced in January 2015 that the election would start on 21 March, with the final run-offs scheduled for 7 May.

Sisi was quick to make his mark on economic policy, by demanding that the deficit in the draft budget for the new financial year, which was to start on 1 July, be reduced from its proposed level of 12 per cent of gross domestic product (GDP). Dimian, the finance minister, had clearly anticipated such an instruction, and he came back with a new budget with a deficit of 10 per cent of GDP. The cuts would be achieved through increases in fuel and electricity prices, which would result in significant reductions in spending on energy subsidies. Prices of petrol, diesel, fuel oil, natural gas and electricity were raised, accordingly (although there was no increase in the price of bottled cooking gas), and Sisi was given credit by international commentators for having the political courage to take such a potentially unpopular decision. These commentators included the International Monetary Fund (IMF), which in November conducted its first formal in-country consultation with Egypt for four years. The government was likely to have been influenced by its main Gulf Arab allies, Saudi Arabia, the United Arab Emirates and Kuwait, which had provided more than $15 billion in aid to Egypt since the removal of Morsi. The actual budget deficit in 2013-14 was 12.8 per cent of GDP, but the tally included $13 billion in Gulf grants entered as revenue; without these grants, the deficit would have been 17 per cent of GDP. The government acknowledged that it could not depend on continuous budgetary support from the Gulf at this level.

As well as signalling its commitment to fiscal reforms, the government launched a drive to promote higher rates of economic growth through public and private investment. At the start of August, Sisi unveiled a scheme aiming to double the capacity of the Suez Canal through building a new, 76-km long, channel. The army engineering corps was entrusted with the management of the project, which attracted criticism for the apparent lack of proper feasibility studies. The canal expansion was linked to a longstanding scheme to create a new economic development zone along the waterway, for the contract to prepare a master plan was awarded to Dar al-Handasah, a well-known regional consultancy firm, in August. This project was to be one of the highlights of an international investment conference that the government planned to host in March 2015.

The government's efforts to attract new investment and to promote a recovery in tourism (following a sharp decline in visitor numbers since the violent events of July and August 2013) risked being compromised by the continued political tensions and periodic outbreaks of violence. During 2014 there were dozens of attacks on police and other security installations in Cairo and other major cities, although most of these were relatively small scale. The main security challenge to the state was in northern Sinai, the base of Ansar Beit al-Maqdis (ABM), a jihadist group including Bedouin tribesmen with grievances against the central state, alongside Islamist fighters from other parts of Egypt and the Arab world. The army stepped up its campaign against ABM during 2014, including the use of attack helicopters and advanced warplanes. On 24 October, 30 Egyptian servicemen were killed in an assault by ABM fighters on their positions outside El-Arish, the largest town in north Sinai. The government claimed that the fighters had made use of the Gaza Strip as a logistical base, and it proceeded to set up a buffer zone in Rafah, on the southern border of the Palestinian territory to counter these activities. More than 1,000 Egyptian families were evicted from their homes in order to make way for this zone.

The October attack in Sinai also prompted Sisi to issue a decree that would allow for civilians to be referred to military tribunals if suspected of attacking or planning to attack any state facility. By the end of 2014, more than 800 civilians had been referred to such tribunals, according to Human Rights Watch, a New York-based human rights agency. The new constitutions adopted in 2012 and 2014 banned the use of military tribunals for trying civilians, except in cases of direct attacks on military facilities. The October decree got round this by defining all state institutions and infrastructure as being part of Egypt's national security fabric.

The Egyptian legal system came under further scrutiny during 2014 as a result of a series of controversial verdicts. These included the issue of hundreds of death sentences by a judge in Minya, to the south of Cairo, to purported members of the Muslim Brotherhood for acts of violence committed in the area in August 2013. There was also heavy media coverage of the trial of three journalists working for the English-language channel of Al-Jazeera, the Qatar-based television station. The three men—Peter Greste, an Australian, Mohammed Fahmy, who held dual Canadian and Egyptian citizenship, and Baher Mohammed, an Egyptian—were convicted on 23 June of falsifying news and harming perceptions of Egypt. Greste and Fahmy were each sentenced to seven years in prison, while Mohammed received a 10-year sentence. Their appeal was upheld by the Court of Cassation on 1 January 2015, and a retrial was ordered, but their request for bail was denied.

David Butter

JORDAN

CAPITAL: Amman   AREA: 88,780 sq km   POPULATION: 6,459,000 ('13)
OFFICIAL LANGUAGE: Arabic
HEAD OF STATE: King Abdullah II ibn al-Husain (since Feb '99)
HEAD OF GOVERNMENT: Prime Minister Abdullah Ensour (since Oct '12)
DEMOCRACY INDEX: 3.76; =122nd of 167   CORRUPTION PERCEPTIONS INDEX: 49; =55th of 175
CURRENCY: Jordanian Dinar (Dec '14 £1.00=JOD 1.10, US$1.00=JOD 0.71)
GNI PER CAPITA: US$4,950, Intl$11,660 at PPP ('13)

JORDAN had to deal with the effects of crises in almost all of its regional neighbours in 2014, as the Syrian conflict ground on, producing a continuous stream of refugees over Jordan's northern border; the Palestinians and Israelis went to war again in Gaza; and much of western and northern Iraq fell under the sway of the extreme jihadist Islamic State in Iraq and Syria (ISIS). King Abdullah II focused on preserving domestic stability, in particular through restricting the activities of Islamist opponents of his rule. He also sought to maximise international and regional economic support for Jordan, on the basis of its strategic importance as an ally to the West. There were no notable domestic political changes during 2014, and Abdullah Ensour remained in his post as prime minister, having been reappointed after the parliamentary election of January 2013.

On 22 April, the lower house of parliament passed a law toughening the state's anti-terrorism measures. The legislation stated that people joining armed organisations or seeking to recruit others for that purpose would be subject to criminal prosecution. The measure was clearly aimed at tackling the issue of Jordanians joining armed groups in Syria, including extreme Islamist factions. The Muslim Brotherhood-affiliated Islamic Action Front attacked the law, claiming that it would be used to suppress activists calling for the overthrow of the regime of Syria's president Bashar Assad.

The offensive by ISIS in northern and western Iraq in June 2014 posed a grave security threat to Jordan. The area of ISIS control extended to the Iraqi-Jordanian border, and the group's success provided inspiration for Jordanian activists sharing its vision of reviving the Islamic Caliphate. Jordan joined the US-led alliance formed to confront the rebel advance, allowing its air bases to be used for Western air strikes, and playing an active role in some of those operations. On 24 December, a Jordanian pilot, Muaz Kasasbeh, was captured by ISIS forces in northern Syria after he had ejected from the F-16 aircraft that he was piloting on a mission against the group. The rebels claimed to have shot down the warplane, but the US military command said that the pilot had ejected after his aircraft suffered technical problems.

The authorities detained dozens of Islamist activists during 2014, but one of the most prominent Islamist figures, Abu Qatada, was released from jail in September after being found not guilty of terrorism offences. He had finally been extradited to Jordan from the UK in 2013 after a prolonged legal battle. Abu Qatada meanwhile, declared his strong opposition to ISIS and its claims of having recreated the Caliphate.

Jordan's peace treaty with Israel remained a focus of much opposition during 2014. One of the issues to arise during the year was the prospect of Jordan becoming a significant importer of natural gas from its neighbour. In February the partners in the Tamar gas field, which had started production off Haifa in 2013, signed an agreement to supply gas to two Jordanian companies, Arab Potash and Jordan Bromine, which operated industrial plants on the Dead Sea. The supplies were scheduled to start in 2016. The deal was relatively small, involving a total of 66 billion cubic feet over 15 years, valued at $500 million. In September, a much larger agreement was announced for the supply of 1.6 trillion cubic feet of gas over 15 years, worth an estimated $15 billion, from the yet-to-be-developed Leviathan field to Jordan's National Electric Power Company. However, that deal was thrown into question at the end of 2014 when Israel's antitrust regulator said that he would recommend the break-up of the consortium that owned the rights to Leviathan. Noble Energy of the US and Israel's Delek were the principal partners in both schemes.

During November, the Jordanian government formally protested to Israel about suspicions that the Israeli government was considering changes to the status of Islamic holy places in Jerusalem, over which Jordan exercised guardianship. On 5 November Jordan withdrew its ambassador to Israel in protest at in incursion by Israeli security forces into the al-Aqsa Mosque as a few hundred Jewish activists sought to assert their claim to be entitled to worship in the compound. According to the 1994 peace treaty between Jordan and Israel, Jews were permitted to visit the compound but not to worship there.

The growth in the number of UN-registered Syrian refugees in Jordan slowed in 2014, reaching 620,000 at the end of the year. During 2013 the number of refugees had increased fourfold to 576,000, as the conflict escalated in the south of the country and around Damascus. The Jordanian government denied reports that it had restricted the entry of Syrians during 2014. Jordan continued to receive considerable aid from the West and from Gulf Arab states to help the government to cope with the impact of the Syria crisis. According to the IMF, the government received budget grants totalling $1.36 billion, including $626 million from the USA, plus $1.8 billion in capital development grants from Gulf donors and $1.6 billion in loans. The economy registered real GDP growth of 3.1 per cent during the year.

David Butter

SYRIA

CAPITAL: Damascus   AREA: 185,180 sq km   POPULATION: 22,845,550 ('13)
OFFICIAL LANGUAGE: Arabic
HEAD OF STATE: President Bashar al-Assad (since July '00)
RULING PARTY: Ba'ath Party
HEAD OF GOVERNMENT: Wael Nader al-Halqi (since Aug '12)
DEMOCRACY INDEX: 1.86; 158th of 167   CORRUPTION PERCEPTIONS INDEX: 20; =159th of 175
CURRENCY: Syrian Pound (Dec '14 £1.00=SYP 287.5, US$1.00=SYP 179.3)
GNI PER CAPITA: US$2,610 ('10), Intl$5,120 at PPP ('12)

SYRIA underwent a fourth year of bitter conflict in 2014, resulting in tens of thousands more deaths and the displacement of several million more of the country's citizens. The regime of President Bashar Assad managed to hold on to much of the central and coastal region of the country, while the splits among rebel forces became deeper. One of the most significant developments was the advances made by the Islamic State in Iraq and Syria (ISIS), an extreme Islamist group with roots in Iraq. In June 2014 the group re-launched itself as the Islamic State (IS), and its Iraqi leader, Abu Bakr Baghdadi, proclaimed himself as the leader of a reborn Islamic Caliphate. The territory under ISIS control spread through much of northern Iraq, up the Euphrates valley to the Syrian border with Turkey. The rise of ISIS, and the threat that it posed to Western-allied governments in Baghdad and Iraqi Kurdistan, prompted the US to form an alliance with regional and European states to confront the group militarily, mainly through air strikes in Iraq, but also including attacks on ISIS positions in Syria. These air strikes played a critical role in enabling Syrian Kurdish forces to beat back an ISIS offensive against Kobane, but they had little impact on other fronts in the Syrian conflict.

At the start of 2014 international efforts to resolve the Syria conflict were focused on organising a conference in Geneva to be attended by representatives of both the regime and the opposition. The talks were to be conducted on the basis of an international agreement reached in Geneva in mid-2012 calling for the creation of a transitional governing body to run the country during negotiations about a long-term political settlement. The conference took place over two rounds—21-23 January and 10-15 February—in Montreux and Geneva. The National Coalition (NC) of Syrian opposition forces, a group made up mainly of political exiles, represented the opposition, while the regime delegation was led by Walid Muallim, the foreign minister. The NC prepared a 24-point statement of principles for the transitional body, which included a call for the removal of all external military forces and foreign fighters from Syria, the deployment of international ceasefire monitors, the distribution of humanitarian aid throughout the country and the preservation of civil state institutions. The regime delegation refused to look at this document, let alone present counter-proposals, and stuck to its position that the only issue to be discussed was how to confront terrorism. The conference broke up without any agreement, and in effect marked the end of any sort of purposeful international diplomatic engagement in political aspects of the Syrian conflict.

In the wake of Geneva 2, Lakhdar Brahimi declared his intention to step down in May from his position as United Nations special envoy on Syria. He was replaced in July by Staffan de Mistura, a Swedish-Italian diplomat with experience in Iraq and Afghanistan. De Mistura started his work in September, and focused on trying to build on the model of a number of local ceasefire negotiations in Homs and in some suburbs of Damascus. The most substantial of these truces had been reached in the Old City of Homs in February, and entailed the evacuation of about 2,500 rebel fighters. De Mistura proposed a variant on this deal in Aleppo, whereby the conflict would be frozen in order to allow for humanitarian aid to be distributed and for local negotiation to proceed with the aim of reaching a broader accommodation. Opposition groups expressed scepticism on the grounds that such a deal would merely allow the regime to refocus its energies on attacking other areas, and they insisted that any local truces would have to be supplemented by wider agreements, in particular for the cessation of regime air raids, including the dropping of explosives-packed barrels from helicopters.

The UN Security Council on 19 February passed a resolution calling for all parties to the conflict to enable the provision of humanitarian aid and relief to all areas where such help was needed. The resolution, 2139 (2014), was approved unanimously, despite reservations expressed by Russia and China during the drafting process about the possibility that it could serve as a pretext for external military intervention against the regime. The final text of the resolution suggested that compromises were made in order to secure the support of Russia and China, notably the inclusion of sections condemning the activities of opposition groups

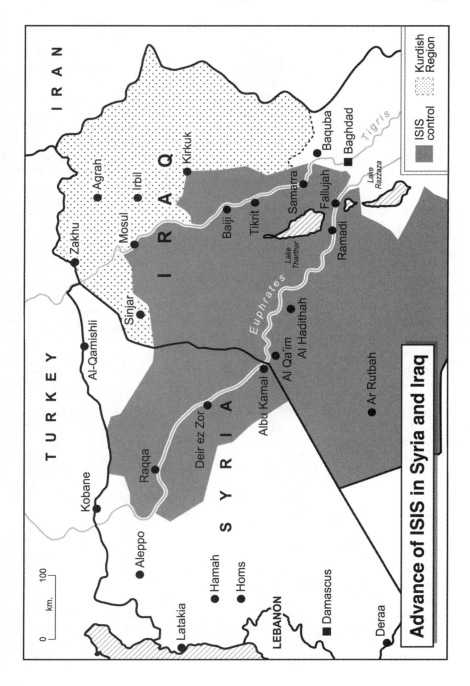

Advance of ISIS in Syria and Iraq

and the exclusion of any reference to specific measures to be taken in the event of non-compliance.

The resolution stemmed from UN concerns at the fate of large numbers of Syrians who had been prevented from receiving humanitarian aid because they had been trapped in rebel-held areas besieged by regime forces, as was the case in the Old City of Homs prior to the local truce. On 14 July the Security Council passed a fresh resolution, 2165 (2014), in light of the failure of all parties to respect the earlier one. The new resolution authorised UN humanitarian agencies and their operational partners to send aid convoys over the Syrian border and across conflict lines within the country, without securing prior approval from the government or other parties in control of these crossing points. However, despite the tougher language, the resolution did not provide for any measures to be taken against the Syrian government or other parties in the event of non-compliance. The resolution said that the UN estimated that there were about 10 million people in Syria in need of assistance, including 6.4 million internally displaced people, and 4.5 million in hard-to-reach areas. These were in addition to the 3 million refugees that the UN had registered in neighbouring countries by the end of 2014, most of them in Lebanon, Turkey and Jordan. The resolution did not make any significant difference to the distribution of aid, which remained heavily dependent on regime co-operation.

The diminishing international interest in a political resolution to the Syria conflict contrasted with the increasing anxiety among Western powers about the growing strength of ISIS. The extremist organisation first made an impact in Syria in early 2013, when it started to attack rebel groups in Raqqa and Aleppo provinces. Baghdadi had also sought, unsuccessfully, to force Jabhat al-Nusra (JN), a group that shared its origins in al-Qaida in Iraq, to pledge allegiance to him. In early 2014, rebel groups managed to drive ISIS out of most of Aleppo province. This campaign cost the lives of an estimated 2,000 rebel fighters, and diverted the energies of the main opposition groups away from confronting the regime. ISIS held on to its main Syrian base of Raqqa, a large town in the north of the Euphrates valley, and sought to build up control of economic assets in northern Syria, in particular oil production, refining and smuggling operations. The Assad regime initially made little effort to curb the activities of ISIS, as the group performed useful functions in tying down rebel forces and in giving substance to the regime's claim that the break-up of Syria would lead to the establishment of an Islamist terrorist base in the region.

In June ISIS launched a campaign to expand its area of control in both Iraq and Syria. Its most dramatic gain was the city of Mosul in Iraq. In Syria, it consolidated its position in the border area of Albu Kamal through co-opting or repressing local tribal groups, and established a corridor from this area to Raqqa by ejecting JN forces from Deir ez-Zor and the surrounding area, largely through negotiation. As a result of these moves, ISIS gained control of a significant part of Syria's oil industry. Prior to the 2011 uprising, Syria had produced 380,000 barrels per day (b/d) of oil, of which about 230,000 b/d was processed in the Homs and Banias refineries to serve the local market, and the remainder was exported from the Banias terminal, on the Mediterranean. Sanctions and the spread of the armed conflict resulted in oil production dwindling from 2012 onwards. Local people, business interests and rebel groups started producing crude oil from the idle fields, and processed it through improvised refineries in the north of the country. Most of this was then smuggled across the border to Turkey. As a result of its June 2014 campaign, ISIS became the dominant player in the Euphrates valley oil business. The fields that fell under its control were producing about 120,000 b/d in 2011, with most of the remainder of Syria's oil fields lying in the north-east corner of the country, which was now under the control of Kurdish groups, with a residual regime presence. Production in the ISIS area was estimated to be about 50,000 b/d in mid-2014, generating revenue of up to $3 million per day, of which a significant portion accrued directly to ISIS. Other sources of wealth for the rebel movement included well-developed extortion operations in Mosul and along the highways in Iraq, hostage ransoms, and plunder from other rebel groups, as well as from the Syrian and Iraqi government and armed forces.

The advance of ISIS was initially checked in Iraq and along the northern stretch of the Iraqi-Syrian border by Syrian Kurdish forces, the People's Protection Units (YPG), many of whose fighters had gained experience fighting the Turkish army as part of the Kurdish Workers Party (PKK). The YPG operated under the political umbrella of the Democratic Union Party (PYD), which had exploited the weakness of the Syrian central state after 2011 to set up autonomous administrations in three cantons in the north of the country: Jazira, in Hasakeh province; Kobane, to the north of Raqqa; and Afrin, north of Aleppo. In July ISIS launched an offensive against the Kobane canton, a wedge of territory surrounded by ISIS-controlled areas. By September, ISIS had seized dozens of villages in the canton, and had advanced to the outskirts of the border town of Kobane itself.

The USA responded to the ISIS campaign by assembling a coalition, including France, the UK, Saudi Arabia, the United Arab Emirates and Jordan, to take military action to stem the group's advances in Iraq. The US and its Arab allies stated that these operations would extend to attacking ISIS targets in Syria. Air raids on ISIS positions began in August, mainly focused on Iraq, but including some attacks on ISIS-controlled oil refineries in Syria. The US also carried out some raids against targets to the west of Aleppo that it identified as belonging to the Khorasan group, a unit within JN and dedicated to preparing terrorist attacks against the West. The raids against JN and the refusal of the US to take any military action against the Assad regime was bitterly criticised by the main rebel groups. In late September the US and its Arab allies started to carry out raids around Kobane in support of the YPG forces (including all-women units, named YPJ) holding out against ISIS attacks. These air assaults enabled the YPG to prevent ISIS from capturing Kobane, but the Islamist group still had a foothold in the town at the end of 2014.

ISIS also attacked a number of Assad regime targets during the second half of 2014, marking an end to the effective truce between the two sides. Several hundred government soldiers were killed as ISIS seized the Tabqa air base, north-west of Raqqa, in August. ISIS also overran a military base on the outskirts of Hasakeh, and launched several assaults on an air base to the west of Deir ez-Zor, although the main part of the base was still in regime hands at year-end. Another target of ISIS assault was the al-Shaer gas field to the east of Homs. This fell into ISIS hands in July before being recaptured by the regime. Syria's natural gas production had not been as badly affected as the oil sector, partly because the main gas fields were in regime-held areas, and partly because natural gas was essential for electricity generation for the entire country, including areas held by rebels or ISIS.

ISIS made a powerful impact on the global media through uploading videos of its execution, apparently by beheading, of several captured Americans and Europeans. The first victim was James Foley, a US photojournalist, whose execution was announced on 19 August. Over the following three months there were four further executions: Steven Sotloff, a US-Israeli journalist; Alan Henning and David Haines, both British aid workers; and Peter Kassig, a US aid worker. The executions were all thought to have been carried out in the vicinity of Raqqa. ISIS also executed hundreds of Syrians, including captured soldiers, rebellious tribesmen and local people convicted by ISIS-administered courts of various misdemeanours.

Apart from the ISIS advances, there were no major changes in the military situation in Syria during 2014. The regime gained some ground in Aleppo and Homs, at the expense of rebel forces operating under the broad framework of the Islamic Front. JN strengthened its position in the north-east province of Idleb after its withdrawal from Deir ez-Zor in July, largely at the expense of the Syrian Revolutionaries Front, led by Jamal Maarouf. Rebels and regime forces continued to fight across battle lines in the eastern suburbs of Damascus, but local truces were negotiated in some outlying areas to the south of the city. Regime forces, backed by Lebanon's Hezbullah, largely held on to territory seized from rebels in the Qalamoun area to the north-west of the capital. In the south, around Deraa, rebels from a newly formed Southern Front, alongside JN, pushed regime forces back towards Damascus, but lacked the capacity to pose a serious threat to the capital.

There were no authoritative figures issued for casualties from the conflict. The Syrian Organisation for Human Rights, a UK-based group which issued regular reports that it said were based on information collated from informants inside the country, announced that it had documented the deaths of about 76,000 people in the conflict during 2014, including some 17,800 civilians, 17,000 rebel fighters (including members of ISIS), and 12,860 members of the Syrian army and regime militias. The UN said in August that it estimated that at least 191,000 people had died in the Syrian conflict by that date. The number of refugees registered with the UN increased by almost one million during 2014 to reach 3.2 million, including 1.16 million in each of Turkey and Lebanon, and 620,000 in Jordan.

David Butter

LEBANON

CAPITAL: Beirut   AREA: 10,400 sq km   POPULATION: 4,467,390 ('13)
OFFICIAL LANGUAGE: Arabic
HEAD OF STATE: acting president Tammam Salam (since Feb '14)
RULING PARTIES: 8 March and 14 March coalition
HEAD OF GOVERNMENT: Prime Minister Tammam Salam (ind) (since Feb '14)
DEMOCRACY INDEX: 5.05; 98th of 167   CORRUPTION PERCEPTIONS INDEX: 27; =136th of 175
CURRENCY: Lebanese Pound (Dec '14 £1.00=LBP 2,349, US$1.00=LBP 1,512)
GNI PER CAPITA: US$9,870, Intl$17,390 at PPP ('13)

IN contrast to the turbulence in the surrounding region, Lebanon had a relatively uneventful year in 2014, as a shared conviction among political leaders of the need to minimise the adverse impact of the continuing conflict in Syria outweighed any tendency to seek to exploit that conflict for political gain. This uneventfulness was also a symptom of the malign effects of the Syria conflict, producing political paralysis, as shown in the failure to elect a new president when the six-year term of Michel Suleiman expired on 25 May.

At the start of 2014 Lebanon's politicians had still not managed to reach agreement on the formation of a new government, following the resignation of Najib Mikati as prime minister in March 2013 and the designation of Tammam Salam as his replacement the following month. On 15 February, agreement was finally reached on the make-up of a new cabinet, based on a formula applied in 2008 whereby each of the main political blocs received one-third of the cabinet seats, and the remaining one-third was made up of a centrist bloc, including the prime minister. The two main blocs were: March 14, including the mainly Sunni Muslim Future Movement, led by Saad Hariri, and the Kataeb, a leading Christian party; and March 8, dominated by the Shia Muslim military/political group, Hezbullah, and including the Free and Patriotic Movement (FPM) led by Michel Aoun, a prominent Christian politician. The centre bloc comprised two nominees of the prime minster, in addition to Salam himself, three nominees of the president, and two supporters of Walid Junblatt, a politician from the Druze minority who had floated between the two main blocs. The structure of the government ensured that it would be impossible for any of the dominant political tendencies to impose their will.

The next challenge facing Lebanon's politicians was the election of a new president. By constitutional custom the president was drawn from the Maronite Christian sect. The election was conducted within parliament, and for a first-round victory the winning candidate needed the votes of two-thirds of the 128 MPs. The polarisation between March 14 and March 8 over the Syria issue meant that there was little chance of the election being successfully completed. Hezbullah and its principal regional backer, Iran, would not tolerate the election of a figure from March 14, which was backed by Saudi Arabia and by Western governments, and has been critical of the involvement of Hezbullah in bolstering the war effort of the Syrian president, Bashar Assad. Likewise, any March 8 candidate would be blocked by March 14. Finding a compromise candidate between these polarised positions proved to be impossible.

Between April and December 2014 there were no fewer than 16 attempts to elect a new president, all of which failed for the lack of a quorum. In the meantime, a revised deadline of November 2014 lapsed for the election of a new parliament, whose mandate had been extended by 17 months in May 2013 after the failure to hold an election. The legislature's mandate was once more extended, until May 2017.

The main impact that the Syrian conflict had on Lebanon was through the massive influx of refugees. The number of Syrians registered by the UN as refugees in Lebanon climbed to 1.16 million by the end of 2014 from 800,000 a year earlier and 130,000 at the start of 2013. The total number of Syrians in Lebanon was at least 250,000 higher than the UN-registered figure. By comparison, the Lebanese population was estimated at about 4.4 million. The government refused to sanction the establishment of formal refugee camps for Syrians in Lebanon, and in October it announced that it had decided to restrict the entry of Syrians. Under the previous system, Syrians were automatically entitled to remain in Lebanon for six months before renewing their entry permit. Henceforth, Syrians would be required to obtain visas, except in urgent cases of humanitarian need.

The hardening of the Lebanese government's position came after fighters from two Syrian groups—Jabhat al-Nusra (JN) and the Islamic State in Iraq and Syria (ISIS)—clashed with Lebanese army forces in August and September in Arsal, a border town that had become one of the largest settlements for Syrian refugees. More than 20 members of the Lebanese security forces were captured by the Syrian Islamist groups, and at least four of them were subsequently executed.

The Syrian conflict and the surge of refugees had a mostly negative impact on the Lebanese economy, placing huge extra burdens on government services and inhibiting investment. There were some positive aspects from the economic standpoint, for example through inflows of capital associated with the shift of Syrian business operations to Lebanon. According to an assessment by the International Monetary Fund (IMF) at the end of the year, real GDP growth was below 2 per cent in 2014. The government's fiscal position showed some improvement, as the budget was expected to show a small primary surplus (excluding debt servicing), as a result of higher than expected transfers of revenue from telecommunications operators, lower capital expenditure and delays in processing salary increases in the public sector. The gross foreign exchange reserves of the central bank rose by about $4 billion during the year to $39 billion. Lebanon's gross public debt remained steady at about 140 per cent of GDP.

David Butter

IRAQ

CAPITAL: Baghdad   AREA: 438,320 sq km   POPULATION: 33,417,476 ('13)
OFFICIAL LANGUAGES: Arabic and Kurdish
HEAD OF STATE: President Fouad Masoum (since July '14) (PUK)
RULING PARTIES: United Iraq Alliance (UIA)
HEAD OF GOVERNMENT: Prime Minister Haider al-Abadi (UIA, Da'wa Party) (since Sept '14)
DEMOCRACY INDEX: 4.10; 113th of 167   CORRUPTION PERCEPTIONS INDEX: 16; 170th of 175
CURRENCY: New Iraqi Dinar (Dec '14 £1.00=IQD 1,776, US$1.00=IQD 1,144)
GNI PER CAPITA: US$6,710, Intl$15,220 at PPP ('13)

IRAQ endured a catastrophic year in 2014, as the deep flaws in the state system created after the 2003 US-led invasion and the overthrow of the Saddam Hussein regime were starkly exposed by the seizure of about one-third of the country by a radical Sunni Islamist movement. The shock of losing Mosul, the country's second-largest city, to forces of the Islamic State of Iraq and Syria (ISIS) in June brought an end to the dominance of Iraqi politics by Nouri Maliki, who was replaced as prime minister by Haider Abadi, and resulted in military intervention by the USA and several regional and international allies to prop up the Baghdad government and the Kurdish Regional Government (KRG). The ISIS advances were also met by increased direct military engagement in Iraq by Iran. By the end of the year, ISIS had been put on the defensive, but it still controlled large parts of Anbar, Salaheddine and Ninewa provinces. The military conflict had little impact on Iraq's oil production, which increased to a record 4 million barrels per day (b/d), but the fall in oil prices put pressure on the government's financial position.

ISIS had its roots in the radical Islamist movements that coalesced into al-Qaida at the end of the 1990s. The group evolved into al-Qaida in Iraq after the 2003 invasion, and later became the Islamic State in Iraq. It suffered setbacks after 2007 when the US enlisted local Sunni tribal groups against it, but it took advantage of the conflict in Syria to regroup in 2012, when it was re-launched as the Islamic State in Iraq and Syria (ISIS) under the leadership of Abu Bakr Baghdadi. During 2013 ISIS had secured control over the northern Syrian town of Raqqa, while in Iraq it had staged a dramatic prison break at Abu Ghraib, outside Baghdad, and seized control of Fallujah, an important town to the west of the capital. ISIS had also built up support among the Sunni population of Iraq's western and northern provinces, exploiting resentment at the sectarianism and corruption of the Shia-dominated Maliki government. ISIS formed alliances with powerful tribal groups and with networks of intelligence officials from the former regime, and it developed financing streams from extortion and protection rackets in Mosul and along the region's highways as well as from oil smuggling in Syria.

Maliki's main focus in the first part of 2014 was on the general election, which was held on April. His strategy was based on maximising his core support among the Shia, and the image of the Sunnis as being dominated by terrorists did no harm to his cause. Maliki's State of Law (SOL) list won 95 of the 328 seats, six more than in the previous election in 2010 (when there were 325 seats in total), and well ahead of any of the other lists. His two main rivals for the Shia vote mustered only 65 seats between them, with 34 going to the list headed by followers of Muqtada Sadr, a populist cleric, and 31 taken by the Islamic Supreme Council of Iraq (ISCI). The Mutahidun list, headed by parliament speaker Usama Nujaifi, did best among parties targeting Sunni votes, and won 27 seats. Ayad Allawi, a former prime minister, was unable to repeat his 2010 success in winning votes for a Shia-Sunni alliance, and his Wataniya list secured only 21 seats. Among the main Kurdish parties there was a shift in favour of the Patriotic Union of Kurdistan (PUK), led by President Jalal Talabani (gravely ill and due to step down after two terms), whose seat tally rose to 21 from 14, but the Kurdish Democratic Party (KDP), led by Masoud Barzani, maintained its ascendancy with 25 seats. On 24 July Fouad Masoum, a Kurdish politician close to Talabani, was elected by the new parliament as Iraq's president.

In order to secure a new mandate as prime minister Maliki needed allies from among the Shia parties, as well as from the Kurdish parties and the Sunnis. Most of the rivals to SOL were critical of Maliki, but there seemed to be little chance of them forging a unified front that would be capable of sidelining him. The deliberations about the formation of the new government were overshadowed by the ISIS offensive in June.

Starting on 5 June groups of ISIS fighters, tribal militias and members of the Naqshabandi group, which included senior figures from the former Baathist regime, staged a series of assaults on several areas in northern and central Iraq, including Samarra, Baquba, Ramadi and Mosul. The largest concentration of Iraqi security forces in the north, at least in theory, was Mosul, where the Second Division of the Iraqi armed forces was stationed, alongside thousands of armed police. However, it later emerged that the actual strength of these forces was much less than it was supposed to be because of systematic corruption, whereby officers would draw payments from the ministry of defence for units that only existed on paper. The assault on Mosul started on 6 June, and four days later the entire city was in ISIS hands. The three generals in command of the security forces in the city had meanwhile departed by helicopter. An offer by the KRG to send Kurdish pershmerga forces to bolster the resistance of the city to the ISIS attack was turned down by Maliki, who claimed that he had matters well in hand.

During the offensive, ISIS took control of the al-Qaim border post with Syria, and published videos of fighters proclaiming as defunct the Sykes-Picot agreement of 1916, which set the framework for the modern state system in the region. On 29 June Baghdadi announced the revival of the Islamic Caliphate set up by the successors of the Prophet Muhammad, with himself at its helm. In keeping with the narrative of modern borders being erased, ISIS rebranded itself as the Islamic State (IS). Both the self-styled name and the concept of the Caliphate contained therein were widely rejected by foreign governments and international bodies.

The retreating Iraqi army in Mosul, Tikrit, Baiji and other areas of northern Iraq left behind large stocks of weaponry that had been supplied by the USA, providing a valuable windfall for ISIS. The jihadist group also laid its hands on large amounts of cash held in the Mosul branch of the Central Bank of Iraq, and gained control over a number of small oil fields and the Mosul dam and hydroelectric power station. However, it failed to secure some other strategic assets. Kurdish forces managed to keep ISIS at bay in the Kirkuk oilfield, the largest in northern Iraq, and ISIS did not manage to seize control of the Baiji oil refinery.

The US had observed the situation in Iraq with mounting concern, but the administration of President Barack Obama made clear that it was not prepared to provide any form of military support unless the new Iraqi government showed commitment to a more inclusive policy towards the Sunni Arab minority. This amounted to setting the condition that Maliki should not become the new prime minister. However, further advances by ISIS forced the hand of Iraq's Western allies. At the start of August ISIS advanced into the Sinjar region, home to the Yazidi minority, ethnic Kurds with their own ancient religious beliefs. Tens of thousands of Yazidis fled their homes in the face of the ISIS onslaught. Some of them made their way to the safe haven of the KRG zone via a Kurdish-controlled pocket in north-eastern Syria, but many were left stranded on desolate mountain-tops. On 7 August Obama announced that the US had started humanitarian air drops to help the Yazidis and that he had authorised US air strikes in order to safe-guard US interests in the KRG. During August the US carried out dozens of air attacks in support of peshmerga forces, and these actions helped to stem the ISIS advance and to drive the jihadist fighters out of the area around the Mosul dam. Iran, meanwhile, stepped up its support to the Iraqi armed forces and Shia militias, as well as providing weapons to the KRG.

The US and Iran reached an effective understanding on the need for a change in the Baghdad government. This external pressure, in particular from the US, was reinforced by Ayatollah Ali Sistani, the supreme religious authority among Iraq's Shia majority, who issued a number of powerful statements calling for national unity and for consensus among Iraq's sects and ethnic groups. By mid-August, faced with a revolt within his own SOL bloc, Maliki recognised that he would not be able to form a new government, and he stepped down from his posi-tion as prime minister on 14 August. The next day SOL nominated Abadi to form the new government, a task that he completed on 8 September. Abadi was a long-time member of the Daawa party who, like many of his colleagues, including Maliki, had spent much of his career abroad. Abadi obtained a doctorate in elec-trical engineering in the UK, where he was based until the 2003 invasion. On his return he was appointed minister of communications, and he was first elected to parliament in 2005. Abadi proceeded to dismiss many of the security command-ers who had been in charge during the ISIS onslaught, and he proposed to set up a national guard to involve Sunnis in ensuring security in their own areas.

The appointment of Abadi was welcomed by the USA, which proceeded to form an international coalition to take military action against ISIS. The coalition included Saudi Arabia, the UAE and Jordan as active partners in air strikes against ISIS in both Iraq and Syria. The UK, France, Australia and Canada agreed to par-ticipate in operations within Iraq, which were sanctioned by the Iraqi government. The US also sent about 1,500 troops to train Iraqi forces, but without any mandate to become involved in combat directly.

The Kurdish parties did not wholeheartedly welcome the appointment of Abadi, as he had previously taken a hard line on the question of the KRG's inde-pendent oil exports. Abadi did not require Kurdish support to secure a vote of confidence in his government from parliament. However, the US and other members of the international coalition urged both the Kurds and Abadi to try to settle their differences. In March the Maliki government had cut off funding from the central government budget for state employees in the KRG, as retribu-tion for the KRG retaining the revenue from its own oil exports. The KRG was normally entitled to 17 per cent of the central government's oil revenue, but the Baghdad government insisted that this could not be paid unless the KRG's oil revenue was managed by the central state oil marketing organisation. The new oil minister, Adel Abdel-Mahdi, took a more conciliatory position than his pred-ecessor on the Kurdish oil issue, and this helped to yield an agreement in November, whereby 150,000 b/d of the KRG's exports, about half of the Kurds' total sales, would be pumped into tanks controlled by the Iraqi State Oil Marketing Organisation (SOMO) at the Turkish terminal at Ceyhan. The agreement also entailed resuming salary payments to civil servants in the KRG. The agreement was subsequently developed to allow for 250,000 b/d of Kurdish oil to be marketed by SOMO and for the KRG to arrange for the export of 300,000 b/d from the Kirkuk field, which was under peshmerga protection.

Iraq's oil production rose from about 3 million b/d at the start of the year to almost 4 million b/d in December 2014. The increase was attributable mainly to additional output from large fields in southern Iraq, in particular the BP-operated Rumaila field. The KRG also made a significant contribution to the overall increase. Oil exports reached a record 2.94 million b/d in December 2014, and averaged 2.5 million b/d over the year as a whole, compared with 2.3 million b/d in 2013. However, export revenue declined at the end of the year as a result of the collapse of oil prices, and the government had to make radical revisions to its revenue projections as it prepared the 2015 budget.

The US-led military intervention assuaged fears that the rise of ISIS would spell the demise of the Iraqi state. However, by the end of 2014 the central government had not made great headway in reasserting its authority over the northern and north-western regions of the country. The KRG had succeeded in driving ISIS out of the Sinjar region, but ISIS still posed a threat to Kirkuk and the Baiji refinery. Abadi's efforts to form a Sunni-based national guard had made little progress, and Shia militias still made up a significant portion of the state's fighting forces. The year was the most violent since the 2006-07 peak of the previous round of sectarian violence. According to the Iraq Body Count, a non-governmental organisation, the number of violent deaths among civilians and irregular fighters (excluding army and peshmerga) was just over 17,000.

David Butter

SAUDI ARABIA

CAPITAL: Riyadh   AREA: 2,000,000 sq km   POPULATION: 28,828,870 ('13)
OFFICIAL LANGUAGE: Arabic
HEAD OF STATE AND GOVERNMENT: King Abdullah bin Abdel-Aziz Al Saud (since Aug '05), also
    Prime Minister
HEIR APPARENT: Crown Prince and Deputy Prime Minister Prince Salman bin Abdel-Aziz Al Saud
    (since June '12)
DEMOCRACY INDEX: 1.82; 160th of 167   CORRUPTION PERCEPTIONS INDEX: 49; =55th of 175
CURRENCY: Saudi Riyal (Dec '14 £1.00=SAR 5.83, US$1.00=SAR 3.76)
GNI PER CAPITA: US$26,200, Intl$53,780 at PPP ('13)

THE nonagenarian king, Abdullah bin Abdel-Aziz Al Saud, took a number of gradual steps to empower younger members of the royal family—a key issue given the advanced age of much of the leadership, in a country where some two-thirds of the population was under 25. In March, he created the new position of deputy crown prince, enabling him to set a longer-term course for the political succession given that the current crown prince, Salman bin Abdel-Aziz Al Saud, was 79. He appointed the 68-year old Muqrin bin Abdel-Aziz Al Saud to the new role, with the approval of the ruling family's Allegiance Council, a body representing the sons of the kingdom's founder, Abdel-Aziz Al Saud. King Abdullah had outlived the previous two crown princes, who, like the current crown prince and his new deputy, were both sons of Abdel-Aziz. In May, Abdullah also appointed his son, Prince Miteb, as commander of the national guard. In December the king reshuffled the Cabinet and made another of his sons, Prince Mishaal, governor of the holy city of Mecca.

In September Saudi Arabia announced it would participate in a US-led military coalition carrying out airstrikes on the Islamic State (ISIS) forces in Syria. Since the extreme Islamist group had captured the Iraqi city of Mosul in June, Saudi Arabia had been increasingly concerned about the threat which it posed. Initially ISIS and other jihadi groups were widely seen in the Gulf as representing a counterweight to the Iranian-backed Shia militias in Syria, and had received extensive private financing and support. However, like al Qaida, the group held the Saudi government to be illegitimate and considered it a target for attack. There were numerous Saudi media reports of local ISIS cells being disrupted, and in November, on the Shia religious festival of Ashura, gunmen linked to ISIS killed eight Saudi Shia worshippers in the mostly Shia Eastern Province. The king and grand mufti condemned the group.

Despite world oil prices falling by nearly half over the course of the year, Saudi Arabia opted not to cut its oil production, and at the December OPEC meeting the oil minister expressed confidence that the oil price would recover. This was consistent with Saudi Arabia's long-term oil policy of seeking to maintain its market share. It generally wanted to avoid the price of oil rising so high that this stimulated investment in alternatives; the recent fall in oil prices had made it more difficult to sustain investment in US shale gas. The move was nonetheless interpreted by some as politically motivated, to add to the economic pressure on Iran.

The country continued to enforce "Saudiisation" policies aimed at tackling unemployment. Officially unemployment stood at 11.8 per cent, but as more women entered the workforce, female unemployment rose to an official rate of 33 per cent by the end of the year.

Jane Kinninmont

YEMEN

CAPITAL: Sana'a   AREA: 527,970 sq km   POPULATION: 24,407,381 ('13)
OFFICIAL LANGUAGE: Arabic
HEAD OF STATE: President Abed-Rabbo Mansour Hadi (since Feb '12)
RULING PARTY: General People's Congress (GPC)
HEAD OF GOVERNMENT: Prime Minister Khaled Bahah (ind) (since Nov '14)
DEMOCRACY INDEX: 2.79; 148th of 167   CORRUPTION PERCEPTIONS INDEX: 19; =161st of 175
CURRENCY: Yemeni Riyal (Dec '14 £1.00=YER 333.9, US$1.00=YER 215)
GNI PER CAPITA: US$1,330, Intl$3,820 at PPP ('13)

IN January Yemen's National Dialogue Conference concluded, with an agreement intended to provide the basis for a new constitution. The 10-month conference brought together representatives of different political and civil society groups, including the main political parties, the Shia Houthi militia and political movement from northern Yemen, and the Hirak separatist movement from the south. Its key recommendations included instituting a system of federalism, though it stopped short of agreeing on the number of regions or their powers; restructuring the appointed upper house of parliament so that half of its members would come from the north and half from the south of the country; holding an inquiry into human rights abuses during the 2011 uprising; and introducing a quota for women in public office. The dialogue conference also agreed that the two-year term of President Abed-Rabbo Mansour Hadi, which had been due to expire in February, should be extended for another year, until the new constitution was completed and elections held. A new Cabinet was appointed, including technocrats and four women (the highest number ever).

UN envoy Jamal Benomar praised the dialogue conference's achievement of a peaceful transition agreement. However, one of the Houthis' envoys to the talks, who sat on the 20-strong group responsible for drafting the final agreement, was shot on the eve of the concluding session. A controversy ensued over whether he had actually endorsed the agreement; a spokesman for the Houthis said the movement rejected it. This placed the whole process in serious jeopardy.

In February President Hadi approved a new federal system based on six regions. The Hirak movement had favoured two—north and south—whereas other groups feared that this would reinforce division by strengthening the separate southern identity. Meanwhile, Hadi postponed the proposed human rights inquiry. Against the backdrop of armed clashes between the Houthis and Salafists, preparations for a new constitution moved slowly and the date for elections remained uncertain.

International donors had long called for cuts in fuel subsidies to reduce the budget deficit and to curb the black market in subsidised oil, from which key members of the elite were alleged to benefit. But when the government reduced fuel subsidies in the middle of the year there were violent protests in the capital, Sana'a, and, repeating a pattern seen in previous years, the government was forced to rescind the cuts. However, the Houthis used the fuel protests to escalate their use of force, seizing control of key sites within the capital in August. Prime Minister Mohammed Salem Basindwa was forced from office and the fighting in Sana'a was ended only after a UN-mediated agreement, which provided for a new government with a prime minister approved by the Houthis.

After a series of disputes over personnel, a national unity government was eventually formed in November under Prime Minister Khaled Bahah. It was immediately undermined, however, by the imposition of UN and US sanctions upon two Houthi commanders and the county's ex-president, Ali Abdullah Saleh. The latter, who had been forced from office in 2012, had formed an alliance of convenience with the Houthis (with whom he had fought when in office), based on shared opposition to the transitional government. Saleh then pulled his party, the General People's Congress, out of the unity government, prompting questions about how long it would last.

Elsewhere, the Houthi continued to make advances against al-Qaida in the Arab Peninsula (AQAP) in southern Yemen, capturing the strategic city of Radmah in October. In the same month AQAP claimed responsibility for a suicide bombing of a Houthi rally in central Sana'a that killed at least 47 people.

Jane Kinninmont

ARAB STATES OF THE GULF

Bahrain

CAPITAL: Manama   AREA: 710 sq km   POPULATION: 1,332,171 ('13)
OFFICIAL LANGUAGE: Arabic
HEAD OF STATE: Sheikh Hamad bin Isa al-Khalifa (since March '99)
HEIR APPARENT: Sheikh Salman bin Hamad bin Isa-al-Khalifa (since March '99)
HEAD OF GOVERNMENT: Prime Minister Sheikh Khalifa bin Sulman al-Khalifa (since Jan '70)
DEMOCRACY INDEX: 2.87; 146th of 167   CORRUPTION PERCEPTIONS INDEX: 49; =55th of 175
CURRENCY: Bahraini Dinar (Dec '14 £1.00=BHD 0.58, US$1.00=BHD 0.38)
GNI PER CAPITA: US$19,560, Intl$36,140 at PPP ('12)

Kuwait

CAPITAL: Kuwait   AREA: 17,820 sq km   POPULATION: 3,368,572 ('13)
OFFICIAL LANGUAGE: Arabic
HEAD OF STATE AND GOVERNMENT: Sheikh Sabah al-Ahmad al-Jaber al-Sabah (since Jan '06)
HEIR APPARENT: Crown Prince Sheikh Nawwaf al-Ahmad al-Jaber al-Sabah
PRIME MINISTER: Sheikh Jaber al-Mubarak al-Hamad al-Sabah (since Dec '11)
DEMOCRACY INDEX: 3.78; 120th of 167   CORRUPTION PERCEPTIONS INDEX: 44; =67th of 175
CURRENCY: Kuwaiti Dinar (Dec '14 £1.00=KWD 0.45, US$1.00=KWD 0.29)
GNI PER CAPITA: US$44,940, Intl$88,170 at PPP ('11)

Oman

CAPITAL: Muscat   AREA: 309,500 sq km   POPULATION: 3,632,444 ('13)
OFFICIAL LANGUAGE: Arabic
HEAD OF STATE AND GOVERNMENT: Shaikh Qaboos bin Said al-Said (since July '70)
DEMOCRACY INDEX: 3.26; 136th of 167   CORRUPTION PERCEPTIONS INDEX: 45; =64th of 175
CURRENCY: Rial Omani (Dec '14 £1.00=OMR 0.60, US$1.00=OMR 0.39)
GNI PER CAPITA: US$25,250, Intl$52,170 at PPP ('12)

Qatar

CAPITAL: Doha   AREA: 11,000 sq km   POPULATION: 2,168,673 ('13)
OFFICIAL LANGUAGE: Arabic
HEAD OF STATE AND GOVERNMENT: Sheikh Tamim bin Hamad Al Thani (since June '13)
PRIME MINISTER: Sheikh Abdullah bin Nasser bin Khalif al-Thani (since June '13)
DEMOCRACY INDEX: 3.18; 139th of 167   CORRUPTION PERCEPTIONS INDEX: 69; =26th of 175
CURRENCY: Qatar Riyal (Dec '14 £1.00=QAR 5.66, US$1.00=QAR 3.64)
GNI PER CAPITA: US$85,550, Intl$123,860 at PPP ('13)

United Arab Emirates (UAE)

CONSTITUENT REPUBLICS: Abu Dhabi, Dubai, Sharjah, Ras Al Khaimah, Fujairah, Umm Al Qaiwin, Ajman
CAPITAL: Abu Dhabi   AREA: 83,600 sq km   POPULATION: 9,346,129 ('13)
OFFICIAL LANGUAGE: Arabic
HEAD OF STATE: Shaikh Khalifa Bin Zayed al-Nahyan (Ruler of Abu Dhabi), President of UAE (since Nov '04)
HEAD OF GOVERNMENT: Gen. Shaikh Mohammed bin Rashid al-Maktoum (ruler of Dubai), Vice-President and Prime Minister of UAE (since Jan '06)
DEMOCRACY INDEX: 2.52; 152nd of 167   CORRUPTION PERCEPTIONS INDEX: 70; 25th of 175
CURRENCY: UAE Dirham (Dec '14 £1.00=AED 5.70, US$1.00=AED 3.67)
GNI PER CAPITA: US$38,620, Intl$58,090 at PPP ('12)

POLITICAL discord within **Bahrain** remained unresolved in 2014. Between January and August the crown prince held talks with opposition societies, including the main legally recognised opposition group, the Shia Islamist Al Wefaq National Islamic Society. The authorities had hoped to end Al Wefaq's boycott of the country's parliament, in force since the 2011 uprising (see AR 2012, p. 205). As a result of the talks, the crown prince said that the next parliament would debate contentious issues including electoral districts, but made no specific promises of reforms. Al Wefaq maintained its boycott and was threatened with legal dissolution on a number of technicalities. Although this was not enforced, the arrest of political dissidents continued.

Parliamentary elections in November recorded an official turnout of 52 per cent, though the figure varied substantially between pro-government areas and (largely Shia) opposition districts, where a boycott was widely observed. Electoral districts were altered by royal decree weeks before the polls, in a move that the authorities claimed was intended to make them more equal. A total of 37 of the 40 seats in the House of Representatives were won by independents, the majority of whom were pro-government. The main established Sunni political groupings won few seats: one for the local affiliate of the Muslim Brotherhood, two for a Salafist association, but none for the Al Fatih Coalition, a largely Sunni movement formed as a counterweight to the largely Shia opposition uprising of 2011.

In June, the US State Department's assistant secretary for human rights, Tom Malinowski, was deported from Bahrain after meeting with opposition groups, in a move that indicated the government's sensitivity to the USA's pro-democracy rhetoric. Nonetheless, the US continued to expand its naval base in Bahrain and Malinowski returned to the country in December. In the same month, the UK announced that Bahrain would be the location of its first permanent military base in the Middle East for three decades, though in reality there was already a semi-permanent British naval presence there.

In **Kuwait** in April, controversy erupted over a videotape that purported to show senior members of the royal family plotting a coup. Local media had been ordered not to report on the recording, and two newspapers that had violated the embargo were suspended. Underlying the commotion was a deeper controversy over the longer-term political succession in Kuwait (after the crown prince, who was 77).

Five MPs resigned from the 50-member parliament after their colleagues rejected a bid to question the prime minister, a member of the royal family, over corruption allegations relating to the videotape. The MPs who resigned included the only woman in parliament, Safa Al Hashem. They were replaced in June through by-elections that were boycotted by most opposition groups. The boycott reflected objections to a new electoral law promulgated by the emir in October 2012, which was seen as disadvantaging the opposition.

In April a coalition of opposition groups launched a "national political reform project" calling for democratic reforms and curbs on the power of the ruling family. One of the most prominent opposition leaders, Musallem al-Barrak, said senior princes had embezzled millions, and was subsequently briefly detained. During 2014 the government revoked the citizenship of 33 people, including the editor of *Alam Al-Youm*, a newspaper seen as sympathetic to the opposition (which was also closed down), and a former opposition MP.

Oman's ruler, Sultan Qaboos travelled to Germany for medical treatment in July and remained there for the rest of the year, prompting increasing speculation about the political succession. The 73-year old sultan had ruled Oman since 1970 and had not appointed a crown prince or prime minister. A royal family council had been charged with determining the political succession after Qaboos's death and, in the event that it could not agree on a candidate, its members were to open a sealed letter from Qaboos containing the name of his preferred successor.

Oman was harder hit by the fall in oil prices than most other Gulf countries, as its limited oil reserves were relatively expensive to extract and process. The fall in revenue prompted officials to float various ideas for rationalising public spending, including a freeze on public-sector promotion and pay, and a tax on remittances by expatriates, who constituted some 1.8 million of Oman's 4 million population. In a similar vein, the government cancelled a number of price controls during the summer, but the sultan rapidly reversed this policy after extensive public criticism on social media.

Qatar faced tensions with other Gulf states in 2014, as Saudi Arabia, the UAE and Bahrain criticised it for "interfering" in regional affairs through what they saw as its support for Islamist and other opposition movements. In March, the three countries withdrew their ambassadors from Doha, saying that Qatar had failed to respect the terms of a 2013 regional security agreement stipulating that Gulf countries would not interfere in each other's affairs. This "interference" was defined very broadly, to include supporting "hostile media" or those whose political influence threatened Gulf stability. In December a rapprochement was reached just before Qatar hosted the annual Gulf Cooperation Council (GCC) summit. Immediately afterwards, Qatar suspended the operations of a television channel that it operated in Egypt, and its state-owned broadcaster, Al Jazeera, became more wary of interviewing anyone from Gulf opposition groups.

Internationally, the country faced criticism for its support of Islamist movements, especially in Syria, and for the often abusive treatment of poorly paid migrant workers. The latter were heavily involved in building the infrastructure for the 2022 football World Cup which had been controversially granted to Qatar.

In September the **UAE**'s air force participated in the US-led campaign of airstrikes against Islamic State (ISIS) fighters in Syria. The move was much publicised, with a photograph of a female UAE pilot giving a "thumbs-up" widely circulated in local and international media, symbolising the country's preferred image as secular, liberal and pro-Western. There were also reports that the UAE and Egypt had jointly carried out airstrikes against Islamist militants in Libya.

In December a US teacher was murdered in Dubai by an Emirati woman, who the authorities said was linked to ISIS. The incident followed calls on jihadi websites for attacks on Western schools and educators.

Investment in property in Dubai slowed after a dramatic 30 per cent rise in 2013, owing to central bank curbs on lending as well as the fall in the oil price. Government spending continued to insulate the economy, and local media reported that half of the 2015 budget would be spent on citizens' welfare and social services, including healthcare and education.

Jane Kinninmont

SUDAN AND SOUTH SUDAN

Sudan

CAPITAL: Khartoum   AREA: 1,886,068 sq km   POPULATION: 37,964,306 ('13)
OFFICIAL LANGUAGES: Arabic, English
HEAD OF STATE: President (Gen.) Omar Hasan Ahmed al-Bashir (since Oct '93), previously
    Chairman of Revolutionary Command Council (since June '89)
RULING PARTY: National Congress Party (NCP)
DEMOCRACY INDEX: 2.54; 151st of 167   CORRUPTION PERCEPTIONS INDEX: 11; 173rd of 175
CURRENCY: Sudanese Pound (Dec '14 £1.00=SDG 8.86, US$1.00=SDG 5.71)
GNI PER CAPITA: US$1,130, Intl$2,370 at PPP ('13)

South Sudan

CAPITAL: Juba   AREA: 619,745 sq km   POPULATION: 11,296,173 ('13)
OFFICIAL LANGUAGE: English
HEAD OF STATE: President Salva Kiir Mayardit (since July '11)
RULING PARTY: Sudan People's Liberation Army (SPLA)
CORRUPTION PERCEPTIONS INDEX: 15; 171st of 175
CURRENCY: South Sudanese Pound (n/a)
GNI PER CAPITA: US$1,120, Intl$2,190 at PPP ('13)

THE year 2014 provided little for either Sudan or South Sudan to celebrate. The two governments maintained the co-operation arrangements they had agreed in September 2012, which provided mutually profitable terms for South Sudanese oil to be exported through Sudan and discouraged the two countries from going to war against each other or quarrelling over issues such as border demarcation. However, each nation continued to face severe political and economic troubles.

In **Sudan** the government and the ruling National Congress Party (NCP) maintained their resolve to dominate power and to defeat the various rebellions in the country on their own terms. In late January President Omar al-Bashir delivered a speech in front of party members and opposition party leaders that was billed as a significant announcement about "national dialogue" and reform, but which in the event seemed much like the government's usual talk.

The tightly controlled process of "dialogue", which the government then launched and continued through the year, duly split opposition parties. Heavy-handed censorship and policing of public debate and the media also gave opposition parties and activists good reason to doubt the government's sincerity and willingness to change. Arrests and harassment of opposition party members and leaders remained common.

Indeed, in May the veteran leader of the Umma Party and twice former prime minister, Sadiq al-Mahdi, was arrested on charges of defaming a pro-government paramilitary force active in Darfur, the Rapid Support Forces, by saying publicly that it ought to be held to account for abuses or crimes carried out by its members. The Umma Party duly suspended its participation in the national dialogue. In June (which marked the 25th anniversary of the coup in 1989 that brought Bashir to power) Sadiq al-Mahdi was released and left Sudan. However, the authorities subsequently barred him from returning to the country after he signed an agreement in Paris with the Sudan Revolutionary Front (SRF)—an alliance of several Darfur rebel groups and the Sudan People's Liberation Movement-North (SPLM-N)—aimed at uniting the "forces of change" in Sudan in order to establish a democratic state.

Meanwhile, the armed rebellions in Blue Nile, South Kordofan and Darfur states remained unresolved, with the army unable to defeat the main rebel groups: the SPLM-N, the Justice and Equality Movement (JEM) and factions of the Sudan Liberation Movement (SLM). Levels of fighting fluctuated, and it was mostly confined to rural areas, with the air force using sporadic aerial bombardment to try to deter villages from hosting rebels. In West Kordofan and Darfur the situation was complicated by inter-communal rivalries: in November some 133 people were killed in an outbreak of fighting between militias from two sub-groups of the Missiriya tribe in West Kordofan.

Negotiations between the government and rebel groups were intermittently held in the Ethiopian capital, Addis Ababa, but African Union mediators were unable to outwit the various parties and their tactics, or end the piecemeal approach of multiple negotiations and dialogue. For its part, the government resisted pressure from rebel groups for Sudan's conflicts and politics to be dealt with under a unified framework of negotiations linked to national dialogue with opposition parties. The Darfur rebels continued to reject a notional peace agreement, signed in Doha in 2011 by the government and a minor rebel faction, the Liberty and Justice Movement.

In **South Sudan** events in the first half of the year continued the downward slide that had started with the political crisis and outbreak of conflict at the end of 2013 (see AR 2014, p. 195). In fighting during January and February, control of Bor, Bentiu and Malakal (the capitals of Jonglei, Unity and Upper Nile states, respectively) repeatedly changed hands between forces loyal to the government of President Salva Kiir and forces opposed to the government and led by Riek Machar, the former vice-president. Thousands were killed in the fighting, with numerous massacres and attacks on civilians occurring, as the crisis took on an inter-ethnic dimension. Within a few months the conflict had displaced more than a million people, rising to some 1.8 million by the end of the year. Many fled into neighbouring states, and some 70,000 people sought protection and shelter at the bases of the UN peacekeeping mission in South Sudan (UNMISS).

International alarm at the escalating conflict led the East African regional Inter-Governmental Authority for Development (IGAD) to push for rapid negotiations. As a result, on 23 January the government and the rebels signed an agreement for a cessation of hostilities and the release of a group of senior political detainees allied to Machar, who were being held by the government. However, momentum in negotiations subsequently slowed, and monitors deployed by IGAD proved unable to prevent the warring parties repeatedly violating the ceasefire and perpetrating "gross violations of human rights", according to a report by UNMISS issued on 8 May.

In May President Kiir and former Vice-President Machar met face-to-face in Addis Ababa and agreed that a "transitional government of national unity" should be formed and an "inclusive" peace process pursued. This effectively meant that negotiations were aimed at producing a deal between that part of the ruling Sudan People's Liberation Movement (SPLM) still loyal to Kiir, and the part that had broken away and was led by Machar and was now referred to as the SPLM-in-Opposition; there was expected to be some role, too, for the SPLM former detainees. This prospect was criticised by many civil society and opposition activists as being unlikely to produce a positive transformation in the new country's predatory politics. With no better alternative in sight, IGAD mediators tried to push the parties forward, nonetheless, but no agreement on the details of a transitional government was reached during the rest of the year.

Amidst their respective political troubles, the economy in neither country fared well in 2014. In Sudan inflation averaged at least 20 per cent, peaking in August at 46 per cent, and the black market exchange rate continued to be some 30 per cent weaker than the official exchange rate. With Sudan making no headway in its search for international debt relief, in September the two countries agreed to postpone again a decision about apportioning Sudan's pre-2011 (pre-partition) sovereign debt, which was believed to be around $45 billion.

In South Sudan the conflict caused oil production in Unity State to be suspended through the year, while production at the Upper Nile oilfields contracted to around 160,000 barrels per day—less than half of what South Sudan produced in 2011 before production was first disrupted. All the same, with the pressure of the conflict, and lax fiscal controls, budgeted spending on the army and defence increased, rising to 4.4 billion South Sudanese pounds, or 39 per cent of total budgeted spending in the financial year 2014-15. As in Sudan, but only more acutely, international aid organisations struggled to help fill the gap in basic services for the poor.

Richard Barltrop

LIBYA

CAPITAL: Tripoli   AREA: 1,759,540 sq km   POPULATION: 6,201,521 ('13)
OFFICIAL LANGUAGE: Arabic
HEAD OF STATE: disputed
HEAD OF GOVERNMENT: Abdallah al-Theni (since Sept '14)
DEMOCRACY INDEX: 4.82; =101st of 167   CORRUPTION PERCEPTIONS INDEX: 18; =166th of 175
CURRENCY: Libyan Dinar (Dec '14 £1.00=LYD 1.86, US$1.00=LYD 1.19)
GNI PER CAPITA: US$10,702, Intl$20,681 at PPP ('13 IMF estimate)

THE year began with abductions and assassinations of Libyan and foreign nationals by *katibas* (ex-rebel militias). This set the pattern for the whole of 2014. The deputy minister for industry, Hassan al-Droui, was shot in Sirte on 11 January. He was the first member of the transitional government to be murdered since the fall of Kadhafi. Then, at the end of the month, Interior Minister Seddik Abdelkarim narrowly escaped an attempt on his life. On 2 January, the bodies of a British oil worker and his partner from New Zealand were found on a beach west of Tripoli. The month also saw militia kidnappings of two Italians working for an infrastructure firm in the Benghazi region on 17 January; a South Korean business representative in Tripoli three days later; and five Egyptian diplomats, including the cultural attaché, on 24 and 25 January. East of Benghazi, on 24 February, seven Egyptian Copts were executed, and on 2 March a French engineer working for an infrastructural company lost his life. Later in the year, the targets shifted to civil rights activists and international aid agency workers, with a Swiss Red Cross representative killed in Sirte on 4 June, the prominent Libyan lawyer and human rights activist, Salwa Bugaighis, murdered at her home on the day of the legislative elections (25 June), and 10 leading Libyan civil rights workers and senior army officers murdered in Benghazi on the "Black Friday" of 19 September.

The struggle for control of Libya's resources revenue that underlay the abductions and killings also prompted the "*Morning Glory* crisis" when, on 9 March, the government deployed troops to prevent the South Korean-flagged tanker of that name from docking in the eastern port of Sidra. As Cyrenaican autonomist militias demanded an increased share of national oil revenues before ending the blockade of ports under their control, the failing government resorted to international assistance. On 17 March, US Navy Seals seized the *Glory* by request of the Libyan government and transferred it to Libyan forces. The crisis left political casualties in its wake: interim Prime Minister Ali Zidan was felled in a parliamentary vote of no confidence on 11 March and his successor, Abdallah al-Theni, served five days in office before suffering an armed attack and resigning in protest on 13 April.

Throughout the year there was an increasingly dangerous rift that gaped ever wider between internationally-recognised government and effective military force. As its end-of-mandate date of 7 February approached, the transitional General National Congress (GNC, the legislature elected in mid-2012) extended its mandate to December 2014, but a week later the authorities were denying that a coup d'état had taken place after a former army general, Khalifa Hiftar, called for the suspension of parliament. Elections for a Constituent Assembly were hastily organised for 20 February to quell the unrest, but produced a paltry 15 per cent turnout. After the chaotic election in the GNC on 5 May of Ahmed Maeteeg as new prime minister, Hiftar embarked upon an offensive, "Operation Dignity", against Islamist militias and the GNC. Bolstered by growing numbers of defectors from the "official" army, Hiftar's offensive led to some of the deadliest clashes seen in Libya since 2011.

Over the coming months, parliamentary chaos deepened with the Supreme Court ruling on 9 June that Maeteeg's election was unconstitutional and attempting to place Abdallah al-Theni back in power. The GNC had finally decreed in late May, under pressure from Hiftar's "Dignity" forces, that elections for a new legislature should be held on 25 June. Though turnout was only 18 per cent, this new 200-member Council of Deputies, in which Islamists were heavily outnumbered by secularists, duly replaced the GNC and provided an internationally-recognised Libyan government. Meanwhile, Hiftar intensified his offensive with air and ground strikes against the Islamist militia, Ansar al-Sharia, in Benghazi. Heavy fighting also broke out between *katibas* for control of Tripoli's airport, partly destroyed by rockets on 13 and 14 July. In late July and early August, Western powers, including the USA, the UK, Germany, the Netherlands and France, progressively closed their embassies and evacuated diplomatic personnel and civilians.

In mid-August the drama took a further internationalist turn as evidence mounted that air strikes on the Islamist militias, who were reportedly supported by Qatar, were, in turn, being backed by the UAE and Egyptian governments, opening the possibility of a further proxy war for control in Libya. On 24 August, the powerful Misrata *katiba* and other militias, collectively calling themselves "Libya Dawn", proclaimed full control of Tripoli's airport and announced an independent Islamist government in opposition to the Council of Deputies. A climate of terror now took hold in Tripoli, as Libya Dawn forces set about rounding up suspected government allies and supporters of the rival Zintan militia, and destroying the homes of GNC officials and journalists thought to be opposed to Dawn's allies in the Libyan Muslim Brotherhood. On 1 September, Dawn took control of the deserted US embassy compound.

Without a secure base, Libya's internationally recognised government took up quarters in the unexpected surroundings of a Greek car ferry docked in the eastern port of Tobruk. On 6 November, its legitimacy was further shattered when the Supreme Court—according to some reports, under an ultimatum from Dawn militias—decreed the legislative elections of 25 June unconstitutional and gave instructions for dissolution of Libya's internationally recognised government.

The year closed with failed army raids to regain control of Sidra and surrounding ports. Apparently doomed to sink deeper into a quagmire of violence, lawlessness and chaos, Libya was increasingly displaying all of the hallmarks of a failed state.

Gabrielle Maas

TUNISIA

CAPITAL: Tunis   AREA: 163,610 sq km   POPULATION: 10,886,500 ('13)
OFFICIAL LANGUAGE: Arabic
HEAD OF STATE: President Beji Caid Essebsi (Call of Tunisia) (since Dec '14)
RULING PARTY: Call of Tunisia
HEAD OF GOVERNMENT: Prime Minister Mehdi Jomaa (ind) (since Jan 14)
DEMOCRACY INDEX: 5.76; 90th of 167   CORRUPTION PERCEPTIONS INDEX: 40; 79th of 175
CURRENCY: Tunisian Dinar (Dec '14 £1.00=TND 2.89, US$1.00=TND 1.86)
GNI PER CAPITA: US$4,360, Intl$10,960 at PPP ('13)

THE resignation of prime minister Ali Larayedh on 9 January, agreed the month before, signalled the compromise made by his Islamist Ennahda party to open the way for Tunisia's new constitution. When the National Constituent Assembly (NCA) passed the document on 26 January, after two hard years of negotiation, the constitution attracted plaudits both at home and abroad. Though there was a nod to the "state undertaking to prevent attacks on the sacred", Article 6 enshrined freedom of conscience; there were also affirmative clauses on women's rights, parliamentary limitations and the role of civil society, and an amendment proposing the Koran and Sunnah (the practices of Islam) as a "principal source of legislation" was rejected before the final draft.

Even with Ennahda's concessions, this consensus had not come without a struggle. As recently as 21 January there had been vehement exchanges and interruptions to sessions of the Assembly over the role of Islam, with member Ibrahim Kassas reportedly shouting "Allahu akbar" ("God is greater") and breaking down in tears after deputies came to blows over a proposed article prohibiting *takfir*, or accusations of apostasy. Secularists argued that in the context of Islamist extremism such accusations were tantamount to incitement to violence; Islamist politicians, including Kassas, stressed that their prohibition would open the way for insults to religion.

On the night of 28-29 January, the Assembly passed a vote of confidence in Mehdi Jomaa's new "government of technocrats". The internationalist leanings of the new administration were clear: ministers' CVs were circulated to the press in Arabic, French and English, and showed backgrounds overwhelmingly in business or university careers rather than politics.

The spring and early summer brought fresh extremist threats. After anti-terrorist units in early February killed three men suspected of orchestrating the 2013 assassinations of Ennahda opponents Chokri Belaid and Mohamed Brahmi, militants disguised as security forces killed four, including two gendarmes, in a presumed reprisal. On the night of 27-28 May, an attack in Kasserine near the Algerian border killed four police agents; the target had been Interior Minister Lotfi Ben Jeddou, who was away at the time. On 13 June, al-Qaida in the Islamic Maghreb (AQIM) claimed responsibility: it was the first time the Islamist group had openly operated in Tunisia since the change of regime in 2011. On 16 July, in what the defence minister called the deadliest attack since independence, two concerted assaults on watch stations (led by both Tunisian and Algerian militants), once again near Kasserine, killed 15 soldiers. Four days later, Jomaa announced that mosques evading the control of the authorities, as well as media sources that published extremist messages, were to be closed.

On 26 October Tunisia held its first legislative elections under the new constitution; fears of extremist violence prompted the posting of around 80,000 troops and security forces to deter attacks. The vote saw Ennahda, which took 28 per cent of the vote, defeated by the 38 per cent cast for erstwhile opposition party, Call of Tunisia (Nida Tounès, NT), with its 87-year old leader, Beji Caid Essebsi, a veteran of both the Bourguiba (1957-87) and Ben Ali (1987-2011) regimes. This victory provoked fears in some quarters of a return to charismatic or even authoritarian politics. The elections for Tunisia's first directly elected head of state were set for 23 November and pitted Essebsi against the incumbent interim president, Moncef Marzouki, who attempted to attract Islamist support but was not officially backed by Ennahda. The first round gave a narrow victory to Essebsi, and the run-off vote on 21 December confirmed this, with 56 per cent cast for Essebsi and 44 per cent for his rival. Marzouki, who had been widely accused of turning a blind eye to extremism, now swung into action with warnings of a single party controlling all offices of power (NT had also been granted the right to appoint Jomaa's successor as prime minister). On 23 December, Marzouki founded a new movement against the "return to dictatorship". Essebsi was sworn in on 31 December.

Gabrielle Maas

ALGERIA

CAPITAL: Algiers   AREA: 2,381,740 sq km   POPULATION: 39,208,194 ('13)
OFFICIAL LANGUAGE: Arabic
HEAD OF STATE: President Abdelaziz Bouteflika (FLN) (since April '99)
RULING PARTIES: National Liberation Front (FLN)-led coalition
HEAD OF GOVERNMENT: Prime Minister Abdelmalek Sellal (since Sept '12)
DEMOCRACY INDEX: 3.83; =118th of 167   CORRUPTION PERCEPTIONS INDEX: 36; =100th of 175
CURRENCY: Algerian Dinar (Dec '14 £1.00=DZD 136.35, US$1.00=DZD 87.80)
GNI PER CAPITA: US$5,290, Intl$12,990 at PPP ('13)

IN Algeria's presidential election of 17 April Abdelaziz Bouteflika, the incumbent since 1999, cast his vote from a wheelchair and won with a reported 81 per cent landslide victory over his rival, Ali Benflis. Stumbling over the oath during his inauguration on 28 April, he had to be removed from the dais and "refreshed" before the ceremony could continue. Having abolished constitutional presidential mandate limits in 2008 in order to allow himself a third term in office, Bouteflika, in an ironic reversal of policy just a month after his 2014 election to a fourth term, announced his intention to reinstate the two-term restriction.

For many, this husk of a president embodied Algeria's predicament of stasis disguised as "stability". As the election approached, this took the shape of a rift between two powerful military factions. One was associated with the army high command and rallied to Bouteflika; the other, supporting Benflis, formed around General Mohamed Mediene (or "Tewfik", as he was commonly known) and the DRS, Algeria's secret intelligence service. In early February the secretary general of the ruling National Liberation Front (FLN), Ammar Saïdani, voiced unprecedented public criticism of Tewfik, while rumours emerged that Bouteflika himself had been unwilling to stand again but was serving as a pawn for his entourage in the factional struggle. Protests from a citizen movement proclaiming—in Arabic, Berber and French—that Algeria had had "Barakat!" (Enough!) of Bouteflika and the old guard were forcefully put down in Algiers and other major cities in the week preceding the election.

On 22 September, the radical Islamist group, Jund al-Khalifa, released a hostage video of French mountain guide, Hervé Gourdel, kidnapped the previous day near the village of Aït Ouabane in the north-eastern region of Kabylia; the group called on France to withdraw from the US-led coalition conducting air strikes against Islamic State in Iraq and Syria (ISIS) in the Middle East. Superseding this, three days later the group's "Message in blood for the French government" showed Gourdel's execution. Kidnappings for ransom had been rife for years in the Djurdjura mountains and forests of Kabylia. But the execution of Gourdel—like the 2013 attack on the In Amenas gas plant—demonstrated the growing power of young, ad hoc groups with a small number of experienced militants, minimal resources and diffuse regional and international allegiances.

Jund al-Khalifa, which had splintered from al-Qaida in the Islamic Maghreb (AQIM) and declared allegiance to ISIS just days before the kidnapping, was by no means unknown to the Algerian army. Its figurehead, the former Armed Islamic Group fighter Abdelmalek Gouri (or Khaled Abu Suleiman by his nom de guerre), had been behind an attack in Iboudrarene 19 April (close to the site of Gourdel's abduction) that had killed 11 soldiers returning from an electoral security assignment. AQIM itself had also orchestrated coordinated attacks on 13 February in Kabylia, around the cities of Boumerdès and Tizi Ouzou. Later in the year, on 13 July, an unclaimed extremist attack had targeted a military convoy in the western Sidi Bel-Abbès region, leaving seven members of the security forces dead. Army roundups and killings of various Jund figures, which began in November, culminated on 22 December in the capture and death of Gouri near Boumerdès, whilst two militants were killed in a separate operation in Tizi Ouzou.

On 26 June celebrations erupted as Algeria qualified for the first time for the knockout stages of the football World Cup. It was not all joy, however: seven people were killed in car accidents during the celebrations after the second and third group-stage qualifying matches, and on 22 June the excitement was too much for one man who collapsed and died during Algeria's second goal against South Korea. World Cup euphoria was also muted by a footballing scandal later in the summer. As he returned to the dressing room after a league match on 23 August, the young Cameroonian striker Albert Ebossé was struck on the head by a missile thrown from the stands, following the defeat of his team Jeunesse Sportive de Kabylie. The injury proved fatal, and the Kabyle team was temporarily banned from playing matches at its home ground of Tizi Ouzou.

On 21 December the defeated presidential candidate Ali Benflis, who had refused to accept the validity of April's election result, made good his promise to found an independent party. In his announcement of the new Talaia El Houriat, he also offered a scathing critique of the bureaucratic formalities that had obstructed registration of the party. Objections had ranged from the party's name to the suspected "individual rather than collective commitment of its members to respect the Constitution"—which was still awaiting a round of revisions promised since 2011 and further delayed on 31 December, after negotiations in the council of ministers failed to reach consensus. The delay, announced Bouteflika, was intended not to serve the regime but to "consolidate the liberties and democracy for which the glorious martyrs of the [1954] November Revolution sacrificed their lives" 60 years before.

Gabrielle Maas

MOROCCO

CAPITAL: Rabat   AREA: 446,550 sq km   POPULATION: 33,008,150 ('13)
OFFICIAL LANGUAGE: Arabic
HEAD OF STATE: King Mohammed VI (since July '99)
RULING PARTIES: Justice and Development Party (PJD)-led coalition
HEAD OF GOVERNMENT: Prime Minister Abdelilah Benkirane (since Nov '11)
DEMOCRACY INDEX: 4.07; 115th of 167   CORRUPTION PERCEPTIONS INDEX: 39; =80th of 175
CURRENCY: Dirham (Dec '14 £1.00=MAD 13.92, US$1.00=MAD 9.00)
GNI PER CAPITA: US$3,030, Intl$7,000 at PPP ('13)

FREEDOM of speech was once again a key issue for Morocco. On 29 May the journalist Ali Anouzla, convicted in 2013 for "material assistance to terrorism" after having published links to an al-Qaida in the Islamic Maghreb (AQIM) video critical of King Mohammed VI (see AR 2014, p. 201), was found guilty on new government-issued charges of defamation and undermining public institutions. Nor did the quest to silence criticism stop at national borders. The Spanish journalist Ignacio Cembrero tendered his resignation on 30 April after 35 years' service at *El País*, after Prime Minister Abdelilah Benkirane brought charges of "apology for terrorism" against him and the paper's former director, for the same alleged wrongdoing as Anouzla.

The year saw some partial progress in the domain of social liberties and family law. On 22 January, after nearly two years of sustained pressure from NGOs and public campaigns following the suicide of 16-year old Amina al-Filali (see AR 2013, p. 202), the parliament finally repealed Article 475 of the penal code, thereby abolishing the immunity previously granted to an "abductor" who married his minor victim. On 18 September, meanwhile, UK national Ray Cole and his Moroccan companion Jamal Wald Nass were arrested for homosexuality and jailed in Marrakesh; police had reportedly searched Cole's phone, email and social media accounts for incriminating evidence. Mounting pressure from a UK-based public campaign saw Cole released and repatriated on 7 October. Although Wald Nass was also freed two days later pending an appeal hearing, many pointed out that leniency came more easily to the Moroccan authorities where the country's external image—and particularly its lucrative tourist industry—were at stake.

On 6 February, nine sub-Saharan migrants drowned while attempting to swim from a Moroccan beach to the Spanish enclave of Ceuta; two weeks later the Moroccan interior minister, Mohamed Hassad, met his opposite numbers from Spain, Portugal and France to discuss the problem. With an estimated 30,000-40,000 migrants on Moroccan soil for transit purposes, and "foreigners' bureaux" already open, on 20 February King Mohammed VI outlined a new policy granting residence rights on proof of five years' residence. Another type of migration was in focus when, on 14 August, the interior minister announced the crushing of an Islamist cell accused of recruiting combatants for Islamic State in Iraq and Syria (ISIS). In a related development, on 15 October the authorities arrested a Moroccan national, resident in France and passing through Casablanca while attempting to join ISIS by way of Turkey.

Moroccan foreign relations were also on show during a diplomatic spat with France early in the year. After petitioning from an anti-torture NGO, the French government on 20 February summoned the head of Morocco's counter-espionage service (DGST), Abdellatif Hammouchi, to testify on torture cases while he was in Paris meeting French officials. Amidst the ensuing accusations, the Spanish actor and Sahrawi rights activist, Javier Bardem, attributed remarks of a distinctly neo-colonialist hue to senior French diplomat Gérard Araud. In 2011, when he was serving as permanent representative of France to the UN, Araud had allegedly described Morocco as being like "a mistress with whom one spends every night, and who must be defended even though there's not much love involved. One looks the other way, in other words." As might be expected, relations cooled considerably.

Gabrielle Maas

WESTERN SAHARA

CAPITAL: El Aaiún   AREA: 284,000 sq km   POPULATION: 567,000 ('13 UN figures)
HEAD OF STATE: President Mohamed Abdelaziz (since Aug '76)
RULING PARTY: Polisario Front
HEAD OF GOVERNMENT: Prime Minister Abdelkader Taleb Omar (since Oct '03)
CURRENCY: Moroccan Dirham [de facto] (Dec '14 £1.00=MAD 13.92, US$1.00=MAD 9.00)

A UK parliamentary delegation visited Western Sahara on 13-16 February; it returned with reports of constant tracking by undercover Moroccan agents and the brutal repression of a peaceful demonstration in El Aaiún calling for the expansion of the remit of the UN Mission for the Referendum in Western Sahara (MIN-URSO) to include human rights monitoring. At a lobbying meeting held in London on 25 February, the prominent Sahrawi rights activist Brahim Dahane drew attention to an agreement quietly implemented in January, whereby lucrative fishing rights in the Western Sahara coastal area were to be made available to EU states—for a fee, paid to Morocco.

In its session of 29 April the UN Security Council extended the mandate of MINURSO—the only UN peacekeeping mission that existed without a human rights component—until 30 April, 2015.

In May, the Sahrawi Youth Movement for Change (YMC) published a video on Al-Arabiya news network claiming that the leadership of the Polisario Front, rather than representing the interests of the Sahrawi people, had in fact systemati-cally embezzled foreign aid funds destined for Sahrawi refugees. YMC also announced that it was creating a military wing in order to divert Polisario attempts to stop its activities, and demanded the replacement of the Front's old guard, including its leader since 1976, Mohamed Abdelaziz.

At the start of November, the ageing Sahrawi rights activist Mbarek Daoudi went on hunger strike in protest against pre-trial detention. Arrested in September 2013, Daoudi claimed to have been coerced into signing a "confession" and, in rapidly deteriorating health, was persuaded to end his strike on 21 December by an oral commitment from the authorities to set the trial date for 25 December.

Gabrielle Maas

VI EQUATORIAL AFRICA

ETHIOPIA—ERITREA—SOMALIA—DJIBOUTI

Ethiopia

CAPITAL: Addis Ababa   AREA: 1,104,300 sq km   POPULATION: 94,100,756 ('13)
OFFICIAL LANGUAGE: Amharic
HEAD OF STATE: President Mulatu Teshome (Oromo People's Democratic Organisation) (since Oct '13)
RULING PARTY: Ethiopian People's Revolutionary Democratic Front (EPRDF)
HEAD OF GOVERNMENT: Prime Minister Hailemariam Desalegn (EPRDF) (since Aug '12)
DEMOCRACY INDEX: 3.83; =118th of 167   CORRUPTION PERCEPTIONS INDEX: 33; =110th of 175
CURRENCY: Ethiopian Birr (Dec '14   £1.00=ETB 31.36,   US$1.00=ETB 20.19)
GNI PER CAPITA: US$470, Intl$1,350 at PPP ('13)

Eritrea

CAPITAL: Asmara   AREA: 117,600 sq km   POPULATION: 6,333,135 ('13)
OFFICIAL LANGUAGES: Arabic & Tigrinya
HEAD OF STATE AND GOVERNMENT: President Isayas Afewerki (since May '93)
RULING PARTY: People's Front for Democracy and Justice (PFDJ)
DEMOCRACY INDEX: 2.40; 155th of 167   CORRUPTION PERCEPTIONS INDEX: 18; =166th of 175
CURRENCY: Nakfa (Dec '14 £1.00=ERN 23.29,   US$1.00=ERN 15.00)
GNI PER CAPITA: US$490, Intl$1,180 at PPP ('13)

Somalia

CAPITAL: Mogadishu   AREA: 637,660 sq km   POPULATION: 10,495,583 ('13)
OFFICIAL LANGUAGES: Somali & Arabic
HEAD OF STATE: President Hassan Sheikh Mohamud (since Sept '12)
HEAD OF GOVERNMENT: Prime Minister Omar Abdirashid Ali Sharmarke (ind) (since Dec '14)
CORRUPTION PERCEPTIONS INDEX: 8; =174th of 175
CURRENCY: Somali Shilling (Dec '14 £1.00=SOS 1,092,   US$1.00=SOS 703)
GNI PER CAPITA: US$107 ('11, UN data)

Djibouti

CAPITAL: Djibouti   AREA: 23,200 sq km   POPULATION: 872,932 ('13)
OFFICIAL LANGUAGES: Arabic & French
HEAD OF STATE AND GOVERNMENT: President Ismail Omar Guelleh (since April '99)
RULING PARTY: Union for a People's Rally for Progress (RPP)
PRIME MINISTER: Abdoulker Kamil Mohamed (RPP) (since April '13)
DEMOCRACY INDEX: 2.96; 144th of 167   CORRUPTION PERCEPTIONS INDEX: 34; =107th of 175
CURRENCY: Djibouti Franc (Dec '14   £1.00=DJF 274.9,   US$1.00=DJF 177.0)
GNI PER CAPITA: US$1,592, Intl$2,915 at PPP ('13 IMF estimate)

THE year in **Ethiopia** was characterised by continuing economic growth and some signs of a loosening of economic control by the government, alongside incidents of political oppression and human rights violations.

Despite endemic poverty and inequality, the Ethiopian economy continued to grow overall at around 9 per cent during the year, and the country received its first sovereign credit ratings of "B1" from Moody's, "B" from both Fitch and Standard & Poor. The minister of finance, Sufian Ahmed, commented that this proved "the country's suitability for investment". After some hesitation, at year's end the government issued a 10-year $1 billion eurobond with a yield of 6.625 per cent that was quickly oversubscribed. The proceeds were to be used to support the development of energy and industrial infrastructure.

The government announced in April that the massive hydroelectric project at Benishangul-Gumuz on the Sudanese border would be entirely government-financed, rejecting offers of Egyptian investment. The project on the Blue Nile, renamed the Grand Ethiopian Renaissance Dam, had earlier caused conflict with Egypt (see AR 2014, p. 204), and talks continued with the downstream countries (Sudan and Egypt) in October, while construction work went on.

At the same time, the United Nations announced that an influx of over 120,000 refugees from South Sudan, intermittent drought and locust swarms meant that food aid was required for 6.5 million people; malnutrition remained a serious and widespread problem.

Several sectors of the economy began to be cautiously opened up to private investment during the year, under pressure from international organisations. Nevertheless, the government maintained tight control over banking, telecommunications and retail distribution, while allowing some foreign management contracts and consultancies.

Ongoing interest in the Ethiopian market of over 90 million people was expressed by such companies as Walmart, Heineken, Visa, Unilever and Nestlé. The IMF warned that massive investment in infrastructural projects such as road-building and hydroelectric dams could not be sustained if private capital was squeezed out. Meanwhile, the government continued to delay its application to join the World Trade Organisation (WTO), a move that required significant privatisation and liberalisation. Trade Minister Kebede Chane commented in May that Ethiopia was "taking one step at a time" and would probably not complete the process even in 2015.

Reporters and bloggers continued to face persecution. Shortly before a visit by US Secretary of State John Kerry in April, the police arrested nine journalists, several of them from the Amharic-language website Zone 9. They were later charged with plotting terrorist attacks. Kerry raised concerns about the incident during his visit. Exiled opposition leader Andargachew Tsige, secretary-general of the Ginbot 7 movement, was arrested and handed over to the Ethiopian authorities while in transit through Yemen. Andargachew, who held joint British and Ethiopian citizenship, was later described by Prime Minister Hailemariam as a "Trojan horse for the Eritrean government to destabilise the country". Amnesty International reported that the government was targeting ethnic Oromo people, up to 5,000 of whom had been arbitrarily arrested, tortured or killed since 2011 for allegedly supporting the separatist Oromo Liberation Front.

The construction of a Chinese-backed 35-km metro rail system—the first in Africa—in the capital, Addis Ababa, neared completion during the year. The system had 41 stations along two axes, running north-south and east-west. The co-pilot of an Ethiopian Airlines flight from Addis Ababa to Rome in February hijacked the aircraft and flew to Geneva, where he climbed out of the cockpit and down a rope to the ground. He then requested political asylum in Switzerland. At the end of the year another pilot fled to Eritrea in a military helicopter gunship.

Eritrea remained isolated internationally under the authoritarian regime of President Isaias Afeworki, one of only three African heads of state not to be invited to the US-Africa summit in Washington, DC in August. In June the United Nations set up a special commission of inquiry into human rights violations, and it was later reported that UN sanctions on Eritrea were to stay in place. The UN claimed that Eritrea supported armed militias in Somalia, Ethiopia and South Sudan.

Eritreans continued to flee in large numbers—as many as 2,000 per month—seeking to avoid open-ended military service, compulsory between the ages of 18 and 50. Italy came under pressure from boats loaded with refugees, many of them Eritreans, trying to reach its shores from North Africa. There were also an estimated 60,000 displaced Africans in Israel, mainly from Eritrea and Sudan.

Army conscripts worked on construction projects in harsh conditions, for less than $30 per month. Others worked in Western mining projects, and in December three refugees filed suit in Vancouver against the Canadian company, Nevshun Resources, alleging human rights abuses and complicity in the use of forced labour at Bisha mine, in which the Eritrean government held a 40 per cent share.

Reliable information on politics as well as data on the Eritrean economy remained hard to find. Even population estimates ranged from 3 to 6 million. Nonetheless, in its 2014 report, the Global Hunger Index classified the food situation as "extremely alarming".

In his speech on Independence Day in May, President Isaias, who reportedly depended increasingly on Ethiopian troops from the rebel Tigray People's Democratic Movement for his security, announced that a new constitution was to be drafted.

Instability in **Somalia** began to have a serious spill-over effect on neighbouring countries, especially Kenya, during 2014, and United States involvement in the country's affairs also increased significantly. Kenyan armed forces flew air strikes against the radical Islamist al-Shabaab group, which controlled large areas of the country, and in October the Kenyans foiled an attempt to infiltrate explosives across the frontier. Al-Shabaab launched several cross-border ambushes and attacks, killing civilians, and in May spokesperson Fuad Mohamed Khalaf threatened Nairobi with "Muslim teenage suicide bombers, explosions and battles". In March al-Shabaab also called for jihad against neighbouring Ethiopia, whose troops served in the African Union (AU) peacekeeping mission in Somalia (AMISOM).

The USA carried out several air strikes and drone attacks on al-Shabaab targets, killing fundamentalist leader Ahmed Abdi Godane in September and Tahliil Abdishakur, the movement's intelligence and security chief, in late December. In July it was revealed for the first time that 120 US military advisers had been secretly deployed inside Somalia since 2007, but had not been used in combat.

Al-Shabaab attacks and bombings continued throughout the year, especially in Mogadishu. In January the well-protected Jazira Hotel was bombed, killing a dozen people; in February Shabaab fighters attacked the presidential compound in an unsuccessful attempt to assassinate President Hassan Sheikh Mohamud. A second assault on the compound in July was repulsed by security forces, and in

November al-Shabaab fired mortar bombs into the complex. An elderly woman parliamentarian and former singer, Saado Ali Warsame, was shot and killed in her car, and various other bombings, killings and attacks, including an assault on parliament itself, cost dozens of lives.

The puritanical fundamentalists banned the use of the Internet, citing the authority of Sharia law, and threatened service providers with violence, even though the group regularly communicated via social media. In October a man was stoned to death for rape in Shabeellaha Hoose region, south of the capital.

The AU peacekeeping force besieged and recaptured the al-Shabaab stronghold of Baraawe on the coast, south-west of Mogadishu, in October, with the militants offering no resistance. The port had been used to export charcoal, mainly to the United Arab Emirates, Oman and Kuwait, providing revenue for the Islamists, but the government immediately halted the trade.

The Somali Federal Government (SFG) filed a case in the Netherlands against Kenya over a contested offshore block with significant oil reserves. The SFG accused a Norwegian company of illegal prospecting off the coast of autonomous Somaliland in the north, and the UN warned that a lack of transparency in the lucrative oil sector risked creating further disputes.

Hunger, malnutrition, high infant mortality, poor access to schooling, and ongoing sexual violence (with AU peacekeepers among those accused) continued to affect the well-being of ordinary Somalis, especially women and children. The rains failed in much of the country, and as many as 3 million people faced the threat of a second famine within three years, with humanitarian funding at only 12 per cent of what was required. In August the UN humanitarian coordinator, Philippe Lazzarini, warned of a "totally preventable" looming catastrophe.

Several hostages held by different groups around the country were freed in 2014. Two Kenyans were rescued in April after being kidnapped by Islamic fundamentalists in 2011, and a German journalist, kidnapped in Galkaayo over two years previously, was released after a ransom was paid. Also in exchange for a ransom payment, seven Indian merchant seamen were freed in October.

Somali pirates attempted 11 attacks in 2014, none of which resulted in the seizing of a vessel; what was initially reported as a successful hijacking in the Red Sea in January turned out to be an Eritrean naval operation against a ship in that country's territorial waters. Nevertheless, an estimated 50 hostages remained in pirate hands, often in precarious conditions.

Controversy dogged the SFG. A presidential advisor was accused by UN monitors of links to Islamist militants, but the government dismissed the allegations. Later in the year, Prime Minister Abdiweli Sheikh Ahmed told his cabinet that he was "ready to accept the resignation of any minister" who was unhappy with his leadership, but in early December he was voted out of office by parliament after a dispute with the President. He was eventually replaced by Omar Abdirashid Ali Sharmarke, who had been prime minister in 2009-10, and who promised inclusiveness and an end to the clan-based infighting.

Government weaponry was found for sale on the open market after the partial lifting of the UN arms embargo in 2013 (see AR 2014, p. 205), and by year's end the UN had authorised the inspection of ships suspected of smuggling weapons.

Strategically located on the 30-km wide Bab el-Mandeb strait at the mouth of the Red Sea, **Djibouti** continued to play an important geopolitical role in anti-terrorist campaigns throughout the year. In May it was reported that the country, which hosted both US and French military bases, had acted as a CIA "black site" for the US extraordinary rendition programme, and that several detainees had been illegally held there. The shortened US Senate report on torture, published later in the year, discounted as false claims that "enhanced interrogation techniques" had thwarted a plot against Camp Lemonier.

In May, President Ismail Omar Guelleh visited Washington, DC, meeting with US President Barack Obama. During the visit, an agreement was signed renewing the lease on Camp Lemonier for another 10 years, at a cost of $38 million a year. President Obama described the base, which had been used to launch drone attacks, as "a critical facility" for US interests in the region. Concerns about the 67-year old President Guelleh's health were reinforced in mid-year when he was flown to Paris to undergo surgery at a military hospital.

In December the government and the opposition USN (Union for National Salvation) reached an agreement for the party to take up eight seats in the 65-member parliament. The USN had boycotted the legislature since the 2013 elections, which it claimed were fraudulent.

In a suicide bombing in Djibouti city late in May, three people were killed and 15 injured in a café; authorities said the attackers were Somalis. In an unrelated incident in August, two people were wounded at the airport when a soldier opened fire, and in November the US government published a "travel advisory" warning visitors of terrorist threats against the country.

The economy in the mainly pastoral country—in its fourth year of drought—continued to rely on revenue from ports and harbours, and from mainly Chinese foreign direct investment. Government policy aimed to turn the country into a regional hub for trade, goods handling and financial services, and pursued an ambitious development programme for infrastructure, including new ports at Tadjourah for potash, and Goubet for salt.

Colin Darch

KENYA

CAPITAL: Nairobi   AREA: 580,370 sq km   POPULATION: 44,353,691 ('13)
OFFICIAL LANGUAGE: Kiswahili & English
HEAD OF STATE AND GOVERNMENT: President Uhuru Kenyatta (TNA) (since April '13)
RULING PARTIES: Party of National Unity (PNU) and Orange Democratic Movement (ODM)
DEMOCRACY INDEX: 5.13; 96th of 167   CORRUPTION PERCEPTIONS INDEX: 25; =145th of 175
CURRENCY: Kenyan Shilling (Dec '14 £1.00=KES 140.8, US$1.00=KES 90.67)
GNI PER CAPITA: US$930, Intl$2,250 at PPP ('13)

ON 5 December, the Office of the Prosecutor (OTP) at the International Criminal Court (ICC) withdrew charges against President Uhuru Kenyatta for his alleged role as an indirect co-perpetrator of crimes against humanity committed during the post-election violence of 2007-08. However, while President Kenyatta lauded the development as proof of his innocence, the OTP insisted that charges were only dropped because it was impossible to fully investigate and prosecute the crimes. The chief prosecutor cited the death, bribery and intimidation of key witnesses and the non-compliance of the Kenyan government in handing over requested records as insurmountable hurdles to a successful prosecution.

This left two Kenyans facing charges at the ICC: Deputy President William Ruto and the Kalenjin vernacular radio presenter, Joshua arap Sang. Ruto and Sang's trial began in September 2013, and 2014 saw the duo travel regularly to The Hague to hear prosecution witnesses. The Kenyan government continued to insist it was complying with the ICC; however, President Kenyatta simultaneously displayed his support for his deputy and Sang, announcing after the withdrawal of the charges against him: "As they say, one case down, two more to go."

The opposition Coalition for Reform and Democracy (CORD) held a series of high profile rallies to protest at the government's alleged undermining of the 2010 constitution and associated reforms, most notably the devolution of power to 46 new county governments. The rallies culminated in the launch of a referendum campaign—dubbed *Okoa Kenya* or "Save Kenya"—which demanded an increase in county government budgets. Soon after, county governors launched a second campaign—*Pesa Mashinani* or "money to the grassroots"—which also demanded more resources for county governments. The fact that governors felt unable to campaign alongside CORD reflected the depth of political division. However, the number of governors who initially came together also revealed the relevance of this new tier of government. In addition to this opposition, the government faced strained relations with vocal human rights organisations and media outlets, since there was the widespread perception that the government was using insecurity as a reason to close the political space.

Insecurity continued to be a problem with high levels of crime, violent cattle raids in pastoralist areas, and a series of terrorist attacks. These included a number of attacks in and around Mpeketoni in Lamu County in June, which left over 60 people dead, and the murder of 64 people in two attacks in Mandera County in November. Al-Shabaab, the radical Islamist group based in Somalia, claimed responsibility for these attacks and argued that they were in retaliation for Kenya's ongoing military presence in Somalia, following Kenya's invasion in early 2012 and the subsequent integration of Kenya's armed forces into the African Union Mission in Somalia (AMISOM).

In addition to the loss of life, these attacks led to a further deterioration in relations between the government and the political opposition, after President Kenyatta blamed local opposition forces for the Mpeketoni attacks. The government's counter-terrorist activities, which included an operation to round up and screen ethnic Somali in Nairobi's Eastleigh area, and the closure of several mosques at the coast—together with allegations of the state's involvement in the murder of a series of radical Islamic clerics—also strengthened a sense of political marginalisation amongst Kenya's Muslims. Finally, the attacks had a direct impact on the country's economy through the extension of travel advisories by a number of foreign governments, which negatively affected tourist numbers and future bookings. Despite these problems, the World Bank forecast in June that the Kenyan economy would expand by 4.7 per cent in 2014. The economy's resilience was linked to investments in large-scale infrastructure projects, the growth of the private sector and development of natural resources. At the same time, many complained of the high costs associated with devolution, endemic corruption, and high levels of inequality, and questioned the benefits brought by economic growth in and of itself.

Gabrielle Lynch

TANZANIA

CAPITAL: Dodoma   AREA: 947,300 sq km   POPULATION: 49,253,126 ('13)
OFFICIAL LANGUAGES: Kiswahili & English
HEAD OF STATE: President Jakaya Kikwete (CCM) (since Dec '05)
RULING PARTY: Chama Cha Mapinduzi (CCM)
HEAD OF GOVERNMENT: Prime Minister Mizengo Pinda (since Feb '08)
DEMOCRACY INDEX: 5.77; 89th of 167   CORRUPTION PERCEPTIONS INDEX: 31; =119th of 175
CURRENCY: Tanzanian Shilling (Dec '14 £1.00=TZS 2,694, US$1.00=TZS 1,735)
GNI PER CAPITA: US$630, Intl$1,750 at PPP ('13)

THE country's next general election, scheduled for 25 October 2015, overshadowed political debate and for the first time the political opposition looked capable of denting CCM's dominance. In October, the country's four main opposition parties—Chadema, Civic United Front (CUF), NCCR-Mageuzi and the National League for Democracy (NLD)—signed a cooperation pact and agreed to field joint candidates in 2015 in a bid to end 50 years of CCM rule. However, many remained sceptical of the ability of an opposition, long wracked by internal divisions, to work together in practice.

These four opposition parties also agreed to reject the government's draft constitution, which was to be put to a national referendum scheduled for April 2015. The constitutional reform process began with the Constitutional Review Act of 2011, which established the Constitutional Review Commission (CRC). The Commission's term ended in March 2014, when it passed a draft to the Constituent Assembly. However, the process was delayed when opposition Assembly members—who had come together in UKAWA, or the Coalition of Defenders of the People's Constitution—staged a walkout. Differences centred on the "union question" and whether Tanzania should continue with a two-government system, as preferred by President Kikwete and CCM, or should adopt a fully federal system with separate governments for Tanzania, Zanzibar and Tanganyika, as demanded by UKAWA.

In contrast to 2013, there was no serious violence between Muslims and Christians. However, many feared that the constitutional referendum and election could escalate tensions, which prompted various efforts to promote dialogue between religious leaders and communities.

Conservationists secured a victory in June, when the East African Court of Justice ruled that the government's plan to upgrade a road in the Serengeti national park was illegal. However, they made less progress in other areas, with Tanzania listed as the largest source of poached ivory (see AR 2014, pp. 438-39). "Operation Tokomeza Two"—an anti-poaching operation—was neither associated with the same excesses, nor with the high profile arrests, of the much-criticised "Operation Tokomeza" of 2013. Meanwhile, the London-based Environmental Investigation Agency released a report that accused Chinese officials and businesspeople of using high level visits to smuggle ivory out of the country.

China had become Tanzania's largest trading partner, and the largest source of investment after the UK. This included investment in ongoing infrastructure projects—such as the Mtwara-Dar es Salaam natural gas pipeline and Kinyerezi Power Station—and plans for a 150-acre logistics hub in Dar es Salaam. However, concerns about a further influx of cheap Chinese goods were raised after Tanzania announced that distribution facilities for the entry of Chinese goods into East Africa would be built before facilities for the export of local goods and resources to China.

The country's economy continued to perform strongly with projected growth rates of 7 per cent for 2014. This was largely due to growth in the transport, communications, manufacturing and agricultural sectors, and to public investment in infrastructure. Further discoveries of large offshore gas deposits raised hopes of higher economic growth rates in future years. However, analysts highlighted how the benefits of growth were limited and poverty levels remained high.

Gabrielle Lynch

UGANDA

CAPITAL: Kampala   AREA: 241,040 sq km   POPULATION: 37,578,876 ('13)
OFFICIAL LANGUAGE: English
HEAD OF STATE: President Yoweri Museveni (since Jan '86)
RULING PARTY: National Resistance Movement (NRM)
HEAD OF GOVERNMENT: Prime Minister Ruhakana Rugunda (NRM) (since Sept '14)
DEMOCRACY INDEX: 5.22; 95th of 167   CORRUPTION PERCEPTIONS INDEX: 26; =142nd of 175
CURRENCY: Uganda Shilling (Dec '14 £1.00=UGX 4,302, US$1.00=UGX 2,770)
GNI PER CAPITA: US$510, Intl$1,370 at PPP ('13)

PRESIDENT Yoweri Museveni's candidacy in the 2016 presidential election, and the perceived presidential ambitions of his prime minister, Amama Mbabazi, dominated political debate. In February, a section of National Resistance Movement (NRM) members of Parliament passed a resolution declaring Museveni to be the party's flag bearer and in September Museveni replaced Mbabazi with Dr Ruhakana Rugunda. Initially, Mbabazi retained his position of NRM secretary general; however, in October he agreed to take a period of "leave" after rumours of his presidential ambitions continued to circulate. Finally, at an NRM National Conference in December, the position of an elected secretary general was removed, confirming Mbabazi's ousting.

With momentum growing around "Support Museveni 2016", the opposition raised claims of voter bribery and wasted resources and opposition leader Kizza Besigye alleged that the government was printing excess money. The opposition also pushed for electoral reforms through six months of regional and sub-regional workshops and consultations, which culminated in a National Consultation Conference (NCC) in November, at which participants agreed to a compact on free and fair elections. However, while NRM had participated in previous consultations, President Museveni's non-attendance at the NCC was widely interpreted as evidence of the government's limited commitment to reforms. Repression of the opposition continued, although the police's active use of the 2013 Public Order Management Act lessened during the year.

The USA continued to lead efforts to arrest leaders of the Lord's Resistance Army (LRA) militia, now largely based in the Central African Republic, for trial at the International Criminal Court (ICC). This culminated in the LRA commander Dominic Ongwen surrendering himself in January 2015. At the same time, President Museveni took advantage of international appearances to publicly criticise the ICC and berate the West for using the Court to punish African leaders, in an effort to mobilise support within Uganda and also to forge alliances with leaders in neighbouring countries.

In February 2014, President Museveni signed into law the controversial Anti-Homosexuality Bill—which rendered the promotion of homosexuality, as well as homosexual acts, a criminal offence—but the Constitutional Court later declared the law invalid. Museveni also signed the Anti-Pornography Act. However, while police stated that the Act did not criminalise mini-skirts, it was dubbed the "anti-mini-skirt act" after Minister for Ethics and Integrity Simon Lokodo said it would help address indecent dressing by women. After the Act was signed, a number of women wearing mini-skirts and some men wearing low-slung trousers were publicly stripped.

Parliament prepared a final draft of the Public Finance Bill with provisions for a separate government account for oil revenues. However, while the Bank of Uganda agreed to publish figures on the Petroleum Investment Fund, analysts criticised plans over the lack of an independent oversight committee and the government's failure to set aside a clear budget to compensate those displaced.

The economy did relatively well with a projected GDP growth rate of 6.6 per cent for 2014. The government also launched a five-year anti-corruption strategy. However, corruption continued to be a significant problem and Uganda fell two places in Transparency International's Global Corruption Index, to 142nd of 175 listed countries worldwide.

Gabrielle Lynch

NIGERIA

CAPITAL: Abuja   AREA: 923,770 sq km   POPULATION: 173,615,345 ('13)
OFFICIAL LANGUAGE: English
HEAD OF STATE AND GOVERNMENT: President Goodluck Jonathan (since May '10; acting president
    since April '10)
RULING PARTY: People's Democratic Party (PDP)
DEMOCRACY INDEX: 3.77; 121st of 167   CORRUPTION PERCEPTIONS INDEX: 27; =136th of 175
CURRENCY: Naira (Dec '14 £1.00=NGN 285.0, US$1=NGN 183.6)
GNI PER CAPITA: US$2,710, Intl$5,360 at PPP ('13)

THE year exposed Nigeria's perilous political, economic and security situation. The presidency demonstrated remarkable apathy in the face of these challenges, but devised new ways of diverting the state's oil revenues and other public assets. With a political base in the country's oil-producing Niger Delta, President Goodluck Jonathan and his associates were well placed to do this. The presence of a plutocracy as the dominant force in Nigeria's political economy was not new. However, the degree of unaccountability and the federal government's brazen contempt for wider national interests was possibly more acute than ever before, certainly since 1999 when the military had relinquished power. There was no longer any pretence to be fighting corruption, nor any institutions empowered to do so. Sanusi Lamido Sanusi, the internationally respected former governor of the Nigerian Central Bank, raised questions about $20 billion in missing oil revenues, but nothing was done. Meanwhile the falling world oil price led to a sharp decrease in the value of the Naira, from 155 to the dollar at the beginning of the year to 180 by the end. Sanusi became the Emir of Kano, succeeding Ado Bayero, who had been Emir since 1953 and had died on 6 June.

Political accountability and socio-economic development were higher in some of Nigeria's 36 states than others. Reforms over the previous eight years under Governor Babatunde Fashola in Lagos state, for example, improved the local infrastructure and economy. Fashola's administration continued to ensure that internally generated revenue from taxation surpassed Lagos state's share of the oil derivation from the federal account. But the megacity still faced major challenges. As in the rest of Nigeria, there were daily electricity outages lasting for hours at a time and widespread poverty. The last poverty rating for Nigeria, in 2010, indicated an upward trend, with 60 per cent of the population living in poverty. This was compounded by rapid population growth and the heavy concentration of wealth in the hands of a relatively small elite. In 2014 the rebasing of the Nigerian economy made it the largest in Africa, but inequalities were widening and some 60 per cent of the population lived on less than $1 per day.

Nigerian politics in 2014 was dominated by the build-up to the presidential election scheduled for February 2015. The People's Democratic Party (PDP), in power since the transition to civilian rule in 1999, nominated the incumbent President Jonathan to stand for a second full term in office. This was expected, but a significant development was the emergence of a potent political opposition in the All Progressives Congress (APC). The APC was formed through an amalgamation of the dominant regional opposition parties from the 2011 election: the Congress for Progressive Change (CPC) and the All Nigeria Peoples Party (ANPP) in the north, and the Action Congress of Nigeria (ACN) in the south-west. Whereas these parties had contested the 2011 elections separately and failed to agree on a common presidential candidate, this time they reached an agreement and merged. This was followed by a steady tide of defections from the PDP to the APC. Five out of a group of seven influential state governors, the "G7", left the PDP and joined the opposition, carrying their states with them. The speaker of the House of Representatives, Aminu Tambuwal, defected in November.

The retired army general, Muhammadu Buhari, won the APC presidential primaries in December. Buhari was a Muslim from Daura, in north-west Nigeria, and had served as military head of state in 1984-85 after the overthrow of Shehu Shagari. He had contested and lost the three previous post-1999 presidential elections—in 2003, 2007 and 2011—but he remained by far the most popular politician in northern Nigeria (except among the northern elite). In previous elections Buhari had carried the northern vote, but had less appeal in the south. In 2014 the opposition APC bridged this regional divide. Buhari's candidacy received northern support and was backed by the political "kingmaker" in the south-west, former Lagos state governor Bola Tinubu, who had a powerful influence over the Yoruba bloc of the APC's elite. Professor Yemi Osinbajo, a lawyer and pastor from the south-west, was selected as Buhari's running mate. With internal cohesion and a credible Muslim-Christian, North-South ticket, the APC election campaign gathered momentum. It had the strategic input of advisors and technocrats with established records in south-western politics, progressive civil society support, and northern support. Faced with the growing possibility of the first democratic transfer of power in Nigeria's modern history, the PDP government attempted to subvert the APC through coercion and by raiding their offices.

In the meantime there was a further collapse of security in large areas of the north. The Nigerian state lost control of a swathe of territory in the north-east in and around Borno and the Lake Chad Basin to Boko Haram ("Westernisation is unlawful"). This was the colloquial name for a jihadist movement that called itself *Jama'at ahl al-sunna li'l da'wa w'al jihad* (Sunnis for Proselytisation and Armed Struggle). An estimated 10,000 people were killed in the insurgency in 2014, making it one of the most deadly in the world. In December the United Nations High Commissioner for Refugees (UNHCR) reported that at least 1.5 million civilians had been displaced by the violence, most of them internally. UNHCR also recorded that 152,000 people had fled north-east Nigeria into Niger, Cameroon and Chad, further increasing the refugee burden in those countries. In August the jihadists captured the town of Gwoza, in south-east Borno, having previously killed the Emir of Gwoza and driven Christians out of the area. They also overran other towns and cities in the region. The crisis exposed the weakness of the Nigerian army, which had often retreated in the face of Boko Haram attacks, leaving the civilian population at the mercy of the insurgents. Boko Haram appropriated the routed military's weapons, including armoured vehicles and tanks, as a matter of routine.

On the night of 14-15 April, Boko Haram abducted more than 270 schoolgirls from the Government Girls Secondary School in Chibok, southern Borno state.

They transported them in a convoy of trucks to the Sambisa forest, a large area of savannah bush that Boko Haram controlled. President Jonathan did not comment on the tragedy for three weeks, until 4 May when the domestic and international outcry became deafening. The following day Boko Haram released a video of the captured Chibok girls, wearing hijabs, and claimed some of them had been converted from Christianity to Islam. Abubakar Shekan, the leader of Boko Haram, said the girls who did not convert would be sold as slaves or held hostage; it was thought the rest were forced to marry Boko Haram fighters. The "Bring Back Our Girls" campaign was a humanitarian response, starting in Nigeria and then spreading worldwide on social media. The Nigerian federal government saw the campaign as a threat. It harassed and sought to discredit its leaders, with the president's wife, Patience Jonathan, even suggesting that the abduction had been fabricated. None of the girls were rescued, although around 50 managed to escape. Boko Haram's abduction of the girls in Chibok was the largest, but neither the first nor the last kidnapping by the insurgents in 2014. In November, the jihadists overran Chibok completely and went on a killing spree, retreating only after soldiers were mobilised to retake it.

The insurgency was not contained in the north-east: hundreds were killed in bombings across northern Nigeria, many by female suicide bombers, a new and disturbing trend that included girls as young as 10. The central market of Jos was again struck with car bombs, killing 120 people on 20 May. In Kaduna, on 23 July, suicide bombers attacked the convoy of General Buhari and, separately, Sheikh Dahiru Bauchi, a Tijaniyya Sufi leader. Both narrowly escaped but at least 82 people died. Boko Haram killed as many as 400 Muslim worshippers during Friday prayers at Kano central mosque on 28 November with bombs and assault rifles, following Emir Sanusi's call on Muslims to rise up against the sect. Boko Haram attacks were a daily occurrence. The Western diplomatic response to the escalating crisis was to encourage the more competent armies of Cameroon, Niger and Chad, whose borders were threatened, to assist the Nigerians. The USA and the UK sent military advisors to help Nigeria, but without structural reforms to improve the country's military capacity, external assistance had only a limited impact.

Adam Higazi

GHANA—SIERRA LEONE—THE GAMBIA—LIBERIA

Ghana

CAPITAL: Accra   AREA: 238,540 sq km   POPULATION: 25,904,598 ('13)
OFFICIAL LANGUAGE: English
HEAD OF STATE AND GOVERNMENT: President John Dramani Mahama (NDC) (since July '12)
RULING PARTY: National Democratic Congress (NDC)
DEMOCRACY INDEX: 6.33; 68th of 167   CORRUPTION PERCEPTIONS INDEX: 48; =61st of 175
CURRENCY: Cedi (Dec '14 £1.00=GHS 4.99, US$1.00=GHS 3.22)
GNI PER CAPITA: US$1,760, Intl$3,880 at PPP ('13)

Sierra Leone

CAPITAL: Freetown   AREA: 71,740 sq km   POPULATION: 6,092,075 ('13)
OFFICIAL LANGUAGE: English
HEAD OF STATE AND GOVERNMENT: President Ernest Bai Koroma (APC) (since Sept '07)
RULING PARTY: All People's Congress (APC)
DEMOCRACY INDEX: 4.64; =107th of 167   CORRUPTION PERCEPTIONS INDEX: 31; =119th of 175
CURRENCY: Leone (Dec '14 £1.00=SLL 6,595, US$1.00=SLL 4,247)
GNI PER CAPITA: US$680, Intl$1,750 at PPP ('13)

The Gambia

CAPITAL: Banjul   AREA: 11,300 sq km   POPULATION: 1,849,285 ('13)
OFFICIAL LANGUAGE: English
HEAD OF STATE AND GOVERNMENT: President (Col) Yahya Jammeh (APRC) (since Sept '96)
RULING PARTY: Alliance for Patriotic Reorientation and Construction (APRC)
DEMOCRACY INDEX: 3.31; 133rd of 167   CORRUPTION PERCEPTIONS INDEX: 29; =126th of 175
CURRENCY: Dalasi (Dec '14 £1.00=GMD 66.93, US$1.00=GMD 43.10)
GNI PER CAPITA: US$510, Intl$1,620 at PPP ('13)

Liberia

CAPITAL: Monrovia   AREA: 111,370 sq km   POPULATION: 4,294,077 ('13)
OFFICIAL LANGUAGE: English
HEAD OF STATE AND GOVERNMENT: Ellen Johnson-Sirleaf, President (since Jan '06)
RULING PARTY: Unity Party
DEMOCRACY INDEX: 4.95; 100th of 167   CORRUPTION PERCEPTIONS INDEX: 37; =94th of 175
CURRENCY: Liberian Dollar (Dec '14 £1.00=LRD 127.3, US$1=LRD 82.0)
GNI PER CAPITA: US$410, Intl$790 at PPP ('13)

SPARED from the outbreak of the Ebola virus that affected the region in 2014, **Ghana** still faced a difficult year economically. As elsewhere in Africa, tourism and travel were affected by fears of Ebola. This impact was worsened by rapidly falling commodity prices for oil, cocoa and gold, the mainstays of Ghanaian export activity. Official projected growth rates were revised downwards several times, and fell below the previous year's growth.

The cedi, Ghana's currency, fluctuated throughout the year, dropping 40 per cent at one point and ending the year down 27 per cent against the US dollar. This combined with rising inflation to exacerbate existing problems of rural and urban underdevelopment, and a stretched middle class. Electricity supply problems meant that power to a number of districts was cut off for up to 12 hours per day, affecting both industry and individuals. Labour strikes and a Ghanaian middle-class "Occupy" protest movement highlighted the widely ranging impact of the financial crisis on different sectors of the economy.

The government and business responded to these poor economic conditions by issuing a $1 billion eurobond and a $1.7 billion cocoa loan. The government also sought assistance from the IMF. In the final quarter of the year, they reached an agreement over a three-year IMF assistance programme and an approved Ghanaian budget, which included a stronger tax regime.

Politically, the move to bring in the IMF was used by the opposition Progressive People's Party (PPP) as evidence of President John Mahama and the ruling National Democratic Congress's (NDC) poor handling of the economic crisis.

Ghana also went to the football World Cup in Brazil in 2014. Although the team finished last in their group, they made international headlines when players threatened to boycott training before their final game against Portugal because of fears that they would not receive their appearance fees from the Ghanaian government. The government sent $3 million to the players on a plane at the last minute and the game went ahead as scheduled.

Sierra Leone's first case of the Ebola virus appeared in May, when a healer who had visited a community in Guinea returned to the country and died. In June, borders with Liberia and Guinea were closed, schools were shut, and quarantines began to be enforced. The number of cases multiplied quickly, however, and by July, Sierra Leone reported more cases than either Liberia or Guinea. In the same month the virus moved to the capital, Freetown. Eventually, every district of the country was affected.

Daytime curfews were imposed in the autumn and public Christmas and New Year celebrations were banned in order to limit the risk of infection. Public health services were overwhelmed, as was the general infrastructure of the country, including sanitation services. Attempts to keep up with the burial of the dead saw overburdened and underpaid workers give up in protest at their working conditions. Nearly 10,000 cases were reported and by the end of the year almost 3,000 people had died from the disease.

As in the other affected countries, the virus had a significant impact on Sierra Leone's economy. London Mining, which was responsible for nearly 15 per cent of the country's annual growth in the previous year, stopped operations for the duration of the outbreak. The agriculture sector was severely affected by restrictions on movement and the World Food Programme was required to step in with emergency food aid. Building projects that relied on Chinese construction workers were halted. Schools and universities were shut.

This was all the more tragic as, at the beginning of the year, Sierra Leone had seemed to be emerging from post-civil war recovery and making clear strides toward sustained economic growth. As a result of Ebola's impact on the economy, projected growth rates of 11.3 per cent at the beginning of 2014 were revised downward to 4.0 per cent and growth rates for 2015 were revised down from 8.9 per cent to -2.0 per cent by the World Bank.

The Gambia avoided the Ebola outbreak, closing its air borders with the affected countries and working with neighbouring Senegal on spreading awareness and monitoring incoming airline passengers. People who had travelled in Sierra Leone, Guinea, Liberia and Mali within the previous 21 days were restricted from entering the country

With tourism throughout the region suffering as a result of the Ebola outbreak, the Gambia had a slow year in terms of economic growth. Tourism dropped by 60 per cent on 2013. Since tourism accounted for 16 per cent of the economy, this contributed to the country missing its target growth rate of 7.5 per cent.

There was relatively little political activity noticed by the international community in comparison to previous years, until 30 December when two Gambian-US nationals attempted to stage a coup whilst President Yahya Jammeh was out of the country. Cherno Njie and Papa Faal were responsible for orchestrating the coup attempt, which quickly failed when members of the military did not join them in attempting to overthrow Jammeh.

The minority leader in government, as well as the United Nations and the USA, condemned the attack. International rights groups worried that this would lead to further restrictions on the rights and freedoms of the country's citizens. The country had made itself notorious in preceding years for its execution of political prisoners. Jammeh visited Washington, DC, in August for the first US-Africa leaders summit, but in October he once again upset European and US observers by issuing a new decree making homosexuality punishable by a life sentence in prison. A report by the NGO, Freedom House, also listed the Gambia as one of the most repressive countries in Africa with regard to Internet access and monitoring of online activity. It was believed that the failed coup would only tighten the strict control over information and increase reprisals for dissent.

In March, the Ebola outbreak that began in Guinea in December 2013 reached Lofa and Nimba counties in **Liberia**. By June, the outbreak reached Monrovia. President Ellen Johnson-Sirleaf imposed a series of emergency measures, including shutting schools, banning football matches, closing international borders, imposing a curfew, and bringing in some troops to cordon off areas of epidemic and enforce quarantines. Unfortunately, the measures taken by the government did not stop the spread of the virus.

In July, Liberian-American Patrick Sawyer died in Nigeria on his way back to Minnesota from Liberia. This was the first recorded case of Ebola in Nigeria. In August, two more US health workers were infected with the disease in Liberia and evacuated. They later recovered in the USA.

On 20 August, a riot broke out in the West Point region of Monrovia. The area had been forcibly quarantined and residents were attempting to leave. Distrust of the government, stemming from the long years of civil war, combined with some misunderstanding of how the disease was spread to create fear amongst the population. A violent confrontation followed with the Liberian national police and the armed forces, and one person was killed. Ten days later, the quarantine was lifted.

By September the World Health Organisation (WHO) identified cases in all but one county of Liberia. However, just as a new, 150-bed clinic was opened in

Monrovia and the United Nations announced that the epidemic was out of control, the number of new cases began to slow. This was attributed to rising awareness of how the disease was spread, including music videos made by local performers with public health messages, and community-based adaptations and sanitation efforts. In November, President Sirleaf ended the state of emergency. In December, a new serum therapy, using the blood of surviving Ebola patients, was introduced in the country.

At the end of the year, Liberia had suffered more than 8,000 cases of Ebola, with nearly 3,500 deaths. Many of the country's health workers were killed by the disease as well—174 doctors and nurses, according to the WHO—leaving the already short-staffed hospital infrastructure in desperate need of additional staff. The impact of the disease on the country's fragile health services raised questions about how to build a better system for the future and how to adapt national rebuilding priorities to reflect the lessons learned from this outbreak.

The disease's toll extended beyond those infected, with small businesses suffering, international trade in decline, and non-Ebola hospital admissions sidelined. The outbreak also had a detrimental effect on the provision of education, with schools closed for more than six months. Unemployment increased, especially amongst the self-employed, but also amongst government workers and teachers, whose offices and schools were shut during the state of emergency. Food shortages resulted from the restrictions imposed on travel between counties in an effort to contain the outbreak. A number of construction projects and foreign investments were put on hold, including the Mount Coffee hydroelectric plant. Major international employers, like the iron-ore mining company ArcelorMittal, stopped operations and evacuated their foreign employees. The tyre manufacturer, Firestone, on the other hand, set up its own clinics and successfully contained the virus amongst its workers and their families in Harbel, where its rubber plantation was located.

With the number of new cases of Ebola slowing, the year 2014 closed with hope that the outbreak would end, but also an awareness that there was much rebuilding to be done.

Bronwen Everill

NIGER—MALI—MAURITANIA—SENEGAL—GUINEA— CÔTE D'IVOIRE—BURKINA FASO—TOGO—BENIN

Niger

CAPITAL: Niamey   AREA: 1,267,000 sq km   POPULATION: 17,831,270 ('13)
OFFICIAL LANGUAGE: French
HEAD OF STATE AND GOVERNMENT: President Mahamadou Issoufou (PNDS) (since April '11)
RULING PARTY: Niger Party for Democracy and Socialism (PNDS)
PRIME MINISTER: Brigi Raffini (since April '11)
DEMOCRACY INDEX: 4.08; 114th of 167   CORRUPTION PERCEPTIONS INDEX: 35; =103rd of 175
CURRENCY: West African CFA Franc BCEAO (Dec '14 £1=XOF 788.44, US$1.00=XOF 476.04)
GNI PER CAPITA: US$410, Intl$910 at PPP ('13)

Mali

CAPITAL: Bamako   AREA: 1,240,190 sq km   POPULATION: 15,301,650 ('13)
OFFICIAL LANGUAGE: French
HEAD OF STATE AND GOVERNMENT: President Ibrahim Bubacar Keita (Rally for Mali, RPM) (since Nov '13)
RULING PARTY: Change Party
PRIME MINISTER: Moussa Mara (Change Party) (since April '14)
DEMOCRACY INDEX: 5.90; 81st of 167   CORRUPTION PERCEPTIONS INDEX: 328; =115th of 175
CURRENCY: West African CFA Franc (see above)
GNI PER CAPITA: US$670, Intl$1,540 at PPP ('13)

Mauritania

CAPITAL: Nouakchott   AREA: 1,030,700 sq km   POPULATION: 3,889,880 ('13)
OFFICIAL LANGUAGES: French & Arabic
HEAD OF STATE AND GOVERNMENT: President General Mohamed Ould Abdelaziz (since Aug '09)
PRIME MINISTER: Yahya Ould Hademine (ind) (since Aug '14)
DEMOCRACY INDEX: 4.17; 111th of 167   CORRUPTION PERCEPTIONS INDEX: 30; =124th of 175
CURRENCY: Ouguiya (Dec '14 £1.00=MRO 455, US$1.00=MRO 293)
GNI PER CAPITA: US$1,060, Intl$2,850 at PPP ('13)

Senegal

CAPITAL: Dakar   AREA: 196,720 sq km   POPULATION: 14,133,280 ('13)
OFFICIAL LANGUAGE: French
HEAD OF STATE AND GOVERNMENT: President Macky Sall (APR) (since April '12)
RULING PARTY: Alliance for the Republic (APR)
PRIME MINISTER: Mohammed Dionne (APR) (since July '14)
DEMOCRACY INDEX: 6.15; 75th of 167   CORRUPTION PERCEPTIONS INDEX: 43; =69th of 175
CURRENCY: West African CFA Franc (see above)
GNI PER CAPITA: US$1,070, Intl$2,240 at PPP ('13)

Guinea

CAPITAL: Conakry   AREA: 245,860 sq km   POPULATION: 11,745,189 ('13)
OFFICIAL LANGUAGE: French
HEAD OF STATE AND GOVERNMENT: Alpha Condé (RPG) (since Dec '10)
RULING PARTY: Rally of the Guinean People (RPG)
PRIME MINISTER: Mohamed Said Fofana (since Dec '10)
DEMOCRACY INDEX: 2.84; 147th of 167   CORRUPTION PERCEPTIONS INDEX: 25; =145th of 175
CURRENCY: Guinean Franc (Dec '14 £1.00=GNF 10,917, US$1=GNF 7,030)
GNI PER CAPITA: US$460, Intl$1,160 at PPP ('13)

Côte d'Ivoire

CAPITAL: Yamoussoukro (official) Abidjan (de facto)   AREA: 322,460 sq km   POPULATION: 20,316,086 ('13)
OFFICIAL LANGUAGE: French
HEAD OF STATE AND GOVERNMENT: President Alassane Ouattara (RDR) (since Dec '10)
RULING PARTIES: Rally of the Republicans (RDR) and Democratic Party of Côte d'Ivoire (PDCI)
PRIME MINISTER: Daniel Kablan Duncan (PDCI) (since Nov '12)
DEMOCRACY INDEX: 3.25; 137th of 167   CORRUPTION PERCEPTIONS INDEX: 32; =115th of 175
CURRENCY: West African CFA Franc (see above)
GNI PER CAPITA: US$1,380, Intl$2,900 at PPP ('13)

Burkina Faso

CAPITAL: Ouagadougou   AREA: 274,000 sq km   POPULATION: 16,934,839 ('13)
OFFICIAL LANGUAGE: French
HEAD OF STATE AND GOVERNMENT: Interim President Michel Kafando (since Nov '14)
PRIME MINISTER: Yacouba Isaac Zida (since Nov '14)
DEMOCRACY INDEX: 4.15; 112th of 167   CORRUPTION PERCEPTIONS INDEX: 38; =85th of 175
CURRENCY: West African CFA Franc (see above)
GNI PER CAPITA: US$670, Intl$1,560 at PPP ('13)

Togo

CAPITAL: Lomé   AREA: 56,790 sq km   POPULATION: 6,816,982 ('13)
OFFICIAL LANGUAGES: French, Kabiye & Ewe
HEAD OF STATE AND GOVERNMENT: President Faure Gnassingbé (RPT) (since May '05)
RULING PARTY: Rally of the Togolese People (RPT)
PRIME MINISTER: Kwesi Seleagodji Ahoomey-Zunu (Patriotic Pan-African Convergence, CPP) (since July '12)
DEMOCRACY INDEX: 3.45; 128th of 167   CORRUPTION PERCEPTIONS INDEX: 29; =126th of 175
CURRENCY: West African CFA Franc (see above)
GNI PER CAPITA: US$530, Intl$1,180 at PPP ('13)

Benin

CAPITAL: Porto Novo   AREA: 112,620 sq km   POPULATION: 10,323,474 ('13)
OFFICIAL LANGUAGE: French
HEAD OF STATE AND GOVERNMENT: President Yayi Boni (since April '06)
RULING PARTY: Cauri Forces for an Emerging Benin (FCBE)
DEMOCRACY INDEX: 5.87; =82nd of 167   CORRUPTION PERCEPTIONS INDEX: 39; =80th of 175
CURRENCY: West African CFA franc (see above)
GNI PER CAPITA: US$790, Intl$1,780 at PPP ('13)

BORDERED on three sides by countries experiencing major security crises, **Niger** deepened its cooperation with African and Western security partners in 2014. The government of President Mahamadou Issoufou had been pressing vocally for tougher international action to counter the threat posed by jihadist militant groups in the Sahara and the Sahel. The absence of state authority in the south of Libya allowed jihadist militant groups to use the region as a supply base from which to traffic weapons and other supplies through northern Niger to groups of fighters in Mali. And from there, the jihadist groups threatened to mount attacks into the west of Niger itself, as they had done in mid-2013. Meanwhile, in north-eastern Nigeria the Islamist group Boko Haram continued its campaign of terror. Issoufou's government was concerned about the risk that this activity could spill over the border into Niger; there were also worries that some Boko Haram fighters might have cultivated Nigérien sympathisers and recruits.

To counter these threats the Issoufou administration was willing to accept the presence of French and US forces, with both basing surveillance drones at Niamey, together with French strike planes. Meanwhile, France established a small forward base at Madama, in the far north, to counter the security threat from southern Libya. The French deployments formed part of Opération Barkhane, a new long-term strategic presence spread across the Sahel region to counter the threat of radical jihadism. Meanwhile, the Nigérien government continued to contribute a substantial troop contingent to the UN's MINUSMA peacekeeping force in Mali. Over the previous two years, President Issoufou had also made use of his contacts among the Touareg to negotiate the release of French hostages held by jihadists in the Malian Sahara and in December he sent an envoy to north-east Mali to secure the release of the sole remaining French hostage in the region, Serge Lazarevic, who was retrieved by Nigérien forces and brought back to Niamey on 9 December.

In May 2014 President Issoufou joined other regional leaders in Paris for talks about coordinating action against Boko Haram in northern Nigeria. Plans began to be made for the creation of a new regional joint force, combining troops from Chad, Niger, Nigeria, Cameroon and possibly Benin. In theory a joint regional security force already existed for the Lake Chad region, but in practice it had functioned only intermittently. By the end of 2014 planning for the new joint force had advanced significantly.

Meanwhile, party politics in Niger became increasingly tense following the breakdown of the political alliance between the government and Hama Amadou, leader of MODEN-FA (Nigérien Democratic Movement for an African Federation) and speaker of the National Assembly. It had become increasingly clear that Amadou had ambitions to challenge Issoufou in the 2016 presidential election. In May, security sources claimed there had been a coup plot and the authorities arrested Hama Amadou's eldest son, Ismaël and some 40 associates.

The speaker and his second wife were also implicated in an official investigation into the purchase of infants born in a Nigérien "baby factory" run by criminals holding girls as sex slaves. Amadou's wife was arrested and the speaker himself fled to Europe after MPs voted to lift his parliamentary immunity.

After the optimism of late 2013—which had seen President Ibrahim Boubacar Keïta elected with a triumphal popular mandate and the international community pledge more than €3 billion in recovery and development assistance (see AR 2014, pp. 221-23)—the year 2014 brought a sobering reality check for **Mali**.

Little progress resulted from the government's initial exploratory talks with the mainly Touareg nationalist rebels: the Azawad National Liberation Movement (MNLA), the High Council for the Unity of Azawad (HCUA) and the Arab Movement of Azawad (MAA). Meanwhile, the government was slow to articulate a clear strategy for rebuilding services in the north and strengthening governance. By the middle of the year, the president's post-election popularity had long since faded, whilst international partners had become disillusioned with the inconsistent performance of his administration.

Keïta had been elected as a strong figure who could be trusted to restore national pride and bring peace to the north of the country. Yet he failed to take advantage of his early popularity and political strength to persuade Malians of the need to make compromises for the sake of national reconciliation. In the early part of the year, the MNLA and HCUA were on the defensive, as the French military and the UN's umbrella peacekeeping force, MINUSMA, built up their positions across the north. This had strengthened the government's negotiating hand for the expected talks over the future of the region. But matters were allowed to drift. In forming his government, Keïta had entrusted the national reconciliation and northern regions portfolio to a close personal confidant, Cheick Oumar Diarrah, who did hold exploratory talks with the northern rebels but who lacked resources and administrative support and proved clumsy in his dealings with northern community leaders.

On the rebel side, too, there were obstacles to progress. Although the MNLA and HCUA had signed the 18 June 2013 Ouagadougou Accord, which affirmed that Mali would remain a united state within its existing borders, these two groups wanted to secure recognition of all or large parts of the north as a distinct, highly autonomous entity—"Azawad". Yet the MNLA and HCUA were supported only by a section of the northern population, notably the Ifoghas Touareg from the Kidal region in the far north east. Among many other strands of the Touareg, such as the Imghad, there was much less interest in the Azawad cause and, frequently, outright resentment of MNLA/HCUA pretentions to speak for all Touareg or all northerners. Armed groups such as the Ganda Izo and Ganda Koy saw themselves as defenders of the interests of settled northern farming communities, such as the Songhai; they were firmly committed to the cause of a united Mali. Indeed, the strength of support for Malian unity among many northerners had been reflected in the December 2013 legislative elections, when most northern towns south of the Sahara itself had seen high voter turnout. Algeria hosted talks in early 2014 in an effort to establish some common ground among the various northern armed factions, but these made little progress and were, in any case, snubbed by the MNLA.

Meanwhile in Bamako the prime minister, Oumar Tatam Ly, was finding it increasingly difficult to press forward with reform of the government machine. A technocrat from the BCEAO (the central bank for the West African franc zone), he encountered obstruction from factional political interests. There was pressure from powerful players in Keïta's Rally for Mali (RPM), who resented the fact that their party had not been given the premiership, even though it had been the main winner in the presidential and legislative elections. Tatam Ly was also reported to be exasperated by the influence exercised by Keïta's son, Karim, an RPM parliamentarian and chair of the National Assembly defence committee. On 5 April, the premier resigned, making public his frustrations.

To replace him, Keïta chose Moussa Mara, the youthful minister of urban affairs, a much more political figure. In 2007 he had come close to toppling Keïta from his Bamako parliamentary seat, but the two men later became allies. Mara's small Yelema (Change) party, with only one seat in the National Assembly, was in no position to challenge the president's political dominance. The reshuffled government team was notable for the creation of portfolios focused on key issues related to the north, such as decentralisation and humanitarian relief. Diarrah was replaced as reconciliation minister by Zaraby Sidi Ould Mohamed, hitherto foreign minister, a Timbuktu Arab who had been a rebel at one stage in the 1990s.

However, Mara—with a career forged in Bamako urban affairs—lacked experience and contacts in the complex northern Mali environment. This became evident on a visit to the Sahara town of Kidal on 17 May, heartland of support for the MNLA and HCUA. Mara failed to include on his agenda goodwill visits to Touareg notables or the leaders of the armed groups, concentrating instead on the local Malian army garrison and the small band of central government civil servants. This one-sided visit provoked protests by Azawad nationalist supporters, a panicky counter-reaction by government security forces and the intervention of MNLA and HCUA fighters, aided by some jihadi militants. Mara had to be rescued by the international forces, whilst the rebels drove the army out of town and repulsed a subsequent government counter-attack. The cost was severe, with about 50 soldiers killed in fighting and several civil servants murdered.

The strategic and political impact was also devastating. The MNLA and HCUA exploited the momentum to seize a string of settlements in the north-east, while the confidence of the Malian army—whose key units had been retrained by a special EU mission (EUTM)—was badly shaken. The respected defence minister, Soumeylou Boubeye Maïga, resigned to defend the honour of his commanders, whom politicians had ordered to launch the ill-fated counter-attack which cost so many soldiers' lives. The UN and French peacekeepers in Kidal remained neutral rather than intervening to support the army, and President Keïta had to invite the incumbent chairman of the African Union, Mauritania's President Mohamed Ould Abdelaziz, to fly to Kidal and negotiate on his behalf to secure a truce with the rebels.

Weakened and humiliated, the Mali government was ill-placed to procrastinate further over peace talks, under a fresh Algerian initiative supported by a wide range of African and international partners. Formal negotiations finally opened in Algiers in July. However, the government was now negotiating from a far weaker position than it would have enjoyed had talks been launched in the early part of 2014. By contrast, the MNLA and HCUA, and an allied MAA faction, had been strengthened in military terms and were full of renewed political self-confidence; groups representing different northern strands of opinion were weak or unrepresented. Throughout subsequent rounds of talks, the MNLA and HCUA remained adamant in demanding a distinct status for the north, as a highly autonomous Azawad entity within an overall federal or confederal Mali. This was far beyond what the government was prepared to offer, or indeed what many elements of the northern Malian population were prepared to accept. By late 2014, these differences were starting to be reflected in the military environment, with the emergence in the Gao region of Gatia (Groupe autodéfense touareg Imghad et alliés), a pro-government militia claiming to represent the interests of the Imghad Touareg.

Meanwhile, jihadist armed groups, excluded from the peace talks, continued to stage regular attacks. Under a new long term strategy for the Sahel and Sahara, the

French established a major permanent base at Gao, and maintained smaller bases at Kidal and Tessalit. They based surveillance drones and warplanes at Niamey in Niger, better placed than Bamako for overflying the Malian Sahara.

The government faced other serious challenges, too. In mid-2014 the IMF suspended its programme of support for Mali after concerns surfaced about the procedures used for military procurement and the purchase of a new presidential jet. The programme was only restored late in the year, after an audit of the transactions ordered by Finance Minister Bouaré Fily Sissoko at the Fund's insistence. This revealed severe financial abuses in the military purchases, and found the jet had been purchased for a competitive price. Nevertheless, the affair seriously damaged President Keïta's image.

However, the Malian authorities demonstrated speed and competence in dealing with two cases of travellers arriving from Guinea with Ebola fever. Most of the contacts of the Ebola patients were rapidly traced; in total, at least six people died, in part due to apparent failings in the controls operated by a clinic where one ill person had been.

In **Mauritania**, the ruling Union for the Republic (UPR) of President Mohamed Ould Abdelaziz sought to build upon its electoral success of late 2013 and consolidate its institutional dominance before the presidential election expected in mid-2014. When outgoing parliamentary speaker Messaoud Ould Boulkheir opted not to seek re-election, the UPR managed to secure the position for its own nominee, fighting off a challenge from the moderate Islamist Tawassoul party. A deal with Boulkheir's Progressive Popular Alliance (APP) also enabled the UPR to secure the chairmanship of the important Nouakchott conurbation council.

As expected, the hardline Democratic Opposition Coordination (COD) alliance decided to boycott the 21 June presidential election. More surprising was the decision of the APP and Tawassoul to stay out of the race; the Islamist party did well in the 2013 elections and had been expected to use the presidential contest to consolidate the new standing of its leader, Mohamed Jemil Ould Mansour, as the leading face of the constitutional opposition. In the event, President Ould Abdelaziz—whose victory was a foregone conclusion—faced four challengers: the parliamentarians Boydiel Ould Houmeid (Al Wiam) and Ibrahima Moctar Sarr (AJD/MR); Marime Mint Moulay Idriss, the sole woman candidate; and Biram Ould Dah Abeid, anti-slavery campaigner and leader of the Initiative for the Resurgence of the Abolitionist Movement (IRA).

Ould Abdelaziz secured an easy victory, with 81.94 per cent of the vote. Subsequently, he appointed a new prime minister in Yahya Ould Hademine, an engineer and latterly transport minister. He replaced Moulaye Ould Mohamed Laghdaf, who had been premier since 2008.

Second place in the presidential election had gone to IRA leader Ould Dah Abeid, with 8.72 per cent. His participation appeared to signal a softening of the sometimes confrontational relationship between his movement and the Mauritanian authorities; but in November he and several colleagues were arrested as they prepared the next phase of a protest over land rights in the southern town of Rosso.

Political life in **Senegal** was dominated by three issues in 2014: the continuing trial on corruption charges of Karim Wade, son of the former president, Abdoulaye Wade; municipal elections; and the efforts of President Macky Sall to deliver tangible improvements in public services, by the mid-point of his expected five year term.

Elected with a hefty 65 per cent of the vote in 2012, and having promised to reduce presidential terms from seven to five years, Sall faced daunting voter expectations for quick results. Yet a number of his most important reforms, such as universal health coverage, would inevitably take a number of years to put into effect.

The president was reminded how quickly voters' enthusiasm could turn sour at municipal elections on 29 June. With rare exceptions—such as the sprawling Dakar suburb of Guédiawaye, where his brother, Aliou, was elected—Sall saw his Alliance for the Republic (APR) and close allies suffer heavy defeats. By contrast, the Socialist Party (PS)—which was part of the ruling coalition, but had been careful to maintain its distinct identity—achieved a crushing victory in Dakar city. A particular shock for the government was the loss of St Louis, the country's second city, to Wade's Senegalese Democratic Party (PDS). Defeated in her political base, Grand Yoff, the prime minister, Aminata Touré, was dismissed by the president, who chose one of his closest advisers, Mohammed Dionne, as her successor.

The main preoccupation for **Guinea** during 2014was the threat posed by the Ebola epidemic, but the country also had to adjust to difficult conditions in the international market for minerals, which affected planned mining schemes. President Alpha Condé had counted heavily on the proposed Simandou iron ore mine in the far south to drive economic rejuvenation and infrastructure development, particularly the construction of a new rail line from the south to the coast.

Guinea was the first country in the current epidemic to report a case of what was later confirmed as Ebola, in December 2013, in the village of Meliandou. About 70 people died as the disease spread to other communities, before the virus was confirmed as Ebola in March 2014. By the middle of the year, Médecins sans Frontières said the epidemic, which had spread to neighbouring Sierra Leone and Liberia, was out of control. A massive international effort achieved substantial progress by the end of the year. Even so, almost 2,700 cases of Ebola had been confirmed in Guinea, and more than 1,600 people had died; the true number of cases was probably two or three times higher than the official confirmed figures.

President Condé continued slowly to advance the process of reform and political normalisation, following the much delayed elections of September 2013, though many problems remained. In July 2014 there were negotiations with the opposition over future arrangements for elections, opposition access to the national media and compensation for the victims of violence.

President Alassane Ouattara of **Côte d'Ivoire** returned home in March, after undergoing treatment for sciatica in France, to face the ongoing challenges of national reconciliation three years after the bitterly confrontational 2010-11 post-election crisis. An early priority was a new census, to prepare a new voters' roll in time for the national elections scheduled for 2015. No such census had been carried out for 16 years, during which time the population had grown and the country had experienced deep political divisions, central to which were questions of identity and nationality. The opposition Ivoirian Popular Front (FPI) called for a boycott of the census; despite a partial thaw in relations between the FPI and the government, attitudes were still marked by mistrust. The opposition was also highly critical of an overhaul of the electoral commission, approved in May by the National Assembly—in which the FPI had no seats, having boycotted the 2011 legislative elections.

Ouattara had sought to reach out to moderate opposition supporters. When he became president in April 2011, after the military defeat of his predecessor, Laurent Gbagbo, some 800 Gbagbo supporters, including many senior FPI figures, had been detained while thousands went into exile in neighbouring countries. The FPI's leader, Pascal Affi N'Guessam, and other senior colleagues were later released and in January 2014 a further 120 detainees were freed, while 1,200 military officers from the Gbagbo regime were welcomed back from exile. But in March the FPI was angered when the government complied with a summons to transfer Charles Blé Goudé, former leader of the pro-Gbagbo Young Patriots movement, to the International Criminal Court (ICC) in The Hague.

The FPI was torn by conflicting influences. Affi N'Guessam had been prepared to engage in dialogue with the government and refocus the party on domestic politics. But there was pressure from loyalist supporters of the party's founder, Gbagbo, to take a much tougher line—reflected in the FPI's decision in September to pull out of the electoral commission. The rift came to a head when—from his prison cell in ICC custody in the Netherlands—former president Gbagbo declared himself a candidate for the party leadership at its planned fourth congress. Affi N'Guessam took legal action to challenge this and on 29 December a court ruled that the former president had failed to present the requisite documents for a valid leadership candidacy. Gbagbo indicated that he would appeal.

There were signs, too, of an internal rift within the Democratic Party of Côte d'Ivoire (PDCI) of former president, Henri Konan Bédié. In 2010, he had come third in the first round of the presidential elections and then thrown his support behind Ouattara. His PDCI was rewarded with a number of major posts in the government when Ouattara finally came to power the following year. In September 2014, after months of speculation, Bédié endorsed Ouattara's candidacy for re-election in 2015 and called for the merger of the PDCI and the Rally of the Republicans (RDR), at least for the next few years. However, many members of the PDCI were unhappy with Bédié's stance; they felt that the party should present its own candidate for the 2015 election.

Rarely in the headlines during the long years of rule by President Blaise Compaoré, **Burkina Faso** burst into the news in the final days of October 2014 when a popular uprising drove one of West Africa's few strongman leaders from power. This cataclysm was sparked by Compaoré's decision to press ahead with a constitutional amendment that would have allowed him to stand for a third term of office. (He had originally come to power through the 1987 putsch that saw the murder of his close revolutionary comrade and predecessor as head of state, Thomas Sankara, see AR 1987, pp. 256-57.)

After a period of authoritarian rule, Compaoré had eventually overseen the introduction of a multi-party system, in which his own position was never seriously challenged. Very occasional protests, and a mutiny by discontented soldiers in 2011, had not fundamentally shaken his hold on power. In late 2013 he revealed plans to alter the constitution so that he could stand again for the presidency in November 2015. He could have used a referendum to secure approval of the constitutional change, but amidst growing signs of civil society opposition to this plan he eventually decided that parliament should legislate instead. But as parliamentarians gathered in the National Assembly building for the necessary debate and vote on 29 October, a popular uprising broke out across Ouagadougou; crowds stormed the building and set fire to it. The security forces, reluctant to use lethal force against the people, could not control the huge protests, while Compaoré sheltered in his presidential palace. During the morning of 31 October, he fled to exile in Côte d'Ivoire.

Military leaders, having seen which way the wind was blowing, had opted not to block the revolution. During several days of tense negotiation with opposition leaders, compromise arrangements for a transitional regime were hammered out. Michel Kafando, a diplomat and former foreign minister, was made interim president, while Lieutenant Colonel Yacouba Isaac Zida, from the presidential guard, became prime minister, with a mandate to prepare the country for new elections in late 2015.

The administration of President Faure Gnassingbé of **Togo** opened the year on a reconciliatory note, by announcing that 13 January would no longer be celebrated as the anniversary of the seizure of power by the late Gnassingbé Eyadéma, father of the current head of state. This decision was welcomed by Gilchrist Olympio, leader of the Union of Forces for Change (UFC), whose own father, Sylvanus Olympio, Togo's first president, had been assassinated in Eyadéma's 1963 coup (see AR 1963, p. 342).

With presidential elections expected in early 2015, the opposition parties began to press for key reforms to create a fairer electoral environment and curtail the duration of the ruling family's monopoly on power. The government was prepared to accept a limit of two consecutive presidential terms, and introduced draft legislation to this effect in June (although parliament then rejected it). But the opposition demanded that the limits should be retrospective, which would mean that Gnassingbé would have to step down in 2015. The government argued otherwise, and—with the ruling Union for the Republic (UNIR) dominating parliament—was in a position to impose its view.

For President Thomas Boni Yayi of **Benin** 2014 proved to be a testing year. It began with a wave of protests and strikes, followed by an awkward setback in a legal dispute, and concluded with the Constitutional Court denying him any hope of a third consecutive term in office.

The sustained trade union campaign of demonstrations finally pressured the president into announcing a rise in the minimum wage in March. Then, on 13 May, the justice and arbitration court of OHADA (the common business law framework for francophone African countries) ordered Benin to pay CFA129 billion (€197 million) to Bénin Control, a company owned by Patrice Talon, a businessman who had been in dispute with the government.

In 2006, Talon had been a prominent supporter of Boni Yayi's presidential election campaign and his businesses subsequently won an important cotton privatisation deal and the contract for import verification at Cotonou port, a major trade gateway for the west African region. But Talon was later accused of trying to poison the president, the port contract was suspended, and he fled into exile. The rift persisted for almost two years, but was brought to an enforced resolution by the momentum of the case at the OHADA court. The day after the court ruling, Boni Yayi announced an official pardon for Talon and five others.

Meanwhile, rumours persisted that Boni Yayi might have hopes of changing the constitution and standing for another term in 2016. But October's revolution in Burkina Faso was a stark warning of what could happened to West African presidents who risked that sort of move. In any case, just three weeks later, on 20 November, Benin's highly respected Constitutional Court declared its total opposition to such a move, ruling that it was not possible to alter Article 42 of the constitution, which imposed the two-term limit.

Paul Melly

CAMEROON—CENTRAL AFRICAN REPUBLIC—CHAD—GABON— CONGO—EQUATORIAL GUINEA

Cameroon

CAPITAL: Yaoundé   AREA: 475,440 sq km   POPULATION: 22,253,959 ('13)
OFFICIAL LANGUAGES: French & English
HEAD OF STATE AND GOVERNMENT: President Paul Biya (since Nov '82)
RULING PARTY: Cameroon People's Democratic Movement (RDPC)
PRIME MINISTER: Yang Philemon (since July '09)
DEMOCRACY INDEX: 3.41; =129th of 167   CORRUPTION PERCEPTIONS INDEX: 27; =136th of 175
CURRENCY: Central African CFA Franc (Dec '14 £1.00=XAF 836.3, US$1.00=XAF 538.5)
GNI PER CAPITA: US$1,270, Intl$2,660 at PPP ('13)

Central African Republic

CAPITAL: Bangui   AREA: 623,000 sq km   POPULATION: 4,616,417 ('13)
OFFICIAL LANGUAGE: French
HEAD OF STATE AND GOVERNMENT: Interim President Catherine Samba-Panza (since Jan '14)
ACTING PRIME MINISTER: Mahamet Kamoun (ind) (since Aug '14)
DEMOCRACY INDEX: 1.49; 165th of 167   CORRUPTION PERCEPTIONS INDEX: 24; =150th of 175
CURRENCY: Central African CFA Franc (see above)
GNI PER CAPITA: US$320, Intl$600 at PPP ('13)

Chad

CAPITAL: Ndjaména   AREA: 1,284,000 sq km   POPULATION: 12,825,314 ('13)
OFFICIAL LANGUAGES: French & Arabic
HEAD OF STATE AND GOVERNMENT: President (Col.) Idriss Déby Itno (MPS) (since Dec '90)
RULING PARTY: Patriotic Salvation Movement (MPS)
PRIME MINISTER: Kalzeubet Pahimi Deubet (since Nov '13)
DEMOCRACY INDEX: 1.50; 164th of 167   CORRUPTION PERCEPTIONS INDEX: 22; =154th of 175
CURRENCY: Central African CFA Franc (see above)
GNI PER CAPITA: US$1,020, Intl$2,000 at PPP ('13)

Gabon

CAPITAL: Libreville   AREA: 267,670 sq km   POPULATION: 1,671,711 ('13)
OFFICIAL LANGUAGE: French
HEAD OF STATE AND GOVERNMENT: President Ali-Ben Bongo Ondimba (since Oct '09)
RULING PARTY: Gabonese Democratic Party (PDG)
PRIME MINISTER: Daniel Ona Ondo (PDG) (since Jan '14)
DEMOCRACY INDEX: 3.76; =122nd of 167   CORRUPTION PERCEPTIONS INDEX: 37; =94th of 175
CURRENCY: Central African CFA Franc (see above)
GNI PER CAPITA: US$10,650, Intl$17,220 at PPP ('13)

Congo

CAPITAL: Brazzaville   AREA: 342,000 sq km   POPULATION: 4,447,632 ('13)
OFFICIAL LANGUAGE: French
HEAD OF STATE AND GOVERNMENT: President Denis Sassou Nguesso (PCT) (since Oct '97)
RULING PARTY: Congolese Labour Party (PCT)
DEMOCRACY INDEX: 2.89; 145th of 167   CORRUPTION PERCEPTIONS INDEX: 23; =152nd of 175
CURRENCY: Central African CFA Franc (see above)
GNI PER CAPITA: US$2,660, Intl$4,720 at PPP ('13)

Equatorial Guinea

CAPITAL: Malabo   AREA: 28,050 sq km   POPULATION: 757,014 ('13)
OFFICIAL LANGUAGES: Spanish & French
HEAD OF STATE AND GOVERNMENT: President (Brig.-Gen.) Teodoro Obiang Nguema Mbasogo (since
    Aug '79)
RULING PARTY: Equatorial Guinea Democratic Party (PDGE)
PRIME MINISTER: Vincente Eyate Tomi (since May '12)
DEMOCRACY INDEX: 1.77; 161st of 167
CURRENCY: Central African CFA Franc (see above)
GNI PER CAPITA: US$14,320, Intl$23,240 at PPP ('13)

THE scale of the threat to northern **Cameroon** from the Nigerian jihadist group, Boko Haram, became graphically apparent during 2014 with an accelerating series of cross-border attacks—a sharp contrast to the occasional kidnappings seen hitherto. As the year went on, the militants increasingly targeted local villages, with mass killings of civilians and, on occasion, the seizure of dozens of hostages. Frequently crossing the porous border using motorbikes, the Nigerian militants passed through rugged terrain where the four-wheeled vehicles of the Cameroonian army were unable to pursue them.

Relations between the two governments took a crucial step forward when both President Paul Biya and his Nigerian counterpart, Goodluck Jonathan, attended a summit of leaders from the region in May to discuss coordinating action against the Boko Haram threat. The meeting took place in Paris, hosted by France's President François Hollande, and also attended by UK Foreign Secretary William Hague and senior US officials. Plans were soon being discussed for a joint force of several thousand troops, with Cameroon, Nigeria, Chad, Niger and possibly Benin all contributing units. However, it took some months for this initial proposal to be turned into a more concrete and detailed plan. One difficulty was linguistic: how to coordinate the operations of forces largely trained and equipped by the French with the Nigerian military, whose main external partners were Anglophone countries.

In 2014, with no formal framework for collaboration with the Nigerian military yet in place, Cameroonian forces were cautious about tackling Boko Haram within Nigeria itself, preferring instead to take muscular action against the militants when they staged raids across the border. These operations resulted in significant casualties on both sides. For example, on 16 October, the army was reported to have killed 107 Boko Haram fighters who had murdered civilians during a cross-border raid. And after a force of 1,000 extremists had seized control of several towns and a military base in Cameroon on 28 December, the government launched its first ever air strikes against the group, to dislodge it from the base.

Internal Cameroonian politics remained characterised by immobilism, with Biya's Cameroon People's Democratic Movement (RPDC) dominating the landscape. The president launched disciplinary action within the party, excluding or suspending a number of activists. He also sought to strengthen its organisation, creating 167 new branches of the RDPC in September (including two abroad, in Chad and in Italy), and preparing an overhaul of the leadership of the party's existing branches.

For the **Central African Republic** (CAR), 2014 opened amidst deep crisis. Caught in a gathering wave of sectarian killing between the Muslim Séléka ("alliance") rebels and the fast-growing Anti-Balaka ("anti-machete") Christian militias, the country had threatened to implode in genocidal violence. But during the final weeks of 2013, in Opération Sangaris, France had deployed a well equipped intervention force of 1,600 troops, to support the small contingent of peacekeepers from regional neighbours known as FOMAC (Military Force for Central Africa), who had been present in the country long-term but who lacked the means to control the situation. Sangaris was soon strengthened to 2,000 troops, backed by air power, while the regional force was upgraded on 19 December, 2013, to a larger African intervention, authorised by the African Union and renamed MISCA (International Support Mission for Central Africa). The African force had an authorised strength of around 6,000 troops mostly from regional neighbours such as Chad, Cameroon and Gabon; but the force also included 850 troops from Burundi, whose soldiers had proved themselves in the impressive African force operating in Somalia (AMISOM).

The African and French forces rapidly established a good working relationship and started the work of stabilising a country with no effective security structure and an enfeebled government. The Séléka rebels, who had taken over the CAR in March 2013, were substantially composed of foreign fighters answerable to mercenary commanders and Janjawid warlords from Darfur in Sudan. Michel Djotodia, the Séléka chief, had proclaimed himself head of state but he had little control over his fighters, who operated autonomously, looting local communities and with no clear agenda for governing the country. Meanwhile, many members of the pre-March 2013 military had begun to join the Anti-Balaka. These had begun as Christian self-defence groups against Séléka killings and persecution, but were already evolving into a sectarian militia with an equally murderous agenda, targeting the CAR's Muslim minority, many of who were living as urban traders in Bangui and other southern towns. In territorial terms, Séléka groups controlled the north and much of the centre of the CAR, while the elements of the Ugandan Lord's Resistance Army were active in the far east, and the Anti-Balaka were increasingly powerful across the south.

After making an initial stabilising impact in Bangui, the international forces slowly began to reach out to southern provincial towns during the early months of 2014. They also started to pursue a programme of disarmament in the capital, where Muslim communities felt increasingly beleaguered. Progress was further hampered by the absence of political leadership: most of the CAR's political class opted to keep a low profile for their personal safety. Djotodia and his prime minister, Nicolas Tiangaye—a respected human rights lawyer—were proving almost totally ineffective. A summit of leaders from fellow member states of ECCAS (the Economic Community of Central African States) insisted they stand aside in January 2014, to allow the CAR's National Transitional Council to elect a new transitional head of state. They chose the mayor of Bangui, Catherine Samba-Panza: she made a promising start, advocating inter-communal reconciliation, but her effectiveness was soon undermined by an ill-considered reliance on advisers, some of whom had links to Séléka.

The international forces endured a difficult period during the early months of 2014, as the Chadian troops were accused of favouring Muslims; the picture was confused by the presence of some Chadian troops in MISCA, while others were present on a bilateral basis. After repeated criticisms, Chad's President Idriss Déby announced in March that he was pulling his troops out of MISCA. But before withdrawing, the Chadians helped many Muslims safely flee the CAR and take refuge in Chad itself. Meanwhile, a European Union force (Eufor-RCA) was also deployed, from April, to support peacekeeping operations and airport logistics in Bangui. In September, the African force was upgraded to full UN status, which ensured a more secure funding basis and allowed the addition of reinforcements from non-African countries.

During the remainder of the year, the international forces gradually extended their control, pushing Séléka out of one town after another. Talks in Brazzaville (Congo) produced a cease-fire agreement between armed groups, which was signed on 23 July, although some elements of Séléka did not participate.

Regional security concerns dominated the agenda for President Idriss Déby Itno of **Chad** during 2014. Having played a key role in the French-led intervention in Mali in 2013, Chadian forces were at the centre of efforts to bring order to the Central African Republic (CAR) in early 2014, and Déby was the driving force behind the regional initiative that forced the resignation of the enfeebled CAR interim president, Michel Djotodia. Chad shared a long border with the CAR, and over recent years Déby had seen the CAR as a key zone of Chadian influence. In early 2014, he had troops deployed in the country as part of the African peacekeeping force (MISCA) and ensured other troops were present on a purely bilateral basis.

Chadian troops assisted the evacuation of Muslim civilians from the CAR at risk of persecution by the Christian Anti-Balaka militia to safety in Chad. But some were accused of acting in a partial manner, harassing Christians and failing to act with the neutrality appropriate for international peacekeepers. Déby, angered by these criticisms, announced in March that he was pulling his troops out of the MISCA force.

As conditions slowly stabilised in the CAR, concern grew about a new regional security threat: the growing strength of the Boko Haram jihadist militants in north-east Nigeria, who had begun to raid neighbouring areas of northern Cameroon. Attacking this part of Cameroon—which was just a narrow band of territory—the militants posed a danger for regional stability and for communities in Chad itself, notably near Lake Chad. During 2014, there was a series of discussions between countries in the region about the creation of a new joint force to take on Boko Haram. Chad, already host to a major French military presence as part of the Opération Barkhane deployment for the Sahel region, was ready to play a key role.

Meanwhile, November brought a reminder of the country's difficult history, with the opening of the trial of 21 former security officers charged with torturing prisoners during the rule of the dictator, Hissène Habré (1982-90).

Although the ruling Gabonese Democratic Party (PDG) had topped the poll in the December 2013 municipal elections in **Gabon**, it secured only 36.2 per cent of the total vote—a warning of the residual strength of support for opposition parties and other critics of the administration of President Ali Bongo Ondimba. Urban discontent was bubbling in the early months of 2014, with customs officials staging a strike in February and students angered by a delay to their grant payments in March. Frequent cuts in water and power supply also fuelled public frustration.

It was in this edgy context that the former foreign minister, Jean Ping, who had returned to Gabon after serving a term as president of the African Union Commission, issued a statement on 1 February indicating that he no longer supported the PDG government. This was widely viewed as signalling a possible challenge to Bongo in the 2016 presidential election.

Bongo's response was to complement the long-running emphasis on his government's provision of public services with a new focus on tackling income inequalities. He overhauled the lavish allowances that since the 1970s had been paid to 9,000 senior officials, using the money saved to finance incentives for a much wider share of the public sector workforce and to fund a new welfare scheme for the unemployed and poor households. The trade unions welcomed the new strategy. In political terms, the president was clearly seeking to marginalise more radical critics, such as senior figures from the banned National Union (UN), as well as Ping.

Another policy in tune with this more egalitarian approach was to tighten supervision of the oil sector. But this did not appear to discourage international investors: in August, under a new offshore licensing round, the government signed seven contracts with six companies—an encouraging outcome for the administration, which was keen to reverse the long term decline in Gabon's oil output. The timing was fortunate, given the sharp slump in global oil prices towards the end of 2014.

In Republic of **Congo** (Congo-Brazzaville), President Denis Sassou-Nguesso began to prepare the ground for his expected bid for re-election in 2016. Existing constitutional rules barred him from doing so, because by 2016 he would have served two consecutive seven-year terms and also be over the age limit. However, there was little doubt that he had ambitions to remain in office: his son Denis-Christel—a senior oil executive—though a member of parliament, lacked serious experience of wielding political power. So, during 2014, the presidential camp began to lobby for a constitutional amendment that would remove the obstacles to a fresh term for the incumbent head of state. Such a change would have to be approved by referendum, but that appeared to pose no serious obstacle in Congo, where elections were carefully managed; the complaints of the emasculated and divided opposition could be sidelined.

Marcel Ntsourou, a once influential military officer and former assistant secretary of the national security council, was sentenced to forced labour for life in September after being convicted of armed rebellion. He had been arrested after a violent security force siege of his home in December 2013. This was his third major trial. In 2005, he had been acquitted of involvement in the mass disappearance of opposition supporters in 1999—the "Brazzaville Beach affair" (see AR 2005, p. 237). In 2013, he had been convicted, but released with a suspended sentence, in connection with the explosion of the Mpila arms depot on 4 March 2012 (see AR 2013, p. 233). The truth about Ntsourou's alleged link to this tragedy never became clear; certainly, he boiled with resentment afterwards, claiming discrimination because of his ethnic background. It was said that the authorities suspected he might be planning a coup.

One of Africa's smallest states, **Equatorial Guinea** nevertheless began to establish itself as a player of some diplomatic weight on the sub-Saharan scene. In June 2014 it hosted the African Union summit; the meeting proved to be a key preparatory step towards the launch of peace talks over the future of northern Mali.

Then, in November, the regime of President Teodoro Obiang Nguema Mbasogo earned goodwill across the continent when it offered to host the African Cup of Nations football tournament. Morocco—the planned host—had pulled out, arguing that because of the Ebola epidemic it could not safely accommodate an event expected to attract sportsmen and spectators from many different countries. The refusal to host Africa's most popular regular sporting event was widely viewed as unreasonable, and even insulting. With the tournament scheduled for the early weeks of 2015, Equatorial Guinea's offer was quickly accepted—a valuable diplomatic coup for a government that, because of its hispanophone cultural background, sometimes seemed distant from mainstream affairs in a continent where inter-governmental engagement was mainly conducted in English and French.

While football bought favourable publicity for the regime, matters of governance were less positive, notably the financial affairs of the president's son, Teodorin Obiang Nguema Mangue, who held the rank of second vice-president. In March he was formally placed under investigation in France, where the authorities had been conducting a lengthy "biens mal acquis" probe into French assets of African presidential families, potentially acquired with the proceeds of corruption. Teodorin was also under investigation in the USA, where a $30 million settlement was reached with the US justice department in October. Under its terms, he was required to sell a villa in Malibu, a Ferrari and six life-size statues of Michael Jackson. Almost two-thirds of the proceeds would be donated to a humanitarian organisation in Equatorial Guinea itself, while the balance would be paid as a fine to the US justice department, which would then pass on the money to worthwhile causes in Equatorial Guinea.

Obiang's regime had shown little tolerance for dissent, but in October it announced an amnesty for past "political offences". This was an overture towards opposition figures and exiled politicians, aimed at tempting them into joining a "national dialogue" with the government, prior to the spotlight that the African Cup of Nations would shine on the country.

Paul Melly

CABO VERDE—GUINEA-BISSAU—SÃO TOMÉ E PRÍNCIPE

Cabo Verde

CAPITAL: Praia   AREA: 4,030 sq km   POPULATION: 498,897 ('13)
OFFICIAL LANGUAGE: Portuguese
HEAD OF STATE: President Jorge Carlos Fonseca (since Sept '11)
RULING PARTY: African Party for the Independence of Cape Verde (PAICV)
HEAD OF GOVERNMENT: Prime Minister José Maria Pereira Neves (since Feb '01)
DEMOCRACY INDEX: 7.92; =27th of 167   CORRUPTION PERCEPTIONS INDEX: 57; 42nd of 175
CURRENCY: CV Escudo (Dec '14 £1.00=CVE 138.4, US$1.00=CVE 89.15)
GNI PER CAPITA: US$3,630, Intl$6,220 at PPP ('13)

Guinea-Bissau

CAPITAL: Bissau   AREA: 36,120 sq km   POPULATION: 1,704,255 ('13)
OFFICIAL LANGUAGE: Portuguese
HEAD OF STATE: President Jose Mario Vaz (PAIGC) (since June '14)
RULING PARTY: African Party for the Independence of Guinea Bissau and Cabo Verde (PAIGC)
HEAD OF GOVERNMENT: Prime Minister Domingos Simoes Pereira (since July '14)
DEMOCRACY INDEX: 1.26; 166th of 167   CORRUPTION PERCEPTIONS INDEX: 19; =161st of 175
CURRENCY: CFR Franc (Dec '14 £1.00=XOF 836.3 US$1=XOF 538.5)
GNI PER CAPITA: US$520, Intl$1,240 at PPP ('13)

São Tomé e Príncipe
CAPITAL: São Tomé   AREA: 960 sq km   POPULATION: 192,993 ('13)
OFFICIAL LANGUAGE: Portuguese
HEAD OF STATE: President Manuel Pinto da Costa (since Sept '11)
RULING PARTIES: Independent Democratic Action (ADI)-led coalition
HEAD OF GOVERNMENT: Prime Minister Patrice Trovoada (ADI) (since Nov '14)
CORRUPTION PERCEPTIONS INDEX: 42; =76th of 175
CURRENCY: Dobra (Dec '14 £1.00=STD 30,293, US$1.00=STD 19,507)
GNI PER CAPITA: US$1,470, Intl$2,950 at PPP ('13)

IN the 2014 Ibrahim index of African governance, **Cabo Verde** retained second place, after Mauritius, in part because of the way its president, Jorge Carlos Fonseca, from the Movement for Democracy (MPD), worked with a prime minister, José Maria Neves, from the other main party, the African Party for the Independence of Cabo Verde (PAICV). Neves had announced that he would not be a candidate in the 2016 elections, and, after much contestation over who should succeed him as party leader, in December the PAICV congress narrowly elected the 35-year old minister of youth, employment and social development, Janira Hopffer Almada, the first woman to be elected to lead the party.

Though tourism was relatively buoyant, the economy remained weak. The government sought to change the labour law in order to increase working hours and make it easier for companies to dismiss workers, but the unions opposed this and called for unemployment insurance. Not only did the number of those out of work increase, but weakness in the eurozone led to lower remittances sent by Cabo Verdeans in Europe. As the national debt reached 95 per cent of GDP, the IMF advised the government to improve its systems for the collection of tax revenue, and reduce spending. The European Commission provided €3 million after destruction caused by a volcanic eruption on the island of Fogo in late November.

At the end of December José Luís Neves, the eldest son of the prime minister, was shot in the capital, Praia, in mysterious circumstances.

In **Guinea-Bissau** the presidential and legislative elections that had been postponed for organisational and financial reasons finally took place in April and May, returning the country to constitutional normality two years after the military coup of April 2012 (see AR 2013, pp. 234-35). After the African Party for the Independence of Guinea Bissau and Cabo Verde (PAIGC) won a majority of seats in parliament, a new government, led by Domingos Simões Pereira, was formed. In the first round of the presidential election José Mario Vaz, the PAIGC candidate, won more votes than an independent candidate, Nuno Gomes Nabiam, but a second round was needed, which Vaz won with 61.9 per cent of the vote. The success of the elections meant the resumption of some of the donor aid that had been cut off after the coup and the lifting of some international sanctions.

In an assertion of his authority as civilian leader, President Vaz in September dismissed the chief of general staff of the armed forces, General Antonio Indjai, the man who had led the April 2012 coup and had been seen as the power behind the transitional government. Indjai was subject to an international arrest warrant for drug smuggling. Prime Minister Pereira told the UN later that month that his government would seek new funding at a planned donors' conference in early 2015. Guinea-Bissau remained one of the poorest countries in the world, with its economy heavily dependent on the export of cashew nuts.

Fortunately, the Ebola epidemic in neighbouring Guinea did not spread to Guinea-Bissau. The government in August closed its borders with Guinea to help prevent this; they were re-opened in December.

Though the small island country of **São Tomé e Príncipe** still hoped to become rich through exploitation of oil deposits in its offshore waters, and continued to allow companies to bid for rights to exploit blocks in those waters, no major discoveries were made in 2014. In the latter part of the year the world price of crude oil dropped significantly, reducing the likelihood that companies would invest large sums in drilling.

In February, when some of the army began a strike for more pay, President Manuel Pinto da Costa played down fears of a possible coup and appointed a new head of the military. The situation stabilised and in June the president made a visit to mainland China that was controversial, for his country retained diplomatic relations with Taiwan. He went on to Angola, where, with the heads of state of the other Lusophone African countries, he helped establish a forum of African Portuguese-speaking nations.

Gabriel Costa remained prime minister until parliamentary and local government elections were held in October, which an African Union observer mission found substantially free and fair. The Independent Democratic Action party (ADI), led by Patrice Trovoada, son of a former president, won 33 of the 55 seats in the National Assembly, giving it the absolute majority it had failed to achieve in the previous election in 2010. The former ruling party, the Movement for the Liberation of São Tomé and Príncipe (MLSTP), won only 16 seats. In late November, Trovoada took office as prime minister for the third time.

Christopher Saunders

VII CENTRAL AND SOUTHERN AFRICA

DEMOCRATIC REPUBLIC OF CONGO

CAPITAL: Kinshasa   AREA: 2,344,860 sq km   POPULATION: 67,513,677 ('13)
OFFICIAL LANGUAGE: French
HEAD OF STATE AND GOVERNMENT: President Joseph Kabila (AMP) (since Jan '01)
RULING PARTIES: Alliance for the Presidential Majority (AMP) coalition
PRIME MINISTER: Augustin Matata Ponyo Mapon (since April '12)
DEMOCRACY INDEX: 1.83; 159th of 167   CORRUPTION PERCEPTIONS INDEX: 22; =154th of 175
CURRENCY: Congo Franc (Dec '14 £1.00=CDF 1,433, US$1.00=CDF 923)
GNI PER CAPITA: US$400, Intl$680 at PPP ('13)

THE government of the Democratic Republic of Congo (DRC), with the grudging support of the international community and of the UN, continued to struggle with chronic problems throughout the year. These included armed conflict in the east spreading to Katanga in the south, popular unrest, severe public health threats, and millions of refugees both inside the country and outside its borders.

In March the UN Security Council renewed the mandate of its mission in the DRC, MONUSCO, for another year, despite concerns about an exit strategy. MONUSCO's troop ceiling was 19,815, alongside observers and police, and including an "intervention brigade". A six-step disarmament, demobilisation and reintegration plan, nicknamed "DDR3", was budgeted at $100 million but remained under-funded and ineffective.

Armed conflict flared in copper-rich Katanga early in the year as the secessionist militia Bakata Katanga engaged government forces (FARDC), destroying homes and displacing 600,000 people. MONUSCO warned that this humanitarian catastrophe had taken aid agencies by surprise, while their attention was turned eastwards to the Kivus. As of March there were 54 armed groups still operating in the Kivus and Ituri, sustaining the humanitarian crisis with two million refugees, high levels of sexual violence, and the collapse of health services. Fears were expressed early in the year of a resurgence of M23, pacified in 2013 (see AR 2013, p.235), but these were not realised. ADF-NALU, a 1,000-strong Islamist group from Uganda that was suspected of links with Somalia's al-Shabaab, killed a senior army commander in an ambush in January. Congolese and Ugandan forces began planning joint counter-operations in April, and by July the USA had blacklisted the group and frozen its assets. In December ADF-NALU was implicated in massacres of civilians in Beni.

Partly because of combat support by the MONUSCO intervention brigade, some militia leaders began to give themselves up, but it was unclear if this was a genuine trend. Paul "Morgan" Sadala was killed near Bunia in April when he tried to escape after surrendering. Justin Banaloki and "Colonel" Mbadhu Adirodhu of the FRPI surrendered together in Ituri, but little was known about other militias. The US repeatedly urged joint UN-FARDC action against the Rwandan Hutu FDLR if they failed to meet disarmament deadlines, while humanitarian organisations expressed concern about possible renewed fighting. In separate trials at the year's end, two senior FARDC officers—Gen. Jérôme Kakwavu and Lt.-Col. Bedi

Engangela—were sentenced to 10 years and life imprisonment respectively for grave human rights violations, verdicts welcomed by the UN as sending a strong message that such crimes would actually be punished.

An Ebola outbreak in Equateur province in August, later traced to bush meat, killed 40 people. The virus strain differed from that in the West African epidemic, and the disease had been contained by mid-November.

Daily life in the DRC remained risky for ordinary Congolese, many of whom died or were injured throughout the year in a variety of situations not directly connected to either rebellion or disease. In January, 11 people were killed in landslides after heavy rain in South Kivu; an explosion at an arms depot in Mbuji-Mayi injured 50 civilians and killed 20; a train derailment in Katanga in April caused 80 serious injuries and 63 fatalities; a power cut during a music concert in a Kinshasa stadium in April provoked a stampede in which 21 people died; and ferryboat accidents on Lake Tanganyika claimed the lives of dozens of passengers. In Ituri, the absence of a police presence after years of conflict created an atmosphere in which petty disputes easily escalated into mob violence and killings, according to local NGOs. In one such incident a dispute over cattle led to 37 deaths in Mutarule village, South Kivu. By contrast, in Kalemie, on the shores of Lake Tanganyika, the police themselves were accused by Human Rights Watch of carrying out summary executions and "disappearances" during anti-gang operations.

Mining remained the principal driver of economic growth, but production slowed in 2014 with a 10 per cent fall in copper prices attributed to unreliable energy supply and uncertainty about planned changes to the investment code. Despite this, the DRC overtook Zambia to become Africa's biggest copper producer during 2014. Seismic surveying also uncovered large reserves of crude oil—around 3 billion barrels—near Lake Albert. A US law intended to force companies to declare that they were not using "conflict minerals" was weakened in litigation, and analysts reported that its impact had been less than hoped for.

Well ahead of the 2016 elections, President Joseph Kabila was rumoured to be considering running for a third mandate, in violation of constitutional term limits. In September, anti-Kabila demonstrations were held peacefully in Kinshasa, but were dispersed with teargas in Goma. Nevertheless, opposition parties struggled to mobilise effectively over the issue, with their leaders squabbling among themselves.

Colin Darch

BURUNDI

CAPITAL: Bujumbura AREA: 27,830 sq km POPULATION: 10,162,532 ('13)
OFFICIAL LANGUAGEs: French & Kirundi
HEAD OF STATE AND GOVERNMENT: President Pierre Nkurunziza (CNDD-FDD) (since Aug '05)
RULING PARTY: National Council for the Defence of Democracy-Forces for the Defence of
    Democracy (CNDD-FDD)
DEMOCRACY INDEX: 3.41; =129th of 167 CORRUPTION PERCEPTIONS INDEX: 20; =159th of 175
CURRENCY: Burundi Franc (Dec '14 £1.00=BIF 2,438, US$1.00=BIF 1,570)
GNI PER CAPITA: US$280, Intl$820 at PPP ('13)

BURUNDI'S political equilibrium was threatened in February, when the ruling National Council for the Defence of Democracy-Forces for the Defence of Democracy (CNDD-FDD) ousted Vice-President Bernard Busokoza of UPRONA and replaced him with Prosper Bazombanza, who lacked his own party's support. The government also attempted to unseat UPRONA's chairperson, Charles Nditije. Subsequently three UPRONA ministers resigned from the Cabinet in protest, leaving the government without minority representation.

The crisis was exacerbated by President Pierre Nkurunziza's planned extra-constitutional candidacy—for the third time—in presidential elections scheduled for mid-2015, and by widespread political violence by the Imbonerakure, CNDD-FDD's militarised youth wing. In March, the government banned jogging groups, fearing they might become political rallies, and in July human rights activist Pierre-Claver Mbonimpa was arrested after discussing claims that Imbonerakure members had undergone military training abroad. Much political tension arose from land disputes, as refugees continued to stream home; the 2014 Global Hunger Index classified levels of hunger in the predominantly agricultural country as "extremely alarming". In October the Tanzanian government eased pressure by granting citizenship, with concomitant land rights, to 160,000 Burundians who had fled there in the early 1970s (see AR 1973, p. 281).

Although the government requested the closure of BNUB, the United Nations Office in Burundi, Secretary-General Ban Ki Moon recommended in January that its mandate be extended for the whole of 2014, as the country moved towards the 2015 elections. BNUB finally closed in December, with opposition leaders describing its departure as "premature". BNUB was replaced by MENUB (UN Electoral Observer Mission), and UN Under-Secretary-General Jeffrey Feltman visited Bujumbura at year's end to discuss the upcoming poll.

In April the government established a Truth and Reconciliation Commission to investigate post-independence conflict. Opposition parties boycotted the vote, accusing CNDD-FDD of bias and "wanting to promote impunity" for perpetrators. The commission was nonetheless constituted in December under the Catholic prelate Jean-Louis Nahimana (who was Hutu), with 11 members, six Hutu, four Tutsi and one Twa.

Heavy rain in Bujumbura in February caused 70 fatalities, destroying 3,500 homes and leaving 15,000 people homeless. Planners blamed the disaster on building in dry watercourses, poor drainage maintenance, and erosion on hillsides stripped of vegetation.

The economy performed poorly: coffee production fell by over 50 per cent from the previous year, to 11,000 tonnes; this was attributed by analysts to government mismanagement, among other factors. Burundi slipped to 159th place in Transparency International's corruption perceptions index, 16 from the bottom, and in May the government revealed that only half the $2.6 billion pledged at a donor conference in 2012 had been released.

In August, 40 bodies were found in a lake on the Rwanda border, but their identities and origins remained unexplained.

Colin Darch

RWANDA

CAPITAL: Kigali   AREA: 26,340 sq km   POPULATION: 11,776,522 ('13)
OFFICIAL LANGUAGES: French, Kinyarwanda & English
HEAD OF STATE AND GOVERNMENT: President Paul Kagame (FPR) (since April '00)
RULING PARTIES: Rwandan Patriotic Front (FPR)-led coalition
PRIME MINISTER: Anastase Murekezi (PSD) (since July '14)
DEMOCRACY INDEX: 3.38; 131st of 167   CORRUPTION PERCEPTIONS INDEX: 49; =55th of 175
CURRENCY: Rwanda Franc (Dec '14 £1.00=RWF 1,072, US$1.00=RWF 691)
GNI PER CAPITA: US$620, Intl$1,430 at PPP ('13)

To mark the 20th anniversary of the genocide that claimed the lives of perhaps one million Rwandans over 100 days in 1994 (see AR 1994, pp. 292-94), President Paul Kagame and UN Secretary-General Ban Ki Moon presided over an emotional commemoration ceremony in a packed Kigali stadium on 7 April. The leaders lit a flame at the city's Memorial Centre, then watched symbolic enactments of the killings and listened to survivors' accounts.

The French government refused to participate in the ceremony, calling renewed Rwandan accusations of complicity in the killings "disgraceful", while characterising its own conduct as "exemplary". Earlier, the trial of accused génocidaire Pascal Simbikangwa opened in Paris; this was the first genocide case to be heard in France, which had been fined in 2004 by the EU's Human Rights Court for delaying such proceedings. In a judgement in Frankfurt in February, Onesphore Rwabukombe, the former mayor of Kiziguro, north-east of Kigali, was sentenced to 14 years for supervising 450 murders. At the International Criminal Tribunal for Rwanda in Arusha, Tanzania, former policeman Augustin Ndindiliyimana was freed on appeal, but was unable to leave the country.

In October a BBC documentary questioned official accounts of the genocide; Rwanda reacted angrily and closed down the corporation's Kinyarwanda radio programmes. The government accused the BBC of "cynicism" and "genocide denial", while a number of British academics and journalists termed the programme "recklessly irresponsible".

Patrick Karegeya, a former intelligence official, was found murdered in a Johannesburg hotel room over the New Year holiday (see AR 2013, p.239); exiled opposition leaders accused the Kagame government of trying to intimidate and silence its critics. The US State Department commented that it was worried about a "succession of what appear to be politically-motivated murders". Western diplomatic criticism of Kagame nevertheless remained muted despite Rwanda's poor human rights record and its military adventurism in the DRC, presumably because of the country's stability and economic growth.

It remained unclear whether Kagame would step down in 2017, with speculation that he might seek a third term fuelled by his refusal to rule this out while speaking in Boston in April.

The economy performed well, with the African Retail Development Index ranking Rwanda the top market in Africa for retail goods. A new investment code planned to offer seven-year tax holidays, and a 50 per cent reduction of corporate tax in strategic sectors. The Fitch ratings agency upgraded Rwanda to "B+" in July, citing average GDP growth of 6.9 per cent during 2009-14 and "a track record of prudent ... fiscal and monetary policy".

In June, the Rwandan army exchanged heavy weapons fire with soldiers from the Democratic Republic of Congo along the border with North Kivu, resulting in several fatalities and angry recriminations.

Colin Darch

MOZAMBIQUE

CAPITAL: Maputo   AREA: 799,380 sq km   POPULATION: 25,833,752 ('13)
OFFICIAL LANGUAGE: Portuguese
HEAD OF STATE: President Armando Emilio Guebuza (Frelimo) (since Feb '05)
PRESIDENT ELECT: Filipe Nyusi (Frelimo)
RULING PARTY: Front for the Liberation of Mozambique (Frelimo)
HEAD OF GOVERNMENT: Prime Minister Alberto Vaquina (Frelimo) (since Oct '12)
DEMOCRACY INDEX: 4.77; =104th of 167   CORRUPTION PERCEPTIONS INDEX: 31; =119th of 175
CURRENCY: Metical (Dec '14 £1.00=MZN 52.8, US$1.00=MZN 34)
GNI PER CAPITA: US$590, Intl$1,040 at PPP ('13)

MOZAMBIQUE'S main opposition party, Renamo, continued to resort to armed violence (see AR 2013, pp. 239-40) throughout the tense run-up to the October presidential and legislative elections. It also simultaneously negotiated with the government over its demands in the two areas of electoral procedure and the make-up of the armed forces. In March the Frelimo government abruptly agreed that several thousand electoral officials could be nominated by political parties, rather than appointed by the electoral commission, but the two sides were unable to reach agreement on what Renamo called "parity" in the army.

Intermittent violence continued until July, with Renamo guerrillas ambushing vehicles on the main north-south highway, attacking trains in Sofala province, and skirmishing with government troops. A unilateral ceasefire was declared by Renamo in May, but ended in June with the party claiming that the government wanted to "capture and kill" its leader, Afonso Dhlakama.

In negotiations, both sides maintained rigid positions and progress was slow, but Renamo announced that it would nevertheless participate in the elections. In May the government facilitated Dhlakama's registration as a voter, a prerequisite for candidates in the presidential elections. The two sides finally signed a formal cease-fire agreement in August, with provisions for foreign military observers from nine countries, and others nominated by the two sides to the conflict. An attached memorandum of understanding declared that Renamo's "residual forces" would be integrated into the army and the police, and that no party should have its own armed forces.

President Armando Guebuza was harshly critical of Dhlakama, whom he termed "a creator of problems", and the former Italian mediator of the 1992 General Peace Accord, Mario Raffaeli, commented that he could not understand Renamo's positions. Dhlakama left his rural base in Gorongosa in September to begin campaigning.

In the elections in October, Renamo performed well, increasing its parliamentary representation by 38 seats to a total of 89 in the 250 seat chamber, while the third party, the Mozambique Democratic Movement (MDM), won 17 seats. The Frelimo candidate for president, Filipe Nyusi, won with 57 per cent of the vote. Nyusi had been Minister of Defence but was a relatively unknown figure politically; even the spelling of his surname varied between different media. Dhlakama rejected the results, claiming victory for himself, but added that "there will be no more war in Mozambique". In November the Assembly of the Republic created a salaried post of Leader of the Opposition, but Dhlakama rejected this too. The Constitutional Council ratified the elections in late December, with some reservations and adjustments. By year's end President-Elect Nyusi had still not formally assumed power. Negotiations on parity in the armed forces continued.

Frelimo manoeuvred to minimise the control of several major cities by the MDM, re-zoning several neighbourhoods in Beira city and insisting that major municipal appointments could only be made by central government.

In November the International Monetary Fund (IMF) described the government's economic performance as "mixed", criticising a fall in productivity in agriculture and fisheries, poor job creation and increasing indebtedness. Several international donors cut back sharply on budget support, with the promised total falling from $400 million for 2014 to $275 million for 2015, at least partly as a result of concerns over the finances of Ematum, the national tuna company. Nevertheless, the gas and coal sectors performed well, and in October the world's largest known deposits of graphite and vanadium—used in batteries and fuel cells—were discovered in Balama North, in Cabo Delgado. Infrastructural development continued with the opening of an international airport in the northern port city of Nacala in December. In a speech in January President Guebuza had stressed the importance of the Nacala rail corridor for landlocked SADC members such as Malawi and Zambia.

In May the independent think-tank IESE (Institute for Economic and Social Research) was evicted from its offices on 15 days notice, and one of its founders, the economist Carlos Nuno Castel-Branco, was questioned by the authorities after a Facebook post in which he criticised the president went viral. In November freedom of information legislation was passed, but parliamentarians removed provisions for an independent information commissioner.

Early in the year, floods and heavy rain displaced hundreds of families in Zambezia province. In November, Inhambane was formally declared to be free of landmines left over from the 16-year conflict with Renamo that had ended in

1992. Seven of the country's 10 provinces were officially categorised as de-mined, with only eight districts remaining to be cleared.

Vicente Ramaya, one of the group of businessmen who ordered the fatal shooting of investigative journalist Carlos Cardoso in 2000 (see AR 2000, p. 267), was gunned down in the street in Maputo in February. Later in the year, a co-conspirator, Momad Assife Abdul "Nini" Satar, was paroled and released for good behaviour after serving only 13 years of a 24-year sentence.

Colin Darch

ANGOLA

CAPITAL: Luanda   AREA: 1,246,700 sq km   POPULATION: 21,471,618 ('13)
OFFICIAL LANGUAGE: Portuguese
HEAD OF STATE AND GOVERNMENT: President José Eduardo dos Santos (MPLA) (since Sept '79)
RULING PARTY: Popular Movement for the Liberation of Angola-Workers' Party (MPLA) heads
    nominal coalition
DEMOCRACY INDEX: 3.35; 132nd of 167   CORRUPTION PERCEPTIONS INDEX: 19; =161st of 175
CURRENCY: Readj. Kwanza (Dec '14 £1.00=AOA 159.10, US$1.00=AOA 102.45)
GNI PER CAPITA: US$5,010, Intl$6,770 at PPP ('13)

As the second-largest producer of crude oil in Africa after Nigeria, and with oil contributing more than three-quarters of all its revenues, Angola, a member of OPEC, was seriously affected by the collapse in the oil price towards the end of the year. The government cut some state expenditures, postponed projects, and put on hold plans to increase production to over two million barrels per day. Fuel subsidies were reduced, thereby increasing fuel prices significantly. President José Eduardo dos Santos called for financial discipline, but the country's budget deficit widened, with the tax reforms introduced in 2014, including a tax amnesty on debts owed before 2013, further reducing government revenue. Though Angola was ranked 161 of the 174 countries on Transparency International's corruption perceptions index for 2014, the government prided itself on the country's stability and development, with the opening of new facilities at the port of Lobito in Benguela province a highlight of the year.

Though housing evictions and demolition of homes continued in Luanda and elsewhere, and protests were quickly suppressed, the government tried to polish its image as it lobbied among the African group at the UN for a non-permanent seat on the Security Council. In October the General Assembly elected Angola to that seat for 2015-16. In November Amnesty International issued a report that accused Angolan security forces of extrajudicial killings and using excessive force against demonstrators. Meanwhile, the main political parties began preparing for the holding of the first-ever local government elections, expected in 2015. The ruling MPLA held an extraordinary Congress to assess the state of its party structures in local communities. The opposition remained divided, with a number of opposition parties riven with factionalism. The media continued to think that Vice President Manuel Domingos Vicente was the most likely successor to the now 72-year-old president, who had been in power for 35 years.

Angola played an increasingly activist role on the African continent, serving in 2014 as president of the International Conference on the Great Lakes Region, hosting PALOP, the organisation of Portuguese-speaking African countries, and announcing in September that it would send peacekeepers to the Central African Republic. Angola's demarcation of its maritime border was, however, rejected by its neighbour, the Democratic Republic of Congo, in April, and, while Angola was one of a group of Southern African Development Community countries that negotiated an Economic Partnership Agreement with the EU, when the negotiations were concluded in July Angola did not sign, merely retaining an option to do so in future.

Christopher Saunders

ZAMBIA

CAPITAL: Lusaka   AREA: 752,610 sq km   POPULATION: 14,538,640 ('13)
OFFICIAL LANGUAGE: English
HEAD OF STATE AND GOVERNMENT: Acting President Guy Scott (PF) (since Oct '14)
RULING PARTY: Patriotic Front (PF)
DEMOCRACY INDEX: 6.26; =70th of 167   CORRUPTION PERCEPTIONS INDEX: 38; =85th of 175
CURRENCY: Zambian Kwacha (Dec '14 £1.00=ZMK 9.88, US$1.00=ZMK 6.36)
GNI PER CAPITA: US$1,480, Intl$3,070 at PPP ('13)

THOUGH 77-year old President Michael Sata disappeared from public view from mid-June, fuelling speculation as to his deteriorating health, the government refused to acknowledge that he was not well. A draft new constitution, in which there was a clear succession plan, was not enacted. In August Sata dismissed his justice minister, Wynter Kabimba, a potential successor with close ties to the vice president, Guy Scott. The ailing Sata, who reappeared only to tell Parliament that he was not dead, then left Edgar Lungu, the defence and justice minister, in charge when he went to the UK for medical treatment. Lungu was for many, especially among the majority Bemba-speakers, the frontrunner to succeed Sata. Though the country's founding leader, the 90-year old Kenneth Kaunda, was among those who participated in celebrating 50 years of independence from the UK in October, Sata was absent. A few days he later died in hospital in London.

A bitter struggle for the succession ensued. As the constitution provided that on the death of the president the vice-president should act until the election, within 90 days, of someone to serve out the rest of the presidential term, Scott took over as acting president and quickly dismissed Lungu as secretary-general of the ruling Patriotic Front (PF). Lungu accused Scott, who was not eligible to become president because his parents were not born in Zambia, of acting illegally, and after riots broke out in Lusaka Lungu was reinstated. In the week before Christmas the two men were reconciled, with Lungu announcing that Scott would actively campaign for him as PF leader in the poll to be held on 20 January, 2015. The main opposition candidate was initially expected to be

Sata's predecessor as president, Rupiah Banda, who had engineered the suspension of the man who had succeeded him as president of the Movement for Multiparty Democracy (MMD), Nevers Mumba, but a court ruling reinstated Mumba as the party's presidential candidate, forcing Banda to withdraw. Other candidates included Sata's widow, his son, the mayor of Lusaka, and Hakainde Hichilema, leader of the United Party for National Development, who had some support from the MMD and those disgruntled by PF rule and infighting and who promised both to woo foreign investors and to ensure the draft constitution was implemented.

During 2014 Zambia's economy was rebased, enlarging it nominally, and investment in infrastructure and agriculture was beginning to pay off, but the bulk of foreign earnings continued to come from mining. In the last months of the year the price of copper, the main export commodity, fell sharply, while the Chamber of Mines lobbied hard against changes to the mining tax regime announced in the budget, on the grounds that they were a disincentive to investment and would put people out of work. Until the end of the year there were hopes that the government would back down on the increases in royalties that were to take effect at the beginning of 2015. If it did not, a major copper mine said it would close, jeopardising 4,000 jobs. But with over half the country's population continuing to live below the poverty line, there was considerable popular support for the mining companies paying more tax.

Christopher Saunders

MALAWI

CAPITAL: Lilongwe   AREA: 118,480 sq km   POPULATION: 16,362,567 ('13)
OFFICIAL LANGUAGE: English
HEAD OF STATE AND GOVERNMENT: President Peter Mutharika (DPP) (since May '14)
RULING PARTY: Democratic Progressive Party (DPP)
DEMOCRACY INDEX: 6.00; 77th of 167   CORRUPTION PERCEPTIONS INDEX: 33; =110th of 175
CURRENCY: Kwacha (Dec '14 £1.00=MWK 733, US$1.00=MWK 472)
GNI PER CAPITA: US$270, Intl$750 at PPP ('13)

THE May presidential, legislative and local government elections were the key political event of the year. Campaigning for these, President Joyce Banda claimed that she had uncovered, and then effectively dealt with, the so-called cash-gate scandal that had broken the previous year (see AR 2014, p. 244), but the austerity measures she was forced to introduce when international donors froze their aid were unpopular. Her main rival, Peter Mutharika, claimed that some of the money siphoned off in the cash-gate scandal had gone to help Banda's election and that she was using state funds for electioneering, and he criticised her hand-outs to poor voters.

When the election took place, many polling stations opened late. Others recorded more votes than there were registered voters. When initial results suggested she had not won, Banda said the election was marred by "serious irregularities" and was therefore "null and void", and she called for another election to be held. The electoral commission rejected this and said it would conduct a re-count. After the high court ruled against a re-count the commission announced that Mutharika had won 36.4 per cent of the vote, Lazarus Chakwera of the Malawi Congress Party (MCP), who was relatively untainted by corruption, 27.8 per cent, and Banda only 20.2 per cent. The MCP, which had supported the idea of a re-count, now said it would challenge the results in court.

Celebrations of 50 years of independence from Britain in July were muted. As president, Mutharika enjoyed immunity from prosecution; he would not be tried for attempting to block Banda from becoming president. The anti-corruption bureau continued its work and in October the first person charged with money-laundering and theft in the cash-gate scandal was jailed, while in December a warrant of arrest was issued for Banda over her alleged involvement in corruption. She had fallen out with the pop-star Madonna, whom Mutharika went out of his way to welcome back to Malawi. Though he and his deputy agreed to postpone vast salary increases, members of Parliament took theirs, though more than half the population continued to live in dire poverty. By the end of the year major Western donors had yet to be persuaded to unfreeze their aid.

Christopher Saunders

ZIMBABWE

CAPITAL: Harare   AREA: 390,760 sq km   POPULATION: 14,149,648 ('13)
OFFICIAL LANGUAGE: English
HEAD OF STATE AND GOVERNMENT: President Robert Mugabe (since Dec '87); previously Prime
    Minister (from April '80)
RULING PARTY: Zimbabwe African National Union-Patriotic Front (ZANU-PF)
DEMOCRACY INDEX: 2.67; 150th of 167   CORRUPTION PERCEPTIONS INDEX: 21; =156th of 175
CURRENCY: Zimbabwe Dollar (Dec '14 £1.00=ZWL 587 US$1.00=ZWL 378)
GNI PER CAPITA: US$820, Intl$1,560 at PPP ('13)

ON 21 February President Robert Mugabe celebrated his 90th birthday. The decisive victory of his Zimbabwe African National Union-Patriotic Front (ZANU-PF) party in the general election the previous July ensured he was also able to celebrate seven consecutive administrations and 34 years of continuous power. Following four years of uneasy coalition the election had delivered complete control of the country to the cabal that had led it since independence in 1980. The crucial two-thirds parliamentary majority enabled the passage of leg-islation unhindered by debate or criticism, and a revised constitution gave the president unprecedented personal authority. The future was up to him. But there was little sign he knew how to handle it.

In the new year the defeated opposition party, the Movement for Democratic Change (MDC), turned on itself. After leading the party through three elections, and coming tantalisingly close to winning one of them (see AR 2009, p. 290), Morgan Tsvangirai finally lost the confidence of his movement. Bitter feuds emerged as cliques supporting Tsvangirai and his former finance minister, the party's secretary-general Tendai Biti, fought for control of the party. Rumours in March of a breakaway initiative led swiftly to the suspension of Biti and his close supporters. The following month the MDC's national council attempted to suspend Tsvangirai as party leader, prompting the retributive expulsion of the Biti dissidents. In June it was reported that Tsvangirai himself had been expelled, a move he promptly denied. The squabbling and confusion merely confirmed the party's growing irrelevance. For individual MDC appointees the costs were high. In January Jacqueline Zwambila, Zimbabwe's retiring ambassador to Australia and a MDC member, declared Mugabe's government "illegitimate" and applied for political asylum in her host country.

Freed from the challenge of an opposition, ZANU-PF identified enemies within its own ranks. The battle to succeed Mugabe—Zimbabwe's longest-running soap opera—entered a vigorous new phase. In the firing line this time was Vice President Joice Mujuru, widow of the liberation war hero Solomon Mujuru (see AR 2012, p. 269) and long-time Mugabe loyalist. In November, after months of briefing against her, Mujuru was deprived of her seat on the central party committee, and the following month she, along with nine other ministers, was dismissed from the cabinet. The basis for the purge was an allegation that the Mujuru faction had plotted against the president and planned his assassination. Mujuru rejected the accusation and declared herself "the fly in a web of lies whose final objective is the destruction of ZANU-PF". On 12 December Mugabe announced the appointment of two new vice presidents, Emmerson Mnangagwa, justice minister and Mujuru's ostensible rival, and the little-known Phelekezela Mphoko, a former diplomat. Mnangagwa, himself the victim of a similar purge in 2004, was named senior vice president, and accepted Mugabe's preferment on his knees at a ceremony at State House. In case it appeared the president was designating his successor, Mugabe remained the declared ZANU-PF presidential candidate for the 2018 election.

A vocal new presence on the political scene was Grace Mugabe, the president's wife. A wealthy landowner and successful businesswoman, Grace Mugabe was awarded a doctorate in sociology by the University of Zimbabwe—of which her husband was chancellor—in September, two months after enrolment. Shortly afterwards she began a "meet the nation" tour. At successive political rallies she excoriated the Mujuru faction for corruption, incompetence and ingratitude, while praising Mnangagwa for his loyalty and discipline. At the ZANU-PF annual congress at the beginning of December Grace Mugabe was confirmed as leader of the party's women's league, propelling her to membership of the core politbureau. Whether as ringmaster, kingmaker or eventual presidential candidate, this was a phenomenal political arrival.

The political drama overshadowed Zimbabwe's dismal economic performance. Notwithstanding a declared 6.4 per cent growth target for the year, the reality of crippling unemployment, falling tax receipts and a halving of foreign investment produced a severe liquidity crisis. Seventy-six per cent of government revenue went to meet the state's salary obligations, at the expense of infrastructure and development. Evidence of a vibrant private sector operating separately within the economy pointed to the ineffectiveness of government fiscal controls. By March the economy was in deflation as manufacturing declined, commodity prices stalled and exports contracted.

As the country defaulted on repayment of its estimated $10 billion external debt the World Bank closed funding options and the IMF established a permanent monitoring presence in Harare. The Chinese government also declined to extend loans beyond its existing $1.5 billion without collateral from mining revenue. By the end of the year the economy was in meltdown, sustained largely by $1.6 billion in annual remittances from two million exiled Zimbabweans, a diaspora which was denied the vote.

During the year the hitherto highly profitable—and controversial—Marange diamond field reported a decline in the quality of its output. The Centre for National Resource Governance, an advocacy Trust concerned with governance issues in respect of the Zimbabwe mining industry, argued that the country could jumpstart the economy by converting the considerable stockpile of diamonds accumulated before approval to sell on the world market under the Kimberley Process. It projected revenue of between $5 billion and $8 billion and a significant boost to jobs if Zimbabwe invested in cutting and polishing diamonds rather than simply exporting the rough stones.

Externally there were some encouraging moves. In February the EU suspended sanctions on 160 ZANU-PF officials, though not those on Mugabe and his family. The president was however granted exemption in April to travel to the EU-Africa summit in Brussels, but declined when travel restrictions were not lifted for his wife. US sanctions saw the exclusion of Mugabe from the first US-Africa summit held in Washington in August. Forty-five other African leaders took advantage of the summit to promote the investment potential of their nations, and attended a state dinner at the White House hosted by President Barack Obama. None saw Mugabe's absence as reason to boycott the event.

Robert Baldock

BOTSWANA—LESOTHO—NAMIBIA—SWAZILAND

Botswana

CAPITAL: Gaborone   AREA: 581,730 sq km   POPULATION: 2,021,144 ('13)
OFFICIAL LANGUAGES: English and Setswana
HEAD OF STATE AND GOVERNMENT: President Lt-Gen. Seretse Khama Ian Khama (since April '08)
RULING PARTY: Botswana Democratic Party (BDP)
DEMOCRACY INDEX: 7.98; 26th of 167   CORRUPTION PERCEPTIONS INDEX: 63; =31st of 175
CURRENCY: Pula (Dec '14 £1.00=BWP 14.80, US$1.00=BWP 9.53)
GNI PER CAPITA: US$7,730, Intl$15,500 at PPP ('13)

Lesotho

CAPITAL: Maseru   AREA: 30,350 sq km   POPULATION: 2,074,465 ('13)
OFFICIAL LANGUAGES: English & Sesotho
HEAD OF STATE: King Letsie III (since Jan '96)
RULING PARTIES: Lesotho Congress for Democracy (LCD)-led coalition
HEAD OF GOVERNMENT: Prime Minister Tom Thabane (All Basotho Convention ABC) (since June '12)
DEMOCRACY INDEX: 6.66; 58th of 167   CORRUPTION PERCEPTIONS INDEX: 49; =55th of 175
CURRENCY: Maloti (Dec '14 £1.00=LSL 18.02, US$1.00=LSL 11.61); South African Rand (Dec '14 £1.00=ZAR 18.02, US$1.00=ZAR 11.61)
GNI PER CAPITA: US$1,550, Intl$3,320 at PPP ('13)

Namibia

CAPITAL: Windhoek   AREA: 824,290 sq km   POPULATION: 2,303,315 ('13)
OFFICIAL LANGUAGES: Afrikaans & English
HEAD OF STATE: President Hifikepunye Pohamba (SWAPO) (since March '05)
PRESIDENT ELECT: Hage Geingob
RULING PARTY: South West Africa People's Organisation (SWAPO)
HEAD OF GOVERNMENT: Prime Minister Hage Geingob (since Dec '12)
DEMOCRACY INDEX: 6.24; 73rd of 167   CORRUPTION PERCEPTIONS INDEX: 49; =55th of 175
CURRENCY: Namibia Dollar (Dec '14 £1.00=NAD 18.02, US$1.00=NAD 11.61), South African Rand (Dec '14 £1.00=ZAR 18.02, US$1.00=ZAR 11.61)
GNI PER CAPITA: US$5,840, Intl$9,590 at PPP ('13)

Swaziland

CAPITAL: Mbabane   AREA: 17,360 sq km   POPULATION: 1,249,514 ('13)
OFFICIAL LANGUAGES: English & Siswati
HEAD OF STATE: King Mswati III (since '86)
HEAD OF GOVERNMENT: Prime Minister Sibusiso Barnabas Dlamini (since Oct '08)
DEMOCRACY INDEX: 3.20; 138th of 167   CORRUPTION PERCEPTIONS INDEX: 43; =69th of 175
CURRENCY: Lilangeni (Dec '14 £1.00=SZL 18.02, US$1.00=SZL 11.61)
GNI PER CAPITA: US$3,080, Intl$6,220 at PPP ('13)

BOTSWANA, Lesotho, Namibia and Swaziland (BLNS), along with South Africa, were constituent members of the Southern African Customs Union (SACU), the world's oldest such body. Owing to the dependence of SACU funds to their budgets, this body was of critical importance to the BLNS states. However, its future was uncertain since South Africa wished to see SACU funds put to more developmental use, rather than as general fiscal transfers. One point of friction, negotiations with the EU for an Economic Partnership Agreement, was resolved with an agreement acceptable to all parties being concluded in July.

Botswana held elections on 24 October. These were conducted against the background of concerns about growing authoritarianism under the presidency (since 2008) of Ian Khama. During the run-up to the elections, several allegations surfaced of state partiality towards the ruling Botswana Democratic Party (BDP), and harassment of the opposition. Among these was the death in a car accident of Gomolemo Motswaledi, secretary general of the opposition coalition, Umbrella for Democratic Change (UDC). The BDP maintained its majority, winning 37 of the 57 directly elected seats, and taking all six of the indirectly elected ones. The UDC took 17 seats. For the BDC, the election represented a loss of 8 seats, and for the UDC a gain of 11. The UDC's support came predominantly from Botswana's urban centres.

Although Botswana had long been regarded as an economic success story in Africa—and was rated the most prosperous country in Africa by the London-based Legatum Institute—concerns existed about its economic prospects. Unemployment stood at around 18 per cent, inequality remained high and Botswana's economy remained vulnerable to global economic difficulties. At his inauguration, President Khama pledged to revitalise Botswana's economy through diversification away from its reliance on diamond mining and by developing its population's skills. To these ends, Botswana attempted to expand its trade relations throughout 2014, building new relationships with investors and potential partners. For example, on the first ever ministerial visit to Bangladesh in December, Minister for the President's Office and Public Administration Dikgang Phillip Makgalemele expressed interest in that country's achievements, which might provide useful lessons to Botswana. He also called for investment from Bangladeshi businesses, and engagement with Bangladeshi NGOs to assist in dealing with Botswana's social problems.

For **Lesotho**, 2014 was dominated by political instability. The country's coalition government, in power since 2012, was riven by tensions between its constituent parties. In particular, the Lesotho Congress for Democracy (LCD), under Deputy Prime Minister Mothetjoa Metsing, appeared dissatisfied with the arrangement and the leadership of Prime Minister Thomas Thabane of the All Basotho Convention (ABC). In March, an opposition legislator attempted to introduce a motion of no-confidence in parliament. This was expected to attract support from the LCD. Metsing was in the meantime under investigation for corruption.

This situation was aggravated by the seeming partiality of Lesotho's security forces, with the army supporting Metsing and the police, Thabane. In June, Thabane suspended parliament for up nine months—an action interpreted variously as a response to the fear of an impending coup, or a means to evade a motion of no confidence—and in August, dismissed the head of the army, Lt-Gen. Tlali Kamoli. In the early hours of 30 August, army personnel reportedly seized key buildings and disarmed the police.

Thabane fled to South Africa calling on the Southern African Development Community (SADC) to intervene. South Africa said that it would not tolerate unconstitutional changes of government, and on 3 September Thabane was escorted back to Lesotho by South African police officers. Under a SADC mandate, South African Deputy President Cyril Ramaphosa was dispatched by the bloc to facilitate a solution. The outcome of this process—the Maseru Facilitation Declaration—included a call for fresh elections in early 2015. However, some observers doubted that this alone would be sufficient, arguing that constitutional and electoral changes, as well as greater professionalisation of the armed forces, were crucial.

Namibia held elections on 28 November. A notable feature of the polls was the use of some 4,000 electronic voting machines—the largest such undertaking in Africa thus far. Although there were complaints about the conduct of the elections, they were generally regarded by observers as free and fair.

The ruling South West African People's Organisation (Swapo) secured some 77 of 96 seats in the National Assembly, while its presidential candidate, Dr Hage Geingob, obtained 87 per cent of the vote. While the election confirmed the overwhelming dominance of Swapo within Namibian politics (the strongest showing by an opposition party, the Democratic Turnhalle Alliance, was only 5 seats), some commentators remarked that these results sat uncomfortably with the severity of the problems confronting Namibia, such as unemployment, corruption, and among the world's most uneven wealth distribution. It remained to be seen whether Geingob, generally regarded as an ideological centrist and technocrat, would be able to deal with these.

Land ownership, an important political issue, was brought into renewed focus prior to the election when activists—including Job Amupanda of the Swapo Youth League—occupied a plot of land in the Windhoek suburb of Klein Kuppe. Termed "affirmative repositioning", this was aimed at demanding expedited land reform and at protesting land sales which supposedly ignored this imperative. Amupanda was suspended from Swapo pending disciplinary charges, but vowed to continue the mobilisation. He subsequently called on young people to submit applications for land, and threatened to embark on large-scale occupations if this issue was not resolved by mid-2015. Towards the end of the year, a separate group of protestors attempted to seize land in Swakopmund.

Political and economic stresses continued in **Swaziland**, Africa's last absolute monarchy, largely around the tightly constricted nature of the society. Widespread poverty and food insecurity—according to the Food and Agricultural Organisation, a quarter of the population was undernourished—continued to dog Swaziland. The heavy dependence of much of the population on subsistence agriculture emphasised the need for land reform, but this was unlikely given the reliance of King Mswati III on the country's traditional leaders (these being custodians of Swaziland's land) to fortify political control.

Swaziland's political arrangements threatened to damage its textile industry. The US government warned that a lack of progress on democratic reform—such as permitting labour unions and employee protests—would exclude it from extension in 2015 of the Africa Growth and Opportunity Act (AGOA), which granted Swazi products preferential access to the US market. As the year progressed, exclusion from AGOA looked increasingly likely. The loss of AGOA benefits would cost an estimated 17,000 jobs. The Swazi government acknowledged the potential damage that loss of AGOA signified, while indicating it would seek markets in Africa and elsewhere to compensate.

Economic problems were paired with regular complaints about repression of dissent. A case that generated widespread attention inside and outside Swaziland involved two journalists, Bheki Makhubu and Thulani Maseko, who were arrested in April after reporting on a case of alleged abuse of power within the judiciary. Subsequently they were sentenced to two years in prison. Critics noted that the case illustrated the lack of liberal freedoms within the country. As the judiciary was essentially both the complainant and adjudicator in the matter, it also demonstrated the collapse of the rule of law. In June, several organisations and activists, including South African Nobel Laureate Desmond Tutu, signed a public letter protesting against the state of the country. But with little prospect of an economic upturn or political reform there was little optimism of a resolution of Swaziland's problems in the foreseeable future.

Terence Corrigan

SOUTH AFRICA

CAPITAL: Pretoria   AREA: 1,219,090 sq km   POPULATION: 52,981,991 ('13)
OFFICIAL LANGUAGES: Afrikaans, English & nine African languages
HEAD OF STATE AND GOVERNMENT: President Jacob Zuma (ANC) (since May '09)
RULING PARTY: African National Congress (ANC)
DEMOCRACY INDEX: 7.90; 29th of 167   CORRUPTION PERCEPTIONS INDEX: 44; =67th of 175
CURRENCY: Rand (Dec '14 £1.00=ZAR 18.02, US$1.00=ZAR 11.61)
GNI PER CAPITA: US$7,190, Intl$12,240 at PPP ('13)

DEVELOPMENTS in South Africa in 2014 turned significantly on the election for the country's national and provincial governments, held on 7 May. These were the fifth set of such polls since the advent of non-racial democracy in 1994. Throughout this period, the country's politics had been dominated by the ruling African National Congress (ANC) whose electoral support had fluctuated at around two-thirds of the vote. While no analysis predicted an electoral defeat for the ANC, a confluence of factors suggested a far more competitive election than had previously been the case, as well as a gradual change in the country's political dynamics.

Foremost among these was the perception of drift and hubris on the part of the government. While part of this was related to a sense of policy drift, and a failure effectively to tackle the country's economic difficulties, another element concerned the president of South Africa and of the ANC, Jacob Zuma, who many observers felt was becoming a liability for the party. This was most graphically illustrated by the ongoing controversy over the upgrading at public expense—costing well above R200m—of his private homestead in Nkandla in KwaZulu-Natal. Shortly before the election, a report by Thuli Madonsela, the country's Public Protector—an office created by the constitution to ensure probity in government—concluded that the project had been undertaken with a reckless attitude towards public funds and that Zuma should be required to pay back a portion of the costs.

The ANC was also facing a more fractious and uncertain support base. Its youth league was largely inactive, following the expulsion of its erstwhile leader, Julius Malema and much of its leadership from the ANC in 2012. In addition, some of its allies in the Congress of South African Trade Unions (Cosatu)—particularly the National Union of Metalworkers of South Africa (Numsa)—opted not to campaign for the ANC in protest against its policy direction, which they felt was insufficiently sensitive to their demands. Both of these groups had traditionally been key contributors to the ANC's election campaigns. (Following the election, Numsa was expelled from Cosatu, and was working on establishing a leftist political party.) In addition, a small group of ANC veterans led an initiative to encourage people to spoil their votes or to vote strategically for smaller parties to register discontent with the ANC.

Opposition parties appeared set to present a more robust challenge than they had previously. The Democratic Alliance (DA)—the official opposition in parliament, drawing its main support from South Africa's racial minorities—controlled a sophisticated and well-resourced electoral machine. It also appeared to be having some success in attracting support among the African population. The Economic Freedom Fighters (EFF), formed by Malema and his allies, ran a highly visible campaign aimed at claiming the mantle of leftist radicalism that the ANC ascribed to itself. While offering vastly different solutions, both sought to capitalise on negative sentiments towards the government's record on employment, poverty alleviation and corruption. The shooting by police of some 34 mineworkers at Marikana in 2012 (see AR 2013, p. 254) remained a key indictment levelled at the ANC, implying that it had lost its moral authority and was reverting to the behaviour of the previous government.

The election saw the ANC take some 62 per cent of the vote, slightly down on the 66 per cent it had received in the previous election in 2009. The DA received some 22 per cent, up from 17 per cent in 2009. It also retained office in the Western Cape with an increased majority. The EFF took just over 6 per cent. The Congress of the People, formed from an earlier breakaway from the ANC and which had polled over 7 per cent in 2009, collapsed to well below 1 per cent, in the wake of severe infighting. Agang SA, a party launched by the internationally renowned academic and activist Dr Mamphela Ramphele, performed poorly, receiving only 0.3 per cent.

The election appeared to show a shift in the political dynamics of Gauteng province, the country's wealthiest and most industrialised. The ANC polled 54 per cent, a decline of some 10 percentage points on its 2009 results. This fall, coupled with dissatisfaction specific to Gauteng, notably the introduction of an electronic tolling system for some major provincial roads, suggested that Gauteng would be a closely contest region in the future.

Following the election, Zuma was re-elected president of South Africa, but remained dogged by the scandal around his Nkandla residence. In August, he announced that reports into the matter from a number of agencies had been reviewed and suggested that the minister of police would decide the amount (if any) for which he would be liable. Critics pointed out that this would place remedial action in the hands of a minister appointed by Zuma, and would allow him to sidestep the highly critical report of the Public Protector. The latter point was important, since recommendations by the Public Protector had generally been regarded as binding. Madonsela objected to this, noting that ministers did not have the power to overrule her decisions, and pointing out that Zuma had not responded to her findings. (The powers of the Public Protector were the subject of a separate court case, which found that while the Public Protector's decisions were not binding in the manner of judicial decisions, they could not be ignored.)

Parliament meanwhile convened its own committee to investigate the matter. This quickly suffered a blow to its credibility when opposition members walked out in protest at the ANC's insistence that the Public Protector's report was not binding, and that Zuma need not appear before the committee. The committee's conclusions were critical of the costs, but absolved Zuma of any responsibility.

Tensions between the ANC and the opposition were noticeably evident in parliament following the election. This was in part due to the overtly confrontational tactics of the EFF, seemingly with little regard as to whether they contravened parliament's rules. However, it was also noted by some observers that this took place against the background of institutions which had been suborned by the ANC, and whose office bearers acted in a partisan fashion. This came to a head in August, as the EFF caucus disrupted presidential question time by chanting "Pay back the Money" in reference to Nkandla. Following this, the ANC suggested that Zuma would return to account to parliament when it had resolved its problems. Furthermore, in November, riot police were ordered into the National Assembly to remove an MP who had called Zuma a "thief" during a debate. This was the first occasion on which police had entered the chamber since the assassination of Dr Hendrik Verwoerd, South Africa's then prime minister, in 1966.

Attempts to broker a "political" settlement to this situation faltered, largely due to opposition insistence that Zuma be censured for avoiding accountability to Parliament. In November, a number of EFF MPs were suspended from parliament for varying terms for the disruption of presidential question time in August. However, this was being taken to the Constitutional Court for review, and the EFF indicated that it would continue to disrupt proceedings if Zuma did not make himself available for questions.

For the DA, its apparent success masked some potentially worrying trends. The emergence of the EFF introduced a serious competitor with an extensive media profile into the opposition space. Some discontent with the party leadership was believed to exist. The departure of former parliamentary leader Lindiwe Mazibuko—once widely viewed as a possible future leader—immediately after the election to study abroad was seen as evidence of conflict with party leader Helen Zille. The latter was in turn regarded by some observers and party members as becoming increasingly authoritarian and intolerant of disagreement. There was also some confusion concerning where the DA stood on important socio-political issues. Where once it had once produced numerous policy proposals and opinion pieces to contribute to public debate, it now produced very few.

Contributing to South Africa's political stresses was a tough economic climate. This was compounded by extensive industrial action, notably a strike in the platinum industry that lasted for some five months, between January and June. In his medium-term budget speech in October, the newly appointed finance minister, Nhlanhla Nene, indicated that GDP would grow by some 1.7 per cent in 2014, around the level of growth achieved in 2013. This would rise marginally to 3 per cent by 2017, which would be insufficient to deal with the widespread poverty or unemployment, which—according to the official definition—stood at some 25 per cent. Noting that "fiscal consolidation can no longer be postponed", he pointed out that government finances were under severe pressure. Funding for new or expanded programmes would be difficult to find, and it was necessary to improve the performance of South Africa's faltering physical, social and governance infrastructure. Negative sentiments about South Africa's future prospects were also increasingly voiced by prominent businesspeople and financial journalists.

Emphasising the difficulties South Africa faced, towards the end of the year, the country's electricity supply system proved unable to meet demand. This resulted in widespread blackouts. Progress on the construction of new power stations at Medupi and Kusile was years behind schedule, but even once they were operating, they would not expand South Africa's generation capacity to the level it required.

In September, it was announced that a cooperation agreement in the nuclear energy field had been concluded between South Africa and Russia. By some accounts this would precede a contract for the construction of eight nuclear power stations over the coming decade, costing some R1 trillion—roughly equivalent to South Africa's annual budget. Although the government disputed this (saying similar agreements would be concluded with other countries), there was widespread concern about the agreement. South Africa's putative development blueprint (the National Development Plan) did not endorse nuclear power, and sources within government reported that the Treasury had warned about the destabilising effect of the spending. The apparent secrecy under which the agreement had been concluded also led to speculation about possible corruption in the deal.

Outside the political realm, the most prominent story of 2014 was the trial of the Paralympic athlete Oscar Pistorius. He had been charged with the murder of his girlfriend, Reeva Steenkamp, in 2013. The trial received extensive international media attention, including live television coverage. It prompted considerable comment on gender based violence, as well as the nature of the justice system—specifically, whether such an expeditious hearing and competent defence would be available to poorer or less prominent people. Pistorius was ultimately found guilty of culpable homicide, and sentenced to serve five years (although he would become eligible for parole after less than a year). There was debate in legal circles as to whether the judge had interpreted certain points of law correctly, and the state was granted leave to appeal, with a view to achieving a conviction for murder.

Terence Corrigan

VIII SOUTH ASIA AND INDIAN OCEAN

IRAN

CAPITAL: Tehran   AREA: 1,745,150 sq km   POPULATION: 77,447,168 ('13)
OFFICIAL LANGUAGE: Farsi (Persian)
SPIRITUAL GUIDE: Ayatollah Ali Khamenei (since June '89)
HEAD OF STATE AND GOVERNMENT: President Hassan Rouhani (since Aug '13)
DEMOCRACY INDEX: 1.98; 157th of 167   CORRUPTION PERCEPTIONS INDEX: 27; =136th of 175
CURRENCY: Iranian Rial (Dec '14 £1.00=IRR 42,097, US$1.00=IRR 27,108)
GNI PER CAPITA: US$5,780, Intl$15,600 at PPP ('13)

ALTHOUGH the new centrist government of President Hassan Rouhani faced some challenges from the conservative-controlled parliament, 2014 was a relatively quiet year politically. There were no elections and the focus of the government, elected in June 2013, was on improving the ailing economy and foreign policy. The government registered success in reducing the inflation rate, which by the end of the year was slightly above 16 per cent, significantly lower than the last year of the previous president Mahmoud Ahmadinejad's tenure. But unemployment remained above 10 per cent. The interim nuclear agreement reached with the five permanent members of the UN Security Council and Germany (P5+1) in November 2013—which released some of Iran's blocked funds on a monthly basis throughout the year and suspended sanctions against the country's vehicle and petrochemical industries—helped the Iranian economy register growth by the Spring quarter of 2014. But the inability to reach a comprehensive nuclear agreement by the November 2014 deadline and rapid drop in oil prices by the end of the year posed serious economic challenges and budget constraints.

Iran and P5+1 did agree to extend the nuclear talks until 1 July 2015. However, deep differences over the number of centrifuges Iran should be allowed to keep as well as the pace and extent of sanctions-relief that the USA would be willing to cede prevented a comprehensive agreement. Although progress was acknowledged, it was unclear how the seemingly irreconcilable differences between the US and Iran that could not be bridged in the past year could be overcome in the future Indeed, each side's expectation for further compromise from the other side continued to be the chief stumbling block to a comprehensive solution. But, in his television appearance immediately after the extension decision, President Rouhani assured the Iranian public that talks would continue and a "final agreement" that would "keep centrifuges and also the wheels of Iranian lives running" would also happen. The fact that Leader Seyyed Ali Khamenei consented to an extension suggested that he also considered the reduction of threats and pressures against Iran as an achievement. All in all, politicians across the political spectrum, with the exception of hardliners, showed unprecedented discipline in their support of nuclear negotiations irrespective of the results. But street-level economic anxiety about the continuation of the sanctions regime underwrote a gradual 10 per cent devaluation of the Iranian currency and a 30 per cent drop in the Tehran Stock exchange by the end of the year.

Foreign policy and security concerns came to the forefront due to the advances that the Islamic State in Iraq and Syria (ISIS) made in Iraq in June. Iran declared the Iraqi Shia holy cities of Karbala and Najaf its red line and immediately sent military advisors to help Kurdish and Iraqi forces arrest the fast movement of ISIS forces. It also supported the change of government in Iraq. Although Ayatollah Khamenei rejected any direct cooperation with the United States in the fight against ISIS, coordination of US air strikes with on the ground Iranian activities was done through the mediation of Iraq's central government as well as the Kurdish regional government. At the same time, Iran and the US remained at odds over their respective anti-ISIS strategies in Syria, with Iran maintaining its solid support for the Bashar Assad government and remaining suspicious of US objectives in Syria.

On the economic front, the second phase of the targeted subsidy plan was initiated through price increases for fuel and utilities in the beginning of the Iranian new year (21 March) without eliciting protests. However, the government was unsuccessful in convincing the relatively well-off from voluntarily withdrawing from the cash grant programme that was initiated during the first phase of subsidy reform. Only 2.4 million people did not re-register for cash grants voluntarily, much lower than the predicted 7-8 million. The failure to make the subsidy plan targeted towards the needy as required by law remained an issue. But the government did institute a universal health insurance programme intended to cover everyone without insurance.

Politically, Rouhani was generally successful in maintaining the support of the reformists, centrists, and even prominent conservatives in his effort to steer the country towards the middle ground. But a loud minority, consisting of hardliners, was able to bring several ministers to the parliament for questioning and eventually even impeach and remove the minister of sciences, research, and technology, Reza Faraji-Dana, in August. The minister came under attack for allowing the return of students and faculty members expelled from universities during Ahmadinejad's tenure. MPs accused Faraji-Dana of acting "against the nation's interests," by allowing forces of "sedition" involved in the post-2009 election protests to return to universities. Lawmakers also bridled at the minister's attempt to probe about 3,000 fellowships granted by the previous government and annul those made to ineligible recipients.

Sensitivity to the potential for the return of political activism to universities prevented the lawmakers from approving Rouhani's two subsequent ministers for this portfolio. Insisting that the time for a securitised climate in the universities was over, Rouhani refused to buckle and kept nominating individuals with similar backgrounds. Parliament eventually approved Mohammad Farhadi, who had been minister during the reformist presidency of Mohammad Khatami.

Dealing with political dissent remained haphazard. Newspapers became more daring in their criticism of the government, judiciary, and instances of corruption, while at the same time two reformist newspapers that had just begun publishing were shut down by the judiciary. More significantly, former presidential candidates Mir Hussein Mussavi (and his spouse) and Mehdi Karribi remained under house arrest without any formal charges issued against them. But public discussions regarding the unconstitutionality of their detention for more than five years became more prevalent. Conservatives and hardliners insisted that the two former presidential candidates must repent and apologise for their role in their post-election protests; something they refused to do. Like the quarrel over Iran's nuclear programme, the deep domestic political cleavages and discords generated out of the contested 2009 election lingered unresolved in 2014.

Farideh Farhi

AFGHANISTAN

CAPITAL: Kabul   AREA: 652,090 sq km   POPULATION: 30,551,674 ('13)
OFFICIAL LANGUAGES: Pushtu, Dari (Persian)
HEAD OF STATE AND GOVERNMENT: President Ashraf Ghani (since Sep '14)
DEMOCRACY INDEX: 2.48; 154th of 167   CORRUPTION PERCEPTIONS INDEX: 12; 172nd of 175
CURRENCY: Afgani (Dec '14 £1.00=AFN 89.34, US$1.00=AFN 57.53)
GNI PER CAPITA: US$700, Intl$2,000 at PPP ('13)

THIS was the year in which the US-led military mission in Afghanistan was formally concluded after more than 13 years of fighting. It marked the end of the longest war in US history, a conflict which had cost the superpower somewhere in the order of $1,000 billion. Around 3,500 coalition troops had died in total—including 2,300 from the USA and 450 from the UK—and large numbers had been wounded (including 20,000 from the USA alone). The conflict was also thought to have killed at least 21,000 Afghan civilians, although this was a loose estimate as no accurate records had been kept of the toll exacted upon those caught up in the crossfire of the war. Victory for the West remained more elusive than ever, with the Taliban insurgents making military gains throughout 2014 and, unusually, continuing the fighting into the harsh winter season. As the flag was formally lowered for the last time at the headquarters of the International Security Assistance Force (ISAF) in Kabul, on 28 December, the future of Afghanistan and its relationship with the West remained shrouded in uncertainty.

Uncertainty had been the year's dominant theme as the clock ticked down towards the scheduled Western withdrawal. Afghanistan's outgoing president, Hamid Karzai, continued to refuse to sign security accords with his US and NATO allies that would guarantee a continued Western military presence in Afghanistan after the formal conclusion of the current mission. Without such support it seemed likely that the Afghan state would be quickly overrun by the insurgents. Yet Karzai, who had long enjoyed an antagonistic relationship with his Western allies, insisted that the signature of the bilateral security accords should be the responsibility of his successor. The problem was that the choice of his successor—a process much heralded as the first time in Afghanistan's history where there would be a peaceful transfer of executive power—proved far from straightforward.

A presidential election was held on 5 April as scheduled. Security was tight and the Afghan government mobilised its entire force of 350,000 troops and police in a bid to prevent polling from being disrupted by the Taliban. There were numerous terrorist attacks and the unusual complaints of electoral malpractice, but the vote went ahead without major disturbance. The count was slow and when results were finally announced on 15 May it appeared that none of the eight candidates had won an overall majority of the vote, thus necessitating a run-off contest. In first place was Abdullah Abdullah, with 45 per cent of the vote. A former foreign minister of mixed Pashtun-Tajik origin, but who was more closely identified as belonging to the latter ethnic group, Abdullah was widely believed to have been the true winner of the 2009 presidential election, which had been stolen by Karzai through the perpetration of electoral fraud on an industrial scale. Abdullah's supporters believed that in this latest contest their man had in fact polled more than the required 50 per cent to win outright and feared that he was being set up to be once again robbed of victory if there was a run-off. In second place was Ashraf Ghani Ahmadzai, with 31.5 per cent, a former finance minister and World Bank technocrat who was a Pashtun, the traditional dominant ethnic group within Afghanistan.

Despite Abdullah's misgivings, the run-off contest was held on 14 June against a background of Taliban attacks. It was also the subject of complaints over malpractice. These came particularly from Abdullah who, within days of the poll, had announced that he was withdrawing his cooperation from the counting process because of the "blatant fraud" that had been perpetrated against him. He cited in particular the apparent sharp increase in turnout for the run-off compared with the initial election. This was particularly pronounced in the Pashtun-dominated eastern and south-eastern provinces (where the most serious of the 2009 fraud had occurred), even though they were wracked by violence from the insurgency. There followed a painfully protracted count. Initial results suggested that Ghani had won by a margin of 56.5 per cent to 43.5 per cent, an outcome utterly rejected by Abdullah. Amid fears that violence could break out between supporters of the rival candidates, thereby igniting a wider ethnic conflict, US Secretary of State John Kerry rushed to Kabul to mediate. He warned both sides that, "Any action to take power by extra-judicial means will cost Afghanistan the financial and security support of the United States and the international community." In mid-July he announced an agreement whereby the two contenders agreed to an audit of all 8 million votes, supervised by international monitors. This process of scrutiny inched forward, beset by delays, inefficiencies and procedural disputes. As it did so, there were suggestions that if the impasse was not soon resolved there could be a coup attempt by a coterie of ministers and officials with ties to the security forces.

Kerry intervened once again and eventually brokered a power-sharing deal which the two candidates publicly endorsed on 21 September. Under its terms, Ghani would become president, presiding over a Cabinet and discharging the strategic functions of government. However, Abdullah would exercise significant day-to-day power through a newly-created post of "chief executive officer", an office that approximated to that of prime minister. With this agreement in place, the Independent Electoral Commission finally announced the end of the electoral process, declaring Ghani's election as president, but declining to specify the final tally of votes. At a ceremony in Kabul on 29 September the two men were sworn in amid heavy security. In his inaugural speech Ghani promised that he would strengthen the rule of law and would "not tolerate administrative corruption in national institutions". He also emphasised that "we need assistance from the international community" but called upon the world to "rethink its strategies" towards Afghanistan.

From the outset Ghani sought to emphasise the difference between his administration and that of his predecessor. During his inauguration he publicly thanked his wife, Rula, a Lebanese Christian whom he had met when they were both students at the American University in Beirut in the 1970s. In a statement that drew warm applause from liberals, he noted that, "She has always supported Afghan women and I hope she continues to do so." It was a marked contrast to Karzai, who had been a consistent apologist for the conservative traditions which discriminated heavily against women in Afghanistan and who, throughout his presidency, had never publicly referred to, or appeared with, his wife at any official event.

Ghani sought to foster closer ties with India and China, encouraging both to involve themselves more closely in Afghanistan, whilst also improving relations with Pakistan. Furthermore he made every effort to distance himself from Karzai's prickly relationship with Afghanistan's Western allies. The new president quickly signed security accords with the USA and NATO that would facilitate the stationing of Western troops in Afghanistan after the expiry of the current military mandate at the end of 2014. He placated the USA further in November by quietly reversing Karzai's 2013 ban on night raids by foreign special forces. The ban—largely ignored in practice by US forces—had been enacted in response to protests over the disruption and civilian casualties associated with the popularly-detested practice of nocturnal anti-insurgency operations which involved intrusions into private homes.

Another area of prompt action by the new president was the reopening in early October of legal proceedings in relation to the Kabul Bank scandal. This 2010 financial scandal, which was emblematic of the corruption associated with the Karzai regime, had seen more than $900 million defrauded from the Bank (most of which had never been recovered), by a group of politically well-connected figures (including one of Karzai's brothers), most of whom had escaped punishment. Ghani's willingness to revisit the case offered a symbolic break from the past, although it remained unclear if the real perpetrators of the fraud would ever be brought to justice.

Unlike Karzai, who had frequently berated the Western powers, Ghani was unafraid to be seen placating them. When UK Prime Minister David Cameron visited Kabul in October, the new president publicly thanked the families of the coalition troops who had "stood shoulder-to-shoulder with us", and promised that "We will remember them." He acknowledged the sacrifices made by those who had "left pieces of their body here" and those who returned home damaged by the "haunting" memories of their wartime service. Significantly, however, he also reminded his allies that they had come to Afghanistan in pursuit of improving their own security, for the "ugly side of globalisation" meant that "We live, whether we like it or dislike it, in an integrated world where global forces, for both good and evil, coexist."

In December the two leaders met again when they hosted the London donors' conference, attended by representatives of 59 countries and numerous non-governmental organisations. The meeting reaffirmed the 2012 Tokyo commitment to provide $16 billion in assistance to Afghanistan during 2015, and sustain support through to 2017 at or near the levels of the past decade. Once again Ghani struck a placatory note, outlining his determination to tackle corruption, achieve economic stability, improve security and uphold women's rights.

However, whilst there was no denying Ghani's good intentions, the effectiveness of his government remained open to question. This stemmed in part from the power-sharing arrangement with Abdullah. Relations between the two men were difficult. Ghani had promised to slim down the country's existing bureaucracy by abolishing and rationalising parallel offices in a bid to improve accountability and efficiency. Yet the reality was that by the end of the year he had still not managed to appoint a Cabinet, as he sought to accommodate the demands of the Abdullah camp (and other powerful figures) for a share in the spoils of office. Furthermore, despite Ghani's laudable cosmetic efforts to combat extravagance and waste, Afghanistan remained hamstrung by a culture of endemic corruption. This had been aggravated by the financial largesse of the Western war effort, which had included lavish but often misspent funds for reconstruction. The culture of corruption was also the product of the country's most lucrative export crop: opium, the production of which continued to rise. According to UN figures the total area under opium poppy cultivation in Afghanistan in 2014 was 224,000 hectares, a 7 per cent increase over the 2013 level, an area that would produce an estimated 6,400 tonnes of opium, which represented a 17 per cent increase on production in 2013.

Ghani also faced the difficult prospect of needing to attempt major reforms whilst Afghanistan faced a growing existential threat from the Taliban insurgency. As the days counted down towards the end of the Western combat mission, coalition troops were increasingly withdrawn and those who remained avoided frontline duties. By contrast, the Afghan security forces suffered record casualties in 2014 as the Taliban stepped up attacks throughout the country, including in Kabul. Government forces suffered more than 5,000 fatalities during the year, a level of attrition that the Pentagon admitted was "not sustainable".

Despite the relentlessly upbeat assessments of the war's progress by Western leaders, it was painfully apparent that the Afghan regime was unlikely to survive without continued Western support. Yet the nature and duration of that support was not clear. As the flag came down on the ISAF operation in late December it was due to be replaced from 1 January 2015 by a new NATO-led mission: Resolute Support. Simultaneously the USA's Operation Enduring Freedom morphed into Operation Freedom's Sentinel. The result was that around 13,500 Western troops, the bulk of whom would be US forces, would remain in Afghanistan. US Defence Secretary Chuck Hagel defined US objectives thus: "We will work with our allies and partners as part of NATO's Resolute Support mission to continue training, advising, and assisting Afghan security forces. And we will continue our counter-terrorism mission against the remnants of al-Qaida to ensure that Afghanistan is never again used to stage attacks against our homeland."

In accordance with the plans finalised by President Barack Obama in May, the size of the US force was due to be scaled down radically in 2015 and 2016, but this would be dependent on the security situation on the ground. In November Obama expanded the remit of the US forces who would remain in Afghanistan by permitting them to conduct counter-terrorism operations not merely against al-Qaida targets but also against the Taliban. They were also permitted to provide ground and air support to Afghan forces where necessary. Thus, despite the flag furling ceremonies and the oft-repeated tributes to the sacrifice of the soldiers who had died, the reality was that the West's military presence in Afghanistan in 2015 would look very similar to that of late 2014. But for how long this would be maintained and whether it would be sufficient to preserve the Afghan regime remained unclear.

And thus the long Western war ended, with a barely audible whimper, amid uncertainty and confusion. It was a far cry from the days when the US-led mission had been defined in the grandiose terms of decisive military victory and the creation of a liberal-democratic state. Obama acknowledged as much after visiting the country in May. "We have to recognise", he said, "that Afghanistan will not be a perfect place and it is not America's responsibility to make it one. The future of Afghanistan must be decided by Afghans. But what the United States can do... is secure our interests and help give the Afghans a chance, an opportunity to seek a long overdue and hard-earned peace."

D.S. Lewis

KAZAKHSTAN—KYRGYZSTAN—UZBEKISTAN— TAJIKISTAN—TURKMENISTAN

Kazakhstan

CAPITAL: Astana   AREA: 2,724,900 sq km   POPULATION: 17,037,508 ('13)
OFFICIAL LANGUAGES: Kazakh & Russian
HEAD OF STATE AND GOVERNMENT: President Nursultan Nazarbayev (since Feb '90)
RULING PARTY: Nur-Otan People's Democratic Party
PRIME MINISTER: Karim Masimov (since April '14)
DEMOCRACY INDEX: 3.06; =140th of 167   CORRUPTION PERCEPTIONS INDEX: 27; =136th of 175
CURRENCY: Tenge (Dec '14 £1.00=KZT 283.4, US$1=KZT 182.5)
GNI PER CAPITA: US$11,380, Intl$20,570 at PPP ('13)

Kyrgyzstan

CAPITAL: Bishkek   AREA: 199,900 sq km   POPULATION: 5,719,500 ('13)
OFFICIAL LANGUAGES: Kyrgyz & Russian
HEAD OF STATE AND GOVERNMENT: President Almazbek Atambayev (SDPK) (since Dec '11)
RULING PARTIES: Social Democratic Party (SDPK)-led coalition
PRIME MINISTER: Djoomart Otorbayev (ind) (since March '14)
DEMOCRACY INDEX: 4.69; 106th of 167   CORRUPTION PERCEPTIONS INDEX: 27; =136th of 175
CURRENCY: Som (Dec '14 £1.00=KGS 91.47, US$1.00=KGS 58.9)
GNI PER CAPITA: US$1,200, Intl$3,070 at PPP ('13)

Uzbekistan

CAPITAL: Tashkent   AREA: 447,400 sq km   POPULATION: 30,241,100 ('13)
OFFICIAL LANGUAGE: Uzbek
HEAD OF STATE AND GOVERNMENT: President Islam Karimov (since March '90)
RULING PARTY: People's Democratic Party (PDP)
PRIME MINISTER: Shavkat Mirziyoev (since Dec '03)
DEMOCRACY INDEX: 1.72; =162nd of 167   CORRUPTION PERCEPTIONS INDEX: 18; =166th of 175
CURRENCY: Sum (Dec '14 £1.00=UZS 3,762, US$1.00=UZS 2,422)
GNI PER CAPITA: US$1,900, Intl$5,340 at PPP ('13)

Tajikistan

CAPITAL: Dushanbe   AREA: 142,550 sq km   POPULATION: 8,207,834 ('13)
OFFICIAL LANGUAGE: Tajik
HEAD OF STATE AND GOVERNMENT: President Imamoli Rahmon (since Nov '92)
RULING PARTY: People's Democratic Party of Tajikistan
PRIME MINISTER: Kokhir Rasulzoda (since Nov '13)
DEMOCRACY INDEX: 2.51; 153rd of 167   CORRUPTION PERCEPTIONS INDEX: 23; =152nd of 175
CURRENCY: Somoni (Dec '14 £1.00=TJS 8.01, US$1.00=TJS 5.16)
GNI PER CAPITA: US$990, Intl$2,500 at PPP ('13)

Turkmenistan

CAPITAL: Ashgabat   AREA: 488,100 sq km   POPULATION: 5,240,072 ('13)
OFFICIAL LANGUAGE: Turkmen
HEAD OF STATE AND GOVERNMENT: President and Prime Minister Gurbanguly Berdymukhamedov
   (since Feb '07)
RULING PARTY: Democratic Party of Turkmentistan (DPT)
DEMOCRACY INDEX: 1.72; =162nd of 167   CORRUPTION PERCEPTIONS INDEX: 17; 169th of 175
CURRENCY: New Manat (Dec '14 £1.00=TMT 4.42, US$1.00=TMT 2.85)
GNI PER CAPITA: US$6,880, Intl$12,920 at PPP ('13)

KAZAKHSTAN suffered three major economic blows in 2014. The first, triggered by
the US government's decision to "taper" its monetary stimulus policy of quantita-

tive easing, resulted in a massive outflow of capital. After months of uncertainty, on 11 February the tenge (**Kazakhstan**'s national currency) was devalued by 18.9 per cent against the US dollar. This benefited exporters, especially in the energy and mining sectors. However, personal savings and pensions lost much of their values; mortgages and other debts rose steeply. Local companies, with no exports, were also severely damaged. There were angry public protests and a run on banks. The government swiftly increased social benefits and salaries, thereby averting serious public unrest. In April, Karim Masimov was reappointed as prime minister, to steer the country through the "difficulties" engendered by the global financial and economic crisis; Masimov had been premier between 2007 and 2012.

In the autumn, Kazakhstan experienced the knock-on effect of Western sanctions against Russia, its co-partner in the nascent Eurasian Economic Union (EEU) (see article on Eurasian Organisations). Bilateral trade slumped. The fall in the value of the Russian rouble put yet more pressure on the tenge, raising fears of a further devaluation (though this did not happen). Simultaneously, Kazakhstan suffered from the dramatic decline in the global oil price. The country's programme of diversification had reduced its dependency on oil exports, but this was still the mainstay of the economy. The effects of the crisis were somewhat mitigated by the National Fund, which had been created in January 2001 specifically to provide a safety net in such circumstances. As of November 2014, the Fund had accumulated $76.8 billion; additionally, the central bank had net gold and foreign exchange reserves of $27.9 billion. Thus, even if the oil price fell as low as $40 a barrel, the government was confident that it would be able to cover its social commitments. Also, to help revitalise the economy, it launched the *Nurly Jol* ("Bright Road") initiative, aimed at stimulating business development.

Relations between Kazakhstan and Russia remained buoyant. Cooperation in defence and security was strengthened. Amongst other provisions, it was confirmed that military facilities such as the Balkhash anti-ballistic missile testing range, located in Kazakhstan and leased by Russia, should be jointly operated. Despite rumours that Russia might withdraw from Kazakhstan's Baikonur Cosmodrome (on lease to Russia until 2050), new plans for joint action were put forward during the year. Senior Kazakh officials acknowledged that they wanted more control over Baikonur's facilities, but stressed that it was vital that Russia remain engaged.

Other Central Asian states were also adversely affected by the economic turmoil in Russia. However, this did not impede the growth of Russian influence in the region. Bilateral ties with **Kyrgyzstan** were boosted by agreements supporting closer political and economic cooperation, in preparation for Kyrgyzstan's accession to the EEU (formally enacted in December, though full membership was temporarily postponed). One of the largest commercial deals was the acquisition by Russia's state-controlled energy company, Gazprom, of the Kyrgyz natural gas network for a symbolic $1; in return, Gazprom assumed debts estimated at $40 million and undertook to invest over $500 million to upgrade the network's infrastructure. In the military sphere, Russia pledged to supply weapons and other military equipment worth $1.1 billion as part of a bilateral armed forces assistance programme; it also upgraded its Kant air base near Bishkek (see AR 2003, p. 335). In **Tajikistan**, Russia's aerospace defence forces completed the modernisation of the Okno ("Window") optical electronic system for space monitoring; upgraded facilities included an improved missile attack warning system. In **Turkmenistan**, the emphasis was on increasing bilateral trade from the current turnover level of $5 billion.

There was also a perceptible improvement in Russo-Uzbek relations. The two countries had signed a strategic partnership agreement in June 2004, but there was often tension between them. By contrast, the visit of President Vladimir Putin to Tashkent in December 2014 was marked by cordiality and mutual respect. One of the outcomes of this meeting was the cancellation of over $860 million of Uzbek debt. Also significant was the signing of the intergovernmental agreement on deepening economic cooperation in 2015-19, which outlined priorities of bilateral interaction. In the commercial sphere, Russia's oil company, Lukoil, made major investments in Uzbek energy projects. According to IMF estimates, **Uzbekistan** was less economically dependent on Russia than other Central Asian states; nevertheless, it topped the list of Uzbekistan's trade partners, with a bilateral turnover of more than $8.3 billion in 2013. This seemed set to increase, as EU sanctions opened up new markets in Russia for Uzbek exports.

In Kyrgyzstan, the US air base at Manas was closed in June, a month before the expiry of the lease (see AR 2014, p. 265). A number of ideas had been mooted for converting it into a civilian airport, under Turkish or Russian management, but at the end of the year the matter was unresolved. Another unresolved issue was the fate of the Kumtor gold mine, the country's largest industrial asset. The Toronto-listed company Centerra Gold owned the mine; Canadian partners held two thirds of the shares and Kyrgyzaltyn (the Kyrgyz national gold company), one-third. Negotiations to increase Kyrgyzaltyn's stake were derailed by opposition politicians, who demanded that the mine be nationalised (see AR 2014, pp. 265-66). In a separate development, under an Ontario court ruling, another Canadian mining company, Stans Energy, was awarded lien (the right to retain possession) of Kyrgyzaltyn's shares in Centerra until the Kyrgyz government settled an outstanding debt. Meanwhile, Kumtor continued to be dogged by allegations of corruption. In May, the former head of Kyrgyzaltyn was arrested and three expatriate managers fled the country, apparently fearing that they would be arrested on "trumped up charges". By the end of the year, Kumtor management problems had cost Kyrgyzstan an estimated $65 million in lost revenue.

The deteriorating situation in Afghanistan prompted widespread regional concern. The NATO-ISAF mission formally ended in December, but the drawdown of foreign troops had begun several months earlier. The Central Asian states unanimously agreed that there could be no military solution to the problems of Afghanistan. However, they were worried by the growing power of the Taliban and other insurgent groups, such as the Islamic Movement of Uzbekistan. Afghanistan, as Uzbek President Islam Karimov put it, seemed to be descending into "permanent instability", characterised by increasing terrorist and extremist activities as well as drug trafficking.

Turkmenistan, which shared a long border with Afghanistan, had already experienced several cross-border incursions; in one such incident, three Turkmen border guards had been killed and several wounded. In response, the Turkmen government strengthened its border defences, but also undertook peace-building initiatives, including a proposal to organise an inter-Afghan national dialogue under UN auspices. Moreover, like other Central Asian states, it provided humanitarian aid to Afghanistan. An important regional project was the construction of the Turkmen-Afghanistan-Pakistan-India gas pipeline (TAPI) (see AR 2009, p. 312). Work was tentatively scheduled to begin in 2018, but many experts regarded the situation in Afghanistan as too volatile for the project to be feasible in the foreseeable future.

Relations with Asia were expanded. In June, the South Korean leader, Park Geun Hye, toured Central Asia and concluded major agreements aimed at deepening political and economic cooperation; the largest new investment was $4 billion to build natural gas-processing plants in Turkmenistan. However, for all the Central Asian states the most important relationship was with China. The visit of Turkmen President Gurbanguly Berdymukhammedov to Beijing in May was marked by the signing of a bilateral treaty of friendship and cooperation; a joint declaration on the development and deepening of the strategic partnership was underpinned by a plan for advancing the bilateral partnership in 2014-18. Other documents included agreements on stable cooperation in the energy sector, especially the safe and stable operation of the Turkmenistan-China gas pipeline (see AR 2010, p. 295). Similarly productive was the visit of China's Premier Li Keqiang to Kazakhstan in December. The two countries agreed to strengthen cooperation in a number of sectors, including trade, transport connectivity, and the processing of energy-related materials. Proposals included the use of Chinese technology in Kazakhstan for the construction of large industrial plants such as steel and glass works, and thermal power stations.

Relations between the EU and the Central Asian states remained stable. In October, an enhanced "partnership and cooperation" pact was negotiated with Kazakhstan. Kazakhstan also expanded ties with several EU members. In June, a strategic partnership agreement was concluded with Hungary and in December, during the French president's visit to Astana, a joint declaration signalled closer bilateral cooperation. In November, Turkmenistan hosted the visit of Italian Prime Minister Matteo Renzi; an important outcome was the 10-year extension of the production sharing agreement with Italian energy company, Eni.

The development of regional transport corridors was a priority for all the Central Asian states. An important event was the inauguration on 3 December of a railway connecting Kazakhstan via Turkmenistan to Iranian ports on the Persian (Arabian) Gulf, thereby providing access to international shipping lines. Initially, the railway would carry between 3 and 5 million tonnes of cargo per year, but it was anticipated that this volume would be doubled in the future. In August, another infrastructural project moved forward when the foreign ministers of Oman, Iran, Turkmenistan and Uzbekistan met in Muscat to sign a quadrilateral "memorandum of understanding on the establishment of the international transport and transit corridor". It was hoped that this railway would become operational in 2015. Transport links to Baltic ports were also attracting attention. In May, the Latvian foreign minister, Edgars Rinkevics, held talks in Ashgabat on prospective land transit and logistics routes; the issue was raised again in December, at the meeting of the intergovernmental Turkmen-Latvian commission on economic cooperation. Latvian cooperation in the development of maritime infrastructure in the Caspian port of Turkmenbashi was also discussed. Kazakhstan, meanwhile, was pursuing ties with the Estonian port of Sillamae. Located close to the borders of the EU and Russia, Sillamae was a convenient distribution hub for transhipment of cargos from Kazakhstan to Europe, the USA and the Commonwealth of Independent States (CIS). The Estonian side offered to provide the Kazakh partners with land for the construction of their own terminal.

The fourth Caspian Summit was held in Astrakhan, Russia, on 29 September. The main outcome was a political declaration, signed by the presidents of the five littoral states, which stipulated that only these states had the right to have armed forces present on the Caspian Sea, thereby pre-empting the basing of any other military forces in these waters. Explicit formulations were set out on such issues as the delimitation of water areas, the seabed and subsoil, as well as the navigation and fishing regimes. Moreover, it was agreed that most of the Caspian Sea basin would remain in the common use of the littoral states. The next summit was scheduled for 2016, to be held in the Kazakh capital, Astana. It was anticipated that this meeting would result in a final agreement on the legal status of the Caspian Sea, an issue that had been under discussion since 1992.

Shirin Akiner

INDIA—PAKISTAN—BANGLADESH—SRI LANKA—NEPAL—BHUTAN

India

CAPITAL: New Delhi   AREA: 3,287,260 sq km   POPULATION: 1,252,139,596 ('13)
OFFICIAL LANGUAGES: Hindi & English
HEAD OF STATE: President Pranab Mukherjee (since July '12)
RULING PARTY: BJP-led National Democratic Alliance coalition
HEAD OF GOVERNMENT: Prime Minister Narendra Modi (BJP) (since May '14)
DEMOCRACY INDEX: 7.69; 33rd of 167   CORRUPTION PERCEPTIONS INDEX: 38; =85th of 175
CURRENCY: Indian Rupee (Dec '14 £1.00=INR 92.93, US$1.00=INR 63.7)
GNI PER CAPITA: US$1,570, Intl$5,350 at PPP ('13)

Pakistan

CAPITAL: Islamabad   AREA: 796,100 sq km   POPULATION: 182,142,594 ('13)
OFFICIAL LANGUAGE: Urdu
HEAD OF STATE AND GOVERNMENT: President Mamnoon Hussain (PML-N) (since Sept '13)
RULING PARTY: Pakistan Muslim League-Nawaz (PML-N)
PRIME MINISTER: Nawaz Sharif (PML-N) (since June '13)
DEMOCRACY INDEX: 4.64; =107th of 167   CORRUPTION PERCEPTIONS INDEX: 29; =126th of 175
CURRENCY: Pakistan Rupee (Dec '14 £1.00=PKR 157, US$1.00=PKR 101)
GNI PER CAPITA: US$1,380, Intl$4,920 at PPP ('13)

Bangladesh

CAPITAL: Dhaka   AREA: 144,000 sq km   POPULATION: 156,594,962 ('13)
OFFICIAL LANGUAGE: Bengali
HEAD OF STATE: President Abdul Hamid (AL) (since April '13)
RULING PARTY: Awami League (AL)
HEAD OF GOVERNMENT: Prime Minister Sheikh Hasina Wajed (AL) (since Jan '09)
DEMOCRACY INDEX: 5.86; 84th of 167   CORRUPTION PERCEPTIONS INDEX: 25; =145th of 175
CURRENCY: Taka (Dec '14 £1.00=BDT 120.98, US$1=BDT 77.91)
GNI PER CAPITA: US$900, Intl$2,810 at PPP ('13)

Sri Lanka

CAPITAL: Sri Jayawardenapura (Kotte)   AREA: 65,610 sq km   POPULATION: 20,483,000 ('13)
OFFICIAL LANGUAGES: Sinhala, Tamil, English
HEAD OF STATE: President Mahinda Rajapaksa (SLFP) (since Nov '05)
RULING PARTY: Sri Lanka Freedom Party (SLFP) heads United People's Freedom Alliance (UPFA)
    coalition
HEAD OF GOVERNMENT: Disanayaka Mudiyanselage Jayaratne (since April '10)
DEMOCRACY INDEX: 5.69; 91st of 167   CORRUPTION PERCEPTIONS INDEX: 38; =85th of 175
CURRENCY: Sri Lankan Rupee (Dec '14 £1.00=LKR 203.8, US$1.00=LKR 131.3)
GNI PER CAPITA: US$3,170, Intl$9,470 at PPP ('13)

Nepal

CAPITAL: Kathmandu   AREA: 147,180 sq km   POPULATION: 27,797,457 ('13)
OFFICIAL LANGUAGE: Nepali
HEAD OF STATE: President Ram Baran Yadav (since July '08)
RULING PARTY: Nepali Congress heads coalition
HEAD OF GOVERNMENT: Prime Minister Sushil Koirala (Nepali Congress) (since Feb '14)
DEMOCRACY INDEX: 4.77; =104th of 167   CORRUPTION PERCEPTIONS INDEX: 29; =126th of 175
CURRENCY: Nepalese Rupee (Dec '14 £1.00=NPR 158.3, US$1=NPR 101.9)
GNI PER CAPITA: US$730, Intl$2,260 at PPP ('13)

Bhutan

CAPITAL: Thimphu   AREA: 47,000 sq km   POPULATION: 753,947 ('13)
OFFICIAL LANGUAGE: Dzongkha
HEAD OF STATE: Dragon King Jigme Khesar Namgyel Wangchuk (since Dec '06)
RULING PARTY: People's Democratic Party
HEAD OF GOVERNMENT: Prime Minister Tshering Tobgay (People's Democratic Party) (since July
    '13)
DEMOCRACY INDEX: 4.82; =101st of 167   CORRUPTION PERCEPTIONS INDEX: 65; 30th of 175
CURRENCY: Ngultrum (Dec '14 £1.00=BTN 98.93, US$1.00=BTN 63.70)
GNI PER CAPITA: US$2,460, Intl$7,210 at PPP ('13)

AFTER a year in which new governments took office in three of its neighbours
(Pakistan, Bhutan and Nepal), 2014 brought a momentous end—after a decade in
power—to the United Progressive Alliance (UPA) coalition government in South
Asia's largest country, India. Narendra Modi, the charismatic but controversial
prime ministerial candidate of the right-wing Bharatiya Janata Party (BJP) capitalised on the widespread dissatisfaction with the lacklustre performance of the
UPA in its second term, to lead the BJP to a remarkably decisive victory. The BJP
thus became the first party in 30 years to win an outright majority in the elections
to the Lok Sabha (the lower house of the Indian Parliament).

The relative peace of the Indian electoral process contrasted with elections in
Bangladesh that were boycotted by the main opposition parties amidst violent con-

frontation, and with a popular agitation in Pakistan to remove the recently elected government of Prime Minister Nawaz Sharif, which was only suspended following a particularly deadly terrorist attack on a school by the Pakistani Taliban. In Sri Lanka, the year closed with President Mahinda Rajapaksa facing an unexpectedly strong challenge after calling an early presidential election.

In **India** the first months of the year were dominated by a general election campaign that had effectively begun in September 2013, as soon as Gujarat Chief Minister Narendra Modi had been named as its prime ministerial candidate by the main opposition party, the BJP (see AR 2014, p. 270). The BJP seized the initiative in a presidential-style campaign that featured a media blitz so successful as to leave the ruling UPA and its main component, the Indian National Congress, looking rudderless and defeated, even before any votes were cast. The 63-year old Modi himself travelled frenetically across the country, addressing nearly 500 rallies in 25 of India's 28 states. This candidate was projected as the face of the BJP nationally, in a manner not seen in India since the days when Jawaharlal Nehru and his daughter, Indira Gandhi, had led Congress to landslide victories in the first four decades after independence. It was an effort that went against the view of most seasoned Indian political observers that elections in India had come to represent the sum of widely divergent patterns of contestation in the country's states, rather than contests that could be swung by national figures.

However, this time across a large swathe of the country the BJP was able to exploit the disenchantment with the UPA government. It did so by combining the effective national projection of "Brand NaMo", through well funded, slickly professional and often innovative political marketing, with the grass-roots efforts of not only its own members but of the Rashtriya Swayamsevak Sangh (RSS), the powerful Hindu nationalist parent organisation. The 45,000 *shakhas* (branches) of the RSS were enthused by the prospect of one of their own—Modi had been a member since childhood—becoming prime minister.

By contrast, not only did Congress seem poorly organised and listless but it was, by most accounts, easily outspent by a BJP that seemed to enjoy the backing of much of corporate India, hoping that a Modi government would be more pro-business and give a decisive push to the slowing pace of economic liberalisation. Up to $5 billion may have been spent on the election, much of it illegal unaccounted or "black" money: the Election Commission seized nearly $50 million in such funds. With 81-year old Prime Minister Manmohan Singh announcing that he would step down after the election, neither Congress Vice President Rahul Gandhi nor his mother, and party president, Sonia Gandhi, decisively took the helm. This left disheartened party workers forlornly hoping that Rahul's younger sister, Priyanka Vadra, might take a greater role, but she limited her efforts to taking charge of the campaign in her mother's and brother's parliamentary constituencies.

In giving his first ever in depth interview (in English) to the television channel, Times Now, in January, the 43-year old Rahul only confirmed the impression that, even after a decade in politics, he remained unsure of his role and unable to articulate a clear message or vision. For his part, Modi, with only a secondary school education, generally spoke to his audiences in plain, forceful Hindi or Gujarati. Fond of referring to Rahul, scion of the Nehru-Gandhi family that had played a leading role in national politics for nearly a century, as *shehzada* (prince), Modi made much of his own relatively humble origins as a onetime tea-stall boy from a backward caste, and of the claim that in a decade his government had transformed Gujarat into a prosperous economic powerhouse and would now do the same for India. Attempts by opponents to portray him as a dangerously divisive figure by holding him responsible for the anti-Muslim riots in Gujarat in 2002 (see AR 2002, pp. 315-16), in which at least a thousand people were killed, were skilfully deflected, with Modi being careful to avoid expressions of hostility towards Muslims. Nevertheless, he emphasised his Hindu identity by choosing to stand for Parliament in Varanasi, the ancient city in Uttar Pradesh regarded as the holiest by the country's nearly one billion Hindus.

A record 66.3 per cent of the world's largest electorate of 834 million voted over nine days in April and May. This represented an 8 per cent rise on the 2009 turnout, with most of the biggest increases in the states of northern and western India where the BJP's support was concentrated and where it won 80 per cent of the seats. It was here that the BJP took 244 of the 282 seats it won nationally (compared to 116 in 2009). This gave it a majority in the 543-seat Lok Sabha, the first overall majority for any party in a general election since 1984. That Modi's appeal was strong but geographically limited was reflected in the fact that the BJP gained a majority with just 31.3 per cent of the national vote, appreciably less than what Congress had won when it suffered landslide defeats in 1977 and 1989. Even more significant, though, was the humiliating reduction of Congress from 206 to 44 seats, albeit still with 19.5 per cent of the popular vote.

Regional parties did well in the south and east: the ruling parties in Tamil Nadu (the Anna Dravida Munnetra Kazhagam (ADMK)), West Bengal (the Trinamool Congress) and Orissa (Biju Janata Dal) swept their states, claiming 37, 34 and 20 seats respectively. In soon-to-be bifurcated Andhra (see AR 2014, pp. 270-71) the Telugu Desam, which had renewed its alliance with the BJP on the eve of the elections and emerged as the ruling party in the rump state of Andhra Pradesh in elections to the state assembly, won 16 seats. In the other part of Andhra, the Telangana Rashtra Samiti won 11 seats. The party had led the successful campaign for a separate Telangana and became the first ruling party in India's newest, 29th, state, on 2 June. Nationally, the two communist parties saw their seat tally halved to a historic low of 10.

Whilst the government formed by Modi was nominally a National Democratic Alliance coalition, the lion's share of posts went to the BJP including all the major portfolios of state. (The NDA coalition included 10 parties allied to the BJP, and held 336 seats in the Lok Sabha; the new government included ministers from five of these parties.) Notable ministerial appointments were Arun Jaitley, a suave corporate lawyer and member of the last NDA Cabinet who had led the BJP in the upper house, the Rajya Sabha, as finance minister (with temporary additional charge of defence); Sushma Swaraj, another ex-Cabinet minister, who had led the BJP in the last Lok Sabha and been one of the few senior BJP leaders initially to oppose Modi's promotion as party leader, as minister for external affairs; and Rajnath Singh, the BJP's president and an RSS veteran who had supported Modi's elevation, as home minister. Five women, in addition to Swaraj, were appointed to the Cabinet—a record number; they included its only Muslim member (as minister for minority affairs). A further expansion of the government in November included the appointment of Manohar Parrikar, highly regarded for his effective performance over two terms as chief minister of the small western state of Goa, as defence minister.

The scale of the BJP's victory enabled Narendra Modi to exert his influence in reorganising his party's leadership. Amit Shah, a close RSS associate, was afforded the opportunity to make a political comeback when he was put in charge of the BJP's campaign in the crucial battleground state of Uttar Pradesh. Shah had been forced to resign as Gujarat's home minister in 2010, after being charged and jailed for the kidnapping and murder in 2005 of an alleged Muslim gangster and terrorist and his wife (see AR 2011, p. 296). Despite being banned by the Election Commission from making speeches in Uttar Pradesh after allegedly inciting violence around the town of Muzaffarnagar in 2013 (see AR 2014, p. 273), his electoral strategy reaped rich dividends, the BJP winning 71 of the 80 Lok Sabha seats from India's most populous state. Shah's reward came in August, when he succeeded Rajnath Singh as BJP party president and appointed a new, younger leadership team, packed with people with an RSS background. The 86-year old former deputy prime minister, Lal Krishna Advani, who had strongly opposed Modi's adoption as the BJP's prime ministerial nominee, was dropped from the party's parliamentary board. At the end of the year, a Mumbai court acquitted Shah of the charges against him for lack of evidence. Shah's case was indicative of a paradox of Indian politics: Modi's rhetoric emphasised clean politics and delivering growth and development, yet one-fifth of his ministers faced prosecution for serious criminal offences. The stock response of Indian politicians was that the charges brought were often mischievous and baseless.

In his first Independence Day speech as prime minister on 15 August, Modi largely focused on uncontentious issues, calling for a 10-year moratorium on caste, communal and regional divisiveness; proposing a scheme to give every citizen a bank account; urging investors to "Come, Make in India"; and calling for a national campaign for public cleanliness and access to toilets for all. However, the rise of the BJP emboldened the forces of Hindu nationalism. When complainants, who included a prominent RSS educationalist, lodged a civil case against the publication of US historian Wendy Doniger's *The Hindus: An Alternative History*, claiming that it disrespected Hinduism, the publisher Penguin responded by withdrawing it from sale in India. In August the *Sarsanghchalak* (supreme guide) of the RSS, Mohan Bhagwat, provoked controversy by suggesting that all inhabitants of Hindustan (India) ought to be regarded as Hindus. RSS-linked groups stepped up their attack against what they described as a "love jihad" campaign by Muslims to seduce and convert Hindu women, while publicising efforts to get Muslims and Christians to "return home" (*ghar vapasi*) to the Hindu fold. In December a BJP junior minister had to apologise to Parliament for making an election speech in

Delhi in which she said that voters had to choose between voting for the sons of the [Hindu deity] Ram or the "illegitimate". Parliamentary proceedings were disrupted by opposition demands that the prime minister make a statement on the row over conversion.

The stunning BJP election victory left demoralised a Congress Party that had been in government for all but 13 of the previous 67 years. Although the party's working committee immediately rejected the post-election resignations of Sonia and Rahul Gandhi, there was widespread disquiet at Congress's dismal performance, which had been so poor that for the first time ever its leader in the Lok Sabha was denied the status of leader of the opposition, having failed to claim the required one-tenth of the seats. Since 19 of Congress's 44 MPs were from the south, Sonia Gandhi chose Mallikarjun Kharge, a former Cabinet minister from the southern state of Karnataka, to lead the party in the Lok Sabha. Kharge was selected in preference to either Rahul or the veteran Kamal Nath, a more formidable figure with nearly three-and-a half decades of parliamentary experience: apart from the Gandhis, he was one of only five surviving Congress MPs from the Hindi-speaking north. It was a sign of the disarray in Congress ranks that in October Shashi Tharoor, a former junior minister and UN under-secretary-general, was dropped as a party spokesperson for having repeatedly expressed appreciation of some of Prime Minister Modi's actions. Tharoor had been a controversial figure since entering politics, having figured in a cricket corruption scandal in 2010 (see AR 2011, p. 294) and in media speculation regarding the mysterious death of his third wife in a New Delhi hotel in January.

The non-Congress opposition was in little better state. Nitish Kumar, the chief minister of Bihar, who had taken his Janata Dal (United) (JD(U)) out of the NDA in 2013 in protest at the BJP's promotion of Modi, resigned after the NDA won three-quarters of the Lok Sabha seats from Bihar. Kumar relinquished his position as chief minister to another member of his party. In an effort to regroup, Kumar allied with Congress and the Rashtriya Janata Dal (RJD) of his long-standing rival, Laloo Prasad Yadav, to fight the BJP in by-elections to the Bihar State Assembly, and won six of 10 seats. Following this minor success, in December the JD(U) and the RJD joined three other parties with whom they shared a Janata socialist tradition—the Samajwadi Party that ruled Uttar Pradesh, and the smaller Janata Dal (Secular) and Indian National Lok Dal—in forming a new party to be called the Samajwadi Janata Dal.

However, the two regional party leaders that had performed best in the general election were preoccupied by their own problems. West Bengal's chief minister, Mamata Banerjee, had to answer allegations in connection with a scam that had resulted in hundreds of thousands of small investors losing over $400 million, after the collapse of the investment operation of the Saradha Group, a consortium which ran many unlicensed financial schemes in eastern India; a minister and MP from Banerjee's Trinamool Congress were arrested in connection with the affair. Tamil Nadu's ADMK chief minister, J. Jayalalitha, was sentenced in September to four years' imprisonment following her conviction by a court in Bengalaru on a 17-year old charge of amassing wealth disproportionate to her known sources of income. Although released on bail after three weeks, she had to vacate her post, and faced being barred from contesting elections for 10 years if unsuccessful in appealing the verdict.

Despite suffering reverses in by-elections to six state assemblies in the autumn, the BJP maintained enough momentum from its general election victory to win state polls in the formerly Congress-ruled states of Maharashtra and Haryana in October, and in the eastern tribal state of Jharkhand in December. It also swept the Hindu-majority region of Jammu, to emerge as the second largest party in Jammu and Kashmir after the People's Democratic Party (PDP). The incumbent Jammu and Kashmir National Conference, with which the Congress had ended a six-year alliance, took third place, losing to the PDP in the mainly Muslim Kashmir Valley. The year ended with the BJP fighting to regain power in Delhi, which had been under governor's rule since February when the Aam Aadmi Party (AAP) of anti-corruption activist Arvind Kejriwal had resigned after just seven weeks in office as a minority administration, in protest at being blocked from introducing an anti-corruption bill.

The slackening in economic growth that had contributed to the unpopularity of Congress and the UPA picked up slightly during the year, to above 5 per cent. Despite high expectations that the new government would move decisively to further liberalise the economy, its first budget was unadventurous. However, there were signals of the direction in which it wanted to go: in his Independence Day speech, the prime minister announced that the Planning Commission, a legacy of once-dominant socialist-style economic planning, would be replaced. In November, an ordinance took initial steps towards ending the four decade-old state monopoly in the coal industry. In May, Hindustan Motors finally ceased production of the Ambassador car, the Indian adaptation of the 1956 Morris Oxford, which had been ubiquitous on the country's roads for four decades until economic liberalisation opened India up to global marques.

There was another significant achievement for the Indian space programme, when, in September, it followed the USA, Russia and the European Space Agency in successfully putting a satellite, *Mangalyaan*, into orbit around the planet Mars. India was the first country to succeed in this challenge at the first attempt.

After witnessing its first change of government through the ballot box in 2013, **Pakistan** went through an year in which the Pakistan Muslim League (Nawaz) (PML(N)) government of Prime Minister Nawaz Sharif was challenged by street protests. They were spearheaded by the Pakistan Tehreek-e-Insaaf (Movement for Justice) (PTI), of ex-cricketer Imran Khan, the third biggest party in the National Assembly, and a Muslim religious leader, Muhammad Tahir-ul-Qadri, who in 2013 had initiated an agitation against the alleged corruption of the previous Pakistan People's Party (PPP) government. After weeks of tension and clashes with police, simultaneous marches by PTI supporters and Qadri's followers, calling for the resignation of the government, set off from Lahore, the capital of Punjab, Pakistan's largest province. They arrived in the national capital, Islamabad, on 14 August, the country's independence day. Qadri and Khan claimed that the 2013 elections had been fraudulent and demanded a fresh poll. With protesters being encamped outside, the National Assembly passed a resolution declaring the demands unconstitutional. The main opposition PPP and other groups supported Prime Minister Sharif against what they saw as dangerously undermining the principle of elected civilian government in a country that had been ruled by the military for nearly half its history. This support was reiterated in a rare emergency joint session of the National Assembly and Senate on 2 September. Most PTI members then resigned from parliament and three people were killed and hundreds injured in a failed attempt to storm the prime minister's house. This action led to the resignation from the PTI of Javed Hashmi, a veteran PML(N) leader who had joined the party in 2011 (see AR 2012, p. 303), becoming its president.

Hashmi implied that Imran Khan's actions had been influenced by the military, but a military statement appealed for calm and for talks to resolve the political crisis. Discussions between the protest leaders and the government broke down, however, over the demand that Nawaz Sharif resign. The chief of the army, General Raheel Sharif (no relation of the prime minister), reportedly overruled calls from some generals to force the prime minister's resignation. In October Tahir-ul-Qadri ended his sit-in outside Parliament after 65 days, saying it had succeeded in awakening the nation. However, Imran Khan's PTI continued with its protest in Islamabad, also staging mass rallies in several other cities until December when the campaign was suspended in the aftermath of the deadly attack by the Pakistani Taliban on a school in Peshawar (see below).

Relations between the government and the military were complicated by a number of issues. One point of tension was the indictment in March by a special court of Pakistan's last military ruler, Pervez Musharraf, who had returned to the country to contest the 2013 elections (see AR 2014, p. 275), on a charge of treason arising from his imposition of emergency rule in 2007. In November the court accepted evidence presented by Musharraf's lawyers that he was not solely responsible for the imposition and that the prosecution should be expanded to include the then prime minister, law minister (Zahid Hamid, also a minister in the current government) and chief justice. This made it more likely that the case would either drag on indefinitely or be abandoned by a weak government which was reluctant to further antagonise the military. Nawaz Sharif was believed to have irked the military establishment by seeking to pursue his own line in dealing with the Pakistani Taliban and trying to improve relations with India and Afghanistan.

The problem of tackling the Pakistani Taliban insurgency, which had claimed about 40,000 lives since 2007, was the major domestic concern for the government. After the death of Taliban leader Hakimullah Mehsud in a US drone strike had aborted possible talks between the Taliban and the government in 2013 (see AR 2014, p. 276), Prime Minister Sharif appointed a four-member commission at the end of January in a renewed attempt to initiate talks. The talks broke down less than three weeks later after a Taliban group said that in retaliation for the killing of their fighters by the army they had executed 23 captured paramilitary personnel. Although at the beginning of March the Taliban announced a new ceasefire in order to revive the talks, and a few days later the prime minister even had breakfast with Taliban negotiators, any chance of progress disappeared in June after the insurgents attacked the international airport in Pakistan's biggest city, Karachi, leaving 36 people, including all 10 attackers, dead. Amidst criticism that the Taliban had simply used the ceasefire to buy time, the military responded to the attack by launching an offensive in the Taliban stronghold of the North Waziristan tribal region, which bordered on Afghanistan, and Parliament approved a Protection of Pakistan bill which granted sweeping new anti-terrorism powers to the security forces. Days before the army offensive, the US resumed its controversial drone strikes in Pakistan's tribal belt after a pause of almost six months. (In February Imran Khan's PTI had called off a three-month blockade of a supply route for NATO forces in Afghanistan in support of its demand for an end to the drone strikes.) The long pause in strikes meant that only 25 were reported during the year, the lowest total since 2007.

Over the following months, while resisting the military offensive, the Tehrik-e-Taliban Pakistan (TTP) showed signs of fragmenting. In May a branch in South Waziristan broke away, to be followed by another breakaway, the Jamaat-ul-Ahrar, in August. In October the TTP spokesman and several other commanders defected and affiliated themselves with Islamic State in Iraq and Syria (ISIS), and one more Taliban splinter, Jundullah, proclaimed its allegiance to IS in November.

Despite the divisions, and the army offensive, the Taliban continued to be able to carry out operations well beyond the tribal belt along the Afghan border. A sailor died in an attack on a naval dockyard in Karachi in September, and in November the Jamaat-ul-Ahrar group claimed responsibility for a suicide bomber who killed 61 people as they returned from watching the daily military parade and flag hoisting at the Wagah border crossing with India, a popular spectacle. In an attack on 16 December that shocked the country and attracted worldwide condemnation, nine gunmen were killed after storming the Army Public School and College in Peshawar, the capital of the province of Khyber Pakhtunkhwa, and massacring 145 people including 132 children. The TTP said that the school was targeted because it served the children of army personnel and in retribution for the offensive in North Waziristan which the army claimed had killed 1,200 militants. However, the attack brought condemnation from the breakaway Jamaat-ul-Ahrar and the Afghan Taliban, as well as the Lashkar-e-Jhangvi, a banned Sunni Muslim militant group that targeted minority Shia Muslims (more than a hundred Shias were killed during the year). The initial government response included ending a six-year moratorium on the execution of militants sentenced to death and the subsequent hanging of six men convicted in connection with a 2003 assassination attempt on the then president, Pervez Musharraf. The government also announced plans to set up new special military courts to try terrorism cases and raise a new anti-terrorism force.

Among those expressing horror at the Peshawar massacre was Malala Yousafzai, the teenage advocate for girls' education who had been seriously injured in a Taliban attack (see AR 2013, p. 278) and thereafter had won international celebrity. In December Malala became, at 17, the youngest ever person to be awarded a Nobel Prize, jointly receiving the Prize for Peace with Kailash Satyarthi, a long-time Indian campaigner against child labour. In September the army had announced that it had captured 10 militants suspected of involvement in the 2012 attack on Malala.

The estimated death toll in the violent conflict in Pakistan remained at roughly the same level as in 2013—about 5,500—but there appeared to be a marked shift in the balance of casualties as a result of the military offensive in North Waziristan, with the number of militants reported killed accounting for the majority of the dead for the first time since 2010. Apart from the Taliban insurgency, other conflicts also rumbled on during 2014. In February, Baloch activists completed a nearly 3,000-kilometre march to Islamabad in protest at the alleged disappearance of thousands of people during the decade-long repression by security forces of insurgents fighting for the autonomy or independence of Balochistan.

Concern about the application of punitive blasphemy laws continued to trouble Pakistan's small Christian minority of about 3 million. In September a policeman killed a Christian pastor who was in custody in Islamabad under a death sentence on a charge of blasphemy, and wounded a 70-year-old British Pakistani with a history of mental illness who had also been condemned to death. Two months later, 45 people were arrested after a mob in a town in Punjab killed a Christian couple accused of desecrating the Koran. In October there was another twist in a case involving Asia Bibi, a Christian woman whose death sentence in 2010 for allegedly insulting the Prophet Mohammad had provoked an international outcry (see AR 2011, p. 300) and was a factor in the assassination in 2011 of the provincial governor of Punjab after he had sought her release (see AR 2012, p. 299). The Lahore High Court upheld her sentence leaving her lawyers to appeal to the Supreme Court.

Blasphemy was also the charge in the sentencing in November, by a court in the autonomous Himalayan region of Gilgit-Baltistan, of Mir Shakeel-ur-Rehman, the owner of Geo News, the country's largest media group. He received 26 years in prison for a broadcast showing people dancing to a song about the wedding of the Prophet Mohammad's daughter. He escaped detention, however, since verdicts by courts in the region did not apply in the rest of Pakistan. The legal action was linked to the military as it had been brought soon after the Geo TV channel blamed the military's Inter-Services Intelligence (ISI) for a gun attack in Karachi, in April, in which Hamid Mir, one of its top journalists and news anchors, was wounded. The Pakistan Electronic Media Regulatory Authority suspended Geo TV for 15 days after it made the accusation, an action that it also took in October against ARY News, a fiercely anti-government television channel, for maligning the country's court system.

In **Bangladesh** the year began in violence. The major opposition parties—the Bangladesh Nationalist Party (BNP) of former prime minister, Begum Khaleda Zia, and the Jamaat-e-Islami, the country's main Islamist party—boycotted elections to the National Assembly, in protest at Prime Minister Sheikh Hasina Wajed's refusal to reverse controversial 2011 legislation that had abolished the practice of conducting general elections under a neutral caretaker administration. Eighteen people were killed on polling day, adding to a toll of over a hundred in the run-up to the ballot. Less than half of the constituencies were contested, and the ruling Awami League (AL) won 234 of the 300 seats in an election shunned by international observers, and in which the official turnout of 51 per cent was the lowest for 35 years. Despite this, Sheikh Hasina insisted that fresh elections could only be considered if the opposition desisted from violent protest. Her long-time rival, Begum Khaleda, claimed that she had been kept under virtual house arrest while more than 300 BNP workers had disappeared or been killed and 22,000 people arrested. In March Begum Khaleda, along with her exiled son and BNP senior vice chairman, Tarique Rahman, and seven others, was indicted on charges of embezzling charitable funds; she faced a possible life sentence if found guilty.

The controversial trials before an International War Crimes Tribunal, set up in 2010, of leaders of the Jamaat-e-Islami in particular continued to provoke recurring violent protest. The defendants faced charges arising from the Pakistani army's violent crackdown during the 1971 independence struggle. In October Ghulam Azzam, the Jamaat's 92-year old former leader, died in hospital before the Supreme Court could hear his appeal against his 90-year sentence. Although the death sentence on one Jamaat leader was commuted to life imprisonment on appeal to the Supreme Court, another was upheld in November. Three more Jamaat figures received sentences of execution, as did a former BNP leader living in exile in Sweden; a local politician, who had been expelled from the AL; and a former minister in the military government of the 1980s. Some 200 people were said to have been killed in protests since the trials began. One of the Jamaat leaders to be sentenced to death was Motiur Rahman Nizami, its serving chief (*Ameer*), who was already facing execution on separate charges. He was among 14 people—including a former deputy interior minister, a former director general of the National Security Intelligence, and a retired major general—who had been sentenced to death by a special tribunal in the port city of Chittagong in January for involvement in a 2004 conspiracy to smuggle arms, it was suspected to separatist insurgents in the Indian state of Assam.

Apart from the Jamaat protests in the streets, the AL government also faced a threat from outlawed militant Islamist groups. In June eight members of one such group, the Harkat-ul Jihad Islami, received judicial death sentences for a series of bomb attacks that had killed 10 people in 2001. In September a 24-year-old Bengali UK citizen, Samiun Rahman, was arrested on suspicion of seeking to recruit people to fight for Islamic State (ISIS) and the al-Qaida-linked Nusra Front in Syria. A month later, an alleged plot to assassinate both Sheikh Hasina and Begum Khaleda was uncovered by Indian intelligence, following the deaths of two members of the banned Jamaat-ul-Mujahideen (JUM) while making bombs in a house in the city of Burdwan in the Indian state of West Bengal. The JUM had carried out a number of attacks across Bangladesh in 2005, but was since thought to have been effectively suppressed. Two people were arrested in the Indian state of Assam in connection with the plot and another four subsequently in Bangladesh.

More than a year after the collapse of the Rana Plaza factory complex in Dhaka (see AR 2014, p. 277), which attracted global attention to the hazardous conditions endured by workers in the lucrative garment industry, 17 people were charged with breaching building regulations. As well as the parents of the owner of the building, they included a local mayor, engineers and three factory owners. In August police forcibly ended a mass hunger strike by workers demanding back pay and a holiday bonus at factories of the Tuba Group, which owned the Tazreen factory where the country's worst factory fire had occurred in 2012 (see AR 2013, p. 279). (After surrendering in February to face homicide charges the Tuba Group's owner was released on bail five months later.) That conditions remained seriously sub-standard across the garment industry was confirmed by inspectors hired by the Accord for Fire and Building Safety in Bangladesh, set up following the Rana Plaza disaster, and joined by more than 180 international clothing brands and retailers. They identified over 80,000 safety issues after initial inspections of 1,106 factories. In spite of the problems affecting the industry, and the chronic power shortages and political instability in the country, the Bangladesh economy grew by an estimated 6 per cent in 2014, with exports—80 per cent of which were accounted for by the garment sector—expected to rise by 10 per cent to over $33 billion.

Domestic politics in **Sri Lanka** continued to be dominated by its authoritarian president, Mahinda Rajapaksa, but by the year's end his hold on power seemed less secure than at any time since he took office in 2005.

Rajapaksa's United People's Freedom Alliance (UPFA) margin of victory was cut in provincial elections in the Southern and Western provinces in March, and Uva in the south-east in September. Opposition parties alleged widespread malpractice and intimidation in polls for municipal councils in the predominantly Tamil Northern Province where the UPFA won most seats in the main city, Jaffna, although the Tamil National Alliance secured a majority in Vavuniya. After attending the swearing in of India's new prime minister, Narendra Modi, in May, Rajapaksa had reaffirmed that his government would not agree to implement in full the Indian-backed 13th constitutional amendment of 1987, which, in an effort to address longstanding Tamil demands for self-government, had stipulated the devolution of power over the police and land to provincial administrations. Nevertheless, in another step towards restoring links between the Tamil areas and the rest of the country five years after the end of the civil war, the railway line between the capital, Colombo, and Jaffna was reopened in October after more than two decades, India having provided credit of $800 million for its repair.

Curbs on the press and tacit encouragement of majority Sinhala Buddhist chauvinism remained features of the Rajapaksa government's effort to maintain its hold on power. Two news websites critical of the government (srilankamirror.com and theindependent.lk) were blocked in May; several media gatherings were prevented from taking place by threats; and, from July, non-governmental organisations were banned from engaging in press activity. Militant Buddhist organisations, such as the Bodu Bala Sena (BBS) (see AR 2014, p. 279) and the Ravana Balaya, continued to campaign against and attack other religions. In June three people were killed and scores injured in attacks on Muslim homes and businesses following provocative speeches by Galagoda Aththe Gnanasara, the secretary general of the

BBS. In September Ashin Wirathu, the leader of the violently anti-Muslim Buddhist "969 movement" in Burma, attended a BBS convention in Colombo and agreed to form an international Buddhist front against militant Islam.

Gnanasara proclaimed that the BBS would dictate the outcome of the next national election through mobilising Buddhists. In November a pliant Supreme Court cleared the way for President Rajapaksa to hold elections a year early by pronouncing that there were no legal impediments to his standing for a third term. Even though the main party of Buddhist monks, the Jathika Hela Urumaya (National Heritage Party), left the government in protest at Rajapaksa's refusal to abolish the powerful executive presidency before fresh elections, a presidential election was called for January 2015.

This was followed by the unexpected resignation of Maithripala Sirisena, the health minister and general secretary of Rajapaksa's Sri Lanka Freedom Party, and his adoption as their joint presidential candidate by most opposition parties, brought together by Maduluwawe Sobitha Thero, a prominent Buddhist monk and the head of a National Movement for Social Justice, formed to promote democratic good governance and the rule of law. By the end of the year, 23 legislators, including several more ministers—among them the leader of the Sri Lankan Muslim Congress—had defected to the opposition.

Notwithstanding a lavishly populist budget and cuts in energy and fuel prices, as well as his control of the state apparatus, and an attempt to exploit the prestige associated with the forthcoming visit to the island by Pope Francis in January 2015, it was clear that, five years after being hailed for crushing the Tamil Tiger insurgency, Rajapaksa faced a formidable challenge. Despite presiding over a country with the highest economic growth in South Asia—estimated at over 7 per cent in 2014, with unprecedented tourist arrivals a significant factor—some of the president's core Sinhala Buddhist supporters appeared to be joining the alienated Tamil and Muslim minorities in turning against the alleged corruption and nepotism of his ruling family clique.

Sri Lanka's international relations continued to be overshadowed by the controversial bloody end to the civil war in 2009 (see AR 2010, pp. 306-08). In March the UN Human Rights Council approved a US-led resolution to open an international war crimes inquiry into alleged violations committed by both sides during the civil war. China and Pakistan opposed the resolution and, unlike in 2013, India abstained from supporting it. An appreciative President Rajapaksa then released 93 Indian fishermen detained for straying into Sri Lankan waters. The Sri Lankan government steadfastly refused to cooperate with the inquiry.

In February, after two months of deadlock, **Nepal's** new Constituent Assembly elected Sushil Koirala, the 76-year old leader of the centrist Nepali Congress, and cousin of three previous prime ministers, to lead a coalition government, which would also include the Communist Party of Nepal (Unified Marxist-Leninist), the second biggest party in the Assembly. However, the Unified Communist Party of Nepal (Maoist) of former rebel leader, Prachanda, refused to join the coalition (see AR 2014, p. 280).

The need to effectively manage the growth of international mountaineering in the Himalayas—a significant source of revenue for the impoverished country—was emphasised by the deaths of 16 Sherpa guides in avalanches in April, followed in October by the deaths of 43 foreign trekkers and their Nepali guides, in what was the worst such disaster to date.

The first foreign visit made by India's new prime minister, Narendra Modi, was to the small Himalayan kingdom of **Bhutan**. His visit in June was seen as demonstrating a desire to reinforce India's position in the subcontinent to counteract the growing economic and political influence of China. He followed it, in August, with a trip to Nepal, the first bilateral visit by an Indian prime minister in 17 years. In Bhutan, Modi laid the foundation of a new 600 mw hydroelectric power station designed to supply power both domestically and to India. He offered Nepal $1 billion in concessional loans to develop its huge hydroelectric potential, as well as communications infrastructure. In October, in the single largest foreign investment scheme to date in Nepal, the Indian GMR Group signed a $1.5 billion deal to build the 900 mw Upper Karnali hydroelectric plant, and a month later India and Nepal signed a deal to build a second $1 billion plant of the same size to generate electricity for both countries from 2021.

INTERNATIONAL RELATIONS OF SOUTH ASIA. After a deterioration in 2013, the prospects for Indo-Pakistani relations initially appeared to improve in the wake of the advent of a new leadership in both countries. Despite his reputation as an aggressive Hindu nationalist, and the stigma of the 2002 Gujarat riots, there were some hopes that Narendra Modi, with his parliamentary majority, might be bolder than Manmohan Singh's lame duck government had been in pursuing better relations with its long-time foe in the interests of strengthening India's position both within South Asia and on the global stage. In an unprecedented gesture, Modi invited the leaders of all the member states of the South Asian Association for Regional Cooperation (SAARC) to New Delhi for his swearing in ceremony. Pakistan's Nawaz Sharif, after hesitating, joined the leaders of Sri Lanka, Nepal, Bhutan, the Maldives and Afghanistan, as well as Prime Minister Navin Ramgoolam, from the Indian Ocean island republic of Mauritius, in attending (Bangladesh was represented by its parliamentary speaker owing to Sheikh Hasina's absence on a visit to Japan). However, the challenge of dealing with the issues dividing India and Pakistan was indicated when, in one of the series of bilateral meetings that the new Indian prime minister had with regional leaders, Modi told Sharif that Islamabad must "abide by its commitment to prevent its territory and territory it controls being used to stage terror attacks on India". Sharif responded by saying that engaging in "accusations and counter-accusations would be counter-productive."

The promise of a new beginning in bilateral relations suffered a setback in August when India called off a visit to Islamabad by its foreign secretary aimed at discussing the resumption of a formal dialogue on bilateral issues, describing meetings that Pakistan's high commissioner in Delhi had had with Kashmiri separatist leaders from the disputed region of Jammu and Kashmir, belonging to the

All Parties Hurriyat Conference and the Jammu and Kashmir Liberation Front, as an effort to interfere in India's internal affairs. Personal gestures such as an exchange of gifts between the prime ministers for each others' mothers and Sharif sending cases of Pakistani mangoes for Modi and other Indian leaders did not preclude them blaming the other for the failure to begin bilateral talks in their speeches to the UN General Assembly in New York in September. The diplomatic standoff was reflected in border tension, with tens of thousands of Kashmiri villagers on either side of the Line of Control being forced to flee their homes in October as Indian and Pakistani forces exchanged artillery fire that left a score of people dead. Addressing a political rally, Prime Minister Modi declared: "The enemy has realised that times have changed and their old habits will not be tolerated." At the end of November, after an attack by gunmen on an Indian army base close to the border left 10 dead, the Indian Home Minister Rajnath Singh accused Pakistan's Inter-Services Intelligence of being behind such attacks. Eleven Indian soldiers and policemen were killed in another attack, just days later, attributed to the Pakistan-based Lashkar-e-Taiba group, which was blamed for the 2008 terrorist attack on Mumbai (see AR 2009, pp. 316-17). The year ended with at least two Pakistani and one Indian soldier being killed in clashes on New Year's eve, making 2014 the worst year for violations of the ceasefire agreed by the two countries in 2003.

The tensions between its two largest members overshadowed the 18th SAARC summit in the Nepalese capital Kathmandu in November. Only after a belated and brief meeting between the Indian and Pakistani prime ministers, did Pakistan sign a framework agreement to create a regional electricity grid, still prevaricating on other agreements on easing road and rail traffic across borders. Pakistan appeared increasingly sidelined at the summit, with India firmly rebuffing a Pakistani suggestion that SAARC consider upgrading the observer status accorded to China and South Korea.

Both India and Pakistan demonstrated greater flexibility in their relations with their other neighbours. In addition to Prime Minister Modi making his first foreign visits to Bhutan and Nepal, in July India accepted a ruling by the Permanent Court of Arbitration in The Hague, under the UN Convention on the Law of the Sea, awarding Bangladesh nearly four-fifths of an area of over 25,000 sq km in the Bay of Bengal, thus opening the way for Bangladesh to explore for oil and gas in the sector. Towards the end of the year, in an apparent reversal of the stand previously taken by the ruling BJP, India also seemed to be moving towards a land exchange deal with Bangladesh affecting enclaves along their land border that could leave India with about 10,000 acres less territory. For its part, the slow improvement in Pakistan's relations with Afghanistan quickened after Ashraf Ghani succeeded Hamid Karzai as president of Afghanistan in September. Ghani, whose predecessor's relationship with Pakistani leaders had always been characterised by mutual suspicion, made what was regarded as a successful first state visit to Islamabad in November. However, there was tension on the frontier between Pakistan's south-western province of Balochistan and Iran, with Pakistan protesting in October at the killing of a security official in firing by Iranian border guards, and allegations by Iran that Sunni militants based in Balochistan had been launching attacks on Iran.

Pakistan's friendliest neighbourly relations continued to be with China, the fourth and largest of the four states with which it shared a border. Although the Chinese president, Xi Jinping, had to postpone a planned visit in September because of the anti-government street protests in Pakistan, Prime Minister Nawaz Sharif visited Beijing in November, promising to be resolute in helping combat the threat from the East Turkestan Islamic Movement that China blamed for attacks in the western region of Xinjiang, and suspected of making use of the lawless tribal area across the border in Pakistan. For Pakistan, increased aid from China was especially welcome at a time when it was nervous about waning US support in the wake of the drawing down of US and other NATO forces in Afghanistan. The Chinese government and banks agreed to finance $45.6 billion worth of energy and infrastructure projects in Pakistan over the next six years in what was dubbed the China-Pakistan Economic Corridor.

In a departure from precedent, China's Xi Jinping began his first official visit to India, in September, not in Delhi but in Ahmedabad, the capital of Prime Minister Modi's home state of Gujarat. As the state's chief minister, Modi had visited China five times and was a keen admirer of its rapid economic development. However, the visit yielded mixed results. Although deals worth $30 billion were reached—including Chinese investment in updating India's huge but ageing railway system and in new industrial parks in Gujarat and neighbouring Maharashtra, and greater access to the Chinese market for Indian pharmaceuticals and agriculture—this was less than had been expected. The atmosphere was soured by actions taken by both sides. A Chinese road construction incursion into the disputed region of Ladakh was raised by Modi during talks with Xi, with the resulting standoff with Indian forces taking two weeks to resolve. For its part, China may well have been piqued by the fact that just as the Chinese president arrived, India's president, Pranab Mukherjee, ended a visit to Vietnam during which agreements reached included one for Indian companies to explore for oil off the Vietnamese coast. India also joined Vietnam in calling for free navigation in the South China Sea, an area in which Vietnam and other countries had long been involved in maritime disputes with China.

China would also have been given pause for thought by the increasing warmth in relations between India and Japan evident when Modi had made his first bilateral visit outside the subcontinent a fortnight earlier. Showing a mutual regard for each other, Modi and Prime Minister Shinzo Abe resolved to strengthen defence cooperation and agreed that the two countries should work as special strategic and global partners. Abe also declared that Japan would aim to invest 3.5 trillion yen in India over the next five years. Japan's desire for more active engagement in South Asia was also indicated by Abe visiting both Bangladesh and Sri Lanka immediately after hosting his Indian counterpart.

The new Indian prime minister's first overseas engagement had been to attend the annual summit of the BRICS (Brazil-Russia-India-China-South Africa) leaders in Fortaleza, Brazil, in July. The summit highlight was the establishment by the

BRICS of a New Development Bank as an alternative to the World Bank, an idea proposed in 2012 (see AR 2013, p. 282). With the five states having equal voting rights despite their economic disparities, it was decided that while the bank's headquarters would be in Shanghai, its presidency would rotate, with India providing the first incumbent.

Modi followed his visit to Japan with one to the USA at the end of September. This held special significance for he had been denied a visitor's visa to the US in 2005, in the aftermath of the 2002 Gujarat riots. A change in the US administration's attitude was signalled before Modi's election victory when, in February, the US ambassador to India travelled to Gujarat to meet him. (In October 2012 the British high commissioner to India had become the first envoy from a leading Western state to do so, see AR 2013, p. 272.) In calling Modi to congratulate him on the BJP's election victory, President Barack Obama also invited him to Washington, DC, and US Secretary of State John Kerry, accompanied by the Commerce Secretary, and Defence Secretary Chuck Hagel, visited India for talks in August. The Obama administration was particularly concerned to begin its dealings with the new government on a positive note given the unexpected strain placed on bilateral relations by the furore occasioned by the circumstances of the arrest, on charges of visa fraud and paying her Indian maid less than the US minimum wage, of Devyani Khobragade, the Indian deputy consul general in New York, at the end of 2013 (see AR 2014, pp. 282-83); Khobragade had been allowed to return to India in January.

In a joint press article published during Modi's visit, the Indian prime minister and the US president described the US-India relationship as "a defining partnership for the 21st century". A highlight of the visit was the superstar welcome that Modi received from a capacity crowd in New York's iconic Madison Square Garden arena. Mainly drawn from among the burgeoning community of well over 3 million Americans of Indian heritage, an increasingly influential and successful group enjoying the highest average per capita income in the US, they also included more than 30 members of the US Congress. In a reflection of the growing importance of the Indian diaspora in the US, Richard Rahul Verma, an Indian-American lawyer, was confirmed as the new US ambassador to Delhi in December. A tangible result of the progress made in Indo-US relations came in November when an agreement between the two countries on food security, protecting India's huge food stockpiles from punitive measures for the time being, paved the way for the adoption by the World Trade Organisation of the Trade Facilitation Agreement, a landmark reform to ease customs restrictions on global trade. Shortly afterwards it was announced that President Obama would be the guest of honour at India's 2015 Republic Day, thereby becoming the first US president to attend the celebration.

Modi joined Obama and other world leaders for the annual East Asia summit in Burma and the G-20 summit in Brisbane, Australia, in November, thereby taking the opportunity to also become the first Indian prime minister to make an official visit to Australia since 1986 and Fiji since 1981. During his visit India and Australia concluded a Framework for Security Cooperation covering defence, counter-terrorism, cyber policy, disarmament and non-proliferation and maritime security.

In September Australian Prime Minister Tony Abbott had visited India for the first time since taking office in 2013, and had sealed a deal under which Australia would supply uranium for India's civil nuclear programme (see AR 2013, p. 283).

Compared with the new Indian government's intensive engagement in Asia and with the USA, there was less traffic with Africa, the Middle East and the EU, although during July and August the French foreign minister and the British deputy prime minister, foreign secretary and Chancellor of the Exchequer all visited India, mainly in an effort to drum up trade. Despite cultivating closer ties with the US, Prime Minister Modi assured Russia's President Vladimir Putin, when he visited Delhi in December, that Russia retained a unique place in Indian foreign policy and would remain India's most important defence partner (although recently overtaken by the US as India's biggest arm supplier, with France and Israel following Russia). Controversially, the prime minister of the new Russian republic of Crimea (which had been detached from Ukraine) accompanied Putin on his visit.

In a shift of emphasis in the Middle East, India notably refrained from condemning Israel's bombing of Gaza in July. Modi, the first Indian prime minister to have visited Israel (he did so as chief minister of Gujarat in 2006), in September met Israel's Prime Minister Binyamin Netanyahu when attending the UN General Assembly session in New York. Despite India being the biggest purchaser of Israeli arms, it was the first time since prime minister Ariel Sharon's visit to India in 2003, when the last BJP-led government of Atal Bihari Vajpayee was in office, that the two countries' heads of government had met.

In July, 46 Indian nurses taken from the Iraqi city of Tikrit following its capture by the Islamic State in Iraq and Syria (ISIS) group were released, but at the end of the year the fate of 39 Indian construction workers, seized after the fall of the city of Mosul to ISIS in June, remained uncertain. ISIS was banned in India in December following the detention of an engineer in Bengalaru accused of running a popular Twitter account for the group. Three months earlier, in a possible reaction to the higher profile gained by the new group, Ayman al-Zawahiri, the leader of al-Qaida, had announced the launch of a South Asian wing to operate from Burma to Kashmir.

James Chiriyankandath

INDIAN OCEAN STATES

The Comoros

CONSTITUENT REPUBLICS: Anjouan, Grande Comore, Mohéli
CAPITAL: Moroni   AREA: 1,861 sq km   POPULATION: 734,917 ('13)
OFFICIAL LANGUAGES: Arabic & French
HEAD OF STATE AND GOVERNMENT: Union President Ikililou Dhoinine, (since May '11)
DEMOCRACY INDEX: 3.52; =126th of 167   CORRUPTION PERCEPTIONS INDEX: 26; =142nd of 175
CURRENCY: Comoro Franc (Dec '14 £1.00=KMF 627.2, US$1.00=KMF 403.9)
GNI PER CAPITA: US$880, Intl$1,560 at PPP ('13)

Madagascar

CAPITAL: Antananarivo   AREA: 587,040 sq km   POPULATION: 22,924,851 ('13)
OFFICIAL LANGUAGES: Malagasy, French & English
HEAD OF STATE AND GOVERNMENT: President Hery Rajaonarimampianina (since Jan '14)
PRIME MINISTER: Kolo Roger (since April '14)
DEMOCRACY INDEX: 4.32; 110th of 167   CORRUPTION PERCEPTIONS INDEX: 28; =133rd of 175
CURRENCY: Malagasy Ariary (Dec '14 £1.00=MGA 4,014, US$1.00=MGA 2,585)
GNI PER CAPITA: US$440, Intl$1,350 at PPP ('13)

Maldives

CAPITAL: Malé   AREA: 300 sq km   POPULATION: 345,023 ('13)
OFFICIAL LANGUAGE: Divehi
HEAD OF STATE AND GOVERNMENT: President Abdulla Yameen (since Nov' 13)
RULING PARTIES: Maldivian Democratic Party (MDP)-led coalition
CURRENCY: Rufiyaa (Dec '14 £1.00=MVR 23.84, US$1.00=MVR 15.35)
GNI PER CAPITA: US$5,600, Intl$9,890 at PPP ('13)

Mauritius

CAPITAL: Port Louis   AREA: 2,040 sq km   POPULATION: 1,296,303 ('13)
OFFICIAL LANGUAGE: English
HEAD OF STATE: President Rajkeswur Purryag (since July '12)
RULING PARTIES: Alliance Lepep
HEAD OF GOVERNMENT: Prime Minister Anerood Jugnauth   (since Dec '14)
DEMOCRACY INDEX: 8.17; =17th of 167   CORRUPTION PERCEPTIONS INDEX: 54; =47th of 175
CURRENCY: Mauritius Rupee (Dec '14 £1.00=MUR 49.28, US$1.00=MUR 31.73)
GNI PER CAPITA: US$9,300, Intl$17,220 at PPP ('13)

Seychelles

CAPITAL: Victoria   AREA: 460 sq km   POPULATION: 89,173 ('13)
OFFICIAL LANGUAGES: Seychellois, English & French
HEAD OF STATE AND GOVERNMENT: President James Michel (SPP, Parti Lepep) (since April '04)
RULING PARTY: Seychelles People's Party (SPP, Parti Lepep)
CORRUPTION PERCEPTIONS INDEX: 55; =43rd of 175
CURRENCY: Seychelles Rupee (Dec '14 £1.00=SCR 21.73, US$1.00=SCR 13.99)
GNI PER CAPITA: US$12,530, Intl$23,270 at PPP ('13)

UNDER the presidency of Ikililou Dhoinine, the political scene in **the Comoros** was unusually calm in 2014, with all eyes focused on the 2016 presidential elections. Constitutional changes came into effect so that local and island legislative elections could be held on the same day. However, the November election date was twice postponed, until January 2015, due to budget restraints and failure to constitute the electoral commission. Potential candidates began to position themselves in anticipation of the 2016 presidential elections. Former president Ahmed Abdallah Sambi formed a new party, called Juwa, to support his presidential bid, although it was not clear that he was eligible to stand as he hailed from Anjouan and the next president should come from Grande Comore. Another former president, Azali Assoumani, also announced his candidature.

Throughout the year the islands suffered from power outages and irregular electricity supplies, reflecting the high oil price and failure to maintain equipment. Having secured debt relief under the IMF's Heavily Indebted Poor Countries (HIPC) scheme, the government was accused of slowing down the promised privatisation of state owned enterprises. The IMF responded by refusing to extend its credit facility. A meeting of the Commission de l'Océan Indien, of which both France and the Comoros were members, was disrupted when the Comoros delegate once again raised the question of the status of the French overseas department of Mayotte, over which the Comoros claimed sovereignty.

After the elections at the end of 2013 **Madagascar** at last had a government recognised by the African Union (AU) and the international community generally. The new National Assembly convened in February, and the president's party, MAPAR, with 49 seats, established a rapprochement with the Ravalomanana Movement (MR) made up of supporters of the former president, Marc Ravalomanana, who had been ousted in a coup in 2009 (see AR 2010, p. 316). The new prime minister, appointed in April, was Kolo Roger, a technocrat with no previous political ties. He formed a government drawn from all parties, including past presidential hopefuls like Roland Ratsiraka. However, permission for the former president to return to Madagascar was not granted. In October Ravalomanana did return and was at once detained and placed under house arrest. This move led the MR to withdraw its support for the government, while splits appeared in MAPAR between supporters of President Hery Rajaonarimampianina and those of the previous acting president, Andry Rajoelina. Power shortages and disruptions undermined the popularity of Roger's precarious government and left the political stability of Madagascar very much in doubt.

The establishment of a legitimate government allowed the AU to lift Madagascar's suspension and for the IMF, the USA and the Francophonie organisation to resume aid. A three-year investment strategy was drawn up allocating funds for infrastructure, health, education, agriculture and the development of luxury eco-tourism.

Following the closely fought and controversial presidential elections in **Maldives** in 2013, the chairman and deputy chairman of the Electoral Commission were dismissed and in March four members of the Commission were given six-month suspended prison sentences. In March, elections were held for the Majlis (the legislature). The Progressive Party, led by former president Maumoon Gayoom, half-brother of the current president, polled 38.8 per cent and won 33 seats, enabling it, together with allies, to control 53 seats in the 85 seat assembly. The Maldivian Democratic Party (MDP, the party of former president

Mohammed Nasheed) polled 30.6 per cent and won 26 seats. The Jumhooree Party saw the greatest increase in popularity, its share of the vote rising to 17.6 per cent with 15 seats. A Commonwealth team monitored the elections and subsequently urged the Majlis to review the election guidelines laid down by the Supreme Court.

On two matters the Maldives authorities were strongly criticised by the UN. In October the Supreme Court prosecuted five members of the Maldives Human Rights Commission after this body had issued a report to the UN; in December two Supreme Court judges were removed by a vote of the Majlis.

Former president Mohammed Nasheed still awaited trial over his dismissal of judges during his period in office, but he remained active on the international stage, attending the Conservative Party conference in the UK and speaking at a business forum in Sri Lanka.

In December a fire at the water treatment plant left the capital without water for a week. Emergency supplies of water had to be sent from India and China.

In **Mauritius**, the ruling Alliance of the Future coalition, made up of the Labour Party and Xavier-Luc Duval's Social Democratic Party (PMSD), had a majority of only five in the legislature but remained secure when, in April, the rival coalition of MMM (Mauritian Militant Movement) and MSM (Militant Socialist Movement) collapsed. However, in June Duval withdrew from the coalition and Prime Minister Navin Ramgoolam was left with a majority of one. Seeking another ally, the Labour Party finally reached agreement with the MMM led by Paul Bérenger. It was widely predicted that this new alliance would win a large majority in the parliamentary elections in December. In the event, the voters caused an earthquake in Mauritian politics. The two opposition parties (MSM and PMSD) formed an electoral pact, called Alliance Lepep, and won 47 seats. Labour and its new ally won only 13 seats with the prime minister losing his seat.

This reversal of what had been predicted was attributed to voters' suspicion of Ramgoolam's proposals to end the "best loser" system that allocated seats on a communal basis and to enhance the power of the presidency. The prospect of Ramgoolam as president and Bérenger as prime minister did not appeal to voters. Some Hindu leaders had openly expressed their opposition to Bérenger. The new government was headed by 84-year old Sir Anerood Jugnauth, a former prime minister and president.

Mauritius remained committed to China's economic trade and cooperation zone as a way of countering the effects of the economic downturn in the eurozone and the staged withdrawal of European sugar quotas.

The dispute between Mauritius and the UK over the sovereignty of the Chagos islands continued, with Mauritius initiating action in April in the Permanent Court of Arbitration against Britain's declaration of a marine reserve surrounding the archipelago. Meanwhile information emerged of the use of the largest island, Diego Garcia, for "extraordinary rendition" flights and the interrogation of terrorist suspects by the USA.

After the **Seychelles** elections in 2011, which were boycotted by the Seychelles National Party (SNP)—the main opposition party, President James Michel's SPP (Parti Lepep) held all but one seat in the National Assembly. The Popular Democratic Movement (PDM), led by David Pierre, held the remaining seat. In spite of defections from his party, Wavel Ramakalawan was re-elected as leader of the SNP, which retained a solid base of support.

Seychelles remained the hub for anti-piracy operations funded by the EU, the USA, China, India and the UAE. In mid-January a counter piracy exercise, Operation Atlanta, was carried out. As a result of these measures, Somali-based piracy almost ceased during 2014.

Tourist numbers were maintained and, as tourism accounted for 25 per cent of GDP, this enabled the Seychelles economy to remain relatively buoyant, in spite of economic problems in the Europe from which 66 per cent of tourists came.

Malyn Newitt

IX SOUTH-EAST AND EAST ASIA

BURMA—THAILAND—MALAYSIA—BRUNEI—SINGAPORE—VIETNAM—CAMBODIA—LAOS

Burma

CAPITAL: Naypyidaw   AREA: 676,580 sq km   POPULATION: 53,259,018 ('13)
OFFICIAL LANGUAGE: Burmese
HEAD OF STATE AND GOVERNMENT: President Thein Sein (since March '11)
RULING PARTY: Union Solidarity Development Party (USDP)
DEMOCRACY INDEX: 2.76; 149th of 167   CORRUPTION PERCEPTIONS INDEX: 21; =156th of 175
CURRENCY: Kyat (Dec '14 Official Rate: £1.00=MMK 1,593, US$1.00=MMK 1,026)
GNI PER CAPITA: US$1,113, Intl$4,344 at PPP ('13 IMF estimate)

Thailand

CAPITAL: Bangkok   AREA: 513,120 sq km   POPULATION: 67,010,502 ('13)
OFFICIAL LANGUAGE: Thai
HEAD OF STATE: King Bhumibol Adulyadej (Rama IX), since June '46
HEAD OF GOVERNMENT: Head of National Council for Peace and Order Prayuth Chan-ocha (ind)
   (since May '14)
DEMOCRACY INDEX: 6.25; 72nd of 167   CORRUPTION PERCEPTIONS INDEX: 38; =85th of 175
CURRENCY: Baht (Dec '14 £1.00=THB 51.21, US$1.00=THB 32.98)
GNI PER CAPITA: US$5,370, Intl$13,510 at PPP ('13)

Malaysia

CAPITAL: Kuala Lumpur   AREA: 329,740 sq km   POPULATION: 29,716,965 ('13)
OFFICIAL LANGUAGE: Bahasa Malaysia
HEAD OF STATE: Sultan Abdul Halim Muadzam Shah, Sultan of Kedah (since Dec '11)
RULING PARTY: National Front (BN) coalition
HEAD OF GOVERNMENT: Prime Minister Najib Razak (since April '09)
DEMOCRACY INDEX: 6.49; 64th of 167   CORRUPTION PERCEPTIONS INDEX: 52; =50th of 175
CURRENCY: Ringgit (Dec '14 £1.00=MYR 5.43, US$1.00=MYR 3.50)
GNI PER CAPITA: US$10,400, Intl$22,460 at PPP ('13)

Brunei

CAPITAL: Bandar Seri Bagawan   AREA: 5,770 sq km   POPULATION: 417,784 ('13)
OFFICIAL LANGUAGES: Malay & English
HEAD OF STATE AND GOVERNMENT: Sultan Sir Hassanal Bolkiah (since Oct '67)
CURRENCY: Brunei Dollar (Dec '14 £1.00=BND 2.05, US$1.00=BND 1.32)
GNI PER CAPITA: US$39,658, Intl$73,823 at PPP ('13 IMF estimate)

Singapore

CAPITAL: Singapore   AREA: 699 sq km   POPULATION: 5,399,200 ('13)
OFFICIAL LANGUAGES: Malay, Chinese, Tamil & English
HEAD OF STATE: President Tony Tan Keng Yam (since Sept '11)
RULING PARTY: People's Action Party (PAP)
HEAD OF GOVERNMENT: Prime Minister Lee Hsien Loong (since August '04)
DEMOCRACY INDEX: 5.92; 80th of 167   CORRUPTION PERCEPTIONS INDEX: 84; 7th of 175
CURRENCY: Singapore Dollar (Dec '14 £1.00=SGD 2.05, US$1.00=SGD 1.32)
GNI PER CAPITA: US$54,040, Intl$76,850 at PPP ('13)

Vietnam

CAPITAL: Hanoi   AREA: 329,310 sq km   POPULATION: 89,708,900 ('13)
OFFICIAL LANGUAGE: Vietnamese
HEAD OF STATE: President Truong Tan Sang (since July '11)
RULING PARTY: Communist Party of Vietnam (CPV)
HEAD OF GOVERNMENT: Prime Minister Nguyen Tan Dung (since June '06)
DEMOCRACY INDEX: 3.29; 134th of 167   CORRUPTION PERCEPTIONS INDEX: 31; =119th of 175
CURRENCY: Dong (Dec '14 £1.00=VND 33,214, US$1.00=VND 21,388)
GNI PER CAPITA: US$1,730, Intl$5,030 at PPP ('13)

Cambodia

CAPITAL: Phnom Penh   AREA: 181,040 sq km   POPULATION: 15,135,169 ('13)
OFFICIAL LANGUAGE: Khmer
HEAD OF STATE: King Norodom Sihamoni (since Oct '04)
RULING PARTY: Cambodian People's Party (CPP)
HEAD OF GOVERNMENT: Prime Minister Hun Sen (since July '97)
DEMOCRACY INDEX: 4.60; 109th of 167   CORRUPTION PERCEPTIONS INDEX: 21; =156th of 175
CURRENCY: Riel (Dec '14 £1.00=KHR 6,289, US$1.00=KHR 4,050)
GNI PER CAPITA: US$950, Intl$2,890 at PPP ('13)

Laos

CAPITAL: Vientiane   AREA: 236,800 sq km   POPULATION: 6,769,727 ('13)
OFFICIAL LANGUAGE: Laotian
HEAD OF STATE: President Choummaly Sayasone (since June '06)
RULING PARTY: Lao People's Revolutionary Party (LPRP)
HEAD OF GOVERNMENT: Prime Minister Thongsing Thammavong (since Dec '10)
DEMOCRACY INDEX: 2.21; 156th of 167   CORRUPTION PERCEPTIONS INDEX: 25; =145th of 175
CURRENCY: New Kip (Dec '14 £1.00=LAK 12,540, US$1.00=LAK 8,075)
GNI PER CAPITA: US$1,460, Intl$4,570 at PPP ('13)

THAILAND'S elected government was removed from office in May, with the country's military leadership subsequently taking control. In Burma (Myanmar), the military maintained its opposition to proposed constitutional changes in advance of parliamentary elections scheduled for 2015. Cambodia's government and opposition came to an agreement in July leading to all National Assembly members agreeing to take their seats a year after legislative elections had returned the ruling party to power. Malaysia's national airline suffered two major disasters, and a third catastrophe struck a Malaysia-based airline, the three air accidents leading to substantial loss of life. Chinese and Vietnamese naval vessels clashed in May in the South China Sea, reflecting long-standing differences over territorial and resource claims.

Thailand's prime minister, Yingluck Shinawatra, was removed from office on 7 May when the Constitutional Court ruled that her transfer of National Security Chief Thawil Pliensree from his position in 2011 had violated the constitution. The following day, the National Anti-Corruption Commission (NACC) found her guilty of negligence in the government's rice subsidy programme (which paid farmers above market rates for their crop); the Court ruled that there was sufficient evidence for her to be indicted and face impeachment by the Senate (and a possible five-year ban from politics).

The prime minister's dismissal followed months of political upheaval. On 7 January the NACC indicted 308 MPs, largely from the prime minister's Pheu Thai

Party, for their attempt to reintroduce a fully elected Senate. In January thousands of people resumed anti-government protests (which had begun in November 2013), blockading intersections and besieging government buildings. The prime minister's invitation to protest leaders and opposition political figures for talks about the possible postponement of elections that were scheduled for 2 February was declined. The continuing political stalemate was accompanied by sporadic acts of violence, including grenade attacks that inflicted several fatalities and other casualties. On 21 January the government imposed a 60-day state of emergency in Bangkok and surrounding provinces.

The election, which went ahead as scheduled, was boycotted by the opposition Democrat Party and was disrupted by protesters, who prevented polling from taking place in a number of constituencies. Lacking a constitutionally mandated quorum, the newly elected Parliament was unable to elect a new prime minister. On 13 February the Constitutional Court rejected a government petition arguing that attempts to block roads and obstruct voting were violations of the law, ruling that the actions exercised the constitutional right to protest. Following further violence, as police sought to reclaim key areas of the capital occupied by anti-government protesters, Prime Minister Yingluck ruled out resigning, again calling for dialogue. On 21 March the Constitutional Court nullified the election, citing the failure of voting to take place on the same day throughout the country. Protest leaders pledged that any subsequent election would be similarly disrupted.

Following the prime minister's dismissal in May, her replacement, Deputy Prime Minister Niwattumrong Boonsongpaisan, stated that new elections, scheduled for 20 July, would be a top priority. Clashes with police continued, with protesters calling for the caretaker government to resign and the Senate to replace it with an appointed administration. On 15 May anti-government protesters interrupted a meeting between the caretaker prime minister and members of the Election Commission, which responded by calling for the July elections to be postponed.

On 20 May the army declared martial law "to preserve law and order", the military leadership initially denying that a coup had taken place. Further protest marches were prohibited. Television stations were placed under military control, with regular programming suspended and all stations broadcasting news from the army's own channel. Patriotic music filled air-time between announcements, until normal programming was restored following public complaints on a page on the social media website, Facebook, set up by the military regime.

The caretaker government initially stated that it welcomed the move to institute martial law and restore order, but on 22 May the army took over the government, suspending the constitution, banning "political gatherings" of more than five people, instituting media censorship and implementing a 10pm to 5am curfew. Key political figures were detained, with the former prime minister (and her replacement) and other Cabinet ministers ordered to report to the military. Other individuals, including politicians, activists, journalists and academics, were also summoned by the military. On 24 May the ruling military council dissolved the

Senate. Subsequently, 13 provincial governors, as well as senior police officers, were transferred from north and north-east regions supportive of former prime ministers Thaksin Shinawatra and his sister Yingluck.

The US government condemned the coup, saying that there was "no justification" for it, cancelling a joint military training exercise, visits by military officers and a police training programme. The coup was also condemned by France and Germany, while Japan termed it "regrettable". The UN secretary-general urged a "prompt return to constitutional, civilian, democratic rule".

Describing itself as the National Council for Peace and Order (NCPO), the regime was led by General Prayuth Chan-ocha, commander-in-chief of the Royal Thai Army. On 27 May General Prayuth stated that the NCPO would hold power "indefinitely", warning citizens not to instigate chaos or criticise his rule. On 31 May General Prayuth identified a three-phase post-coup process: reconciliation; a temporary constitution and appointment of an interim prime minister and Cabinet; and, finally, elections. Subsequently, the military initiated various events, including street parties and weekly concerts, as part of a "Festival for Returning Happiness to the People". General Prayuth began making a weekly radio broadcast, "Bringing Back Happiness to the Nation" and wrote lyrics to a patriotic ballad—"Return Happiness to Thailand"—which was played regularly on radio and television and made available on the website, YouTube. On 11 June the military ordered TV regulators to ensure that the 2014 football World Cup would be broadcast at no cost to viewers as part of the "Return Happiness" campaign. The nationwide curfew was also ended. Free screenings were provided in June for a patriotic movie, *The Legend of King Naresuan Part V*; thousands of free movie tickets were distributed for Mother's Day (12 August). In July the military issued an order instructing the ministry of education to promote 12 traditional "core values", including gratitude to parents, love for the nation and the monarchy, and pride in Thai culture.

On 22 July a temporary constitution was adopted, barring from the Cabinet anyone who had been a member of a political party in the three previous years; military and government officials remained eligible, however. On 31 July the military government appointed an interim National Legislative Assembly, dominated by active and retired military officers. On 21 August the Assembly unanimously elected General Prayuth—the sole candidate—as prime minister. On 31 August a Cabinet was appointed, with active or retired senior military officials in more than one-third of the positions. On 4 September the Cabinet met the King (in a Bangkok hospital), marking the formal start of its administration. General Prayuth retired from military service on 30 September. A 250-member advisory National Reform Council was endorsed by the King on 6 October. On 4 November a 36-member committee was appointed, charged with producing a constitution that would allow the country to return to civilian rule in late 2015 or early 2016.

Despite the "happiness" campaign, martial law remained in place through the year and there were punishments for journalists and pro-democracy activists who expressed critical views. In November journalists launched a social media campaign aimed at stopping media intimidation, in response to the dismissal of a television newsreader after government officials objected to her coverage.

Thailand's political upheaval was accompanied by ongoing violence in the insurgency in the Muslim-majority southern provinces, with car bombs and other attacks producing death and injury to police, soldiers and civilians, as well as damage to school buildings and other properties. The King's health also remained fragile; his planned appearance on 5 December, marking his 87th birthday, was cancelled, as the monarch remained in Bangkok's Siriraj Hospital, to which he had been admitted in October. A poet and pro-Thaksin activist, Kamol Duangphasuk, opposed to the lèse majesté law punishing critics of the monarchy, was shot and killed on 23 April.

The sluggish pace of the reform process in **Burma** attracted international criticism, with little if any progress made in 2014 towards further democratic change or the consolidation of peace agreements with armed ethnic groups.

As chairman of ASEAN (the Association of South-East Asian Nations), the Burmese government hosted several hundred meetings and conferences, including the ASEAN and East Asia summits in November. Further investment was made in infrastructure in the capital, Naypyidaw, to enhance conference and accommodation facilities. Parliamentary by-elections scheduled for November were cancelled. Suggested changes to the electoral system for 2015—to introduce proportional representation (PR)—were supported by the pro-government Union Solidarity and Development Party and opposed by the opposition National League for Democracy and by ethnic parties. A change to PR for the upper house was approved; the lower house voted to retain the first-past-the-post constituency representative system.

Proposed revisions to the country's constitution met resistance from the government and the military leadership: opposition leader Aung San Suu Kyi remained ineligible for the presidency, and Suu Kyi's efforts to bring about an end to the military's veto over constitutional amendment proposals proved futile, despite over five million signatures to a petition in support of such a measure. On 31 May, in his monthly radio speech, President Thein Sein stated that constitutional changes would be made "under the right conditions and at the appropriate time in harmony with society's political, economic and social needs". The president and the army chief, Senior-General Min Aung Hlaing, rejected a proposal, endorsed in a joint session of Parliament, for six-party talks on constitutional reform, involving the president, the army chief, Suu Kyi, the speaker of each house of Parliament, and a representative of the ethnic parties.

Ethnic groups' political demands included the adoption of a federal system giving their groups greater autonomy. Efforts to achieve a comprehensive and permanent ceasefire between the military and all rebel ethnic forces continued to prove elusive, however, and during the year there were intermittent clashes between the military and several ethnic armies.

The issue of the ethnic minority Rohingya Muslims continued intractable, with the government's stance—that members of the group were not to be regarded as citizens—attracting persistent international criticism. The government rejected discussion of the Rohingya at the first meeting of ASEAN foreign ministers to be hosted by Burma, describing the matter as an internal affair. Many Rohingya remained displaced, confined to refugee camps following communal violence between Rohingya and Buddhists. The country's first nationwide census since 1983 was conducted between 30 March and 10 April. Individuals seeking to identify as "Rohingya" were not permitted to do so. In November the USA urged the government to draft a new plan to allow Rohingya to become Burmese citizens and to do away with a proposal to send them to detention camps if they refused to identify themselves as Bengalis. On 29 December, the UN General Assembly approved a resolution urging that Rohingya be provided "full citizenship", recognised under the name "Rohingya" and be allowed to move freely throughout the country.

The Myanmar National Human Rights Commission Law was enacted in March. This governed the process of appointments to the commission (established in 2011) and procedures for handling reports of abuses of human rights. Issues involving the government and the news media arose during the year, with several journalists arrested and prosecuted for publishing stories of which the government disapproved. Individuals who protested against journalists' prison sentences were also prosecuted. The country's interim Press Council met with the president in August and urged him to intervene over what it described as growing threats to media freedom.

In March a report to the US Congress stated that Burma remained one of the few countries still purchasing weapons from North Korea in violation of UN sanctions. In May President Barack Obama notified leaders of Congress that he was renewing the National Emergencies Act, allowing the continuance of some economic sanctions whilst also permitting some US business investment. In June Burma became the 150th country to endorse the Declaration of Commitment to End Sexual Violence in Conflict, the announcement coming just ahead of a global summit on the issue being held in London. In September al-Qaida leader Ayman al-Zawahiri announced the formation of a new branch of the Islamist militant group, Al Qaida in the Indian Subcontinent, listing Burma amongst the places to be targeted.

In June the Pyu archaeological site, covering the remains of three ancient cities, became the country's first to receive UNESCO World Heritage status.

Malaysia's national airline suffered two extraordinary disasters in 2014, each involving substantial loss of life. In both cases, the causes of the accident remained unresolved or disputed. Plans were announced in August for a restructuring of the airline.

On 8 March, Malaysia Airlines flight 370 (MH370), en route from Kuala Lumpur to Beijing, disappeared after flying far off course. Seventeen days later the prime minister stated that the airliner had ended its flight in the southern Indian Ocean and that none of the 239 people on board could have survived. Despite an extensive search operation, the aircraft was not found. The airline, and the Malaysian government, were strongly criticised (particularly by China:

most of those on board were Chinese citizens) for all aspects of the way they had handled the situation, ranging from communication with the relatives of those on board (including flight crew and passengers), to the investigation of the aircraft's disappearance.

On 17 July, Malaysia Airlines flight 17 (MH17), from the Netherlands to Kuala Lumpur, was shot down over an area of eastern Ukraine controlled by pro-Russian separatists with the loss of all 298 people on board, the majority of them Dutch citizens (see the article on Ukraine). This time, criticism was directed at the airline for its decision—contrary to the procedures adopted by other carriers—to continue flying over the area rather than take a different route. The Malaysian government was involved in subsequent efforts to gain access to the crash site, which was situated in a conflict zone, in order to obtain the flight recorders and recover the bodies of those killed in the incident. Responsibility for the shooting down of the aircraft was widely thought to lie with the pro-Russian separatists, though none of the several investigations into the disaster had issued its conclusions as of the end of the year.

A third air catastrophe, involving a low-cost airline based in Malaysia, occurred on 28 December when AirAsia flight 8501, from Indonesia to Singapore, went missing with 162 people on board; debris from the aircraft was found in the Java Sea two days later.

Limitations on freedom of expression in Malaysia were evident in the prosecution and imprisonment of students, opposition politicians (including Members of Parliament), activists and academics under the country's 1948 Sedition Act. Although Prime Minister Najib Razak had stated in 2013 that the government planned to replace the law (enacted under British rule) with measures supporting greater freedom of speech, it was subsequently decided to revise and strengthen the statute instead. In June, the prime minister sued an independent news website for allegedly defamatory comments made about him and his ruling party, the first such action taken by a Malaysian prime minister against a media organisation.

In January, Islamic authorities seized several hundred Bibles from a Christian group because of their use of the word "Allah". The raid followed a court ruling of October 2013 that the Arabic word was reserved for use by Muslims. This ruling had overturning a 2009 decision by a lower court that had allowed a Roman Catholic newspaper printed in Malay to use the word (see AR 2014, p. 294).

On 7 March the opposition's de facto leader, Anwar Ibrahim, was convicted and sentenced to five years in prison, with the Court of Appeal voting unanimously to overturn his 2012 acquittal on a charge of sodomy. The ruling, criticised by Anwar's supporters and by international human rights groups, barred Anwar from running for a seat in the Selangor state assembly; winning the contest would give him the opportunity to become chief minister of the country's most heavily populated state. Anwar's wife, Wan Azizah Wan Ismail, replaced him as a candidate in the 23 March by-election, which she won. On 28 October the Federal Court of Malaysia, the country's highest court, held hearings on Anwar's appeal but reserved judgment following closing statements on 7 November.

The governments of both Malaysia and the Philippines took action against Islamists—members of the Abu Sayyaf group—who participated in incursions (involving armed abductions) into Sabah, in Malaysia's north Borneo. In July a member of Malaysia's police was killed and another kidnapped. Maritime patrols were increased in an effort to deter kidnapping raids.

On 16 October Malaysia was elected to the UN Security Council for the first time since 1998, winning unopposed a seat allocated to a country from the Asia Pacific. In December monsoon rains led to the evacuation of more than 160,000 people from their homes.

The introduction of Sharia law in **Brunei** on 1 May led to international criticism and protests, including the cancellation of star-studded events at the Beverly Hills Hotel in California, which was owned by the Brunei Investment Agency, a government-owned corporation. The protests focused on punishments mandated by Sharia law that included death by stoning for adultery and for same-sex relationships, amputations for theft, and lashes from a rattan cane for drunkenness. The Beverly Hills city council called on Brunei's government either to change the law or divest itself of the hotel. The US government also expressed concern; the Sultan of Brunei, however, defended Sharia law as consistent with the Koran and the strengthening of Islam.

On 30 April the Sultan announced that implementation of the first phase of the Sharia penal code order would begin on 1 May, with jail sentences and fines to be imposed for offences such as pregnancy outside marriage or failure to perform Friday prayers. The second phase, relating to theft and alcohol consumption, would introduce corporal punishment; the third phase—for offences including adultery, sodomy and "insulting the Koran"—the death penalty.

The UN Human Rights Council characterised some of the penalties, such as stoning, as "cruel, inhuman or degrading treatment or punishment". The code was also criticised by the International Commission of Jurists, which anticipated serious human rights violations if it were implemented. The Sultan ordered his citizens in February to cease criticising the plan in social media, indicating that doing so would lead to punishments once the code came into force.

In February, Indonesian defence officials withdrew from an air show in **Singapore** after Singapore had objected to Indonesia's decision to name one of its warships *KRI Usman Harun*. The name honoured two Indonesian commandos, Usman Haji Mohamed Ali and Harun Said, executed in Singapore in 1968 for their part in a 1965 bombing in the country that had killed three people and injured 33 others (see AR 1965, p. 96). Indonesia described its decision as consistent with its practice of naming vessels after the country's "heroes" and rejected "intervention from any other country". In April, following Singapore's suspension of military relations, the commander of Indonesia's armed forces apologised for harming "sensitivities" but indicated that Indonesia would not reverse its choice of name for the ship. Singapore's defence minister, welcoming the apology, announced that bilateral defence cooperation would be resumed. Relations were further strained in

September when Singapore's air quality dropped to unhealthy levels as a result of annual forest burnings in Indonesia. In August Parliament enacted the Transboundary Haze Pollution Act, allowing fines against entities, both local and international, that produced air pollution crossing Singapore's borders.

In November Singapore's High Court ruled in favour of Prime Minister Lee Hsien Loong in a defamation case brought against a blogger (an Internet diarist) who had posted messages alleging that the prime minister had criminally misappropriated moneys from the Central Provident Fund—the compulsory, state-run, social-security savings scheme. This was the first time that the prime minister had sued an online critic, whose request for a trial was denied by the court, which ruled that there was "no triable defence" in the case.

The government announced a range of initiatives in November intended to make Singapore an energy efficient, data-connected "smart nation".

On 7 May war veterans, communist leaders and diplomats gathered in Dien Bien Phu to mark the 60th anniversary of the victory over French forces that brought about **Vietnam**'s independence and the end of French rule throughout Indochina (Vietnam, Laos and Cambodia). The following day, Chinese ships rammed into and fired water cannon at Vietnamese vessels trying to disrupt China's installation of an oil rig in the disputed South China Sea. Several boats were damaged and several Vietnamese injured. On 10 May, at Vietnam's request, ASEAN issued a statement expressing "serious concerns" over what had occurred. On 27 May a Vietnamese fishing boat sank after colliding with a Chinese vessel.

The conflict with China brought protests and riots throughout Vietnam. More than a dozen factories believed to be Chinese-owned were attacked and set on fire. At least two Chinese workers died and dozens were injured. More than 1,000 Vietnamese were arrested for their involvement. Thousands of Chinese workers were evacuated from Vietnam by ship and hundreds of other Chinese nationals crossed the border into Cambodia. In June Vietnam began making payments in compensation to nearly 140 businesses owned by Chinese and Taiwanese corporations.

In July a group of 61 Communist Party members issued a letter criticising the government's alleged mishandling of relations with China, calling for greater openness, development of "a truly democratic, law-abiding state" and a reduction in Vietnam's economic reliance on China. The prime minister and the Central Committee of the Communist Party issued statements condemning China, and the National Assembly concluded its June session with a statement declaring that China's placement of the oil rig violated Vietnam's sovereignty as well as international law. On 15 July China withdrew the rig from disputed waters, at least temporarily bringing the crisis to a close.

The oil rig incident revealed weaknesses in Vietnam's naval capabilities and led to rapid efforts to upgrade. In August Japan indicated that it would provide Vietnam with radar equipment and naval vessels to assist with patrols and surveillance. Several submarines were purchased from Russia, and India extended a $100 million export credit to Vietnam for defence and security purposes, promising to expedite the sale of patrol boats to strengthen Vietnam's naval defences. On 2 October the United States announced that it was partially lifting its 30 years' arms embargo in order to strengthen Vietnam's coastguard capability.

In October, Chinese and Vietnamese leaders agreed to use an existing border dispute mechanism to find a solution to their territorial dispute. Vietnam's government filed a statement with the Permanent Court of Arbitration at The Hague on 11 December, in which it fully "rejected China's claims" over islands in the South China Sea, supporting the case brought by the Philippines.

On 1 January the prime minister issued a New Year's message emphasising the values of democracy and the rule of law, with a government able to do "only things that the law allows". In November, continuing the practice begun in 2013, the National Assembly assessed the performance of senior government members. Both President Truong Tan Sang and Prime Minister Nguyen Tan Dung received votes of "high confidence", the 64 per cent awarded to the prime minister being a significant improvement over his score in 2013 (43 per cent). Vietnam's government maintained its limited tolerance for political dissidents, with prosecutions of bloggers who had posted articles critical of the government.

Cambodia's opposition Cambodia National Rescue Party (CNRP) agreed on 22 July to end its year-long parliamentary boycott, which it had embarked upon after the disputed July 2013 elections (see AR 2014, p. 289). An agreement between the prime minister, Hun Sen, and the opposition leader, Sam Rainsy, provided for various electoral and constitutional reforms, and the post of first vice-president of the National Assembly was allocated to the CRNP vice-president, Kem Sokha. On 8 August MPs from the governing and opposition parties attended the National Assembly together for the first time since the elections. Implementing their agreement, the parties formalised the establishment of a new commission to tackle corruption, which was to be chaired by the CNRP. They also committed themselves to make changes to the existing government-controlled National Election Committee.

The party leaders' agreement to work together had been preceded by months of discord and protests over the 2013 election, which the CNRP claimed to have won. There were also violent protests by workers in garment factories demanding improved wages and working conditions. In September armed troops were deployed in Phnom Penh as further rallies were held, reviving the garment workers' campaign for higher wages. On 12 November the monthly minimum wage for garment workers was raised by 28 per cent, a decision criticised by unions seeking a larger increase. There were also protests by (and prosecutions of) land rights activists.

In January the United Nations and the Cambodian government agreed to continue to fund the special tribunal (the Extraordinary Chambers in the Courts of Cambodia, ECCC) that was hearing cases against former Khmer Rouge head of state Khieu Samphan and the regime's main ideologist, Nuon Chea. On 7 August the two were found guilty of crimes against humanity and sentenced to life in prison. Proceedings in a second trial, on charges of genocide, were begun on 30 July. On 25 November the sessions were suspended until January 2015 in response to threats of a boycott from the lawyers working on an appeal in the earlier crimes against humanity trial (see AR 2014, p. 296).

In January filmmaker Rithy Panh's *The Missing Picture* became the first Cambodian film to receive nomination for an Academy Award, in the best foreign language film category. Set in the 1970s Khmer Rouge period and based on the filmmaker's 2013 book *The Elimination*, the film used clay figures to depict a family and nation gripped by genocide, reflecting the filmmaker's own experience of loss and survival.

In September Cambodia signed an agreement with Australia to accept refugees detained on Nauru. The Cambodian government described the arrangement as part of its obligation as a signatory to the UN refugee convention and related protocols, and stressed that all refugees coming to the country must do so voluntarily. Resettlement costs were to be met by Australia.

In October Sorn Seavmey became the first Cambodian ever to win a gold medal at an Asian Games.

In June the government of **Laos** announced new Cabinet appointments following the death in an air crash on 17 May of the defence minister (also a deputy prime minister and a member of the Politburo of the ruling Communist Party). Fatalities also included the minister of public security and the mayor of the capital, Vientiane.

In September, reflecting the steadily growing use in Laos of mobile telephones and the Internet, a decree was issued that threatened criminal penalties against anyone spreading "false" information aimed at discrediting the government or the Communist Party.

In December, the four-nation Mekong River Commission (MRC)—representing Laos, Cambodia, Thailand and Vietnam—held public consultations on the development of the Don Sahong hydroelectric power project in the Siphandone area of southern Laos, near the border with Cambodia and Thailand. Vietnam and Cambodia expressed concerns about the possible impact upon fishing and agriculture and urged a delay in construction. Laos claimed that MRC rules requiring consensus on dam projects along the mainstream Mekong River did not apply to the Don Sahong dam, which was to be built on one of the river's several channels.

Stephen Levine

INDONESIA—PHILIPPINES—TIMOR-LESTE

Indonesia

CAPITAL: Jakarta   AREA: 1,904,570 sq km   POPULATION: 249,865,631 ('13)
OFFICIAL LANGUAGE: Bahasa Indonesia
HEAD OF STATE AND GOVERNMENT: President Joko Widodo (DP) (since Oct '14)
RULING PARTY: Democratic Party (DP)
DEMOCRACY INDEX: 6.82; 54th of 167   CORRUPTION PERCEPTIONS INDEX: 34; =107th of 175
CURRENCY: Rupiah (Dec '14 £1.00=IDR 19,329, US$1.00=IDR 12,447)
GNI PER CAPITA: US$3,580, Intl$9,260 at PPP ('13)

Philippines

CAPITAL: Manila   AREA: 300,000 sq km   POPULATION: 98,393,574 ('13)
OFFICIAL LANGUAGE: Filipino
HEAD OF STATE AND GOVERNMENT: President Benigno "Noynoy" Aquino III (since June '10)
RULING PARTY: Liberal Party (LP)
DEMOCRACY INDEX: 6.41; 66th of 167   CORRUPTION PERCEPTIONS INDEX: 38; =85th of 175
CURRENCY: Philippine Peso (Dec '14 £1.00=PHP 69.47, US$1.00=PHP 44.73)
GNI PER CAPITA: US$3,270, Intl$7,820 at PPP ('13)

Timor-Leste

CAPITAL: Dili   AREA: 14,870 sq km   POPULATION: 1,178,252 ('13)
OFFICIAL LANGUAGES: Portuguese, Tetum & Bahasa Indonesian
HEAD OF STATE: President Taur Matan Ruak (since May '12)
RULING PARTIES: National Congress for Timorese Reconstruction (CNRT)-led coalition
HEAD OF GOVERNMENT: Prime Minister Kay Rala Xanana Gusmao (CNRT) (since Aug '07)
DEMOCRACY INDEX: 7.24; 43rd of 167   CORRUPTION PERCEPTIONS INDEX: 28; =133rd of 175
CURRENCY: US Dollar (Dec '14 £1.00=USD 1.55)
GNI PER CAPITA: US$3,580, Intl$6,410 at PPP ('13)

THE dominating events in **Indonesia** during 2014 were the elections for the legislature, in April, and, more significantly, for the presidency, in July. The results of these marked, in prospect at any rate, something of a departure from Indonesia's long-established culture of government by entrenched elite. The year also saw Indonesia assailed by a number of natural and not so natural disasters. The national economy, though subdued during 2014, remained reasonably robust and stable.

The elections for the 560-seat People's Representative Council, held on 9 April, provided a preliminary guide to the prospects of the main aspirants for the presidency in July. As expected, the Indonesian Democratic Party of Struggle (the PDI-P) led the field. The PDI-P was the party of former president (and daughter of the country's founding head of state) Megawati Sukarnoputri, who remained its leader. The party luminary attracting most interest, however, was Joko Widodo, the governor of Jakarta province and the PDI-P's presidential hopeful. Widodo, a furniture dealer from a modest provincial background, had a reputation for personal integrity and was largely immune to the growing distrust of the established political elite.

In the event, the performance of PDI-P was not as strong as had been predicted (19 per cent of the vote and 109 seats). Golkar, the "national" party of the old Suharto regime, came an unexpectedly strong second (15 per cent and 91 seats), while Gerindra, the party of Widodo's main rival in the presidential race, Prabowo Subianto, the former commander of Indonesia's notorious special forces, finished third (with 11.5 per cent of the vote and 73 seats). Support for the Democratic Party of the outgoing president, Susilo Bambang Yudhoyono, slumped dramatically from 21 per cent of the vote in the previous election in 2009 to 10 per cent (61 seats). This reflected widespread disillusionment with Yudhoyono's failure to make any real inroad into the country's institutionalised corruption, despite his own relatively untainted reputation.

In the wake of the parliamentary elections both Widodo's PDI-P and Prabowo's Gerindra scrambled to make alliances in order to meet the legal requirement for a threshold of 25 per cent of votes (or 20 per cent of parliamentary seats) before a party could nominate a presidential candidate. This hurdle having been successfully overcome by both parties, the presidential election was held on 9 July. The prospects of the two candidates appeared too close to call. Shortly after voting was completed Widodo claimed a narrow victory over Prabowo, though the latter doggedly refused to concede defeat, claiming electoral fraud. Fortunately, quite realistic fears that the political stand-off might lead to violence in the streets between supporters of the two candidates proved unfounded. The official electoral commission eventually confirmed the result as 53 per cent (71 million votes) for Widodo against 47 per cent (62.5 million votes) for Prabowo on a turnout just short of 70 per cent. Widodo—or "Jokowi" as he was popularly known—was formally inaugurated as president on 20 October.

The result contrasted sharply with previous President Yudhoyono's near-landslides in his two presidential campaigns in 2004 and 2009 (see AR 2004, p.317 and AR 2010, p.329). Widodo's narrow victory was not perhaps the best basis from which to begin the sort of root and branch reform of Indonesian public life that was required to meet the expectations of his supporters. Moreover, Widodo faced potential legislative difficulties in implementing a reform programme. The party coalition negotiations that followed the parliamentary elections in April had in fact put Prabowo's Gerindra party in a stronger position in the legislature than Widodo's PDI-P. Initial reaction to the outcome of the presidential election from Indonesia's foreign allies was generally favourable, however, with congratulations from the leaders of key regional neighbours Singapore and Australia being notably warmer than diplomatic courtesies would require.

The Indonesian economy in 2014 was only marginally affected by the uncertainties around the elections. The contested outcome caused a small depreciation in the rupiah and a temporary slip in share prices. More generally the Indonesian economy slowed slightly in 2014 with GDP growth, at 5.3 per cent, the lowest in four years. This was an expected outcome of government economic management aimed at restraining domestic demand and controlling inflation (which stood at 5.8 per cent in 2014). But the cooling of the economy was also due to a drop in export earnings, though this was to an extent balanced by a reduction in imports. More positively, the fight against inflation was aided by particularly good domestic harvests in 2014. Indonesia's international currency reserves grew during the year and the rupiah-US dollar exchange rate improved.

Indonesia's position on the eastern arc of the Pacific "ring of fire" was much in evidence during 2014. In January Mount Sinabung, in North Sumatra, erupted repeatedly, leading to the evacuation of 20,000 local inhabitants. The following month it was the turn of Mount Kelud in eastern Java, though here the greater impact was environmental rather human, with debris washed into river systems. January also saw Jakarta subjected to damaging flooding, after a long period of continuous rainfall, resulting in the temporary displacement of over 100,000 residents. February brought the now customary forest fires in Sumatra, most likely as a result of unregulated land clearance for the extension of plantations. The environmental impact of these fires was widespread and had in the past led to diplomatic tensions with neighbouring Singapore (see AR 2014, p.300).

At the very end of the year, on 28 December, AirAsia flight 8501 from Surabaya in Java to Singapore crashed into the Java Sea off Indonesian Borneo with the loss of all 162 people on board. Indonesia undertook the air and sea operation to locate and recover the remains of the aircraft and the bodies of its passengers.

During 2014 the **Philippines** continued to be challenged by problems of political violence and by an apparently ever-growing tally of corruption scandals. Foreign policy was beset by ongoing conflicts with China over sovereign rights in the South China Sea. The country faced, as it had in most recent years, a series of climate-based disasters. More positively, the national economy appeared to be following a stable route to moderate growth.

The year began with skirmishes between national security forces and Bangsamoro Islamic Freedom Fighters (BIFF) in the restive southern island of Mindanao. A relatively new element in the panoply of armed resistance movement in the Philippines, BIFF had broken away from the long-established Moro Islamic Liberation Front (MILF) when the latter negotiated an autonomy deal with the central government which fell short of total independence (see AR 2013, p.302). The fighting, which cost about 40 lives, followed closely on MILF's signing of a framework agreement with the central government on 25 January. The substantive settlement was finalised at a ceremony in Manila on 27 March attended by President Benigno Aquino, the MILF leader Al Haj Murad Ebrahim, and the Malaysian prime minister, who had been closely involved in the peace negotiations. The continued activities of BIFF were a source of worry for the main parties to the settlement.

In March clashes broke out with a more venerable anti-government movement, the Marxist New People's Army (NPA), in Davao, also in the Mindanao region. A few weeks later Benito Tiamzon, chairman of the Philippines Communist Party and secretary-general of the NPA, was arrested along with his wife and a number of close lieutenants. Whatever the prospects for peace with the Islamic separatists of Mindanao, it seemed clear that the decades-long conflict with the NPA was far from resolution.

Throughout the year security forces also confronted elements of Abu Sayyaf (AS), perhaps the most radical (and most internationally networked) Islamist group within the anti-Manila organisations operating in the southern Philippines. AS continued with its longstanding tactic of kidnapping foreigners for ransom which, in April, included two Chinese citizens.

(c.19 August) US journalist James Foley, who was taken prisoner in Syria, is the first of a series of Western hostages to be beheaded by the jihadist group ISIS (Frame from ISIS video - Public Domain)

(11 August) Yazidi refugees near their home region of Sinjar, in Iraq, flee towards the Syrian border in an attempt to escape genocide at the hands of ISIS fighters (REUTERS/Rodi Said)

(2 August) Israelis watch the progress of the incursion into Gaza by their armed forces (REUTERS/Siegfried Modola)

(21 October) Health workers in Freetown, Sierra Leone, remove the body of a victim of the Ebola virus (REUTERS/Josephus Olu-Mamma)

(11 August) Palestinians in Beit Lahiya sit outside the ruins of their apartment block, destroyed in the Israeli offensive into the Gaza Strip (REUTERS/Suhaib Salem)

(26 May) An Egyptian woman casts her vote at a polling station in Cairo during the presidential election (REUTERS/Mohamed Abd El Ghany)

(16 July) A supporter of Scottish independence poses with a flag in Edinburgh while campaigning in the run-up to the referendum in September (REUTERS/Paul Hackett)

(10 November) Japanese Prime Minister Shinzo Abe shakes hands with Chinese President Xi Jinping during a frosty meeting on the sidelines of the APEC summit in Beijing (REUTERS/Kim Kyung-Hoon)

(28 March) Supporters of Abdullah Abdullah attend a political rally in northern Afghanistan during the campaign for the presidential election in April (REUTERS/Ahmad Masood)

(16 May) Hindu nationalist Narendra Modi receives a garland from supporters in Gujarat, prior to being sworn in as prime minister of India following his general election victory (REUTERS/Amit Dave)

(8 July) Germany's Thomas Mueller battles with Brazil's Bernard during the 2014 World Cup semi-final at the Mineirao stadium, in Belo Horizonte, in which Germany thrashed the host nation 7-1 (REUTERS/Francois Xavier Marit/Pool)

(5 March) Local women watch Russian soldiers assemble near a Ukrainian military base in Perevalnoe during Russia's annexation of Crimea (REUTERS/Thomas Peter)

At a more venal level of anti-state activity, attempts by the government of President Aquino to tackle the corruption evident at virtually all levels of public life continued. Although these made no rapid or dramatic impact on practices which were tightly woven into Filipino social and political culture, there were signs of some improvement amidst growing public resentment . A major focus of anti-corruption investigators during 2014 was misuse of the Priority Development Assistance Fund (PDAF). This was a budget held and controlled by individual legislators designed to support small development projects in their constituencies. The opportunities for its misuse were evident. A number of investigations were begun against legislators during the year with the judicial authorities showing a new determination to pursue them to prosecution. One positive sign was an improvement, though a limited one, in the standing of the Philippines in Transparency International's Corruption Perceptions Index: its index rating rose from 34 in 2012 to 38 in 2014 (on a scale of 100).

The fraught issue of sovereign rights in the South China Sea (or the "West Philippines Sea" as the government termed it) was prominent in Philippines foreign policy in 2014 (see AR 2014, p.301). China continued to lay claim to the major part of the maritime area which was rich in mineral resources. It backed its position with aggressive naval patrolling. At the end of March the Philippines government submitted a lengthy and detailed memorandum setting out its case to the International Tribunal for the Law of the Sea. President Aquino had long sought to build international support in the dispute. The issue dominated his discussions with other regional leaders at the Association of Southeast Asian Nations (ASEAN) summit in Burma in May. It was also on the agenda during the visit to the Philippines of US President Barack Obama in April. The two presidents used the occasion to sign an "Enhanced Defence Cooperation Agreement" permitting the use by US forces of Philippines military bases. The major purpose of this was to enable joint action against Islamist insurgency in the Philippines itself and in the broader South-East Asian region.

In 2014 the country continued to suffer repeated assaults at the hands of an increasingly unpredictable climate. In January tropical storm Agaton struck Mindanao causing around 70 deaths and displacing some 170,000 residents. Later, in July, typhoon Glenda hit Manila killing about 100 and causing severe infrastructural damage in the capital. Two months later Manila suffered again when tropical storm Mario struck. Other extreme weather events brought destruction to various parts of the country in September (typhoon Luis) and December (typhoon Ruby and typhoon Jangmi).

The national economy remained relatively stable during 2014, showing a satisfactory level of GDP growth of 6.2 per cent with inflation reasonably under control at 4.4 per cent. Concern over corruption had an impact on economic performance, however, as government agencies reduced spending in the face of worries about the misuse of funds.

The protracted wrangle over the agreement signed by the **Timor-Leste** government with Australia over exploitation of oil and gas resources in the Timor Sea went to the International Court of Justice (ICJ) in January. Timor-Leste sought to renegotiate the original treaty which it had long considered to be inequitable. The specific issue in contention at the ICJ was the seizure by Australia of documents held by the Canberra-based lawyer acting for Timor-Leste in its renegotiation attempt (see AR 2014, p.302). In an interim order the ICJ instructed Australia not to make use of any seized material but declined to order its return. Hearings resumed in September and were continuing at the end of the year. In an ironic twist, Indonesia, against whose militia gangs Australia had intervened in 1999 to guarantee Timor-Leste's independence (see AR 1999, p.348), awarded its highest national honour—the Adipurna Star—to Timor-Leste's prime minister and former anti-Indonesian resistance leader Xanana Gusmão.

In October all foreign judges (mostly from other Portuguese-speaking countries) employed in Timor-Leste's legal system were unexpectedly ordered to leave the country. The move was criticised by the United Nations Human Rights Council amidst fears that this political interference in the judicial sector would diminish Timor-Leste's already less than enthusiastic pursuit of offenders from the violence of 1999.

The economy performed well during 2014, driven on by high levels of government expenditure which were underwritten by income from the disputed oil and gas exploitation with Australia. There was a dramatic fall in inflation from the double digit figures of recent years to about 4 per cent. GDP growth, excluding oil and gas income, stood at an impressive 8 per cent.

Norrie MacQueen

PEOPLE'S REPUBLIC OF CHINA—HONG KONG—TAIWAN

People's Republic of China

CAPITAL: Beijing   AREA: 9,598,088 sq km   POPULATION: 1,357,380,000 ('13)
OFFICIAL LANGUAGE: Mandarin Chinese
HEAD OF STATE AND GOVERNMENT: President Xi Jinping (since March '13)
RULING PARTY: Chinese Communist Party (CCP)
PARTY LEADER: Xi Jinping (since Nov '12)
POLITBURO STANDING COMMITTEE: Xi Jinping, Li Keqiang, Zhang Gaoili, Yu Zhenghsheng, Zhang Dejiang, Wang Qishan, Liu Yunshan
CHAIRMAN OF CENTRAL MILITARY COMMISSION: Xi Jinping (since Nov '12)
PREMIER: Li Keqing (since March '13)
DEMOCRACY INDEX: 3.00; 143rd of 167   CORRUPTION PERCEPTIONS INDEX: 36; =100th of 175
CURRENCY: Renminbi denominated in Yuan (Dec '14 £1.00=CNY 9.66, US$1.00=CNY 6.22)
GNI PER CAPITA: US$6,560, Intl$11,850 at PPP ('13)

Hong Kong SAR

CAPITAL: Victoria   AREA: 1,092 sq km   POPULATION: 7,187,500 ('13)
CHIEF EXECUTIVE: Leung Chun-Ying (since June '12)
ADMINISTRATIVE SECRETARY: Carrie Lam (since June '12)
DEMOCRACY INDEX: 6.42; 65th of 167   CORRUPTION PERCEPTIONS INDEX: 74; =17th of 175
CURRENCY: Hong Kong Dollar (Dec '14 £1.00=HKD 12.05, US$1.00=HKD 7.76)
GNI PER CAPITA: US$38,420, Intl$54,260 at PPP ('13)

Taiwan

CAPITAL: Taipei   AREA: 35,980 sq km   POPULATION: 23,374,000 ('13 National Statistics Taiwan)
OFFICIAL LANGUAGE: Chinese
HEAD OF STATE AND GOVERNMENT: President Ma Ying-jeou (KMT) (since May '08)
RULING PARTY: Kuomintang (KMT)
PREMIER: Mao Chi-kuo (KMT) (since Dec '14)
DEMOCRACY INDEX: 7.57; 37th of 167   CORRUPTION PERCEPTIONS INDEX: 61; =35th of 175
CURRENCY: New Taiwan Dollar (Dec '14 £1.00=TWD 49.30, US$1.00=TWD 31.75)
GNI PER CAPITA: US$20,924, Intl$41,538 at PPP ('13 IMF estimate)

THROUGHOUT 2014, China kept to its target of around 7.5 per cent growth. But its leaders, in particular President Xi Jinping and chief macroeconomist Premier Li Keqiang, were frank about the future prospects for growth in the country. For them, the message was to undertake reforms so that the country's productivity and its efficiency could be improved, even while growth continued to flat line around 7 per cent or even fall beneath it. Wage rises, ongoing since 2012, meant that China was no longer the place to consider as a manufacturing centre for making export products cheaply, with multinationals and even Chinese companies increasingly looking to Vietnam, India or other places. Growing social welfare costs, pension costs and the general rise in expectations of living standards all fuelled this imperative to change the country's growth model. Throughout the year, exports rose and fell depending on the month; for the first time in two years the central bank also raised interest rates. One of the continuing anomalies of the modern Chinese economy was that there was little reliable data on such fundamental factors as real unemployment or government debt. Regarding the first, the official figure of around 3 per cent hardly shifted from year to year, showing that it was a purely notional figure which bore little relation to reality. For the second, Western analysts guessed that the real figure for the ratio of public debt to GDP was in the region of 250 per cent, placing it on a par with hugely indebted countries like Japan. But, again, solid data was lacking.

A symbolic moment for China in 2014 was its ranking as the world's largest economy with regard to at least one measure: that of purchasing power parity, which looked at the relative power of currencies within their respective economies. This was an estimate produced by the IMF and the World Bank. Another first, perhaps even more meaningful, was that China invested almost as much outwardly throughout the year as it received as inward investment. It became a major investment player in the Middle East, in Africa, and even made inroads into Europe where its companies, state and non-state, bought significant assets in countries ranging from the UK to Poland. The market within which it experienced the greatest challenges was the USA, where political distrust of any corporation linked to China caused impediments. Huawei, the telecoms company, experienced particular problems. It was accused, despite spending great sums on lobbying companies in Washington, DC, of being a security threat and was barred from government contracts. The great exception to this was the successful listing on the New York Stock Exchange in October of the Alibaba company, established over a decade earlier by former English teacher from Zhejiang province Jack (Ma) Yun. Overnight, he became Asia's richest man, according to

Forbes, overtaking Hong Kong's Li Ka Shing, and his company became the fifth-largest globally in terms of market capitalisation. If there was one brand carrier for the face of modern Chinese business that everyone could buy into, literally, then this was the company.

China's economic footprint was seen elsewhere, too, in the establishment in October in Beijing of an Asian Infrastructure Investment Bank, sponsored by the Chinese government but with over 20 regional partners. Once more, this was guided by a desire from Beijing to undermine the hegemony of US-dominated institutions like the World Bank, the IMF, or even the Asian Development Bank. Instead, this fund was presented as something run by Asians for Asians. During the annual Asia Pacific Economic Cooperation (APEC) summit held in early November, the Chinese government also promoted an Asian free trade zone, and once more this was interpreted as a counterblast to the Trans-Pacific Partnership (TPP) being promoted by the USA, which did not include China.

Xi Jinping once more provided the overarching narrative for this foreign economic and diplomatic activism by his concept of "the New Silk Road". The extent of this idea, modelled on the ancient trade route which had evolved almost two millennia earlier, embraced areas as diverse as the Middle East, where China continued to source over 50 per cent of its imported oil; Russia, with which China signed a major energy deal in May, when President Vladimir Putin—isolated from the USA and the EU because of his actions in Crimea—visited Shanghai; and maritime areas extending deep into the Pacific and Indian Oceans.

Beyond economic friendliness and stressing mutually beneficial outcomes, 2014 was a remarkable year for seeing Chinese leaders diversifying their international contacts. Xi Jinping took the lead in this, too, visiting the EU in March and addressing the European Commission. Remarkably, this was the first time that a Chinese head of state had done so. Speaking in Bruges at the College of Europe during this visit, he characterised EU-China relations as those between "civilisational partners", a flattering term that recognised their immense trading and economic importance to each other whilst also leaving space to admit that, in terms of values, they often disagreed with each other. The fact remained, however, that the EU was China's largest intellectual property partner, and this kind of exchange mattered deeply to Beijing.

On top of this, Xi was also able to visit India, a country with which China had a famously complex relationship, and the sole land neighbour with which it still had a border dispute. Appositely, the day that Xi arrived in New Delhi there were reports of Chinese military incursions across one of the disputed border areas. This did not stop him signing, with the new, popularly elected Indian Prime Minister Narendra Modi, a series of deals amounting to a projected total of $20 billion. A little earlier, Premier Li Keqiang had also undertaken a visit across a group of African countries and managed to sign deals for a similar amount. For Li, the message was that China was a non-judgemental friend, and one that understood the challenges of being a developing country better than the preaching West, which expected too much and gave too little.

Heedful of not neglecting Latin America, a major supplier of energy and resources to China, Xi attended the 6th BRICS summit in April, held in Brazil. The summitry activism continued later in the year, when, in the space of a week, China hosted the APEC summit in Beijing attended by US President Barack Obama and 21 other national leaders, and then Xi went to the G-20 summit, hosted by Australia in Brisbane. Afterwards, he undertook three successful state visits: one to Australia itself, where he witnessed the signing of a free trade agreement which had been almost a decade in preparation, before going on to New Zealand and Fiji. Through all these meetings his most singular achievement was to accept, in partnership with the USA, a major climate change agreement whereby China set 2030 as the year in which its emissions would peak. That the world's two largest polluters were able to arrange such a deal was a major achievement and managed to embarrass the Australian government, which had remarkably staged a major summit without this issue featuring prominently on the agenda.

The less positive side of China's diplomacy lay in its relations with its closest neighbours. China continued to test, provoke or irritate the countries with which it was in dispute over its maritime borders. Japan and Vietnam came in for particular attention, with a massive oil rig owned by China pushing deep into waters claimed by Vietnam, prompting unpleasant riots in Saigon and Hanoi against interests perceived to be Chinese (even though this sometimes targeted what in fact turned out to be Taiwanese or overseas Chinese projects). With Japan, simmering nastiness throughout the year, sometimes resulting in sea vessels and planes from either side harrying each other, was only partially dispelled when Japanese Prime Minister Shinzo Abe met with Xi Jinping in Beijing in November during the APEC summit. Their look of frosty antipathy when shaking hands became an Internet hit. But for the first time since Xi came to power in late 2012 he was at least talking to his Japanese counterpart. This counted as progress. It was helped by a declaration from the Japanese side which amounted to an unprecedented public acknowledgement that there was dispute between the two countries over the sovereignty of the Senkaku Islands, the group of uninhabited, Japanese-administered, islands in the East China Sea (called the Diaoyu Islands by China), which lay at the heart of the maritime dispute.

The one neighbour which Xi seemed unwilling to spend much time on or reach out to was the Democratic People's Republic of Korea (DPRK). Remarkably, Xi visited South Korea during 2014, but had showed no inclination to follow precedent and go first to North Korea. The disappearance of the DPRK's young leader, Kim Jong Un, in September, for over a month, was widely interpreted as an attention-grabbing tactic by a country anxious to continue receiving some sign of solidarity from its largest economic and political partner. But the bottom line seemed clear. Unlike the previous leadership of Hu Jintao, Xi Jinping had no tangible link with the DPRK and appeared unwilling to spend much time expending energy on building one. Nor, despite being in power for almost three years, had Kim Jong Un yet made a visit to Beijing.

Domestically, 2014 was the year in which it became clear, both inside and outside the country, that Xi had managed to consolidate his power and was the dominant leader of his generation in ways that seemed to far exceed the powers invested in his predecessor, Hu Jintao, at the start of his period in office over a decade earlier. Xi seemed to chair every significant strategic and political body, and to control almost every significant lever of power. He even mandated the issuance, in September, of a book of his speeches with a Maoist-style cover and colour plates of him during domestic inspection tours or foreign visits, grandly entitled *The Governance of China*. This outlined his principal philosophy. The main thrust of his public words was to make the ruling Chinese Communist Party (CCP) truly representative of the aspirations of the Chinese people, and to modernise its internal accountability and functioning.

Part of this was evident in the anti-corruption campaign, launched by Xi in the immediate aftermath of his accession to the leadership in late 2012 and which continued unabated throughout 2014. As the year proceeded, a number of new targets were felled, from General Xu Caihou, a former deputy chair of the Central Military Commission who, despite having terminal cancer, was formally prosecuted for corruption in August, to the largest target of all, former Standing Committee Politburo member and head of domestic security, Zhou Yongkang. The latter's case had been an ongoing issue in China ever since the fall of the man regarded as his chief protégé, Bo Xilai, in March 2012 (see AR 2013, pp. 306-07). But the consensus of expert opinion before Zhou was formally placed under investigation by the Central Discipline and Inspection Commission (CDIC), China's key anti-corruption unit, in mid-2014, was that the precedent of prosecuting a former member of the political super-elite was not one that the current leaders would want to set. This was dispelled when it was announced in early December that Zhou had been formally put forward for criminal prosecution.

The official news agency, Xinhua, gave a remarkably frank account of the charges against him, stating that he had "used his position to give illegal benefits to many people, and took bribes directly and via his family members; abused his position to help his family members, mistresses and friends gain huge profits through business activities at the cost of state assets; leaked party and state secrets; severely breached regulations of corruption by taking a great amount of assets belonging to other people; committed adultery with a number of women, and traded money and power for sexual advantages." Along with Zhou went a range of former cronies and family members, some from his time in the national state oil sector. Throughout this high risk process, Xi appeared to maintain the support of all his colleagues and the public. For although Zhou was the highest-ranking Chinese leader to face corruption charges since the foundation of the People's Republic, he was also widely regarded as a violent, unattractive and venal character. In choosing the right kind of enemy to bring down, Xi seemed to have displayed excellent political instincts.

At the end of the year it was confirmed that Ling Jihua, once the closest advisor to former General Secretary Hu Jintao, was also under investigation. Ling had been seen as a contender for the highest office until his career had been derailed by his attempt to cover-up the death of his son, Ling Gu. The latter had perished after crashing his Ferrari at high speed in an accident which also severely injured his two naked female passengers, to the authorities' embarrassment. News that Ling was the subject of official investigation followed anti-corruption action against a number of his family and was preceded by the announcement that he had been dismissed from his post as head of the United Front Work Department, which managed relations between the CCP and non-party elite. His close relationship with Hu meant that the move against him was largely interpreted as a direct rebuke to the leadership of the previous decade. It was also confirmation that under the ruthlessly effective Wang Qishan, the head of the CDIC, there were few limits to the scope of corruption investigations.

Part of the bite to the anti-corruption campaign was clearly linked to the sense, from leaders' speeches and their actions, that China was in a moment of semi-crisis, with falling growth and huge sustainability issues that needed to be addressed. Figures like Zhou were adversaries in this, trying to feed their own personal networks rather than working for the greater good of the country. Xi's rallying call throughout 2014 was the phrase, originally used in late 2013, of "The China Dream". Achievement of this dream—to be a strong, rich, prosperous country—was threatened by the heedless behaviour of corrupt officials. Throughout the year Beijing and Shanghai, along with other major cities, were blighted with terrible smog. Water resources became critically low. The push to increase urban residents from 52 per cent of the population in 2013 to over 70 per cent within a decade also meant that the infrastructure and sustainability of cities needed to be organised to accommodate the needs and living requirements of this vast swathe of people. Towards the end of the year, Xi himself referred to two centennial goals towards which the Party was steering China: the celebration in 2021 of the hundredth anniversary of the Communist Party's foundation, and the achievement of middle-income status the same year, whereby per capita GDP of about $14,000 would put China on the same level as mid-level developing countries in the rest of the world.

In order to achieve this new kind of China, the Fourth Plenum (of the 18th CCP Congress), held in October, focused on the development of the Chinese legal system. For this, the clear ambition was not to create a Western system where an entity like a Supreme Court could hold the Party to account externally, but rather to fashion a defined area where legality in the country was more predictable, even though the pre-eminence of the Party was maintained. In areas like commerce, or even civil cases, therefore, the courts needed to modernise, becoming more professional and efficient. But the legal system itself would still, it was clear, be under the guidance and ultimate control of the Party. The Plenum statement phrased this as "perfecting law with Chinese characteristics". The fact that such a concept was regarded by most experts in jurisprudence in the rest of the world as inherently contradictory was of little interest to Chinese policy makers. For them, the main thing was to have some kind of stronger sense of legality as a means of ensuring stable economic and political development during the tough transition China was about to make. As one phrase put out in late 2014 put it, "Stability is bliss!"

Proof of the limits of support for universal rule of law could be found in the rough treatment given to rights lawyers who were seen to be contesting the legitimacy of the Party. Attempts by one group—as the 25th anniversary of the Tiananmen Square massacre of June 1989 approached—to hold a small commemorative event were met with harsh reprisals. Pu Zhiqiang, a civil rights lawyer, was taken in soon after this event, and formally handed over to prosecutors in November.

Perhaps the most extreme example of the unwillingness of the Party authorities and their courts to tolerate any form of opposition was that of Ilham Tohti, a Beijing-based Uighur who had been a courageous and outspoken critic of central government policy towards his native Xinjiang Autonomous Region. Tohti was arrested early in the year when attempting to board a flight to the USA to take up a temporary academic position there. While his teenage daughter was allowed to board the flight, he himself was taken into custody, and in September handed a life sentence for separatism charges. If this were not enough, the assets and property of his family in Xinjiang were also confiscated. Amnesty International condemned his two-day trial as an "affront to justice" and US Secretary of State John Kerry stated that it was a "harsh" outcome, asking the Chinese government to reconsider it.

Behind Tohti's treatment was the issue of Xinjiang itself, an area that had seen a number of deeply unpleasant incidents in recent years connected to the Uighur separatist campaign. This trend continued in 2014. Amongst the worst incidents was an attack at Kunming train station on 1 March by a group of separatists armed with knives, who killed 29 people and wounded 143 others. In both April and May there were car bomb attacks in Xinjiang's capital, Urumqi, which left dozens dead, prompting the central government to convene a number of meetings on how to handle the situation there. An added worry for the central government was the links between some local groups and international Islamic extremist activists.

Unlike Xinjiang, in Tibet the situation remained more stable, even though self-immolation by separatist protesters continued during the year, albeit at a reduced rate. Well over a hundred people had sacrificed their lives in this way since 2009. It was reported in early October that Tibet's exiled spiritual leader, the Dalai Lama, had participated in informal talks with representatives of the central government concerning the possibility of allowing him to make a visit to his homeland after more than half a century in exile. The Dalai Lama—who had met with President Obama at the White House in February, an event which, even shorn of the ceremony traditionally afforded a head of state, had provoked predictable fury in Beijing—emphasised that nothing had been agreed, but indicated that he had an "optimistic view" of President Xi.

In addition to this, there was the challenge of the management of Hong Kong Special Administrative Region (see below) and the impact of the Sunflower Movement in Taiwan (see below).

All of these many issues suggested that, whatever readers might have felt about the literary merits of Xi Jinping's *The Governance of China*, they would have to agree that the complexity of this task meant that his book had merited its 500-plus pages.

In the **Hong Kong Special Administrative Region** 2014 was the year in which Hong Kong's government was expected to conclude its consultations on the best system by which to elect a chief executive in 2017, and to make an announcement on its findings. An online petition, set up earlier in the year by pro-democracy groups, tried to feed into this process by showing that the 5 million eligible voters in the city were mostly supportive of a one-person, one-vote system, something that they felt had been promised in the handover agreements signed between the UK and China, when Hong Kong reverted to mainland sovereignty in 1997.

The central government in Beijing made its own contribution to this debate in late May when the State Council issued a White Paper on Hong Kong just before Premier Li Keqiang travelled to the UK. In this document, the principle of supreme decision-making power for Hong Kong lying with the National People's Congress, China's legislature, was set out starkly. The paper also gave short shrift to the idea that the opinions of outsiders—like the UK or the USA—were of any import for deciding the city's political destiny. This event in particular marked a sea change in the mood, both in the city and the outside world, towards China's intentions. As one local newspaper editorial summarised the White Paper, its message was clear: China is in charge now, and no one needs to interfere.

When the final proposal for which electoral system would be in place in 2017 was presented in September, it managed to fulfil the pro-democrats' worst expectations. A system was outlined whereby a specially appointed committee of about 1,400 people would select two or three candidates to put forward for election by the full electorate. Such a managed system immediately aroused local opposition, with the "Occupy Central" movement attracting massive student support, and over 50,000 people protesting in one day. The remarkable difference between the 2014 Occupy Central and previous forms of public protest in Hong Kong was that, rather than petering out, the movement continued deep into December, and was only dispersed by police and bailiffs in order to free up highways and restore functioning transport to the city on 9 December.

The Hong Kong 2014 Umbrella Revolution, so named because of the vast numbers of umbrellas used early on in the movement by participants who took part despite torrential rains, showed a side of Hong Kong that the world had seldom seen. The mood of protesters was not helped by the highly inept response of serving Chief Executive C.Y. Leung, who simply dealt with their demands by declaring that the outcome they had was the best deal they could expect from Beijing and they needed to accept this. Leung proceeded to suffer from perhaps the worst ratings of any of the three Hong Kong leaders who had been in office since 1997.

Despite this turmoil, business sentiment in the city remained positive, showing something of the resilience of the place. Those looking for a silver lining in the events of late 2014 were able to point to the fact that the protests had been orderly and civil. The stark political reality, however, was that Hong Kong was now largely on its own, with any outside interventions—by the UK in particular—being met with icy indifference. Hong Kong seemed to show most vividly the ways in which China was more confident and assertive. Attempts in December by a delegation of British Members of Parliament to undertake a visit to the territory in order to interview participants and produce a report on the status of democracy in Hong Kong were blocked by the local authorities, despite British nationals usually being granted visa-free entry for six months. This, more than anything, symbolised a China that had grown uninterested in any further lectures from its former colonial masters. But by the end of 2014, uncertainty still reigned over precisely which system Hong Kong would finally have in 2017.

In eerie symmetry with the campaign on the mainland, at the end of December Rafael Hui, former chief secretary of the city, was indicted for massive corruption and sentenced to seven years in prison. He was proved guilty of misappropriation of funds, and misuse of his official position. His mistress even complained about how he had given her so many gifts she had not known what to do with them. He was put on trial alongside the billionaire businessman Thomas Kwok, who was sentenced to five years. It seemed either side of the border that life was getting tougher for groups previously thought to be above the law, though in Hong Kong's case there was a long and distinguished record, dating back to the 1970s, of clamping down on corruption, meaning that it managed to maintain its record as one of the world's cleanest places to do business.

Those in **Taiwan** who watched events in Hong Kong evidently drew their own conclusions about what to think of an arrangement that promised "one country, two systems", and yet where power so evidently lay finally within the "country" portion of the equation rather than the "systems" element. For Taiwan many of the issues that had been significant in Hong Kong had an impact on domestic politics and views of how to manage relations with an increasingly assertive mainland. Some 600 direct flights a week between the island and China, and over 3 million visitors coming as tourists, were the immediate tangible impact of the closer links that had been encouraged by President Ma Ying-jeou since his election in 2008. Closer political relations, too, were happening, with the first visit ever by a high level mainland official—Zhang Zhijun, minister of the Taiwan affairs office on the State Council—to the island in June, despite loud protests by some opponents.

Despite these warm atmospherics, public opinion in Taiwan was out of step with the political leadership of the ruling Kuomintang (KMT). In March, with public approval ratings of around 9 per cent, President Ma attempted to secure parliamentary approval for the Cross Strait Service Trade Agreement. This was one of the agreements flowing from the earlier landmark Economic Cooperation Framework Agreement (ECFA), but in the much more contentious areas of finance and the service sector, where many of Taiwan's best quality employment lay. Angry at the tactics used by the government to push through the agreement hastily, a number of students and protesters broke into the Legislative Yuan building, occupying it before being forcibly evicted. This precipitated a mass rally at the end of March, which saw over 100,000 people march through Taipei. The Ma administration's response to this "Sunflower Movement"—so named by the protesters' adoption of sunflowers as a symbol of their aspirations—was to shelve the agreement pending more consultations.

The political price paid by the KMT came in the latter part of the year, however, during local elections in November which saw over 22 municipal and provincial seats contested. Of these, only six remained in KMT hands by the end of the evening, most with greatly reduced majorities. Strongholds like Taipei City, almost always in the hands of the KMT, fell to an independent regarded as closer to the opposition Democratic Progressive Party (DPP). Protest votes across the island combined anger at the over-closeness to the mainland by Ma with dissatisfaction over Taiwan's economic performance. Despite posting growth of almost 4 per cent during 2014, the simple fact was that wages had remained stagnant for almost two decades. Professionals were working for the same salaries as they had in the late 1990s, despite housing and living costs continuing to rise inexorably.

Adding to the challenges, Ma had to face a Chinese government whose leader, Xi Jinping, remained insistent upon discussing greater polity unity between the two states. While Beijing had made no overt pronouncement prior to the November elections, Xi had stated a month before that the "one country, two systems" rubric was perfectly viable as a means of handling Chinese reunification. Ma condemned this, insisting that such a notion was unworkable. For it seemed clear that the identity of Taiwanese people had become more strongly defined and, therefore, the concept of reunification with a state which had just dealt so summarily with Hong Kong and its electoral ambitions was, to put it lightly, highly unattractive.

Kerry Brown

JAPAN

CAPITAL: Tokyo   AREA: 377,910 sq km   POPULATION: 127,338,621 ('13)
OFFICIAL LANGUAGE: Japanese
HEAD OF STATE: Emperor Tsugu no Miya Akihito (since Jan '89)
RULING PARTIES: Liberal Democratic Party (LDP)-led coalition
HEAD OF GOVERNMENT: Prime Minister Shinzo Abe (LDP) (since Dec '12)
DEMOCRACY INDEX: 8.08; 20th of 167   CORRUPTION PERCEPTIONS INDEX: 76; =15th of 175
CURRENCY: Yen (Dec '14 £1.00=JPY 187.25, US$1.00=JPY 120.58)
GNI PER CAPITA: US$46,140, Intl$37,630 at PPP ('13)

THE year began with the Liberal Democratic Party (LDP)-led government of Prime Minister Shinzo Abe enjoying a level of popularity unusual among Japanese premiers in recent years. He remained committed to the radical economic programme that he had pursued—widely dubbed "Abenomics"—since coming to power at the end of 2012. The first two elements of this—a large fiscal stimulus and a huge round of quantitative easing—had been adopted in 2013 and had been effective in making some progress towards ending Japan's persistent problem of deflation. The third, and in many ways most significant element, structural reform, remained yet to be convincingly addressed. Nevertheless, Abe began 2014 in buoyant mood, telling the World Economic Forum in Davos that his policies were enabling Japan "to break free from chronic deflation," and boasting that, "I have broken through the notion that certain reforms could never be carried out."

Behind the bravado, however, there lay real uncertainty, with economists divided over whether Abe's high-risk strategy would deliver long-term success. There was economic growth, certainly. Official data in February showed GDP had grown by 1 per cent (annualised) in the final quarter of 2013, thereby taking overall economic growth for the year to 1.6 per cent. However, exports rose sluggishly and the quarter-on-quarter level of private consumption increased by a mere 0.5 per cent. This latter statistic was particularly ominous as it suggested that there was, as yet, no evidence of the sustained wage rises which Abenomics needed if it was to achieve stable growth whilst remaining acceptable to the electorate. From the outset of his administration Abe had dragooned the Bank of Japan (BoJ), the central bank, into adopting a target of 2 per cent for inflation. And whilst this had not yet been achieved, the loose monetary policy at the heart of Abenomics had succeeded in creating some inflationary pressure. But the prospect of increasing consumer prices without a concomitant rise in wages was politically toxic for the government's chances of securing re-election. Thus, tentative evidence in March that basic pay for average Japanese employees had increased for the first time in 22 months (albeit more than offset by a decline in bonuses and overtime, which meant that average take-home earnings actually dropped by 0.2 per cent) was seized upon by the government as evidence of progress.

A further problem for the government lay in a rise in the level of the consumption tax (a flat-rate sales tax), from 5 per cent to 8 per cent, which was scheduled for 1 April. It was the first of a two-stage increase, with the second rise, to 10 per cent, due in October 2015. The rises had been agreed by Abe's predecessor as a step towards addressing Japan's chronic level of public debt (currently running at around 245 per cent of GDP), and Abe had decided to honour the pledge. However, the move was replete with political and economic risk. The planned rise was deeply unpopular with the electorate and the previous increase (from 3 to 5 per cent in 1997) had been the catalyst for tipping a fragile economic recovery back into recession. Nevertheless, the increase went ahead as scheduled and initially all seemed well. In fact, the rush by consumers to make purchases before the tax increase meant that GDP grew in the first quarter by an annualised rate of 6.7 per cent, the sixth consecutive quarterly rise and the largest recorded since mid-2011.

In June Abe unleashed the third "arrow" of his economic programme: structural reform. He sought to go beyond the reforms announced in mid-2013, which had been criticised as overly cautious and lacking coherence. This time he promised changes to tax policies (including a cut in corporation tax), government pension fund investments, corporate governance, and labour regulations, and the adoption of measures to stabilise the declining population at around 100 million and to boost the labour force through the encouragement of female employees and foreign nationals. Once again, however, he faced criticism that the policies were too vague and that he had pulled back from his commitment to restructure the notoriously protected Japanese agricultural sector, a key constituency of LDP support. Many of his proposals would also require separate legislation or would be left in the hands of new "special economic zones", which would be empowered to cut red tape in a range of areas.

By August the result of the consumption tax rise had made itself evident, as the official data showed that GDP had shrunk by 1.7 per cent (an annualised rate of 6.8 per cent) in the second quarter, the sharpest contraction since the disastrous 2011 earthquake and tsunami. It was the first significant quarterly fall since Abe had come to power, but the government dismissed it as a transient and anticipated effect of the consumption tax rise. The data also showed that the inflation rate was falling and that real wages had dropped by 3.2 per cent (annualised) in the second quarter, the sharpest fall in more than four years. With the looming threat of a return of deflation and recession, it seemed that Abenomics was running out of steam. The evidence of the opinion polls also showed that the popularity of the government was in sharp decline.

In addition to the faltering economy, public disenchantment with the government was exacerbated by two of Abe's other key policies. The first was his determination to restart the country's nuclear power plants, which had been mothballed in the aftermath of the 2011 Fukushima nuclear disaster (see AR 2012, pp. 340-44). He reiterated his strong belief in nuclear power in February when he unveiled a new energy strategy that amounted to a clear break from the 2012 pledge of Prime Minister Naoto Kan to phase out nuclear power in its entirety. The details of the "appropriate energy mix" advocated by Abe, in terms of the proportion of nuclear power, fossil fuel and renewables, was vague, but the plan certainly envisaged the reopening of closed reactors and the likelihood of constructing new ones.

In economic terms this made sense. Prior to the Fukushima disaster nuclear power had accounted for 30 per cent of Japan's electricity generation. The burden of making good this shortfall for a country that lacked reserves of fossil fuel had meant increased imports of oil and gas, which had had an adverse effect on the economy. Although it made economic sense to restart the idle reactors, however, it was politically toxic. Nuclear power remained deeply unpopular. The Fukushima accident had been badly handled from the start. Evidence continued to accumulate during 2014 of the poor operating practices of the Fukushima plant's owner, the Tokyo Electric Power Company (Tepco), prior to the tsunami; its inadequate response, together with that of the government, in the immediate aftermath of the accident; and Tepco's largely incompetent and less than transparent efforts to deal with the long-term impact of the disaster. The year saw further revelations about the extent of the nuclear meltdown, as well as the level of contamination of the land and sea around the Fukushima facility. Thus, the long, slow process of decommissioning the stricken plant continued, but did so without any public faith in the probity or efficiency of Tepco. The company was accused of using low paid and unskilled workers for the decommissioning operation, an economy measure deemed to be responsible for causing (or failing to spot) serious leaks from the vast quantities of contaminated water being stored at the site. The overall result was that large swathes of land remained uninhabitable with many former residents continuing to live in temporary accommodation.

The combined effect of the tsunami and nuclear accident had forced the evacuation of some 470,000 people. At the time of the commemorative ceremonies on 11 March to mark the third anniversary of the huge earthquake which had sparked the disaster, some 267,000 of these evacuees remained in temporary housing. Although Abe promised to speed up the reconstruction process, the widespread perception was that the government's efforts remained slow, limited in scope, inefficient and underfunded. There was also a widespread acceptance—backed by the evidence of the investigations into Fukushima—that the roots of the disaster lay in the lack of regulatory oversight. This was directly linked to the traditionally close relationship between Japanese politicians, bureaucrats and corporate interests, which was itself in part a product of the long period of almost unbroken LDP rule in the post-war era. As such, Abe faced an uphill task in convincing the public to trust and accept the nuclear industry, particularly as the decision to restart the mothballed reactors required the consent of local governments.

There was also widespread public distrust of another key Abe policy goal: reform of Japan's pacifist constitution. Foisted upon Japan by the USA in the aftermath of catastrophic military defeat, Article 9 forever renounced the use of war. Thus it was seen by many right-wing nationalists as a symbol of Japan's humiliating capitulation of 1945, and its revision had long been an Abe goal. The route to amending the constitution was arduous, as it required a two-thirds majority in each house of the Diet (the legislature) and a majority at a subsequent referendum. Nevertheless, Abe began making preparations by securing legislation in June to lower the minimum age of voter participation from 20 to 18 years, in a move that sought to counteract the stronger support amongst older voters for the maintenance of Article 9.

He also pursued the easier option of changing policy and moving to reinterpret the existing constitution. In April the government had announced a new weapons export policy that would permit Japan to engage in the joint development and production, and the export, of weapons, a departure not merely from the current embargo on exporting military hardware but also from the pacifism embodied in Article 9. The constitution also prohibited the existence of a Japanese standing army, navy or air force, although this was in practice circumvented through a linguistic sleight of hand which allowed the establishment of a powerful military in the form of "Self-Defence Forces" (SDF). However, severe limits circumscribed how these could be used. Overseas deployment by the SDF was rare and had been limited to logistical tasks, humanitarian relief, and non-combat peacekeeping duties where, humiliatingly, unarmed Japanese military personnel had to be guarded by soldiers from other countries. But in May a panel of security experts—empowered by Abe to examine the limits on overseas combat missions by SDF forces—found in favour of a reinterpretation of the constitution that would legitimatise the principle of collective self-defence, whereby Japan could provide military assistance to its allies. After finally convincing his own party—and, with greater difficulty, New Komeito, the LDP's junior coalition partner whose Buddhist base made it strongly pro-pacifist—to accept this, Abe succeeded on 1 July in adopting it as government policy. This meant that once the necessary legislation had been enacted, the SDF would be empowered to assist allies if there was a "clear danger" which constituted "an imminent threat to Japan's survival" or the lives and rights of its people. Under such circumstances the "minimum level of force necessary" could be exercised, provided that other means of neutralising the threat had failed. The new policy would also enable the SDF to use weapons in UN-approved peacekeeping operations.

Abe adopted the policy in the face of street protests—a rarity within Japan—in Tokyo and other cities, and amid consistent opinion poll evidence that the change was opposed by more than half of the electorate and supported by only around one-third. Opponents feared that the stipulations whereby force could be used were intentionally vague in order to give the government maximum discretion in deciding whether to participate in military engagements, and that the policy represented a dangerous step towards a return to militarism. Abe acknowledged that it was the greatest recalibration of Japan's military posture since the Second World War, but insisted that it decreased rather than increased the chances of Japan's involvement in a war. In a televised national address he promised that Japan would "never again" wage war, and that although it would stand squarely beside its US ally, Japan would "absolutely not go into combat in wars like the Gulf war and Iraq".

Abe's stance on the constitution was indicative of his wider support for right-wing revisionism with regard to Japan's wartime record. He was the patron of a number of controversial figures known for denying the well-documented and notorious 1937-38 Nanking massacre by Japanese troops in China, or advocating the restoration of the divinity of the Emperor, or denying the use by the Japanese military of sex slaves—known euphemistically as "comfort women"—who had been forcibly conscripted from occupied countries. In 1993 Japan had formally apologised over the issue of "comfort women", issuing what became known as the "Kono statement", named after the then Cabinet secretary. This was particularly reviled by Japanese nationalists as an example of Japan's self-abasement in the post-war period through its willingness to participate in "apology diplomacy". In March Abe commissioned a panel to examine the circumstances of the Kono statement, and although this reported in June that the historical evidence underpinning it was accurate, it also revealed the extent to which the statement had been the product of protracted negotiations between Japan and South Korea, motivated not by a desire to address the past but rather a diplomatic move to improve bilateral relations.

Collectively, these issues, together with subjects such as the revision of school textbooks concerning Japan's record in Asia in the 1931-45 period, or the visit by Cabinet members to the Yasukuni shrine (a Shinto memorial to the country's war dead, which included executed war criminals), were touchstones of the wider question of Japan's relationship with its own recent past. As such they were keenly watched by those on the alert for signs of nascent Japanese militarism and were issues of particular sensitivity in countries such as China and South Korea which had suffered most from the brutality of Japanese military occupation. Abe's revisionist steps provoked predictable condemnation from neighbouring countries which accused Japan of whitewashing its wartime record as it reverted to policies redolent with its dark past. For many Japanese, too, Abe's revisionism was a source of anxiety, for Japan, as the world's only victim of attack by atomic weapons, had a unique insight into the horrors of modern warfare.

Thus, for a combination of reasons, by mid-2014 Abe's government was suffering a sharp decline in popularity. This was demonstrated in July by its defeat in the gubernatorial election in Shiga prefecture, where it had been expected to win comfortably. In the event, Taizo Mikazuki, an anti-nuclear candidate backed by the opposition, defeated Takashi Koyari, a former bureaucrat at the ministry of economy, trade and industry, the LDP's favoured candidate. Significantly, the contest saw a markedly low turnout by supporters of New Komeito. Acknowl- edging defeat, LDP secretary-general Shigeru Ishiba accepted that the govern- ment's decision on collective defence had been a critical factor in determining the outcome of the election.

Abe sought to reinvigorate his flagging administration with a Cabinet reshuffle on 3 September which saw him replace 12 ministers whilst preserving the Cabinet's right-wing, nationalist sheen. The new line-up increased the number of women to five, a figure that equalled the largest ever quota of female ministers. The move was a clear attempt by the prime minister to improve his standing with women voters, whose support had lagged behind that of men throughout his administration. How- ever, in the following month two of the women were forced to step down amid alle- gations that they had contravened regulations on election campaign spending. Such scandals had been routine in the era before Abe's government but these were the first to have affected the current prime minister. The speed with which he replaced the compromised ministers seemed to indicate his determination not to allow his administration to become tarnished by the traditional slur of "money politics".

Nevertheless, the government continued to struggle as data released in Novem- ber, rather than showing the anticipated return to growth, in fact confirmed that Japan had entered economic recession. On top of the revised contraction of 7.3 per cent in the second quarter, the preliminary third quarter figures showed an annualised fall of 1.6 per cent in GDP (later revised to 1.9 per cent). Abe responded quickly, announcing on 18 November that the next scheduled rise in the consumption tax would be delayed until April 2017, but promising that it would then go ahead "without fail". He also announced a general election for the House of Representatives on 14 December, a contest which he characterised as a referendum on Abenomics. He defended his economic policy but acknowledged that there were "divided opinions" and "resistance" to it, and called for an unequivocal endorsement of his "growth strategy" via the "voice of the people".

It was less of a political gamble than it appeared. The election offered Abe the chance to exploit the deep disarray and demoralisation within the opposition Dem- ocratic Party of Japan (DPJ), which was running at around only 10 per cent in the opinion polls and had not recovered from the chaotic taste of government which had ended with its decisive ejection from office in 2012 at the election that had brought Abe to power. The prospect of victory (the LDP was polling around 37 per cent in the polls) offered Abe the hope of heading off any challenge to his leader- ship within the party, whilst also giving him a mandate to push ahead with struc- tural economic reform. Furthermore, even if the party lost seats, its strong show- ing in the 2012 election ensured that there was every likelihood that it would retain a comfortable majority in the House.

In the event, the snap election—which saw turnout of only 52.7 per cent, the lowest recorded in the post-war era—delivered a comprehensive victory. The government won 326 seats (compared with 325 in 2012) in the 475-member lower chamber, thereby retaining the two-thirds "supermajority" which enabled it to overcome opposition from the House of Councillors (the upper chamber). The LDP lost three seats but this was more than offset by New Komeito gains. The prime minster welcomed the vote of confidence in Abenomics, a policy which he insisted had "ended the dark stagnation of two or three years ago". He acknowledged, however, that though progress had been made, the job was only half complete. He promised to make greater efforts to raise household incomes as he continued to pursue growth by stimulating domestic demand. At the end of the year he unveiled a new stimulus package which was smaller in scale (3,500 billion yen) but more specifically targeted than its predecessors. The government also announced that it had reached an agreement with Keidanren, the country's largest employers' group, to cut corporate tax rates in return for a commitment by employers to make "maximum efforts" to raise pay levels in 2015.

Thus, as the year ended, it appeared that Abenomics, far from being a spent force, was very much alive and kicking, although its long-term outcome remained uncertain.

In terms of foreign relations, it was a relatively quiet year for Japan. Its traditional ally, the USA, generally welcomed Japanese moves towards greater military participation as Japan was seen not as a potential enemy but as a reliable ally and a counterweight to the growing regional bellicosity of China. President Barack Obama visited Japan in April and affirmed the US-Japan military alliance, noting that its defence commitment covered all territory administered by Japan, including the Senkaku Islands (known in China as the Diaoyu islands), over which China claimed sovereignty.

As for Japan's Asian neighbours, relations were stable, despite the regular accusations that Abe was steering his country back towards its militaristic past. There was no progress in Japan's territorial disputes with Russia, South Korea or China, but nor did they get worse. China continued to make frequent naval and aerial incursions in the vicinity of the Senkaku Islands and on a number of occasions Chinese fighters passed within 30 metres of Japanese aircraft, leading to Japanese diplomatic protests. Other Chinese provocations included the seizure in April of a Japanese merchant ship, which had docked in China, in pursuit of a reparations claim dating back to the Sino-Japanese war (1937-45). But in general, China's actions against Japan were less recklessly aggressive than in 2013. There was even a face-to-face meeting between Prime Minister Abe and Chinese President Xi Jinping, on 10 November, when the former was in Beijing to attend an APEC summit. It was their first meeting since they had assumed the leaderships of their respective countries and it was characterised by a grim and joyless handshake. Their meeting was preceded by a statement that acknowledged their different positions on the sovereignty of the Senkaku Islands without either side making any concession on the vexed issue.

Although the points of dispute, not least the poisonous legacy of the past, remained unresolved, overall, Sino-Japanese relations were more stable than in recent years. Perhaps this was significant progress, particularly when compared with the beginning of 2014 when Abe had warned the audience at Davos that, "The dividend of growth in Asia must not be wasted on military expansion." He appealed for "a mechanism for crisis management as well as a communication channel" between the armed forces of Japan and China, and noted that, "If peace and stability were shaken in Asia, the knock-on effect for the entire world would be enormous." He likened Sino-Japanese relations to those between Germany and Britain prior to the outbreak of war in 1914 and warned that any "inadvertent" conflict would have catastrophic global consequences. It was a chilling analogy, delivered on the centenary of a war that was still leaving its mark upon the world, despite the disappearance of the last of those who had fought in it.

D.S. Lewis

SOUTH AND NORTH KOREA

South Korea

CAPITAL: Seoul   AREA: 99,260 sq km   POPULATION: 50,219,669 ('13)
OFFICIAL LANGUAGE: Korean
HEAD OF STATE AND GOVERNMENT: President Park Geun Hye (since Feb '13)
RULING PARTY: Saenuri Party (formerly GNP)
PRIME MINISTER: Jung Hong Won (Saenuri) (since Feb '13)
DEMOCRACY INDEX: 8.06; =21st of 167   CORRUPTION PERCEPTIONS INDEX: 55; =43rd of 175
CURRENCY: Won (Dec '14 £1.00=KRW 1,704, US$1.00=KRW 1,098)
GNI PER CAPITA: US$25,920, Intl$33,440 at PPP ('13)

North Korea

CAPITAL: Pyongyang   AREA: 120,540 sq km   POPULATION: 24,895,480 ('13)
OFFICIAL LANGUAGE: Korean
HEAD OF STATE: Eternal President (ceremonial) Kim Il Sung [died 1994]; Kim Jong Un (since Dec '11)
RULING PARTY: Korean Workers' Party (KWP)
HEAD OF GOVERNMENT: Premier Pak Pong Ju (since April '13)
DEMOCRACY INDEX: 1.08; 167th of 167   CORRUPTION PERCEPTIONS INDEX: 8; =174th of 175
CURRENCY: North Korean Won [official rate] (Dec '14 £1.00=KPW 2.02, US$1.00=KPW 1.30)
GNI PER CAPITA: US$506 ('11) [UN data]

THE drama that marked 2013, at least as far as the Democratic People's Republic of Korea (DPRK, North Korea) was concerned (see AR 2014, pp. 321-23), was not repeated. Yet the year was not without its moments. In April, the Republic of Korea (ROK, South Korea) saw its second worst-ever ferry disaster, when the MV *Sewol* sank with the loss of 304 known dead and nine missing; most of those lost were schoolchildren. Grief turned to anger at the government's inadequate handing of the tragedy. Developments affecting the North did not match the *Sewol*, but the repercussions from the fall and execution of Jang Song Taek at the end of 2013, a UN enquiry into the country's human rights, a long disappearance from public view of Kim Jong Un, the leader since December 201, and a cyber attack on Sony Pictures, blamed on North Korea, all made an international impact.

South Korea. President Park Geun Hye's second year in office turned out to be much like her first. She enjoyed a better press abroad than she did at home, where her choice of ministers and advisers was seen as flawed and her performance somewhat lacklustre. Events surrounding the sinking of the *Sewol* highlighted the problems. The ship's crew seemed primarily concerned with saving themselves and gave instructions that led to many being trapped and drowned. Search and rescue organisations were slow in responding, while fishing boats and other craft were quickly on the scene. Distraught parents were manhandled by the police at the scene of the disaster and later during protests. As the story unfolded, it emerged that officials appeared to have connived at the bypassing of safety regulations.

Park did not visit the memorial altar set up in Anson, the town near Seoul which lost some 250 children and staff in the disaster, until 29 April, 13 days after the ferry sank. There she issued her first public apology for the failings highlighted by the incident. She accepted the prime minister's offer to resign in order to take responsibility for the incident, and dismissed her national security adviser and the head of the National Intelligence Service (NIS). The effect of this was somewhat marred, however, by her inability to find a replacement prime minister. Two candidates withdrew under criticism, and Prime Minister Jong Hong-won agreed to remain. Park's popularity in the polls dropped, which did not bode well for the local elections in early June. But the opposition seemed unable to fully capitalise on the government's difficulties. The local elections reflected this, with each side doing well in its traditional areas of support, and the opposition gaining one more seat than the government in the race for provincial governors and mayors. It was not a ringing endorsement of anybody.

The repercussions of the tragedy lingered on during the rest of the year, overshadowing many events. Thus, the families of those lost were invited to a special Mass held when Pope Francis visited South Korea in August, and protests continued to the end of the year. By then there was another indictment of corporate Korea and its standards. Early in December, Helen Cho was served nuts in a bag rather than on a plate on a Korean Air (KA) aeroplane taxiing to the runway in New York. Cho, an executive vice-president of the airline and daughter of the chairman, ordered the aeroplane to turn back, demanding that the chief steward leave. By the end of the year, she had resigned from KA and apologised, but was on trial for endangering aircraft safety along with another executive who had tried to organise a cover up. Transport ministry officials also came under scrutiny. One was arrested and others were disciplined.

The role of the NIS was another subject of constant debate. This centred on its alleged interference in the 2012 presidential election (see AR 2014, p. 320), even though those then at the top had been removed. The question of the National Security Law and the pursuit of those who were deemed to be pro-North Korea loomed large. After a year's deliberation, the Constitutional Court ordered the dissolution of the left-wing United Progressive Party (UPP) on the grounds that it was dominated by a pro-North Korean organisation, the first time since the founding of the ROK that a party had been so dissolved. For some, this was a rousing victory over pro-North Korean activists. Others thought it showed the increasingly authoritarian trend of President Park's government.

MONGOLIA

CAPITAL: Ulan Bator   AREA: 1,566,500 sq km   POPULATION: 2,839,073 ('13)
OFFICIAL LANGUAGE: Halh (Khalkha) Mongolia
HEAD OF STATE: President Tsakhiagiyn Elbegdorj (DPM) (since June '09)
RULING PARTY: Democratic Party of Mongolia (DPM)
HEAD OF GOVERNMENT: Prime Minister Chimed Saikhanbileg (DPM) (since Nov '14)
DEMOCRACY INDEX: 6.51; 63rd of 167   CORRUPTION PERCEPTIONS INDEX: 39; =80th of 175
CURRENCY: Tugrik (Dec '14 £1.00=MNT 2,922, US$1.00=MNT 1,881)
GNI PER CAPITA: US$3,770, Intl$8,810 at PPP ('13)

DISPUTES between the Mongolian government and the British-Australian mining company, Rio Tinto, over financing for the vast Oyu Tolgoi (OT) copper mine dominated 2014. The government, which owned 34 per cent of the Oyu Tolgoi project, had been engaged in a long-running dispute with the mining company over management fees, cost over-runs, and $127 million in tax demands dating from 2010-12. Without the resolution of these issues, Rio Tinto refused to fund the $5.4 billion underground expansion of the mine, wherein lay 80 per cent of the project's value.

This uncertainty contributed to investors' wariness over dealing with Mongolia. Foreign direct investment fell by 60 per cent in the first half of 2014, on top of a 52 per cent fall in 2013; GDP growth also slowed, to 5.3 per cent in the first part of the year, compared with the 17.5 per cent growth seen in 2011. Meanwhile, the economy suffered from the fall in the global price of coal—still Mongolia's main export—as demand from China contracted. The currency, the tugrik, lost value and a credit crunch brought the hitherto breakneck rate of economic expansion to a halt. Hard currency reserves fell by two-thirds. Domestic spending had risen sharply in 2013 in an attempt to reinvigorate the economy, but in 2014 the government tried to reverse these measures, which included mortgage subsidies and a price stabilisation programme, in order to rein back spending.

The economic crisis prompted the removal in November of Prime Minister Norov Altankhuyag of the Democratic Party, who narrowly lost a no-confidence vote (by 36 votes to 30 in the 76-seat Great Hural, the legislature). The opposition People's Party (MPP) had called the vote, and was supported by some members of the prime minister's Democratic Party (DPM). The government had been shaky since a decision in August to reduce the number of ministries from 16 to 13 had prompted a number of ministers to resign in protest, including those leading the foreign affairs and mining sectors.

The Altankhuyag government was replaced in December by a Cabinet of technocrats, led by Chimed Saikhanbileg of the DPM, formerly the Cabinet office minister.

China and Russia both offered economic assistance, leading to concerns in the country that Mongolia might have to soften its foreign policy strategy of seeking a "third neighbour"—an international partner to balance relations with its two giant physical neighbours: Russia and China. The "third neighbour" was not specified, however, beyond being one of the "advanced democratic countries", which, most obviously, meant the USA, Japan or South Korea. Particular importance thus attached to the visit in April of US Defence Secretary Chuck Hagel, who arrived at the end of his tour of the Far East. This first visit by a US defence secretary since 2005 acknowledged Mongolia's role in US-led military operations in Afghanistan and Iraq, and the efforts it had made to adapt the Mongolian Armed Forces (MAF) to the functions of a peacekeeping force. Since 2002 Mongolia had deployed over 5,000 personnel in 15 global peacekeeping operations, which represented a significant commitment given the size of its population. At the end of his visit, Hagel received the traditional Mongolian gift of a horse and named the animal "Shamrock"—hoping, perhaps, to revive Mongolia's good luck.

Wendy Slater

X AUSTRALASIA AND THE PACIFIC

AUSTRALIA

CAPITAL: Canberra   AREA: 7,741,220 sq km   POPULATION: 23,130,900 ('13)
OFFICIAL LANGUAGE: English
HEAD OF STATE: Queen Elizabeth II (since Feb '52)
GOVERNOR-GENERAL: Sir Peter Cosgrove (since March '14)
RULING PARTIES: Liberal-National coalition
HEAD OF GOVERNMENT: Prime Minister Tony Abbot (Liberal Party) (since Sept '13)
DEMOCRACY INDEX: 9.13; 6th of 167   CORRUPTION PERCEPTIONS INDEX: 80; 11th of 175
CURRENCY: Australian Dollar (Dec '14 £1.00=AUD 1.91, US$1.00=AUD 1.23)
GNI PER CAPITA: US$65,520, Intl$42,540 at PPP ('13)

AUSTRALIA spent its first full year since 2006 under the stewardship of a conservative government, ending a period of rotating and warring Australian Labor Party (ALP) leadership. The new government soon found itself stymied by economic headwinds, an uncooperative Senate and a poorly received first budget. Aiming at medium term deficit reduction, the budget was widely perceived as socially inequitable. As a result, Prime Minister Tony Abbott endured a rapid decline in his personal standing.

Proposals to restrict unemployment assistance for people under 30, to raise the pension age to 70, for a co-payment on basic medical services and to deregulate university fees all stalled in the Senate. Fuel tax, however, was increased and a temporary high income levy passed with opposition support. Over 2014, the fiscal position worsened with declining export commodity prices. The currency consequently weakened, although it remained overvalued according to the Reserve Bank. Exacerbating fiscal concerns, wages were stagnant in real terms, for only the second time in recent decades.

Various policies of the previous administration were overturned or trimmed. The mining profits tax was removed and the ambitious NBN (a fibre-optical national Internet system) scaled-down. Dominated by climate change sceptics, the new government repealed its predecessor's carbon pricing and emissions trading system. Australia thus became the first nation to backtrack on pricing greenhouse gas emissions. In its stead, an A$2.5 billion fund for businesses to implement carbon reduction measures was established. The government also disbanded a climate action loans scheme and sought to reduce the target for renewable energy generation.

The febrile nature of contemporary politics was illustrated in mining magnate and MP Clive Palmer whose eponymous Palmer United party held veto power over all legislation. By year's end that bloc had split, with Senator Jacqui Lambie abandoning it to reject all government bills in protest against a miserly pay offer to defence personnel. The Senate also attracted attention when, for the first time in 110 years, the High Court ordered a fresh election. The re-election, in May, affected six Western Australian senators. It followed an administrative loss of votes cast in the 2013 general election.

At state level, anti-corruption hearings engulfed the New South Wales government. Investigations began with shady commercial dealings involving former ALP figures, then shifted to circumvention of donation limits by conservative politicians and property developers. Ten Liberal Party MPs resigned or were suspended. Premier Barry O'Farrell also resigned after having to correct his evidence about a congratulatory bottle of vintage wine received from a lobbyist.

In Queensland, the Liberal-National Party experienced collapsing voter confidence just two years after winning a record majority. A brace of by-elections recorded anti-government swings of 17 per cent. Amongst a raft of causes was a battle with lawyers and civil libertarians. This included a furore over a new chief justice whose fellow judges felt was so ill-equipped for appointment that they boycotted his swearing-in.

Out of office almost everywhere, the ALP retained government in South Australia in March, despite again achieving under half of the two-party preferred vote. Then, in November it regained power in Victoria, after just one term in opposition. Melbourne, once the home of mercantile capitalism, was firmly declared "the progressive capital" of Australia after a decades-long drift to the Left.

International affairs loomed larger than at any time since the 2003 Iraq war. Military advisers were committed as part of a US led-effort to counteract Islamic State (ISIS) forces in Iraq. In mid-December an Iranian cleric turned refugee took hostages in a central Sydney café, purporting to align himself with ISIS. In the ensuing siege and commando raid, the gunman and two patrons were killed.

A further 36 Australian residents died in the shooting down, over Ukraine, of Malaysian Airliner MH17. Australia was at the forefront of attempts to force Russia to aid recovery efforts and offer compensation. Prime Minister Abbott vowed to "shirtfront" Russian President Vladimir Putin, sparking diplomatic curiosity and mirth over the meaning of this sporting term for a physical confrontation.

Three major bilateral trade agreements were entered. The first two were with South Korea and Japan. The most significant was with China. Building on the A$150 billion annual relationship, Chinese tariffs on energy products and some agricultural goods would be removed and its financial services market opened to Australian firms. In return, China's private sector would gain greater freedom to invest in Australian enterprises and property.

The longstanding issue of asylum seekers arriving by unauthorised boats (see AR 2014, p.326) was politically muted by hardline policy. Naval exclusions, the interception and turning back of vessels, and a refusal to accept such refugees or offer permanent protection visas stemmed boat arrivals, whilst harming Australia's humanitarian reputation internationally. Asylum seekers were repatriated to Sri Lanka and one was bludgeoned to death by locals during a riot in an Australian run detention centre on Manus Island, in Papua New Guinea. Cambodia agreed to relocate other detainees, triggering UNHCR concerns about Australia shirking its responsibilities.

In November, Brisbane hosted the annual G-20 meeting of leaders of the world's largest 20 economies. Due to the tyranny of distance, co-operative policing and a heatwave, the event was not marked by violent protests, unlike previous meetings. Leaders agreed to aim for a world economic growth rate of 2.1 per cent and—to the host nation's chagrin—to commit funding to a Green Climate Fund to assist poorer countries respond to global warming. The G-20 summit also brought addresses to the Australian parliament by China's President Xi Xinping, India's Prime Minister Narendra Modi, and UK Prime Minister David Cameron, as well as the first state visit by a French President.

November also saw the death, at the age of 98, of former Prime Minister Gough Whitlam (see Obituary). Whitlam's state memorial was over-subscribed fourfold. Well-wishers heard Indigenous orator Noel Pearson hail Whitlam as Australia's "Great White Elder". Obituaries reflected on the pivotal role his short-lived reforming government had played in modernising Australia.

Whitlam had been a prominent centraliser rather than federalist. But in mid-year the High Court affirmed limits on the spending power of the national government, striking down a scheme for direct funding of chaplains in state schools. The decision included legal rhetoric sympathetic to state autonomy, after 90 years of centralising developments in the law and national life.

Moves by libertarian Senator David Leyjonhelm to legalise gay marriage were delayed, pending conservative MPs being granted a conscience vote on the issue. The High Court proved more liberal, in finding that people who identified as neither male nor female but as "intersexual" were entitled to birth certificates reflecting that. Knighthoods and damehoods were reinstated under the Order of Australia, despite lampooning by republicans. The first two recipients were the outgoing and incoming Governors-General.

Early in 2014, Australian cricket enjoyed its third ever "whitewash" in a five-test "Ashes" series against England. There was no such glory for the men's soccer team, which lost all three of its games in the World Cup finals in Brazil. By year's end, sport spelt grief rather than entertainment. For a second consecutive year one of the world's premier horse races, the Melbourne Cup, was marred by the death of horses. Two died, sparking nationwide debate about the ethics of horse racing. Then in late November, international cricketer Phillip Hughes died after being struck in the neck by a ball, whilst batting in an inter-state match. Mourning led to the postponement of international matches in Australia and the UAE.

Graeme Orr

PAPUA NEW GUINEA

CAPITAL: Port Moresby   AREA: 462,840 sq km   POPULATION: 7,321,262 ('13)
OFFICIAL LANGUAGES: Pidgin, Motu & English
HEAD OF STATE: Queen Elizabeth II (since Feb '52)
GOVERNOR-GENERAL: Sir Michael Ogio (since Feb '11)
RULING PARTY: People's National Congress (NPC)-led coalition
HEAD OF GOVERNMENT: Prime Minister Peter O'Neill (since Aug '12)
DEMOCRACY INDEX: 6.36; 67th of 167   CORRUPTION PERCEPTIONS INDEX: 25; =145th of 175
CURRENCY: Kina (Dec '14 £1.00=PGK 4.00, US$1.00=PGK 2.58)
GNI PER CAPITA: US$2,010, Intl$2,430 at PPP ('13)

THE rich and colourful pageant that is Papua New Guinea (PNG) politics continued in 2014 with alliances shifting between the country's bewildering array of parties. Prime Minister Peter O'Neill's hold on power remained more or less secure, however, with his longevity in office marking him out as one of PNG's small elite of political survivors.

PNG's long anticipated export of liquid natural gas (LNG) from its extensive reserves began in 2014. Significantly, Japanese Prime Minister Shinzo Abe added PNG to his regional tour of Australia and New Zealand in July. He promised extensive bilateral aid for infrastructural development in PNG in return for a secure supply of gas for Japan. China too, which O'Neill visited in November for the 22nd APEC summit, also expressed strong interest in procuring gas from PNG.

The arrangement with Australia whereby intercepted asylum seekers were detained in camps in remote parts of PNG rather than being permitted to make landfall in Australia, continued to cause controversy in both countries. In February an Iranian refugee was beaten to death by guards and more than 70 were injured during disturbances at the largest camp on Manus island, where some 1,300 people were being held in very poor conditions. The UN High Commissioner for Refugees had strongly and repeatedly criticised the plight of the incarcerated refugees.

Corruption continued to cause difficulties for aid and development. In January the Australian government withdrew its long-standing funding of pharmaceutical procurement after the PNG government took over the process, awarding high value tenders to dubious suppliers.

The economy performed well in 2014, principally on the back of gas revenues, actual and prospective. The agricultural sector also flourished due to sharp rises during the year in major PNG export commodities (notably coffee, cocoa and copra). Inflation remained high, however, at 6 per cent, while overall GDP growth outside the mineral and mining sector was low, at 1.6 per cent.

Norrie MacQueen

NEW ZEALAND

CAPITAL: Wellington   AREA: 267,710 sq km   POPULATION: 4,470,800 ('13)
OFFICIAL LANGUAGE: English
HEAD OF STATE: Queen Elizabeth II (since Feb '52)
GOVERNOR-GENERAL: Sir Jeremiah Mateparae (since Aug '11)
RULING PARTY: National Party (NP)
HEAD OF GOVERNMENT: Prime Minister John Key (NP) (since Nov '08)
DEMOCRACY INDEX: 9.26; 5th of 167   CORRUPTION PERCEPTIONS INDEX: 91; 2nd of 175
CURRENCY: New Zealand Dollar (Dec '14 £1.00=NZD 1.99, US$1.00=NZD 1.28)
GNI PER CAPITA: US$35,550, Intl$30,750 at PPP ('12)

PRIME Minister John Key won a third consecutive term as he led his National Party to a decisive victory over its main rival, the opposition Labour Party. The parliamentary elections, held on 20 September, returned National to office with 60 seats (an increase of one from 2011) in the 121-seat Parliament and 47 per cent of the vote. Labour's 32 seats were a loss of two, its 25 per cent share of the vote representing its lowest proportion since 1922.

Key announced his new Cabinet on 6 October, having completed confidence agreements with the same three small parties as in 2008 and 2011: ACT and United Future, which won one seat apiece, and the Maori Party, which won two seats. The government's 64 parliamentary seats gave it a comfortable majority over a fragmented opposition comprising three parties: Labour; the Greens (which won 14 seats, as in 2011); and the populist New Zealand First party, which increased its support, winning 8.7 per cent of the vote and 11 seats (up from eight in 2011).

The decline in Labour's support led to an immediate challenge to party leader David Cunliffe, who was chosen in September 2013 using selection rules that eliminated the parliamentary caucus's exclusive control over the choice of party leader. While initially seeking to retain his post, on 13 October Cunliffe announced that he would not be participating in a new leadership vote. On 18 November Andrew Little was elected Labour's leader, defeating three rivals for the position.

Cunliffe was not the only election casualty. The Mana Party's sole MP was defeated in his electorate (voting district), and an electoral partnership between Mana and a new political entity, the Internet Party, inspired by a controversial immigrant, Kim Dotcom, failed to win support (achieving only 1.4 per cent of the vote). The Conservative Party's 3.97 per cent share of the vote also proved insufficient to achieve parliamentary representation, falling short of the 5 per cent required of parties without an electorate seat.

The campaign was not without controversy. The Conservatives' leader, Colin Craig, attracted attention by expressing scepticism about whether US astronauts had ever actually walked on the Moon. A book based on leaked emails and launched at the outset of the campaign, alleging "dirty tricks" involving collusion between the government and right-wing bloggers (Internet diarists), led to the resignation on 30 August of a senior Cabinet minister. The Internet-Mana campaign's televised "Moment of Truth" event (staged five days before the election) brought together Kim Dotcom and US journalist Glenn Greenwald, Edward Snowden (the former US National Security Agency (NSA) analyst, in Russia), and WikiLeaks founder Julian Assange (in Ecuador's embassy in London), in an effort to link New Zealand's intelligence agencies and Prime Minister Key with the NSA. While defending cooperation between New Zealand and US agencies, Key denied that New Zealand's intelligence services were engaged in mass electronic surveillance of New Zealanders. Following the election, day-to-day responsibilities for the intelligence agencies were transferred to the attorney-general, with the prime minister assuming the new portfolio of minister for national security and intelligence.

There were positive developments in the economy. A government budget surplus was predicted for the first time since 2008. In March, China agreed to permit direct trading of New Zealand's currency against China's, New Zealand becoming only the sixth country to have that status. New Zealand's AA credit rating was reaffirmed by Fitch Ratings in July, its economic outlook upgraded from "stable" to "positive". In December a free trade agreement was signed with South Korea, the country's sixth largest export market.

Security concerns featured both within the country and internationally. New Zealand's HMNZS *Canterbury* participated in the US-led RIMPAC (Rim of the Pacific) military exercise (26 June-1 August), the first time that a New Zealand naval vessel had been permitted to berth at the US Navy Base at Pearl Harbor since the anti-nuclear policy was introduced in 1984. The prime minister met US President Barack Obama at the White House in June, their talks focusing on economic and security issues. The prime minister indicated his support for US air strikes against terrorists in Iraq so long as they were at the request of the Iraqi government.

In October the government raised New Zealand's threat level (from "very low" to "low"), meaning that a terrorist attack was regarded as "possible but not expected". Security was tightened at entrances to Parliament in the wake of shootings at Canada's Parliament on 22 October. In December Parliament enacted legislation intended to prevent New Zealanders from leaving the country to join Islamic State (ISIS) and from returning to carry out terrorist attacks, increasing the powers of the Security Intelligence Service and strengthening ministerial authority to cancel passports.

In February the minister of foreign affairs summoned the Japanese ambassador to express the government's displeasure at the entry into New Zealand's exclusive economic zone of a Japanese whaling support vessel. In March a limited number of sanctions were announced against Russia in response to its annexation of Crimea, including a travel ban against specified individuals and deferment of action on a possible free trade agreement. In May a Malaysian diplomat accused of assault with intent to rape was offered diplomatic immunity and allowed to leave the country, returning in October to face trial following requests to Malaysia's government for him to do so. On 16 October New Zealand was elected to a two-year term on the UN Security Council, beginning in January 2015, winning a first-ballot victory to secure a seat it had last held in 1993-94.

Other events and achievements, both individual and national, made an impact. A 10-day tour in April by Prince William, Catherine (née Kate Middleton) and the nine-month old Prince George attracted widespread interest and warm media coverage. New Zealand athletes won 45 medals, including 14 gold (and the team's 600th Games medal) at the 20th Commonwealth Games (23 July-3 August). In January New Zealand singer-songwriter Lorde won two Grammy Awards for her song "Royals", including Song of the Year. In April New Zealand golfer Lydia Ko was chosen by *Time* magazine as one of the world's 100 most influential people and in November she won the LPGA Tour's rookie of the year award, the youngest golfer (at age 17) to do so. In December film director Sir Peter Jackson was presented with his own star on the Hollywood Walk of Fame and his film *The Hobbit: The Battle of the Five Armies*—the last of *The Hobbit* trilogy—was given its world premiere in New Zealand.

Separate proposals for improved connections (by monorail or by tunnel) linking South Island tourist attractions Queenstown and Milford Sound were rejected by the minister for conservation because of concerns about their environmental impact and economic viability. In August the Hikurangi Marine Reserve was established as a sanctuary for whales, dolphins and seals, becoming the country's largest marine reserve. In April New Zealand was ranked as the world's most socially advanced country by the Social Progress Imperative, a US-based non-profit organisation which assessed societies' capacity to meet citizens' basic human needs. In October the government announced that New Zealanders would be given the opportunity to decide whether to retain the country's current flag, the prime minister expressing support for a change to better reflect the country's independent status and national identity.

Stephen Levine

PACIFIC ISLAND STATES

Fiji

CAPITAL: Suva   AREA: 18,270 sq km   POPULATION: 881,065 ('13)
OFFICIAL LANGUAGES: Fijian, Hindi & English
HEAD OF STATE: President Ratu Epeli Nailatikau (since July '09)
RULING PARTY: Fiji First party
HEAD OF GOVERNMENT: Prime Minister Commodore Voreqe "Frank" Bainimarama (since Jan '07)
DEMOCRACY INDEX: 3.61; 124th of 167
CURRENCY: Fiji Dollar (Dec '14 £1.00=FJD 3.10, US$1.00=FJD 1.99)
GNI PER CAPITA: US$4,430, Intl$7,610 at PPP ('13)

Kiribati

CAPITAL: Tarawa   AREA: 810 sq km   POPULATION: 102,351 ('13)
OFFICIAL LANGUAGES: English & Kiribati
HEAD OF STATE AND GOVERNMENT: President Anote Tong (since July '03)
RULING PARTY: Pillars of Truth
CURRENCY: Australian Dollar (Dec '14 £1.00=AUD 1.91, US$1.00=AUD 1.23)
GNI PER CAPITA: US$2,620, Intl$2,780 at PPP ('13)

Marshall Islands

CAPITAL: Dalap-Uliga-Darrit   AREA: 180 sq km   POPULATION: 52,634 ('13)
OFFICIAL LANGUAGES: English & Marshallese
HEAD OF STATE AND GOVERNMENT: President Christopher Loeak (since Jan '12)
CURRENCY: US Dollar (Dec '14 £1.00=USD 1.55)
GNI PER CAPITA: US$4,200, Intl$4,620 at PPP ('13)

Federated States of Micronesia

CAPITAL: Palikir (Pohnpei)   AREA: 700 sq km   POPULATION: 103,549 ('13)
OFFICIAL LANGUAGE: English
HEAD OF STATE AND GOVERNMENT: President Emanuel "Manny" Mori (since May '07)
CURRENCY: US Dollar (see above)
GNI PER CAPITA: US$3,430, Intl$3,840 at PPP ('13)

Nauru

CAPITAL: Domaneab   AREA: 21.4 sq km   POPULATION: 10,000 ('13 UN figures)
OFFICIAL LANGUAGES: Nauruan & English
HEAD OF STATE AND GOVERNMENT: President Baron Waqa (since June '13)
CURRENCY: Australian Dollar (see above)
GNI PER CAPITA: US$6,746 ('11) [UN data]

Palau (Belau)

CAPITAL: Koror   AREA: 460 sq km   POPULATION: 20,918 ('13)
OFFICIAL LANGUAGE: English
HEAD OF STATE AND GOVERNMENT: President Tommy Remengesau (from Jan '13)
CURRENCY: US Dollar (see above)
GNI PER CAPITA: US$10,970, Intl$14,540 at PPP ('13)

Samoa

CAPITAL: Apia   AREA: 2,840 sq km   POPULATION: 190,372 ('13)
OFFICIAL LANGUAGES: English & Samoan
HEAD OF STATE: Tupua Tamasese Tupuola Tufuga Efi (since June '07)
RULING PARTY: Human Rights Protection Party (HRPP)
HEAD OF GOVERNMENT: Prime Minister Tuilaepa Aiono Sailele Malielegaoi (since Nov '98)
CORRUPTION PERCEPTIONS INDEX: 52; =50th of 175
CURRENCY: Tala (Dec '14 £1.00=WST 3.78, US$1.00=WST 2.44)
GNI PER CAPITA: US$3,430, Intl$4,840 at PPP ('13)

Solomon Islands

CAPITAL: Honiara   AREA: 28,900 sq km   POPULATION: 561,231 ('13)
OFFICIAL LANGUAGE: English
HEAD OF STATE: Queen Elizabeth II (since Feb '52)
GOVERNOR-GENERAL: Sir Frank Ofagioro Kabui (since July '09)
RULING PARTY: Democratic Coalition for Change
HEAD OF GOVERNMENT: Prime Minister Manasseh Sogavare (since Dec '14)
CURRENCY: Solomon Islands Dollar (Dec '14 £1.00=SBD 11.85, US$1.00=SBD 7.63)
GNI PER CAPITA: US$1,610, Intl$1,810 at PPP ('13)

Tonga

CAPITAL: Nuku'alofa   AREA: 750 sq km   POPULATION: 105,323 ('13)
OFFICIAL LANGUAGES: Tongan & English
HEAD OF STATE: King Tupou VI (since March '12)
RULING PARTY: Friendly Islands Democracy Party
HEAD OF GOVERNMENT: Prime Minister Akilisi Pohiva (since Dec '14)
CURRENCY: Pa'anga (Dec '14 £1.00=TOP 3.02, US$1.00=TOP 1.95)
GNI PER CAPITA: US$4,490, Intl$5,450 at PPP ('13)

Tuvalu

CAPITAL: Fongafale   AREA: 26 sq km   POPULATION: 9,876 ('13)
OFFICIAL LANGUAGE: English
HEAD OF STATE: Queen Elizabeth II (since Feb '52)
GOVERNOR-GENERAL: Sir Iakoba Taeia Italeli (since April '10)
HEAD OF GOVERNMENT: Prime Minister Enele Sopoaga (since Aug '13)
CURRENCY: Australian Dollar (see above)
GNI PER CAPITA: US$6,630, Intl$5,990 at PPP ('13)

Vanuatu

CAPITAL: Port Vila   AREA: 12,190 sq km   POPULATION: 252,763 ('13)
OFFICIAL LANGUAGES: English, French & Bislama
HEAD OF STATE: President Baldwin Londsdale (ind) (since Sept '14)
RULING PARTY: Vanua'aku Pati (VP)-led coalition
HEAD OF GOVERNMENT: Prime Minister Joe Natuman (VP) (since May '14)
CURRENCY: Vatu (Dec '14 £1.00=VUV 162.6, US$1.00=VUV 104.7)
GNI PER CAPITA: US$3,130, Intl$2,840 at PPP ('13)

ELECTIONS in **Fiji** on 17 September were the country's first since 2006 (when the government was removed in a military coup led by Voreqe "Frank" Bainimarama). Bainimarama's newly established Fiji First party won a majority—32 seats—with two other parties also achieving representation: Social Democratic Liberal Party (SODELPA), with 15 seats, and the National Federation Party, with three. Bainimarama was sworn in as prime minister on 22 September. Parliament convened on 6 October, electing Dr Jiko Luveni as speaker and SODELPA's leader Teimumu Kepa as leader of the opposition; they were the first women to hold these positions in Fiji. Following the election the Commonwealth ended Fiji's suspension (introduced in 2009) and foreign governments lifted sanctions.

Parliamentary elections in **Tonga** on 27 November were the second held since a more democratic system was introduced in 2010. On 29 December, Parliament elected veteran pro-democracy campaigner 'Akilisi Pohiva as prime minister; he became the first People's Representative (and the first commoner) to be elected to the position.

In February Joy Kere became the **Solomon Islands'** first woman ambassador with her appointment as high commissioner to New Zealand. In May the governor-general, Sir Frank Kabui, was re-elected by Parliament for a second five-year term. A more accurate electoral roll using biometric voter registration contributed to the country's highest ever voter turnout (89.9 per cent) in parliamentary elections on 19 November.

The incumbent prime minister, Gordon Darcy Lilo, was defeated in his electorate (voting district) after having served three terms in Parliament and three years as prime minister. On 9 December former prime minister Manasseh Sogavare (2000-01; 2006-07), representing the Democratic Coalition for Change, was elected prime minister.

Following 12 April legislative assembly elections Toke Talagi was re-elected **Niue**'s premier. The **Cook Islands'** 9 July parliamentary elections left Henry Puna of the Cook Islands Party as prime minister, pending the results of recounts, electoral petitions and by-elections.

In March, Sonia Lagarde was elected the first woman mayor of **New Caledonia**'s capital, Nouméa. Following elections in May to the three provincial assemblies, Cynthia Ligeard was elected president but was forced to resign in December. On 31 December, the Congress re-elected the 11-member government but failed to elect a new president.

French Polynesia's President Gaston Flosse was removed from office on 5 September following the denial of his appeal against a 2013 conviction on corruption charges and the refusal of France's president to grant him a pardon. Edouard Fritch was elected president by the Assembly on 13 September. Flosse was also removed from his seat in the French Senate, on 17 September, just before his term was due to expire; his ruling Tahoeraa Huiraatira Party's candidates won the territory's two seats in the French Senate at the end of the month.

On 19 January **Nauru**'s president dismissed the country's resident magistrate and its chief justice. In May three opposition MPs were suspended from Parliament for comments critical of the government's actions, made to foreign news organisations, and a further two opposition MPs were suspended in June. The MPs' appeal against their suspensions was dismissed by the Supreme Court in December. In August a new chief justice and two other members were appointed to the Supreme Court, with Elizabeth Hamilton-White becoming the court's first woman member. In September Emma Garo was appointed resident magistrate, the first woman to hold this position.

Vanuatu's Parliament elected Joe Natuman prime minister on 15 May after the incumbent, Moana Carcasses, was defeated on a no-confidence motion. In September, Vanuatu's electoral college chose Father Baldwin Lonsdale, a priest in the Anglican Church, as the country's eighth president. On 25 November, following allegations that Carcasses was providing funds to MPs to gain their support for a further no-confidence vote, Parliament voted to suspend him and 15 other MPs for alleged bribery; the Supreme Court ruled the suspensions invalid a week later.

In February the nomination of Jamil al-Sayyed as the **Marshall Islands'** ambassador to UNESCO was withdrawn, following disclosure that the former head of Lebanon's security services had spent four years in prison (2005-09) on suspicion of involvement in the 2005 assassination of Lebanon's prime minister, Rafik Hariri.

Incumbent governors and delegates to the US House of Representatives won November's elections in the **Commonwealth of the Northern Mariana Islands (CNMI)** and **Guam**. However, in **American Samoa** Aumua Amata Radewagen defeated the incumbent to become the territory's first woman delegate to the US House of Representatives. In local ballot initiatives, CNMI voters amended the constitution to allow land ownership by US citizens with "at least some degree" of Chamorro or Carolinian descent, rather than the previous stipulation of 25 per cent; Guam's electors voted to legalise marijuana for medical purposes.

Shooting incidents took place intermittently in **West Papua** involving Indonesian soldiers and insurgents. Political prisoners released from prison in July and August included Forkorus Yaboisembut, president of the organisation calling itself the Federal Republic of West Papua, who had been arrested in 2011, and Victor Yeimo, chairman of the National Committee for West Papua, jailed in May 2013.

Pacific island states' involvements in international affairs continued to span a wide range of issues.

In May Nauru lodged an application to join the International Monetary Fund, seeking to become the organisation's 189th member. The cost of journalists' visa applications to Nauru was substantially increased following negative coverage about asylum seekers sent to the island by Australia. In May asylum seekers who had been granted refugee visas began to be released from detention. In June the first asylum seekers convicted of rioting in 2013 at the Nauru detention centre were sentenced and received prison sentences. Protests resumed in September following Cambodia's decision to accept refugees from Nauru in return for Australian financial aid.

In January Samoa legislated to declare Samoan the country's official language (in addition to English). Samoa hosted the Third International Conference on Small Island Developing States from 1-4 September—the largest international meeting ever held in the country—on the theme of "Island Voices, Global Choices". The conference urged action on a range of issues, including climate change, sustainable energy, food security and health.

On 5 March Niue ratified the Comprehensive Nuclear-Test-Ban Treaty, becoming the 162nd country (and the 12th Pacific Islands Forum member) to do so. On 1 May Tonga's marines returned from Afghanistan following their seventh (and final) tour of duty. In June, Samoa ratified the Arms Trade Treaty (adopted in 2013), being the first Pacific Island country to do so. On 28 August, 45 Fijian soldiers serving as part of a UN peacekeeping mission on the Golan Heights were taken hostage by an al-Qaida-linked rebel group, the Al-Nusra Front, on the Syrian side of the Golan Heights. On 11 September the soldiers were released, crossing into the Israeli side.

In April, the Marshall Islands government initiated legal action against all nine nuclear-armed states for failing to pursue negotiations required by the 1968 Nuclear Non-Proliferation Treaty. The lawsuit demanded that talks begin towards a convention banning nuclear weapons. In November the French Polynesia assembly passed a resolution asking France for compensation for environmental damage caused by the nuclear weapons tests it had carried out between 1966 and 1996, and for its continued occupation of Fangataufa and Mururoa atolls, acquired by France for the tests.

Efforts continued towards increasing the energy independence of island states, and protecting ocean environments. In January an agreement was signed with the government of the United Arab Emirates for the construction of a solar grid system in Vanuatu's capital, Port Vila. In March a solar-powered desalination plant was opened in Palau. Construction was begun in September on solar powered energy projects, funded by New Zealand, in the Cook Islands and Tuvalu. In December the Pacific islands' largest solar array was completed in Samoa.

In February Palau's entire exclusive economic zone (EEZ) was declared a marine sanctuary and all commercial fishing within it banned. In June Kiribati announced that it would expand its Phoenix Islands protected area, and in September US President Barack Obama issued a proclamation expanding the Pacific Remote Islands Marine National Monument, established in January 2009, from 87,000 square miles to 490,000 square miles, banning commercial fishing and energy exploration within the protected area to create the world's largest marine sanctuary. In May Vanuatu's government protested to France over New Caledonia's marine reserve, the Natural Park of the Coral Sea—formally established in April covering New Caledonia's entire EEZ—because of its inclusion of the Matthew and Hunter Islands (claimed by both France and Vanuatu).

Tonga was the only Pacific country to compete in the 2014 Winter Olympics in Sochi. It did not win a medal (in the luge event). In July athletes from Pacific Island states belonging to the Commonwealth took part in the Commonwealth Games in Glasgow, David Katoatau's gold medal in weightlifting being the first medal to be won by a Kiribati athlete at a Commonwealth Games. Athletes from Fiji, Nauru and Samoa won silver and bronze medals.

Pacific leaders continued to raise concerns about global warming, describing climate change as a weapon of mass destruction. In September Marshall Islands' poet Kathy Jetnil-Kijiner, chosen to speak as the representative from civil society at the opening ceremony of the UN's one-day Climate Summit 2014, offered a poem ("Dear Matafele Peinem") written to her seven-month old daughter about the threat to small islands. The summit was told by Pacific representatives that island nations remained determined to survive but needed action to reverse global warming if they were to do so.

Stephen Levine

XI INTERNATIONAL ORGANISATIONS

UNITED NATIONS AND ITS AGENCIES

DATE OF FOUNDATION: 1945   HEADQUARTERS: New York, USA
OBJECTIVES: To promote international peace, security and co-operation on the basis of the equality
of member-states, the right of self-determination of peoples and respect for human rights
MEMBERSHIP (END-'14): 193 sovereign states
SECRETARY GENERAL: Ban Ki Moon (South Korea) (since Jan '07)

IN 2014 the United Nations had to grapple with new crises in Gaza and Ukraine; the Ebola virus epidemic; the ever-increasing spread of terrorist groups throughout the world, many with enhanced military capabilities and radical appeal; and the issue of how to improve protection for civilians in war zones.

INSTITUTIONAL DEVELOPMENTS: The theme of the General Debate at the 69th session of the **UN General Assembly**, which convened on 16 September, 2014, was "Delivering on and implementing a transformative post-2015 Development Agenda".

The Assembly, in the second part of the 68th and the first part of the 69th session, discussed in a range of formats: the revitalisation of the work of the General Assembly; the reform and strengthening of the Economic and Social Council; the effective functioning of the human rights treaty system; a mobility framework for United Nations staff; the responsibility to protect; human rights and the rule of law; conditions conducive to the spread of terrorism; the biennial review of Global Counter Terrorism Strategy; indigenous peoples; the state of racial discrimination; improving the coordination of efforts against the trafficking of people; the humanitarian situation in the Syrian Arab Republic; the sovereignty of Ukraine: declaring that the referendum in Crimea to join Russia was invalid and the annexation of Crimea illegal; the Ebola epidemic; climate change and many facets of the post-2015 development agenda.

Sam Kahamba Kutesa, the foreign minister of Uganda, was elected president of the 69th session of the General Assembly on 11 June. The General Assembly on 16-17 October elected Venezuela, New Zealand, Spain, Angola and Malaysia as new **non-permanent members of the Security Council** for two-year terms, beginning on 1 January, 2015. All were elected on the first ballot, bar Spain, which needed three rounds of voting to defeat Turkey. The new members would replace Argentina, Australia, Luxembourg, South Korea and Rwanda.

The **UN Security Council** held 263 meetings: 241 public and 22 private, and 167 consultations. It adopted 63 resolutions (all but three being unanimous), two of which—on Ebola, and terrorist acts—attracted the largest number of co-sponsors (134 and 104, respectively) in the history of the Council.

Two draft resolutions were vetoed: the first, concerning Ukraine, by the Russian Federation, with China abstaining, on 15 March; the second, on Syria, by China and the Russian Federation on 22 May; and a draft resolution on the Middle East, including the Palestine question, failed to be adopted on 30 December because it received only eight votes—nine were needed (in the absence of a veto)—with two against and five abstentions.

The Council issued 28 presidential and 138 press statements. It created a new peacekeeping force and a new sanctions regime. It terminated three United Nations political missions and the joint OPCW-UN (Organisation for the Prohibition of Chemical Weapons-UN) mission in Syria. The Council despatched two visiting missions: to Mali on 1-3 February; and to Belgium, the Netherlands, South Sudan and Somalia on 8-14 August. These reported on 26 February and 19 August, respectively.

EBOLA: The Council on 18 September held its first-ever emergency meeting on a health issue: the **Ebola epidemic**. It wanted to draw attention to the urgency of the crisis: the speed of the spread of the virus; the scale of the loss of lives; and the economic, social, humanitarian, political and security consequences for the three most affected West African states of Liberia, Sierra Leone and Guinea. It also wanted to prevent the isolation of these three states and to galvanise the greatest possible co-ordinated, international response.

During the meeting, the secretary general, who had already appointed his own special envoy for Ebola, announced that he would establish the UN Mission for Ebola Emergency Response (UNMEER), which would have five priorities: stopping the outbreak, treating the infected, ensuring essential services, preserving stability and preventing further outbreaks.

The Council adopted Resolution 2177(2014), determining that the unprecedented extent of the Ebola outbreak in Africa constituted a threat to international peace and security. The Council on 14 October received a briefing from officials and representatives from the affected states, who expressed concern that the international aid which had been offered was insufficient to stop the spread of the disease. The Council held a further debate on 21 November and issued a Presidential Statement (S/PRST/2014/24), reiterating the need for continued efforts against the disease.

TERRORISM: The Council held seven meetings, including one at head of state level; approved six Resolutions (2133; 2160; 2161; 2170; 2178; 2195) and two presidential statements (S/PRST/2014/14 and S/PRST/2014/23) as it sought, and assessed the efficacy of, countermeasures against the evolving multifaceted threat posed by terrorist entities associated with **al-Qaida** in Somalia, Yemen and states in the Maghreb and Sahel regions and, in particular, the **Islamic State in Iraq and Syria (ISIS)** (also known as ISIL), and the **al-Nusra Front**. These were engaging in a brutal military campaign initially to establish a "caliphate" in Syria and Iraq.

The main thrust of these resolutions and presidential statements was that the Council first condemned ISIS and the al-Nusra for the recruitment of foreign terrorist fighters, whose presence was exacerbating conflict and contributing to violent radicalism. Then it encouraged states to identify and propose additional foreign fighters and recruiters for possible designation by sanctions committees 1267 and 1989, concerning al-Qaida and associated individuals. The Council was considering listing any individual or entity associated with al-Qaida and supporting them, including through the Internet, social media or any other means.

The Council also asked states to share information in order to identify foreign terrorist fighters and to understand their patterns of travel, including evasive travel routes. It asked states to share practices in evidence-based traveller risk assessment and border screening, in order to fulfil their obligation of preventing the movement of terrorist groups, particularly those benefiting from transnational crime. It also urged states to persuade citizens at risk of being recruited not to travel to Iraq and Syria; to have laws that permitted prosecution of their nationals who attempted to travel for terrorist purposes; and to develop effective counter-narratives to the terrorists' violent extremist propaganda and incitement on the Internet and social media.

The Council sought to disrupt the financial flows to terrorists, reminding states that their nationals were not to finance or engage directly or indirectly in trade in oil and oil products derived from oilfields and pipelines in Syria and Iraq controlled by ISIS; that their nationals were not to donate to ISIS and al-Nusra; that members should take appropriate measures to prevent the trade in items of archaeological, historical, cultural and religious importance which had been illegally removed from territory controlled by ISIS and al-Nusra; and that states should secure the safe release of hostages without paying ransoms and without making political concessions.

The Chair of the 1373 Counter-Terrorism Committee, at the request of the Council, analysed the principal gaps in states' abilities to stem the flow of foreign terrorist fighters and which would have to be rectified if the flows were to be stemmed. Areas of concern included the legal and judicial frameworks, law enforcement and border controls; countering the financing of terrorist movements; combating violent extremism; and complying with human rights obligations and the rule of law.

SYRIA: The Security Council discussed four elements of the continuing horrific civil war in **Syria**: a political solution, humanitarian assistance, international law, and chemical weapons.

Any hope that a political solution would be achieved through the Geneva Conference talks (Geneva 2), held in Montreux and Geneva on 22-31 January and 10-15 February, quickly evaporated. Lakhdar Brahimi, the joint special representative of the UN and the Arab League, reported that he achieved his aim in the first round—keeping the government and opposition delegations in the room. But there was no political dialogue: the government representatives wanted to talk about terrorism; the opposition was focused on the main provision of the 2012 Geneva Communiqué: the formation of a transitional government to replace the administration of President Bashar Assad.

On 10 February the meetings resumed with an agenda prepared by Brahimi. The points for discussion comprised: (i) ending violence and fighting terrorism; (ii) the transitional governing body; (iii) national reconciliation and national dialogue; and (iv) national institutions between continuity and change. Brahimi wanted the first two items to be discussed in parallel, which was acceptable to the opposition but not to the government delegation. This delegation demanded that the agenda be discussed in succession and that terrorism had to be discussed before common ground could be achieved. Brahimi believed that the government delegation's demands were simply delaying tactics, that discussions were futile. He therefore ended the talks, invited both parties to reflect on how the Geneva process could achieve momentum, and said that a further round should take place only if there was a genuine political will to negotiate. He also believed that the forthcoming Syrian presidential election in June would prevent negotiations for the foreseeable future. Brahimi resigned on 31 May. His successor—but only as special representative of the UN, and not the Arab League—was Staffan de Mistura, a veteran United Nations official who was appointed on 10 July. No further discussions took place. The special representative therefore sought to reduce violence against civilians in the urban areas by seeking agreements on freezing the fighting.

The monthly reports of the under-secretary general for humanitarian affairs on the suffering of civilians caused by indiscriminate bombing and shelling, siege tactics, the denial of food and medicine, and the obstruction of the few aid convoys permitted indicated that the parties to the conflict—particularly the Syrian government—were not heeding the terms of the presidential statement of 2 October, 2013 (S/PRST/2013/15). The Council, therefore, on 22 February in Resolution 2139(2014) demanded that all parties promptly allow rapid, safe and unhindered access for United Nations agencies, including across conflict lines and across borders, to ensure that humanitarian assistance reached people in need by the most direct routes throughout Syria. When the secretary general, who had been asked to report every 30 days on the implementation of the resolution, stated that the steps that had been taken by the parties had not had the desired effect, the Council on 14 July in Resolution 2165(2014) authorised access without state consent. Access to Syria would be through four border crossings, where a UN mechanism would monitor that the convoys were humanitarian and would inform the Syrian authorities. These provisions, which would have lapsed after 180 days, were renewed by Resolution 2191(2014) on 17 December until 10 January 2016

On 22 May China and the Russian Federation vetoed a draft resolution, sponsored by 65 states. This would have referred the widespread violations of human rights and international humanitarian law by the Syrian government and its militias, and by non-state armed groups in Syria since March 2011, to the prosecutor of the International Criminal Court.

The Council received monthly briefings from the special coordinator for the joint mission of OPCW-UN, Sigrid Kaag, on the implementation of Resolution 2118 (2013)—the destruction of Syria's *declared* chemical weapons programme. Although Syria failed to meet the 30 June deadline, the special coordinator was able to report on 4 September that—despite amendments to the original declaration, government obstruction and delays, and the difficult security situation—96 per cent of Syria's *declared* chemical weapons stockpile had been destroyed.

Although the mission would end on 30 September, she would continue to brief the Council on residual issues. The successor mission from the OPCW would monitor verification, discuss possible discrepancies in the original declaration, oversee the destruction of 12 chemical production facilities, and a fact-finding team would investigate the possible use of chlorine gas as a chemical weapon.

ISRAEL/PALESTINE: **Israel** conducted a 50-day air, ground and naval military campaign against Gaza in retaliation for the firing of rockets from **Palestine** into southern Israel and to destroy the tunnel system and the military infrastructure of the Palestinian movement, Hamas. It was estimated by the United Nations that 2,205 Palestinians were killed and 18,000 housing units destroyed, leaving 108,000 Palestinians homeless. It estimated that 71 Israelis were killed.

The Council met on six occasions in July and once in August, including emergency and urgent meetings to receive secretariat briefings in New York and from the field on the evolving crisis. The Council—constrained by the threat of a US veto if any substantive criticism was made of Israel—had to express what degree of agreement it could reach through partial statements to the press, full press statements and one presidential statement (S/PRST/2014/13). The central elements of these were: grave concern at the loss of civilian lives and casualties; welcoming the efforts of international partners to improve the humanitarian situation and of Egypt to secure a long-term ceasefire; the need to respect international humanitarian law, including the protection of civilians and of United Nations and other humanitarian facilities; and the need to return to negotiations (the US-brokered talks having collapsed in April) with the aim of a two-state solution and a permanent peace.

In September the United Nations helped to negotiate with the governments of Palestine and Israel the "Gaza Reconstruction Mechanism". This was intended to allow large-scale reconstruction to take place in Gaza, whilst meeting Israeli security concerns about the use of construction and other "dual use" material.

UKRAINE: The Security Council between February and December held 27 public and private meetings on **Ukraine**—the largest number devoted to any item on its agenda. This was a reflection of the importance of the issue. How could the Council respond to the behaviour of **Russia**, a permanent member, who, in response to a change of government in Kiev, flouted the principles of the Charter and of international law: first by annexing part of the territory of Ukraine on 18 March; then by providing unacknowledged assistance of soldiers, matériel and leadership in April and May to armed pro-Russian separatists in the Donbas region of eastern Ukraine; and later in the year by markedly increasing such assistance, to repel Ukrainian armed forces whenever they appeared to be retaking territory.

From the outset members of the Council sought a diplomatic solution to the crisis in **Crimea**; the secretary general was encouraged to use his good offices to the full, including sending envoys to Ukraine and seeking a coordinated international response to maintain a united and stable Ukraine. On 15 March a draft Resolution was introduced, which was intended to prevent further escalation, to uphold the sovereignty, unity and territorial integrity of Ukraine, to reaffirm core United Nations principles about the non-use of force in international relations, and to confirm that any referendum held in Crimea would have no validity. Russia was forced to veto the draft (China abstained), which indicated the degree of its international isolation.

Although there was now a sharp difference within the Council, the majority of members were able to use meetings to persuade Ukraine to address the concerns of its Russian-speaking citizens, particularly in eastern Ukraine; to support the Secretariat's watching brief, with its regular updating of the changing issues; to encourage the range of diplomatic efforts to reach agreement between the parties; to hold the parties to the international commitments that they had made, particularly the Minsk Protocol; to sustain the role of the OSCE mission which provided impartial information on men and matériel moving across even the small part of the Ukraine-Russia border that it was allowed to monitor in eastern Ukraine; and to draw attention to any restriction on the monitors' freedom of movement and their area of operation, threats to their security, and interference with their aerial reconnaissance equipment.

The shooting down on 17 July of Malaysia Airlines Flight MH17 over territory controlled by separatists induced the Council to adopt unanimously Resolution 2166(2014) on 21 July. This demanded accountability, full access to the site and a halt to military activities in the area. Although initial investigations showed that the plane was hit by "high energy objects", responsibility was disputed.

PEACEKEEPING: The Council did not respond to a request from **Libya** for a stabilisation force. Presumably, this was because it would be difficult to establish a mandate, given the internal political and military turmoil; and because it was difficult to know what troops might be available and whether the force might be attacked from within by militias, or from without by terrorists and criminals seeping through Libya's porous borders.

On 10 April the Council established the United Nations Multidimensional Integrated Stabilisation Mission in the **Central African Republic** (MINUSCA) for one year with an authorised strength of 10,000 military and 1,800 police. The protection of civilians would be its top priority. The transfer of authority from the African Union-led MISCA to MINUSCA took place on 15 September. There were shortfalls in the deployment of MINUSCA: it was not expected to achieve 80 per cent of its authorised troop level until December, nor would it have 90 per cent of its formed police units before January 2015. The transport of equipment to the mission was delayed by poor infrastructure and an absence of competent contractors.

The Council reviewed and where necessary adjusted the size and the mandate of a number of missions. The secretary general prepared a strategic assessment, which identified three major constraints on the ability of UNAMID to achieve its mandate in the changing conditions in **Darfur**. These included the lack of co-operation by the government, major shortfalls in the capabilities of several troop and police contingents, and deficiencies in co-ordination within the mission and between the mission and the United Nations country team. The Council, in Resolutions 2148(2014) of 3 April and 2173(2014) of 27 August, decided that the mission should be streamlined by withdrawing 355 troops and 1,287 police; that it should concentrate only on its core roles: protection of civilians, humanitarian assistance and supporting the peace process; and that any other tasks not related to these should be discontinued.

On 27 May, in Resolution 2155(2014), the Council revised the mandate of UNMISS to enable it better to address the changing political, security, humanitarian and human rights elements of the predominately inter-ethnic civil war in **South Sudan**. The Council decided that, as in Darfur, the mission should concentrate upon core roles. These comprised the protection of civilians—the force was already protecting upwards of 85,000 displaced civilians on its bases with the attendant external and internal security problems, ethnic tension and health issues; monitoring and investigating human rights; facilitating the delivery of humanitarian assistance; and supporting the agreement for the cessation of hostilities. The mission would no longer engage in state-building activities. But, unlike in Darfur, the authorised troop and police levels remained the same: 12,500 troops and 1,323 police, which, however, had yet to be reached.

The mandate in **Mali** was reviewed, rather unusually, in an informal interactive dialogue on 10 November between members of the Council and the secretariat. There was serious concern about the number of casualties that the mission had suffered in the north of Mali, where the number of French troops had been reduced and the Malian armed forces withdrawn, after convoys, personnel and bases had been subject to a range of attacks from armed groups with links to terrorists and criminals. The Council members called for continued bilateral training and equipping of MINUSMA contingents. (The USA, for example, had offered to share its knowledge, gleaned from its military campaign in Afghanistan, on countermeasures against improvised explosive devices.) The Council also called for the secretariat to enhance the capabilities of the mission and to take all steps needed to implement the mission's existing robust mandate.

In a presidential statement of 5 November, the Council called for MONUSCO (the UN mission in the **Democratic Republic of Congo**), including the intervention brigade and the Congolese armed forces, to prepare immediately for military action. The FDLR (Democratic Forces for the Liberation of Rwanda) and other armed groups had failed to disarm and continued to violate human rights in eastern Congo; the secretariat had also given permission for MONSUCO to act unilaterally, if necessary.

MINURSO, the mission for the referendum in **Western Sahara**, had its authorised strength increased by 15 troops. Two peacekeeping operations had reductions: MINUSTAH, in **Haiti**, by 2,651 troops and UNOCI, in **Côte d'Ivoire**, by 1,700 troops, partly to ensure that governments took responsibility for security, partly to reduce costs, and partly to release resources for possible use elsewhere. The proposed reduction for the force in **Liberia** (UNMIL) was postponed because of the Ebola epidemic.

There was an important Peacekeeping Summit on the fringes of the General Assembly, where commitments were made by member states to increase the number of suitably trained and equipped military personnel available for peacekeeping.

The secretary general appointed a high level panel on UN peace operations to consider how these activities should adapt to new demands and what capabilities and resources were needed for adaption. On 20 November, the Security Council held an informal interactive dialogue with the chair of the panel, José Ramos Horta. The Council members presented a range of priorities to the panel for consideration including whether peacekeeping principles needed to be revised to accommodate new operating environments where there was often no peace to keep; the need for high quality planning by the secretariat; the provision of clear and achievable objectives in the mandates; the rapid deployment of trained and equipped personnel, especially in crisis situations; the elimination of dual command systems; the enhancement of military capabilities to help peacekeepers achieve the central feature of many missions—the protection of civilians; the need to use force in defence of the mandate; the establishment of performance and accountability standards, especially in robust operations; and the improvement of relations with regional organisations.

ECONOMIC SANCTIONS: The Council established one new sanctions regime: a travel and asset freeze against any individual or entity whose actions threaten the peace and security of **Yemen**. (This brought the number of sanctions regimes to 15—the highest in the history of the United Nations.) The Council also authorised marine interdiction against vessels believed to be violating the arms and charcoal sanctions against **Somalia** and against shipping believed to be transporting illicit oil from **Libya**. It expanded the sanctions against the **Central African Republic** to include a travel ban and assets freeze; it eased the sanctions against **Côte d'Ivoire** and Somalia by partially lifting the arms embargos and by removing the ban on the sale of Côte d'Ivoire rough diamonds; and it decided that it would keep sanctions against **Liberia** under continuous review, and would take into account, when deciding whether to modify or lift the measures, the threat posed by the Ebola virus. In an attempt to increase transparency, chairmen of sanctions committees briefed in public, rather than in private, meetings of the Council on the reports of their panels of experts.

The Council discussed for the first time since 2006 how it might improve the design, implementation and evaluation of sanctions. This had been encouraged by a high level review, sponsored by the governments of Australia, Sweden, Greece, Finland and Germany, which in turn had prompted a report by the United Nations interagency working group on sanctions. The findings of both informed the debate. Members of the Council, however, were unable to reach a consensus on a resolution.

MILITARY FORCES: The Council authorised mandates for the European Union operation in the **Central African Republic** until 15 March 2015; the French forces in support of MINUSCA until 30 April 2015; for the French forces in **Côte d'Ivoire** and in **Mali** until 30 June 2015; for AMISOM in **Somalia** until 24 October 2015; for maritime interdiction of charcoal and arms to prevent violations of sanctions against Somalia until 24 October 2015; for states and regional organisation combating piracy and armed robbery at sea off the coast of Somalia until 12 November 2015; and for EUFOR ALTHEA in **Bosnia** until 11 November 2015.

Finally, the Council welcomed the agreement between NATO and the Afghan government to replace from 1 January 2015 the International Security Assistance Force (ISAF) with a new NATO-led mission, "Resolute Support"—which was non-combat—to train and assist the national security forces of **Afghanistan**.

David Travers

UNITED NATIONS PEACEKEEPING MISSIONS 2014

MISSION	Established	Present Strength	Renewal Date
UNTSO: United Nations Truce Supervision Organisation	May 1948	155 military observers; 86 international civilians; 135 local civilians. Total personnel: 376. Fatalities: 50. Budget: $74,291,900 (2014-15)	
UNMOGIP: United Nations Military Observer Group in India and Pakistan	January 1949	43 military observers; 22 international civilians; 47 local civilians. Total personnel: 112. Fatalities: 11. Budget: $19,647,100 (2014-15)	
UNFICYP: United Nations Peacekeeping Force in Cyprus	March 1964	858 military; 66 civilian police; 37 international civilians; 111 local civilians. Total personnel: 1,072. Fatalities:182. Budget: $ 59,072,800, including voluntary contributions of one-third from Cyprus and $6.5 million from Greece	31 January 2015
UNDOF: United Nations Disengagement Observer Force	June 1974	930 military; 53 international civilians; 107 local civilians. Total personnel: 1,090. Fatalities: 46. Budget: $48,019,000	30 June 2015
UNIFIL: United Nations Interim Force in Lebanon	March 1978	10,238 military; 282 international civilians; 603 local civilians. Total personnel: 11,123. Fatalities: 307. Budget: $509,554,400	31 August 2015
MINURSO: United Nations Mission for the Referendum in Western Sahara	April 1991	26 military; 194 military observers; 5 civilian police; 88 international civilians; 164 local civilians; 12 UN volunteers. Total personnel: 489. Fatalities: 15. Budget: $55,990,080	30 April 2015
UNMIK: United Nations Interim Administration Mission in Kosovo	June 1999	8 military observers; 8 civilian police; 113 international civilians; 211 local civilians; 26 UN volunteers. Total personnel: 366. Fatalities:55. Budget: $42,971,600	Established for an initial period of 12 months; to continue unless the Security Council decides otherwise

UNITED NATIONS PEACEKEEPING MISSIONS 2014 *continued*

MISSION	Established	Present Strength	Renewal Date
UNMIL: United Nations Mission in Liberia	September 2003	4,308 military; 113 military observers; 1,417 civilian police; 397 international civilians; 856 local civilians; 194 UN volunteers. Total personnel: 7,285. Fatalities: 189. Budget: $427,319,800	30 September 2015
UNOCI: United Nations Operation in Côte d'Ivoire	April 2004	6,086 military; 180 military observers; 1,367 civilian police; 337 international civilians; 698 local civilians; 153 UN volunteers. Total personnel: 8,821. Fatalities: 120. Budget: $493,570,300	30 June 2015
MINUSTAH: United Nations Stabilisation Mission in Haiti	June 2004	4,957 military; 2,256 civilian police; 344 international civilians; 1,169 local civilians; 129 UN volunteers. Total personnel: 8,855. Fatalities: 176. Budget: $500,080,500	15 October 2015
UNAMID: African Union/ United Nations Hybrid Operation in Darfur	July 2007	12,614 military; 220 military observers; 3,035 civilian police; 1,005 international civilians; 2,891 local civilians; 295 UN volunteers. Total personnel: 20,060. Fatalities: 212. Budget: $639,654,200 (1 July—31 December 2014)	30 June 2015
MONUSCO: United Nations Organisation Stabilisation Mission in the Democratic Republic of the Congo	July 2010	19,463 military; 490 military observers; 1,083 civilian police; 920 international civilians; 2,751 local civilians; 465 UN volunteers. Total personnel: 25,172. Fatalities: 85. Budget: $1,398,475,300	31 March 2015
UNISFA: United Nations Interim Security Forcei for Abye	June 2011	3,946 military; 97 military observers; 23 civilian police; 120 international civilians; 72 local civilians; 22 UN volunteers. Total personnel: 4,280. Fatalities: 17. Budget: $318,925,200	28 February 2015

UNITED NATIONS PEACEKEEPING MISSIONS 2014 *continued*

MISSION	Established	Present Strength	Renewal Date
UNMISS: United Nations Mission in the Republic of South Sudan	July 2011	10,251 military; 164 military observers; 1,018 civilian police; 834 international civilians; 1,372 local civilians; 411 UN volunteers. Total personnel: 14,050. Fatalities: 32. Budget: $580,830,4000 (1 July—31 December 2014)	30 May 2015
MINUSMA: United Nations Multidimensional Integrated Stabilisation Mission in Mali	March 2013	8,461 military; 1,033 civilian police; 513 international civilians; 469 local civilians; 119 UN volunteers. Total personnel: 10,595. Fatalities: 44. Budget: $830,701,700	30 June 2015
MINUSCA: United Nations Multidimensional Integrated Stabilisation Mission the Central African Republic	April 2014	7,469 military; 91 military observers; 1,125 civilian police; 174 international civilians; 106 local civilians; 18 UN volunteers. Total personnel: 8,983. Fatalities: 2. Budget: $253,424,400 (1 July—31 December 2014)	30 April 2015

NOTES.

Number of peacekeeping operation since 1948   69

Current Peacekeeping Operations   16

Total number of personnel serving in the 16 peacekeeping operations   122,729

Total number of fatalities in all UN peace operations

(includes peacekeeping operations, political and peacebuilding missions) since 1948   3,315

Different Categories of personnel serving in the 16 peacekeeping missions as of 31 December 2014:

Military troops, observers and civilian police   103,798 (89,607 troops; 12,436 civilian police; 1,755 military observers)

Countries contributing uniformed personnel   122

International civilian (30 September 2014)   5,325

Local civilian (30 September 2014)   11,762

UN volunteers   1,844

Approved budgets for the period 1 July 2014 to 30 June 2015: about $7.06 billion.

(This figure includes funds for the United Nations Support Office for the AU Mission in Somalia (UNSOA), the support account for peacekeeping operations and the United Nations Logistics Base in Brindisi in Italy.)

Outstanding contributions to peacekeeping as of 31 December 2014: about $1,28 billion

UNTSO and UNMOGIP are funded from the United Nations regular biennial budget. The costs to the United Nations of the 14 other current peacekeeping operations are financed from their own separate accounts on the basis of legal binding assessments on all Member States. For these missions budget figures are for one year July 2014 to June 2015 unless otherwise specified.

(Sources: United Nations Background note 31 December 2014; United Nations current peacekeeping operations website and United Nations press releases.)

UNITED NATIONS POLITICAL AND PEACEBUILDING MISSIONS 2014

MISSION	Established	Present Strength	Current Authorisation
UNSCO: Office of the United Nations Special Coordinator for the Middle East	1 October 1999	Special Coordinator for the Middle East Peace Process and / Personal Representative of the Secretary General to the Palestine Liberation Organisation and the Palestinian Authority: Robert H. Serry (Netherlands). 28 international civilians; 30 local civilians	
UNOWA: Office of the Special Representative of the Secretary General for West Africa	29 November 2001	Special Representative of the Secretary General: Said Djinnit (Algeria). 22 international civilians;19 local civilians; 3 military advisers	31 December 2016
UNAMA: United Nations Assistance Mission in Afghanistan	28 March 2002	Special Representative of the Secretary General: Nicholas Haysom (South Africa). 336 international civilians; 1,154 local civilians; 14 military advisers; 2 civilian police; 69 UN volunteers	15 October 2015
UNAMI: United Nations Assistance Mission for Iraq	14 August 2003	Special Representative of the Secretary General for Iraq: Nickolay Mladenov (Bulgaria). Staff are based in Iraq, Jordan and Kuwait. 349 international civilians; 474 local civilians; 270 military; 2 civilian police	31 July 2015
UNSCOL: Office of the United Nations Special Coordinator for Lebanon	16 February 2007	Special Coordinator for Lebanon: Derek Plumbly (UK). 18 international civilians; 57 local civilians	
UNRCCA: United Nations Regional Centre for Preventive Diplomacy for Central Asia	10 December 2007	Special Representative of the Secretary General: Miroslav Jenca (Slovakia). 7 international civilians; 2 local civilians	

UNITED NATIONS POLITICAL AND PEACEBUILDING MISSIONS 2014 *continued*

MISSION	Established	Present Strength	Current Authorisation
UNIOGBIS: United Nations Integrated Peacebuilding Office in Guinea-Bissau	1 January 2010	Special Representative of the Secretary General: Miguel Trovoada (São Tomé and Príncipe). 48 international civilians; 57 local civilians; 2 military advisers; 13 civilian police; 6 UN volunteers	28 February 2015
BNUB: United Nations Office in Burundi	1 January 2011	Special Representative of the Secretary General: Parfait Onanga-Anyanga (Gabon). 43 international civilians; 59 local ivilians; 1 military adviser; 1 civilian police; 3 UN volunteers	31 December 2014. (to be replaced by UN electoral mission when mandate terminated)
UNOCA: United Nations Regional Office for Central Africa	1 January 2011	Special Representative of the Secretary General: Abdoulaye Bathily (Senegal). 14 international civilians; 8 local civilians; 1 military adviser	31 August 2015
UNSMIL: United Nations Support Mission in Libya	16 September 2011	Special Representative of the Secretary General: Bernardino Leon (Spain). 150 international civilians; 77 local civilians; 4 civilian police; 3 UN volunteers	13 March 2015
UNSOM: United Nations Assistance Mission in Somalia	3 June 2013	Special Representative of the Secretary General: Nicholas Kay (UK). 58 international civilians; 21 local civilians; 5 military advisers; 3 civilian police; 7 UN volunteers	28 May 2015

NOTES:

Missions completed in 2014:

UNIPSIL: United Nations Integrated Peacebuilding Office in Sierra Leone: 1 October 2008 to 31 March 2014.

BINUCA: United Nations Integrated Peacebuilding Office in Central African Republic. 1 January 2010 to 10 April 2014.

Number of Missions: 11

Personnel:

Uniformed personnel	321
International civilian personnel (31 July 2014)	1,073
Local civilian personnel (31 July 2014)	1,958
United Nations volunteers	88
Total number of personnel serving in political and peacebuilding missions:	3,440

(UNAMA in Afghanistan is directed and supported by the Department of Peacekeeping Operations.)

Sources: United Nations Political and Peacebuilding Missions Fact Sheet 31 August 2014; United Nations resolutions, press releases and websites of individual departments and missions.

CURRENT UNITED NATIONS SANCTIONS REGIMES 2014

Sanctions Regime	Arms	Travel	Asset	Commodities	Natural Resources	Sanctions Committee: Current Authorization	Expert Panel: Current Authorization	Notes
751 (1992) and 1907 (2009) Committee concerning **Somalia** and **Eritrea**	X	X	X	X: charcoal		30 October 2015	30 November 2015	Commodity interdiction permitted
1267 (1999) and 1989 (2011) Committee concerning **Al Qaida** and associated individuals and entities wherever located	X	X	X				17 December 2017	The Office of the Ombudsperson which assists the committee in considering de-listing requests had its mandate extended until 17 December 2017
1518 (2003) Committee concerning **Iraq**	X		X					
1521 (2003) Committee concerning **Liberia**	X	X	X			9 September 2015	9 October 2015	
1533 (2004) Committee concerning the **Democratic Republic of the Congo**	X	X	X		gold, wildlife products	1 February 2015	1 February 2015	

CURRENT UNITED NATIONS SANCTIONS REGIMES 2014 *continued*

Sanctions Regime	Arms	Travel	Asset	Commodities	Natural Resources	Sanctions Committee: Current Authorization	Expert Panel: Current Authorization	Notes
1572 (2004) Committee concerning **Côte d'Ivoire**	X	X	X			30 April 2015	30 May 2015	
1591 (2005) Committee concerning the **Sudan**	X	X	X				13 March 2015	
1636 (2005) Committee concerning **Lebanon**		X	X				Special Tribunal for Lebanon	
1718 (2006) Committee concerning the **Democratic People's Republic of Korea**	X	X	X	Items, Materials, Equipment, Goods and technology related to nuclear ballistic missile and other weapons of mass destruction programmes. Luxury Goods to DPRK			5 April 2015	Commodity interdiction permitted

CURRENT UNITED NATIONS SANCTIONS REGIMES 2014 *continued*

Sanctions Regime	Arms	Travel	Asset	Commodities	Natural Resources	Sanctions Committee: Current Authorization	Expert Panel: Current Authorization	Notes
1937 (2006) Committee concerning the Islamic Republic of **Iran**	X	X	X	Any item or financial service that could contribute to Iran's nuclear proliferation activities or the development of nuclear weapon delivery systems			9 July 2015	
1970 (2011) Committee concerning **Libya**	X	X	X	Any attempt illicitly to export crude oil			13 April 2015	Member states permitted to inspect on the high seas vessels attempting illicitly to export crude oil from Libya.
1988 (2011) Committee concerning any individual, group, undertaking and entity designated as or associated with the **Taliban** in **Afghanistan**	X	X	X				17 December 2017	

CURRENT UNITED NATIONS SANCTIONS REGIMES 2014 *continued*

Sanctions Regime	Arms	Travel	Asset	Commodities	Natural Resources	Sanctions Committee: Current Authorization	Expert Panel: Current Authorization	Notes
2048 (2012) Committee concerning **Guinea-Bissau**		X						
2127 (2013) Committee concerning the **Central African Republic**	X	X	X			28 January 2015	28 January 2015	
2140 (2014) Committee concerning **Yemen**		X	X			26 February 2015	26 March 2015	

NORTH ATLANTIC TREATY ORGANISATION (NATO)

DATE OF FOUNDATION: 1949   HEADQUARTERS: Brussels, Belgium
OBJECTIVES: To ensure the collective security of member states
MEMBERSHIP (END-'14): Albania, Belgium, Bulgaria, Canada, Croatia, Czech Republic, Denmark,
   Estonia, France, Germany, Greece, Hungary, Iceland, Italy, Latvia, Lithuania, Luxembourg,
   Netherlands, Norway, Poland, Portugal, Romania, Slovakia, Slovenia, Spain, Turkey, UK, USA
   (total 28)
SECRETARY GENERAL: Jens Stoltenberg (Norway) (since Oct '14)

IN late February 2014, in the aftermath of the Ukrainian revolution, pro-Russian protests in Crimea led to Russian forces and their proxies occupying strategically important areas of the Crimean peninsula. In March a referendum provided the questionable rationale for Russia's annexation of Crimea. Pro-Russian demonstrations in the Donbas region of eastern Ukraine also prompted covert Russian intervention. By late 2014 several thousand Russian troops were deployed inside Ukraine with many more poised on the Russian side of the border (see the article on Ukraine in this volume).

The challenge to the European order was stark: contrary to decades of expectation, European borders had been changed by armed force. The challenge to NATO was especially vivid. Although the West had, arguably, misunderstood and mishandled Russia since the end of the Cold War, and although Ukraine was not a member of the Alliance, Russia's readiness to use armed force against its neighbour called NATO's credibility into question. NATO had reinvented itself since the end of the Cold War as the sponsor of strategic stability in Europe, working with former adversaries. This claim no longer carried much weight. Russia made use of so-called "new generation warfare"—a combination of civil action and intimidation with the deniable use of conventional military forces, all orchestrated by a strategic communication campaign drawing heavily on the high-minded rhetoric of democratisation and humanitarian intervention. Actions in Crimea and eastern Ukraine seemed to leave NATO with little, if anything to say or do; the Alliance's bluff had been called.

Although some saw in these events the beginning of a "new Cold War", NATO's response was more cautious. Alliance air forces flew surveillance missions to monitor Russian military activity and an "air policing" operation was launched over Estonia, Latvia and Lithuania. Naval vessels were deployed to the Baltic and the Mediterranean and military exercises took place in northern and central Europe.

Events in Ukraine also focused attention on NATO's 2014 summit meeting. Scheduled for early September in Newport, Wales, the summit had been intended to review the Alliance's involvement in (and departure from) Afghanistan. Unsure as to the value of the exercise, some NATO officials had taken to describing the event as "the unnecessary summit". In what would prove to be an excess of expectation, others saw the summit as NATO's most significant meeting since the breach of the Berlin Wall in November 1989.

Several declarations were made at Newport, and several initiatives launched. At the suggestion of the UK, the Alliance adopted an "Armed Forces Declaration"—

a military covenant for the Alliance, setting out the proper relationship between societies and their armed forces. A "Declaration on the Transatlantic Bond" was unequivocal about "Russia's illegal, self-declared 'annexation' of Crimea and Russia's continued aggressive acts in other parts of Ukraine." A "Readiness Action Plan" would improve NATO's preparedness and readiness, and Alliance leaders also pledged to "reverse the trend of declining defence budgets" and to "move towards the existing NATO guidance of spending 2 per cent of GDP on defence within a decade".

Newport also saw the announcement of a Very High Readiness Joint Task Force (VJTF). This was the latest step in the evolution of the NATO Response Force (NRF), announced at the Alliance's Prague Summit in November 2002 (see AR 2002, p. 396). NATO's supreme allied commander Europe at the time had described the ambition of the NRF in the following terms: "NATO will no longer have the large, massed units that were necessary for the Cold War, but will have agile and capable forces at Graduated Readiness levels that will better prepare the Alliance to meet any threat that it is likely to face in this 21st century." The NRF had three elements: a command and control element; an Immediate Response Force of about 13,000 troops (comprising land, sea, air and special forces); and a pool of reinforcements. Since its inception, the NRF had been little used: two security missions in 2004 (the Athens Olympic Games and the presidential election in Afghanistan), and two humanitarian missions (Hurricane Katrina in 2005 and the Pakistan earthquake in 2006). The NRF was not, however, used when Estonia (a NATO member) faced a massive assault on its critical cyber infrastructure in 2007. Nor was it called upon when Georgia (not a NATO member, but a member of the Alliance's Partnership for Peace since 2005) was in armed conflict with Russia in 2008. Unsurprisingly, the NRF was not called upon in response to conflict in Crimea and eastern Ukraine.

In spite, or possibly because of this lacklustre record, NATO saw fit at Newport to reinvigorate the NRF with the VJTF. Described by UK Prime Minister David Cameron as a "spearhead force", the VJTF would, like its parent, comprise land, sea, air and special forces and would be deployable within a few days, anywhere in the world and "particularly at the periphery of NATO's territory". Following approval of the concept by NATO defence ministers, the force was expected to begin a training and exercise programme towards the end of 2015. The size of the VJTF remained unconfirmed, although it was expected to comprise about 4,000 troops.

If a force of this size were even to begin to be credible, it would have to be both capable and deployable. Ukraine and Syria were both "at the periphery of NATO territory", but it was not clear that the VJTF (or indeed the larger NRF behind it) would have the capability to influence the outcome of either conflict. Neither was it clear that NATO governments would be willing to deploy forces on such missions.

Thus, 2014 was not a good year for European stability, and neither was it a good year for NATO's credibility and solidarity. In spite of its various deployments, decisions and initiatives, the Alliance seemed to have been wrong-footed by

Russia. By the end of the year, with the constraints on NATO's strategic capacity having been demonstrated, the United States could be forgiven for judging the defence effort of its European allies to be as risible as it had long suspected.

Paul Cornish

ECONOMIC ORGANISATIONS

International Monetary Fund (IMF)
DATE OF FOUNDATION: 1945   HEADQUARTERS: Washington DC, USA
OBJECTIVES: To promote international monetary co-operation and to assist member states in establishing sound budgetary and trading policies
MEMBERSHIP (END-'14): 188 members
MANAGING DIRECTOR: Christine Lagarde (France) (since July '11)

World Bank (International Bank for Reconstruction and Development (IBRD) and International Development Association (IDA))
DATE OF FOUNDATION: 1944   HEADQUARTERS: Washington DC, USA
OBJECTIVES: To make loans on reasonable terms to developing countries with the aim of increasing their productive capacity
MEMBERSHIP (END-'14): 188 members
PRESIDENT, WORLD BANK GROUP: Jim Yong Kim (USA) (since July '12)

World Trade Organisation (WTO)
DATE OF FOUNDATION: 1995 (successor to General Agreement on Tariffs and Trade, GATT)
HEADQUARTERS: Geneva, Switzerland
OBJECTIVES: To eliminate tariffs and other barriers to international trade and to facilitate international financial settlements
MEMBERSHIP (END-'14): 160 members
DIRECTOR GENERAL: Roberto Azevêdo (Brazil) (since Sept '13)

Organisation for Economic Co-operation and Development (OECD)
DATE OF FOUNDATION: 1961   HEADQUARTERS: Paris, France
OBJECTIVES: To promote economic growth in member states and the sound development of the world economy
MEMBERSHIP (END-'14): Australia, Austria, Belgium, Canada, Chile, Czech Republic, Denmark, Estonia, Finland, France, Germany, Greece, Hungary, Iceland, Ireland, Israel, Italy, Japan, South Korea, Luxembourg, Mexico, The Netherlands, New Zealand, Norway, Poland, Portugal, Slovakia, Slovenia, Spain, Sweden, Switzerland, Turkey, UK, USA (total 34)
SECRETARY GENERAL: Angel Gurría (Mexico) (since June '06)

INTERNATIONAL MONETARY FUND (IMF). For most IMF members and the organisation's director general, Christine Lagarde, there was considerable disappointment, and increasing irritation, throughout the year at the continued refusal of the US Congress to ratify the Reform of the Fund's system of quotas and governance that had been agreed in 2010 (see AR 2011, pp. 401-402). Although Congress rejected the Reform in March, it was still hoped that approval might be obtained before the end of the year. But despite repeated appeals from the Obama administration, Congress made it clear in December that it would refuse to ratify the Reform if the administration included it in the federal budget bill, several members insisting that the US should not increase its exposure to the IMF. Lagarde then declared that "as requested by our membership", specifically by the Group of Twenty-Four (G-24) "emerging market and developing economies" (EMDC) finance ministers and the International Monetary and Financial Committee (IMFC), alternative ways to promote the Reform and ensure that the Fund continued to have adequate resources would be explored. The Executive Board was expected to take up the question of alternatives and to prepare a report to the board of governors by the end of January 2015.

In a series of lectures and speeches throughout the year, the director general placed the problems of the IMF Reform in the wider context of a global economy that had become integrated to a high level but at the same time was becoming more dispersed or fragmented "in terms of power, influence and decision-making. The changing distribution of economic power was a big factor in "the tendency to grow apart", but also important were the increased power of multinational companies, which controlled some two-thirds of world trade, and the legacy of tensions from the financial and economic crisis of 2008. The system of global governance and multilateral cooperation had failed to adjust to these changes in the structure of the global economy. This was a world, she suggested, in her Dimbleby Lecture in February, that could lead to "more indecision, impasse and insecurity—the temptations of extremism"—and she pointedly compared the current period with the imbalances and tensions of 1914 which opened the gateway to "30 years of disaster". The challenge now, indeed the obligation, was to "choose the ethos of 1944 over 1914" and to construct a "new multilateralism".

Despite the failure to ratify the Reform, the Fund's two standby credit lines—comprising a number of countries committed to providing the Fund with short-term loans when required—had been strengthened in 2012 ensuring that funds would be available for new lending (see AR 2013, p. 381). The doubling of quotas together with the enlarged credit lines, however, were intended to create a global "firewall" to enable the Fund to react effectively in the event of another major financial crisis, a need which, in the light of the director general's analysis of tensions and fragilities in the global economy, remained. Nevertheless, the Fund's estimate of its reserves available for future lending—its "forward commitment capacity"—was SDRs 244 billion at the end of 2014, some 10 per cent less than a year earlier but still higher than in 2012. Notable in 2014 was the reduced level of lending to the eurozone: Portugal's arrangement ended in May which left only those with Cyprus and Greece. At the end of the year the eurozone's share of outstanding credit from the Fund's General Resources Account (GRA), the principal lending facility, was just under 30 per cent compared with 54 per cent a year earlier. Total lending fell quite sharply in 2014, to SDR11.1 billion from SDR14.3 billion in 2013. This was largely in the GRA but there was also a fall in concessional loans (from SDR800 million in 2013 to SDR500 million). Repayments were again very high, at nearly SDR26 billion, a reflection of the winding down of the very high levels of lending in 2009-12, with the result that net lending was negative.

With the reduction in lending to the eurozone the Fund's focus shifted more towards the support of developing countries and Eastern Europe. New arrangements, of up to $18 billion in total, were made for Chad, Georgia, Grenada, Seychelles, Ukraine and Yemen. Technical assistance and training accounted for about a quarter of the Fund's total activity in 2014, most of it directed to low-income developing countries.

One important event was the Fund's response to the Ebola crisis in West Africa. Reports on the growing scale of the epidemic had appeared in March, but it was not until 8 August that the World Health Organisation (WHO) classified the outbreak as "an extraordinary event" and declared a Global Health Emergency. In mid-September IMF staff proposed support of some $127 million for the three countries most directly affected by the epidemic, namely, Guinea, Liberia and Sierra Leone, countries that were already receiving assistance under the IMF's regular programmes. On 26 September, the Executive Board approved $130 million of emergency assistance: $41 million for Guinea, $49 million for Liberia and $40 million for Sierra Leone. It was reckoned this would meet about 40 per cent of their needs for balance of payments and fiscal financing.

These estimates of financing needs, which already assumed large reductions in the forecasts of GDP growth in 2014, assumed that the epidemic would be more or less under control by the first quarter of 2015. By the end of October, however, this appeared optimistic and at the IMF-WB meetings in October, the IMFC urged the Executive Board to expand the Fund's zero-interest lending to low-income countries and the US treasury secretary called for more funds for the three countries, including debt write-offs. At the summit of G-20 leaders in November, the Fund proposed a further $300 million package of interest-free loans and debt relief. On 23 December, the Executive Board extended the waiver of all interest on the Fund's concessional loans—the third such extension since 2009—and was expected to approve the $300 million programme in January 2015. (On the Ebola crisis, see also World Bank, below.)

Another agreement that received a lot of publicity in 2014 was the Stand-by Arrangement for Ukraine. The country had requested IMF support at the end of February and by the end of March a staff level agreement was in place for a two-year agreement of $14-18 billion that would contribute to Ukraine's estimated financing needs of $27 billion over the same period. The rest was to come from the EU and the USA. The Executive Board approved the stand-by at $17 billion (SDR10.97 billion) at the end of April with an immediate disbursement of SDR2.058 billion. The Fund admitted that there were "many risks to the programme" and that the degree of uncertainty was very large. A second disbursement was approved in late August, taking the total to SDR2.97 billion (about $4.51 billion). By September, however, doubts were being raised about the bailout programme and in December, with the economic situation in Ukraine declining, it became clear the Fund would be unable to disburse any more money until confidence was restored in the sustainability of the country's debt.

Forecasts for the world economy in 2014 and 2015, in the Fund's *World Economic Outlook* (WEO), were steadily lowered through the year. In January, global GDP in 2014 was forecast at 3.7 per cent but by the end of the year that had been lowered to 3.3 per cent. For 2015, the forecast was cut from 4 per cent in July to 3.5 per cent by the end of the year. The deterioration in 2014 reflected a weaker outlook in emerging and developing economies (from 5.1 per cent to 4.4 per cent) and a weakening of an already poor outlook in the advanced economies (from 2.2 per cent to 1.8 per cent). In the spring the Fund's economists were "cautiously optimistic" that the brakes on the recovery were easing, particularly in the USA. By the end of the year there were fears that recovery was about to stall in the euro-zone, with the added risk of price deflation, and of an increased risk of economic spillovers from the turmoil in the Middle East and Ukraine. For the Fund's economists, the weaker outlook required monetary policy to avoid a rise in interest rates, an acceleration of financial reform and, given the prospect of reduced rates of potential output growth in many countries, greater attention to supply-side measures. The latter included traditional IMF recommendations of more flexible labour markets, trade liberalisation and smaller government, but infrastructure investment was highlighted as a means of boosting employment and wages in the short run and raising productive capacities in the longer run.

Among other developments during 2014, the government of Nauru applied to become a member of the IMF on 9 May. The IMF's resident representative in Afghanistan, Wabel Abdallah, was among 20 people killed in a bomb attack in Kabul in January. It was the first time that the IMF had lost a staff member in such circumstances.

WORLD BANK (WB). The year was marked not by celebration of the WB's 70th anniversary but by the controversial efforts of the president, Jim Yong Kim, and the Bank's top management to introduce the structural and operational changes judged necessary to support the new strategy for the World Bank Group (WBG) that had been approved in 2013 (See AR 2014, pp. 382-383.) (For a brief description of the five bodies that constituted the WBG, see AR 2009, p. 411.)

A major change in the WB's approach to development was to reduce the emphasis on countries and regions in favour of increasing and exploiting its expertise across specialised areas, from agriculture to finance, from education to water supply. There were, in addition to these "Global Practices", "Cross Cutting Solution Areas" such as climate change, that required international cooperation and integration across several specialised areas. Acting along these lines would transform the institution into a "Solutions World Bank Group".

The programmes involved restructuring the six regional divisions of the Bank—frequently criticised as operating as isolated silos—into 14 "global practices", specialising in the areas noted above. The discontent of the staff, which spilled over into a demonstration in the atrium of the WB's headquarters in October, appeared to be focused more on the management of the reform rather than the overall objective: a survey of staff revealed genuine confusion as to what was expected of them. The revelation that the Chief Financial Officer was to receive a "special skills premium" on top of his salary, despite the slow progress in finding $400 million of savings in the $2.6 billion administrative budget, did little for morale, nor did the expenditure of $12.5 million on outside business consultants. As a number of commentators in developing countries were keen to point out, an organisation that had been lecturing them for decades on how to reform their administrative and financial institutions appeared unable to restructure itself. The end of the process was still not in sight at the close of the year and there was uncertainty about the likely scale of cuts in the salaried staff of over 12,000.

Despite the confusion over implementation, many people inside and outside the WB still regarded the president's reform as desirable and the shift in emphasis— that included addressing global externalities, such as climate change, the spread of infectious diseases, and natural resource conservation—very welcome. Kim declared that the restructuring of the Bank, the most extensive in decades, would be counted a success if the demand for its advice and lending increased.

Commentators had for some time claimed that the WB was losing "competitiveness" to other sources of finance and that it risked becoming irrelevant for many middle-income developing countries. It was certainly the case that lending to these countries had been falling before the economic crisis (see AR 2008, p. 392). After a sharp rise in 2009 and 2010, lending resumed its decline as developing countries were able to access the international capital markets at low interest rates and without WB conditionality, thanks to the "unconventional monetary policies" in several advanced economies. Nevertheless, from 2008 the WB was making commitments of some $40 billion a year, which was hardly irrelevant, and in 2014 they were above the pre-crisis average. Although down from the exceptionally high level of 2010, commitments rose nearly 30 per cent in 2014 (to $40.8 billion, against $58.7 billion in 2010), gross lending rose 19 per cent and net lending (net of repayments) by 26 per cent (to $18.9 billion).

A feature of the last five years was the growing share of IDA concessional lending to the poorest countries, from a low point of 25 per cent of the WB total in 2010 to more than 54 per cent in 2014. This shift was broadly consistent with the new strategic focus on reducing poverty and boosting the incomes of the bottom 40 per cent. The regional distribution of WB lending was still dominated by sub-Saharan Africa and South Asia (India, Pakistan, Bangladesh) with each taking 26 per cent of the total in 2014 and this in turn reflected their dominance (84 per cent) of the IDA's concessional lending. IBRD commitments were more concentrated on East Asia, Europe and Central Asia, and Latin America (22 per cent to 25 per cent each) but the shares of the Middle East and North Africa doubled between 2012 and 2014 (from 7 to 14 per cent) as did that of South Asia (from 6 to 12 per cent). About two-thirds of the WB's loans in 2014 went to three broad economic sectors, namely, transport, water sanitation and flood protection. Surprisingly, commitments to health and other social services were halved between 2010 and 2014 (from $6.8 billion to $3.4 billion) and accounted for just over 8 per cent of the total last year.

The other source of WBG finance, the IFC, focused on the private sector, where lending commitments and disbursements had averaged $15.2 billion and $8.1 billion per year, respectively, since 2010. In 2014, $17.3 billion was committed on the IFC account while another $5.1 billion was raised from other entities as a result of IFC's direct involvement. Thus, in June, IFC provided $90 million of credit risk protection to support a $2 billion portfolio of loans made by Crédit Agricole to emerging markets including for infrastructure projects in Egypt. The provision of such protection by the IFC generated a higher level of lending by others than would otherwise have been the case, but some bank regulators were concerned that such transactions might conceal rather than share risk.

The regional distribution of IFC financing was less concentrated than that of the WB, with 19-20 per cent going to each of four regions and 9-10 per cent to South Asia and the Middle East and North Africa respectively. In October the Compliance Adviser Ombudsman (CAO) reported on the extent to which IFC had complied with its 2012 audit of its investments through intermediaries (see AR 2014, p. 384). It found that, despite a positive response by the IFC ,"important findings remained unaddressed" and the CAO repeated that the IFC still did not have a systematic methodology for determining whether the implementation of an Environmental and Social management system could actually achieve the IFC's objectives of doing no harm or improving such outcomes on the ground. Some critics feared that competition from the new BRICS bank, the New Development Bank, as well as other regional banks, might lead to a lowering of safeguards. In December such fears appear to have led the US Congress to include in the federal spending bill a requirement that the US director on the WB's Executive Board be instructed to oppose any weakening of the existing environmental and social standards.

The WB itself put more emphasis on initiatives that would involve cooperation rather than competition with other providers of finance. An example in 2014 was the Global Infrastructure Facility (GIF) that was launched in October and to which the Bank's governors approved the transfer of a $15 million surplus from the IBRD. The WB president described the GIF as essentially a platform that would combine resources from the WB with those from other development banks, including the Asian Infrastructure Investment Bank launched in November, as well as private sector and capital market institutions. In approving the GIF the board of governors was concerned about the "potential for reputational risks" and called for strong oversight from the board and for the GIF to "draw upon the Bank's standards, safeguards and procurement processes".

Despite academic questioning of poverty lines, the WB introduced its first *Global Monitoring Report 2014/2015: Ending Poverty*, an annual review of progress in reducing inequality, written jointly with the IMF and with contributions from the OECD. It covered not only the WB's twin goals but also the status of the UN's Millennium Development Goals (MDGs). While the MDGs referred to the developing countries, monitoring of the bottom 40 per cent of income earners was extended to all countries.

The WBG mobilised just under $1 billion in 2014 to assist the west African countries hardest hit by the Ebola epidemic. This included emergency funds of $518 million from IDA and at least $450 million mobilised by the IFC to support trade, employment and investment in the three countries. The IDA funds were used to help bolster public healthcare systems. Just over half of IFC funds went to a rapid response programme to secure supplies of essential goods and services, and to maintain businesses where possible; the rest went to finance projects in a post-crisis recovery programme. Unprepared for such an outbreak, the human and economic costs were immense, with more than 8,000 deaths and huge reductions in economic activity. WB forecasts made in June for GDP growth in 2015 were 4.3 per cent in Guinea, 6.8 per cent in Liberia and 8.9 per cent in Sierra Leone; the WB's latest forecasts were -0.2 per cent, 3.0 per cent, and -2.0 per cent, respectively. Despite the severe impact on the three countries, the impact on the rest of Africa was still limited at the end of the year.

For several decades, mainstream economics had been dominated by a model of decision-making that described rational actors taking optimal decisions in their own interest, guided by prices formed in free markets, and producing favourable outcomes for society as a whole. The basic assumptions of this model were questioned in the WB's flagship publication, the *World Development Report 2015: Mind, Society and Behaviour*, published in December. Reviewing a large body of research in behavioural economics, together with areas such as cognitive science and anthropology, it cast doubt on the idea that behaviour generally reflected rational choices. Instead, decisions were the result of a more complicated process: short-term reactions, psychological and social influences all played a role in particular contexts, and understanding this was crucial for successful policies. It remained to be seen whether this pointed to an eventual paradigm shift in the WB's approach to economic development or to more subtle ways of selling the traditional model.

WORLD TRADE ORGANISATION (WTO). After 12 years of minimal and halting progress in the Doha Round of trade negotiations, the agreement on Trade Facilitation (TFA) at the Ministerial Conference at Bali in December 2013 was hailed as a sign that the Round was not doomed to fail and that significant progress might be expected in 2014 in dealing with the more numerous and more complex parts of the Doha Development Agenda (DDA).

In early February, the WTO's director general, Roberto Azevêdo, set out the two major tasks of the membership for the year: one, to implement by the end of July the TFA agreed in Bali; and two, to prepare a well-defined programme on the remaining DDA issues by the end of the year. For the developing country members this meant a focus on agricultural and economic development issues and the concerns of the Least Developed Countries (LDCs); their understanding was that "binding outcomes" on these issues were the objective and that they would receive the same degree of attention from the developed countries as had been given to the TFA at Bali.

Implementing the TFA consisted of three steps: first, the legal review or editing of the text, which was completed in May and formally approved in July; second, agreeing a draft protocol to insert the TFA into the WTO Agreement; and third, notification of the measures that each developing country would designate for implementation once the TFA entered into force. Seemingly straightforward, implementing the TFA quickly ran into an impasse for reasons that were familiar from the setbacks of previous years. First, the African members decided that they would accept the TFA only on a provisional basis and proposed that the Protocol should reflect the language of the original Doha Ministerial Declaration, namely, that all outcomes "shall be treated as part of a single undertaking" and that early agreements "may be implemented on a provisional or a definitive basis". Secondly, India, unhappy at what it regarded as a lack of engagement by the developed countries with the rest of the DDA, declared it would be unable to join the consensus on the Protocol unless there was a firm commitment to a permanent solution to the issue of public stockholding for food security (see AR 2014, p. 386). India was supported by other developing countries many of which, such as China, also had similar stockholding policies. The USA, together with the EU, Japan and Australia, refused to engage with other issues unless the TFA was fully implemented and threatened to take it outside the WTO if agreement was not reached inside.

The deadlock continued until the middle of November when India and the US suddenly announced that they had reached an agreement, one that was subsequently adopted by the General Council at the end of November. Stockholding would not be challenged under the Agreement on Agriculture until a permanent solution to the issue was agreed and adopted (the Bali decision was for an interim arrangement pending a permanent solution to be reached by July 2015). It was not clear whether challenges might still arise under other WTO Agreements. As for the TFA, that would enter into force when two-thirds of the 160 members had confirmed their acceptance, with a deadline set for July 2015. In July, the WTO launched a facility to provide technical assistance and "capacity-building support" to developing countries and LDCs to help them meet their commitments under the FTA. The funding appeared to be on a voluntary basis by WTO donor members, so its scale was uncertain as was its likely duration. The World Bank, the OECD and parts of the UN system offered assistance, but it was far from clear that sufficient funds would be available to finance large infrastructure projects such as ports.

The director general once again declared that the negotiations were "back on track" and that commitment to the multilateral system had been renewed. He looked forward to a "big year" for the WTO in 2015 when a permanent solution for public stockbuilding should be reached by end-December and a post-Bali work programme for concluding the Doha Round should be agreed by July. Whether a repeat of the paralysis of 2014 could be avoided, however, was questionable.

Against a background of weakening growth in world trade—the secretariat's spring forecasts of 4.7 per cent and 5.3 per cent growth in 2014 and 2015 respectively were lowered to 3.1 per cent and 4.0 per cent in September—the WTO continued to worry about the growth of trade restrictions while admitting that the protectionist reaction to the 2008 crisis had been quite muted compared with similar events in the past. Between May and October 2014, WTO recorded 93 new restrictions by the G-20 countries affecting some 0.8 per cent of their imports. The number of new measures had not increased over the previous six months and a positive trend was that tariff reductions exceeded the number of increases. Altogether, the total number of restrictions introduced by the G-20 countries since October 2008 had reached 1,244 by mid-October, affecting about 4 per cent of world imports. The net impact on world trade, allowing for measures withdrawn and for new liberalisation, would be rather less than suggested by that figure.

Another concern was the relationship between the multilateral trading system and regional trade agreements. By mid-October the WTO had been notified of 253 regional arrangements but there were another 63 that had not been notified. Detailed information of such arrangements was clearly necessary for the WTO to determine whether they were consistent with WTO rules and the multilateral trading system.

On 10 December the General Council formally adopted the Protocol of Accession to the WTO of the Republic of Seychelles. After a 20-year process the negotiations were concluded in October. When its parliament ratified the Protocol, the Seychelles would become the WTO's 161st member.

ORGANISATION FOR ECONOMIC CO-OPERATION AND DEVELOPMENT (OECD). In the spring the OECD's *Economic Outlook* expected the world economy to strengthen in 2014 and 2015. Secretary General Angel Gurría told the assembled OECD ministers in May that the "advanced economies are gaining momentum and driving the pickup in global growth, while once-stalled cylinders of the economic engine, like investment and trade, are starting to fire again". The world economy was forecast to grow by 3.4 per cent in 2014, rising to 3.9 per cent in 2015, GDP in the eurozone would rise by 1.2 per cent and 1.7 per cent respectively, and the US economy would accelerate from under 2 per cent to 2.6 per cent. For the OECD countries as a whole, a rather heterogeneous group, growth was expected at 2.2 per cent in 2014, rising to 2.8 per cent in 2015. The risks to the outlook seemed better balanced than in 2013.

This relatively positive, albeit modest, improvement in the outlook began to weaken by late spring and early summer and in its November *Economic Outlook* the secretariat concluded that the world economy was "stuck in low gear" and painted a less optimistic picture. Unemployment rates remained generally very high, estimates of potential output were being lowered, and there was a growing divergence of monetary policies and of economic performance, both within and between the advanced and the emerging market economies. The world economy was now expected to grow by 3.3 per cent, less than forecast a year earlier (3.6 per cent), and the OECD countries by 1.8 per cent (against 2.3 per cent). Once again, a small improvement was expected in 2015—3.7 per cent for the world economy, 2.3 per cent for OECD—but these were still lower than the forecasts of November 2013 or May 2014. Major uncertainties included the financial risks from heavily indebted emerging market economies and the possibility of a "prolonged stagnation" in the eurozone.

Such prospects had usually led the OECD to urge member countries to further "structural reform" in order to boost economic growth, but OECD's new chief economist, Catherine Mann, said that a "stronger policy response is needed particularly to boost demand. That will mean more action by the ECB and more supportive fiscal policy, so that there is space for deeper structural reforms to take hold". This was a rare suggestion from one of the leading multilateral institutions that the weakness of demand was part of the problem and that the direction of causation between structural reform and economic growth might be the reverse of the ruling orthodoxy or, at least, that the two might be mutually supportive.

At their annual Ministerial Council Meeting (MCM) in May the ministers and representatives of the 36 member countries plus the EU agreed that a global recovery was under way and shared the secretariat's assessment of the weaknesses and risks in the outlook. The MCM, however, focused not on the conjuncture but on the reforms required to make their individual economies and the global system both more resilient in the face of shocks and more inclusive. Inclusive growth has been part of the MCM's agenda for several years but 2014 saw the issue of increasing inequality and its impact on economic growth receiving much greater attention. The MCM emphasised "appropriate flexibility and security in labour markets and relevant education and skills programmes" as ways of achieving inclusive growth and supported specific policies to promote gender equality and youth employment, to cope with the issues arising from ageing populations and to assist the integration of migrants. Systemic resilience required a range of reforms from rebuilding public trust through greater openness, transparency and accountability of governments and the private business sector, not the least through measures to combat corruption and the undermining of national tax systems through the use of tax havens and other devices. Climate change was a major global risk to the resilience of all economies and the MCM adopted the OECD Ministerial Statement on Climate Change. While many of the MCM's concerns were focused on what many economists would call market failures, ministers emphasised their belief in the power of free trade and foreign investment as key drivers of growth and job creation and their resistance to "all forms of protectionism".

In March, the OECD Governing Council decided to suspend "for the time being" the accession process for the Russian Federation. At the same time, the Council agreed to respond positively to a request from Ukraine to strengthen its existing cooperation with OECD to help it face its current "public policy challenges".

Paul Rayment

NON-ALIGNED MOVEMENT AND DEVELOPING COUNTRIES

Non-Aligned Movement (NAM)

DATE OF FOUNDATION: 1961 HEADQUARTERS: rotating with chair
OBJECTIVES: Originally to promote decolonisation and to avoid domination by either the Western industrialised world or the Communist bloc; since the early 1970s to provide an authoritative forum to set the political and economic priorities of developing countries; in addition, since the end of the Cold War, to resist domination of the UN system by the USA.
MEMBERSHIP (END-'14): Afghanistan, Algeria, Angola, Antigua and Barbuda, Azerbaijan, Bahamas, Bahrain, Bangladesh, Barbados, Belarus, Belize, Benin, Bhutan, Bolivia, Botswana, Brunei, Burkina Faso, Burma (Myanmar), Burundi, Cambodia, Cameroon, Cape Verde, Central African Republic, Chad, Chile, Colombia, Comoros, Congo, Côte d'Ivoire, Cuba, Democratic Republic of the Congo, Djibouti, Dominica, Dominican Republic, East Timor, Ecuador, Egypt, Equatorial Guinea, Eritrea, Ethiopia, Fiji, Gabon, the Gambia, Ghana, Grenada, Guatemala, Guinea, Guinea-Bissau, Guyana, Haiti, Honduras, India, Indonesia, Iran, Iraq, Jamaica, Jordan, Kenya, Kuwait, Laos, Lebanon, Lesotho, Liberia, Libya, Madagascar, Malawi, Malaysia, Maldives, Mali, Mauritania, Mauritius, Mongolia, Morocco, Mozambique, Namibia, Nepal, Nicaragua, Niger, Nigeria, North Korea, Oman, Pakistan, Palestine, Panama, Papua New Guinea, Peru, Philippines, Qatar, Rwanda, St Kitts and Nevis, St Lucia, St Vincent and the Grenadines, São Tomé and Príncipe, Saudi Arabia, Senegal, Seychelles, Sierra Leone, Singapore, Somalia, South Africa, Sri Lanka, Sudan, Suriname, Swaziland, Syria, Tanzania, Thailand, Togo, Trinidad and Tobago, Tunisia, Turkmenistan, Uganda, United Arab Emirates, Uzbekistan, Vanuatu, Venezuela, Vietnam, Yemen, Zambia, Zimbabwe (total 120)
CHAIRMAN: President of Iran Hassan Rouhani (from Aug '13)

Group of 77 (G-77)

DATE OF FOUNDATION: 1964 HEADQUARTERS: UN centres
OBJECTIVES: To act as an international lobbying group for the concerns of developing countries
MEMBERSHIP (END-'14): All NAM members, except Azerbaijan, Belarus and Uzbekistan, are members of the G-77; 16 other countries (Argentina, Bosnia & Herzegovina, Brazil, Costa Rica, El Salvador, Kiribati, the Marshall Islands, Micronesia, Nauru, Paraguay, Samoa, the Solomon Islands, South Sudan, Tajikistan, Tonga, Uruguay) are also G-77 members (total 133).
CHAIR: Bolivia (2014); South Africa (2015)

THE three main meetings of developing countries in 2014 were the 17th conference of foreign ministers of the **Non-Aligned Movement (NAM)** in Algiers, 26-29 May; a commemorative meeting in Bolivia, 14-15 June, for the 50th anniversary of the formation of the G-77; and the 38th annual meeting of the foreign ministers of the **Group of 77 (G-77)** in New York, on 26 September.

The NAM foreign ministers aimed to address the full range of current global issues, by updating the declaration from the 2012 summit in Tehran. Despite three months of drafting work, by the Co-ordinating Bureau in New York, consensus could not be achieved on 18 of the 800 paragraphs. Divisions on the Syrian crisis continued (see AR 2013, p. 391), but they now acknowledged the scale of the conflict, in a strong call for humanitarian assistance to support the neighbouring host counties Jordan, Lebanon, Iraq and Egypt, accommodating Syrian refugees. In a delicate compromise, the ministers condemned the use of chemical weapons "in" Syria, without mentioning who had used the weapons.

In Algiers, there was a very different perspective on terrorism from that of the European countries facing occasional small-scale attacks. The NAM denounced terrorism, particularly its association with religion, and rejected the concept of terrorism sponsoring-states. Developing countries were the main victims of terrorism: the NAM condemned the sustained onslaughts by terrorists in Syria, Lebanon, Yemen, Iran, Iraq, India, Pakistan, Sri Lanka, Algeria, Nigeria, Kenya, Somalia and Mali. The declaration also called for "measures to prevent the use of new platforms, including the Internet, digital social networking and mass media, in spreading extremist religious thoughts and ideas". Although the "Islamic State" terrorist movement (ISIS) had in January established a presence in the Iraqi city of Fallujah, its significance was not generally understood initially. By September, the UN Human Rights Council held a special session on the situation in Iraq. The Iranian representative, speaking on behalf of the NAM, declared in the debate that ISIS had committed war crimes and crimes against humanity.

Although the Non-Aligned normally opposed any use of force in bilateral disputes, they were deeply divided over Russia's annexation of the Ukrainian territory of Crimea. On 27 March, when a UN General Assembly resolution was passed saying that the referendum held in Crimea on joining the Russian Federation had no validity, only 42 NAM members voted in favour, while 49 abstained. Of the 10 countries voting with Russia against the resolution, nine were from the NAM. Consequently, with these divisions, no joint position was adopted. Also, due to strict application of the NAM principle of consensus, the Algiers conference was unable to endorse ASEAN criticisms of Chinese oil exploration in the South China Sea.

The conflict over Palestine became substantially worse in 2014, with tensions over religious sites from February onwards, the breakdown of peace negotiations in April, the killing of three Israeli settler youths in June, detention of Palestinian leaders, rocket attacks on Israel, and the intense and sustained bombardment of Gaza by Israeli forces in June and July. The developing countries responded with anger in their regional organisations, and a series of strong statements by the NAM conference in Algiers and the NAM Bureau in New York. In addition, measures were taken to strengthen Palestinian statehood. In April, the NAM welcomed the announcement that President Mahmoud Abbas had signed letters of accession to 15 multilateral treaties. The year ended with efforts to obtain a UN Security Council resolution specifying that Israel must withdraw from the Occupied Territories within two years. This was expected to obtain a majority vote, but on 30 December two members of the Non-Aligned, Nigeria and Rwanda, defected. By abstaining, they produced a shock defeat for the draft resolution. The next day Abbas responded by signing a further 17 treaties, including the Statute of the International Criminal Court.

Following the revelation by Associated Press in April that the US government had from 2010 to 2012 run a "Cuban Twitter" network, called ZunZuneo, the NAM adopted a special Declaration on Information and Communication Technologies, which strongly rejected the illicit use of social networks and called for "safeguarding cyberspace". Sustained support by both the Non-Aligned and the G-77 for Cuba, against the diplomatic and economic blockade by the United States, had won increasing support in South America. The ALBA group of 11 countries, all of which were NAM members, had said in 2012 that they would boycott the next Summit of the Americas in 2015, if Cuba were not invited. In September, the

Panamanians announced they had invited the Cubans. On 17 December, US President Barack Obama admitted that the policy of isolating Cuba had failed and instead had "isolated the United States from regional and international partners".

The commemorative meeting of the G-77 in Bolivia adopted a long declaration, but it contained no new initiatives. The attempt to maintain a programme of activities to promote South-South co-operation was quietly abandoned. The G-77 had finally become no more than a very active caucus group at United Nations meetings.

The main achievement of the G-77 in 2014 was to push through a UN General Assembly resolution on 9 September, endorsing the case for establishing a global multilateral framework for international debt restructuring, and a second resolution on 29 December, that specified the arrangements for three negotiating sessions at the UN in 2015. Given the opposition from the USA, the UK, Germany and Japan, the prospects for agreeing a legal text were poor. Long-standing, generalised appeals for transfer of technology, to enable environmentally sound development, had been translated into a series of UN "structured dialogues". The process concluded in July 2014, with the G-77 arguing for the establishment of a UN operational programme, while most of the developed countries did not wish to go further than information exchange and co-ordination of activities. The question was carried forward to the Assembly's debate, due in February 2015, on the "Post-2015 Development Agenda".

In September, South Sudan joined the G-77, increasing its membership to 133 countries (excluding China), but it did not claim a seat in the NAM, which remained with 120 members.

Peter Willetts

THE EUROPEAN UNION

DATE OF FOUNDATION: 1957   HEADQUARTERS: Brussels, Belgium
OBJECTIVES: To promote peace, its values and the well-being of its peoples
MEMBERSHIP (END-'14): Austria, Belgium, Bulgaria, Croatia, Cyprus, Czech Republic, Denmark, Estonia, Finland, France, Germany, Greece, Hungary, Ireland, Italy, Latvia, Lithuania, Luxembourg, Malta, Netherlands, Poland, Portugal, Romania, Slovakia, Slovenia, Spain, Sweden, United Kingdom (total 28)
PRESIDENT OF EUROPEAN COMMISSION: Jean-Claude Juncker (Luxembourg) (since Oct '14)

IF there has been one word commonly associated with the European Union, that word is "crisis". Most of those crises have been internal ones: major rows between the Member States, often with the United Kingdom prominent in the mêlée. The year 2014 was different. There was no existential crisis of the kind which hit the eurozone after the banking collapse of 2008. Instead, there was one big and enduring drama: that of Russia's behaviour towards Ukraine and the European Union's reaction to it.

That is not to say that the year was serene. Far from it. Public disaffection with the European Union throughout the member countries was widespread. It was hard to separate what could justifiably be laid at the door of the European Union from what was going on within each nation's economic and political stories. But, of course, the perceived inadequacy of many of Europe's individual leaders fed the perception of a lack of collective leadership from the European Council, the EU's top decision-making body. Into that vacuum of leadership stepped the European Parliament, in what was the only real internal drama of the EU's year.

The biggest of the domestic dramas which fuelled the wider story, and potentially the most serious, was the possible separation of Scotland from the rest of the United Kingdom. The Scottish referendum of 18 September was not just an existential moment for the UK. It produced nervous jitters around the rest of Europe. Contrary to the assertions of Alex Salmond, Scotland's first minister, there was no doubt that, if Scotland had voted for independence, the Scottish government could not have assumed that membership of the EU was theirs by right. Under the rules of the EU Treaties, Scotland would, as a new country, have had to apply to join. That application could, formally, only have been lodged after independence had actually taken place. Accession could only have taken place with the consent of the governments of all the Member States. There were dire warnings—from José-Manuel Durão Barroso, the president of the European Commission, and from Herman van Rompuy, the president of the European Council—that Scotland would find it hard to gain entry to the club.

Neither man had any authority to express such a view. Under the EU Treaties, an independent Scotland would have had every right to apply to join, and it would have been a travesty for a democratic country, whose citizens had enjoyed the rights of EU membership for over 40 years, to be denied. But van Rompuy, as a senior politician from Belgium, was expressing, not a considered judgement, but a fear that the break-up of the United Kingdom would encourage the already serious fissiparous tendencies in his own country. The Commission president, for his part, was probably conscious of the huge implications for Spain, the neighbour of his own native Portugal. The Spanish government, one of the worst affected by the eurozone crisis, and with unemployment running at close to 25 per cent throughout 2014, was facing its own constitutional crisis with pressure from Catalonia for full independence. Unlike the British government, the Spanish government asserted that any referendum in Catalonia on the issue of independence would be illegal. When a referendum was nonetheless held in November 2014, 80 per cent of the 2.3 million voters who participated expressed their support for independence.

President Barroso may also have been concerned at the possibility that an independent Scottish government could be applying for EU membership in 2017 just as a government in London was putting to the rest of the UK the question whether or not to remain an EU member. Would Scotland be trying to get in just as England was trying to get out? Or might England be in and Scotland out?

The result of the referendum resolved these issues, for a period at least. But the degree of nervousness that the Scottish referendum provoked in the rest of the EU was a measure of a wider sense of political insecurity in almost all the member countries.

In France, that country's domestic problems were exacerbated by the degree to which her president, François Hollande, became an object of national embarrassment because of his very public, so-called private life. Underlying this was a much more serious concern about France's weak economic performance, her inability to do more than flat-line in terms of growth, her government's belated attempts at economic rigour and her ongoing argument with the European Commission over the French government's failure to meet the deficit targets required under eurozone rules (see the article on France).

One effect of this drama was to inflict grave damage to the Franco-German relationship. Ever since the post-war reconciliation of the two countries effected by the Franco-German Treaty of 1963, negotiated by President Charles de Gaulle and Chancellor Konrad Adenauer, France and Germany had provided the driving force of European integration. Together, in the late 1970s, President Valéry Giscard d'Estaing and Chancellor Helmut Schmidt pioneered the currency exchange-rate mechanism which was the forerunner of the single currency, itself brokered between French President François Mitterrand and German Chancellor Helmut Kohl. Even when there was little personal affinity, as between President Jacques Chirac and Chancellor Gerhard Schroeder, the two leaders recognised that their common interest had to compel them to settle differences and to provide an agreed vision for the rest of the EU. Neither personally nor politically did that kind of relationship exist between President Hollande and German Chancellor Angela Merkel. They had no liking for each other and few points of political convergence.

For the first time in the history of the European Union, therefore, 2014 saw Germany emerge unchallenged as the Union's leader. This provoked both apprehension and relief among other Member States. The relief came from the fact that, alone among eurozone countries, Germany's economy was still growing, albeit haltingly. Without Germany, there would be no eurozone. Relief came, too, from the fact that Angela Merkel was genuinely committed to the success of the European project. Her leadership was clear and firm, but not authoritarian. The apprehension came from the fact that, at the heart of the European Union, lay reconciliation between France and Germany and the productive partnership that resulted from it. That partnership had stalled. Nor could the UK fill the void, since most of Britain's partners saw her as only tenuously committed to continued EU membership. So, historical fears of German domination of Europe—albeit by peaceful means—resurfaced. They were exacerbated by the continuing problems of the eurozone as a whole.

The abiding problem of the eurozone, since the 2008 crisis, was the conflict between rigorous action to control deficits, on the one hand, and the vital need to promote growth and employment, on the other. The early signs in 2014 were positive, as Ireland and Portugal began to turn around their economies and as Greece, too, on the back of an exceptionally harsh recovery plan and some resurgence in its tourist trade, re-established its credit worthiness. But as the year progressed, growth stalled. The average eurozone rate of inflation towards the year's end was 0.3 per cent, set against the target of the European Central Bank (ECB) of 2 per cent. In June, European leaders concluded that "fiscal consolidation must continue in a growth-friendly and differentiated manner". But the ECB hesitated, not least in the face of German resistance, to deploy quantitative easing to inject more money into the collective economy. In this deflationary climate, 11 of the Member States had double-digit rates of unemployment, rising to as high as 25 per cent in Spain and Greece.

It was scarcely surprising, therefore, that in these two countries what would once have been considered fringe political parties surged in popularity: Syriza in Greece and Podemos in Spain, both with levels of support high enough to make them very significant contenders in national elections in 2015. Elsewhere in the European Union, populist parties thrived, with two of them—UK Independence Party (UKIP) in Britain and the National Front (FN) in France—topping the polls in the elections to the European Parliament in May.

The European Parliament elections provided a perfect example of how the European Union could engender its own dramas without engaging the emotions of its citizens. Under the terms of the EU Lisbon Treaty of 2009, while it remained the responsibility of the heads of state or government collectively to nominate the president of the new European Commission (to take office at the end of October 2014), they were enjoined to do so "taking account" of the results of the European Parliament elections.

The Socialist group in the Parliament, under the leadership of German politician Martin Schulz, decided to put forward a leading candidate who, if the Socialist group formed a majority in the Parliament following the elections, would be their candidate to become president of the European Commission. In the case of the Socialists, it was to be Schulz himself. The purpose was two-fold: firstly to increase the power of the European Parliament vis à vis the other EU institutions and, secondly, to seek to engage public interest in the elections, with the notion that, in choosing to vote for a particular party, electors were also able to influence the choice of Commission president.

Other political groupings in the Parliament followed suit. The European People's Party (EPP), representing the centre-right, chose as their candidate Jean-Claude Juncker, former prime minister and finance minister of Luxembourg. German Members of the European Parliament (MEPs) from Angela Merkel's Christian Democratic Union (CDU) formed the biggest single entity within the EPP. Merkel herself was not keen on the whole process but was powerless to stop it.

Turnout in the elections, held between 22 and 25 May, was 42.5 per cent across the European Union, slightly down on the turnout at the last such elections in 2009 and an all-time low since the first elections to the EP in 1979, when turnout across the European Community was 62 per cent. Exit polls suggested that the ability to have a say in the choice of Commission president had had little resonance. In the UK and France, populist, anti-immigrant parties defeated traditional, mainstream ones. Populist parties also did well in Spain, Greece, Portugal, Denmark, Austria, Hungary and Sweden, but less well than previously in the Netherlands and the Czech Republic. Overall, the EPP was the largest group in the Parliament, but without an overall majority. A deal was quickly done whereby the Socialist grouping agreed to support Juncker's candidacy for the presidency of the European

Commission in return for EPP support for Schulz's candidature to become the President of the European Parliament.

In the face of very low enthusiasm for Juncker's candidacy among the EU heads of government, there was nonetheless a fatalistic sense of inevitability that the European Council should bow to the will of the European Parliament. Only British Prime Minister David Cameron set his face firmly and publicly against Juncker's candidacy. However, he did so on grounds that were not calculated to appeal to other EU heads of government: namely that Juncker was too much in favour of political integration and was not a moderniser. Chancellor Merkel appeared, briefly, to support Prime Minister Cameron's reservations, but she immediately ran into a firestorm in Germany, with both press and members of her own party accusing her of flying in the face of democracy. She quickly backed down and left Cameron to battle alone.

By now, it was too late for opponents of Juncker to rally round the more sub-stantive objection to his nomination: namely that, by nominating as Commission president a candidate chosen in advance by the European Parliament, the heads of government were failing to respect their obligations under the EU Treaties to put forward the best possible candidate "taking account" of the election results. In other words, instead of the heads of government choosing a candidate for the European Parliament to approve, they were simply rubber-stamping the Parlia-ment's choice.

The British prime minister maintained his opposition and risked provoking another impasse by leaking to the media his intention to invoke the Luxembourg Compromise in order to block Juncker's candidacy. The so-called "Luxembourg Compromise" was a political statement made by the French government in 1966, after it had failed to block the introduction of more decision-making in the EU by majority vote instead of unanimity. The statement asserted that when, on any leg-islative decision, a Member State declared that it had a very important national interest at stake, then discussion should continue until agreement was reached, i.e., that no vote should be taken. Neither then, nor subsequently, was this statement of practice supported by the majority of other Member States, although the UK signed up to it in 1972 as part of the price of French agreement to British acces-sion to the European Community.

So, in May 2014 Cameron's threat to invoke the Luxembourg Compromise, in order to block Jean-Claude Juncker's candidature to be European Commission president, provoked anxious heart searching in Paris. On the one hand, argued Pres-ident Hollande's advisers, it was hard to accept that there was any special British national interest at stake; nor was this the kind of legislative decision for which the Luxembourg Compromise had been designed. On the other hand, the French gov-ernment took seriously the risk that, if Cameron were humiliated, it would only bring closer the danger of Britain leaving the European Union altogether.

In the end, President Hollande announced that, in the event that the British prime minister should invoke the Luxembourg Compromise, France would not support him. Notwithstanding that decision, the Luxembourg Compromise remained, so Hollande asserted, "unassailable".

Faced with this decision, Cameron did not invoke the Luxembourg Compromise when heads of government met on 27 June to endorse Juncker's candidature. He did, however, insist on a vote, in which only one other leader voted with the UK to oppose the nomination. The overall outcome looked like a humiliating defeat for Cameron. But, rather on the model of one of his admired predecessors, Margaret Thatcher, if Cameron had not been able to "trounce" Europe, he had at least been seen to "defy" Europe, and domestic reaction on the whole gave him credit for standing up for what he believed in. In this, he was helped by the fact that the other European leaders had chosen Juncker without evident enthusiasm.

As for Juncker himself, he was, in public at least, magnanimous in victory. It was reportedly not the job he wanted, which was to succeed Herman van Rompuy as president of the European Council, a task for which his experience and working habits made him well suited. But, as an experienced and long-serving EU head of government, Juncker was also acutely aware of the massive task he had assumed at a time when public confidence in the EU institutions—in all Member States—was low; when the European economy was in the doldrums; and when the relative power of the European Commission vis à vis the Council of Ministers and, more especially, the European Parliament, was weaker than at any previous time in the EU's history. Juncker's first task was to secure the approval of the European Parliament for his appointment as Commission president and, at the same time, to signal to the EU as a whole that he had understood the magnitude of his task.

When he appeared before the 751 newly-elected MEPs on 15 July, Juncker presented what he called "A New Start for Europe: My agenda for jobs growth, fairness and democratic change". There were, he said, 10 policy areas which must be tackled by the new Commission. He undertook to mobilise up to €300 billion of additional private investment in the economy, focusing on broadband and energy networks, transport infrastructure, education, research and innovation. He promised a deeper and fairer internal market, including completion of the single market in services. But services alone, he argued, could not be the basis for renewed growth. His ambition was to see industry's weight in the EU's GDP brought back from its current level of 16 per cent to 20 per cent by 2020. Within the first six months of its mandate, the new Commission would take ambitious legislative steps to create a connected digital single market, capable of generating up to €250 billion of additional growth during the five years of the Commission's mandate. He promised a "capital markets union", allied to strict implementation of the new banking supervisory rules already introduced. He undertook to negotiate a "fair and balanced trade agreement with the USA". But he would not "sacrifice Europe's safety, health, social and data protection standards or our cultural diversity on the altar of free trade".

In a Europe of shared values, Juncker promised to entrust one commissioner with specific responsibility for the implementation of the Charter of Fundamental Rights. He acknowledged that the risk of an uncontrolled influx of illegal migrants from third countries must be tackled, but was clear that this could only be done through shared responsibility and solidarity among the Member States. Perhaps in the knowledge that migration between Member States, and the fear of more migration with further EU enlargement, was a neuralgic issue for many EU governments, Juncker undertook that, while current enlargement negotiations would continue, there would be no further enlargement over the next five years.

Finally, Juncker promised to be a president of the Commission in the interest of all. With British fears of being discriminated against outside the eurozone, Juncker undertook to work "with everyone—whether in the euro or not, whether in the Schengen agreement or outside, whether supportive of deeper integration, or not". Europe must move forward as a Union, but all did not have to move at the same speed. Those who wanted to move further, faster, should be able to do so.

Juncker's presidency was endorsed by a comfortable cross-party majority of MEPs. He set about choosing the members of the new Commission: 28 of them, one each from each member country. He had promised to the EP that he would come up with a gender-balanced list.

It was a testing task. Under the rules, each member government of the EU nominated a commissioner in consultation with the Commission president, who had to try to achieve a degree of political balance as well as balance between large and small Member States in the allocation of portfolios. Once completed, the new Commission had to be approved by the European Parliament, following a set of hearings in which each candidate commissioner was questioned by those MEPs with particular interests in his or her area of responsibility. The EP could not reject individual candidates, but it could—and had done so in the past—refuse to endorse the Commission as a whole, if it continued to contain an individual nominee of whom the Parliament disapproved.

After some weeks of intensive juggling, Juncker announced his proposed team of 28, comprising 19 men and nine women. Four of them were former prime ministers, four were former deputy prime ministers, and 19 had other ministerial experience. Seven members of the outgoing Commission were reappointed. Eight of the new team were former MEPs; 11 of the new team had an economic background and eight a foreign relations background. Their political affiliations were also mixed: 14 were from the centre-right, eight were social democrats, and one was Liberal, one a European Conservative (the UK's Lord Hill). The average age of the new team was 49.

In order to cope with the fact that, with a complement of 28, there were more commissioners than substantive jobs to go round, Juncker proposed that there should be seven vice-presidents who would supervise the work of overlapping areas of responsibility. In other words, each of the vice-presidents would have oversight of the work of up to seven commissioners, in groupings covering: jobs, growth, competiveness and investment; the digital single market; deeper and fairer economic and monetary union; better regulation, inter-institutional relations; rule of law and Charter of Fundamental Rights, subsidiarity and relations with national parliaments; budget and human resources; and energy. The high representative of the Union, Italy's Federica Mogherini, would cover foreign and security policy, as laid down by the EU treaties, but would in addition, as a Commission vice-president, have oversight of migration, transport, trade, development and neighbourhood policy. No legislative proposal could come before the full Commission for approval without first being vetted by the relevant supervising vice-president. The Dutch former foreign minister, Frans Timmermans, was to be the senior of the vice-presidents with an overall watching brief. At the same time, there would be a reorganisation of the directorates general of the Commission (the European civil service) to reflect the new political structure.

Ingenious as it was, the proposed restructuring raised obvious questions about workability. Would, for example, a "big beast" like Pierre Moscovici of France, a former finance minister, now with responsibility for the senior economic portfolio, be willing to work closely and, in a sense in a subordinate capacity, with Jyrki Katainen of Finland? Much would depend on personalities. But some commentators with experience of previous commissioners judged that, without direct line authority, the vice-presidents, all from small Member States, would have difficulty establishing their authority. The reorganisation of directorates general would take time and make it harder for the new Commission to hit the ground running.

In the ensuing hearings in the European Parliament, four candidates, in particular, were given a hard time: Pierre Moscovici because of France's failure to implement the deficit rules of the eurozone; Spain's Miguel Arias Cañete, because of a perceived conflict of interest between his energy and climate change portfolio and his previous links with energy companies; Alenka Bratusek of Slovenia because she had effectively nominated herself while she was outgoing prime minister; and Jonathan Hill (Lord Hill) of the UK.

Bratusek failed to satisfy MEPs that she had sufficient knowledge of her portfolio and they declined to give her their approval. After some behind the scenes activity, she chose to resign and was replaced by Violeta Bulc, whose credentials were far from obvious but who secured approval. Cañete was obliged to give additional undertakings to convince MEPs of his impartiality. Lord Hill faced a second hearing. This was partly because he had failed to satisfy MEPs that he had sufficient knowledge of his portfolio, and partly because he was assumed—as the nominee of David Cameron—to be hostile to the European Union. On both scores, Lord Hill was able to satisfy his critics at a second hearing.

Approval of the new Commission team was further delayed because of disagreement among EU leaders, when they met at the end of July, over the twin posts of president of the European Council and high representative. Some doubted whether Mogherini had sufficient foreign policy experience; others (from east and central Europe) feared that she would not be robust in dealing with the Russians over Ukraine. Eventual agreement (in August) to her appointment was balanced in political terms by the appointment of Poland's former prime minister, Donald Tusk, as the new president of the European Council. At the same time, Commission President Juncker made it clear that he would devote less time to overseas engagements (including bilateral summits) than had his predecessors.

October saw the approval of the new Commission by the European Parliament and the departure of the old team. Six hundred pages of self-analysis by the Barroso Commission of their achievements could not disguise the fact that Barroso's second term had been dominated by the 2008 financial crash and by the Commis-

The members of the Juncker Commission (2014-19)

Jean-Claude Juncker (Luxembourg)	*Commission President*
Frans Timmermans (Netherlands)	*First Vice President; Better Regulation, Inter-institutional Relations, the Rule of Law, and the Charter of Fundamental Rights*
Federica Mogherini (Italy)	*High Representative of the Union for foreign affairs and security policy; Vice-President of the Commission*
Kristalina Georgievna (Bulgaria)	*Vice-president; Budget and Human Resources*
Andrus Ansip (Estonia)	*Vice-president; Digital Single Market*
Maros Sefcovic (Slovakia)	*Vice-president; Energy Union*
Valdis Dombrovskis (Latvia)	*Vice-president; Euro and Social Dialogue*
Jyrki Katainen (Finland)	*Vice-president; Jobs, Growth, Investment and Competitiveness*
Günther Oettinger (Germany)	*Digital Economy and Society*
Johannes Hahn Austria	*European Neighbourhood Policy and Enlargement Negotiations*
Cecilia Malmstrom (Sweden)	*Trade*
Neven Mimica (Croatia)	*International Co-operation and Development*
Miguel Arias Cañete (Spain)	*Climate Action and Energy*
Karmenu Vella (Malta)	*Environment, Maritime Affairs and Fisheries*
Vytenis Andriukaitis (Lithuania)	*Health and Food Safety*
Dimitris Avramopoulos (Greece)	*Migration, Home Affairs and Citizenship*
Marianne Thyssen (Belgium)	*Employment, Social Affairs, Skills and Labour Mobility*
Pierre Moscovici (France)	*Economic and Financial Affairs, Taxation and Customs Union*
Christos Stylianides (Cyprus)	*Humanitarian Aid and Crisis Management*
Phil Hogan (Ireland)	*Agriculture and Rural Development*
Jonathan Hill (UK)	*Financial Stability, Financial Services and Capital Markets Union*
Violeta Bulc (Slovenia)	*Transport*
Elzbieta Bienkowska (Poland)	*Internal Market, Industry, Entrepreneurship and SMEs*
Vera Jourova (Czech Republic)	*Justice, Consumers and Gender Equality*
Tibor Navracsics (Hungary)	*Education, Culture, Youth and Sport*
Corina Cretu (Romania)	*Regional Policy*
Margrethe Vestager (Denmark)	*Competition*
Carlos Moedas (Portugal)	*Research, Science and Innovation*

sion's relative marginalisation as emergency measures to rescue the banking system were put in place. The main drivers in managing subsequent events had been the member governments of the eurozone, the European Central Bank and the president of the European Council, Herman van Rompuy.

Van Rompuy had proved to be an inspired choice. As a politician from one of the smaller member states, he did not threaten the power or egos of the larger countries. He did not seek the limelight. Fluent in French, English and German, he proved adept at working the telephones and brokering deals. Cameth the hour, cameth the man. Van Rompuy worked hard at his relationship with the president of the Commission; the two were oxen yoked to the same plough. But Commission President Barroso was ever mindful that the Commission headed by one of his predecessors, Jacques Santer, had lost office because it lost the confidence of the European Parliament. Barroso lived in fear of a vote of no confidence from the European Parliament. It also fell to him to preside over a Commission of 27 members, the largest in the history of the EU. He was the leader of an orchestra where getting musicians to play in unison, let alone in tune, was already an achievement.

Juncker was quick to act on his promise of an agenda based on growth and jobs. Barely a month into the five-year term of the new Commission, he launched an investment plan aimed at increasing European GDP and creating new jobs. The plan was built on three main strands: the creation of a new European Fund for Strategic Investment (EFSI), guaranteed with public money, to mobilise at least €315 billion of additional investment over three years from 2015 to 2017; the establishment of a project pipeline, coupled with an assistance programme, to channel investments where they were most needed; and a roadmap to make Europe more attractive for investment, including by removing regulatory bottlenecks.

The Juncker plan was endorsed by EU heads of state or government when the European Council met in December, for the first time under the presidency of Donald Tusk. The leaders called for the implementation of the new investment plan to begin within six months. They also called for the creation of an Energy Union to connect networks across national frontiers; for greater efforts to complete the internal market in goods and services; for better integration of capital markets; and for better regulation, and better enforcement of EU laws.

The brevity of the meeting and of the conclusions were widely commended. But many of the steps for which the heads of government called had been regular items on the agendas of the European Council since Margaret Thatcher first took up the cudgels of economic reform in the 1980s.

One area where the EU did remain in the vanguard was that of climate change. At the end of October, the European Commission reported a decrease in EU emissions of greenhouse gases of 1.8 per cent in 2013 compared to 2012. A few days previously, the European Council had committed the EU to achieving at least a 40 per cent domestic reduction in greenhouse gases by 2030.

The year closed, as it had almost begun, with the European Union holding its breath over its relationship with Russia over Ukraine. Ukraine had long been a potential candidate for accession to the EU, though its capacity for the economic and political reform that was necessary for a productive relationship with the EU had been tested, and often found wanting. With the west of Ukraine leaning politically and geographically towards the EU, and the east of the country leaning towards Russia; with Russia's President Vladimir Putin eager to redress the humiliation of the break-up of the old Soviet empire; and with Ukraine's President Viktor Yanukovych bent on turning his back on association with the EU, the stage had been set for what followed.

The forced departure of President Yanukovych in February in the face of anti-government and pro-EU demonstrations was followed by Russia's annexation of Crimea. In early March, the EU heads of government suspended bilateral talks with Russia on visa matters, as well as discussion on a new EU-Russia Agreement, and the preparations for participation in the G-8 summit in Sochi. Later in the month, the EU imposed the first of a gradually escalating series of measures against Russia. Instead of the planned G-8 summit in Sochi, the G-7—without Russia—met in Brussels in June. The EU-Russia summit was cancelled; bilateral talks with Russia on a number of issues were suspended.

Asset freezes and visa bans were put in place in respect of well over a hundred individuals, and more than 20 Russian entities had their assets in the EU frozen. The EU imposed a ban on goods originating in Russia-annexed Crimea and Sevastopol, and new EU investment in both places was banned in key transport, telecommunications and energy sectors. EU nationals and companies were barred from buying or selling long-term financial instruments issued by five major state-owned Russian banks, three major Russian energy companies and three major Russian defence companies. The import and export of arms was embargoed.

At the same time, the EU stepped up its relationship—political, financial and economic—with the new government in Ukraine, completing the signature of all parts of the EU-Ukraine Association Agreement in June. However, at Russia's insistence, one element of the agreement (the lowering of Ukrainian tariffs on EU goods) was delayed from taking effect.

So the year 2014 ended with an apprehensive stand-off with Russia; with Ukraine still in internal conflict; with Greece's place in the eurozone in doubt; and with a fragile European economy in a jittery global economy, on whose "dashboard", in Prime Minister David Cameron's words, the warning lights were flashing. Economic fragility had contributed to the rise of populist parties. Human rights in one Member State, Hungary, had come under threat. Turkey, hitherto a candidate for EU membership, appeared to be headed towards elected dictatorship.

There was a strong sense among the EU heads of government that coherent leadership was more than ever necessary, and more than ever hard to achieve.

Stephen Wall

COUNCIL OF EUROPE AND OSCE

Council of Europe

DATE OF FOUNDATION: 1949   HEADQUARTERS: Strasbourg, France
OBJECTIVES: To strengthen pluralist democracy, the rule of law and the maintenance of human
    rights in Europe and to further political, social and cultural co-operation between member
    states
MEMBERSHIP (END-'14): Albania, Andorra, Armenia, Austria, Azerbaijan, Belgium, Bosnia &
    Herzegovina, Bulgaria, Croatia, Cyprus, Czech Republic, Denmark, Estonia, Finland, France,
    Georgia, Germany, Greece, Hungary, Iceland, Ireland, Italy, Latvia, Liechtenstein, Lithuania,
    Luxembourg, Macedonia, Malta, Moldova, Monaco, Montenegro, Netherlands, Norway,
    Poland, Portugal, Romania, Russia, San Marino, Serbia, Slovakia, Slovenia, Spain, Sweden,
    Switzerland, Turkey, Ukraine, UK (total 47)
SECRETARY GENERAL: Thorbjorn Jagland (Norway) (since Oct '09)

Organisation for Security and Co-operation in Europe (OSCE)

DATE OF FOUNDATION: 1975   HEADQUARTERS: Vienna, Austria
OBJECTIVES: To promote security and co-operation among member states, particularly in respect of
    the resolution of internal and external conflicts
MEMBERSHIP (END-'14): Albania, Andorra, Armenia, Austria, Azerbaijan, Belarus, Belgium, Bosnia &
    Herzegovina, Bulgaria, Canada, Croatia, Cyprus, Czech Republic, Denmark, Estonia, Finland,
    France, Georgia, Germany, Greece, Holy See (Vatican), Hungary, Iceland, Ireland, Italy,
    Kazakhstan, Kyrgyzstan, Latvia, Liechtenstein, Lithuania, Luxembourg, Macedonia, Malta,
    Moldova, Monaco, Mongolia, Montenegro, Netherlands, Norway, Poland, Portugal, Romania,
    Russia, San Marino, Serbia, Slovakia, Slovenia, Spain, Sweden, Switzerland, Tajikistan,
    Turkey, Turkmenistan, Ukraine, UK, USA, Uzbekistan (total 57)
SECRETARY GENERAL: Lamberto Zannier (Italy) (since July '11)

THE **Council of Europe** and its associated agencies had a challenging year. Chief
among those challenges was the situation in Ukraine. In April, the Parliamentary
Assembly (PACE) voted after a long and heated debate, by 145 to 21, with 22
abstentions, to suspend Russia from several of its major activities for the remainder of 2014. Russia countered by cutting its financial contribution. The Assembly
was also notified of allegations that Russia and several Central Asian member-
states had attempted to influence members' votes with lavish gifts and trips. These
allegations were unresolved but, more generally, corruption in a variety of forms
and at a variety of levels was a recurring theme in the year's work. The president
of the Group of States Against Corruption (GRECO) voiced concern about the
inadequacy of legal and financial resources and even a lack of political will to
combat corruption.

In similar vein, the Parliamentary Assembly voiced concern about breaches of
civil liberties and discrimination against minorities in several member-states One
of these was Azerbaijan, whose president, Ilham Aliyev, was the current chairman
of the Council's committee of ministers. His claim that "all fundamental freedoms
are respected" in his country could be given little credence. Activists protested but
Aliyev served his term.

The Ukraine crisis presented the **Organisation for Security and Cooperation
in Europe (OSCE)** with the biggest challenge and the largest deployment of
personnel in its history. A special monitoring mission was formed in March and

reported daily from the field, including border and ceasefire monitoring and the humanitarian dimension of the conflict. This was not easy: forces on the ground were often uncooperative and in the spring one team was held prisoner by a separatist militia for four weeks. In July, an OSCE team was approaching Donetsk when Malaysia Airlines flight MH17 was downed, but obstruction and inability to operate freely in a war zone led to the team's withdrawal until adequate access could be secured. However, OSCE observers were able to monitor the country's presidential and parliamentary elections—apart from Crimea and Donetsk and Lugansk regions, which were in rebel hands and where polling did not take place (see the article on Ukraine). From September, OSCE worked with Russia and Ukraine in a Tripartite Contact Group, charged with finding ways of stabilising and de-escalating the situation and, where possible, negotiating a solution.

Ukraine was not the only place where OSCE personnel encountered physical danger. Its election monitors in Afghanistan had to withdraw temporarily to Istanbul when their hotel in Kabul was bombed. Their report noted that the ground was better prepared than previously but added drily that there was "still a long way to go". Much the same could have been said of polls held in several other countries. In Bulgaria, Uzbekistan, Hungary, Croatia, Turkey and FYR Macedonia corruption or bias in favour of the ruling party (or both) were endemic. In several countries reforms had made the electoral process more efficient without its becoming more democratic: old habits died hard. By contrast, reports on Denmark, Norway and Latvia found few failings of consequence.

Martin Harrison

AMERICAN AND CARIBBEAN ORGANISATIONS

Organisation of American States (OAS)

DATE OF FOUNDATION: 1951   HEADQUARTERS: Washington DC, USA
OBJECTIVES: To facilitate political, economic and other co-operation between member states and to
    defend their territorial integrity and independence
MEMBERSHIP (END-'14): Antigua & Barbuda, Argentina, Bahamas, Barbados, Belize, Bolivia, Brazil,
    Canada, Chile, Colombia, Costa Rica, Cuba, Dominica, Dominican Republic, Ecuador, El
    Salvador, Grenada, Guatemala, Guyana, Haiti, Honduras, Jamaica, Mexico, Nicaragua,
    Panama, Paraguay, Peru, St Kitts & Nevis, St Lucia, St Vincent & the Grenadines, Suriname,
    Trinidad & Tobago, USA, Uruguay, Venezuela (total 35)
SECRETARY GENERAL: José Miguel Insulza (Chile) (since May '05)

Union of South American Nations (UNASUR)

DATE OF FOUNDATION: 2008   HEADQUARTERS: Quito, Ecuador
OBJECTIVES: To improve political and economic integration in the region, and defence co-operation
MEMBERSHIP (END-'14): Argentina, Bolivia, Brazil, Chile, Colombia, Ecuador, Guyana, Paraguay,
    Peru, Suriname, Uruguay, Venezuela (total 12)
SECRETARY GENERAL: Ernesto Samper Pizano (Colombia) (since Aug '14)

Organisation of Ibero-American States (OEI)

DATE OF FOUNDATION: 1957   HEADQUARTERS: Madrid, Spain
OBJECTIVES: To promote the development of regional projects in education, science, technology and
    the arts
MEMBERSHIP (END-'14): Andorra, Argentina, Bolivia, Brazil, Chile, Colombia, Costa Rica, Cuba,
    Dominican Republic, Ecuador, El Salvador, Equatorial Guinea, Guatemala, Honduras, Mexico,
    Nicaragua, Panama, Paraguay, Peru, Portugal, Puerto Rico, Spain, Uruguay, Venezuela (total 24)
SECRETARY GENERAL: Alvaro Marchesi Ullastres (Spain)

Caribbean Community (CARICOM)

DATE OF FOUNDATION: 1973   HEADQUARTERS: Georgetown, Guyana
OBJECTIVES: To facilitate economic, political and other co-operation between member states and to
    operate certain regional services
MEMBERSHIP (END-'14): Antigua & Barbuda, Bahamas, Barbados, Belize, Dominica, Grenada,
    Guyana, Haiti, Jamaica, Montserrat, St Kitts & Nevis, St Lucia, St Vincent & the Grenadines,
    Suriname, Trinidad & Tobago (total 15)
ASSOCIATE MEMBERS: Anguilla, Bermuda, British Virgin Islands, Cayman Islands, Turk & Caicos
    Islands (total 5)
SECRETARY GENERAL: Irwin LaRocque (Dominica) (since Aug '11)

THERE were a series of high profile meetings during the year. The first came in
early June when the 44th General Assembly of the **Organization of American
States (OAS)** met in Asunción, Paraguay. Two issues dominated the proceedings.
The first was the proposal by Ecuador to reform the Inter-American Commission
on Human Rights (IACHR). The second was Brazil's desire for a resolution supporting equal access to all aspects of public life for everyone regardless of race,
gender, or sexual orientation. Both proposals were controversial and divided
opinion among OAS members and civil society groups alike. After two days of
discussions a final declaration was agreed. The two proposals were included but
both were watered-down considerably. On the IACHR, a resolution was passed
calling for changes to the way in which the body functioned, but there was no
mention of a potential move of its headquarters to Latin America or to limit its
funding. Similarly a "human rights, sexual identity and orientation" resolution
was approved, but with many reservations and formal objections from 11 countries, including the USA and Paraguay. Another reason why these resolutions had
limited impact was because of their non-binding nature.

On 4 December the **Union of South American Nations (UNASUR)** met for
a two-day summit. On day two Unasur's new headquarters were inaugurated in
Mitad del Mundo. Unasur delegations were scheduled to begin working in the
building in January, along with the new secretary general, Ernesto Samper, a
former Colombian president. Speaking at the inauguration, Samper said that he
would move quickly to "a process of convergence" with other regional blocs,
so that South America could project itself on the world stage as a "new fourth
bloc, the South-South bloc," to compete against the likes of the USA, the EU
and Asia. However, perhaps greater work was needed on Unasur itself. At the
summit meeting little was achieved, and clear divisions were seen between the
heads of government in terms of how the organisation should develop.
Ecuador's President Rafael Correa talked about the need to implement grand
integration schemes, such as a regional currency, while Peru's President

Ollanta Humala was more pragmatic, calling for a focus on "productive diversification and the search for new markets". These different approaches meant that Unasur's performance continued to disappoint.

Two other meetings worth noting also took place in December. The **Organisation of Ibero-American States (OEI)**, a grouping including Spain, Portugal and 21 Latin American countries, met and agreed an Ibero-American Erasmus exchange programme. This provided student scholarships and allowed for the free movement of professors and researchers. However, a number of heads of government did not attend, including Bolivia's President Evo Morales, who said he had no interest in attending something created by "Spanish monarchs for their own interests". The second was the **Caribbean Community (CARICOM)**-Cuba summit, in Santiago de Cuba. However, the outcomes were disappointing. The *Jamaica Gleaner* newspaper, for example, criticised the summit for avoiding the key issues facing the region.

Peter Clegg

ARAB ORGANISATIONS

League of Arab States (Arab League)
DATE OF FOUNDATION: 1945   HEADQUARTERS: Cairo, Egypt
OBJECTIVES: To coordinate political, economic, social and cultural co-operation between member
   states and to mediate in disputes between them
MEMBERSHIP (END-'14): Algeria, Bahrain, Comoros, Djibouti, Egypt, Iraq, Jordan, Kuwait, Lebanon,
   Libya, Mauritania, Morocco, Oman, Palestine, Qatar, Saudi Arabia, Somalia, Sudan, Syria
   (suspended), Tunisia, United Arab Emirates, Yemen (total 22)
SECRETARY GENERAL: Nabil al-Araby (Egypt) (since May '11)

Gulf Co-operation Council (GCC)
DATE OF FOUNDATION: 1981   HEADQUARTERS: Riyadh, Saudi Arabia
OBJECTIVES: To promote co-operation between member states in all fields with a view to achieving
   unity
MEMBERSHIP (END-'13): Bahrain, Kuwait, Oman, Qatar, Saudi Arabia, United Arab Emirates (total 6)
SECRETARY GENERAL: Abdullatif bin Rashid al-Zayani (Bahrain) (since April '11)

THE shortcomings of pan-Arab organisations were cruelly exposed in 2014 as they failed to exert any significant influence on the multiple crises that beset the region: the brutal war in Syria; the rise of the Islamic State in Iraq and Syria (ISIS); the break-up of Libya; the war in Gaza; and the Houthi assault on the central government in Yemen. One rare achievement was a Saudi Arabian-engineered reconciliation within the **Gulf Co-operation Council (GCC)**, which paved the way for the organisation to hold its annual summit conference in Qatar with all six member states represented.

The **Arab League** held its annual summit in Kuwait on 25-26 March. The fractious tone of the meeting was reflected in the disagreement over whether to issue a final communiqué. The hosts got round this problem by referring to the statement issued at the end of the conference as the Kuwait Declaration. One of the main issues of dispute was the role of Qatar in regional political affairs. Shortly before the conference, Saudi Arabia, the UAE and Bahrain had all withdrawn their ambassadors from Doha on the grounds that Qatar was supporting subversive Islamist movements in other Arab countries, in particular Egypt, where Qatar had been the main backer of the Muslim Brotherhood president, Mohammed Morsi before he was ousted by the Egyptian army in July 2013. Qatar was also accused by fellow Arab states of backing extreme Islamist groups in Syria, which had undermined the capacities of the main rebel groups fighting against the forces of the Syrian president, Bashar Assad. The Arab League had suspended the membership of the Syrian government in 2011.

The Arab League's formal involvement in diplomatic efforts to resolve the Syria crisis came to an end with the resignation in May of Lakhdar Brahimi as the joint UN-Arab League special envoy on Syria. Both Brahimi and his predecessor, Kofi Annan, who had resigned in August 2012, operated under a joint mandate from the UN and the Arab League, whereas the new Syria envoy, Staffan de Mistura, solely represented the UN.

The Arab League did not make much impact on the conflict between Israel and the Palestinian Hamas group in Gaza in July and August 2014, but it lent its support to a resolution presented to the UN Security Council at the end of the year, calling for a three-year deadline to be set for the establishment of a Palestinian state. The resolution narrowly failed to garner the required support of a minimum of nine of the council's 15 members. The Arab League agreed in January 2015 to back the drafting of a new resolution on similar lines.

The other main Arab political organisation, the GCC, was riven by the dispute between Qatar, on one side, and Saudi Arabia and the UAE, on the other, for much of the year. In November, King Abdullah of Saudi Arabia convened a meeting of leaders of GCC member states in Riyadh in an effort to clear the air. As a result, Saudi Arabia, the UAE and Bahrain agreed to return their ambassadors to Doha, and Qatar agreed to rein in its support for the Muslim Brotherhood and to close down a channel of the Al-Jazeera television network that was dedicated to reporting on Egypt. This agreement paved the way for the Doha GCC summit to go ahead on 8-9 December. The meeting focused on supporting long-term efforts to integrate the economies of the six member states.

David Butter

AFRICAN ORGANISATIONS

African Union (AU)

DATE OF FOUNDATION: 2001   HEADQUARTERS: Addis Ababa, Ethiopia
OBJECTIVES: To promote the unity, solidarity and co-operation of African states, to defend their sovereignty, to promote democratic principles, human rights and sustainable development and to accelerate the political and socio-economic integration of the continent
MEMBERSHIP (END-'14): Algeria, Angola, Benin, Botswana, Burkina Faso, Burundi, Cameroon, Cape Verde, Central African Republic (suspended), Chad, Comoros, Congo, Côte d'Ivoire, Democratic Republic of Congo, Djibouti, Egypt, Equatorial Guinea, Eritrea, Ethiopia, Gabon, the Gambia, Ghana, Guinea, Guinea-Bissau, Kenya, Lesotho, Liberia, Libya, Madagascar, Malawi, Mali, Mauritania, Mauritius, Mozambique, Namibia, Niger, Nigeria, Rwanda, São Tomé and Príncipe, Senegal, Seychelles, Sierra Leone, Somalia, South Africa, South Sudan, Sudan, Swaziland, Tanzania, Togo, Tunisia, Uganda, Western Sahara, Zambia, Zimbabwe (total 54)
CHAIR OF AU COMISSION: Nkosazana Dlamini-Zuma (South Africa) (since July '12)

Southern African Development Community (SADC)

DATE OF FOUNDATION: 1992   HEADQUARTERS: Gaborone, Botswana
OBJECTIVES: To work towards the creation of a regional common market
MEMBERSHIP (END-'14): Angola, Botswana, Democratic Republic of Congo, Lesotho, Madagascar, Malawi, Mauritius, Mozambique, Namibia, Seychelles, South Africa, Swaziland, Tanzania, Zambia, Zimbabwe (total 15)
EXECUTIVE SECRETARY: Stergomena Lawrence Tax (Tanzania) (since Aug '13)

Economic Community of West African States (ECOWAS)

DATE OF FOUNDATION: 1975   HEADQUARTERS: Abuja, Nigeria
OBJECTIVES: To seek the creation of an economic union of member states
MEMBERSHIP (END-'14): Benin, Burkina Faso, Cabo Verde, Côte d'Ivoire, the Gambia, Ghana, Guinea, Guinea-Bissau, Liberia, Mali, Niger, Nigeria, Senegal, Sierra Leone, Togo (total 15)
PRESIDENT OF THE COMMISSION: Kadré Désiré Ouedraogo (Burkina Faso) (since March '12)

THOUGH the 22nd **African Union (AU)** summit, held in January at the AU's headquarters in Addis Ababa, Ethiopia, had as its theme "agriculture and food security", both then and in late June, when the AU heads of state met for the 23rd summit at a plush conference centre in Malabo, Equatorial Guinea, security issues dominated discussions. AU Commission chair Nkosazana Dlamini-Zuma was among those who warned that the growth of terrorism was a threat to African prosperity, peace and integration.

Boko Haram's attacks in northern Nigeria drew international attention in April when over 200 girls were kidnapped by the Islamist militants. An AU force, 22,000 strong, continued to battle al-Shabaab in Somalia, with some success towards the end of the year, but neighbouring Kenya, involved militarily against al-Shabaab, suffered a number of terrorist incidents.

The conflict in South Sudan continued, despite AU mediation efforts through the Intergovernmental Authority on Development (IGAD); tensions remained high, too, in the Central African Republic, where an African-led International Support Mission to the Central African Republic (MISCA) set up a humanitarian corridor to facilitate supplies reaching those in need. The AU's Peace and Security Council discussed the resurgence of violence in the Darfur region of Sudan and called for negotiations between the rebels and the government.

Towards the end of the year, the AU called on the international community to help restore stability in Libya.

No substantial progress was made in rendering operational the African Standby Force and its Rapid Deployment Capability, or the African Immediate Crisis Response Capacity (see AR 2014, p. 409). On the other hand, the **Economic Community of West African States (ECOWAS)**, having aided the transition in Burkina Faso, hailed the relative political stability of its region. After lifting its 2013 suspension of Egypt, the AU welcomed President Abdel-Fattah Sisi at the Malabo summit.

During the year there was much talk of how to begin to integrate the AU's "Agenda 2063" blueprint—a call for action to develop the continent, unveiled at the 50th anniversary, in 2013, of the founding of the Organisation of African Unity—into both national plans and those of the eight sub-regional economic communities recognised by the AU.

Critics said that the AU was slow to recognise the damage to the continent from the spread of the Ebola virus in West Africa and to coordinate action against it. After the AU summit in 2013 had agreed that leaders in office should have immunity from prosecution for serious crimes, the decision by the prosecutor of the International Criminal Court in December to withdraw charges against President Uhuru Kenyatta of Kenya for lack of evidence was thought likely to mute somewhat the AU's long-standing criticisms of the court (see AR 2014, p. 410). The 22nd AU summit adopted a maritime action plan and set 2015-25 as the "Decade of African Seas and Oceans". While measures taken against pirates off the East African coast had proved successful, a new threat emerged in West African waters.

At a BRICS summit in Brazil it was agreed that the African regional centre of the BRICS New Development Bank would be in South Africa. ECOWAS made plans to introduce a common external tariff from the beginning of 2015, and South Africa continued to promote a free trade agreement linking the **Southern African Development Community (SADC)**, the Common Market for Eastern and Southern Africa and the East African Community. The SADC summit held in Zimbabwe in August saw the 90-year old Robert Mugabe take over as chair of the sub-regional body. Though the summit hailed the completion of the Hashim Mbita project on the history of liberation in the region, no funds were made available to print the outcome of the research.

Christopher Saunders

EURASIAN ORGANISATIONS

Conference on Interaction and Confidence-Building Measures in Asia (CICA)

DATE OF FOUNDATION: 1994   HEADQUARTERS: Almaty, Kazakhstan
OBJECTIVES: To enhance peace, security and stability in Asia
MEMBERSHIP (END-'14): Afghanistan, Azerbaijan, Bahrain, Bangladesh, Cambodia, China, Egypt, India, Iran, Iraq, Israel, Jordan, Kazakhstan, Kyrgyzstan, Mongolia, Pakistan, Palestine, Qatar, Russia, South Korea, Tajikistan, Thailand, Turkey, UAE, Uzbekistan, Vietnam (total 26)
EXECUTIVE DIRECTOR: Gong Jianwei (China)

Eurasian Economic Union

DATE OF FOUNDATION: 2014   HEADQUARTERS: Moscow, Russia
OBJECTIVES: to guarantee the free movement of goods, services, capital and labour between member states
MEMBERSHIP (END-'14): Armenia, Belarus, Kazakhstan, Kyrgyzstan (pending), Russia (total 5)
CHAIRMAN OF EURASIAN COMMISSION: Viktor Khristenko (Russia)

Shanghai Co-operation Organisation (SCO)

DATE OF FOUNDATION: 2001   HEADQUARTERS: Beijing, China
OBJECTIVES: To strengthen mutual trust and good-neighbourly relations among member states
MEMBERSHIP (END-'14): China, Kazakhstan, Kyrgyzstan, Russia, Tajikistan, Uzbekistan (total 6)
OBSERVER MEMBERS: Afghanistan, India, Iran, Mongolia, Pakistan (total 5)
SECRETARY GENERAL: Dmitry Mezentsev (Russia) (since Jan '13)

Collective Security Treaty Organisation (CSTO)

DATE OF FOUNDATION: 2002   HEADQUARTERS: Moscow, Russia
OBJECTIVES: To further co-operation and develop joint structures in security, defence and intelligence
MEMBERSHIP (END-'14): Armenia, Belarus, Kazakhstan, Kyrgyzstan, Russia, Tajikistan (total 6)
SECRETARY GENERAL: Gen. Nikolai Bordyuzha (Russia) (since April '03)

Commonwealth of Independent States (CIS)

DATE OF FOUNDATION: 1991   HEADQUARTERS: Minsk, Belarus
OBJECTIVES: To facilitate economic and humanitarian integration between member states
MEMBERSHIP (END-'14): Armenia, Azerbaijan, Belarus, Kazakhstan, Kyrgyzstan, Moldova, Russia, Tajikistan, Turkmenistan, Uzbekistan, Ukraine (total 11)
EXECUTIVE SECRETARY: Sergei Lebedev (Russia) (since Oct '07)

THERE were parallel and potentially rival developments in Eurasian organisations in 2014. The first major event was the fourth summit meeting of the **Conference on Interaction and Confidence-Building Measures in Asia (CICA)**, held on 20-21 May in Shanghai, hosted by China, the current holder of the chairmanship. Founded by Kazakhstan in 1994, CICA was conceived as an Asian equivalent of the Organisation for Security and Cooperation in Europe (OSCE), with members from South, South-East and East Asia, also the Middle East. The May summit was notable for the emphasis on "Asian-ness", echoing the declarations of the 1955 Bandung Conference (or Afro-Asian Conference, see AR 1955, p. 165). Chinese President Xi Jinping stressed that Asian problems should be solved by Asians themselves and proposed the creation of a multilateral Asian security structure.

On 29 May, the heads of state of Belarus, Kazakhstan and the Russian Federation signed the **Eurasian Economic Union (EEU)** treaty. It was subsequently ratified by the national parliaments and would come into force on 1 January 2015. The main aim of the treaty was to guarantee the free movement of goods, services, capital and labour between member states. Concurrently, the **Eurasian Economic Community (EurAsEc)** which, in addition to the EEU members included Tajikistan, Kyrgyzstan and Uzbekistan, was phased out. Armenia joined the EEU in October; Kyrgyzstan signed the accession Treaty on 23 December but would not become a full member for several months. Tajikistan's position was unclear; Turkmenistan and Uzbekistan rejected the idea of membership. The EEU was interpreted by some analysts as a Russian attempt to counter Chinese influence in Central Asia.

On 12 September the annual summit of the **Shanghai Cooperation Organization (SCO)** was held in Dushanbe, the Tajik capital. President Xi took advantage of this meeting to make his first official visit to all five Central Asian states. He emphasised the strategic importance of the region for China and during the SCO summit announced a credit packet of $5 billion for the implementation of joint projects.

The **Collective Security Treaty Organisation (CSTO)** announced in June that it was suspending efforts to "facilitate dialogue" with NATO, though it confirmed that it intended to develop relations with the OSCE. The regular summit meeting of the **Commonwealth of Independent States (CIS)** was held in Minsk in September. Unsurprisingly, Ukraine's President Petro Poroshenko was absent, but the Ukrainian ambassador to Belarus did participate. Other CIS events included the Ashgabat Council of Heads of Government meeting in Turkmenistan in November, at which the implementation of CIS Free Trade Agreement was analysed.

On 24 October, ministers of the 10-member **Central Asia Regional Economic Cooperation (CAREC)** programme met in Astana, Kazakhstan's capital, and endorsed the joint Trade Policy Strategic Action Plan 2013-17. The proceedings were somewhat overshadowed by the simultaneous launch in Beijing of the **Asian Infrastructure Investment Bank (AIIB)**. The new institution had a registered capital of $100 billion (double the initial proposal), most of which was provided by China, with smaller contributions from other members, including Kazakhstan and Uzbekistan. The AIIB was widely seen as a challenge to the activities of the **Asian Development Bank**, the main sponsor of the CAREC programme, which was dominated by the USA and Japan.

Shirin Akiner

ASIA-PACIFIC ORGANISATIONS

Association of South-East Asian Nations (ASEAN)

DATE OF FOUNDATION: 1967   HEADQUARTERS: Jakarta, Indonesia
OBJECTIVES: To accelerate economic growth, social progress and cultural development in the region
MEMBERSHIP (END-'14): Brunei, Burma (Myanmar), Cambodia, Indonesia, Laos, Malaysia,
    Philippines, Singapore, Thailand, Vietnam (total 10)
SECRETARY GENERAL: Le Luong Minh (Vietnam) (since Jan '13)

Asia-Pacific Economic Co-operation (APEC)

DATE OF FOUNDATION: 1989   HEADQUARTERS: Singapore
OBJECTIVES: To promote market-oriented economic development and co-operation in the Pacific
    Rim countries
MEMBERSHIP (END-'14): Australia, Brunei, Canada, Chile, China, Hong Kong, Indonesia, Japan,
    South Korea, Malaysia, Mexico, New Zealand, Papua New Guinea, Peru, Philippines, Russia,
    Singapore, Taiwan, Thailand, USA, Vietnam (total 21)
EXECUTIVE DIRECTOR: Allan Bollard (New Zealand) (since Jan '13)

Asian Development Bank (ADB)

DATE OF FOUNDATION: 1966   HEADQUARTERS: Manila, Philippines
OBJECTIVES: To improve the welfare of the people in Asia and the Pacific, particularly the 1.9
    billion who live on less than $2 a day
MEMBERSHIP (END-'14): REGIONAL MEMBERS: Afghanistan, Armenia, Australia, Azerbaijan,
    Bangladesh, Bhutan, Brunei, Burma (Myanmar), Cambodia, China, Cook Islands, East Timor,
    Fiji, Georgia, Hong Kong, India, Indonesia, Japan, Kazakhstan, Kiribati, Kyrgyzstan, Laos,
    Malaysia, Maldives, Marshall Islands, Federated States of Micronesia, Mongolia, Nauru,
    Nepal, New Zealand, Pakistan, Palau, Papua New Guinea, Philippines, Samoa, Singapore,
    Solomon Islands, South Korea, Sri Lanka, Taiwan, Tajikistan, Thailand, Tonga, Turkmenistan,
    Tuvalu, Uzbekistan, Vanuatu, Vietnam (total 48); NON REGIONAL MEMBERS: Austria, Belgium,
    Canada, Denmark, Finland, France, Germany, Ireland, Italy, Luxembourg, the Netherlands,
    Norway, Portugal, Spain, Sweden, Switzerland, Turkey, UK, USA (total 19)
PRESIDENT: Takehiko Nakao (Japan) (since April '13)

South Asian Association for Regional Co-operation (SAARC)

DATE OF FOUNDATION: 1985   HEADQUARTERS: Kathmandu, Nepal
OBJECTIVES: To promote collaboration and mutual assistance in the economic, social, cultural and
    technical fields
MEMBERSHIP (END-'14): Afghanistan, Bangladesh, Bhutan, India, Maldives, Nepal, Pakistan, Sri
    Lanka (total 8)
SECRETARY GENERAL: Ahmed Saleem (Maldives) (since March '12)

Pacific Islands Forum (PIF)

DATE OF FOUNDATION: 1971 (as South Pacific Forum)   HEADQUARTERS: Suva, Fiji
OBJECTIVES: To enhance the economic and social well-being of the people of the Pacific, in support
    of the efforts of the members' governments
MEMBERSHIP (END-'14): Australia, Cook Islands, Fiji, Kiribati, Marshall Islands, Federated States of
    Micronesia, Nauru, New Zealand, Niue, Palau, Papua New Guinea, Samoa, Solomon Islands,
    Tonga, Tuvalu, Vanuatu (total 16)
SECRETARY GENERAL: Meg Taylor (Papua New Guinea) (since July '14)

THE 25th summit of the **Association of South-East Asian Nations (ASEAN)** was
held in November in Naypyidaw, Burma on the theme "Moving Forward in Unity
towards a Peaceful and Prosperous Community". The 9th East Asia Summit took

place on 13 November. The meetings noted efforts to achieve an ASEAN Economic Community by the end of 2015, and to agree on procedures to deal with confrontations in the South China Sea, where competing claims involving China and several ASEAN nations remained a source of tension.

The 22nd **Asia-Pacific Economic Cooperation (APEC)** summit was held in Beijing on 10-12 November. Asia-Pacific leaders agreed to make progress towards a new free trade zone—the Free Trade Area of the Asia-Pacific—which was strongly backed by China. The summit issued a "Leaders' Declaration"—the "Beijing Agenda for an Integrated, Innovative and Interconnected Asia-Pacific"—which reflected the APEC summit's theme, "Shaping the Future through Asia-Pacific Partnership". The Chinese government took steps to improve Beijing's air quality prior to the APEC summit, imposing restrictions on the use of motor vehicles, closing public schools, state-run businesses and factories, and encouraging residents to leave the city.

The **Asian Development Bank (ADB)** held the 47th annual meeting of its board of governors in Astana, Kazakhstan, from 2-5 May on the theme of "The Silk Road: Connecting Asia with a Changing World". On 24 October China launched the Asian Infrastructure Investment Bank, a rival to the ADB.

The 18th **South Asian Association For Regional Co-operation (SAARC)** summit was held from 26-27 November in Kathmandu, Nepal—the organisation's first summit since 2011—under the theme of "Deeper Integration for Peace and Prosperity". The eight member states signed the "SAARC Framework Agreement for Energy Cooperation" and agreed to a 19th summit in Pakistan in 2016.

The 45th **Pacific Islands Forum (PIF)** summit was held on 29-31 July in Palau, and issued "The Palau Declaration on 'The Ocean: Life and Future'—Charting a Course to Sustainability", which emphasised initiatives to protect the world's oceans. Dame Meg Taylor (of Papua New Guinea) was appointed PIF secretary-general, the first woman to hold this position. Tokelau was admitted as an Associate Member. Fiji was reinstated following parliamentary elections in the country, but declined to renew its PIF participation pending a reassessment of the role of Australia and New Zealand. The Pacific Islands Development Forum, launched by Fiji in 2013 (comprising PIF members other than Australia and New Zealand), held its second summit in Fiji in June under the theme of "Green Growth in the Pacific—Building Resilient and Sustainable Futures".

In June, the Melanesian Spearhead Group rejected an application for membership by the West Papua National Coalition for Liberation, advising West Papuans to reapply through a fully representative organisation. The 20th Micronesian Chief Executives Summit was held in June in Yap, Federated States of Micronesia (FSM), with the theme "One Heartbeat, Diversity Is Our Strength", stressing the unifying power of the ocean for Micronesian peoples. The 14th Micronesian Presidents' Summit was held in July in Pohnpei, FSM. In September the FSM, Marshall Islands and Palau signed a treaty establishing the Micronesian Trade and Economic Community.

Stephen Levine

XII THE INTERNATIONAL ECONOMY IN 2014

THE world economy continued to expand in 2014 but only along the low growth path that had emerged from the depression of 2008-09. At the start of the year there were cautious forecasts of a stronger rate of recovery but by mid-year such expectations had largely diminished. In the event, global GDP, at market exchange rates, grew by some 2.6 per cent compared with 2.5 per cent in 2013 and with forecasts at the end of 2013 of around 3 per cent. Using purchasing power parities, which give more weight in the total to developing and emerging market economies, global GDP rose by about 3.3 per cent, also virtually unchanged from 2013 and against forecasts of some 3.7 per cent. These were of course estimates based on provisional data for the major advanced economies and "guesstimates" for many other countries but the general picture of a relatively slow and uncertain rate of recovery from the worst economic crisis since at least the 1930s was unlikely to be revised significantly.

There were, however, large fluctuations in quarterly rates of growth within the year in some of the larger advanced economies, notably the United States, Japan and Germany, with swings from positive to negative growth and back again, which complicated life for policy makers and the financial markets. Despite its fluctuating output, the US grew significantly faster than most of the other advanced economies, notably Japan and the eurozone, although within the latter there were large differences between the individual members. Among the developing and emerging market economies, rates of growth remained relatively high in East Asia but nevertheless decelerated as China continued its transition to a lower, alternative growth path. Only in South Asia was growth faster than in 2013, largely because of India. In Africa there were large differences among individual countries but overall the average growth rate was more or less stable. In contrast there was a sharp deceleration of growth rates in much of Latin America, in part a reflection of weak commodity markets, and also in the Commonwealth of Independent States (CIS) where geopolitical tensions, a severe slowdown in Russia and spill-overs from the Ukrainian crisis affected most of the region.

With sluggish growth in all but a few advanced economies and a slowdown in much of the developing and emerging market world, there were concerns that differences in macro-economic policies, especially between the United States and the eurozone, would heighten tensions in the foreign exchange and international capital markets. Towards the end of the year there were a number of warnings about the risks of "currency wars", especially in the US, where the dollar appreciated sharply against a range of currencies and where a number of members of Congress were pressing for measures to counter alleged "currency manipulation". Net private capital flows to developing and emerging economies fell in 2014 but most of the decline was due to outflows from Russia. With central banks still holding down interest rates close to zero, however, inflows to other developing and emerging economies continued, with investors frantically searching for higher yields and borrowers attracted by lower capital costs. With very high levels of foreign currency debt held by the corporate sector in a number of countries including China, Brazil, Mexico and India, the risks to financial stability from changing expectations about interest rates remained high. The US Federal Reserve ended its quantitative easing programme in October and was expected to start raising interest rates at some time in the course of 2015, even though the sharp decline in the price of oil from mid-year, together with the appreciation of the dollar, was expected to keep US inflation below the Federal Reserve's target.

At the end of the year there was little prospect of the global economy moving away from the low growth path of the past four years. The major international institutions were forecasting a modest acceleration in global GDP to 3 per cent (or 3.5 per cent with purchasing power parity weights), a rate that a year earlier was being forecast for 2014. There was disagreement as to how far the collapse in the price of crude oil—a fall of nearly 50 per cent between June and December— might help to lift the overall growth rate: on balance it was likely to raise real incomes and household spending in a number of oil-importing countries but was unlikely to overcome a combination of policy mistakes and deep-seated structural obstacles that were seen as restraining a faster rate of recovery. A broader and controversial question that received a lot of attention from economists and commentators during the year was whether the low growth rates since the recession of 2008-09 signalled the onset of a prolonged period of secular stagnation.

Not surprisingly, given the weak growth of world output, **world trade** also continued to grow slowly, and by less than forecast earlier in the year: the volume of merchandise trade rose by nearly 3.5 per cent, slightly more than in 2013 (just under 3 per cent) but still well below the trend rate of around 7 per cent in the 20 years to 2007. The improvement was largely due to stronger growth in the United States and to a recovery in the EU where import volumes had fallen in the two previous years. Since the EU accounted for about one third of world imports, and given the weak outlook for economic growth in the eurozone, the region was likely to remain a constraint on a more rapid recovery of world trade. The developing economies, especially in East Asia, continued to increase their share of world trade in manufactures mainly at the expense of the EU, whose share of the world total fell from 44 per cent in the mid-1990s to around 37 per cent, and the United States. The increased share of trade between the developing countries, together with the long established fact of developed countries exporting most of their merchandise to one another, emphasised the increased regional concentration of trade within the global economy.

Primary commodity prices showed some signs of stabilisation in the first half of 2014 but from mid-year resumed the downward trend that had been under way since their post-recession peak in 2011. The principal exception was crude oil, for which the price had remained relatively stable from 2011 to mid-2014. Over the 12 months to December, the UNCTAD commodity price index fell by just over 8 per cent in US dollar terms, or just over 3 per cent in SDRs. Most commodity prices, however, remained above their average levels during the boom of 2003-08 and many were still relatively close to the peaks of 2008. The decline in 2014 affected most product groups: food prices fell on average by about 4 per cent in the 12 months to December, agricultural raw materials by nearly 17 per cent and mineral ores and metals by 14 per cent.

Among the industrial products there were some large price falls—46 per cent for iron ore, for example—but the "shock" of the year was the collapse in the price of crude oil from just under $112 per barrel (p/b) in June to just over $62 p/b in December, and it was still falling at the turn of the year (price of UK Brent, Light Blend). This was the third largest oil price collapse in 30 years— only those in 1985-86 and 2008 were larger—and reflected both a slowdown in the growth of demand and a large increase in supply, including from non-OPEC producers such as the United States and Canada. Fears that supply might be disrupted by rising political tensions in Ukraine and military activity in Iraq were short-lived. The decline accelerated in the last quarter, especially after the decision by OPEC, on 27 November, that in order to preserve its share of the world market it would not support the price by reducing supply: between November and December, the average monthly price fell by just over 20 per cent.

The slow pace of economic recovery, large margins of unused capacities in many of the advanced economies, and falling commodity prices all helped to ensure that **global inflation** remained more or less unchanged at an average rate of around 3 per cent, although as usual there were significant differences between countries. In the advanced economies the rate ranged from 2.7 per cent in Japan to 1.9 per cent in the USA and 0.7 per cent in the EU. Monetary policies remained accommodative and although there was discussion about raising interest rates in the US and the UK, following the collapse of the oil price, any tightening of policy was postponed until sometime in 2015 in the US and *sine die* in the UK. The uncertainty that faced policy makers was whether the oil price fall would have a one-off effect on the headline rate or whether it would influence consumers' expectations and increase the risk of a prolonged fall in the core inflation rate. In Japan, monetary policy was set to prevent a slowdown in the inflation rate, while in the eurozone expectations in December were that the ECB would act early in 2015 to counter what was seen as a growing risk of deflation. Consumer prices in the eurozone fell by 0.2 per cent in the 12 months to December, the first decline since October 2009. Inflation in 2014 was essentially a problem for individual countries such as Egypt, Argentina and Venezuela where the annual rates accelerated to 10, 25 and 68 per cent respectively. In Iran, another "outlier", inflation more than halved to just under 18 per cent.

The slow recovery of the world economy meant that many of the most severe economic and social problems facing policy makers arose in the **labour markets**. The International Labour Organisation (ILO) estimated that there were 61 million fewer jobs available in 2014 than there would have been had global output growth not been hit by the crisis of 2008-09. Global unemployment in 2014 stood at 201.3 million or just under 6 per cent of the labour force. There were falls in unemployment in the advanced economies but they were quite

small, except in the United States and the UK. In the EU the jobless rate averaged 11 per cent but there were no significant reductions in Southern Europe
where rates averaged 25 and 27 per cent in Spain and Greece, while double digit
rates (18 to 28 per cent) persisted in South East Europe. Among the developing
economies, unemployment remained relatively low and stable in Asia, at 4 to 5
per cent, but such figures were less significant than elsewhere because of the
very high levels of informal employment, over 80 per cent in India for example.
Some of the highest rates of unemployment were in the Middle East and North
Africa (MENA) where the average was unchanged at just under 12 per cent. One
of the most disturbing features of the situation in MENA was the youth (15 to
24 years) unemployment rate which remained stuck at an average of just under
30 per cent and where ILO surveys showed very high rates (50-90 per cent) of
young people engaged in the informal sector amid falling wage levels and poor
working conditions. In the EU, the jobless rate for the young was 21.4 per cent
at the end of the year and ranged from 7.2 per cent in Germany to more than 50
per cent in Greece and Spain.

In the **foreign exchange markets** the principal development in 2014 was the
appreciation of the US dollar, encouraged by the improving outlook for economic
growth and, from October, renewed expectation of a move to higher interest rates
by the Federal Reserve. The dollar index (a basket of six advanced economy currencies), was at a four-year high in November. The dollar rose 10 per cent against
the euro from May to November as the outlook pointed to monetary policies in the
US and eurozone moving in opposite directions.

The scale of the **current account imbalances** continued to diminish although
their distribution among the principal economies remained much the same as in
previous years. The sum of the absolute balances was around 3.5 per cent of
global GDP, down from 5.6 per cent in 2006. The US still had the largest deficit,
at 2.5 per cent of GDP (or $430 billion) while Germany had the largest surplus
at about 7 per cent of its GDP. China's surplus, which was the world's largest
before the crisis at just over 10 per cent of GDP, was under 2 per cent in 2014.
The IMF did not regard the current scale of imbalances as an immediate risk to
financial stability and there was more confidence than in previous years that part
of the reduction was due to structural changes and not just to the fall in demand.

The recovery of the **United States** economy, relatively slow compared with previous upturns from recession but relatively fast compared with most of Europe and
Japan, continued through 2014, with an acceleration of growth in mid-year and a
slowdown in the last quarter that was rather more abrupt than expected. For the
year as a whole, GDP rose by 2.4 per cent against 2.2 per cent in 2013. The slowdown in the last quarter—an annualised rate of 2.2 per cent against 5 per cent in
the third—reflected, for the most part, poor international trade data and lower government spending. The recovery was accompanied by a very weak growth of
wages, but strong gains in employment together with low interest rates and abundant liquidity supported the recovery of domestic borrowing and consumption.
The unemployment rate at the end of the year was 5.6 per cent, a marked but slow

improvement on the peak rate of 10 per cent in 2009. Fixed investment for the year as a whole rose by some 2.5 per cent but strengthened during the year. Given the strong position of the corporate sector—very low ratios of debt to earnings, cash holdings of over $3 trillion, and record low rates of long-term interest rates—the potential at the end of the year for an acceleration of fixed investment appeared to be strong, but that also depended on the prospects for aggregate demand, domestic and foreign, and greater certainty about economic policy. A long-standing problem in the United States has been the failure of wages to keep up with productivity growth, and in July the IMF, in its Article IV Consultation, suggested the US increase the minimum wage and enlarge the earned income tax credit in order to provide extra support to demand.

In **Japan** the economy remained weak despite unprecedented efforts to end two decades of low growth and price deflation. The "three-arrows strategy" consisted of a large fiscal stimulus, aggressive monetary easing by the Bank of Japan, and structural reforms to boost competitiveness, but by the end of 2014 it was still not very successful. For the year as a whole GDP growth was just 0.4 per cent, against 1.5 per cent in 2013, and for much of the year domestic demand was struggling to recover from the effects of the rise in the sales tax (VAT) in April. After a boom in consumption in the first quarter, with households anticipating the tax rise, the economy went into recession from April to September, and although there was an upturn in the last quarter it was much weaker than expected. The measures raised the headline inflation rate for 2014 to around 2.7 per cent but, as the core rate was reckoned to be much lower, the Bank of Japan introduced a further monetary stimulus in October. The recovery at the end of the year was still not strong enough to generate enough demand to end deflation or to enable the government to start reducing its large deficit of nearly 8 per cent of GDP.

Growth in **Western Europe** continued to be held back by the eurozone where fiscal austerity, somewhat less severe than in previous years but still counter-productive in the opinion of many economists, was maintained despite weak demand, high levels of unemployment and increasing fears of deflation. Private sector debt levels, although reduced, remained a constraint on consumer spending and investment, and a large number of banks still needed to strengthen their balance sheets following the ECB's stress tests and asset quality reviews. The exit from recession occurred in the second quarter of 2013 but the pace of recovery was weak and uncertain: it decelerated in the second quarter of 2014, stabilised in the third, and strengthened again in the fourth. For the year as a whole, aggregate GDP rose by 0.9 per cent, a modest rebound from the declines of -0.8 and -0.5 per cent in 2012 and 2013. Outside the eurozone, economic growth was more robust in the UK (3.1 per cent), Poland (3.4 per cent), Romania (3.1 per cent) and just under 3 per cent in Hungary, Latvia and Lithuania. For the EU as a whole, GDP rose by 1.3 per cent against zero in 2013.

Concern at the sluggish pace of recovery and its associated vulnerability to external setbacks, such as the Ukrainian crisis and the "blowback" from sanctions on Russia, led to increased calls for more action to boost growth. Germany's attachment to its zero budget deficit policy and its unwillingness to adjust its exceptionally large current account surplus attracted criticism from political leaders in France, Italy and the United States, as well as an appeal from the IMF for a loosening of policy to revive activity in the eurozone, but with little effect. In December there were general strikes against austerity in Belgium and Italy and by the end of the month the Greek government was forced to call a general election which the anti-austerity party, Syriza, was predicted to win early in the New Year.

In November, the European Commission proposed a €315 billion infrastructure investment programme to promote stronger growth but at the end of the year details of the strategy were still under discussion. The pressure for policy action was largely focused on the ECB which had been active during the year in buying covered bonds and asset backed securities. But it was the very low take-up by the banks of its second offer of low-interest, four-year loans that underlined the stagnation of the economy: the problem was weak credit demand, not liquidity. Instead, the combination of tight fiscal policy and the fall in the inflation rate, which turned negative in December, led to calls for the ECB to act against deflation with large-scale purchases of government bonds, or quantitative easing. When the president, Mario Draghi, said in November that the ECB should act to boost inflation "without delay", it was generally assumed that quantitative easing was imminent. It was not announced in December but expectations were high that it would be early in the New Year. The end-year forecasts for eurozone growth in 2015 were about 1.3 per cent and for the EU 1.7 per cent.

Outside the EU, the economies of **South-East Europe**, the western Balkans, suffered a number of setbacks and their average growth rate was under 1 per cent compared with just under 2.5 per cent in 2013. Severe flooding in May in Bosnia & Herzegovina and in Serbia severely damaged housing, transport infrastructure and telecommunications with the result that annual GDP growth slowed sharply in Bosnia & Herzegovina (from 2.5 to 1.5 per cent) and turned negative in Serbia (from 2.5 per cent to -0.8 per cent). Growth accelerated in the Former Yugoslav Republic of Macedonia, to 3.5 per cent, the strongest in the region, helped by a large rise in exports. All countries in the region suffered high rates of unemployment (18 to 28 per cent of the labour force), large public debts and fiscal deficits, as well as large current account deficits. Reconstruction in the flood- affected areas and other infrastructure projects were expected to strengthen growth in 2015 but, given the constraints of the region's serious structural problems, its economic prospects remained closely tied to those of the European Union, both as an export market and as a source of workers' and other remittances. A major upset was the sudden decision by Russia in early December to cancel South Stream, the $50 billion pipeline project to bring gas to Europe via the Black Sea and which had been seen as both improving energy security and providing major investments in the region. (The cancellation followed the European Commission's insistence that the pipeline should not be monopolised by Gazprom.)

Economic growth slowed down throughout the **Commonwealth of Independent States (CIS)** largely because of the severe deterioration in the Russian economy which slowed through the first three quarters of the year and then tipped into recession in the fourth, the result of the large fall in the oil price and of economic sanctions combining with the country's long-standing structural problems. With oil and gas accounting for some two-thirds of Russian exports and about a quarter of general government revenue, the fall in the oil price had a major impact, both directly and via the multiplier effects on other industries. Western economic sanctions, applied from March, inter alia, restricted access to the international capital markets and contributed to the general deterioration in the climate for investment. Fixed investment fell (by some 3 per cent) and domestic consumption rose by only 2 per cent (just under 4 per cent in 2013); the main support to GDP was net exports, mainly because the volume of imports fell 6 per cent in the wake of a nearly 50 per cent depreciation of the rouble. The currency crisis led to a sharp rise in an already high rate of inflation to more than 11 per cent and to very high interest rates which, in turn, led to stress on the banking system by raising the proportion of non-performing loans. Russia's GDP rose by just 0.4 per cent against 1.3 per cent in 2013 and end-year forecasts pointed to a fall of some 4 to 5 per cent in 2015.

The situation in Russia had important consequences for the other CIS countries. For the net importers of oil and gas (Armenia Belarus, Kyrgyzstan, Moldova, Tajikistan and Ukraine) the benefits of lower fuel prices were significantly offset by reduced exports to and workers' remittances from Russia. For those with the closest economic links to Russia—Armenia and Belarus for example—their currencies were under considerable pressure in December. GDP growth in the fuel-importing countries (excluding Ukraine) ranged between 1.5 per cent (Belarus) and 5.8 per cent (Tajikistan). Among the oil exporters, GDP slowed under the influence of lower oil prices and the impact of the Russian slowdown and the Ukrainian crisis.

The economy of Ukraine was in a parlous state. GDP fell sharply as the military conflicts greatly damaged its industrial economy in the regions of Donetsk and Lugansk: the destruction of productive capacities helped to account for the limited impact of the 50 per cent or so depreciation of the hryvnia against the US dollar on the large current account deficit. International reserves were down to one month's imports at the end of December, government debt rose rapidly and many banks were declared insolvent. GDP fell by a "guesstimated" 7 to 8 per cent and another large fall was expected for 2015. The government's room for policy manoeuvre was very limited and clearly needed a stabilisation and structural reform programme with international support, but neither had been clearly formulated by the end of the year. An agreement with the IMF was under negotiation and, if successful, additional funds were promised by the USA and the EU.

Despite some deceleration, **East Asia** remained the fastest growing region of the world economy with an average rise in GDP of just over 6 per cent compared with 6.4 per cent in 2013. The Chinese economy, which accounted for about two-thirds of the region's GDP, slowed to 7.4 per cent from 7.7 per cent in both 2012 and 2013. This was more or less in line with the Chinese government's aim of moving onto a lower growth path that would give greater weight to household consumption and the service sector and move away from its reliance on high-pollution industries and on construction. Concerns that slower growth in China would have a major adverse effect on the rest of the region were not borne out: growth did weaken in some countries for domestic reasons or weak global export demand but except in Thailand the deceleration was not great and in several countries growth ranged between 3.4 per cent (South Korea) and 6.4 per cent (Philippines). Forecasts at the end of the year pointed to faster growth in 2015 in South Korea, Indonesia, Singapore and Thailand despite a further slowdown in China. Monetary policy was accommodative and in general there was scope for fiscal policy to support activity. A significant change in fiscal policy was the start in most of the region at removing the large subsidies to fuel prices, a policy urged by the IMF and World Bank facilitated by the global fall in the price of crude oil.

Economic growth in **South Asia**, in contrast to most other regions, strengthened in 2014, the average increase in GDP rising to 4.9 per cent from just over 4 per cent in 2013. The improvement was led by India, which accounted for around 70 per cent of regional output, with growth of 5.5 per cent against 4.7 per cent in calendar year 2013. (India's official GDP data were published on a fiscal year basis.) The newly-elected Indian government in May launched a wide-ranging reform programme which was well under way by the last quarter and, after several mediocre years, fixed investment began to strengthen and there were the beginnings of recovery in manufacturing and construction. In Bangladesh and Sri Lanka, household consumption and fixed investment helped to maintain strong rates of GDP growth of between 6 and 8 per cent. In Pakistan, strong private and public consumption sustained growth of close to 5 per cent but the economic fundamentals remained uncertain in the face of worries over security and low rates of fixed investment. In Iran, after two years of substantial falls in GDP, the partial lifting of sanctions and some improvement in macroeconomic balance helped a return to positive growth, albeit at a modest 2 per cent.

Labour markets were relatively stable but as vulnerable employment, i.e. unpaid family and own account workers, was very high in much of the region, this only underlined the challenge facing development policies. Annual inflation rates fell sharply, on average from nearly 15 per cent in 2013 to under 10 per cent, helped by the falling price of oil, moderate demand pressures, and stable monetary policies. Fiscal policy supported growth but budget deficits of some 4 per cent of GDP (India) to 7 per cent (Pakistan) suggested this would not be maintained for much longer, although reductions would be difficult as large proportions of government spending were on price subsidies and the military. Current account positions were improved by strong export growth and increased workers' remittances.

In **Western Asia** economic growth weakened, but more sharply for the net fuel importers (2.1 per cent against 3.8 per cent in 2013) than for the net fuel exporters (4.2 per cent to 3.5 per cent). For the oil exporters, particularly members of the Gulf Cooperation Council (GCC), growth held up reasonably well despite the fall in oil prices, partly due to stronger demand from East Asia and partly because of increased government spending. Given their financial resources and continued support for domestic infrastructure investment, growth in the GCC countries in 2015 was expected to return to rates of over 4 per cent. Despite efforts to "nationalise" employment in GCC countries, increased labour demand, skill mismatches among the youth of the region, and the increased levels of violence in Iraq, Syria and Yemen, led to increased inflows of immigrants and refugees who filled job vacancies but also added to higher levels of unemployment.

Any assessment of the situation in Iraq could only be tentative given the limited data available, especially concerning the non-oil sectors and the effects of the disruption in the north of the country. However, production in the major oil fields in the south increased by some 6 per cent to November. The World Bank estimated that GDP fell by 2.7 per cent against a rise of just over 4 per cent in 2013. Social as well as economic pressures were underlined by the number of displaced persons rising to two million or 6 per cent of the population. Assessing the economic situation in Syria was even more fraught given the intensity and scale of the violence in the country as well as the impact of sanctions. The UN estimated that the country's GDP had fallen by some 40 per cent between 2010 and the end of 2013. There was little doubt that swathes of the country's capital infrastructure and other capital stock had been destroyed and another double-digit fall of GDP was not implausible. UNHCR estimated that in July there were 6.5 million internally displaced persons in Syria, 30 per cent of the population, and the UN's Office for the Coordination of Humanitarian Affairs (OCHA) reckoned another 20 per cent of the population, including 150,000 refugees from Iraq, needed humanitarian assistance.

The violence and social distress in Syria led to considerable tensions in Jordan and Lebanon where GDP growth rates of 3.5 per cent and 1.8 per cent respectively, mainly driven by government spending and the construction sector, were insufficient to meet the demands of hosting more than 3 million refugees, equivalent to 25 per cent and 10 per cent of the local populations and, according to UNHCR, the largest refugee movement since World War II. (Given the problems of collecting reliable statistics, the actual numbers of refugees were probably higher.) In the face of growing financial and social strains, both Jordan and Lebanon (and also Turkey) tightened their border controls on Syrian refugees and the inflows appeared to have been reduced through the year. The current account deficits of Jordan and Lebanon edged higher, to just over 11 per cent and 8 per cent, and they continued to rely on remittances and foreign aid for finance.

The spillovers from Syria and Iraq also touched Turkey, the largest economy in the region, and where GDP growth slowed from just over 4 per cent in 2013 to 2.7 per cent. This mainly reflected weaker private consumption and fixed investment which in turn followed the tightening of monetary policy from January in order to check inflation and a depreciating exchange rate. Despite the loss of some exports to Iraq, the trade balance improved and the current account deficit was smaller than in 2013.

In **North Africa** the economic outlook remained deeply influenced by political and security tensions but there were signs of improved confidence in Egypt, Tunisia and Morocco: manufacturing output and exports increased and although capital flows to the region slowed, Morocco and Tunisia were able to raise funds on the international capital markets, Morocco with support from an IMF programme. Nevertheless, nervousness over geopolitical risks left foreign direct investment well below the levels preceding the Arab Spring. Overall there was a slight improvement in economic growth (excluding Libya), mainly due to Egypt where GDP rose from some 2 per cent in 2013 to just under 3 per cent and a small improvement to 3 per cent in Algeria, but there was some deceleration in Morocco and Tunisia (to 3 and 2.3 per cent). (In Libya, GDP collapsed by more than one fifth, following a decline of around 14 per cent in 2013.) These rates of growth were still well below what was needed for a significant reduction in the high levels of unemployment. Recorded unemployment rates ranged from just over 9 per cent in Morocco to 16 per cent in Tunisia but the significance of such statistics was limited given the size of the informal economy. The high and chronic rates of youth unemployment, estimated at over 50 per cent in Tunisia and still higher in Egypt, were indicators of the scale of casual work, not of young men waiting at employment exchanges. There was some relief from the fall in the global price of food which was a major component of household spending.

The economies of **Sub-Saharan Africa** continued for the most part to grow steadily with an average rise in GDP of around 4.5 per cent, slightly higher than in 2013. There was a wide range of experience, from the Ebola stricken countries in West Africa to 10 countries growing at 5 to 6 per cent and another eight at between 6.3 and 9 per cent. South Africa's GDP rose by just 1.5 per cent against a revised 2.2 per cent in 2013, its worst performance in five years and a reflection of increased labour unrest and continual power cuts due to ageing and poorly maintained electric power systems. Growth, however, was robust in some of the region's low-income countries (for example Cote d'Ivoire (9 per cent) and Mozambique (just over 7 per cent)) while the largest economy, Nigeria, grew by some 6 per cent with support from a strong non-oil sector. Across much of the region activity was driven by large-scale infrastructure investment in power generation, transport, ports etc., expansion of service sectors and increased agricultural output. On average, fiscal deficits were around 2.5 per cent of GDP and current account deficits around 3 per cent, about the same as in 2013. Several countries, including Angola, Botswana and Nigeria, had current account surpluses of around 4 to 8 per cent of GDP, all somewhat smaller than in 2013, but for the deficit countries their debt burdens caused few problems in a context of strong growth and concessional interest rates. Commodity price falls led to currency depreciation in several countries including Nigeria and Ghana. The Ebola epidemic in West Africa was a major shock for the region, the consequences of which were still uncertain at the end of the year. For the countries directly affected, Guinea, Liberia and Sierra Leone, the economic dislocation was considerable with all the key sectors hit by labour absenteeism, the closure of markets, and large constraints on cross-border trade and the movement of people. Earlier forecasts for the three economies in 2014 were all greatly reduced and the outlook for 2015 was for declining GDP in all three, although the extent of the decline was dependent on the epidemic ending and on the scale of the promised financial assistance. Despite the severity of the epidemic, the economic impact on the rest of West Africa was reckoned to be relatively minor at the end of the year, although were the disease to spread to Ghana and Senegal major disruption to the regional economy would be likely.

In **Latin America and the Caribbean** economic growth was estimated at between 0.8 and 1.3 per cent, the smallest increase since 2009. There were however large differences among this group of economies: South American growth averaged just 0.7 per cent, Mexico and central America 2.6 per cent, and the Caribbean 3.8 per cent. The overall slowdown was heavily influenced by weak or negative growth in some of the region's largest economies: Argentina (-0.2 per cent), Brazil (0.2 per cent) and Venezuela (-3.0 per cent). In Brazil, the region's largest economy, the impact of falling commodity prices and external demand was amplified by severe drought affecting agricultural output, falling investment and uncertainty surrounding the presidential election. Despite some positive factors (a bumper soy harvest), Argentina's economy was faced with a shortage of dollars, a large fiscal deficit, and, at 25 per cent, one of the highest inflation rates in the world. In July despite long-running negotiations with a group of US hedge funds which refused to join the restructuring of the debt after the 2001 crisis, it partly defaulted on its international debt payments, thus weakening its credit rating and access to the international financial markets. Elsewhere, GDP growth was in the range of 4 to 5 per cent in Bolivia, Colombia, Ecuador and Paraguay, while for Mexico and central America activity improved in the wake of the recovery of the US economy. Growth in the Caribbean also remained relatively high, reflecting stronger demand in the US and rising incomes from tourism.

The weaker economic situation resulted in a slower pace of job creation, although that was reflected more in lower labour force participation rates than high unemployment rates. Rising levels of formal employment contributed to reduced income inequality in recent years but data published by the UN's Economic Commission for Latin America and the Caribbean (ECLAC) showed that for the first time in a decade income poverty reduction had stagnated and that some 3 million people fell below the poverty line in 2014 and that another 1.5 million were expected to do so in 2015.

Inflation increased on average from just over 7 to just over 10 per cent, but the trend had been rising since mid-2012. The differences within the region were marked, with accelerating inflation in south America (Argentina and Venezuela at the extremes of 25 and 68 per cent) but more moderate rates elsewhere. Monetary policy was mostly directed at reducing inflation to central bank target rates while for most of the region the scope for fiscal stimulus was limited by rising government deficits. At the end of the year, the outlook was for only a modest improvement in the regional growth rate, to around 2 per cent.

Beyond the annual "ups and downs" of the global economy were many systemic issued that stretched beyond the calendar year. There is room here to mention only three that became more worrying or prominent in 2014. First was the question of whether the global financial system was more stable and better able to withstand shocks on the scale of those in 2008—and the answer at the end of 2014 was "possibly not". Banks in the advanced economies were judged to be safer with higher capital ratios, increased regulation of risk management, governance and transparency, and the withdrawal from investment activity by a number of universal banks. The Basel III process to improve the sector's ability to absorb shocks was largely completed although some key matters (net funding and leverage ratios) remained to be settled. But while progress was made the process of reform was not complete and it was doubtful whether the system as a whole was safer and better functioning. The banks were stronger but not strong enough to fully perform their basic function of supporting the real economy: the IMF estimated that 40 per cent of advanced economy banks (70 per cent in the eurozone) were not strong enough to risk lending for productivity and employment-creating investment. At the same time, the poorly regulated shadow-banking system (asset management companies, mutual funds etc.) was financing considerable investment in a range of financial assets across many countries. The $40 trillion or so placed by advanced economy investors in fixed income securities in the emerging economies both tightened the financial links between them and left them highly vulnerable to geopolitical shocks or the normalisation of US monetary policy, a vulnerability that was amplified by what the IMF described as the "illusion of liquidity" created by these investment flows. Thus, the real economy was still being held back by weak banks, while the potential for another international financial crisis was increased by the financial risk-taking of the shadow banks. This appeared to be a priority area for closer cooperation between regulators in the advanced and in the emerging market economies.

Second, the high levels of inequality of income and wealth that have developed in the last 30 years or so have been noted here before and have already been the subject of studies by the international economic institutions in the last few years and by academic economists for much longer. Popular awareness of the issue and of the need to do something about it, however, increased considerably in 2014 with the publication of an Oxfam study showing that 85 billionaires owned as much wealth as half the global population and of Thomas Piketty's *Capital in the Twenty-First Century*, a major economic-historical study of the evolution of inequality over three centuries and which, unusually for a heavyweight, academic work was a best seller. Piketty's main focus was on the tendency for the returns to capital to be higher than the rate of economic growth and, with current signs of a return to 19th century levels of wealth concentration, he proposed a wealth tax. The international institutions, especially the IMF and the OECD, published several studies showing that current levels of inequality were a curb on economic growth and both concluded that redistribution policies had not had a negative effect on growth. At the World Bank-IMF annual meetings, there was a broad consensus on the need to reduce inequality. The governor of the Bank of England, Mark Carney, warned in May that inequality was undermining social mobility and the basic social contract of fairness, and in October the chair of the US Federal Reserve, Janet Yellen, declared that widening inequality was incompatible with US values and the "high value Americans have traditionally placed on equality of opportunity". Despite widespread agreement that inequality was a problem, however, there was less agreement on how to solve it. The OECD emphasised the importance of raising educational opportunities for children from poor backgrounds in the bottom 40 per cent (not just the bottom 10 per cent) as well as support for the most vulnerable, and the IMF saw fiscal policy making a useful contribution. Although it was clear that inequality would not be reduced to acceptable levels by market forces, it was unclear how such specific measures would be effective in the continued presence of excessive financialisation and the unfettered movements of international capital. The emphasis on "inclusive capitalism" by international institutions, and a number of politicians, businessmen and central bank governors was a sign of unease that the prevailing orthodoxies of neo-liberalism might be starting to undermine the system itself.

And third, the general framework of international co-operation continued to suffer multiple strains, in part because of geopolitical tensions, such as the crises in Ukraine and the Middle East, all of which had economic consequences, but also because longer standing problems had not been addressed (see AR 2013, pp. 378-80). A prominent example of the latter was the continued failure to agree the 2010 reforms of the MF (see International Organisations, IMF) which left the organisation caught between the frustration and discontent of the emerging market and developing countries (EMDCs) on the one hand and the obduracy of the US Congress on the other, a situation that threatened the Fund's role at the centre of the international financial system. A similar lack of willingness to compromise and to respect the interests of other members was apparent in the WTO, where subsets of the membership sought, often in a secretive manner, to pursue their own objectives in plurilateral groups that effectively undermined the basic multilateral principles of transparency and inclusiveness. Given the high degree of integration of the world economy the only realistic way to maintain political and economic stability was to co-operate, but that depended on restraint both by the more powerful and by coalitions of smaller powers. The distinction between the national (private) and global (public) interest was largely abandoned in the pursuit of globalisation based on unfettered market forces, but that approach was meeting increasing resistance from nationalist protests at the effects of austerity in Europe or at the narrowing of domestic policy space in both advanced and developing economies by international finance. Most developing countries felt increasingly vulnerable to the transmission of shocks within a global system that lacked effective mechanisms to handle the destabilising effects of policy changes in the advanced economies. Most of these points were made by the managing director of the IMF, Christine Lagarde, in her repeated calls for a renewal of international co-operation in the spirit of 1944 rather than the 1920s, a "new multilateralism" that would renew the commitment to the concept of the global public good and the implicit need for restraint in the pursuit of national interest. It was clear that many of the challenges facing the world economy were global and that there was no alternative to a co-operative and multinational response if countries were to achieve their individual objectives. The big test for such co-operation in 2015 would be whether a global agreement to limit greenhouse gas emissions would be signed in Paris in December. That was one area where 2014 at least provided some grounds for optimism, namely, the bilateral agreement between China and the US on reducing their emissions and the framework agreement for the Paris negotiations agreed between Europe, China and the US in Lima in December.

Paul Rayment

XIII THE SCIENCES

MEDICAL, SCIENTIFIC AND INDUSTRIAL RESEARCH

MEDICAL AND BIOLOGICAL SCIENCES. The most recent deadly Ebola epidemic started in March in the West African state of Guinea and spread to the nearby states of Sierra Leone and Liberia and, to a much lesser extent, to Nigeria and Senegal. The virus *Zaire ebolavirus* was identified as the cause of the epidemic, the largest of the 22 Ebola outbreaks since the virus was co-discovered in 1976 by Peter Piot, then of the Institute of Tropical Medicine in Antwerp.

The virus was found to have originated in the fruit bat and to be transmitted to humans via close contact with infected bush animals, including chimpanzees and forest antelope, or bush meat. Human to human transmission is known to occur mainly through direct, unprotected physical contact with bodily fluids of symptomatic individuals, including corpses. There was no evidence of airborne transmission in humans. Early symptoms, which were similar to malaria, included headache, fatigue, sore throat, fever and muscle soreness, progressing to sudden high fever, vomiting blood, lethargy and bleeding from the nose, mouth, eyes and anus. Late symptoms include seizures, loss of consciousness, massive internal bleeding and death from systems failure. Treatment was directed to early diagnosis, quarantining and rehydration. There was, to date, no specific cure or vaccine.

The epidemic spread at an alarming rate, in part because of the inadequacy of the rudimentary, ill-equipped national health systems with few medical staff and hospital beds, and in part because of the cultural reluctance of many inhabitants to accept the severity of the disease, and their distrust of medical assistance.

The medical charity, Médicins sans frontières (MSF), was the earliest international group to offer help; by the end of June its leaders were warning the World Health Organisation (WHO) that the epidemic was out of control. Two months later WHO accepted that the outbreak was a public health emergency, by which time 2,274 cases had been identified and 961 people had died. In mid-September the UN Security Council took the unprecedented step of declaring the epidemic "a threat to international peace and security ... which unless contained, may lead to further instances of civil unrest, social tensions and deterioration of the political and security climate". The Security Council established the UN Mission for Ebola Emergency Response (UNMEER).

By mid-October the number of known cases reported by WHO had risen to 8,914 and were doubling every 16 to 30 days. UNMEER planned field military and civilian response teams from the USA, the UK, and the EU. The UN had appealed for $1 billion, and although the initial uptake was slow major commitments came from the USA, the UK and the EU, with lesser amounts from across the world. By the end of the year, community care centres and field hospitals had been established and the institution of necessary impersonal burial systems had begun to create some impact. The WHO ruled that it was ethically acceptable to give untested drugs to patients infected with Ebola. An experimental drug ZMapp was successfully given to a few infected aid workers and vaccine clinical trials began. At the end of 2014 WHO reported that more than 14,000 people had been infected, of whom over 6,900 had died.

Many questions have been raised concerning this epidemic. For example: why did WHO take so long to recognise its severity? Why were nations, in particular China, reluctant to give significant financial support? Why had vaccines not been produced during earlier epidemics? Many commentators concluded that answers may lie within the regional context: these West African countries were among the poorest nations in the world; had been stricken with political internal conflict; had poorly developed health infrastructures; and did not attract significant international investment. The periodic epidemics of Ebola, although severe, had not hitherto been sufficiently large to attract major pharmaceutical companies to invest in vaccine research and production.

The threat to humanity from drug resistant infections was considered by a group of the UK's most eminent medical experts to be greater than that of climate change. In England alone 5,000 deaths each year were attributed to antibiotic-resistant strains of disease. Professor Dame Sally Davies, the chief medical officer, and Dr Jeremy Farrar, director of the Wellcome Trust, warned that the world was facing an apocalyptic scenario in which people would die from routine infections because effective drugs would not be available. Highlighting the prospect of a growing number of drug-resistant infections, the overuse and misuse of antibiotics, and the fact that no new class of antibiotic had been developed since 1987, they called for the creation of an international group of experts to champion the development of new forms of antibiosis.

Alternative ways of destroying bacteria focused on the breakdown of the impenetrability of the bacterial cell wall by endolysins. The first such endolysin made available for human use on the intact skin was claimed by Micreos, a Dutch biotechnical company, to be equally as effective in killing methicillin-resistant Gram-positive *Staphylococcus aureus* (MRSA) as methicillin-susceptible *Staphylococcus aureus* (MSSA), and did not affect beneficial bacteria. For those Gram-negative organisms with thicker impenetrable outer membranes (such as *gonococcus*, *salmonella* and *E. Coli*) and *M. Tuberculosis* a different approach was promoted by Professor Changjong Dong of the University of East Anglia. Dong identified a protein called LptD that was created by these bacteria to reinforce the outer wall. By blocking this protein, he postulated that the defensive wall would be weakened thus increasing the vulnerability and death of the bacteria.

At the end of 2014 a new, hitherto unreachable source of antibiotics was discovered in the soil by a team from the North Eastern University in Boston, Massachusetts, led by Professor Kim Lewis. By using an electronic chip to grow the microbes in the soil, the team was able to isolate their antibiotic chemical compounds. The antibiotic, named Teixobactin, had been found to be effective (in mice experiments) against common bacterial infections including *Cloistridium difficile*, *M. Tuberculosis* and *Staphylococcus aureus*.

A breakthrough in the challenge of eliminating the necessity for all type l, and 10 per cent of type ll, diabetics to inject insulin was proposed by Professor Douglas Melton of Harvard University, with the publication of a paper in the journal *Cell* entitled "Generation of Functional Human Pancreatic _ Cells in Vitro". This represented the culmination of 22 years' research in this field by Melton, prompted by his son's early diagnosis of type l diabetes. Starting with both embryonic and induced pluripotent stem (iPS) cells Melton and his team succeeded in generating insulin-producing pancreatic _ cells, which would provide an unprecedented cell source for transplantation therapy. They created a scalable differentiation protocol that could generate hundreds of millions of glucose-responsive _ cells that resembled human islet _ cells by gene expression and ultrastructure and, on transplantation, ameliorated hyperglycaemia in diabetic mice. Crucially, a single production line of cells would be used to treat all patients, rather than necessitating individual genetic matching. This was achieved by placing cells in a porous capsule that allowed insulin to diffuse out but protected cells from attacks by the body's immune system. Melton reported that his team was in the last stages of animal testing in non-human primates.

Artificial red blood cells, derived from iPS cells (from adult skin cells or blood cells), had been created by a team at the Scottish National Blood Transfusion Service, University of Edinburgh, led by Professor Marc Turner. A trial planned for 2016 was likely to involve patients with thalassemia, a disorder of red blood cells that required regular transfusions. Artificial red blood cells, which would contain entirely new cells, would be made from individuals with the relatively rare universal type O negative blood group that could be transfused into almost any patient.

Progress in the field of sensory-enhanced prosthetic limbs (see AR 2013, p. 429) was reported by Dr Max Ortiz Catalan of the Chalmers University of Technology, Gothenburg, Sweden. He described a male amputee patient who had been living for more than a year with an osseo-integrated sensory-enhanced prosthetic arm that enabled him to perform tasks such as tying shoe laces, using an electric drill, catching objects and, most importantly, meant he was able to retain his job as a truck driver. The prosthesis was only disconnected when he took a shower.

Perhaps sooner than had been anticipated in 2012 (see AR 2012, p.431), olfactory ensheathing cells (OECs) were successfully used to span across a spinal cord injury site in a human. Olfactory nerves were known to be the sole continually regenerating nerves in the central nervous system. OECs provided a pathway along which cells grew and rerouted themselves. Professor Geoffrey Raisman of the Institute of Neurology, University College, London, in collaboration with Pawel Tabakow, a Polish neurosurgeon working in Wroclaw, reported the case of a Polish patient who had suffered a complete severance of his spinal cord as a result of a stabbing injury. The patient had one of his brain's two olfactory bulbs removed, from which OECs were harvested and cultured. A fortnight later these cells were transplanted into his spine using 100 microinjections across the injury site. A small piece of nerve from his ankle was also grafted on to the injury site to provide a scaffold for the spinal neurons to extend, guided by the

OECs, and reconnect with the other side. A year after surgery, the patient was able to walk between parallel bars with a walker and wearing short callipers. He had noticed some return of sensation in his bladder and bowel. Raisman cautiously stated that more patients must be treated to ensure that this case was not an isolated success story.

In September a Swedish woman who had received a transplanted uterus (see AR 2012, p. 429) became the first to give birth to a healthy baby boy. Professor Mats Brannstrom of the University of Gothenburg reported that the woman had been born without a uterus and had received a donor uterus from a post-menopausal family friend, who had given birth to two children. The transplanted uterus had survived because of immunosuppressant medication and therefore would in due course be removed because of the dangers of long-term use of these drugs. Although this successful delivery solved the last untreated form of female infertility, questions were raised about the realism of the medical risks, expense, and potential ethical issues associated with male to female transgendered persons.

A Japanese woman in September received the first medical treatment based on induced pluripotent stem (iPS) cells eight years after they were discovered by the Nobel Prize winner Shinya Yamanaka in 2006 (see AR 2008, p. 448; AR 2009, p. 466). The iPS cells, reprogrammed from skin cells taken from the woman's arm, were transformed into retinal epithelial cells to treat her age-related macular degeneration (AMD)—a condition that affected thousands of older people worldwide and which often resulted in blindness. This technique, which did not involve the destruction of embryos, was developed by the ophthalmologist Masayo Takahashi at the RIKEN Centre for Developmental Biology in Kobe. A patch of cells measuring 1.3 by 3 millimetres was grafted into the eye in order to cover the retina, patch up the epithelial layer and give support to the remaining photoreceptors. Takahashi indicated that the success of the graft would not be judged until a year had elapsed.

The Nobel Prize in Physiology or Medicine was one half awarded to the British-American neuroscientist Professor John O'Keefe and the other half jointly to the Norwegian husband and wife team, May-Britt Moser and Edvard I. Moser, for "their discoveries of cells that constitute a positioning system in the brain"—an "inner GPS" that makes it possible to orient ourselves in space and demonstrated a cellular basis for higher cognitive function. O'Keefe, a US-born scientist who had worked at University College London since the 1960s, discovered in 1971 the first component of this positioning system in rats, by showing that certain cells in the hippocampus were always activated when the rat was at a certain place in a room. Other hippocampal nerve cells were activated when the rat moved to other places in the room. O'Keefe concluded that these "place" cells, as he named them, not only formed a map of the rat's position in the room but also, by generating numerous maps, enabled the rat to create a memory of an environment which was stored as a specific combination of place cell activities in the hippocampus. The Mosers, who in the mid-1990s were postdoctoral visiting scientists with O'Keefe before moving to the Norwegian University of Science and Technology in Trondheim in 2005, discovered the second component of the brain's positioning system.

This was an area close to the hippocampus called the entorhinal cortex. Here, certain cells, which they named "grid cells", were activated in a unique spatial pattern that collectively constituted a coordinate system that permitted spatial navigation. They found that the grid cells formed circuits with the place cells in the hippocampus, thus constituting a comprehensive positioning system in the brain.

Neil Weir

ASTRONOMY. After a journey taking more than 10 years and covering 6.4 billion km, the *Philae* lander detached from its mothership *Rosetta* on 12 November and started a 7 hour descent onto comet 67P Churyumov-Gerasimenko, 405 million km from Earth. *Rosetta* had been orbiting round the comet since August. Although *Philae* was hailed as the first comet-landing, in fact Japan's *Hayabusa* probe had touched down briefly on a comet in 2004 (see AR 2005, p. 403).

Water and organic chemicals may have been carried to Earth by comets, so analysis of the surface was eagerly awaited. Carbon-containing molecules including methane, methanol and carbon dioxide were detected in the dust, but the deuterium (heavy hydrogen) content of the water was markedly different from that found on Earth. Stunning photographs of kilometre-high cliffs were sent back from the comet, but unfortunately the lander rolled into the shade of one of these, leaving it without enough solar energy to stay active. The European Space Agency hoped that as the comet moved closer to the Sun the solar panels might again be illuminated allowing more data to be obtained.

More conventional exploration of the Solar System continued during the year. Plumes of methane gas were detected on Mars by NASA's *Curiosity* rover (see AR 2012, p. 463). Methane had been found before (see AR 2009, p. 469; AR 2010, p. 453), but the localised nature of these plumes was unusual. Enceladus, one of Saturn's moons, was thought the most likely place in the Solar System for life to be found, and this view was strengthened in April when NASA's *Cassini* space probe found an ocean 40 km below the surface of its southern pole. Observations of the movements of belts of rock in the outer regions of the Solar System suggested that there was a large, unknown planet orbiting the Sun three times further out than Pluto.

An intriguing and very heavy planet outside the Solar System was discovered on 2 June. Kepler-10c was over twice the size of Earth, but 17 times as heavy. This was significant because it had been thought that the gravity of large planets would attract gases during formation so that all large planets would be light and gaseous, but Kepler-10c was very dense indeed. Distant stars in the Milky Way were detected, 775,000 and 900,000 light-years from Earth, dramatically extending the known size of our galaxy.

Commercial space travel suffered a major setback when a test flight of *Virgin Galactic SpaceShipTwo* (see AR 2008, p. 450; AR 2011, p. 453) broke up shortly after launch on 31 October, killing one of the pilots. Preliminary investigation indicated that the air-braking descent device deployed too early, but it was not known why.

CHEMISTRY. Graphene continued to be the focus of research and its properties were even more valuable than originally thought. Its ability to conduct heat was found to be almost unlimited, disobeying the usual law of heat transfer, as the longer the sheet of graphene, the more heat could be transferred per millimetre. Graphene was also found to allow protons to pass through, but was impermeable to other gases, an important property in developing clean energy technology. Samsung, the South Korean conglomerate, developed a new method of growing large areas of high-quality single-crystal graphene on silicon wafers, suitable for the production of transistors. In September scientists at the University of Cambridge manufactured a flexible display screen, a long-awaited usage of graphene.

An Israeli company developed a battery which stored charge in nanodots of bio-organic peptide molecules, which it was claimed could recharge a mobile phone in seconds and an electric car in minutes.

Further confirmation of the heaviest element yet, with an atomic weight of 117, was found in May, when a team in Germany created four atoms of it by firing calcium atoms into Berkelium.

A team of researchers in California managed to break carbon dioxide molecules into solid carbon and oxygen gas using short-wave UV light. This was a dramatic finding because it showed that not all oxygen in the atmosphere needed to have been produced by plants. This synthesis might make it possible to develop space-suits that did not require oxygen tanks.

Cows had long been blamed for generating methane, a potent greenhouse gas. Residents of Rasdorf, Germany, experienced more immediate problems in January, when a cowshed exploded because of the build-up of bovine-produced methane.

The Nobel Prize in Chemistry was awarded jointly to Eric Betzig (Janelia Research Campus, Howard Hughes Medical Institute, USA), Stefan W. Hell (Max Planck Institute for Biophysical Chemistry, Gottingen, and German Cancer Research Centre, Heidelberg) and William E. Moerner (Stanford University) "for the development of super-resolved fluorescence microscopy". It had been assumed that optical microscopes could never have a better resolution than half the wavelength of light. This work circumvented the limitation, allowing optical microscopes to develop into the nanodimension.

ARCHAEOLOGY. Zig-zag patterns carved on a mollusc shell found in Indonesia were dated, on 4 December, as 430,000 years old, ascribing them to a period long before the emergence of modern humans or Neanderthals. They were probably made by *Homo erectus*, showing that decoration—considered to be modern behaviour—was very much older than had been thought. The earliest previously known engraving was dated 75,000 years old.

Footprints in rocks by a beach in Happisburgh, Norfolk, in the UK, were found to be 800,000 years old, the oldest known outside Africa. Previously archaeologists had thought hominids came to Europe only 300,000 years ago.

DNA extracted from the tooth of a 7,000-year old skeleton found in Spain showed that pre-agricultural man was dark-skinned and blue-eyed. He was lactose intolerant and would have had difficulty digesting starch, confirmation that digestion developed as man moved into agriculture.

Survey results of the landscape around Stonehenge, announced in September, showed many more structures than expected (see AR 2011, p. 452). The survey found 17 previously unknown burial pits, henges and circles, and the remains of a 33 metre-long building thought to be 1,000 years older than the Stonehenge circle itself, dated around 2500 BC. The area had been developed over a very long period of time and was probably used by ordinary people, not as a special site for high priests, as had been previously thought. The bluestones used for the well-known circle were found to have exceptional sonic properties when tapped with hammer-stones, perhaps explaining why they were brought from Wales rather than using local stone.

The only known Roman wooden toilet seat was unearthed at Vindolanda, a Roman fort in Northumberland. Marble toilet seats from this period were common finds in Europe but archaeologists were not sure whether wood was used only in Britain or whether the cold, wet conditions meant that Britain was the only area where it was preserved.

There were several major dinosaur discoveries. On 16 May palaeontologists in Argentina dug up bones of a *titanosaur*, the largest dinosaur ever found. Its gigantic thigh bones suggested an overall length of 40m and height of 20m, and a weight of 77 tonnes. A dinosaur in Portugal was the largest predator every found in Europe. At 10 metres long, its size approached that of *Tyrannosaurus rex*. Fossilised trackways in Canada showed that *tyrannosaurs* probably hunted in packs.

Other important fossil finds were a carnivorous plant dated around 40 million years ago, and identification of the biggest bird ever to have lived: *Pelagornis sandersi*, with a wingspan of over 7 metres.

A tiny fragment of zircon found in Western Australia and dated to 4.4 billion years ago was the oldest known piece of the Earth's crust; it provided evidence that a solid crust formed shortly after the Earth was made.

PHYSICS. There was excitement in March when a team analysing data from a telescope at the South Pole announced that they had detected ripples in space dating back to the birth of the universe. These gravitational waves seemed to provide evidence of the Big Bang theory and the subsequent inflation of the universe. However, the effect of space dust had been underestimated in the calculations and by September the conclusions were withdrawn.

Tentative suggestions of the first signal of dark matter were announced in December when physicists in Leiden spotted a weak and atypical photon emission in X-rays from space.

Physicists in Ontario announced in September that they had managed to entangle three photons, instead of the usual two. The three photons had the same strange properties of entanglement that meant that measuring the properties of one immediately determined the properties of the others, no matter the distance between them.

Nuclear fusion continued to be an important area of research, and for the first time scientists succeeded in developing the conditions for fusion inside a tiny pellet of fuel. On 12 February the Lawrence Livermore National Laboratory, California, achieved a major breakthrough by getting out more fusion energy from a fuel pellet than had been put in.

The Nobel Prize in Physics was awarded jointly to Isamu Akasaki (Meijo University and Nagoya University, Japan), Hiroshi Amano (Nagoya University), and Shuji Nakamura (University of California) for their work in inventing efficient blue LEDs (light-emitting diodes), a development which "has enabled bright and energy-saving white light sources".

Lorelly Wilson

INFORMATION TECHNOLOGY

THE year 2014 marked the 50th anniversary of the computer language BASIC, which had been designed by John Kemeny and Thomas Kurtz to be easily learned by students at Dartmouth University. Twenty-five years later, BASIC would become a core part of personal computing, installed on almost every home computer. In 1975, Bill Gates, Paul Allen, and Monte Davidof developed a version of BASIC for the Altair computer, the first product by the software company Microsoft. In 2014, BASIC was ranked as the 14th most popular programming language in use, just two positions behind the HTML language that formatted documents on the World Wide Web.

In business, venture capital funding grew in influence in 2014, reaching levels similar to the heights of the 2001 "Dot Com era", with $47.3 billion going to young US companies, especially in California, which attracted 57 per cent of the funding. The technology industry accounted for one-third of firms exiting venture funding to become publicly-traded; healthcare businesses constituted most of the remaining two-thirds. New York City ro se in prominence, attracting more than $12 billion in venture funding, mostly to Internet and mobile technology companies. The European startup industry also continued to grow, as £3.7 billion in venture funding was invested in 855 young companies, with 38 per cent based in the UK and 18 per cent in Germany.

Many hobbyist electronic devices reached wider audiences in 2014. An international community of designers, academics, and enthusiasts used 3D printing technology to design low-cost, custom-made hand prostheses for $50. Users entered their arm dimensions into a website and receive personalised, customisable designs that could be printed to make their own "Cyborg Beast" prosthetic hand. First developed in 2013, 3D printed firearms became viable in 2014 with the development of ammunition that could be used repeatedly in the same gun. In Japan, courts sentenced a defendant to two years in prison for manufacturing, selling, and publishing designs for 3D printed revolvers. Policy concerning flying drones was also contentious in 2014, especially after Internet retailer Amazon and University of Cincinnati researchers made progress on competing package delivery systems that used autonomous flying robots. Fitness tracking systems also became more widespread in 2014 when Apple added HealthKit to its phones and tablets, integrating a market of formerly-unconnected personal fitness tracking sensors into a single platform for tracking personal health. Oculus Rift, makers of a head-mounted virtual reality display, were acquired by the social network company Facebook, for $2 billion; their developer kits were used by film-makers to showcase the cinematic possibilities of virtual reality.

Revelations on US and UK government surveillance, leaked in 2013 by former National Security Agency contractor Edward Snowden, continued to unfold in 2014, as privacy became a key question for governments and the technology industry worldwide. In January, the *Guardian* reported that US and UK intelligence agencies had indiscriminately monitored 200 million text messages per day without a warrant. Leaks also showed that UK intelligence collected video conversations in bulk, applying facial recognition indiscriminately to at least 1.8 million people and collecting large amounts of sexually explicit private communications. The UK Parliament responded to the leaks through an emergency bill passed in a single day that retained and expanded the powers of British intelligence to force communications companies to carry out large-scale surveillance, after the European Court of Justice ruled these surveillance practices to be a breach of privacy. In the US, President Barack Obama promised to end bulk collection of citizen telephone metadata, after multiple independent government advisory groups suggested changes to intelligence-gathering practices. As the year ended, debate continued on US changes, focusing mostly on telephone information rather than Internet communications. In Brazil, citizens collaboratively drafted legislation for a "Marco Civil da Internet", an Internet "Bill of Rights", that limited data collected from Brazilian Internet users and held international technology companies accountable to Brazilian law. The bill was passed in April.

The Brazilian Marco Civil also addressed the policy issue of "network neutrality." Proponents of network neutrality argued that the Internet should be treated as a common carrier resource like telephones, water, electricity, or roads, and that companies had no right to inspect or discriminate the price or quality of a connection based on the details of a customer's activities. Communications companies, on the other hand, argued for the right to carry out "deep inspection" of Internet communications, to differentiate charges based on customer activity. The Brazilian Marco Civil affirmed the network neutrality position. In the USA, the Federal Communications Commission (FCC), also considered regulating the Internet as a public utility. US citizens became aware of this issue when cable Internet provider Comcast reduced the Internet speeds of their competitor, Internet film service Netflix, early in the year, with the result that many customers could no longer easily watch films from Netflix. When FCC chairman Tom Wheeler suggested that he might side with communications companies, citizens submitted over 4 million comments to the FCC, the largest number of public comments ever submitted to a US regulator, mostly in support of network neutrality.

Long-term debates about the ethics of data, privacy, and computer algorithms expanded in 2014 through a series of high profile research publications and policy debates. In Europe, court rulings and regulations established a "right to be forgotten", in which individuals could suppress information about themselves from search results. This requirement was met with widespread criticism after it was used to prevent public criminal records and news articles from being accessible on search engines. Another algorithm under public scrutiny was the "NewsFeed" of the social network company, Facebook. Researchers at Facebook and Cornell University conducted an experiment, finding that messages from friends had an "emotion contagion" effect on the positivity or negativity of a person's own posts. Publication of this research led to public concern about the power of Facebook to influence their emotions and beliefs by choosing what messages to show. Other research highlighted privacy risks associated with personal data. Massachusetts Institute of Technology (MIT) researcher Yves de Alexandre Montjoye demonstrated that private persons could be re-identified in anonymised datasets with information from four mobile phone call locations or four transaction receipts. Privacy was also an important component of EU regulation, with the European Parliament passing General Data Protection Regulation proposals for consideration by the Council of Europe. Previous regulations had focused on safe storage of personal data, while the new proposals would require individual consent for each intended use of personal data.

Online harassment dominated discussion of social technologies in 2014. In February, game developer Dong Nguyen was forced to take down the popular videogame "Flappy Bird" after consistent, large-scale harassment online. In September, nude photographs stolen from the phones of celebrities were released on discussion sites Reddit and 4chan and were spread widely. In one case, harassers barraged Zelda Williams, daughter of actor Robin Williams, with images of her father's body and accusations that she had caused his death. Harassment against Anita Sarkeesian was part of a wider GamerGate controversy online, sparked from dissatisfaction among many videogame fans at a growing demographic inclusion within an industry that previously underrepresented groups like women, LGBTQ, and minority groups. GamerGate supporters organised large scale harassment and misinformation campaigns to push these groups out of the videogame industry, sending threats, releasing personal information, and convincing advertisers to stop funding media outlets that featured minority groups. GamerGate participants carried out their campaign across a wide range of online social platforms, including the social networks Twitter and Facebook, the discussion sites Reddit and 4chan, the crowdfunding site Indiegogo, and the knowledge repository Wikipedia. Attackers took advantage of the weakness of platforms to defend their users from coordinated harassment. Despite these problems, social media was also used to organise productive, large-scale cooperative responses to major societal issues. On Facebook, hundreds of thousands of people challenged their friends to film themselves dumping buckets of ice on their heads while also donating to medical research; the initiative raised $100 million in 30 days.

Interaction with technological personalities grew to prominence in 2014. In the film *Her*, directed by Spike Jonze and released widely in 2014, a lonely writer undergoing divorce, develops an emotional and sexual relationship with "Samantha", an artificial intelligence. Later in the year, the startup company Jibo raised $27.3 million from pre-sales and investors to mass-produce a home robot personality to sit on counter-tops. In October, Western television audiences were introduced to virtual music performers when Hatsune Miku, a popular Japanese female 3D holographic performer with a computer generated voice, performed on *The Late Show* with David Letterman. Robotic telepresence, in which a person moves and speaks in a space through a robot, also rose to prominence in 2014. Edward Snowden, who obtained Russian residency after leaking reports of US and UK surveillance activities, attended high profile events in the USA and UK through a telepresent robot in order to avoid being arrested. That same year, researchers tested the telepresent People's Bot to support journalism, provide scholarships at international events, and carry out democratic representation for people unable to attend physical meetings.

J. Nathan Matias

THE ENVIRONMENT

THE nations of the world have now spent more than a quarter of a century grappling with the threat of global climate change, since they first addressed the issue collectively in 1988 at the Toronto Conference on the Changing Atmosphere; but the more they have sought agreement, the more agreement has seemed impossible to find. Great hopes were raised, therefore, when towards the end of 2014 China and the United States, the two key players—the two biggest emitters of carbon dioxide and other greenhouse gases which were causing the atmosphere to warm, suddenly and unexpectedly announced a climate accord.

Unveiled in Beijing on 12 November by US President Barack Obama and Chinese President Xi Jinping, during a visit by Obama to attend the Asia Pacific Economic Cooperation (APEC) conference in the Chinese capital, the agreement formally recognised climate change as "one of the greatest threats facing humanity" and affirmed that the two countries would work together to try to secure, at the United Nations Climate Conference in Paris in December 2015, a treaty to cut carbon emissions, which would be legally binding on all countries. Furthermore, they both announced targets of their own to bring emissions down, which went far beyond anything that either nation had previously contemplated. The US set a goal to reduce its CO2 by 26-28 per cent from 2005 levels by 2025, while China adopted a target of having its soaring emissions peak, and then start to fall back, "around 2030"—the first time the world's biggest polluter had set any sort of specific date for its greenhouse gases to stop increasing.

Some environmentalists and diplomatic observers asserted that, welcome though they were, these commitments did not go far enough to meet the UN's aim of limiting global warming to the recognised danger threshold of 2 degrees Celsius (3.6 degrees Fahrenheit) above pre-industrial levels; but the demarche, which had been negotiated in secret and took the rest of the world by surprise, was generally seen in an enormously positive light. There were two main reasons for this. Firstly, China and the US were themselves the biggest emitters in the world, contributing between them about 45 per cent of the carbon going into the atmosphere each year—the Chinese about 29 per cent and the US about 16 per cent. (The third biggest emitter in 2014 was India, with about 7 per cent and rising, meaning that more than half of all emissions came from just three nations, none of which had hitherto been covered by a binding emissions reduction treaty.)

The second reason for the warmth of the welcome was that not only were the US and China the biggest polluters, they had long been the biggest obstructers of any comprehensive climate agreement—the US had fatally undermined the first such, the Kyoto protocol of 1997, by withdrawing from it under the Republican President George W. Bush in 2001, while the Chinese, who at the time saw a world climate agreement as potentially restrictive of their runaway economic growth, largely obstructed the second attempt at a treaty at the Copenhagen climate conference in 2009. (A senior UK official told correspondents at the time: "This conference has been systematically wrecked by the government of China".) The accord announced in Beijing in November reflected changing political and economic realities. This time a Democrat was in the White House; and there was much suggestion that President Obama was beginning to see successful action on climate as an issue which would help define his legacy. In China, there was a growing recognition that global warming presented real threats to the People's Republic itself, combined with a slowing of economic growth and an increasing willingness to tackle the calamitous air pollution affecting China's cities, caused by the unlimited expansion of fossil fuel power plants, mainly fired by coal.

That the two great nations might jointly perform a volte-face, therefore, and declare themselves both believers in the seriousness of the global warming threat, and proponents of a comprehensive climate deal to tackle it, produced a remarkable burst of optimism. This reinforced the hope which had begun the previous month, on 24 October, when the 28 member states of the EU had agreed on the boldest target to cut carbon emissions in history, with a stated goal of reducing them by "at least" 40 per cent on 1990 levels by 2030.

During the year there had been mounting pressure—political and scientific—for such moves. On 23 September the UN held a high-level Climate Summit at its headquarters in New York which was addressed by, among others, President Obama, UK Prime Minister David Cameron, French President François Hollande, and the Hollywood actor Leonardo di Caprio. There was a universal recognition of the seriousness of the problem, although less in the way of specific commitments. Two days earlier, there had been worldwide grass roots demonstrations in a series of rallies, collectively named "The People's Climate March", which involved hundreds of thousands of people taking to the streets in cities from London and Brussels to New York and Melbourne, and demanding action from governments.

Even more pressure on political leaders to act came from the three-part Fifth Assessment Report (AR5) of the UN's Intergovernmental Panel on Climate Change (IPCC), whose first part—on the state of climate science, declaring that man-made global warming was "unequivocal"—had been published in September 2013 (see AR 2014, pp. 562-63). The second part, on the likely impacts of climate change around the world, published at the end of March, caused an international stir, as it painted a dramatic picture of damage and loss across the globe, from failing food supplies to inundations of coastal cities, especially in Asia. The day after its publication, US Secretary of State John Kerry called on the world to "act dramatically and quickly," warning that the "costs of inaction are catastrophic." The third part of the report, published in April, on the measures which could be taken to counter the warming, said that low-carbon energy would have to triple by 2050 if there were to be any chance of holding temperatures below the two-degree threshold, and that fossil fuels would need to be phased out altogether by the end of the century. The warnings contained in all three parts were repeated and re-emphasised in the AR5 Synthesis Report, which was released in Copenhagen in November and endorsed by 195 countries, meaning that, although disbelief in man-made warming of the atmosphere was still expressed by some so-called climate sceptics, no government doubted the reality of the phenomenon.

Strong support for the idea of a warming atmosphere came during the year from observation as well as prediction. Two US agencies, NASA (the National Aeronautics and Space Administration) and NOAA (The National Oceanic and Atmospheric Administration) separately affirmed that 2014 was the warmest year in the global record dating back to 1880, with temperatures 0.69C (1.24F) above 20th century averages. In the UK, the Met Office said that 2014 was the warmest year in all-UK records dating back to 1910, and the warmest in the Central England Temperature series, the world's longest-running such data set, dating back to 1659. According to the World Meteorological Organisation, 2014 saw "exceptional heat and flooding in many parts of the world" (flooding being another expected consequence of climate change, as a warming atmosphere holds more moisture), with record rainfall in many regions of South America and Eastern Europe. By the end of the year, the cause of the trouble, the globally-averaged CO_2 level in the atmosphere, had reached 399 parts per million (when measurement began on Mauna Loa, the Hawaiian volcano, in 1958, the level was 315 ppm).

However, all this scientific and political pressure did not make for success in the principal climate negotiating forum, the annual Conference of the Parties, or COP, of the UN's Framework Convention on Climate Change, this year being COP20, held in late November and early December in Lima, Peru. COP20 was meant to clear the way for COP21 in Paris in December 2015, the meeting at which a new global climate treaty was due to be signed, but so little progress was made in the tortuous, not to say sclerotic, negotiating process, involving nearly 200 different players, that all the hard decisions were kicked down the road to Paris. If the US-China climate deal had not been reached, the outlook would have been very pessimistic as the year ended; as it was, there was guarded optimism.

Yet had Presidents Obama and Xi not reached their accord, something else would have been the most notable environmental event of 2014: the publication in the journal *Science* on 18 September of a paper overturning 20 years of assumptions about the future growth of the world's population. Written by an international team of demographers—led by Patrick Gerland, of the United Nations Population Division in New York, and Adrian Raftery, of the University of Washington, in Seattle—it was entitled "World population stabilization unlikely this century", and it challenged the long-held belief that human numbers would peak at about 9 billion in 2050, and then stabilise. Instead, the new analysis asserted, there was an 80 per cent probability that population would continue increasing to between 9.6 and 12.3 billion by 2100, with most of the increase expected in sub-Saharan Africa, where fertility rates were remaining very high, partly because of the lack of women's education, and partly because of lack of access to contraception services. "Because rapid population increase in high-fertility countries can create challenges ranging from depletion of natural resources to unemployment to social unrest, the results of this study have important policy implications," the paper said in studiously understated language. In fact, it was prefiguring a potentially catastrophic increase in the human pressures on the Earth, which a growing number of studies said were already exceeding the planet's capacity to withstand them. Indeed, one of the most dramatic of such analyses appeared only 12 days after the Gerland-Raftery report, on 30 September.

The *Living Planet Report* of the World Wide Fund for Nature (WWF) asserted that more than half of the world's wild animals had disappeared in the previous 40 years. It calculated that since 1970, the total number of vertebrates—mammals, birds, fish, reptiles and amphibians—had shrunk by a remarkable 52 per cent, and that loss of biodiversity was reaching "critical levels". The decline was computed by looking at 10,000 different vertebrate populations and using the data to create a "Living Planet Index" to reflect the status of vertebrates as a whole. Another index in the report illustrated the "ecological footprint" of humanity, concluding that to sustain the scale at which human society was using up natural resources would now need one-and-a-half Earths. Another significant marker of human destruction came in new figures for deforestation: a paper in the journal *Nature Climate Change*, published on 29 June by Belinda Arunarwati Margono, formerly in charge of data gathering at Indonesia's ministry of forestry, calculated that in 2012 Indonesia had lost 840,000 hectares of its primary forest compared to 460,000 hectares in Brazil, thus making Indonesia the most rapidly "deforesting" country on earth.

In the UK, 2014 was notable environmentally for the extremely wet and stormy weather of January and February, which brought devastating floods to the low-lying ground of the Somerset levels and also to the Thames valley to the west of London, affecting suburban towns such as Sunbury. It was the wettest January on record. In February storms were so severe that the main railway line from Exeter to west Devon and Cornwall was washed away at Dawlish, leaving the extreme far west of the country cut off, in rail terms; it was April before the line was repaired, at a cost of £35 million.

The two principal environmental controversies during the year were the arguments over the extraction of shale gas by hydraulic fracturing, or fracking, and the continuing cull of wild badgers initiated by the government in an attempt to limit the incidence of bovine tuberculosis in cattle herds, of which badgers were known to constitute a reservoir. The conflict over fracking was continual between the Conservative ministers in the coalition government—who were enthusiastic about the technology and its potential benefits, with David Cameron announcing in January that his government would go "all out for shale"—and a mounting opposition, which spread beyond organised environmental pressure groups concerned at the climate effects of a new fossil-fuel industry, and included many people who feared widespread damage to the landscape from drilling. The badger cull, which had begun in 2013, resumed in early September and the government announced on 18 December that, over a six-week period, 274 badgers had been killed in Gloucestershire and 341 in Somerset. Animal welfare groups were vociferous in their criticism.

Perhaps the most singular event of the year was the rechristening of Britain's environment movement as a whole, which was testily referred to as "the Green Blob" by the sometime environment secretary, Owen Paterson, who was sacked in the government reshuffle of 15 July, to be replaced by Liz Truss. In a newspaper article after his dismissal, Paterson said that by the Green Blob he had meant "the mutually supportive network of environmental pressure groups, renewable energy companies and some public officials who keep each other well supplied with lavish funds, scare stories and green tape". He contended: "This tangled triangle of unelected busybodies claims to have the interests of the planet and the countryside at heart, but it is increasingly clear that it is focusing on the wrong issues and doing real harm while profiting handsomely." Some commentators suggested that the principal function of the Green Blob in 2014 had been to swallow up Mr Paterson himself.

Michael McCarthy

XIV THE LAW

INTERNATIONAL LAW

THE issue that dominated the international peace and security agenda in 2014 was, once again, the possibility of a military intervention in the Middle East: this time not against President Bashar Assad of Syria, although not in his support either. The US-led coalition launched air raids to stop the advance of the Islamic State of Iraq and Syria, known as ISIS or ISIL. The coalition could rely on the consent of Iraq as far as the legality of the use of force in the territory of that country was concerned. But military action in Syria required a different explanation. According to one view, it was justified under the doctrine of humanitarian intervention as a response to the gross human rights violations perpetrated by ISIS; according to another view, Iraq's right of self-defence permitted such action given that ISIS's aggression against Iraq originated from Syrian territory. These two views were not mutually exclusive. The United Kingdom chose to participate in operations in Iraq but not in Syria because of Parliament's opposition to intervention in Syria a year earlier. Violations of the law of armed conflict of an ever more gruesome and barbaric nature were widely reported in this latest Middle Eastern war. The question of who was responsible for the atrocities posed less difficulty than in other situations, given ISIS's eagerness to disseminate evidence of its brutalities on the Internet.

Elsewhere in the Middle East, a new conflict between Israel and Hamas in Gaza flared up in the summer of 2014. The UN Human Rights Council appointed a commission of enquiry in order to investigate all possible violations of international humanitarian law and international human rights law. The Palestinian bid for statehood continued but a round of peace talks sponsored by US Secretary of State John Kerry ended in April with no results.

There were various armed conflicts outside the Middle East, too, but these generally remained local or regional affairs. An exception was the war in Eastern Ukraine which had significant repercussions for Russia's relations with the West. Russia's annexation of Crimea attracted almost universal condemnation.

In 2014 the **International Court of Justice (ICJ)** ruled in two cases. In *Whaling in the Antarctic* (Australia v. Japan: New Zealand intervening), the Court held that Japan's whaling programme was in breach of a number of provisions of the International Convention for the Regulation of Whaling. In particular, the Court found that, although the programme included scientific elements, it was not conducted *"for the purposes of"* scientific research and that it therefore breached Article 8 of the Whaling Convention. The second case decided by the ICJ concerned a maritime delimitation dispute between Peru and Chile that had its origins in the War of the Pacific fought by Peru, Chile and Bolivia at the end of the 19th century. The Court accepted Chile's position on the relevance of the

1952 Santiago Declaration for the demarcation of the maritime boundary, but only insofar as the first part of the boundary was concerned. Peru's position prevailed in respect of the rest. In the end, each country had reason both to celebrate and to lament the outcome of the case.

The Marshall Islands instituted proceedings against all nine states (USA, Russia, the UK, France, China, Israel, India, Pakistan, North Korea) known or believed to possess nuclear weapons. The Marshall Islands contended that each of these states violated the obligation to pursue negotiations in good faith towards nuclear disarmament. This obligation was contained in Article 6 of the Treaty on the Non-Proliferation of Nuclear Weapons, to which some—but not all—of the nine nuclear-armed states were parties. The case against all but three of those states (India, Pakistan, UK) was removed from the register of the Court because no basis for jurisdiction other than the consent of the potential respondents existed and such consent was not given.

Of concern to the activities of the ICJ was a decision of the Italian Constitutional Court at the end of 2014. The Italian Court found that it could not give effect to the 2012 judgment of the ICJ in *Jurisdictional Immunities of the State* (Germany v. Italy). In that judgment, the ICJ had found that the decisions of Italian courts awarding compensation in lawsuits brought against Germany for war crimes committed in World War II violated the law of state immunity (see AR 2013, pp. 443-44).

Three new judges were elected to the ICJ in 2014: Mr James Richard Crawford, an Australian national; Mr Kirill Gevorgian, a Russian national; and Mr Patrick Lipton Robinson, a Jamaican national. The election of James Crawford, widely regarded as one of the leading international lawyers of his generation, was welcomed within the growing community of international law scholars and practitioners.

Meanwhile, two important awards were rendered by arbitral tribunals under the auspices of the **Permanent Court of Arbitration** in The Hague. The first case, brought under the United Nations Convention on the Law of the Sea (UNCLOS), concerned the delimitation of the maritime boundary between Bangladesh and the Republic of India. The second case was a dispute between former shareholders of Yukos Oil Company and the Russian Federation. The claim, which was brought under the Energy Charter Treaty, had great economic and political significance. Yukos was a Russian oil and gas company bought by the Russian oligarch Mikhail Khodorkovsky from the Russian government in the mid-1990s. In October 2003 Khodorkovsky was arrested in Russia. Yukos was broken up for alleged unpaid taxes shortly thereafter, before being eventually declared bankrupt. The arbitral tribunals established to handle the different Yukos claims concluded that the Russian Federation had taken measures which were equivalent in effects to expropriation and breached the Energy Charter Treaty. Notwithstanding some reduction in the damages on account of contributory fault on the part of the claimants, $50 billion were awarded in damages against Russia, making this the largest award of its kind in history.

The **International Tribunal for the Law of the Sea (ITLOS)** delivered only one judgment in 2014. In *M/V "Virginia G" Case* (Panama v. Guinea-Bissau), the Tribunal held that the confiscation by Guinea-Bissau of a vessel flying the flag of Panama had violated the UNCLOS. The Tribunal also found in favour of Panama in respect of the claim that Guinea-Bissau had failed to notify Panama of the detention and arrest of the vessel, but it rejected the Panamanian contention that excessive force had been used by the authorities of Guinea-Bissau.

Elections were held for one-third of the judges sitting on ITLOS. The seven new judges came from Iceland, Japan, Korea, Mexico, Poland, South Africa and Tanzania. In October Judge Vladimir Golitsyn (Russian Federation) was elected as president of the Tribunal and Judge Boualem Bouguetaia (Algeria) as vice-president for the period 2014-17 by the members of the Tribunal.

There were also important developments in the field of international criminal law. In March, Trial Chamber II of the **International Criminal Court** (ICC) found Germain Katanga, a former Congolese commander of the Patriotic Resistance Front in Ituri (FRPI), guilty of war crimes and a crime against humanity but acquitted him of charges of rape, sexual slavery and using children under the age of 15 years to participate actively in hostilities. He was sentenced to 12 years of imprisonment. This was the second conviction in the history of the ICC, following the 2012 conviction of Thomas Lubanga Dyilo (see AR 2013, p. 446). In December, the Appeals Chamber of the ICC confirmed the verdict and sentence in the Lubanga case.

The ad hoc International Criminal Tribunals established to deal with international crimes committed in the former Yugoslavia and during the Rwandan genocide were approaching the third decade of their activity.

The **International Criminal Tribunal for the former Yugoslavia** had completed almost all its work: fewer than 10 trials and appeals remained on its docket, involving the last 20 defendants and appellants (out of a total of 161 indicted). The Appeals Chamber delivered two judgments. The first was in the case of Sainovic et al., one of the largest and most complex cases to be decided by the Yugoslav Tribunal. The appellants were four former senior officials of the Federal Republic of Yugoslavia ("FRY") and Serbia, who had been convicted of various offences committed against civilians in Kosovo between March and May 1999. The appeals were partially successful, leading to reductions in the sentences for Nikola Sainovic (former deputy prime minister of the FRY) from 22 to 18 years of imprisonment; for Sreten Lukic (former Serbian ministry of the interior staff in Pristina) from 22 to 20 years of imprisonment; and for Vladimir Lazarevic (former commander of the Pristina Corps) from 15 to 14 years in prison. The 22-year sentence for the former commander of the 3rd Army of the Army of Yugoslavia, Nebojsa Pavkovic, was confirmed. The second judgment of the Appeals Chambers was in the case of Vlastimir Dordevic who had been assistant minister of the Serbian ministry of internal affairs and chief of its public security department. The Appeals Chamber reduced the sentence from 27 years to 18 years in prison.

The **International Criminal Tribunal for Rwanda** completed its first-instance case load in 2012. It was expected to deliver its final judgment in August 2015 and to shut down by the end of September 2015. In 2014, the Appeals Chamber delivered final judgments in several cases. Among the most prominent was that of the chairman of Rwanda's ruling party during the genocide and his deputy (Edouard Karemera and Matthieu Ngirumpatse). The Appeals Chamber reversed some of the findings of the Trial Chamber, but confirmed the convictions for direct and public incitement to commit genocide; genocide, extermination and rape as crimes against humanity; and murder as a serious violation of Article 3 common to the Geneva Conventions. The sentence of life imprisonment was confirmed. The Appeals Chamber also ruled on the appeal of Augustin Bizimungu, former chief of staff of the Rwandan Army, against his conviction. The sentence of 30 years of imprisonment was confirmed. In the case of Ildéphonse Nizeyimana, who had been a captain at the military training facility during the genocide, the Appeals Chamber upheld some of the convictions but reversed others. Among the victims of Nizeyimana had been Rosalie Gicanda, wife of King Mutara III of Rwanda and effectively Rwanda's last living queen at the time of her assassination. In the *Military II* case, the Appeal Chambers examined the convictions of Augustin Ndindiliyimana, who as a major general and former chief of staff of the Rwandan gendarmerie had been one of the most senior figures to be sentenced by the Tribunal. The Appeal Chambers reversed the Ndindiliyimana convictions that had been based on his superior responsibility over the gendarmerie, finding that Ndindiliyimana did not exercise the required effective control.

The **European Court of Human Rights** remained the busiest human rights court in 2014. Among its most important judgments was *S.A.S. v France*, where the Court found that the French law *"prohibiting the concealment of one's face in public places"* did not violate the European Convention on Human Rights. The law had been the object of intense debate in France and beyond, and criticised by some Muslim groups. The Court accepted the argument made by France that the law was a proportionate measure aimed at ensuring the protection of the rights of others and guaranteeing minimum conditions of "living together" in society.

Another case concerning sartorial matters and human rights was *Gough v UK*. Stephen Gough had been incarcerated repeatedly since 2006 for refusing to wear any clothes in public. Gough, who had been found not to suffer from any mental illness, alleged that his human rights to private life and to free expression were violated. The Court found no breach of such rights, in a judgment that did not stand out for the quality and clarity of its reasoning.

In *Hassan v UK*, the Court returned to the difficult relationship between the law of armed conflict and international human rights law. The question was whether internment in conformity with the Third and Fourth Geneva Conventions could nonetheless breach Article 5 of the European Convention on Human Rights protecting the right to liberty and security. The Court interpreted Article

5 in a manner that was consistent with the powers granted to States under the Geneva Convention. In essence, it added a further ground for detention to those expressly mentioned in that provision. It held that the right of *habeas corpus*, which was also protected under Article 5, had to be interpreted in light of the law of armed conflict. The Court seemed to suggest that its approach was limited to international armed conflict. The *Hassan* case far from settled all the complex issues related to the application of human rights law in wartime. It remained unclear, for example, whether States had authority to detain in non-international armed conflicts—an issue at the heart of litigation pending before the English courts.

Guglielmo Verdirame and Noam Zamir

EUROPEAN UNION LAW

WHEN the first paragraphs emerged in 2013 about a proposed EU free trade treaty (FTA) with the United States they evoked no particular interest. Such treaties were nothing new, not even when they involved trading partners in distant continents far from the EU's "near abroad". The FTA with South Korea dated back to 2010. But during 2014 there suddenly emerged a vehement campaign opposing this Transatlantic Trade and Investment Partnership (TTIP) (called Transatlantic Free Trade Agreement (TAFTA) in the US).

The core of the opposition appeared to be a fear that the treaty's procedures would allow powerful (US) corporations to sue EU governments, to dismantle consumer safeguards and public services, particularly in the health sector, in favour of private economic interests. The mechanism for attaining this end would be the Investor-to-State Dispute Settlement (ISDS) system, which was aimed to protect the security of foreign investments. ISDS was provocative because it relied on arbitration, done in secret by commercial arbitrators, and not on open adjudication in courts by legally trained judges.

The agitation against the ISDS caused the European Commission to delay progress on the negotiations in order to meet these issues and deflect what by the end of the year had become a powerful political pressure. At the same time, however, it had been negotiating a parallel FTA with Canada, the Comprehensive and Economic (or Canada-EU) Trade Agreement (CETA), which also contained ISDS provisions that were opposed by Canadians on identical grounds, fearing (this time, EU) corporations attacking their public, especially health, services. CETA was, however, off the radar of the EU agitators and its text was agreed by both parties (the EU Member States as such were not involved) in September ready for formal signature the following spring.

Both treaties formed part of wider international strategies. CETA was part of the EU-Canada comprehensive strategic partnership, the other, non-mercantile, strand of which was the Strategic Partnership Agreement (SPA) initialled by

Canada and the EU also in September, three weeks before CETA. It covered foreign policy, crisis management, the Arctic and internal policy areas such as education and transport. TTIP was in parallel to the US Trans-Pacific Partnership series with Australia and others. A yet wider context was the potential Trade in Services Agreement (TISA), which was being negotiated by 23 members of the World Trade Organisation (WTO) and for which the EU published its negotiation position papers during 2014. Here, too, fears were being expressed about its potential negative impact on public health services.

The EU-South Korea FTA of 2010 had also contained arbitration provisions for the settlement of disputes but they were traditional in form and applied only to disputes between the contracting parties, i.e. states or state equivalent (the EU). ISDS as embodied in TTIP and CETA was original in this context in that it gave private parties status to initiate and pursue disputes directly against the contracting parties (and not via their governments) and thereby pursue their private interests, hence the sensitivity of the protesters. In July the EU enacted Regulation 912/2014 to deal with the financial consequences for the EU and/or its Member States following a successful arbitration claim under any future ISDS provisions, which would include both CETA and TTIP.

The EU association agreement with Ukraine which had been aborted just before its signing ceremony in 2013 was eventually signed in two parts in March and June 2014 (an unusual process). This very far-reaching treaty, although described as creating an association, in reality was a free trade agreement in disguise and contained the express aim to convert within 10 years into a Deep and Comprehensive Free Trade Agreement (DCFTA), a new form of EU relationship which was also being discussed in relation to Jordan and Egypt. It was massive (more than 2,000 pages) and contained very detailed social, legal and other policy requirements. Like the Serbian association treaty before it (see AR 2014, p. 449) it was clearly intended to align the country, as far as was possible outside actual membership, on the EU constitutional treaties and the Union acquis. Similar but less far-reaching association agreements were also signed with Moldova and Georgia.

Of great importance for the future development of the European project has been the proposal for the EU as such to accede to the European Convention on Human Rights. This was specifically authorised, indeed mandated, by the Lisbon Treaty. The draft text of a treaty to enable this to happen was agreed in 2013 (see AR 2014, p. 451) but could not progress beyond that until, in particular, the European Court of Justice (ECJ) had ruled on its constitutional propriety. It finally delivered its Opinion in December 2014 and, disappointingly, it was negative. In an earlier Opinion in 1996 the Court had already rejected such a move on the grounds that the EU had no competence to do so. That objection was removed by the Lisbon Treaty. The objection this time was centred on the special nature of the relationship between the Member States themselves and with the EU; but underlying that was the perennial problem of the status of the Court itself and the maintenance of its monopoly of power to adju-

dicate on EU matters. The Opinion was subtle and long (80 pages). It was preceded in June by the "View" of Advocate General Juliane Kokott, which was
equally long plus a further 20 pages of endnotes and very scholarly and which
concluded in favour of the proposals. The Commission would now have the
task of incorporating the Court's criticisms and re-obtaining the necessary con-
sents from the various stakeholders.

The third dramatic constitutional event of the year was the much heralded
"United Kingdom opt-out" which also had a Lisbon dimension. Article 10(4) of
Protocol 36 to the Lisbon Treaty allowed the UK to in effect opt out of pre-
Lisbon acts in the field of police and judicial cooperation in criminal matters en
bloc. This it did, with the result that those acts ceased to apply to the UK as from
1 December 2014. However, Article 10(5) of the Protocol allowed the UK to
request to opt back in for some or all of them, which it did in respect of 29 out
of the total of 88 contained in the original block opt-out. In addition, a further
15 pre-Lisbon acts had been amended after Lisbon and so could not be included
in the opt-out but would remain automatically binding on the UK. The whole of
this procedure was embodied in a series of four Decisions and one Council list
published on 27 November and 1 December.

The justice system generally began a new phase with the beginning of a series
of strategies in 2014 replacing earlier plans that had expired in 2013. Thus the
new e-justice strategy 2014-2018 replaced the previous action plan and saw a
Decision in June on an e-justice portal system; the Justice Programme 2014-
2020 continued three expiring programmes on drug prevention, criminal justice
and civil justice; the programme on Rights, Equality and Citizenship 2014-2020
replaced three expiring programmes on anti-discrimination and gender equality.

At Luxembourg the European Court of Justice followed the revision of its
rules of procedure the previous year by revising its "supplementary rules" and
its practice directions (procedural guidance to litigants), while the Civil Service
Tribunal revised all its documentation (rules of procedure, Instructions to the
Registrar and practice directions) in May. The ramifications of the new Unified
Patent Court began to be felt as its unique character needed to be considered
within the system of enforcement of foreign judgments. Consequently, a new
concept was invented for the purpose, that of "common court", which would
apply not only to the Unified Patent Court but also to the Benelux Court of Justice (which acted as a form of unified patent court for the three Benelux countries). This was done by adding four new Articles to the Brussels I Regulation
on Jurisdiction and Enforcement of Judgments. Also relevant in this connection
was the "ratification" by the EU in December of the 2005 Hague Convention on
Choice of Court Agreements. The Convention would now come into force in
2015 and provide a mini-code for EU Member States on clauses in commercial
contracts regarding the choice of court.

The attempt to define the rights of defendants in criminal proceedings following the introduction of the European Arrest Warrant and in face of the UK's
adamant refusal to countenance a general directive to that effect continued its

piecemeal path. Two Recommendations (which were not binding and so could evade the objections of Member States) were adopted on procedural rights for vulnerable defendants and on legal aid in criminal proceedings. At the same time the development of a European legal area continued with the adoption of Regulation 655/2014 on transnational orders for the preservation of evidence.

Finally, in the field of commercial law, a new Market Abuse Regulation on abuse of insider information, together with a Directive on criminal and other penalties for its breach, were adopted in April. In November a far-reaching Directive was adopted governing the use in national courts of the action for damages for breach of competition law.

Neville March Hunnings

LAW IN THE UNITED KINGDOM

No sooner were the Scottish referendum votes counted than Prime Minister David Cameron sought to seize the agenda (see the articles on Scotland and the UK). He said that the West Lothian question—whereby non-English MPs were allowed to vote on English laws—"requires a decisive answer".

Legal aid was introduced on the recommendations of the Rushcliffe Committee, which reported in 1945 (see AR 1948, p. 465). The Legal Aid, Sentencing and Punishment of Offenders Act 2012 (see AR 2012, p. 451) drastically reduced the provision of legal aid; it provided the Lord Chancellor with powers to limit legal aid yet further. In the approach to the 800th anniversary of Magna Carta, Chris Grayling sought to exercise these powers. Particularly controversial was a regulation purportedly limiting (with a few exceptions) the provision of legal aid to "residents", which meant those who had been in the UK for a continuous period of 12 months. In *Public Law Project v The Secretary of State for Justice*, the Administrative Court declared the regulation unlawful. Lord Justice Moses concluded that Grayling's legal argument amounted "to little more than reliance on public prejudice". In another judgment, the president of the Family Division of the High Court, Sir James Munby, called the current state of affairs on access to justice "both unprincipled and unconscionable".

The underlying problem was highlighted by *Coventry v Lawrence*, a case twice heard by the Supreme Court in 2014. The substance concerned the tort of nuisance. A complicated case, the key question was whether an injunction could be ordered to restrain the number of races at a popular motor racing venue. The orthodox view—that a landowner is, prima facie, entitled to injunctive relief—was affirmed. The second case concerned the costs. The successful claimants had spent over £1,000,000 en route to their ultimate victory. These costs were not obviously the responsibility of the respondents: they lost in the Supreme Court, but they won in the Court of Appeal (that is: their argument was not risible). Lord Neuberger expressed "grave concern" about the costs and the hope "that those responsible for civil justice in England and Wales are considering what further steps can be taken to ensure better access to justice".

It was a bumper year for private law in the Supreme Court. In *Williams v Central Bank of Nigeria* the limitation period for claims in knowing receipt and dishonest assistance was considered. The court held that a limitation period of six years applied. For over a century lawyers had debated whether fiduciaries who accepted bribes held the bribes on trust—of practical importance in case of fiduciary insolvency or appreciation in value of the subject matter of the bribe. In *FHR European Ventures LLP v Cedar Capital Partners LLC* it was held that they did. The arguments were finely balanced. The Court thought it "useful to have a judgment ... which is right because it is final", and took the route they thought would best promote certainty. Another important case concerned remedies against trustees who mismanaged funds. In *AIB Group (UK) Plc v Mark Redler & Co Solicitors* the Court stepped away from the approach of Australia and Hong Kong, holding that remedies for breach of trust are in principle not distinct from those for breach of common law obligations like contractual duties. The case would likely find favour with professional insurers; it would be less well received by beneficiaries of trusts. Finally, in *Hounga v Allen* and *Les Laboratoires Servier v Apotex Inc*, the Court gave conflicting judgments on the law of illegality. The actual results in the cases were comparatively unimportant. (Although the former case overruled a much-criticised decision that a trafficked migrant worker could not claim damages for race discrimination.) The important distinction was in approach. While Lord Wilson, in *Hounga*, seemed willing to countenance balancing of various policies, Lord Sumption (who did not cite *Hounga*) regarded illegality as a rule that did not admit such balancing.

Two important cases considered whether the European Convention on Human Rights (ECHR) conflicted with domestic criminal law. The European Court of Human Rights held, in *Vinter, Moore and Bamber v United Kingdom*, that prisoners must have "a prospect of release" in order for domestic law to comply with Article 3 of ECHR. Yet in the UK some prisoners were sentenced to whole life terms. In *Attorney General's Reference (No.69 of 2013)* Lord Thomas held that such sentences were ECHR compliant. The reason was that the justice secretary had to review whether exceptional circumstances justified releasing the prisoners. In doing so, he had to have regard to the ECHR. The practical effect was that a discretion to consider whether there were such exceptional circumstances became a duty. In *R (T) v Secretary of State for the Home Department* the Supreme Court examined the law on disclosure of criminal records. If a potential employer asked about a job applicant's record, the state would disclose all convictions and cautions, regardless of relevance to the job application. An applicant—who had received a caution when, aged 11, he had stolen a bicycle—challenged this as inconsistent with Article 8 of the ECHR (on the right to respect for private and family life). The Supreme Court unanimously upheld the challenge.

When a court must balance two values—for instance, free speech and national security—how much weight, if any, should they give to a decision of the executive branch on the issue? This enduring question was crucial to *R. (on the application of Lord Carlile of Berriew QC) v Secretary of State for the Home Department*. The applicant sought judicial review of the ban on entry to the UK of a "dissident Iranian politician". The Supreme Court (Lord Kerr dissenting) refused the application. The important differences between the Justices concerned the route to that conclusion, and in particular the proper way both to defer accordingly to decision makers while also protecting individual rights. An analogous question arose in *Shergill v Khaira*. Courts are in general reluctant to adjudicate on the validity of religious beliefs. But the Supreme Court held that they would adjudicate on private rights even if doing so required consideration of religious claims.

The High Speed Two (HS2) rail project (see AR 2013, pp.11; 486) was scrutinised in *R. (on the application of Buckinghamshire CC) v Secretary of State for Transport*. The applicant argued, first, that the government should have conducted an environmental impact assessment into HS2 and the "reasonable alternatives" and, second, that the procedure adopted for the proposals did not comply with an EC Directive. These arguments, uninteresting in themselves, were rejected by the Supreme Court. More interesting were the reflections on what would have been the case had the EC Directives indicated otherwise. What if the EC Directive required the Court to scrutinise the legislative process? The Court affirmed the UK Parliament's sovereignty and, as Article 9 of the Bill of Rights 1689 would indicate, that the judiciary had no power to inquire into the quality of Parliament's deliberations. Lords Neuberger and Mance endorsed Lord Justice Laws's suggestion, in *Thoburn v Sunderland City Council*, that some statutes are entrenched against implied repeal.

Mrs Sandiford was convicted of drug smuggling in Bali and sentenced to death. In *R (on the application of Sandiford) v Secretary of State for Foreign and Commonwealth Affairs* she challenged the secretary of state's refusal to pay for her legal assistance. The Supreme Court held that she was not within the jurisdiction of the UK for the purposes of the ECHR. Jurisdiction was primarily territorial. At common law, the government's policy of refusing funding was not irrational. So Lindsay Sandiford remained on death row without financial support of the government.

Section 1 of the Suicide Act 1961 decriminalised suicide. But Section 2 of the same Act makes complicity in another's suicide a criminal offence. In *R. (on the application of Nicklinson) v Ministry of Justice* a number of applicants argued that the provision was inconsistent with their right (under Article 8 of the ECHR) to respect for private life. Nine Justices heard the case; all gave judgments; few were wholly consistent. A majority of 7-2 (Lady Hale and Lord Kerr dissenting) dismissed the case. Lord Neuberger, Lady Hale, Lords Mance, Kerr and Wilson held that the Court had jurisdiction to make a declaration of incompatibility. Lords Neuberger, Mance and Wilson declined to issue such a declaration; they thought it best to give Parliament another chance to examine the law in question. Lady Hale and Lord Kerr would have issued such a declaration. The remaining Justices concluded that the legality turned on issues that Parliament was better able to decide and, in particular, a judgment about the relative importance of the right to commit suicide and the right of the vulnerable to be protected from pressure to commit suicide. For these Justices the question was: how much risk is acceptable? Such a question, they reasoned, was better suited to Parliament as the representative organ of the constitution. Meanwhile, Lord Falconer's Assisted Dying Bill passed its second reading in the House of Lords without a vote; 126 peers spoke on the issue.

Frederick Wilmot-Smith

LAW IN THE USA

In *Bahlul v. United States*, the United States Court of Appeals for Washington, D.C. made a ruling in the case of Ali Hamza al Bahlul, a Yemen native who had participated in the planning and execution of the 11 September 2001 terrorist attacks. Al Bahlul had been captured in Pakistan in December 2001 and transferred to, and detained at, the US prison camp at Guantanamo Bay, Cuba, where he had been convicted and sentenced to life imprisonment by a military commission for conspiracy, material support and solicitation to commit terrorist acts, which were made crimes under the Military Commission Act of 2006. The Court of Appeal ruled that, under the ex post facto clause in the US constitution (which prohibits prosecution for acts not crimes when they were committed), he could not be prosecuted for material support and solicitation, since these were not crimes before the 2006 law. But it found that he could be convicted for conspiracy, as federal statutes already made different conspiracies crimes. In *Aamer v. Obama* the same court ruled that terrorists suspects detained at the Guantanamo Bay facility could file a petition for a writ of *habeas corpus* to challenge their forced feeding, notwithstanding that the Military Commissions Act expressly denied the courts jurisdiction to receive such petitions and that the purpose of such petitions was to secure release from unlawful detention. However, the court also held the forced feeding was lawful.

The federal courts continued to review a variety of state law restrictions on voting rights adopted in the wake of the 2013 decision of the US Supreme Court, in *Shelby County v. Holder*. Laws that required voters to provide photograph identification when voting in person, and which were in effect in 30 states, were challenged in federal courts in North Carolina, Texas and Wisconsin. Such laws were held to violate the US constitution and the Voting Rights Act of 1965 in the Texas and Wisconsin cases but not in the North Carolina case; the Court of Appeals for the Fourth Circuit upheld this last decision. Measures that restricted registration and voting on election day, disqualified ballots delivered in the wrong districts, limited the number of days and hours for voting prior to election day, expanded the right of voters to challenge the qualifications of other voters at the time of voting, eliminated the discretion of local officials to keep the polls open for an additional hour in extraordinary circumstances, and barred the early registration of persons below the minimum voting age were challenged in federal courts in North Carolina and Ohio. In the North Carolina case, the fourth circuit appeals court enjoined the restriction on registration and voting on election day and the disqualification of ballots delivered in the wrong district. In the Ohio case, the Court of Appeals for the Sixth Circuit upheld the issue of a preliminary injunction against the measures reducing the number of early voting days and ordered that the hours for voting during these days be uniform. The Supreme Court stayed the injunctions in both cases. Officials in Arizona and Kansas asked the US election assistance commission to modify the federal voter registration form to require individuals who completed the form to provide documentary proof of their citizenship. The request sought to circumvent the 2013 decision of the Supreme Court, in *Arizona v. Inter Tribal Council of Arizona, Inc.*, which held that states could not require information in addition to that required by the commission's form. The commission refused to modify its form as requested, and the Court of Appeals for the Tenth Circuit upheld the commission's decision *in Kobach v. U.S. Election Assistance Commission.*

The federal courts continued to review new state laws that restricted abortion practices. A Mississippi law, that required physicians who performed abortions in the state to have admitting privileges in a hospital in the state, was held by the Court of Appeal for the Fifth Circuit to be an unconstitutional burden on the right to an abortion, as it would have the effect of closing the state's last abortion clinic. A new Texas law that required abortion clinics to comply with standards for ambulatory surgical centres was upheld by the same court, even though it would result in closing all but seven clinics in the state. The Supreme Court stayed the order pending appeal. An Arizona law that required the use of abortion-inducing medications to comply with the protocols approved by the US food and drug administration was held invalid by the Court of Appeals for the Ninth Circuit, because the law had the effect of prohibiting the use of one of the two medications used in non-surgical abortions.

A California trial court ruled, in *Vegara v. California*, that the state laws which gave tenure to teachers—making their employment permanent after 18 months, their dismissal costly and complex, and their layoff subject to seniority rules—violated the students' rights to equal educational opportunities because grossly ineffective teachers were assigned to schools with a higher proportion of low-income and minority students. The court stayed the ruling pending an appeal, because of its disruptive potential. A similar lawsuit was filed in New York after the court issued its decision.

The fourth, seventh, ninth and tenth circuits appeals courts and federal district and state courts held invalid laws prohibiting same-sex marriages in a number of states, and the Supreme Court declined to hear appeals in those cases in which appeals to it were made. Same-sex marriages were allowed in 36 states by the end of 2014. The sixth circuit appeals court, however, upheld such laws in three states. This decision was appealed to the Supreme Court, which had not decided whether to hear the case.

A \$2.4 million jury verdict in favour of landowners against Aruba Petroleum, Inc. for intentionally creating a private nuisance—by drilling for oil in the Barnett Shale, Texas, using hydraulic fracturing (fracking)—and causing the associated physical and mental suffering, drew mixed reactions. Energy lawyers expected the verdict to be reversed, while plaintiff lawyers suggested it could inspire similar cases.

Robert J. Spjut

XV RELIGION

In 2014 the three Abrahamic religions were seldom out of the news: levels of conflict were particular high, especially in the Middle East, with acts of sometimes extreme violence frequently being perpetrated in the name of religion. At the same time, however, there were signs of reconciliation and efforts at inter-faith dialogue on issues of mutual concern such as human trafficking and slavery.

CHRISTIANITY. The year saw further consolidation of the new style of leadership of the Roman Catholic Church exercised by Pope Francis who celebrated his first anniversary in March. Reminding the faithful in his Lent message of the importance of poverty, he spoke later in the year about the "legitimate redistribution of wealth", and more symbolically he washed the feet of disabled people on Maundy Thursday. In February he announced the appointment of 19 new cardinals, drawn mainly from the developing world. Franz-Peter Tebartz-van Elst, Bishop of Limburg in Germany (often referred to as the "Bishop of Bling"), who had spent €31 million on his residence, was deprived of office in March. Francis's international Council of nine cardinals met regularly, spending a considerable amount of time in planning for the Extraordinary Synod of Bishops on the family, which was to be "more dynamic and participatory" and was scheduled for October. As part of the preparation, on St Valentine's Day (14 February), the Pope received 10,000 engaged couples in St Peter's Square. Responding to the extensive questionnaires which had been sent out to laity by the different conferences of bishops, the participating bishops were instructed by Francis to "speak clearly, listen with humility, and accept with an open heart". The conversations ranged across issues of sexuality, divorce and family life, revealing a diversity of opinion which, with an unprecedented degree of openness, was recorded in the proceedings. Although there was no new teaching, the "complexity" of the contemporary world was acknowledged and a more accepting approach to homosexuals and divorcees only narrowly failed to receive a two-thirds majority. God, Francis maintained, was "not afraid of new things". At times, however, Francis could sound somewhat more naïve. In June, for instance, he told childless couples not to substitute dogs and cats for children.

As well as canonising two of his predecessors (John Paul II and John XXIII) and beatifying a third (Paul VI), Francis undertook a busy schedule of travel, visiting South Korea in August, Albania in September, and Turkey at the end of November. He also made a memorable visit to the Holy Land in May, where he met with Jordanian, Palestinian, and Israeli leaders, beginning somewhat unusually in Jordan. He prayed by the security or separation wall, as well as the Western Wall in Jerusalem, and issued a joint declaration with the Ecumenical Patriarch of the Orthodox Church, Bartholomew. Their plea for peace fell on deaf ears as violence erupted in the Gaza Strip in July. Francis interrupted one of his Sunday homilies with the unscripted cry: "Please stop. I ask you with all my heart. It's time to stop. Please stop." In June in the United States the Presbyterian Church, one of the largest mainline denominations, voted to disinvest from three multinationals that were said to promote violence in the Occupied Territories.

Issues of sexuality continued to divide the churches. On St Valentine's Day, the Church of England bishops issued a statement opposing same-sex marriage (although it was later revealed that 22 bishops had refused their support). Despite this, a number of clergy married their long-term same-sex partners, which tested the authority of the bishops. Gene Robinson, the first openly gay bishop in the Anglican Communion—the third largest Christian grouping—whose consecration had provoked a crisis in the church, divorced his partner of 25 years. Justin Welby, Archbishop of Canterbury and worldwide Anglican leader, who had visited each of the 38 provinces of the Anglican Communion in his first year in office, commented pessimistically in December that the Communion might well not survive divisions over sexuality. In the United Methodist Church in the USA, charges were dropped against a pastor, Thomas Ogletree, former Dean of Yale Divinity School, for conducting his son's same-sex wedding. Also in the United States Fred Phelps, controversial pastor of the Westboro' Baptist Church in Topeka, Kansas, and pioneer of the "God hates fags" campaign, died in March and was soon afterwards accused by his son Nate of mental and physical abuse. Other prominent Evangelicals fell victim to temptation: Pastor Bob Coy of Florida's second largest megachurch, Fort Lauderdale's Calvary Chapel, resigned in April over "moral failings" which included extra-marital affairs and use of pornography. Similarly, Mark Driscoll, a prominent pastor in Seattle, was accused of major flaws in leadership which led to the dissolution of the Mars Hill network of megachurches.

A number of women made a particular mark on the churches in 2014. In a foray into popular culture, the Sicilian religious Sister Cristina Scuccia won an Italian music contest, "the Voice of Italy". Less positively, in Maryland, USA, on 27 December the suffragan (assistant) Episcopal bishop, Heather Cook, was arrested after a hit and run car accident while under the influence of alcohol and was forced to resign. After a very long process, the Church of England finally passed legislation in November to allow women to be ordained bishop. Shortly afterwards the first appointment was announced, of Libby Lane as suffragan bishop in the Diocese of Chester.

By December the Church of England had decided that it was in terminal decline and sought emergency funding to train more clergy. After seeking advice from bankers who had led their own organisations into financial crisis, it also sought to introduce expensive management courses for its future senior leaders.

Most churches faced sexual abuse claims: the former papal nuncio to the Dominican Republic, Jozef Wesolowski, was deprived of his orders after child abuse claims. In March Pope Francis announced the members of a commission charged with addressing issues of child abuse. Of the eight members, four were women, one of whom had been abused by a priest as a 13-year old. In the Church of England an enquiry into a former Dean of Manchester, the late Robert Waddington, revealed a string of abuse allegations which had not been taken seriously and which prompted the resignation of the former Archbishop of York, David Hope (Lord Hope of Thornes), as an honorary assistant bishop.

Somewhat surprisingly, 12 leaders of the autonomous Orthodox churches announced that an ecumenical council would be convened in Istanbul in 2016, the first in 1,200 years. At the same time, the Orthodox world faced significant conflict, especially in Ukraine where the pre-existing divisions between those loyal to the Kiev Patriarchate and those loyal to Moscow mirrored the political divide which had led to armed conflict and the annexation of Crimea by Russia in March.

Inter-religious conflict escalated in the so-called Islamic State (ISIS)-dominated areas of Syria and Iraq, where the indigenous Christian communities were threatened with extinction. In this context, the troubled Syrian Orthodox Church gained a new patriarch, Mor Ignatius Aphrem II. In Nigeria the Islamist Boko Haram group kidnapped a group of 276 girls from a boarding school in April, which prompted an outspoken response from Justin Welby, who had earlier worked in Nigeria. In February the Archbishop had visited South Sudan, following the escalation of violence and the massacre of Christians. There was international outrage after Meriam Ibrahim, a Christian mother, was forced to give birth in shackles in a Sudanese prison; this eventually led to her release. On a more positive note, a number of leaders from across the faiths gathered in Rome in December to launch a campaign (the "Global Freedom Network") opposing slavery and human trafficking; the movement was the initiative of Archbishop Welby and Pope Francis.

Mark D. Chapman

JUDAISM. In many respects, 2014 was a year of challenges for Judaism and world Jewry, both new and renewed. There were distinct developments in the three predominant areas of world Jewry (Israel, Europe and the United States), which pointed to challenges that ranged from distinctly political issues to developments at the heart of Judaism and Jewish cultural life.

In so far as the challenges faced by Jews in 2014 were novel, most were experienced by Israel's Jews. In particular, it had become increasingly clear that the aftermath of the Arab Spring of 2011 had radically altered the region and Israel's place within it. Once more, negotiations conducted between Israel and the Palestinian Authority led by Mahmoud Abbas broke down, as the Palestinian Authority returned to its agenda of employing applications to international agencies to put pressure on Israel, while the government of Binyamin Netanyahu returned to settlement building and rejected the release of Palestinian prisoners. In Gaza, too, events took their predictably violent turn, with renewed Hamas rocket fire leading to a summer of heavy Israeli bombardments that caused Palestinian casualties totalling more than 2,000. On other "fronts", however, Israel faced a markedly new situation. In Egypt, the new government of Abdel Fattah el-Sisi proved an ally against Hamas, joining Israel's attempt to isolate the Islamists. Ties with Jordan and Saudi Arabia, too, were strengthened, in common opposition to the Iranian nuclear project. It was Syria, however, that provided the most unpredictable and uncertain challenges for Israel. The Israeli-Syrian border on the Golan Heights—Israel's calmest since the Israeli-Syrian cease fire of 1974—erupted into a chaotic battlefield of Shia Hezbullah and Sunni al-Nusra Front radicals, both ultimately seeking to establish a basis for operations against Israel. This new and uncertain situation in Syria, where behind Hezbullah and al-Nusra lurked an even more dangerous enemy in the form of Islamic State (ISIS), would likely be one of Israel's biggest challenges in 2015.

In Europe, by contrast, the challenges that 2014 posed to the Jewish people were all too familiar. In a culmination of trends that had extended for more than a decade, tensions between Muslim immigrants and both the Jewish and autochthonous populations burst into episodes of open violence. In Brussels, for example, a French national, Mehdi Nemmouche, who had been a jihadist fighter in Syria, opened fire on employees and visitors at the city's Jewish museum in May, killing four. The incident, which followed a number of similar attacks in France during previous years, caused consternation in the wider Jewish community and fears for its future. In this regard, the worries felt by European Jews were not limited to the threat of Islamist radicals. For this threat in turn precipitated a growth in support for far-Right political parties opposing themselves to Europe's Muslim community and aiming to gain politically from the attacks on Europe's Jews. To the Jewish community itself, however, this far-Right "support" presented the unpalatable dilemma between calling attention to the jihadist threat and associating with former and current anti-Semites. One issue that brought this tension to the surface was the attempt among some European countries to ban the institution of kosher butchery known as *Shechitah*. In February Denmark put into effect a ban on ritual slaughter (on the grounds of animal welfare) that affected both Jewish and Islamic practices. In December, a similar Polish decision taken in 2013 was overturned by the courts as unconstitutional. Whilst portraying themselves as sympathetic to Jewish issues, many of Europe's far-Right parties supported efforts to ban *Shechitah*, a stance ostensibly aimed at the Muslim religious practice of halal slaughter but which directly affected Jewish religious practice as well.

In the United States, the challenges that 2014 posed to the Jewish community were more directly cultural than political (although there were inevitably close connections between the two areas). In particular, the central issue for the American-Jewish community was how to bridge a growing gap between the American-Jewish establishment and a new, more progressive generation of American Jews. There were differences on various issues, not least the relationship between American Jewry and Israel. While much of the establishment had traditionally taken a staunchly Zionist attitude, a younger, more liberal generation questioned Israel's policies and, more specifically, the unqualified US support for them. In 2014, two developments brought this tension to the fore. First, there was the rejection in February by the Conference of Presidents of Major American Jewish Organizations of the new, progressive Zionist organisation, JStreet. This raised questions over the claim of the Conference of Presidents to represent America's Jews. Secondly, there was the issue of rising sympathy with the Boycott, Divestment and Solidarity (BDS) movements on US college campuses, which had also provoked fractious debates between America's older and younger generations of Jews. Such divisions would probably widen in 2015, given the broken relationship between the Netanyahu government in Israel and the Obama administration, if not the wider Democratic Party.

David de Bruijn

ISLAM. The apparently inexorable rise of Salafist extremism was a major theme in a number of Muslim countries. Most notably the group often known as the Islamic State in Iraq and Syria, or Islamic State (ISIS), startled observers with its rapid capture of a string of major towns and cities in eastern Syria and northern Iraq in the early summer. Its leader, Ibrahim Awad al-Badri, styling himself Abu Bakr al-Baghdadi, proclaimed himself caliph on 4 July during a sermon at the Nur al-Din Zangi mosque in Mosul. Despite air attacks by a variety of countries, the group maintained its hold on its territory and began to solicit the allegiance of violent Salafist groups elsewhere in the Islamic world.

The ISIS occupation resulted in the persecution, death or flight of almost all religious minorities, particularly Christians, Yazidis and Shia Muslims. The Sunni population also saw its leadership and institutions assailed. The leading imam of Mosul, Sheikh Muhammad al-Mansuri, an internationally-known Koranic scholar, was executed along with 12 other imams of the city for refusing to subscribe to ISIS ideology or acknowledge its authority. Executions of other Sunni religious leaders were reported elsewhere in ISIS-held territory. In Mosul, the branch campus of the Imam Azam Islamic University of Baghdad was taken over by ISIS militants and the scholars and students forced to relocate to Irbil, outside ISIS control. Scholars in the occupied region reported that traditional Sunni Islam was being replaced by a hard-line version of Salafism.

ISIS was condemned by Sunni Islam's mainline leadership. In October an open letter signed by over a hundred senior scholars condemned ISIS for its "extremism" and its misreading of scripture. The International Union of Muslim Scholars, an Islamist-leaning body chaired by Egyptian scholar Yusuf al-Qardawi, also attacked ISIS and derided its claim to represent a legitimate caliphate. Even many Salafist political hardliners joined the chorus of condemnation: leading Jordanian radical activist Abu Muhammad al-Maqdisi, recently released from prison, instructed ISIS to "reform yourselves, repent, stop killing Muslims and distorting the religion". Grand Mufti of Saudi Arabia Abd al-Aziz Al al-Sheikh also denounced ISIS by identifying its members as followers of Kharijism, a seventh-century extreme sect which carried out assassinations of its enemies.

The targeting of non-Salafist scholars and theologians was not confined to ISIS-controlled territory. In Kenya, Sheikh Mohammed Idris, chairman of the country's Council of Imams and Preachers, was killed in his mosque in Mombasa. Another victim, Sheikh Salim Bakari Mwarengi, was also assassinated near a Mombasa mosque. Altogether it was thought that more than 20 imams opposed to Salafist radicalism were killed in Kenya. Scholars were likewise targeted in Nigeria, where the Boko Haram group also targeted major Sunni mosques, killing over 120 worshippers during Friday prayers at the main mosque in Kano, and planting bombs in mosques in Maiduguri and other towns. And on 30 July, the 74-year old imam of the main mosque in Kashgar in western China was stabbed to death by three assailants.

The growth of extremism prompted several governments to impose tight restrictions on Muslim practice. In China, members of the Uighur minority under the age of 18 were legally forbidden to observe the fasting month of Ramadan. In the Arab world existing restrictions on sermons were tightened. In Tunisia the fall of the moderate Islamist Ennahda party heralded the reintroduction of state control of mosques. Saudi Arabia installed recording equipment in every mosque in order to monitor sermons. In Egypt the Sisi government decreed that all sermons must cover a weekly topic prescribed by the state, and must be delivered only by graduates of state-approved institutions. The country's approximately 7,000 Salafi mosques were also taken under state control following reports that a sermon had been preached criticising the government's issuing of interest-bearing bonds.

In Europe, anxieties remained over radical tendencies in some Muslim communities, particularly with reports of young Muslims travelling to the Middle East to join ISIS. In Britain, controversy attended a series of government inspections of state schools in Birmingham, which had allegedly been infiltrated by Islamist radicals. The report documented a number of conservative Muslim practices in some schools, but concluded that there was no evidence of radicalisation. The inquiry, widely seen as hostile to Muslim concerns, drew criticism from the National Association of Head Teachers, and was said to have reinforced isolationist elements in the Muslim community.

In Austria a draft law was proposed which would place a range of restrictions on the country's Muslim minority, including the imposition of a single German translation of the Koran, and a prohibition on the acceptance by Muslim charities of financial support from abroad. Muslim and human rights activists protested that this would alienate the community and might run afoul of European human rights legislation. In Germany, anti-Muslim marches led by the new Dresden-based organisation Pegida (Patriotic Europeans against the Islamisation of the Occident) attracted up to 10,000 participants. Elsewhere, violent pressure against Muslim minorities continued in the Central African Republic, China, Burma, Sri Lanka and the Crimea.

Tim Winter

XVI THE ARTS

OPERA

FEW critics could have imagined, as they settled into their seats at Glyndebourne for the opening show of the 2014 festival in May, that the major talking point to emerge from the ensuing afternoon of entertainment would be critics themselves. When five newspaper reviews went heavy on the physical appearance of young mezzo Tara Erraught's Octavian (adjectives included "chubby", "dumpy" and "unsightly"), many in the wider media were horrified. Some critics stood firm: Erraught should have been better costumed and directed in order to fulfil her dramatic function, said one. Others dug themselves deeper holes: "I'm no misogynist, some of my best friends are female," chirruped another. The fact that all five were white men of a certain age was not lost on the rapidly growing hoard of onlookers.

The commotion prompted a healthy argument about criticism, casting, and what contemporary audiences want and expect from opera productions. Mezzo Alice Coote penned a furious opinion piece protesting that opera is "ALL about the human voice". But many, critics included, took a broader view: that opera's primary purpose is a theatrical one, which involves imperatives both dramatic and physical as well as musical. The whole debate—possibly the first surrounding a particular aesthetic element of the opera tradition since social media embedded itself fully into the discourse—felt like a salutary check for the opera world, forced to ask itself what it was doing and why. If members of the public felt compelled to formulate their own critical appraisals and moral standpoints on Tara Erraught's performance—as did many of them, much to the horror of the professional critics—so much the better.

Unfortunately for the show's director Richard Jones, the whole affair rather overshadowed his typically punchy *Der Rosenkavalier* production, broadcast over the Internet by the *Telegraph* (a burgeoning trend in 2014). In this 150th anniversary year of Richard Strauss, there were both duds and hits at Covent Garden, notably a sprawling production of *Ariadne auf Naxos* from Christof Loy which did little to enliven or clarify the work's twisting dramatic threads, and an intense, deeply moving *Die Frau ohne Schatten* in which Claus Guth made his UK directorial debut. After all the questions that had arisen out of the Glyndebourne debacle, here was a master class in how to develop an arresting, contemporary stage language born from the notes in the score, whatever the quality of the singing—which happened to be generally brilliant.

Only the notes in the score were on offer at two late-in-the-season BBC Proms, which presented Strauss's two most coruscating operas in concert on consecutive days in August. *Elektra* under Semyon Bychkov and *Salome* under Donald Runnicles proved many a critic's festival highlight. There was no Strauss across town at English National Opera (ENO), but an extremely eventful year nonetheless: the world premiere of *Thebans* by Julian Anderson (generally successful if slightly unbalanced), and a landmark production of Berlioz's mammoth *Benvenuto Cellini* directed by Terry Gilliam that proved an undeniable "event".

Regrettably, the political machinations backstage at the London Coliseum would prove no less epic. First came the surprise announcement that music director Edward Gardner would depart in 2015, the damage limited by the fact that his replacement, Mark Wigglesworth (an astute choice), had already been lined up. Then came the news that the Arts Council would be reducing its grant to the company by 29 per cent, but ENO had a riposte to that, too: it had actively negotiated the cut with the Arts Council and could unveil new changes to its business model to stay robust, including the staging of an annual musical. But the ensuing pressures led to management scraps, and as 2014 drifted into 2015 the company lost both its chairman and its executive director.

In the face of managerial, financial and political turmoil, opera companies elsewhere reacted with surprising resolve and creativity. San Diego Opera, which faced immediate shut-down in March, was saved by a crowd-funding campaign two months later; the worrying dispute between performing and technical unions and the management of the Metropolitan Opera in New York was resolved with a healthy dose of pragmatism that bodes well for the future. For the hundreds of smaller opera companies from Berlin to Bangkok, the age of austerity seemed to be prompting more agility and creativity. One effect of this was that more people of more backgrounds experienced their wares. "Australian opera is more plugged into the community than before," wrote the director of the ever-flexible Opera Queensland, Lindy Hulme, in the *Guardian*. "The artform is genre-bending with co-creations of all kinds; the possibilities are as limitless." She seemed to be speaking for smaller opera companies everywhere.

Likewise, in Britain the more nimble opera groups flourished in 2014. Birmingham Opera Company's immersive tent-in-a-park staging of Mussorgsky's *Khovanskygate* (usually called *Khovanshchina*) became a chilling criticism of state power and one of the hottest tickets of the year. English Touring Opera—which took up to nine shows a year from Belfast to Truro, all masterminded by a full-time staff of 12—picked up the Olivier Award for outstanding achievement in opera after a string of productions that punched way above their weight. Opera North was notable for particularly effective productions of two operas at either ends of the "scale" scale: Monteverdi's *L'Incoronazione di Poppea*, directed with delicious immorality by Tim Albery, and Wagner's *Götterdämmerung*, sung and played in an unusually atmospheric concert at Leeds Town Hall. After a critically lukewarm response to its troubled "concept season", "Fallen Women", Welsh National Opera scored a coup with Schoenberg's unfinished biblical epic *Moses und Aaron*, which travelled triumphantly from Cardiff to Covent Garden. North of the border Scottish Opera continued to lurch from point of intense anger to standing industry joke—no orchestra, no chorus, no music director—but it did manage to open a new café and foyer at Glasgow Theatre Royal. Further east, the Edinburgh Festival organised a staging of "Hobo composer" Harry Partch's music drama *Delusion of the Fury*, for which Ensemble MusikFabrik had to reconstruct, learn and perform on replicas of Partch's madcap invented instruments.

The opera world lost two great leaders in 2014. Belgian director Gerard Mortier (died 8 March) was a controversial figure right up to his resignation from Madrid's Teatro Real in 2013 and a man who singularly revitalised that and many other opera houses. In contrast, George Christie (died 7 May) rarely courted controversy but founded the institution which had ensured that the opera world absolutely did so in 2014: Glyndebourne.

Andrew Mellor

CLASSICAL MUSIC

IT had taken the best part of four centuries, but in 2014 a woman was finally appointed principal conductor of a major European capital's flagship symphony orchestra. Susanna Mälkki was to take the reins of the Helsinki Philharmonic in her native city from September 2016, following a vote of approval from the town council at the end of August 2014. The news came three days after Mälkki had conducted Mozart's *The Marriage of Figaro* at the Finnish National Opera in a production directed by a woman and programmed by a female intendant under a female general director who reported to a female chair: Finland had precedents in this area, and they clearly helped.

Mixed with the general sense of wellbeing that the classical music world had done something to correct its inherent sexism came the acknowledgement that it had taken far too long and that one appointment hardly represented a seismic shift. In the UK the glass ceiling was finally shattered with Judith Weir's appointment as Master of the Queen's Music. Once more, it was a case of "talented individual gets a deserved job". But while the political implications and symbolic status of that position should not be underestimated, it was a far more straightforward (and less democratic) process than that of the appointment of a principal conductorship at one of the UK's self-governing symphony orchestras.

If Britain were to nurture more female conducting talent, the National Youth Orchestra (NYO) might well have something to do with it. The organisation had launched the career of Sir Simon Rattle and began the year at Leeds Town Hall by introducing another standout talent, the composer Larry Goves (himself an NYO alumnus). His piece *The Rules* was not just another glitzy, button-pushing new work for another competent orchestra, but a delightful act of musical subversion aimed squarely at the youths who were giving it life for the first time.

Further north, Lars Vogt's delicate but fierce performance of Beethoven's Emperor Concerto with the Scottish Chamber Orchestra proved that the Edinburgh Festival still counted home-grown creativity among its highlights. But Vogt was increasingly known as a conductor, too, and 2014 saw him replace Northern Sinfonia's principal conductor of 12 years, Thomas Zehetmair. The Gateshead-based orchestra hoped that Vogt, a player-conductor like his predecessor (and a UK resident) would deliver the mixture of brilliance and care that had come to characterise the ensemble over the last decade.

There were moves, too, over at the Ulster Orchestra, and also troubles. The orchestra's chairman raised the alarm in October with claims that the ensemble would close unless a rescue plan was approved by Belfast City Council, which it duly was. This produced a sigh of relief, particularly as the orchestra got the hard bit right in 2014 by appointing talented young principal conductor Rafael Payare, a product of Venezuela's El Sistema musical training programme. The appointment was made long before 2014's most incendiary classical music book—Geoffrey Baker's *Orchestrating Venezuela's Youth*—which rigorously questioned El Sistema's programme of "social action through music" and put a juddering halt to the endless party that surrounded the Simón Bolívar Orchestra's (SBO's) world tours.

That was not before the SBO's sister ensemble, the Teresa Carreño Youth Orchestra, visited the Royal Festival Hall in London, brushing shoulders with a temporary studio erected by BBC Radio 3 from which the station broadcast day and night for two weeks. It was one of the "last hurrahs" from Roger Wright, who announced his departure as controller of the station (and the Proms) to replace Jonathan Reekie at Aldeburgh Music. Wright was in turn replaced at Radio 3 by Alan Davey of Arts Council England, though the Proms directorship remained vacant in 2014.

Up in the Royal Festival Hall auditorium in March, the Harrison & Harrison organ played in all its departments for the first time since it had been removed for refurbishment in 2005, forming the centrepiece of a festival of organ music. The general consensus among knowledgeable organ aficionados was that the distinctive "sound" of the Harrison instrument had not been lost and that the timbral qualities had been vastly improved by cleaning, re-voicing and re-configuration.

In the same space there were landmark performances from Antonio Pappano and his Orchestra of the National Academy of St Cecilia (Verdi's Requiem) and a much-praised Brahms Symphony Cycle from the Philharmonia and Andris Nelsons. But the series did not start with Nelsons, who fell ill days in advance of the first concert. Enter stage left Hannu Lintu, a Finn making his UK debut, who conducted Brahms's First Symphony and First Piano Concerto to critical delight. Sir Simon Rattle was back at the same hall in May for a searing performance of Haydn's *The Creation* with the Orchestra of the Age of Enlightenment, as speculation continued as to whether he would succeed Valery Gergiev at the London Symphony Orchestra (LSO)—and whether that orchestra could bypass the fact that Rattle disliked the Barbican Centre by building him a new concert hall.

With LSO concerts under Gergiev at the Barbican increasingly fraught with the idea and reality of protest (given Gergiev's closeness to Russia's President Vladimir Putin), and sometimes bordering on the lacklustre, the LSO was looking to its guest conductors to conjure the magic. No bad thing, perhaps, when one was on the hunt for a new boss. (John Eliot Gardiner was particularly mesmerising in

Mendelssohn.) But Barbican plaudits had to go to the BBC Symphony Orchestra, who spiced their season by incorporating celebrations of the music of Villa-Lobos and the start of a cycle of Carl Nielsen's symphonies, both under principal conductor Sakari Oramo.

The North West remained a powerhouse for musical invention in 2014. The BBC Philharmonic in Manchester explored rare repertoire and commissioned some of its own, including *SET* by Gary Carpenter, a concerto for jazz drummer and saxophonist. Down the M62 the Royal Liverpool Philharmonic Orchestra gave the world premiere of Michael Nyman's Symphony No 11, dedicated to the victims of the Hillsborough disaster, in Liverpool Cathedral; Philharmonic Hall further down Hope Street remained closed for a major internal refurbishment, looking stunning at its reopening just before Christmas.

It seemed that the whole music world was united at the start of 2014 when its gentle, generous godfather, Claudio Abbado, died following a long illness. The conductors Lorin Maazel and Rafael Fruhbeck de Burghos also died this year, both having worked almost until the end. With appointments for young maestros at the Hallé (Ryan Wigglesworth) and City of Birmingham Symphony Orchestra (Alpesh Chauhan), it was not hard to wonder whether—and hope that—we could still nurture and deliver other musicians capable of the astonishing communicative power of these conductors, whatever their sex.

Andrew Mellor

ROCK AND POP MUSIC

It was the year of the charm offensive in pop. The most successful performers all made a virtue of being conventionally groomed and rather nice. Sam Smith released his first album, *In the Lonely Hour*, on 26 May, one week after his 22nd birthday. In December it became the first and last album of the year to sell 1 million copies in both the UK and the USA, part of a global overnight success story which transformed the clean-cut, London-born singer from a young hopeful into the brightest new star of the year. His compatriot, Ed Sheeran, 23, released his second collection, *x*, which became the only other new album to sell a million copies in the UK, thereby consolidating the ginger-haired troubadour's status as a one-man super-band. Meanwhile, the demure US star Taylor Swift, 24, sold 1 million copies of her fifth album, *1989*, within one week of its release in October. It duly became the biggest-selling album of the year in the USA, just ahead of the soundtrack to the Walt Disney film *Frozen*, released in 2013.

To sell musical recordings in these quantities was an increasingly rare accomplishment. Indeed, as sales of recorded music continued to fall across the board in whatever format—physical CDs, digital downloads, single tracks, albums—Smith, Sheeran and Swift were the only acts to sell 1 million copies of a new album in either the UK or the USA.

Only two areas of music retailing—at opposite ends of the spectrum—saw an improvement. Sales of vinyl records (*all* vinyl records combined) exceeded 1 million copies in the UK for the first time since 1996 (and reached 9.2 million in the USA). News of this belated upswing prompted celebrations out of all proportion to the tiny sliver of market share (barely 2 per cent) for which vinyl now accounted. More significant was the rapidly accelerating trend for consumers to access music via online streaming services—such as Spotify and Pandora—whose volume of traffic increased by 65.1 per cent in the UK and by 54 per cent in the USA. However, the revenue per unit generated by this latest delivery system was tiny compared to that earned from even the dwindling sales of digital downloads let alone physical CDs. So while the convenience and economy of being able to listen to music on demand was plainly a blessing for consumers, this latest revolution—from buying and owning music to streaming it online—triggered another steep loss of revenue for the music industry and the artists which it supported.

Receipts from live concerts continued to make up for much of this financial shortfall. The Anglo-Irish boyband One Direction mounted the highest-grossing tour of the year—including a three-night stand at Wembley Stadium—taking a total of $282.2 million from 69 shows, followed by Justin Timberlake ($184.7 million) and the Rolling Stones ($165.1 million). The average price of a ticket to see the Stones was now $191.42 and it may be no coincidence that while listeners had grown accustomed to accessing recorded music for next to nothing, audiences were now more willing than ever before to pay top dollar for a live concert experience.

If the concert was by a star as reclusive as Kate Bush, then a sell-out could be guaranteed at virtually any price. Bush's return to the limelight—35 years after her first and only previous tour—for a run of 22 shows, beginning on 26 August in the 5,000-capacity Hammersmith Apollo in London, was described as an "ecstatic triumph" by one reviewer and words to much the same effect by everyone else. But even this late-blooming phenomenon was trumped, in terms of media coverage anyway, by the appearance of the country legend Dolly Parton at the Glastonbury festival in June. "I grew up on a farm," Parton, 68, reminded her fans, "So this mud ain't nothin' new to me." She sang beautifully and played guitar, melodian, banjo and saxophone, handing the festival a publicity coup which outranked even the "controversial" booking of heavy metal overlords Metallica to close the show on the Pyramid Stage on Saturday night.

Happy by Pharrell Williams—released in November 2013—was the best-selling single in both the USA (6.45 million copies) and the UK, where it reached No.1 on three separate occasions and became the most downloaded song of all time. Pharrell's contagious ode to optimism became a cultural phenomenon, inspiring people all over the world to make their own "tribute" versions of the promotional video. But the song's message of goodwill did not impress the authorities in Iran, who declared one such video made on the rooftops of Tehran to be "vulgar" and condoning "illicit relations". The Iranian director and dancers in the video were each handed down suspended sentences of six months in prison and 91 lashes. Not so happy.

Band Aid returned, 30 years after the original event, with a new recording of *Do They Know it's Christmas?* to raise funds this time for victims of the Ebola crisis in Western Africa. Bob Geldof looked spectacularly knackered as he and Midge Ure rallied the latest Who's Who of UK pop to the cause, including Paloma Faith, Ellie Goulding, One Direction, Rita Ora, Olly Murs, Emeli Sande, Ed Sheeran, Sam Smith, Jessie Ware and, making his third appearance on one of these records, Bono.

U2 released their long-awaited new album, *Songs of Innocence*, a decent enough collection of songs which, thanks to a promotional deal with Apple, was distributed willy-nilly, free of charge to iTunes subscribers. This heady marketing cocktail of largesse and hubris resulted in 33 million people apparently accessing the album in its first week of release, a phenomenon described by Apple CEO Tim Cook as "the largest album release of all time", but a somewhat Pyrrhic victory for all that.

The folk singer and political activist Pete Seeger died aged 94 on 27 January (see Obituary) and the bass player, singer and harmonica player Jack Bruce became the first member of 1960s supergroup Cream to take a final bow, aged 71 on 25 October. The mighty roar of Joe Cocker, 70, immortalised with a little help from his friends in the Woodstock movie, fell silent on 22 December.

David Sinclair

BALLET AND DANCE

THERE were three significant areas of focus for dance in 2014: Shakespeare-inspired productions in conjunction with the 450th anniversary of his birth, echoes of the 1914-18 war, and the 25th anniversary of the death of the great 20th century choreographer Frederick Ashton. Choreographers Crystal Pite and Alexander Whitley showed new authority in their creations; however, the production that remained in the memory was Ballet Rambert's *Event*, a new staging, in June and July, of Merce Cunningham's legendary *Events*, for which Jeannie Steele, teacher and one of the preservers of Cunningham's choreography, pieced together fragments of the 10 Cunningham works that Rambert had danced. Performed across studios on two floors of the company's new London base, with fresh and stylish costumes and cloths by Gerhard Richter and a new score played live by Philip Selway, Adem Ilhan and Quinta, the work allowed the audience to move at leisure between the performance spaces. In this *Event* Rambert was seen to best advantage. Their May season of revivals was enjoyable, but the November programme of recent creations featured three works that each outstayed its welcome.

English National Ballet's (ENB's) programme in tribute to the fallen of the 1914-18 war was given the umbrella title *Lest We Forget*. It was great for the company to commission new works from three of the UK's most interesting choreographers—Liam Scarlett, *No Man's Land*; Russell Maliphant, *Second Breath*; and

Akram Khan, *Dust*—although George Williamson's reworking of his 2012 *Firebird* seemed quite out of place. ENB also conveniently forgot earlier responses to war that had previously enriched their repertoire (including Antony Tudor's *Echoing of Trumpets* and works by Christopher Bruce such as *Land*). Khan's *Dust*, a bleak landscape populated by humans transformed into a machine from which individuals emerged, attracted most attention, particularly after it was powerfully performed at the Glastonbury Festival. Scarlett had his dead warriors descending a ramp, echoing the Shades of the 19th century work, *La Bayadère*, while the women "canaries" of the munitions factories conjured up memories of love and loss. The downside of such a programme was that a similar mood was created by all three choreographers.

All worked elsewhere in 2014 with Khan joining forces with Israel Galván to explore the similarities and contrasts between the dance and music of Spanish flamenco and Indian kathak in *TOROBAKA*. Scarlett's work was presented internationally. For The Royal Ballet he created *The Age of Anxiety*, inspired by W.H. Auden's poem of the ennui experienced by a quartet of lonely characters in 1940s America. He was admirably served by his dancers—Bennet Gartside as Quant; Steven McRae the sailor, Emble; Tristan Dyer as an Air Force medical officer, Malin; and Laura Morera as the department store buyer, Rosetta—as well as the settings from seedy bar to New York skyline by his designer John Macfarlane.

Birmingham Royal Ballet presented a programme called *Shadow of War* with works ranging from Kenneth MacMillan's *Fin du Jour,* showing brittle 1930s society swept away in 1939, to David Bintley's *Flowers of the Forest,* with its lament for the dead of the Battle of Flodden. The most significant work in the triple bill was *Miracle in the Gorbals*, Gillian Lynne's evocation of Robert Helpmann's 1944 creation. Lynne had danced in the original and acknowledged that her career had been influenced by Helpmann but little of the original choreography could be recalled. Using the original plot, a reconstruction of Edward Burra's set of the Glaswegian slum and Arthur Bliss's score, the production drew attention to Helpmann's place in the development of dramatic ballet. The addition of the sound of bombs falling to introduce the work seemed superfluous.

Sarasota Ballet, based in Florida, presented a festival honouring Sir Frederick Ashton. Their director, Iain Webb, and his wife and assistant director, former ballerina, Margaret Barbieri, had danced in many of Ashton's ballets and had the ability to impart their knowledge of his style to their dancers. Presenting eight ballets plus further gala divertissement, Webb and his team showed just what strong commitment could achieve. The festival included panels and presentation from other experts but it was the performances of familiar and lesser-known works that impressed. To enjoy the rarely performed, Rimbaud-inspired, Cecil Beaton-decorated *Illuminations* with Ricardo Graziano as the poet, alongside the technically challenging *Birthday Offering*, created for a septet of ballerinas, and the witty variety-theatre based *Façade*, and with the dancers really understanding the ballets, was thrilling. To see again *Valses Nobles and Sentimentales* and *Sinfonietta* was a delight and the performance of Ashton's skating ballet, *Les Patineurs*, with Logan Learned as the virtuoso Blue Boy, was exhilarating.

Under Webb's leadership this regional US company had made its mark not only as America's leading interpreter of Ashton's work but by building up a distinctive repertory that was performed with conviction.

Birmingham Royal Ballet also presented *Façade* and *Les Rendezvous* (unfortunately in the Anthony Ward designs rather than earlier ones by William Chappell) with the rarer *Dante Sonata* as well as *La Fille mal gardée*; American Ballet Theatre added Ashton's *Cinderella* to their repertoire. The Royal Ballet left their tribute programme to October-November but it was worth the wait. It consisted of four major ballets: *Scenes de Ballet*; *Five Brahms Waltzes in the manner of Isadora Duncan*; *Symphonic Variations;* and *A Month in the Country*. Both the pure classical and narrative ballets were well performed and two Russian dancers were stunning. Vladimir Mutagirov, who looked good in a number of Royal Ballet productions including *A Winter's Tale* and *Manon*, was a superb interpreter of the central man in the non-narrative *Symphonic Variations*, while Natalia Osipova was delightful as the frustrated and flirtatious Natalia Petrovna in *A Month in the Country*. Osipova was delightful in several ballets, even saving Alistair Marriott's dated and clichéd *Connectome*. She was also revengeful in Arthur Pita's *Facada*, one of three works in a showcase programme, *Solo for Two*, presented with Ivan Vasiliev.

The Royal Ballet had presented two of Ashton's ballets earlier in the year. In *Rhapsody*, the young dancers Francesca Hayward and James Hay reassured lovers of Ashton's work that his style was being handed on. Hayward had a triumphant year with a memorable debut as the amoral, eponymous Manon in Kenneth MacMillan's popular ballet. Ashton's *The Dream* was presented in June. Again it was Osipova as a thistledown Titania who impressed, although The Royal Ballet fielded two impressive teams of human lovers. At the same time, New York City Ballet presented their refurbished *A Midsummer Night's Dream* by George Balanchine. This was less successfully presented in London by the Maryinsky who also performed Leonid Lavrovsky's Soviet *Romeo and Juliet*. Danced *Romeo and Juliet*s ranged from Krzysztof Pastor's production of a mid-20th century Italian-based version for Scottish Ballet, in which the action confusingly took place over seven decades, to Mats Ek's monochrome *Juliet and Romeo*, set in an unspecified time and place within the confines of rapidly rearranged corridors marked out by corrugated walls, presented by the Swedish Royal Ballet.

Christopher Wheeldon's *A Winter's Tale*, with a score by Joby Talbot, designs by Bob Crowley and projections by Daniel Brodie (a co-production by The Royal Ballet and the National Ballet of Canada), was the most important danced Shakespeare of 2014. This kept faith with the original play although the jolly folk dancing of a Mediterranean Bohemia in Act II needed tightening. Edward Watson played the tortured jealous Leontes, with Lauren Cuthbertson portraying a dignified Hermione, but it was Zenaida Yanowsky's consoling Paulina who provided a strong core to the production.

During 2014 London also revealed a new ability to mix companies in single programmes to create more varied evenings. Sadler's Wells drew on their community work and artists in residence for their Elixir Festival, designed to show that age should be no barrier to dance. Almost all the performers were over 60 including

Mats Ek, Ana Laguna, Dominique Mercy and the Wells's own seniors performing group. Most entertaining was the presentation organised by Jonathan Burrows, which included former dancers of London Contemporary Dance Theatre and Sadler's Wells Royal Ballet dancing reminiscences of their careers.

Within the area of professional/community dance links, Scott Ambler's *Lord of the Flies*, a version of William Golding's novel, successfully recruited young boys to join the professionals of Matthew Bourne's New Adventures at venues around the UK. *See the Music, Hear the Dance*, a programme at Sadler's Wells, presented choreography by Wayne McGregor, Karole Armitage, Alexander Whitley and Crystal Pite in response to music by Thomas Adès. Pite's *Polaris*, with a cast of 58 student dancers joining her company of six, created a stupendous finale with echoes of a *Rite of Spring*. Whitley's *The Grit in the Oyster* was less impressive than his *Kin* for Birmingham Royal Ballet or his own programme at the Linbury Theatre in which the integration of technology enhanced his production. Justin Peck at New York City Ballet continued to develop with *Everywhere We Go* to a commissioned score from Sufjan Stevens for 25 dancers, appearing as a community from which individuals and couples emerged for brief moments in the limelight.

Jane Pritchard

NEW YORK AND LONDON THEATRE

2014 will be remembered as the year in which the British theatre seemed in thrall to all things American even as the US theatre—if New York's output was any gauge—decided that it could do without the usual slew of British imports, at least until the autumn. In London, American titles kept the volume of openings across the UK capital in overdrive, whether one was referring to time-honoured classics dusted down and refreshed (*A Streetcar Named Desire*, *The Crucible*, *A View From the Bridge*), erstwhile Broadway hits (the Theresa Rebeck play *Seminar*, which starred Roger Allam in the role originated on Broadway by Alan Rickman), or the usual plethora of musicals, of which a revival of the Stephen Sondheim-John Weidman show *Assassins* was by some measure the year's best.

Indeed, throughout much of the summer, a veritable crash course in the American canon was available to London theatregoers, courtesy of the concurrent stagings, at playhouses located minutes away from one another, of *The Crucible*, Arthur Miller's 1953 play set during the Salem witch trials in 17th century Massachusetts, and *A Streetcar Named Desire*, Tennessee Williams's celebrated portrait of a psyche in meltdown. Seen at the Old Vic and Young Vic theatres, respectively, both productions significantly looked beyond Britain for their choice of directors. *The Crucible* was the work of the Canada-based South African, Yael Farber, who had impressed London in 2013 with a post-apartheid staging of the August Strindberg classic *Miss Julie* (here re-titled *Mies Julie*), while *Streetcar* was staged by Benedict Andrews, an Australian director based in Iceland, who was represented on the New York stage soon after *Streetcar* with a characteristically polarising production of the Jean Genet play *The Maids*, starring Cate Blanchett and Isabelle Huppert.

For *Streetcar*, Andrews placed the audience on all sides of an ever-rotating set which meant that one or another part of the action was partially obscured at all times—a deliberate provocation in keeping with Andrews's desire to shatter an audience's complacency. Farber's *Crucible* was a leisurely production that ladled on atmosphere at the expense of pacing: early previews ran close to four hours, though the running time was trimmed by opening night and the play garnered nine five-star reviews—an impressive achievement by anyone's reckoning. Better than both of these—and considerably shorter—was the Belgian director Ivo van Hove's hurtling reclamation of a second Miller play, *A View from the Bridge*, this one starring Mark Strong in a ferocious return to the London stage as the Brooklyn longshoreman, Eddie Carbone, who is destroyed by extremes of passion. (The staging, played without an interval, transferred from the Young Vic to the West End for a commercial run in February 2015.) Performed on a stripped-back stage with virtually no set and the cast appearing barefoot, Miller's play had never before seemed quite so primal in its embrace of a range of feelings for which there are no words. (Although there had been previous brilliant productions of the same play in the capital, with Ken Stott and Michael Gambon acclaimed in the role that brought Strong extensive plaudits this time around.)

If these three shows constituted a fairly mighty US trifecta, there was plenty more to make British spectators wonder whether they might have inadvertently hopped on a trans-Atlantic flight without realising it. The tiny Finborough Theatre in Earl's Court, south-west London—seating capacity 50—unearthed a play, *Rachel*, written by the Boston-born Angelina Weld Grimké in 1916, that was merciless in its appraisal of the plight of black Americans amidst a social structure that had no idea how to accommodate them. One could quibble about a few of the performances, but there was no denying the service performed by the director, Ola Ince, in allowing audiences a rare glimpse of what is believed to have been the first play professionally produced by an African-American writer. Adelayo Adedayo took the title role of a young, educated black woman who surrenders to an abiding pessimism that the play confronts head-on.

Other American titles included *Rapture, Blister, Burn*, Gina Gionfriddo's play about three generations of women adjusting to the various "isms" of the day, and David Lindsay-Abaire's *Good People*, a riveting portrait of the class divide that starred the tiny yet formidable Imelda Staunton as the tough-minded single mother, Margie—the same part that won a 2011 Tony Award on Broadway for the role's American originator, Frances McDormand. Staunton returned later in the year, this time at the Chichester Festival Theatre in the Sussex countryside south of London, to play the defining mother in perhaps all US musicals: Momma Rose in a rare UK revival of *Gypsy*, the 1959 Jule Styne (composer)-Stephen Sondheim (lyricist) collaboration based on the memoirs of the famed stripper Gypsy Rose Lee, who happened to be the grasping, aggressive Rose's comely and canny daughter. (Like *A View from the Bridge*, the production was also picked up for a commercial transfer to the West End during 2015.) It was the redoubtable Sondheim, this time functioning as his own composer as well as lyricist, who was responsible for the London year's most galvanic musical—a scorching revival at the Menier Chocolate Factory in south London of the take-no-prisoners show, *Assassins*, focusing on the various men (and women, as well) who over time had either attempted to assassinate a US president or, in several cases, had succeeded. The director, Jamie Lloyd, reconceived this demanding show as a sort of funfair run both aground and amok, complete with a clown-faced proprietor (Simon Lipkin) to lead us into a world where the gun speaks more volubly—and tragically—than words ever could.

Where was the British theatre in all this? Everywhere in evidence, notwithstanding a trans-Atlantic immersion that helped explain why it was that so many US television shows and films featured British actors playing Americans. (On the celluloid front, surely the reigning champ in that regard was the civil rights-themed film *Selma*, which cast Britons as the American president Lyndon Johnson, Alabama governor George Wallace, civil rights leader Martin Luther King, and his wife Coretta Scott King.) The bijou Donmar Warehouse in Covent Garden may have ended the year with a revival of the 1990 Tony Award-winning Broadway musical *City of Angels*—a production notable for sets that seemed to reach right the way up to the ceiling—but its standout productions were in fact a new James Graham play, *Privacy*, in which audiences were invited upon entering the theatre to turn their phones on as opposed to off, and *My Night with Reg*, a gorgeous revival from the director Robert Hastie of Kevin Elyot's 1994 tragicomedy about love and lust in the shadow of AIDS. (Elyot died on 7 June at age 62 within only weeks of the first preview of the play, which gave the revival the added feel of a commemoration and a celebration of its writer's gifts.) The Almeida—north London's answer to the Donmar—featured its own ad hoc US season with the inclusion of the Anne Washburn play *Mr Burns*, and the 1938 Thornton Wilder Pulitzer prize-winner, *Our Town*, among its season. But it was a new British play, *King Charles III*, that struck critical and commercial gold, transferring to the West End and setting its sights on a New York transfer to follow. Tim Pigott-Smith played the heir to the throne in a play that starts in the immediate aftermath of the death of his mother, Queen Elizabeth II, an event that, at the time of the play's run, seemed some while off yet. The monarch was a tireless 88 while the play was running and showed no signs of passing the crown to her 66-year-old eldest son. Rupert Goold, that play's director, returned later in the year with a new musical, *Made in Dagenham*, based on the 2010 film of the same name, which might have been better (or at least less cynical) if it had not been one of two autumn musicals to all but demand that audiences stood and cheered. The show included a number late in the second act called "Stand Up" that asked us to do precisely that, a ploy echoed by the London version of the Tony-winning Broadway entry *Memphis*, a slack piece of work redeemed by blazing star turns from Irishman Killian Donnelly and English singer-songwriter Beverley Knight.

The National Theatre, long-considered the engine room of the British theatre, broadened its geographical horizons still further, turning in the second half of the year toward the local premiere of the off-Broadway musical *Here Lies Love*, a through-sung piece about Imelda Marcos, the widow of the former Philippine president Ferdinand Marcos, and to the little-known Croatian writer Tena Stivicic's *3 Winters*, a multi-generational drama refracting the shifts in Eastern European place names and politics through a family home that adapts in varying ways to the changing times. The latter's author was revealed to be the wife of the noted Scottish actor Douglas Henshall, so her appearance out of nowhere was not in fact as much of a surprise as it had seemed at first. And in a curtain-raiser of sorts as to what one might expect from his National Theatre regime to follow, the National's artistic director designate Rufus Norris opened an empathically conceived, wholly absorbing stage adaptation by Sir David Hare of the Katherine Boo book, *Behind the Beautiful Forevers*, which told of a community of slum-dwellers living underneath the flight path of the airport in Mumbai, India.

In New York itself, it was a National Theatre production, from summer 2012, that stormed Broadway in early-autumn 2014 with the arrival at the Barrymore Theatre of *The Curious Incident of the Dog in the Night-Time*, Simon Stephens's adaptation of the Mark Haddon novel about a challenged teenager who wants to solve the mystery of the title, even as he attempts to reassemble his fractured family. In downtown Manhattan, well away from the box office pressures of Broadway, Englishman Jonny Donahoe was garnering his own set of raves for a solo play, *Every Brilliant Thing*, that included the audience in Donahoe's imaginative canter through the many reasons to embrace life in a scenario prompted by talk of depression and suicide. A second (and older) Englishman, the New York-based Tony-winning performer Jim Dale, was the subject and sole player of an affectionate autobiographical venture, *Just Jim Dale*, in which the wiry veteran of many a play and musical gave off-Broadway's Laura Pels Theatre something of the feel of a largish living room as he looked back amiably over his life and art.

Elsewhere in New York, Lily Rabe and Hamish Linklater, a real-life couple off-stage with several dual credits to their names, reunited onstage over the summer in Central Park to play Beatrice and Benedick in an al fresco staging of *Much Ado About Nothing*, from the prolific director Jack O'Brien, that by rights ought to have been considerably more charming and winning than it was. The same venerable director did far better later in the year with a lesser script: Terrence McNally's *It's Only A Play*, a piece of theatrical navel-gazing that was spun by O'Brien into star-studded gold, helped no end by the lustre of leading players Nathan Lane and Stockard Channing—two of the best that Broadway had to offer. And the trend toward turning every third film (or so it seemed) into a stage musical saw the successive misfires of *Bullets over Broadway*, *Rocky*, and *Heathers*, though the first of the three did at least announce a star's birth in the person of Nick Cordero, a fleet-footed Canadian playing a gun-toting heavy. Cordero managed to do a mean tap dance and look effortlessly cool all the while.

Cordero deserved the Tony Award nomination that came his way in an otherwise poor showing for that much-anticipated venture, but Broadway's annual prize-

giving ceremony was dominated by two of the most seismically exciting performances in many a year. Former Tony Awards host Neil Patrick Harris on this occasion picked up his own trophy for playing the transgender rock phenomenon that
is Hedwig in an all-stops-out revival of the musical *Hedwig and the Angry Inch*,
which saw a glammed-up Harris baring his all, emotionally and physically. And at
the still-young age of 44, Audra McDonald on Tony night made history as the first-
ever performer to win six Tonys, this time for her soul-searing performance as
Billie Holliday in *Lady Day at Emerson's Bar and Grill*, a feat of acting so raw
and pure that one felt grateful to be in its presence. No one could possibly imagine what the mighty McDonald could possibly do for an encore, but everyone
knew that whatever it was, they wanted to be there to find out.

Matt Wolf

CINEMA

WHEN Colin Welland, writer of the Oscar-winning *Chariots of Fire*, told his
audience that "the British are coming" all those years ago, he spoke truer than
he knew. Ever since 1982, albeit with some notable gaps, the British had more
than pulled their weight at the Oscar celebrations. It happened again for the films
of 2014, when Eddie Redmayne, hitherto respected more as an excellent character actor, won the 2015 Best Actor Academy Award for his performance as
Stephen Hawking in *The Theory of Everything*. There were plenty more British
nominations; Hollywood has always respected Britain's capacity to produce fine
performances in good films. Whereas the rest of Europe and the world generally
had to be content with nominations for the Best Foreign Film, Britain was not
regarded as foreign at all.

There were, however, disappointments. Mike Leigh's extraordinary *Mr Turner*,
in which Timothy Spall turned in a magnificent performance as the eccentric but
brilliant painter, got nothing, though many thought it the most original British film
of the year, if only as a portrait of Victorian times freed of the cobwebs of cliché.

Elsewhere, there was a fully deserved Best Actress award for Julianne Moore,
possibly the most consistently notable female performer in America, for her part
as a woman with early dementia in *Still Alice*, one of the bravest US films of the
year. But Best Film and Best Director went to *Birdman* and Mexican director Alejandro Inarritu. This had Michael Keaton as a washed-up Hollywood star trying to
make his way again in the theatre. It was an original, funny and lively movie but
hardly a classic. In fact, there were not many classics on display this year, but
enough good films to make 2014 seem well above average.

One of them was undoubtedly Richard Linklater's *Boyhood*, a 12-year labour of
love about a young man progressing from childhood into adolescence. Its four-
hour length made it a difficult prospect for exhibitors but *Boyhood* did well enough
to convince the Academy voters that it deserved several nominations. This was
more than *Selma*—the story of the final months of Martin Luther King—was able

to manage, despite a powerful performance from David Oyelowo which surely deserved at least an Oscar nomination. But, as a commentator observed accurately enough, the Academy voters were predominately white males and their average age was over 60. Another original American film was Wes Anderson's *The Grand Budapest Hotel*, in which Ralph Fiennes played the concierge of a ski resort hotel, where a succession of elderly women become his prey until one, after leaving him a precious painting, is discovered to have been murdered. The film proved the most successful that Anderson had made and, even if its fey humour sometimes curdled, its production design was outstanding.

Perhaps the most controversial American films of 2014 were *Foxcatcher* and *American Sniper*. *Foxcatcher*, directed by Bennett Miller, had comedian Steve Carell in the serious role of a rich tycoon intent on training up Channing Tatum's promising wrestler for the Olympics. Essentially the story of a violent murder, the film was based on a true story but quite unlike most Hollywood thrillers. *American Sniper* was Clint Eastwood's most popular film so far as director, made at the age of 82, and also based on a true story. It had Bradley Cooper as Chris Kyle, the US Navy Seal who became a formidable sniper but who, after four tours of duty, went home unable to adapt to civilian life. The controversy surrounded the fact that Eastwood made Kyle an exemplary figure, protecting his country from its enemies; this approach was heavily criticised by some as overly patriotic.

If Britain and the USA had good years, the rest of the world was not far behind. Three films stood out. One was *Winter Sleep*, the Turkish winner at the Cannes Festival, directed by Nuri Bilge Ceylan. This three-hour long conversation piece had a former actor holed up in an Anatolian hotel with his younger wife and newly divorced sister, and showed how an arrogant man can receive his comeuppance when others no longer fear him. This psychological study had considerably more power than one might suspect, with Ceylan proving himself one of the best half-dozen directors working today.

There were two other outstanding films. *Leviathan* by Andrey Zvyagintsev had a fisherman trying to protect his ancestral home from a corrupt local mayor, who was determined to destroy it and build a new church in its place in order to win the local election. Despite the friendship and efforts of a young lawyer from Moscow, the fisherman is totally unable to win a battle of wills against what seems to be a totally corrupt society. The film, winner of the foreign award at the Golden Globes, received stunning reviews everywhere except in Russia, where the official line was that it was unpatriotic and exaggerated in its criticism of the country under President Vladimir Putin. Many cinemas there refused to show the film, even though Zvyagintsev was known as an outstanding director with many awards to his name after making films like *The Return* and *Elena*.

The third exceptional film, *Ida*, by Pawel Pawlikowski, beat both *Leviathan* and *Winter Sleep* to the Academy's Foreign Film Oscar. Made in a daring black and white, it told the story of a young novitiate in 1960s Poland, who discovers from her one remaining relative that she is Jewish and has an uncomfortable family history. Beautifully made, *Ida* was as much a cinematographer's film as a director's, and may have won the Academy vote because of the accusations of anti-Semitism now rolling around Europe.

Documentaries flourished during 2014, and the Academy was right to award *Citizenfour* its accolade in that section. The film's subject was Edward Snowden, whom director Laura Poitras and reporter Glenn Greenwald met after travelling to Hong Kong to see the mysterious figure whose evidence of mass government surveillance in the USA caused such a sensation. The film was not so much a tribute to a brave man as disturbing proof that he was right. Two other documentaries of note, both by the distinguished veteran Frederick Wiseman, ought to be celebrated. The first was *Berkeley*, a fascinating glimpse of how the Californian university operates in straightened times; and *National Gallery*, a discursive look at the operation of a national institution, also facing financial constraints. Another outstanding work was *The Overnighters* by Jesse Moss, which portrayed how a pastor in North Dakota controversially opens his church's doors to some of the desperate men, often war veterans, chasing jobs in the state's oilfields. Criticised for his efforts, the pastor continues to attempt to save the lives if not the souls of America's poverty-stricken down and outs.

Among performers who died in 2014 were Robin Williams, American actor and comedian (see Obituary); Philip Seymour Hoffman, Oscar-winning American actor; Lauren Bacall, actress and wife of Humphrey Bogart (see Obituary); Shirley Temple, Hollywood superstar of the 1920s and 1930s (see Obituary); and American stars Mickey Rooney, Eli Wallach, and James Garner; Anita Ekberg, Swedish star of Fellini's *La Dolce Vita*; Louis Jourdan, French actor and Hollywood leading man; Billie Whitelaw, distinctive British actress; Elaine Stritch, American singer and actress; Bob Hoskins, popular British actor; Sid Caesar, American comedian; Maximilian Schell, German actor and director; and Richard Kiel, Bond villain.

Film-makers who left the scene included Richard Attenborough, scion of the British film industry as actor, director and producer, and Oscar winner for *Gandhi* (see Obituary); Mike Nicholls, American director who made *The Graduate* and *Silkwood*; Harold Ramis, who directed *Groundhog Day*; and American producer Sam Goldwyn Jr.

Derek Malcolm

TELEVISION AND RADIO

THE year 2014 saw major international corporate deals in the broadcasting industry that also turned up the volume on what has been called the increasing Americanisation of British and European media.

One of the most eye-catching, if not the largest in value, was the purchase by Viacom, owners of MTV, of Channel 5, in a deal worth £450 million, from *Daily Express* owner Richard Desmond. This was the first time that a US group had bought a UK free-to-air public service broadcaster. At around the same time,

All3Media, one of the largest British independent producers, founded by former Granada Television executives, was bought by Discovery and Liberty Global for £500 million. In the wave of consolidation, which was seen as a frenetic international battle to control viewers' eyeballs and purses everywhere, Discovery also bought the Eurosport TV business and the Scandinavian television company, SBS. Liberty Global, owned by John Malone, which in 2013 had spent £15 billion buying the cable group Virgin Media in the UK, also added the Dutch cable group Ziggo and took a 6 per cent stake in ITV for £484 million. Many analysts believed that a full bid for ITV, the UK's leading commercial broadcaster, could not be ruled out.

The catalogue of deals continued when Scripps Networks, an American specialist in food and leisure channels, bought 50 per cent of the multi-channel operator, UKTV. It would also like to buy the other half, owned by the BBC—if it got the chance.

US media group, AMC Networks, the company behind the hugely successful series *Mad Men* and *Breaking Bad* and which in early 2014 paid £660 million for the European multi-channel business, Chellomedia, bought a 49.9 per cent stake in BBC America.

Unsurprisingly, Rupert Murdoch was active in the deal-making merry-go-round and created an international £1.3 billion "super-Indy" by putting together British, Dutch and American production companies: Shine, makers of *MasterChef*; Endemol of *Big Brother* fame; and Core Media, producers of *American Idol*. The new, combined business would be run by Sophie Turner Laing, a former Sky executive. Murdoch also engineered a £7 billion deal, which netted him £5 billion, in which he sold his stakes in Sky Deutschland and Sky Italia to BSkyB, the British satellite broadcaster. Murdoch's 21st Century Fox would retain a 36 per cent stake in the enlarged group, renamed Sky, which was likely to expand as a European pay-TV powerhouse. However, the biggest deal of all, a £52.8 billion Fox bid for Time Warner, slipped through Murdoch's fingers as Time Warner shareholders voiced their opposition.

If all of that was not enough, the USA's two largest cable operators, Comcast and Time Warner Cable, agreed a £29.8 billion merger and AT&T, the US telephone company, pulled off a £32 billion acquisition of DirectTV, the US satellite TV group. Both deals were, however, subject to regulatory approval.

The US moves in the UK broadcasting industry attracted the attention of David Abraham, the Channel 4 chief executive, in the annual MacTaggart lecture at the Edinburgh International Television Festival. Abraham expressed fears that British television could "wither" under the influence of American media moguls such as Murdoch and Malone. Malone could end up owning ITV; the enlarged Sky, effectively controlled by Murdoch, had combined revenues more than three times the size of the entire UK television industry, the Channel 4 executive emphasised. In his lecture, Abraham appealed to British regulators and politicians to act decisively to protect the UK's unique blend of public and commercial broadcasters in the face of the American "gold rush." Abraham added: "Stay silent and our special system may wither. Once gone, it will never come back."

Channel 4 reported a loss of £15 million in 2013, although Abraham described the deficit as "planned" because of greater investment in programmes and digital operations. The broadcaster's total share of audience fell to 11 per cent from 11.5 per cent in 2011, with the core Channel 4 network down to 6.1 per cent from 6.6 per cent. In a forward looking initiative, Abraham also announced the creation of a £20 million Growth Fund to take minority stakes in middle-sized independent producers to help them expand—a first for the public service broadcaster.

During the year the BBC spent a lot of time thinking about its structure and future, although negotiations over the licence fee and a new Royal Charter would only get under way after the general election in May 2015. However, the initial decisions, forged by the realities of a revenue squeeze flowing from a frozen licence fee, which could get worse after the next funding round, were dramatic enough. The Corporation decided that BBC3, the channel aimed at young adults, would go on-line-only in autumn 2015 and admitted that the decision had been brought forward to save money. This change was opposed for downgrading a "valuable voice" of youth culture and dissent, and the decision remained to be ratified by the BBC Trust.

The very existence of the Trust itself was uncertain—a judgement accepted by its chair, Rona Fairhead, the former chief executive of the *Financial Times*. She had been chosen to lead the Trust after Chris Patten (Lord Patten of Barnes), responsible for appointing George Entwistle who had lasted just 54 days as BBC director-general, stood down in May because of ill-health. Fairhead, a controversial appointment because of her lack of political or broadcasting experience and her connections with the Conservative party, told MPs in September that she would be surprised if the BBC Trust survived in its present form beyond the renewal of its Charter in 2016.

The scale of the task she faced in the coming negotiations became all too apparent when Michael Grade (Baron Grade of Yarmouth), a former chairman of the BBC, made it clear he wanted to see a much smaller Corporation. In evidence to the House of Commons committee on culture, media and sport, in February, the Conservative peer said that the BBC was "far too big" and should outsource most of its programmes, including dramas and documentaries, to the private sector and concentrate instead on news. It was an opening shot in the battle for the future shape of the Corporation.

The BBC's director-general Tony Hall (Baron Hall of Birkenhead) appeared to get some of his retaliation in first. Fifty per cent of the BBC's non-news commissions already went out for competition, but the Corporation was under pressure to go further. In July Lord Hall announced what he called "a competition revolution". The 50 per cent quota would go and all BBC production, apart from news-gathering, would be open to competition from the private sector. In what many saw as the most fundamental change in the BBC's 92-year history, Hall said that the present system of "managed competition" would end. In future, independent production companies, who already made popular BBC programmes such as *The Great British Bake-Off* and *Sherlock*, would be able to compete for almost all commissions, while BBC Production could also make programmes for other broadcasters. "Competition works just as you would expect. We do well. Others have to compete. They raise their game. They challenge us. We respond. Competition spurs us all on," said Hall, who acknowledged that under the present system it was getting harder to retain talented people within the BBC.

The financial pressures on the BBC could be seen even in the more "protected" area of news-gathering when James Harding, director of news and former editor of *The Times*, warned of more cuts. Harding said in July that 415 jobs in the news sector would go as part of an £800 million savings plan, although the net loss would be 220 following the creation of new posts.

The BBC was likely to face another embarrassing blow in 2015 when former High Court judge, Dame Janet Jones, was due to publish her inquiry into the sexual abuse allegations against once popular presenter, Jimmy Savile. The report, expected to be hard-hitting, was presaged by prison sentences imposed on former high-profile BBC broadcasters Stuart Hall and Rolf Harris, who were convicted in 2014 of sexual assaults on under-age girls.

The BBC could face another financial setback following a review set up by the new secretary of state for culture, media and sport, Sajid Javid, into decriminalising non-payment of the BBC licence fee. A large number of MPs opposed prison sentences—of which there were around 50 a year—for failing to pay fines for not having a television licence. The BBC argued that any change in the law could cost it up to £200 million per year in unpaid licence fees. Javid, the first Muslim Cabinet member and a rising star in the Conservative party, was appointed in April after Maria Miller had resigned as culture secretary following an accusation that she had funded a home for her parents at tax-payers' expense.

ITV, helped by award-winning programme successes such as *Broadchurch*, continued its growth under chief executive Adam Crozier. In the six months to June, for example, the company increased its revenues by 7 per cent to £1.2 billion and pre-tax profits rose by 40 per cent to £250 million. ITV caused a stir with a submission to MPs suggesting that a slice of the BBC licence fee should be used to help fund the news services of rival broadcasters.

The commercial broadcaster failed to make much of an impact with the relaunch of its breakfast show, *Good Morning Britain*, but it did manage to do something to reverse the transatlantic flow of acquisitions. It moved into US reality television with a £237 million deal to take 80 per cent of Leftfield, the company which made programmes such as *Pawn Stars*, *Bridal Bootcamp* and *Real Housewives of New Jersey*.

This was also the year when local television, the brainchild of former culture secretary Jeremy Hunt, got off the ground. Fourteen out of more than 30 planned stations were launched in cities such as Bristol, Cardiff and Norwich. The biggest launch was London Live, a TV channel owned by the *Independent* newspaper group. Initial viewing figures were modest, reaching a first night peak of 59,000 viewers and questions remained over the financial viability of local television in the UK.

It was a very strong year for radio in the UK, with the number of adults aged 15 and over listening to radio at least once a week rising to 48.4 million, or 91 per cent. This was the highest proportion since the current system of measuring listenership had been introduced in 1999.

Radio 4 scored a weekly record reach of 11.2 million, up from 10.8 in 2013. BBC Radio 6 Music, which the BBC hierarchy had tried to close down, hit its biggest ever audience of more than 2 million. On the commercial side, Absolute 80s, featuring bands such as Duran Duran and Human League, helped to make the station the most popular digital-only UK radio service with more than 1.4 million listeners a week.

While complimenting the radio industry in continuing to reach more than 90 per cent of adults a week, listening for an average of 21 hours a week, Ed Vaizey, minister of state for culture and the digital economy, highlighted a potential problem. Speaking at the Radio Festival 2014, Vaizey noted figures from Ofcom, the communications regulator, which suggested a fall in listening in the 15-24 age group from 18.7 hours a week in 2007 to 15.5 hours in 2013. The reason? Probably that the young were consuming more of their media from the Internet and social media.

It was also announced in 2014 that the planned switchover from analogue to digital radio would be delayed until 2022, partly because of cost but also the relatively slow uptake of digital radio.

There were a number of influential departures from broadcasting. In the UK Jeremy Paxman decided that it was time to end a 25-year stint presenting the BBC's current affairs programme, *Newsnight*. Paxman, who left with critical words for the BBC, could end up presenting Channel 4's general election coverage.

In the US it was all-change in the battle of the late-night talk-show hosts. In February Jay Leno, host of NBC's *The Tonight Show*, departed, whilst David Letterman, host of CBS's *Late Show*, in April announced his intended retirement. His last show was to be in May 2015.

Worldwide, more than 1 billion people were believed to have watched the football World Cup final in Brazil between Germany and Argentina. In the UK the World Cup final drew 20.6 million.

There were, however, some worries for traditional broadcasters. According to Ofcom, which in December appointed Sharon White as chief executive following the retirement of Ed Richards, teenagers were watching around half the amount of live television each day compared with adults and were increasingly turning to online sites such as YouTube, Vimeo and Vine.

The year 2014 was also marked by the expansion of video services such as Netflix, which launched in six new European countries during the year. On the news front, online news services such as Vice and Buzzfeed began offering journalistic alternatives to conventional news broadcasters, aiming primarily at young adults. But one service seen as a threat to network TV in the US, Aereo, failed following a legal challenge. The Supreme Court ruled that Aereo, which allowed subscribers to receive live over-the-air television via aerials, breached the copyright of the US networks.

Evidently, in 2015 observers of the communications and broadcast industries would be watching carefully to see whether the wave of consolidation, and with it the "Americanisation" of British media, would continue—or even accelerate.

Raymond Snoddy

VISUAL ARTS

IF 2013 was the year of the outsider in the visual arts, with a host of exhibitions dedicated to untrained and unknown artists, 2014 was the year the established names fought back. Foremost among these was Britain's cultural behemoth, the Tate. Sir Nicholas Serota, the Tate's director, topped *Art Review*'s influential "Power 100", the magazine lauding his role in helping the institution to "punch above its weight in the global network of influence". The Tate has "come to epitomise almost all the elements of the current 'global' art world, where the distribution of art is arguably now more important than its production", said the magazine. Earlier in the year, Serota had co-curated Tate Modern's blockbuster exhibition, "Henri Matisse: The Cut-Outs"—its first show to attract more than half-a-million viewers—which focused exclusively on Matisse's use of cut paper as his primary medium, and scissors as his chief implement, in the late 1940s. The exhibition was a sensation, receiving near unanimous five-star reviews from the critics. "Nothing can prepare you for the joyous brilliance—and scale—of Matisse's late, great work, proliferating from one gallery to the next like some super-abundant garden", eulogised the *Guardian*'s Laura Cumming. Equally as popular with the public as it was with the critics, a record-breaking 560,000 people viewed the exhibition.

The late style of another great artist was the subject of the National Gallery's major exhibition of the year. Organised in conjunction with the Rijksmuseum, Amsterdam, "Rembrandt: The Late Works" was the first time an exhibition had been dedicated to the latter work of the master of the Dutch Golden Age. Examining radical developments in the artist's painting as he grew older—self-scrutiny, observations of everyday life, experimentation with technique—the show was as well received as Matisse at the Tate. "This brilliant, brave blockbuster reveals the true Rembrandt—a man at the end of his tether. It is a shocking and cathartic journey through the tragedy of his fall," said Jonathan Jones in another *Guardian* five-star review.

Completing a triumvirate of landmark exhibitions, and epitomising the fashion for lateness throughout the year, was "Late Turner: Painting Set Free" at Tate Britain. As with Matisse and Rembrandt, "Late Turner" received a highly favourable critical reception, indicating that 2014 was either a vintage year for major gallery shows, or that there was a softening within the famously hard-nosed world of art criticism. Coinciding with Turner at the Tate was the release of the biographical film *Mr Turner*, for which the director Mike Leigh was awarded the Palme d'Or at the Cannes Film Festival.

Predictably, it was another bumper year for the art market, which had grown in value from €18.6 billion in 2003 to €47.4 billion in 2013, according to the 2014 TEFAF *Art Market Report*. In the first six months of 2014, revenues had already reached 88 per cent of the 2013 total. The extent of this growth was emphasised in November when Christie's Evening Sale of Contemporary Art in New York realised a staggering $853 million, the highest total achieved for any auction, in any category, and setting new records for the artists Ed Ruscha, Peter Doig, Georg

Baselitz, Cindy Sherman and Cy Twombly in the process. The sale was led by Andy Warhol's 1963 silkscreen of Elvis Presley, appropriating a publicity image for the movie *Flaming Star*, in which the singer is shown as a cowboy with a gun. "Contemporary art collectors can be summed up in a word right now: Insatiable", said the *Wall Street Journal*'s Kelly Crow following the sale.

Warhol was once again the top-selling artist of the year, as collectors bought 1,295 works by the pop-art pioneer, worth a combined total of $653.2 million. Auction sales worldwide rose 10 per cent to $16 billion, the second-highest figure on record. Just a single living artist, Gerhard Richter, 82, featured in the 10 top-selling artists of the year, with no female artists making the list. There were, however, some signs of change in the perennially male-centric art market. In November, when the Georgia O'Keeffe Museum in Santa Fe, New Mexico, sold *Jimson Weed/White Flower No. 1*, 1932, at Sotheby's New York to benefit its acquisitions fund, the painting fetched $44.4 million, smashing its pre-sale estimate of $10 million to $15 million and comfortably surpassing the previous record for a female artist. Perhaps the most surprising auction result of the year also went to a female artist: *Le Passage*, 1956, by the American surrealist painter Kay Sage carried the lowest pre-sale estimate—£70,000-£90,000—of any work in Sotheby's February sale of Impressionist, Modern and Surrealist Art in London. The painting soared to an incredible £4,338,500, nearly 50 times the pre-sale estimate. Despite these encouraging signs for female artists in the art market, it was once again a work of art by a male artist that ranked as the most expensive sold at auction in 2014. Alberto Giacometti's *Chariot*, 1951-52, sold for $101 million in November at Sotheby's in New York .

Away from the commercial arena, an artistic movement as yet untapped by the auction houses continued to take the contemporary art scene by storm. Grouped under the catch-all moniker of "post-internet art", an expanding group of young artists who had grown-up immersed in the technology of the world wide web were creating works of art by using the Internet as their toolbox: from YouTube videos and labyrinthine web pages to animated GIFs (an image format) and Instagram snapshots. Although this thriving scene had been bubbling under the surface for a number of years, led by artists such as Cory Arcangel in the USA and the "Lucky PDF" group in Britain, 2014 was the first time this emerging mode of artistic practice gained widespread institutional support. New York's Museum of Modern Art dedicated one of its forums on contemporary photography to post-internet art; Beijing's Ullens Center for Contemporary Art staged the exhibition "Art Post-Internet"; and the Museum of Modern Art in Warsaw presented "Private Settings: Art after the Internet". London's Serpentine Gallery even launched its first digital commission, *AGNES*, by Cécile B. Evans. *AGNES* existed only on the Serpentine's website and, in the words of the gallery, "will accompany you on your digital encounter ... like a person, she cannot be experienced in totality through a single encounter". For the moment, works such as *AGNES* that challenge the traditional forms and languages of fine art had yet to find a footing in the major collections of the world's museums, but it would be interesting to see how these institutions adapted in future to accommodate the inevitable growth in the digital age of post-internet art.

One of these institutions may well be the Yuz Museum, Shanghai, which opened in May and was designed by the superstar architect Sou Fujimoto. The Yuz housed the private collection of the Chinese-Indonesian billionaire and avid art collector, Budi Tek. Tek told *The Art Newspaper* that he intended the museum to "be a kind of a platform to meet East and West: our own slogan, clearly stated, is to 'draw the world's attention to Shanghai'". Works in the permanent collection of the 9,000 sq m museum included Xu Bing's *Tobacco Project Shanghai*, 2004, a 40ft rug woven from around half-a-million cigarettes.

The trend for vast new museums to house the bulging collections of private organisations and individuals was also evident in the opening of the Fondation Louis Vuitton in the Bois de Boulogne in Paris. The $143 million museum, designed by Frank Gehry, was due to house a combination of works owned by LVMH and its chairman Bernard Arnault (see the article on Architecture). Overcoming years of legal wrangling with local councils and pressure groups over the effect that the building would have on the local environment, in an agreement reached with the city of Paris for the plot, ownership of the museum will revert to Paris in 55 years.

Looking to the future, it is clear that the ways in which we create, experience and consume art will continue to move towards online and digital models. Sotheby's announced that it would be partnering with the online auction website, Ebay, due to launch in spring 2015, in the hope of reaching a new constituent of collectors among the website's 145 million shoppers; Christie's already offered "click and buy" options on certain objects through its website. Other websites, such as Artsy, were linking up with major galleries to "make all the world's art accessible to anyone with an Internet connection". Artists could share new works directly and instantaneously with their audience, completely negating the need for a traditional gallery model. Without doubt, it is this technological acceleration that will transform the artistic landscape in the coming years.

Toby Skeggs

ARCHITECTURE

"ARCHITECTURE, not architects" declared Rem Koolhaas, whose curatorship of the 14th Venice Architecture Biennale claimed to eschew the cult of the "starchitect" and instead focus the attention of the Biennale on the "fundamentals" of architecture itself.

The critical response to the *rappel a l'ordre* contained in Koolhaas's Venetian summary of the state of architecture was mixed. Nonetheless, this dialectic between architecture's return to essentials on the one hand, versus the egotism and vanity of famous architects and their clients on the other, stood as something of a theme for the year 2014. This polarity emerged, perhaps, from a global sense of crisis—economic, security—and a flirtation with austerity, which, as the architectural writer Jeremy Till pointed out, had been refracted from economic ideology to aesthetics, and appeared as a stylistic tic in architecture.

Austerity as an aesthetic was present in Sir David Chipperfield's stripped-back office building at One Pancras Square, part of London's King's Cross redevelopment and completed at the beginning of 2014. Despite its asceticism it nevertheless captured something of the mysterious character of King's Cross station, with its great latticed cast-iron columns and expressed concrete floor slabs.

Asceticism was not a description that could be applied to MVRDV's Markthal in Rotterdam: an extruded horseshoe portal of 230 flats covering an artisanal market, all built over the city's largest underground car park. Here, the unashamedly garish internal decoration by Dutch artists Arno Coenen and Iris Roskam celebrated cornucopia: the fecund excess of nature.

At the far extreme of the spectrum, Frank Gehry's structure for the Fondation Louis Vuitton opened in Paris in October (see the article on Visual Arts). Sited contentiously in the otherwise protected enclaves of the Bois de Boulogne, the project brought together the runaway egos of Gehry and the Vuitton billionaire, Bernard Arnault, with repulsive effect.

One particular phenomenon encapsulated by that project was the annexation of public spaces and institutions by private or corporate interests. This spatial development was itself reflected in the Western phenomena of shrinking national state expenditure, contrasted with the growing wealth of the super-rich. As the civic realm was diminished, the powerful elites were increasingly becoming the patrons of architecture.

This phenomenon was more than evident in London. While the Olympic Park, in post-games mode, finally re-opened to the public with a garden design by James Corner Field Operations—the landscape designers responsible for New York's High Line park—a number of other publicly-sponsored projects seemed to involve the loss of truly civic space in the city. Vanity projects characterised what could be the final year of Mayor of London Boris Johnson's reign, with a series of schemes that rarely seemed to develop beyond the sales pitch.

The proposed £500 million recreation of Joseph Paxton's Crystal Palace (destroyed by fire in 1936), through the agency of the mysterious ZhongRong Group, began the year with the announcement of a stellar shortlist to create what Johnson described as "an extraordinary new landmark for the city". By the year's end the project appeared to have stalled. Likewise, in November, Transport for London, the mayoral transit authority, had to announce that there were no regular users of the "Emirates Air Line", the heavily sponsored cable car linking North Greenwich to the Royal Docks.

The Garden Bridge—a Thames crossing proposed in central London designed by Thomas Heatherwick—was given planning consent against a general outcry that £60 million of public money was being spent on a structure which the organisers described both as a park and a bridge, but which would be privately managed, with no access at night nor open to cyclists. The bridge would be closed 12 times a year to host corporate events, and groups of more than eight people would have to apply in advance for consent to cross.

Mayor Johnson's ultimate fantasy—a replacement for Heathrow airport built on an artificial island in the outer reaches of the Thames estuary and known, inevitably, as "Boris Island"—appeared to have been dealt a death blow. The government's Airports Commission to review the location of London's expanded hub airport excluded the island (designed by Foster and Partners) as an option in their inquiry in the autumn.

122 Leadenhall Street—a tower designed by Rogers Stirk Harbour + Partners, popularly known as "the Cheesegrater"—opened in the City to general approval, most particularly of the "public" space that the tower created at its base: with tall buildings this is normally such a compromised environment. Delight was tempered when bolts the size of a human forearm started to fall from the 48-storey structure, prompting general replacement. In contrast, Rafael Vinoly's "Walkie Talkie", at 20 Fenchurch Street, promised a public space in the form of a garden at its summit. When it opened at the end of the year, this was found to have poor views and a chill environment.

The annexation of public space by private development was not confined to London, with much attention turning to the north of the UK. In Manchester the Central Library reopened after many years of refurbishment, but the opening was accompanied by controversy. The City Council had enclosed Library Walk—one of the city's best loved and most distinctive spaces, running between the Central Library's curved flank and the echoing curve of the Town Hall Extension—in a glass lobby designed by Ian Simpson Architects. Objections to the Council's desire to stop up this right of way led to a public inquiry. Further south, the Stirling Prize-shortlisted Library of Birmingham, designed by the Dutch practice Mecanoo, was hit by savage budget cuts which led to campaigners fearing that the building could become "a shell". Mecanoo's building replaced John Madin's brutalist Birmingham Central Library, completed in 1974, the demolition of which began at the end of 2014.

The Chancellor of the Exchequer made a speech in Manchester in June, calling for the city to become a "northern powerhouse" linked by transport investment, and followed that up with an announcement, in his Autumn Statement, of £78 million funding for a theatre and arts venue to be called The Factory. Meanwhile, Liverpool's Everyman Theatre, by Haworth Tompkins architects, triumphed in the Stirling Prize against a strong shortlist of public buildings, including a new school of architecture at Manchester University by Fielden Clegg Bradley Studios, and the Saw Swee Hock Student Centre for the London School of Economics. O'Donnell & Tuomey, the Dublin-based architects of the latter, had become serial runners-up for the prize after having been shortlisted five times; ironically, both partners worked for the eponymous James Stirling. Offering some recompense, Sheila O'Donnell and John Tuomey's work was recognised by the award of the Royal Institute of British Architects (RIBA) 2015 Royal Gold Medal.

The RIBA also acknowledged, through the award of honorary fellowships, the significant educational contribution of Dalibor Vesely and Peter Carl to the discipline. Together with Joseph Rykwert, winner of the Royal Gold Medal in 2013, they had established an influential programme at the University of Cambridge, founded in an understanding of history and philosophy of architecture within broader culture.

The huge and growing issue of the availability and affordability of housing in the UK was generally acknowledged to have reach the status of a crisis. Renewed interest in the 19th-century utopian idea of the Garden City was brought into focus by the topic of the 2014 Wolfson Economics Prize, backed by the right-wing think-tank, Policy Exchange. The prize posed the question: "How would you deliver a new Garden City which is visionary, economically viable, and popular?" Entrants were asked to demonstrate how a new city could be built without "a single penny of public money". Meanwhile, visitors to the UK Pavilion at the aforementioned Venice Biennale were reminded of a different tradition: the idea of the enabling state, expressed though the post-war planning and Keynesian economic stimulation that had established Britain's New Towns and other innovations, and which, in retrospect, addressed many of the problems experienced today.

The great advocate of British planning, Sir Peter Hall, died at the end of 2014, a year which saw some other significant losses to the discipline: the architect Kathryn Findlay died as the year began, followed by the maverick Viennese Hans Hollein and Sir Richard MacCormac, past president of the RIBA and founder of the Practice of MacCormac, Jamieson & Prichard.

In terms of losses of significant architecture over the year, in May, fire at Charles Rennie Mackintosh's Glasgow School of Art was fortunately brought under control quickly, although significant damage was caused to the School's library: one of the most highly wrought spaces. A public campaign to save London's Smithfield Market from bland redevelopment as an office quarter was successful, with ministers upholding a planning inspector's recommendation to refuse planning permission. In Portland, Oregon USA, Michael Graves defended his postmodern icon, The Portland Building, against threats of demolition.

Tom Holbrook

LITERATURE

THE titles of books are all important to their chances in the market place. In 2014 there were some curious choices. Two of the books on the Man Booker long-list went for minimalism: *J* by Howard Jacobson and *Us* by David Nicholls. Other titles of novels were positively lyrical: *To Rise Again at a Decent Hour* by Joshua Ferris, *All That is Solid Melts into Air* by Darragh McKeon, *Colourless Tsukuru and His Years of Pilgrimage* by Haruki Murakami. Poets have always gone for poetic namings and did not disappoint this year, with Kevin Powers's *Letter Composed During a Lull in the Fighting* and with Niall Campbell calling his new collection *Hebridean Moon*—a more romantic title than the pragmatic appellation of Dannie Abse's last book, *Ask the Moon*. The most exotic of all titles—in poetry or prose—was Rosemary Tonks's *Bedouin of the London Evening*.

A careful selection of title, often accompanied by superb cover designs (the art of the book illustrator continued to delight), were means of showing that the printed book was far from dead, threatened though it was by the ever increasing dominance of reading by Kindlelight. Literary festivals in the United States and the United Kingdom both reported record attendances, book groups continued to mushroom, and there were fewer convulsions in the publishing industry as firms developed survival strategies. It did not stop some of them elaborating bizarre ideas to capture readers. Of these the HarperCollins Austen Project was one of the strangest. Reputable writers were invited to "update" Jane Austen's master-pieces. Thus the world gained a second *Sense and Sensibility* by Joanna Trol-lope, a new *Northanger Abbey* (spoof of a spoof?) by Val McDermid, a revi-sioned *Emma* by Alexander McCall Smith, and another *Pride and Prejudice* by Curtis Sittenfeld. As the respected critic Robert McCrum commented of the McDermid book, it showed "every sign of a professional writer putting her foot to the floor in first gear".

A more traditional means of promoting books—entering them for prizes—was as effective a method as ever. The Man Booker Prize for Fiction written in the Eng-lish language underwent the most fundamental change in its rules since it was established in 1969, with the admission for the first time of American entries. After much examination of the remit of the Prize, it was decided that its pre-eminent rep-utation internationally would be at risk if its eligibility criteria were restricted to novels from Britain, other parts of the Commonwealth, and Ireland, as hitherto had always been the case. Opening the Prize up not only to work from the United States, but potentially from any nation where English was a language of publish-ing currency, such as the Philippines or Sudan, was opposed by a number of prominent authors in the UK itself, who felt that American writing in particular might swamp everything else. They need not have feared because the final short list of six books had only two by American writers: Joshua Ferris and Karen Joy Fowler. Although the number of entries for the Prize from traditional Common-wealth sources was reduced, the final winner of the Man Booker Prize was, for the second year, from the Antipodes, the brilliant Australian novelist Richard Flana-gan, whose *Narrow Road to the Deep North*, cited by the six judges as a master-piece, was the most popular as well as most respected win for many years. After much cavilling in recent times that the Prize had slightly lost its way, the change of direction in the rules and the quality of the short list were felt to have put it back on track. Indeed, a new award called the Folio Book Prize came into existence in 2014 as a direct response to gathering criticisms of the Man Booker, but, though it made a good choice by honouring the underestimated American writer George Saunders, it was felt by many to have been wrong-footed by the reinvigoration of the older prize.

One of the surprises of the Man Booker lists was the omission of Donna Tartt's best-selling work, *The Goldfinch*, first published in 2013; it garnered much atten-tion elsewhere, however, and won the Pulitzer Prize for fiction. It was possibly the most widely read serious novel of the year. More controversially, Martin Amis, who continued to miss out on the major awards, aroused a lot of interest with *The*

Zone of Interest, a book that tackled the nearly impossible task of humanising the people who ran Auschwitz. Understanding the motivation of those who commit acts of extreme cruelty in the name of the state or a religious idea or a code of honour was arguably one of the imperatives of the year, as news headlines were so often taken up with horrific stories of fanatical executions and terrorist attacks in many parts of the world. Just as *Narrow Road to the Deep North* explored the psyche and obligations of the commandants of the Japanese prisoner of war camps in the Second World War, so Amis looked at Nazi behaviour in the same period. His attempts to blend moral comment with documentary accuracy and a measure of comedy misfired, though his ambition was worthy.

Chimamanda Ngozi Adichie was felt to have more than fulfilled her promise as a much lauded young writer with *Americanah*, a story linking Africa and the US. Ali Smith's *How To Be Both* was shortlisted for several awards, though missed out on the principal ones. It was, however, recognised as a complex work on the nature of aesthetic appreciation, set in two time zones and remarkably wise about grief, youth and gender. Other established novelists who were felt to have written at the top of their game were Peter Carey, Rachel Cusk, Dave Eggers, Richard Ford, Siri Hustvedt, Ian McEwan, Joseph O'Neill, Marilynne Robinson (completing her *Gilead* trilogy), Colm Tóibín, Christos Tsiolkas, Sarah Waters and Tim Winton.

As always, much of the excitement in the literary year lay with identifying possible "big names" of the future. Jessie Burton with *The Miniaturist* sold hugely for a first-time novelist, getting fully into the private life behind closed doors of a house in Amsterdam, imaginatively blending an intriguing interiority with an international perspective. Yvonne Owuor and Zia Haider Rahman were two new Commonwealth writers of distinction, and Neel Mukherjee was seen as joining the pantheon of brilliant Indian talents with *The Lives of Others*, which certainly had the most harrowing opening section of any book in the year: a man driven by poverty to slaughter his wife and children before killing himself. It was deservedly shortlisted for the Man Booker Prize.

In the popular as opposed to literary press, Hilary Mantel, who in 2014 was given the high national honour of a damehood, aroused outraged condemnation for the title story of a new collection called *The Assassination of Margaret Thatcher*. Literalists failed to acknowledge either the imaginative adventure or the incipient satire of the tale. Less controversially, Mantel had a brilliant year with her two Man Booker Prize-winning novels, *Wolf Hall* and *Bring Up the Bodies*, not only continuing to sell well but dramatised both for the stage by the Royal Shakespeare Company, with successful seasons in Stratford-upon-Avon and the West End of London, and for television in a series due for screening in 2015. Perhaps not since the era of Charles Dickens had contemporary successes in novel form been so immediately transposed into other media.

The Nobel Prize for Literature went to a prominent French novelist, Patrick Modiano. Beloved in his own country, he was little known elsewhere but there was general acceptance that he was a worthy winner whose fiction deserved to be better known. His subject matter was very often the influence of memory on individual conduct.

It was a strong year for poetry. John Burnside confirmed his major talent with his collection *All One Breath*. Equally proficient as a novelist, Burnside won awards and was increasingly seen as the major Scottish writer of the day, following the death in 2013 of Iain Banks. Simon Armitage extended his range with a staged play at the Globe Theatre in London on the theme of the last days of Troy. Lavinia Greenlaw's *A Double Sorrow* provided a new take on Chaucer's *Troilus and Criseyde*. Hugo Williams was thought to have produced his best poems in years in *I Knew the Bride* and there was much admiration for Michael Longley's *The Stairwell*, produced late in his career but on a par with his best work. Sadly two collections, those of Dannie Abse and Sebastian Barker, were to be their last, as both writers died. Both left behind a formidable body of poetic achievement.

In the field of biography Andrew Roberts's approving revaluation of Napoleon made a big impact. Hillary Rodham Clinton wrote an autobiography, *Hard Choices*, which cynics thought was geared to a likely presidential bid, though by common agreement it was not comparable to the memoir, *Dreams from My Father*, which Barack Obama had published at an equivalent time prior to his election to the supreme office. John Lahr was thought to have done Tennessee Williams proud with his biography, luridly sub-titled *Mad Pilgrimage of the Flesh*. Of books on royalty, always a popular genre, A.N. Wilson's new life of Queen Victoria was the best regarded.

The year saw the death of many outstanding writers, in addition to Abse and Barker. P.D. James was considered the best British crime writer since Agatha Christie, whose conventions she subtly subverted. Baroness James of Holland Park, as she became, was a great public servant as well as a writer who converted genre into literature. Her occasional departures from a contemporary crime format, notably in her final novel *Death Comes to Pemberley*, where she almost trumped Jane Austen in elegant nuance, or in *The Children of Men*, where she surmised a world which had lost the ability to procreate, were in their way imaginative masterpieces.

Two giants of contemporary writing, both Nobel laureates, also died: South Africa's Nadine Gordimer and Colombia's Gabriel Garcia Márquez. Gordimer's liberal advocacy in the era of apartheid was massively influential politically. It almost outshone her literary distinction, but generations to come will most likely read her novels and short stories as humane dissections of inter-racial relationships. Márquez was one of the major authors of the two centuries in which he lived. His *Love in the Time of Cholera* was a defining book of its time, helping to establish "magic realism" as a key post-modernist critical term.

The most prominent American author to die in 2014 was Maya Angelou. Known as much for the colourfulness of her life as for her often autobiographical writing, she had inspired more than one generation with her uncompromising determination that women, and particularly black women, should be given the same opportunities as men, and particularly white men. She was one of the iconic figures of her age.

Other major authors on the world stage whose deaths were reported included Canadian writer Mavis Gallant, Indo-Pakistani Khushwant Singh, and American

Amiri Baraka, previously known as LeRoi Jones. In Britain two of the most criti-cally influential intellectuals of the second half of the 20th century, Richard Hog-gart and Karl Miller, also died.

(See Obituary for P.D. James, Nadine Gordimer, Gabriel Garcia Márquez, Maya Angelou and Richard Hoggart).

There was much debate throughout the year as to whether young people in the Western world were turning away from reading. Book sales, despite the competi-tion of electronic delivery, were not notably down. It was not only book groups and literary festivals that flourished, but creative writing courses in universities bur-geoned. Whether, however, people under 25 had caught the reading habit was a matter of great concern to older people. It will be some years hence before we know the true impact on reading of increasing addiction to portable technology. Governments were aware of the issue, but whether they, or the media, or parents, had any solutions was still to be seen.

Alastair Niven

Among the publications which made a mark in 2014 were:

FICTION. Chimamanda Ngozi Adichie, *Americanah* (Fourth Estate); Martin Amis, *The Zone of Interest* (Cape); Greg Baxter, *Munich Airport* (Penguin); John Boyne, *A History of Loneliness* (Doubleday); Jessie Burton, *The Miniaturist* (Picador); Peter Carey, *Amne-sia* (Faber); Teju Cole, *Every Day is for the Thief* (Faber); Michal Cunningham, *The Snow Queen* (Fourth Estate); Rachel Cusk, *Outline* (Faber); Lydia Davis, *Can't and Won't* (Hamish Hamilton); Emma Donoghue, *Frog Music* (Picador); E.L. Doctorow, *Andrew's Brain* (Random House); Helen Dunmore, *The Lie* (Hutchinson); Dave Eggers, *The Circle* (Penguin); Michel Faber, *The Book of Strange New Things* (Canongate); Joshua Ferris, *To Rise Again at a Decent Hour* (Viking); Richard Flanagan, *The Narrow Road to the Deep North* (Chatto & Windus); Richard Ford, *Let Me Be Frank With You* (Bloomsbury); Adam Foulds, *In the Wolf's Mouth* (Cape); Damon Galgut, *Arctic Summer* (Atlantic); David Gilbert, *& Sons* (Fourth Estate); Niven Govinden, *All the Days and Nights* (The Friday Project); David Grossman, *Falling Out of Time* (Cape); Romesh Gunesekera, *Noontide* Tol (Granta); Philip Hensher, *The Emperor Waltz* (Fourth Estate); Siri Hustvedt, *The Blazing World* (Sceptre); Howard Jacobson, *J* (Cape); Cynan Jones, *The Dig* (Granta); A.L. Kennedy, *All the Rage* (Cape); Hanif Kureishi, *The Last Word* (Faber); Jonathan Lethem, *Dissident Gardens* (Cape); Paul Lynch, *The Black Snow* (Quercus); Audrey Magee, *The Undertaking* (Atlantic); Hilary Mantel, *The Assassination of Margaret Thatcher* (Fourth Estate); Ben Marcus, *Leaving the Sea* (Granta); Valerie Martin, *The Ghost of the Marie Celeste* (Weidenfeld & Nicholson); Peter Matthiessen, *In Paradise* (Oneworld); Armistead Maupin, *The Days of Anna Madrigal* (Doubleday); Ian McEwan, *The Children Act* (Cape); Darragh McKeon, *All That is Solid Melts into Air* (Viking); Dinaw Mengestu, *All Our Names* (Sceptre); Susan Minot, *Thirty Girls* (Fourth Estate); David Mitchell, *The Bone Clocks* (Sceptre); Lorrie Moore, *Bark* (Faber); Neel Mukherjee, *The Lives of Others* (Chatto & Windus); Haruki Murakami, trans. Philip Gabriel, *Colourless Tsukuru and His Years of Pilgrimage* (Harvill Secker); Okey Ndibe, *Foreign Gods, Inc* (Soho Press); David Nicholls, *Us* (Hodder & Stoughton); Joseph O'Neill, *The Dog* (Fourth Estate); Yvonne Owuor, *Dust* (Granta); David Park, *The Poets' Wives* (Bloomsbury); Glenn Patterson, *The*

Rest Just Follows (Faber); Georges Perec, trans. David Bellos, *Portrait of a Man* (MacLehose); Kate Pullinger, *Landing Gear* (self-published ebook); Zia Haider Rahman, *In the Light of What We Know* (Picador); Marilynne Robinson, *Lila* (Virago); Donal Ryan, *The Thing About December* (Doubleday Ireland); José Saramago, trans. Margaret Jull Costa, *Skylight* (Harvill Secker); Ali Smith, *How To Be Both* (Hamish Hamilton); Graham Swift, *England and Other Stories* (Simon and Schuster); Bilal Tanweer, *The Scatter Here is Too Great* (Cape); Colm Tóibín, *Nora Webster* (Viking); Christos Tsiolkas, *Barracuda* (Atlantic); Sarah Waters, *The Paying Guests* (Virago); Tim Winton, *Eyrie* (Picador); Gerard Woodward, *Vanishing* (Picador).

POETRY. Dannie Abse, *Ask the Moon* (Hutchinson); Simon Armitage, *Paper Aeroplane: Selected Poems 1989-2014* (Faber); Sebastian Barker, *The Land of Gold* (Enitharmon Press); Fiona Benson, *Bright Travellers* (Cape); Rachel Boast, *Pilgrim's Flower* (Picador); John Burnside, *All One Breath* (Cape); Niall Campbell, *Hebridean Moonlight* (Bloodaxe); David Constantine, *Elder* (Bloodaxe); Carol Ann Duffy, with art work by Stephen Raw, *Ritual Lighting: Laureate Poems* (Picador); Paul Farley, *Selected Poems* (Picador); Louise Gluck, *Faithful and Virtuous Night* (Carcanet); Lavinia Greenlaw, *A Double Sorrow* (Faber); David Harsent, *Fire Songs* (Faber); Mimi Khalvati, *The Weather Wheel* (Carcanet); August Kleinzahler, *The Hotel Oneira* (Faber); Michael Longley, *The Stairwell* (Cape); Thomas Lux, *Selected Poems* (Bloodaxe); Bill Manhire, *Selected Poems* (Carcanet); Kevin Powers, *Letter Composed During a Lull in the Fighting* (Sceptre); Robin Robertson, *Sailing the Forest* (Picador); Karen Solie, *The Living Option: Selected Poems* (Bloodaxe); Rosemary Tonks, *Bedouin of the London Evening* (Bloodaxe); Hugo Williams, *I Knew the Bride* (Faber); Rowan Williams, *The Poems of Rowan Williams* (Carcanet).

BIOGRAPHY AND AUTOBIOGRAPHY. Anita Anand, *Sophia: Princess, Suffragette, Revolutionary* (Bloomsbury); Scott Anderson, *Lawrence in Arabia: War, Deceit, Imperial Folly and the Making of the Modern Middle East* (Atlantic); Adam Begley, *Updike* (HarperCollins); James Booth, *Philip Larkin: Life, Art and Love* (Bloomsbury); Tracy Borman, *Thomas Cromwell: The Untold Story of Henry VIII's Most Faithful Servant* (Hodder & Stoughton; John Campbell, *Roy Jenkins: A Well-Rounded Life* (Cape); David Cannadine, *George V: The Unexpected King* (Allen Lane); Helen Castor, *Joan of Arc: A History* (Faber); Hillary Rodham Clinton, *Hard Choices* (Simon and Schuster); Guy Cuthbertson, *Wilfred Owen* (Yale); Dan Davies, *In Plain Sight: The Life and Lies of Jimmy Savile* (Quercus); Jonathan Fenby, *The General: Charles de Gaulle and the France He Saved* (Simon and Schuster); Lyndall Gordon, *Divided Lives: Dreams of a Mother and Daughter* (Virago); John Guy, *Henry VIII: The Quest for Fame* (Allen Lane); Lucinda Hawksley, *The Mystery of Princess Louise: Queen Victoria's Rebellious Daughter* (Chatto & Windus); Mark Kishlansky, *Charles I: An Abbreviated Life* (Allen Lane); John Lahr, *Tennessee Williams: Mad Pilgrimage of the Flesh* (Bloomsbury); Richard Mabey, *Dreams of the Good Life: The Life of Flora Thompson and the Creation of Lark Rise to Candleford* (Allen Lane); Helen Macdonald, *H is for Hawk* (Cape); Ben MacIntyre, *A Spy Among Friends: Kim Philby and the Great Betrayal* (Bloomsbury); Patrick McGuinness, *Other People's Countries: A Journey into Memory* (Cape); Barry Miles, *Call Me Burroughs: A Life* (Twelve); Stephen Parker, *Bertolt Brecht: A Literary Life* (Bloomsbury); Claudia Roth Pierpont, *Roth Unbound: A Writer and His Books* (Cape); Helen Rappaport, *Four Sisters: The Lost Lives of the Romanov Grand Duchesses* (Macmillan); Andrew Roberts, *Napoleon the Great* (Allen Lane); Anthony Sattin, *Young Lawrence: Portrait of the Legend as a Young Man* (John

Murray); Daniel Schreiber, *Susan Sontag* (Northwestern UP); Michael Smith, *Shackleton* (Oneworld); Boel Westin, trans. Silvester Mazzarella, *Tove Jansson: Life, Art, Words* (Sort of Books); Edmund White, *Inside a Pearl: My Years in Paris* (Bloomsbury); A.N. Wilson, *Victoria: A Life* (Atlantic); Michael Zantovsky, *Havel: A Life* (Grove Atlantic); Philip Ziegler, *George VI: The Dutiful King* (Allen Lane).

GENERAL. Lisa Appignanesi, *Trials of Passion: Crimes in the Name of Love and Madness* (Virago); Sybille Bedford, *Pleasures and Landscapes* (Daunt Books); Jessie Childs, *God's Traitors: Terror and Faith in Elizabethan England* (Bodley Head); Linda Colley, *Acts of Union, Acts of Disunion*(Profile); Peter Conrad, *How the World Was Won: The Americanization of Everywhere* (Thames & Hudson); Terry Eagleton, *Culture and the Death of God* (Yale); Irving Finkel, *The Ark Before Noah: Decoding the Story of the Flood* (Hodder & Stoughton); Christopher Frayling, *The Yellow Peril: Dr Fu Manchu and the Rise of Chinaphobia* (Thames & Hudson); Frank Furedi, *First World War: Still No End in Sight* (Bloomsbury); Glenn Greenwald, *No Place to Hide: Edward Snowden, the NSA and the Surveillance State* (Hamish Hamilton); Nick Groom, *The Seasons: An Elegy for the Passing of the Year* (Atlantic); James Hall, *The Self-Portrait: A Cultural History* (Thames & Hudson); Walter Isaacson, *The Innovators: How a Group of Inventors, Hackers, Geniuses and Geeks Created the Digital Revolution* (Simon and Schuster); Naomi Klein, *This Changes Everything* (Allen Lane); Tom Lawson, *The Last Man: A British Genocide in Tasmania* (Tauris); Andro Linklater, *Owning the Earth: The Transforming History of Land Ownership* (Bloomsbury); Neil MacGregor, *Germany: Memories of a Nation* (Allen Lane); Justin Marozzi, *Baghdad: City of Peace, City of Blood* (Allen Lane); Richard Overy, *The Bombing War: Europe 1939-45*(Allen Lane); Philip Parker, *The Northmen's Fury: A History of the Viking World* (Doubleday); Nikil Saval, *Cubed: A Secret of the Workplace* (Doubleday); Muriel Spark, ed. Penelope Jardine, *The Golden Fleece*: *Essays* (Carcanet); Charles Spencer, *Killers of the King: The Men Who Dared to Execute Charles I* (Bloomsbury); Jon Tonks, *Empire* (Dewi Lewis); Adam Tooze, *The Deluge: The Great War and the Remaking of the Global Order 1916-1931* (Allen Lane); Marina Warner, *Once Upon a Time: A Short History of the Fairy Tale* (O.U.P.).

XVII SPORT

ASSOCIATION FOOTBALL Fears that the World Cup in Brazil might not live up to expectations were allayed as the country staged a memorable tournament. Civil unrest had troubled the dress rehearsal event, the 2013 Confederations Cup, and there were concerns about delays in finishing work on the stadiums, but the competition ran smoothly. Exciting new players emerged from unlikely countries and some traditional powerhouses made early exits. Ultimately, however, two heavyweights contested the final, Germany edging out Argentina.

The early stages were a triumph for many less heralded teams. Costa Rica and Uruguay qualified at the expense of England and Italy. Colombia, Chile, Algeria and the USA also reached the knock-out phase, while Spain, Russia and Portugal were among those that fell at the first hurdle. England were knocked out at the group stage for the first time for 56 years. Roy Hodgson's team were beaten 2-1 by Italy in their opening match and lost by the same margin to Uruguay, for whom Luis Suarez scored twice. Even before their concluding goalless draw against Costa Rica, England knew they would be on their way home. Suarez bit the shoulder of Italy's Giorgio Chellini in Uruguay's final group match and was subsequently banned from football for the next four months.

Brazil kicked off the tournament with a 3-1 victory over Croatia, with Neymar scoring twice, but their limitations had been evident in a goalless draw with Mexico. In the second round they needed penalties to beat Chile. The hosts reached the semi-finals with a 2-1 victory over Colombia, but Neymar was carried off on a stretcher with a back injury and missed the rest of the tournament. The semi-finals produced arguably the most remarkable match in World Cup history as Germany beat Brazil 7-1. It was Brazil's first home defeat in a competitive match for 39 years. Brazil's woes were compounded when they were beaten 3-0 by the Netherlands in the play-off for third place.

Argentina reached the final by beating the Netherlands on penalties after a goalless draw and extra time. The final was goalless until Mario Götze scored the winner after 113 minutes. Argentina scorned several chances, but Germany deserved their fourth World Cup triumph. Joachim Löw, the coach, and Philipp Lahm, the captain, exemplified the team's all-round excellence in technique, organisation and tactics. Argentina's Lionel Messi was named player of the tournament.

FIFA's decision to award the 2018 and 2022 World Cups to Russia and Qatar, respectively, continued to cause controversy. The world governing body commissioned a report into possible corruption in the bidding process but refused to publish its findings in full. Michael J Garcia, FIFA's chief investigator, resigned in protest.

Qualifying began for the 2016 European Championship. England won their first four matches, while Scotland, the Republic of Ireland, Northern Ireland and Wales all ended the year well placed to qualify. San Marino ended a run of 61 straight defeats when they held Estonia to a goalless draw.

Manchester City, coached by Manuel Pellegrini, won the Premier League title for the second time in three years. Liverpool finished second and would have won the title but for some late slip-ups. Manchester United dismissed David Moyes, the successor to Sir Alex Ferguson as manager, before the end of his first season. Louis van Gaal replaced him. In the summer Manchester United broke the British transfer record by signing Angel di Maria from Real Madrid for £59.7 million. Arsenal won the FA Cup final, coming from behind to beat Hull City 3-2. Manchester City won the League Cup final, beating Sunderland 3-1. Arsenal, Manchester City and Chelsea all reached the knock-out stage of the 2014-15 Champions League.

Real Madrid won the Champions League, beating Atletico Madrid 4-1 in the final in Lisbon. Atletico led until Sergio Ramos equalised in the 90th minute. Sevilla won the Europa League, beating Benfica 4-2 on penalties after the final had finished goalless after extra time. Barcelona were banned by FIFA from signing any players for two transfer windows after being accused of not complying fully with rules over the signings of some of their most promising young recruits. Meanwhile nine clubs in Europe were found guilty of breaches of UEFA's Financial Fair Play rules.

Neil Lennon resigned as manager of Celtic after leading the club to three successive Scottish Premiership titles. St Johnstone claimed the first major trophy in their 130-year history when they beat Dundee United 2-0 in the final of the Scottish Cup. Aberdeen beat Inverness Caledonian Thistle on penalties to win the Scottish League Cup after the final had finished goalless. Liverpool retained their Women's Super League title while Arsenal won the Women's FA Cup for the second successive year by beating Everton 2-0 in the final.

WINTER OLYMPICS AND WINTER PARALYMPICS   Russia's determination to erase the memory of its worst ever Winter Olympics in Vancouver in 2010 was rewarded by a hugely successful Games in the Black Sea resort of Sochi. In the build-up there had been much publicity about the Russian government's attitude towards homosexuality and other human rights, but a memorable fortnight of competition helped to rewrite the headlines. Most competitors, officials and spectators considered the Games a success, even if some found it strange to walk to some venues in shirt sleeves under a blazing sun.

Russia had finished 11th in the medals table in Vancouver. Athletes were subsequently recruited from other countries, including a short-track skater from South Korea, Ahn Hyun-soo, who went on to win three gold medals, competing as Viktor An. Russia topped the medals table, winning 13 golds, ahead of Norway and Canada. Norway's Ole Einar Bjoerndalen won a record 13th Winter Games medal when he helped his country to the biathlon team mixed relay title. Austria's Matthias Mayer took the men's downhill skiing gold, while the women's gold was shared by Slovenia's Tina Maze and Switzerland's Dominique Gisin as an Olympic ski race finished in a dead-heat for the first time in 78 years. Britain won four medals, equalling the country's best Winter Olympics performance. Lizzy Yarnold won Britain's second successive gold in the skeleton event, while the men's curling team took silver. The British women's curling team won bronze, as did Jenny Jones in the snowboard slopestyle event.

Britain enjoyed their most successful Winter Paralympics, winning six medals, including five in Alpine skiing to go with the wheelchair curling team's bronze. Kelly Gallagher claimed Britain's first gold on snow when she won the Super G for the visually impaired with her guide, Charlotte Evans. The visually impaired skier Jade Etherington and her guide, Caroline Powell, became the most decorated Britons at a single Winter Games when they won three silvers and a bronze.

COMMONWEALTH GAMES The "Friendly Games" built on their reputation as large crowds enjoyed some excellent competition in Glasgow. The Games drew some big names, like Usain Bolt and Sir Bradley Wiggins, but also provided a stage for exciting newcomers like the diminutive gymnast, Claudia Fragapane, who became the first Englishwoman to win four gold medals at a single Commonwealth Games for 84 years.

Bolt competed only in the sprint relay, in which he led Jamaica to gold. The individual 100m gold medal went to another Jamaican, Kemar Bailey-Cole. England won a surprise gold in the 4 x 400m relay as Matt Hudson-Smith held off the Bahamas, the Olympic champions, on the final leg. The English long jumper Greg Rutherford added Commonwealth Games gold to his Olympic gold, while Botswana's Nijel Amos surprised David Rudisha, the Olympic champion, in the 800m. Two Welsh athletes, Gareth Warburton and Rhys Williams, withdrew after failing drugs tests.

Wiggins's attempt to win a first Commonwealth Games gold ended in disappointment when England's team pursuit squad were beaten into second place by Australia. Lizzie Armitstead, who had won silver four years previously and at the London Olympics, won the women's road race, while Geraint Thomas took the men's event. Australia were the most successful team in the swimming pool, winning 19 gold medals, but Ben Proud, aged 19, won two golds, as did another English teenager, Adam Peaty. Fran Halsall also won two golds to take her career total to nine. Ross Murdoch surprised his fellow Scot, Michael Jamieson, to win the 200m breaststroke. South Africa's Chad Le Clos won a record-equalling seven medals. Tom Daley retained his title in the 10m platform diving.

England dominated the gymnastics, winning the men's and women's team events. Max Whitlock and Fragapane added golds in the individual all-round competitions. In rhythmic gymnastics, Frankie Jones of Wales rounded off her career by winning six medals. Australia's women denied England hockey gold by equalising in the last 10 seconds and then winning on penalties. England ended Australia's 28-year run at the top of the medals table. Glasgow also staged 22 Para-Sport medal events, across five different sports. David Weir, six times a Paralympic champion, won his first Commonwealth title in the T54 1500m.

CRICKET The year ended in tragedy when the Australian batsman Phil Hughes died after being struck in the neck by a ball. Hughes, who was wearing a helmet, was hit by a bouncer from Sean Abbott in a Sheffield Shield match. He never regained consciousness. The Australia captain, Michael Clarke, paid a moving tribute at Hughes's funeral.

The sport's attention had also been focused on Australia at the start of the year. The Ashes had already been decided before England lost the Fifth Test to suffer only their third whitewash in 131 years. England finally won their first international match of the tour after 91 days in the fourth one-day international in Adelaide, but lost the series 4-1. Andy Flower, England's head coach, resigned and was eventually replaced by Peter Moores, who had been sacked from the same post in 2009. Within days of Flower's resignation, Kevin Pietersen's international career was ended by the England management and selectors, who considered his influence disruptive. In his autobiography later in the year Pietersen denounced many of his former colleagues, particularly Flower and Matt Prior, the wicketkeeper.

England won a one-day series in the West Indies but lost to the same opponents in a three-match Twenty20 series just before the World Twenty20. Sri Lanka won the World Twenty20 title in Bangladesh, beating India in the final. England lost to New Zealand, beat Sri Lanka but went out after losing to South Africa and the Netherlands. Australia won the women's final, beating England by six wickets.

England began their home summer by losing to Sri Lanka in a one-day series and a two-Test series. In the drawn First Test, 23-year-old Joe Root became the youngest Englishman to score a double century at Lord's, while Gary Ballance scored his maiden Test hundred. On a thrilling final day Sri Lanka avoided defeat when their last batsman, Nuwan Pradeep, survived the final over. Sam Robson and Moeen Ali hit maiden Test centuries in the Second Test at Headingley but could not prevent a 100-run defeat.

England won their summer series against India 3-1 after a remarkable turnaround, Alastair Cook's team having trailed 1-0 after the Second Test. The drawn First Test at Trent Bridge featured two remarkable last-wicket partnerships. Bhuvneshwar Kumar and Mohammed Shami added 111 for India's tenth wicket, but were upstaged when James Anderson and Root shared a last-wicket partnership of 198, a record for Test cricket. India won the Second Test by 95 runs to claim their first victory at Lord's for 28 years. England ended a run of 10 Tests without a victory when they won the Third Test by 266 runs. They won the Fourth Test by an innings and 54 runs and the Fifth by an innings and 244 runs to complete a sequence of three Test wins in 21 days. India won the one-day series that followed. At the end of the year England lost a one-day series in Sri Lanka 7-2.

Graeme Smith, South Africa's captain, announced his retirement after a home series defeat to Australia. New Zealand's Corey Anderson struck the fastest one-day international century off just 36 balls, while India's Rohit Sharma hit the highest one-day international score with 264. Lou Vincent, a former New Zealand Test batsman, was banned for life by the England and Wales Cricket Board after admitting 18 breaches of its anti-corruption regulations covering one match in 2008 with Lancashire and two in 2011 with Sussex. Naved Arif, the former Sussex all-rounder, was also banned for life after an investigation into match-fixing.

Yorkshire won the county championship for the 31st time. Warwickshire were Twenty20 champions, while Durham won the Royal London One-Day Cup, beating Warwickshire in the final. The England women's team won their Ashes series in Australia. England won the only Ashes Test by 61 runs and the first one-day international by seven wickets, but Australia won the next two. England completed their Ashes triumph when they won the first of three Twenty20 matches. England's women completed a fifth successive limited-overs win when they beat South Africa 3-0 in a Twenty20 series in England.

RUGBY Brian O'Driscoll ended his international career in fitting fashion as Ireland won the Six Nations Championship. A dramatic final day began with Ireland, France and England all in with a chance of victory. England won 52-11 in Italy, but Ireland finished ahead on points difference after beating France 22-20 in Paris in O'Driscoll's 141st Test match. A thrilling finale saw France denied a late try on video evidence. It was a closely fought championship from the opening weekend, when France beat England 26-24 thanks to a late try by Gaël Fickou. That was England's only defeat. Stuart Lancaster's team beat Scotland 20-0 at Murrayfield, ended Ireland's hopes of a Grand Slam with a tense victory at Twickenham and beat Wales to win the Triple Crown. Wales beat France in Cardiff, but Italy and Scotland struggled throughout. The only win by either team came when Scotland beat Italy 21-20 with a late drop goal by Duncan Weir.

In the summer England lost all three Tests in New Zealand. The hosts won the First Test 20-15 against an England team without 14 players who played in the Premiership final. New Zealand won the Second Test 28-27, England scoring two late tries. New Zealand won the Third Test 36-13 as Julian Savea scored three tries to take his tally against England to seven in four matches. South Africa won a two-Test series against Wales but needed a late penalty try to win the Second Test 31-30. New Zealand won the southern hemisphere's Rugby Championship, but their 22-match unbeaten run ended with a 27-25 defeat in South Africa.

England began their autumn campaign with narrow defeats to New Zealand and South Africa, but ended a run of five successive defeats by beating Samoa and then Australia. Wales lost 28-33 to Australia despite scoring four tries against the Wallabies for the first time in 39 years. They then stumbled to an unconvincing victory over Fiji before losing to New Zealand and beating South Africa. Ireland demonstrated their growing strength under Joe Schmidt, beating South Africa, Georgia and Australia. Scotland beat Argentina and Tonga but lost to New Zealand.

Jonny Wilkinson retired. He kicked 13 points in Toulon's 23-6 victory over Saracens in the Heineken Cup final in Cardiff in his penultimate match. In his last match Toulon beat Castres 18-10 in the final of the Top 14 in France. Northampton beat Saracens 24-20 in the Premiership final at Twickenham and beat Bath 30-16 to take the Amlin Challenge Cup. Exeter Chiefs won the first major trophy in their 143-year history when they beat Northampton 15-8 in the final of the LV= Cup. England won the Women's World Cup in France, beating Canada 21-9 in the final.

In rugby league, St Helens ended their run of five successive defeats at Old Trafford when they beat Wigan Warriors 14-6 in the Grand Final. Wigan's Ben Flower was sent off for punching and was banned for six months. Leeds Rhinos ended a run of six successive defeats in Challenge Cup finals when they beat Castleford 23-10. Sydney beat Wigan 36-14 in the World Club Challenge. New Zealand won the Four Nations title, beating Australia 22-18 in the final in Wellington.

TENNIS Until 2014 the "Big Four" of men's tennis—Roger Federer, Rafael Nadal, Novak Djokovic and Andy Murray—had won 34 of the previous 35 Grand Slam titles. However, this was the year when the next generation made some break-throughs. Although Stan Wawrinka was 29 when he won the Australian Open, beating an injured Nadal in the final, his achievement inspired younger players. Marin Cilic won the US Open, beating another new face, Kei Nishikori, in the final, and Milos Raonic, Grigor Dimitrov and Ernests Gulbis all reached Grand Slam semi-finals for the first time.

Djokovic reclaimed the world No 1 position when he won Wimbledon for the second time, beating Federer 6-7, 6-4, 7-6, 5-7, 6-4 in a high-quality final. The Serb finished the season by winning the World Tour Finals. Federer made a fine comeback following a frustrating year in 2013. He won more matches (73) than any other player and led Switzerland to their first Davis Cup triumph. Nadal won his ninth French Open, beating Djokovic in the final, but lost to Nick Kyrgios, an Australian teenager, in the fourth round at Wimbledon, missed the US Open with a wrist injury and ended his season early because of appendicitis. Murray rebuilt confidence following back surgery, won three titles in the autumn and became the first Grand Slam champion to appoint a woman (other than a family member) as his coach when Amélie Mauresmo replaced Ivan Lendl. Murray led Britain to their first Davis Cup World Group win for 28 years with a victory over the United States in San Diego.

Serena Williams ended the year as world No 1, though that had appeared unlikely after she lost to Ana Ivanovic in the fourth round in Melbourne, to Gar-bine Muguruza in the second round in Paris, and to Alizé Cornet in the third round at Wimbledon. Order was restored at the US Open, where Williams beat Caroline Wozniacki in the Dane's first Grand Slam final for five years. Williams's 18th Grand Slam title matched the tallies of Chris Evert and Martina Navratilova. Williams also won the season-ending WTA Finals in Singapore. Li Na won the Australian Open, beating Dominika Cibulkova in the final, but retired later in the year because of injury. Maria Sharapova won her second French Open, beating Simona Halep in the Romanian's first Grand Slam final. Petra Kvitova claimed her second Wimbledon title, crushing Eugenie Bouchard, another Grand Slam final debutant, 6-3, 6-0 in the tournament's shortest final for 31 years.

GOLF Rory McIlroy became the first player from the United Kingdom to win back-to-back majors with victories in the Open at Royal Liverpool and the US PGA Championship at Valhalla. McIlroy dominated the Open from the start and led by six strokes after the third round. The final day, nevertheless, was not straightfor-ward after late charges by Sergio Garcia and Rickie Fowler, who eventually fin-ished only two strokes adrift. With nine holes to play in the final round of the US

PGA Championship McIlroy was three shots off the lead, but he overtook Phil Mickelson, Fowler and Henrik Stenson to win by one stroke. Bubba Watson took the Masters for the second time, coming from behind to claim the Green Jacket after Jordan Spieth let slip a two-shot lead in the final round. Germany's Martin Kaymer won the US Open at Pinehurst by eight strokes.

Europe won the Ryder Cup for the fourth time in a row, defeating USA 16.5-11.5 at Gleneagles. Justin Rose was the outstanding European performer, winning three of his five matches and halving the other two. Patrick Reed and Spieth were the best US performers, but too many of their big guns failed to fire. McIlroy said Paul McGinley had been "the most wonderful captain", but there was no such unity in the opposition camp. Mickelson criticised Tom Watson, the US captain, saying he could not understand why the team had strayed from the "winning formula" that Paul Azinger had employed as captain in 2008.

Women's golf featured some remarkable performances by teenagers. Lexi Thompson won the Kraft Nabisco Championship, while another 19-year-old, Kim Hyo-Joo, won the Evian Championship. Lydia Ko, aged 17, claimed the richest prize in LPGA history ($1.5 million) by winning the season-ending CME Group Tour Championship and the order of merit. At 18, Britain's Charley Hull became the youngest woman to top the European order of merit. Michelle Wie secured her first major when she won the US Open, Inbee Park successfully defended her title in the LPGA Championship and Mo Martin won the Women's British Open at Royal Birkdale. However, arguably the year's most significant female victory came when the Royal and Ancient Golf Club of St Andrews voted to admit women members for the first time in its 260-year history.

ATHLETICS   Britain topped the medals table at the European Championships in Zurich, winning 12 golds. Mo Farah won the 5,000m and 10,000m to become the first athlete to win that double at Olympic, world and European level. James Dasaolu won the 100m and Adam Gemili the 200m as Britain took the men's sprint double for the first time for 24 years. Golds were also won by Tiffany Porter (100m hurdles), Jo Pavey (10,000m), Martyn Rooney (400m), Eilidh Child (400m hurdles), Greg Rutherford (long jump) and three relay squads (men's 4 x 100m and 4 x 400m and women's 4 x 100m). France finished second in the medals table and Germany third. France's Mahiedine Mekhissi-Benabbad won the 1500m but was disqualified after winning the 3,000m steeplechase, when he ripped off his shirt in the finishing straight and waved it aloft.

Britain won six medals at the World Indoor Championships at Sopot in Poland. Richard Kilty won the 60m in his first appearance as an individual competitor at a major championships. The men's 4 x 400m relay team and Katarina Johnson-Thompson (long jump) won silver and there were bronzes for Andrew Osagie (800m), Porter (60m hurdles) and the women's 4 x 400m relay squad. Kenya's Wilson Kipsang won his second London Marathon in three years, while Farah became the first British man to win the Great North Run for 29 years.

Asafa Powell, the former 100m world record holder, and Sherone Simpson, his training partner, had 18-month suspensions for doping offences reduced to six months by the Court of Arbitration for Sport. Tyson Gay was banned for a year and forfeited the Olympic silver medal he won as part of the USA's 4 x 100m relay team at the London Olympics after testing positive for an anabolic steroid. Oscar Pistorius, the South African Paralympic and Olympic runner, was sentenced to five years in prison for the manslaughter of his girlfriend, Reeva Steenkamp. Pistorius claimed he had shot her because he believed she was an intruder in his house.

MOTOR SPORT   Formula One thrives on rivalries and the tussle between Lewis Hamilton and his Mercedes team mate, Nico Rosberg, was the central theme of the season. Hamilton claimed his second world title by winning 11 grands prix, but the championship was not decided until the final race. The rivalry came to the fore at the Monaco Grand Prix, where Hamilton suggested that Rosberg might have deliberately ruined his final effort in qualifying by going off the track, bringing out the yellow flags. At the Hungarian Grand Prix Hamilton refused to follow team orders to allow Rosberg to overtake him and in the Belgian Grand Prix the two men collided. Mercedes took unspecified action against Rosberg after he admitted culpability. Rosberg kept his title hopes alive by winning the penultimate grand prix in Brazil. He was faster than Hamilton in qualifying at the concluding race in Abu Dhabi, but the Briton won convincingly as his rival suffered technical problems.

Hamilton had claimed the title once before, in 2008. He was the fourth Briton, after Graham Hill, Jim Clark and Jackie Stewart, to win the world championship more than once and became the most successful British driver when he passed Nigel Mansell's total of 31 wins. He was named the BBC's Sports Personality of the Year. Daniel Ricciardo, who won three races in his first season with Red Bull, was third in the drivers' championship and Williams's Valtteri Bottas fourth. Mercedes won their first constructors' title, while Ferrari failed to win a race for the first time since 1993. The year ended with grave concerns over Jules Bianchi, the Marussia driver, who suffered severe brain injuries after crashing at the Japanese Grand Prix.

Bernie Ecclestone, the chief executive of Formula One and the most powerful figure in the sport, was involved in a remarkable bribery case in Germany. Ecclestone was accused of paying a German banker $44 million to ensure that some shares in Formula One would be sold to his preferred bidder. After months of inconclusive testimony the trial ended when Ecclestone agreed to pay a record sum of €100 million.

France's Sébastien Ogier retained the world rally championship, holding off his Volkswagen team mate, Jari-Matti Latvala. Argentina's Jose Maria Lopez won the world touring car championship. Audi won the Le Mans 24 Hours for the 13th time in 16 years through Benoît Tréluyer, Marcel Fässler and André Lotterer. On two wheels Marc Marquez won a record-breaking 13 races to retain his MotoGP world title ahead of Valentino Rossi. Britain's Tom Sykes failed to take back-to-back World Superbike titles after France's Sylvain Guintoli won both races on the final weekend in Qatar.

CYCLING   Vincenzo Nibali became the seventh Italian to win the Tour de France. The 29-year-old Sicilian benefited from the retirements of Chris Froome and Alberto Contador, who suffered injuries in crashes. Britain's Mark Cavendish also pulled out after crashing on the first day, though his withdrawal did not dampen the spirits of the watching public. The first three days of the race were held in the UK in front of huge crowds, particularly in Yorkshire, which staged the "Grand Départ". The Tour has not been won by a French rider since 1985, but Jean-Christophe Péraud and Thibaut Pinot finished second and third respectively.

Contador won the Vuelta ahead of Froome, while Sir Bradley Wiggins captured a major trophy that had hitherto eluded him when he won the time trial at the world championships in Spain. Britain won five medals at the track world championships in Colombia. The British won gold in the women's team pursuit, while Joana Rowsell took the women's individual pursuit. Laura Trott and Becky James won silver in the omnium and bronze in the keirin respectively. James and Jess Varnish won bronze in the team sprint. Britain's men did not win a medal for the first time since 1998.

BOXING   Floyd Mayweather stretched his unbeaten record to 47 fights when he beat Marcos Maidana for the second time in the year to retain his World Boxing Council (WBC) and World Boxing Association (WBA) welterweight and WBC super-welterweight titles. Wladimir Klitschko retained his four heavyweight world titles with victories over Alex Leapai and Kubrat Pulev.

Carl Froch successfully defended his International Boxing Federation (IBF) and WBA super-middleweight titles when he knocked out his fellow Briton, George Groves, at Wembley. Britain's Kell Brook and Carl Frampton both won world titles. Brook beat Shawn Porter to claim the IBF's welterweight crown while Frampton took the IBF super-bantamweight title when he beat Kiko Martinez. Scotland's Ricky Burns suffered his first defeat in seven years when he lost his World Boxing Organisation (WBO) lightweight title to Terence Crawford.

HORSE RACING   Aidan O'Brien became the first trainer to saddle the Derby winner three years in a row when Australia, ridden by Joseph O'Brien, won at Epsom. Australia also won the Irish Derby and the Juddmonte International at York. The Derby runner-up, Kingston Hill, gave trainer Roger Varian, jockey Andrea Atzeni and owner Paul Smith their first Classic victory in the St Leger. Night of Thunder, ridden by Kieren Fallon, won the 2000 Guineas in Richard Hannon's first Classic as a trainer. Miss France, ridden by Maxime Guyon and trained by André Fabre, won the 1000 Guineas. The trainer John Gosden and jockey Paul Hanagan enjoyed their first victories in the Oaks as Taghrooda triumphed at Epsom. Treve, trained by Criquette Head-Maarek, won the Arc de Triomphe in Paris for the second year in a row. The trainer Philip Fenton was suspended for three years by the Irish Turf Club for possessing steroids and other banned substances.

Richard Hughes was champion jockey on the Flat, while Tony McCoy won his 19th National Hunt title. Barry Geraghty had a fine Cheltenham, riding Jessica Harrington's Jezki to victory in the Champion Hurdle and Jonjo O'Neill's More

Of That to a triumph in the World Hurdle. Lord Windermere, trained by Jim Culloty and ridden by Davy Russell, won the Gold Cup, while Sire De Grugy, trained by Gary Moore and ridden by his son Jamie Moore, won the Queen Mother Champion Chase. Pineau de Re, ridden by Leighton Aspell and trained by Dr Richard Newland, won the Grand National.

MISCELLANEOUS Britain finished second in the medals table at the world rowing championships in Amsterdam behind New Zealand, winning golds in the women's pair, men's four, men's eight and LTA mixed coxed four. Britain went one better at the European championships in Belgrade, topping the medals table with two golds, four silvers and two bronzes. Oxford recorded the biggest winning margin in the Boat Race since 1973 when they beat Cambridge by 11 lengths. British swimmers won 24 medals, including nine golds, to claim their best ever haul at the European Swimming Championships in Berlin. Fran Halsall won three golds and a bronze. Adam Peaty set a world record of 26.62sec in the 50m breaststroke.

Charlotte Dujardin excelled at the World Equestrian Games in Caen. Dujardin and her horse, Valegro, won the individual and freestyle dressage gold medals and helped Britain take the team silver behind Germany. Britain won the team three-day event silver, again behind Germany. Mark Selby won the world snooker championship, beating Ronnie O'Sullivan 18-14 in the final. Michael van Gerwen beat Peter Wright 7-4 to claim the Professional Darts Corporation's World Championship for the first time.

The Seattle Seahawks trounced the Denver Broncos 43-8 in the most one-sided Super Bowl for 21 years. The San Francisco Giants won baseball's World Series for the third time in five years by beating the Kansas City Royals 4-3. The San Antonio Spurs won their fifth National Basketball Association title, beating the Miami Heat 4-1.

Paul Newman

XVIII OBITUARY

Attenborough, Richard (b. 1923), renowned British actor, director, producer and philanthropist. Born into an academic and cultured family in Cambridge, Attenborough attended Wyggeston Grammar School for Boys in Leicester and showed early promise as an actor. He won a scholarship to the Royal Academy of Dramatic Art (RADA) in 1940 and had achieved several notable stage performances prior to joining the RAF. His first film role was a minor but memorable part in Noël Coward's *In Which We Serve* (1942), where he played a cowardly stoker who deserts his post. It was the first of some 65 film roles during his long career. He received great acclaim for his portrayal as the small-time and deeply psychotic gangster, Pinkie, in *Brighton Rock* (1947), an adaptation of Graham Greene's memorably disturbing novel. He also continued to make stage appearances, including as an original cast member of Agatha Christie's *The Mousetrap*, which opened in the West End in 1952 and went on to become the world's longest running play. Other memorable film performances came in *The Great Escape* (1963), his first Hollywood success; *The Flight of the Phoenix* (1965); and, most chillingly, as the serial killer Christie in *10 Rillington Place* (1971). From the 1960s he also produced films and in 1969 made his directorial debut with an artistically innovative adaptation of the World War I satirical musical *Oh! What a Lovely War*. He was to direct a further 11 movies including *Young Winston* (1972); *A Bridge Too Far* (1977), a star-studded epic about the ill-conceived Arnhem wartime air assault; and *Cry Freedom* (1987), a powerful anti-apartheid account of the life of Steve Biko. During the 1980s he was finally also able to realise an 18-year ambition to produce and direct a biography of the life of India's most famous son. *Ghandi* (1982), starring Ben Kingsley as the eponymous hero, was filmed on an epic scale and used over 300,000 extras. It proved a major critical and commercial success, winning eight Academy Awards, including those for best film, best director and best leading actor. Although Attenborough continued to produce and direct movies until 2007, his final two decades were taken up increasingly by his work for a vast range of professional bodies and charities in the fields of arts, education and health, and towards the end of his life he suffered from ill health. He received many honours during his lifetime including a CBE (1967), a knighthood (1976), and a life peerage (1993), after which he sat on the Labour benches as Baron Attenborough of Richmond upon Thames. Died 24 August.

Angelou, Maya (b. 1928), US writer, poet, feminist and civil rights campaigner. Born as Marguerite Annie Johnson in St Louis, Missouri, her parent separated whilst she was an infant. At the age of eight she was raped by her mother's boyfriend and his subsequent murder traumatised her to such an extent that she stopped speaking for five years. Reading the work of great authors aloud was later prescribed as a form of therapy, which also had the effect of giving her a love of the rhythm of language. Difficult teenage years culminated in the birth of a son when she was only 17, but afterwards she achieved success as a professional calypso dancer, adopting the name Maya Angelou. In the early 1960s she moved to Africa with a lover and then spent several years on the continent working as a journalist and exploring her black heritage. She returned to the USA in 1965 where, as a close friend of Malcolm X, she was increasingly involved in the civil rights struggle. Encouraged by the writer James Baldwin, Angelou wrote a first volume of autobiography, *I Know Why the Caged Bird Sings* (1969), which won her international recognition for its vivid portrayal of her childhood set against the racial segregation of the American South. In the years that followed she wrote a torrent of songs, musical scores, screen plays, poetry, articles and short stories, whilst also trying her hand at acting, directing, producing and working as a professor of literature at a university in North Carolina. She also wrote further volumes of autobiography—*Gather Together in My Name* (1974); *Singin' and Swingin' and Gettin' Merry Like Christmas* (1976); *The Heart of a Woman*

(1981); *All God's Children Need Travelling Shoes* (1986); *A Song Flung Up to Heaven* (2002);and *Mom & Me & Mom* (2013)— although none received the same acclaim as her first volume. From the 1990s Angelou was a regular on the literary and lecture circuits, where her imposing frame and expressive voice imbued her recitations with a resonant power. In 1993 she received wide publicity when she was invited to write and recite a poem for the inauguration of President Bill Clinton, and in 2011 she was awarded the Presidential Medal of Freedom by President Obama. Died 28 May.

Bacall, Lauren (b. 1924), US actress renowned for her sultry looks and husky voice. Born as Betty Joan Perske to Jewish parents in New York, Bacall adopted the family name of her mother, by whom she was raised after her parents divorced. She received an expensive education courtesy of a rich uncle and made her acting debut in 1942, at the age of 17, with a minor role in a Broadway play. Her striking good looks also made her a teenage fashion model, and she appeared on the cover of *Harper's Bazaar* in March 1943. As a result of that image, she was signed up as an actress by Hollywood film director Howard Hawks who changed her name to Lauren, and whose wife coached her in style, manners, taste. A vocal coach was also used to lower the pitch of her voice, transforming it from nasal drawl to her trademark smoky purr. Her film debut was alongside Humphrey Bogart in *To Have and Have Not* (1944), where her nervousness caused her to lower her chin against her chest and tilt her eyes upwards towards the camera, creating what became known as "that look". The film catapulted her into instant stardom and set a personal style which was to forever define her public image. She married Bogart, who was 25 years her senior, in 1945, and collaborated with him in several other successful film noir projects: *The Big Sleep* (1946), *Dark Passage* (1947), and *Key Largo* (1948). Although she made a number of films in the 1950s, including successes such as *How to Marry a Millionaire* (1953), none achieved the same level of acclaim. Her career took second place to that of her husband and to the demands of the two children she bore him.

She also turned down numerous roles which she considered too insubstantial, thereby acquiring a reputation amongst film-makers of being "difficult". Bogart died in 1957 and shortly afterwards Bacall appeared in her last critically-acclaimed major role in *North West Frontier* (1959). Thereafter her film appearances tended to be cameos, although she played more substantial parts on stage. She also worked in television and was the spokesperson for a number of commercial interests, although she also remained, throughout her life, an outspoken liberal. She received an Honorary Academy Award in 2009 and continued working until shortly before her death. Her final role, appropriately, was a guest voiceover in an episode of the iconoclastic animation *Family Guy* in 2014. Died 12 August.

Benn, Anthony (Tony) Wedgewood, (b. 1925), radical British socialist, veteran Parliamentarian, formidable orator and voluminous diarist. Tony Benn was born in London into a patrician family—both of his grandfathers had been Liberal MPs and his father served in the same capacity before crossing the floor to the Labour Party in 1928. He held ministerial office and in 1942 reluctantly gave up his seat in the House of Commons in order to be raised to the peerage as Viscount Stansgate, a decision that was to have profound consequences for his second son, Tony. The latter was educated at Westminster school and then studied Philosophy, Politics and Economics at New College, Oxford. His education was interrupted by wartime service in the RAF (1943-45), and he graduated in 1948. He entered Parliament at a by-election for Bristol South East, formerly the seat of Sir Stafford Cripps, in November 1950. A centre-left member of the Labour Party, Benn's parliamentary career was threatened in 1960 when his father died and—his elder brother having been killed in 1944—he inherited the family title and was thus disqualified from membership of the House of Commons. He won the resulting by-election in 1961 but was debarred from taking his seat and thereafter fought a tenacious three-year battle for the right to give up his title. Eventually the Peerage Act became law in July 1963 and Benn became the first person to use it to renounce a title. In the following month he won re-election to his seat in the Commons. Benn's struggle—and particularly his harnessing of mass support to enact constitutional change—accelerated his own process of left-wing radicalisation. He served as Postmaster General and then Minister of Technology in the Labour governments of 1964-70, and then, after Labour regained office, as Secretary of State for Industry (1974-75) and Secretary of State for Energy (1975-79). He was increasingly at odds with his ministerial colleagues from the centre-right party establishment, however, particularly over his calls for mass militancy, greater state ownership and more fundamental forms of democratic participation. After Labour's decisive election defeat of 1979 Benn became the standard bearer of the radical Left. Unfettered by office, he advocated a vision of revolutionary socialism derived not from Marxist economic materialism but from a tradition of English radicalism that included non-conformists and dissenters such as the Levellers, the Chartists and the Suffragettes. His efforts contributed to the ongoing polarisation of British party politics and hastened the fracturing of the Labour Party along ideological lines. In September 1981 he contested the deputy leadership of his party, losing by a tiny margin to Dennis Healey. It was to prove the high-water mark of his party career as his popular appeal was undermined by the triumph of Thatcherite conservatism in the 1980s and a ruthless campaign of personal vilification undertaken by the press. Benn was defeated in the 1983 general election (contesting an alternative Bristol seat after Bristol South East had been abolished by boundary changes) and by the time that he returned at a by-election (in Chesterfield, in 1984), Neil Kinnock had replaced Michael Foot as Labour leader. Kinnock began the long process of moving the party to the Right, a process that deracinated Labour's radical roots and culminated in the ideologically-shriven return to government of "New Labour", under Tony Blair, in 1997. Amidst the change, Benn remained true to his radical vision, advocating a range of unfashionable but humanitarian causes, and retaining the respect of those who believed that politics should amount to more than the sum of opinion polls and the wisdom of spin doctors. Even those

who disagreed with his views recognised his sincerity and acknowledged his principled endorsement of Parliament's role as a check on executive power and his refusal to denigrate the character of his opponents. As the tide of passing years drew him further from the possibility of exercising power his image softened, evolving from dangerous demagogue to national institution, instantly recognisable by his distinctive voice, dry humour, and fondness for a mug of tea and his pipe. Marginalised within the Westminster establishment, he stood down at the 2001 general election "in order to spend more time on politics". Thereafter, for the remainder of his life he gave speeches, wrote books, pamphlets and articles, published volumes of his diaries, and promoted a range of causes, including steadfast opposition to the "imperialist" wars in Iraq and Afghanistan. Died 14 March.

Bradlee, Ben (b. 1921), US journalist who, as executive editor of the *Washington Post*, broke the Watergate scandal which brought down President Nixon. Bradlee was born into a patrician family in Boston and as a child contracted polio. He graduated from Harvard in 1942 and, after wartime service in the navy, pursued a career in journalism. He worked as a reporter on the *Washington Post*, served as a press attaché at the US embassy in Paris in 1951, and in 1952 joined the staff of the Office of US Information and Education Exchange (later the US Information Agency), which supplied news stories for use by the CIA. He returned to the US and worked for *Newsweek* before rejoining the *Post* and becoming editor in 1965. Despite his close connections to the intelligence community, Bradlee followed the example of the *New York Times* in 1971 in publishing the "Pentagon Papers", leaked documents which contained embarrassing revelations concerning US policy in Vietnam. Under Bradlee's leadership the *Post* was renowned for its opposition to the Nixon administration. This was spectacularly demonstrated in 1972 when Bradlee supported the investigative efforts of two of the newspaper's junior reporters, Bob Woodward and Carl Bernstein, in their hunch that the mysterious break-in at the Watergate headquarters of the Democratic Party could be traced back to the White House. The story proved to be a sensation and ultimately forced the resignation of Nixon in 1974 and the trial and imprisonment of several of his aides. It also transformed the *Washington Post* from a local to an international newspaper. However, Bradlee also presided over one of the worst scandals involving the newspaper when in 1981 it was shown that a Pulitzer prizewinning article about a black child heroin addict had been concocted by a reporter, Janet Cooke. Although he remained at the paper's helm until his retirement in 1991, and remained involved with it as vice president at large until his death, he was shaken by the disgrace which had emanated from the affair. As late as 2006 he expressed dread that the name of the errant reporter would appear in his obituaries. Bradlee wrote two books about his friend and fellow Harvard alumnus, John F. Kennedy: *That Special Grace* (1964) and *Conversations With Kennedy* (1975). In 2007 he received the French Legion of Honour and in 2013 the US Presidential Medal of Freedom. Died 21 October.

Brady, James (b. 1940), former White House press secretary who became an advocate of gun control after being shot. Brady was born in Centralia, Illinois, and graduated in political science and communications from the University of Illinois in 1962. After teaching and working in public relations in his home state, he moved to Washington, DC, in 1973 where he held a series of appointments in the department of housing, the budget office and the Pentagon. Later, his adroit performance as a press officer for Republican presidential nomination candidate John Connally won him recognition and he was appointed as White House press secretary by the winner of the 1980 presidential contest, Ronald Reagan. His life changed forever on 30 March 1981, however, when he was one of four people (including Reagan) who were shot by John Hinckley outside the Washington Hilton Hotel during an attempted assassination of the president. Brady was the most seriously injured, having been shot in the head, and although he survived he was left partially paralysed with permanent neurological damage. After a long process of rehabilitation Brady and his wife Sarah became high-profile

advocates of gun control, a contentious political issue in a country where the right to bear arms is enshrined within the Constitution. Despite fierce opposition from the powerful gun lobby, the Brady Handgun Violence Prevention Act (widely known as the Brady Law) was eventually passed by Congress and signed into law by President Bill Clinton in February 1994. Although shorn of some of its original provisions, the legislation imposed background checks on those purchasing firearms. Notwithstanding loopholes and subsequent legal challenges, and an ongoing debate over the effectiveness of the law, the legislation has been widely credited with reducing the USA's high incidence of gun violence. Both James and Sarah Brady received a range of honours for their efforts, and in 1996 the former was awarded the Presidential Medal of Freedom. Died 4 August.

Carter, Rubin "Hurricane" (b. 1937), imprisoned US boxer immortalised by Bob Dylan's 1975 protest song *Hurricane*. Born in Clifton, New Jersey, Carter committed numerous juvenile crimes and spent much of his youth in detention. He joined the army in 1954 and began to box, but was discharged after 21 months for disciplinary infractions. He returned to New Jersey and served various terms in prison, culminating in a four-year sentence in 1957 for a series of muggings. He resumed boxing upon his release in 1961, becoming a professional fighter renowned for his ferocious left hook. Although only 5 feet 8 inches tall—shorter than most middleweights—his aggressive style resulted in many knockouts, making him a crowd favourite and earning him the nickname "Hurricane". By 1963 he had established himself as a leading contender for the middleweight title, but in 1964 he lost to the then champion, Joey Giardello, in a title fight in Philadelphia. Carter continued boxing, notching up a career total of 40 fights with 27 wins (19 total knockouts), 12 losses, and one draw. He was a controversial figure, however, within an America still strictly segregated along racial lines. He was outspoken and flamboyant, and was the subject of persistent allegations of violent conduct outside the ring. In the early hours of 17 June, 1966, two black men opened fire in a white bar in

Paterson, New Jersey, killing the bartender and two patrons and grievously wounded a fourth. Carter and a companion were arrested in the vicinity but released after the survivor of the shooting failed to identify them. Four months later, however, they were charged with the murders after being identified by Alfred Bello and Arthur Dexter Bradley who had been trying to burgle a nearby factory at the time of the shooting. The two petty criminals were offered reduced sentences in exchange for their identification of Carter as the murderer, and their testimony was crucial to the all-white jury's conviction of the boxer in 1967. Sentenced to life imprisonment, Carter continued to protest his innocence and whilst incarcerated wrote an autobiography, a copy of which was sent to Bob Dylan who later visited him. Dylan turned Carter's case into an international cause célèbre by writing (together with Jacques Levy) a scorching eight-and-a-half-minute protest song which he recorded and played at a number of benefit concerts. Against the high-energy rhythm of driving guitars and vaulting electric violin, Dylan howled poetic lyrics that flayed the racism of a US justice system which had conspired to wrongfully convict an innocent man. The song was recognised as a brilliant piece of art and was widely played, although it was also criticised for having sanitised Carter's criminal record. Carter was awarded a retrial in 1976, but whilst free was accused of violent and unsavoury conduct which discredited him in the eyes of many of his celebrity supporters. At the new trial the prosecution argued that the 1966 murders had been a racially motivated revenge attack for an earlier shooting at a black bar in Paterson. Although Bradley and Bello had rescinded their original testimony, the latter—who had looted a cash register at the murder scene—then recanted this recantation. Carter was reconvicted and once again sentenced to life in prison. A lengthy appeals process ensued, until a federal judge in 1985 once more quashed the conviction, arguing that there had been "grave constitutional violations" in a prosecution "predicated upon an appeal to racism rather than reason, and concealment rather than disclosure". The authorities chose not to seek a third trial and Carter was released from prison. He moved to Toronto where he spent the remainder of his life campaigning on behalf of wrongfully convicted prisoners, an effort which won him several awards. In 1999 he was the subject of a commercially successful Hollywood movie starring Denzel Washington, but the film was marred by its distortion and falsification of many of the facts in his complex life. In 2011, the year that he was diagnosed with cancer, Carter wrote another autobiography, *Eye of the Hurricane*, which included a foreword by Nelson Mandela. Died 20 April.

Cavendish, Deborah (b. 1920), Dowager Duchess of Devonshire and the last surviving member of the famous Mitford sisters. The youngest of seven children (six of whom were girls) of Lord and Lady Redesdale, Deborah Mitford was born at Asthall Manor, Oxfordshire, and received a patchy education at home. Like her sisters, Deborah inherited the characteristic Mitford accent (including its extraordinary vowel sounds) and the private language which they called "Boudledidge". She did not, however, share their glamour and notoriety—Nancy became a successful novelist; Diana married fascist leader Sir Oswald Mosley; Unity enjoyed a close relationship with Hitler and shot herself upon the outbreak of war; and Jessica, a communist, became a journalist. By contrast, Deborah—who described herself as the slowest and dimmest of the brood—was more mundane, preferring domesticity and country matters to the perils of ideology. She came out as a debutante in 1938 and in 1941 married Lord Andrew Cavendish, the younger son of the 10th Duke of Devonshire. Following the death of his brother in combat in 1944, Cavendish inherited his father's title in 1950, whereupon Deborah became Duchess of Devonshire. Amongst the many properties inherited by the couple was Chatsworth House, a stately pile with 297 rooms (and 397 windows), set in 1,000 acres of the Peak District. The couple lived there from 1959 and Deborah oversaw the huge task of restoring the house, in the process transforming Chatsworth into a business and a (tastefully) branded commodity. By 2013 the house was attracting 644,000 paying visitors per year, many of whom also contributed to the family coffers by purchasing refreshments, souvenirs and produce from the estate. The success of the business, together with the sale of land, other houses, and heirlooms, cleared the crippling debts which had been inherited with the title. It also made Chatsworth a much-emulated model for the creation of a financially self-sustaining stately home. Along the way she endured personal hardship, including three children who died at birth and a husband who struggled with the temptations of young women and alcohol, but in public she maintained an aristocratic insouciance. In addition to showing great flair for managing the Chatsworth business, the Duchess wrote a number of books on the house and estate, as well as on farming (particularly her love of poultry) and cookery. After the death of her husband in 2004, she published a number of private letters, including many between the Mitford sisters, and wrote a memoir, *Wait for Me!... Memories of the Youngest Mitford Sister* (2010). Died 24 September.

Duvalier, Jean-Claude (b. 1951), infamous former dictator of Haiti. Born in Port-au-Prince, Duvalier was the son of François Duvalier, the physician known as "Papa Doc" who ruled Haiti from 1957 to 1971 and whose dictatorial regime was notorious for its violence, corruption, paranoid personality cult, and gross human rights abuses. The young Duvalier led a privileged and indolent life distinguished only by his obesity, a physical characteristic made more marked by the malnourished poverty of the mass of Haiti's population. In 1971 his dying father named him as his successor, and he subsequently succeeded to the post of "president for life", thereby becoming— at the age of 19—the world's youngest president. Nicknamed "Baby Doc", Duvalier performed some ceremonial functions but assiduously ensured that the process of government did not interfere with his playboy lifestyle, preferring to leave administrative matters in the hands of his mother, Simone, and his elder sister, Marie-Denise. Under his presidency there were some cosmetic changes in Haiti's dictatorship and greater support from many Western countries, particularly the USA. The dark heart of Duvalier absolutism remained unaltered, however, and Haiti continued to be the poorest country in the Western hemisphere. In 1980 Duvalier married Michèle Bennett-Pasquet, a prominent representative of Haiti's elite mulatto community which Papa Doc had so ruthlessly subdued. The energetic new First Lady, when not occupied by shopping orgies in Paris, quickly dominated her hapless husband's regime. She exiled her mother-in-law and thereafter appointed and reprimanded ministers, determined policy, and presided over a vast network of corrupt business interests which vastly increased the wealth of her family. She maintained her opulent lifestyle even as food riots gripped the country in 1985 and developed into a wider revolt which the regime's fearsome mechanism of state terror could not subdue. With the US government having withdrawn its support, the Duvaliers fled their palace in February 1986, being flown by the US Air Force to exile in France. They lived in luxury on the $100 million fortune which they had looted from their country, although as a result of their divorce in 1993 Duvalier lost most of his wealth. He eventually returned to Haiti in January 2011 and resumed a luxurious lifestyle in the capital. Although he faced theoretical corruption charges, the combination of a sympathetic president and Haiti's corrupt legal system meant that little action was taken to hold him to account for his crimes. Died 4 October.

Eusébio da Silva Ferreira (b. 1942), widely regarded as the greatest African footballer in the history of the game. Eusébio was born in Lourenço Marques (now Maputo) in Mozambique, which was at the time a Portuguese colony. He grew up in poverty until signing for the local Sporting Clube de Lourenço Marques at the age of 15. Word of his prodigious footballing talent led to him being recruited by Benfica, the champions of Portugal and Europe. Eusébio arrived in Portugal in December 1960 and made his first team debut in June 1961, scoring a hat trick. At the end of that season Benfica retained the European Cup, defeating the mighty Real Madrid, led by the legendary Ferenc Puskas. Eusébio scored twice in the 5-3 victory and at the end of the game Puskas exchanged shirts with him in a gesture that was seen as the anointing of his heir as football's greatest player. In the years that followed Benfica finished as runners up in the European

Cup in 1963, 1965 and 1968. On the last occasion they lost to Manchester United with Eusébio, displaying the gentlemanly conduct which characterised his career, warmly congratulating the English goalkeeper who had saved his shot towards the end of normal time and thus denied Benfica victory. In all, during his 15 years at the club, Eusébio scored an astonishing 473 goals in 440 competitive games, won 11 league titles and five Portuguese cups, was top scorer on seven occasions in the Portuguese league, and won the European Golden Boot twice. At international level he represented Portugal for 12 years, making his debut in 1961 and going on to win 64 caps and score 41 goals. He was the greatest player at the 1966 World Cup in England He scored twice in Portugal's 3-1 victory over the trophy's holders, Brazil, and inspired Portugal's remarkable recovery from 3-0 down against North Korea, scoring four of their five goals. Portugal lost in the semi-finals to England, in a game that the hosts rescheduled at the last moment, forcing the Portuguese team to make a train journey on the night before the match. The English side tightly marked the great man—though he still scored from the penalty spot—and eventually won 2-1. Eusébio wept as he left the pitch, causing the game to be remembered in Portugal as "Jogo das Lágrimas" (the "game of tears"). Portugal finished in third place, the country's best ever World Cup showing, and Eusébio was the tournament's top scorer. But he was never again to grace the World Cup finals. In the mid-1970s he, like many aging football stars, plied his trade in the North American Soccer League. In retirement he lived in Portugal but made frequent trips to Mozambique—by then an independent country—where he always received a hero's welcome. Died 5 January.

Finney, Tom (b. 1922), thought by many to be the greatest all-round English footballer of any era. Finney was born in Preston, a stone's throw away from Deepdale, the ground of Preston North End. It was the club that he was to represent throughout his career. Although a sickly child, he showed early promise as a footballer and was offered a contract by Preston, despite measuring only 4 feet 9 inches in height. His father, however, insisted that he learn a trade and so he signed for Preston as an amateur part-timer whilst at the same time becoming an apprentice plumber, a profession that he continued to practise throughout his sporting career. Finney did eventually turn professional but this coincided with the outbreak of war, for the duration of which normal football was suspended. He was called up in 1942 and served as a tank driver in North Africa and Italy, occasionally finding time to play football in army tournaments. He was demobilised quickly—for plumbers were in demand in post-war Britain—and made his long-delayed debut for Preston on 31 August 1946, the opening day of the post-war football season. It was the first of 473 league and cup appearances for the club in a career that lasted until 1960 and saw him score 210 goals. A left footer with great natural pace and balance, he played principally on the right wing but was capable of shining in any forward position, creating and scoring goals, and in his later years played as a centre forward. In addition to his speed and versatility he possessed immense footballing intelligence, an attribute recognised by Stanley Matthews—the other English footballing giant of the post-war era—when he described Finney as one of only five players in history who, "blessed with awesome talent", could " dictate the pace and course of a game". In 1946 Finney also made his first of 76 appearances for England, during an international career that lasted until 1958 and saw him score a (then) record of 30 goals. He participated in the World Cup finals of 1950, 1954 and 1958, but England did not progress beyond the quarter finals. Neither did Preston win any trophies during the Finney years, with the club finishing as runners-up in league and cup, although Finney did receive the Footballer of the Year award in 1954 and 1957. Amid the financial excess of the modern game it is hard to comprehend the degree to which Finney practised his dazzling skills in an era when even the best footballers earned humble wages. Thus, upon retiring from the game in 1960, he returned to his plumbing business. He also became president of the club that he had served so loyally, and served as a magistrate and chairman of his local health authority. He was knighted in 1998. Died 14 February.

García Márquez, Gabriel (b. 1927), Colombian novelist and journalist who won the Nobel Prize. He was born in the small town of Aracataca and was subsequently educated in Bogotá, where he unhappily studied law before abandoning it at the age of 20 to pursue his ambition to write. Whilst writing fiction in his spare time he worked as a successful journalist whose willingness to seek the truth sometimes made him unpopular with the authorities. He also lived in Venezuela and in Europe before settling in Mexico in 1961. His first novel, *Leaf Storm* (*La Hojarasca*), had been published in 1955 and by the mid-1960s he had established a critical, although not a hugely popular, reputation. His profile was raised massively by his fourth novel, *One Hundred Years of Solitude* (1967), a multi-generational family saga which sold more than 30 million copies. It combined fact and fantasy and became hugely influential in establishing the success of magical realism as a major literary genre within Latin American writing. Financially secure at last, García Márquez returned to live in Europe as something of a literary celebrity. He enjoyed a wide circle of friends, including Cuban president Fidel Castro, and was an outspoken opponent of US imperialism and the right-wing dictatorships which cursed his native sub-continent. He built on his literary success with further critically acclaimed novels: *The Autumn of the Patriarch* (1975); *Love in the Time of Cholera* (1985); *The General in His Labyrinth* (1989); and *Of Love and Other Demons* (1994). He also wrote novellas including *Chronicle of a Death Foretold* (1981), and a range of non-fiction. His work was characterised by verve and imagination but also by great tenderness and compassion. Throughout his life he remained a socialist and was true to his belief that writers had a duty to speak out boldly on political issues, but he never allowed his work to be diminished through becoming a vehicle for ideological propaganda. In 1982 García Márquez became the first Colombian to receive the Nobel Prize in Literature, accepting it with characteristic modesty as an award to Latin American literature as a whole. Died 17 April.

Gordimer, Nadine (b. 1923), South African anti-apartheid activist and writer who won the Nobel Prize. Gordimer was born near the small mining town of Springs, in East Rand, the child of secular Jewish immigrant parents. Initially she was educated at a Catholic school before her mother removed her, "for strange reasons of her own", after which she was schooled at home. She read voraciously and began writing at an early age, publishing children's stories in 1937 and then, at the age of 16, her first adult fiction. She studied at the University of Witwatersrand for a year, making her first friendships which transcended the "colour bar", and then moved to Johannesburg in 1948 where she remained for life. During the following years she wrote numerous short stories for South African and, later, international, literary magazines, including, from 1951, the *New Yorker*. During her long career she wrote several hundred short stories, publishing a number of critically acclaimed collections including *Not for Publication* (1965); *Livingstone's Companions* (1971); *Jump* (1991); *Loot* (2003); and *Life Times* (2011). In addition to her mastery of the short-story genre, she was a prolific novelist. Her first, *The Lying Days* (1953), was semi-autobiographical, and was followed by *A World of Strangers* (1958), *Occasion for Loving* (1963), and *The Late Bourgeois World* (1966), a body of work that quickly established her reputation as an acute observer of the corrupting impact of colonialism. Her later books were more modernist in style—*A Guest of Honour* (1970); *The Conservationist* (1974) (which won the Booker prize); *Burger's Daughter* (1979); *July's People* (1981); *A Sport of Nature* (1987); and *My Son's Story* (1990)—but equally political in scope. Her unflinching opposition to the institutionalised racism of the South African state meant that her books, whist garnering awards in other countries, were often banned or censored at home. Nevertheless, she remained in her country of birth and was courageous in her opposition to apartheid. In addition to exposing its moral bankruptcy through her work, she was also politically active, joining the African National Congress when it was still an illegal organisation and clandestinely assisting its activities. Even after the collapse of apartheid Gordimer remained an outspoken and radical voice with novels such as *The House Gun* (1997); *The Pickup* (2001); *Get a Life* (2005); and *No Time Like the Present* (2012). She dealt with issues such as migration, corruption, inequality and alienation within the newly democratic South Africa. Her fearlessness led to some of her work again being banned, although when she became the country's first winner of the Nobel Prize for Literature in 1991 her reputation was such that she achieved a degree of immunity from the wrath of those in authority who were discomforted by her uncompromising analysis of the impact of public politics upon personal morality. She was showered in international honours and awards but remained, even in old age, an uncompromising radical. Died 13 July.

Hall, Stuart (b. 1932), British campaigner, author and academic who popularised the field of cultural studies. Born in Kingston, Jamaica, Hall attended a prestigious local school and in 1951 won a Rhodes Scholarship to Merton College, Oxford where he obtained an MA in English. After university he worked as a teacher and in the field of adult education and was active in campaigning for a number of left-wing causes including the Campaign for Nuclear Disarmament. Together with several other socialist intellectuals Hall founded the *New Left Review* in 1960, and was its first editor, helping to create its position as one of the world's most influential journals of political science. In 1964 Hall was invited by Richard Hoggart to join the Centre of Contemporary Cultural Studies at Birmingham University and in 1968 he succeeded Hoggart as the Centre's director. In 1979 he joined the Open University as a professor of sociology and over the following decades was also associated closely with the journal *Marxism Today*. He retired from the Open University in 1997, but remained active in range of fields, including serving on the Runnymede Commission on the Future of Multi-Ethnic Britain from 1997 to 2000, and as a Fellow of the British Academy from 2005. Throughout his career Hall published many collaborative books, articles and lectures and made frequent television appearances including as the writer and presenter of a history of the Caribbean. A fine orator and fierce debater, Hall was never one for pettiness or vilification, displaying a personal style that was unfailingly generous and courteous. His was an intellectual Marxism that recognised the failures of the Left's cult of "statism" and its role in inad-

vertently abetting the rise of the "authoritarian populism" of Margaret Thatcher. He was also a great proponent of Gramsci's work on political hegemony and used it to provide intellectual rigour to the sometime amorphous field of cultural studies, the interdisciplinary perspectives of which drew on literary theory, linguistics and cultural anthropology. Died 10 February.

Hoggart, Richard (b. 1918), English author and academic pioneer of cultural studies. Hoggart was born into extreme poverty in Leeds and was orphaned at an early age. He won a scholarship to Cockburn grammar school and in 1936 gained a scholarship to Leeds University and achieved a first class degree in English. After wartime service in the Royal Artillery, he worked as a staff tutor at the University of Hull from 1946 to 1959. It was during this time that he wrote the book for which he would be best known: *The Uses of Literacy: Aspects of Working Class Life* (1957), a study of working class culture and its debasement under the assault from banal mass media and consumerism. The book, which was in many respects deeply prescient, was hailed as a seminal work and became a foundation stone in the rise of cultural studies as an academic discipline. Hoggart rapidly became a significant figure within the loose intellectual association that became known as the New Left. He served as a lecturer in English at the University of Leicester (1959-62), when he also appeared as a decisive defence witness at the *Lady Chatterley* obscenity trial in 1960; professor of English at Birmingham University (1962-67), where he founded the Centre for Contemporary Cultural Studies; assistant director of UNESCO (1971-75); and Warden of Goldsmiths, at the University of London (1976-84). In all he wrote more than a dozen books, edited a number of others, as well as producing pamphlets, reports and reviews. He was also active on innumerable public bodies and committees—including the Arts Council and the Royal Shakespeare Company—especially where he saw an opportunity to make education in general—and literature and the arts in particular—available to the widest possible audience. In his later works he lamented the erosion of moral authority and the rise of "cultural relativism". Died 10 April.

Hogwood, Christopher (b. 1941), British musician, conductor and musicologist who was a leading figure in the movement for the revival of early music. Born in Nottingham, Hogwood went to Pembroke College, Cambridge, in 1960 to study classics and music. It was here that he came under the pioneering influence of figures such as Charles Cudworth, Thurston Dart and Mary Potts. After a post-graduate year in Prague as a British Council scholar, in 1965 he became a joint founder of the Early Music Consort with fellow Pembroke alumnus David Munrow. The ensemble's recordings for BBC period dramas brought success, and Hogwood also enhanced his growing reputation through writing and presenting a music magazine programme on BBC Radio 3. In 1973 he founded his own group, the Academy of Ancient Music (AAM), which specialised in using period instruments to perform Baroque and early Classical music. His interpretations were pioneering and sometimes radical, but were based on painstaking scholarship through which he attempted to return to the music as it had been in its original composition. To this end he corrected publishing errors, evaluated the relevance of later revisions, and attempted to discern the original intentions of a composer. As director of the AAM for over 30 years he eschewed the traditional authoritarianism of conductors, preferring instead an egalitarianism which he characterised as "democracy to the point of anarchy". From the early 1980s he conducted regularly in the USA and from 1986 to 2001 was artistic director of Boston's Handel and Hayden Society. In addition to working as a conductor with numerous orchestras around the world, he continued to record and play using a range of piped and strung instruments. One of his favourites was the clavichord, an instrument much favoured historically by composers because of its expressive qualities. From 1983 he also conducted a range of operas and staged concerts which mixed early music with neo-Baroque and neo-Classical responses by composers such as Casella, Respighi and Stravinsky. He retired as director of the AAM in 2006 but continued his connection as emeritus director. He also continued to work on a range of other projects even though his final years were undermined by ill health. He received numerous honours, including a CBE in 1989, and held a range of academic positions including honorary professor of music at the University of Cambridge. Died 24 September.

Howard, Elizabeth Jane (b. 1923), English novelist acclaimed for her story-telling skills and sharp observation of human character. Born into a privileged family in London, Howard, who was educated at home by a governess, had a difficult and distant relationship with her mother. In 1942 she married the naturalist and war hero Peter Scott, with whom she had her only child, Nicola, in 1943. Her first novel, *The Beautiful Visit* (1950), won the John Llewellyn Rhys Prize in 1951. In the same year she left her husband and daughter and thereafter had a series of clandestine affairs, her lovers including Laurie Lee and Cecil Day-Lewis, both of whose wives were amongst her circle of friends. She continued to write novels, short stories, articles, television and screen plays, as well as editing several anthologies. Howard's output was too often dismissed as "women's fiction", a condescending tag that did not acknowledge her skill in creating narrative tension, depth of character and memorable dialogue. It was true, however, that much of her fiction was set in upper-middle-class English society and reflected the sort of mistaken judgements, misguided passions and tangled relations that so defined her own life. After a brief and unhappy second marriage, Howard enjoyed a long relationship with follow novelist Kingsley Amis, whom she met at the Cheltenham literary festival of 1962. Initially an extra-marital affair, their relationship later became public and the two married in 1965. Whilst running a large and chaotically Bohemian household, and appeasing the often insensitive demands made upon her by Amis, Howard maintained her glamorous and intelligent image. She even found time to write, with notable novels including *Something in Disguise* (1969) and the wryly comic *Getting It Right* (1982). She was also instrumental in fashioning the literary tastes and skills of her indolent teenage stepson, Martin Amis, who later acknowledged her contribution to his distinguished writing career. In 1980 she finally left her controlling husband. Thereafter she lived alone, in reduced circumstances, but achieved literary success with the much acclaimed *Cazalet Chronicle* set in the England of 1937-47. This tetralogy of novels—*The Light Years* (1990), *Marking Time* (1991), *Confusion* (1993) and *Casting Off* (1995)—drew heavily upon her own youthful experience and formed the basis of a successful television series. In 2002 she published a frank autobiography, *Slipstream*, and in 2013 published a fifth Cazalet novel, *All Change*. Died 2 January.

James, P.D. (b. 1920), English writer who specialised in popular crime fiction. Born in Oxford and raised in Cambridge, Phyllis Dorothy James was a bright child but was denied the opportunity of higher education by her father's opposition to education for girls. She married in 1941 and pursued a post-war career as a National Health Service administrator in order to support her family after her husband, a doctor, had returned from wartime service with a serious psychiatric disorder. She began writing in her spare time at the age of 40. Her first novel, *Cover Her Face* (1962), involved a murder in a country house being solved by a gentleman poet-policeman. It was a formula which harked back to the golden age of crime fiction, as epitomised by Agatha Christie. It was also a format which James was to use throughout her prolific literary career, with the exception of *The Children of Men* (1992), a futuristic satire. She claimed not to feel constrained by her adherence to the crime genre and wrote sufficiently well for Kingsley Amis to describe her as "Iris Murdoch with murder". In all she produced 19 novels between 1962 and 2011, many of which were adapted for television. She also wrote several nonfiction books including an autobiography, *Time to Be in Earnest* (1999). She received numerous honours from universities and other institutions and in 1983 was appointed OBE. She served as a governor of the BBC, a magistrate, a member of the board of the British Council, and chairman of the literary advisory panel of the Arts Council. In 1991 she became a Conservative life peer as Lady James of Holland Park. Died 27 November.

Jaruzelski, Wojciech Witold (b. 1923), soldier-politician who was the last leader of the communist regime in Poland. Born in Kurów, in south-

east Poland, into a landed family, Jaruzelski received a Jesuit education. When Poland was invaded in 1939 the family fled to Lithuania but was later deported by the Soviet regime to Siberia. After a period of forced labour, the young Jaruzelski joined a Polish division of the Red Army in 1943 and distinguished himself in action. In 1948 he joined the ruling (communist) Polish United Workers Party and thereafter achieved further army and civil promotions, becoming chief of staff in 1964, minister of defence in 1968, and a member of the Politburo. A stern and authoritarian figure, and now holding the rank of general, he presided over the use of Polish troops to assist in the Soviet-led crushing of the pro-democracy movement in Czechoslovakia in 1968, and the violent suppression of Polish strikers and food rioters in 1970. He was seen as a reliable figure by the Soviet government, and became Polish prime minister and head of the ruling party in 1981. Immediately he was faced with the growing threat posed by the Solidarity movement. Led by Lech Walesa, Solidarity had begun as a free trade union in 1980 but rapidly became a mass movement which was demanding free elections. With the country torn by strikes and unrest, in December 1981 Jaruzelski staged what was in effect a military coup. He imposed martial law and in the following year banned Solidarity. He ruled with an unsympathetic severity—epitomised by his stern personal style and trademark dark glasses—which caused outrage in the West. In the years that followed, however, he sought to relax military rule and to foster a dialogue of reconciliation with the Catholic Church and Solidarity leaders. He stepped down as prime minister and minister of defence in 1985 and became state president. But his regime was unable to overcome continuing pro-Solidarity protests. Furthermore, with the accession of Mikhail Gorbachev as a new and reformist Soviet leader, Jaruzelski seemed increasingly to belong to a bygone era. In the face of Solidarity's relentless rise to power, Jaruzelski stepped down as party leader in 1989 and president in 1990. During his long retirement he apologised for the excesses of martial law but justified his coup on the grounds that it was the only way to prevent a Soviet invasion of Poland. Historians tended to disagree with this self-serving claim that, ultimately, he had been merely a Polish patriot. Nevertheless, his increasing ill health meant that he managed to evade later attempts to hold him responsible for the crimes of his much derided regime. Died 25 May.

Mango, Andrew James (b. 1926), British writer who was an internationally recognised authority on Turkey. Born into an Anglo-Russian Levantine family in Istanbul, when the Republic of Turkey was in its infancy, Mango was fluent in English, Russian, Greek, and French as well as Ottoman and modern Turkish. His polyglotism landed him a job as a translator in the press office of the British Embassy in Ankara during World War II and in 1947 he emigrated to Britain. He studied at London University's School of Oriental and African Studies, and took a PhD in Persian literature. His passion for politics and international affairs led him to join the Turkish section of the World Service whilst still a student, and he went on to become head of the South East European Service. He was a regular visitor to Turkey throughout his life and his erudite analysis— often dispensed with wit and conversational good humour—was much sought after by politicians, diplomats, academics and fellow journalists. He was awarded numerous Turkish honorary doctorates and the Turkish Distinguished Service Medal. He also frequently appeared on Turkish television, often being greeted with affection and respect by leading Turkish politicians and statesmen. He retired from the BBC in 1986 but remained a leading authority on Turkey. He continued to write widely and in 1999 published his masterly *Atatürk: The Biography of the Founder of Modern Turkey*. Other notable books included *Turkey and the War on Terrorism*, (2005) and *From the Sultan to Atatürk: Turkey—The Peace Conferences of 1919-23 and Their Aftermath* (2009). Although sometimes his views were controversial—he denied that the mass killing of Armenians had amounted to genocide and defended the military coups of 1960 and 1980 as having been necessary to avoid civil war—his scholarship was beyond reproach. For more than 50 years he also contributed to *The Annual Register*, in which capacity his loyalty, professionalism and knowledge of his subject will be greatly missed by the book's current editors. Died 6 July.

Mayall, Rik (b. 1958), English alternative comedian, actor and writer. Born in Harlow, Essex, Richard Mayall attended the King's School, Worcester, before studying drama at Manchester University. It was there that he met a number of those with whom he would collaborate during his career, including Lise Mayer, Ben Elton, and his long-time comedy partner, Ade Edmondson. During the early 1980s Mayall and Edmondson gained a growing reputation with their "20th Century Coyote" double act at The Comedy Store. Their high-octane and anarchic humour, although sometimes vacuous and puerile, was irreverent and chimed perfectly with the rise of the "alternative" stand-up comedy movement. The two also appeared as "The Dangerous Brothers" and from 1982 enjoyed success in the television series *The Comic Strip Presents...* At the same time the pair achieved great acclaim with *The Young Ones*, a sitcom written by Elton, Mayall, and Mayer. Set in a shared student house, it drew comedy from the squalor of their Manchester days, and veered wildly between tasteless slapstick and grotesque hilarity. Mayall also continued as a stand-up performer and appeared in a range of TV comedies including successes (most notably, the *Blackadder* series) and failures (such as *Hardwicke House*, which was withdrawn from TV after only two episodes in 1987 because of a flood of negative reaction). Mayall also had success in the long-running sitcom *The New Statesman* (1987-92), in which he played a reptilian and repulsive Tory MP, Alan B'Stard, and *Bottom* (1991-95) where he and Edmondson once again engaged in violent slapstick comedy as two flatmates living on the dole. In 1998 he suffered a severe accident when he crashed his quad bike near his home in Devon. He survived and eventually returned to work making stage appearances, participating in a number of mostly insubstantial films, and continuing his lucrative voiceovers for film and advertising. Died 9 June.

Paisley, Ian Richard Kyle (b. 1926), Northern Ireland politician and Protestant clergyman. Born in Armagh, the son of a Baptist pastor, Paisley was ordained by his father in 1946. He was deeply conservative, abhorring homosexuality, opposing abortion, and demonstrating an almost pathological loathing of Catholicism—which he denounced as the religion of the "Antichrist"—and Irish nationalism, which he saw as an existential threat to the tradition of Ulster Unionism. In 1951 he split from the Presbyterian Church in Ireland and founded the Free Presbyterian Church, an evangelical body that emphasised a literal interpretation of the Bible. Paisley achieved national stature in the 1960s through his uncompromising opposition to the civil rights movement launched by the marginalised Catholic minority in Northern Ireland. Paisley's ugly rhetoric inflamed Protestant extremists and inspired violence on the streets. He served several short prison sentences and was widely believed to have close connections to the paramilitary wing of Unionism, particularly the Ulster Volunteer Force, which perpetrated acts of terrorism against Catholic civilians. In April 1970 he was elected to the Stormont parliament, for Bannside, and at the June UK general election entered Parliament as the member for North Antrim. In the following year he founded the Democratic Unionist Party (DUP), which he was to lead for almost four decades. He fiercely opposed the 1973 Sunningdale Agreement on power-sharing and was instrumental in fomenting the Protestant violence and civil disorder that brought about its collapse in 1974. Thereafter he continued to pursue parliamentary and extra-parliamentary tactics. In 1979 he added a seat in the European Parliament to his portfolio of legislative seats, and in 1981 founded the Third Force, a Protestant militia committed to fighting the IRA and resisting nascent talks between the British and Irish governments. These talks led to the 1985 Anglo-Irish Agreement, which gave the Irish government an advisory role in Northern Ireland. However, it was not until 13 years later that a power-sharing government in Northern Ireland, as envisaged by the Anglo-Irish Agreement, came about with the signing of the 1998 Good Friday Agreement. Unsurprisingly, the accord and the peace process to which it was linked, were opposed by Paisley. Nevertheless, the peace process stumbled on, driven by war weariness on all sides. Eventually Paisley, now approaching 80 and suffering from a serious heart ailment, was persuaded to join it even though it meant working with those whom he had spent a lifetime hating.

The DUP, which had become the largest party in the Northern Ireland assembly, in 2006 signed the St Andrews Agreement which opened the way for a power-sharing executive. In a remarkable volte face, in March 2007 Paisley appeared publicly with Sinn Féin president Gerry Adams to announce that they had reached a deal. A devolved government was duly formed in May. Paisley, as chief minister, went on to enjoy a surprisingly cordial relationship with his deputy, former IRA commander Martin McGuinness, a partnership that won widespread respect and became affectionately known as the "Chuckle Brothers". Having played a key (if somewhat late) role in securing the permanence of the peace agreement, Paisley retired as chief minister and leader of the DUP in 2008. He did not contest his Westminster seat at the general election of 2010, instead becoming a life peer, Baron Bannside. With his health failing he stepped down from his religious ministry in January 2012. Died 12 September.

Pillinger, Colin (b. 1943), English scientist who helped popularise astronomy. Pillinger was born into a working class family in Kingswood, South Gloucestershire, and attended the local grammar school before studying chemistry at University College Swansea. After completing a PhD he served as a senior research associate in the Department of Earth Sciences at Cambridge University. He moved to the Open University in 1984, working as a senior research fellow and then, from 1991, as professor in interplanetary science. From 1996 to 2000 he was Gresham Professor of Astronomy at Gresham College, a post once held by Sir Christopher Wren. Like Wren, Pillinger was interdisciplinary in his approach to science, He combined his background in organic chemistry with his passion for astronomy and geology, and aimed to inspire widespread public interest in space science as a means of understanding the origins of life. He was best known as a leading figure for the *Beagle 2* project which aimed to land a craft on Mars in order to collect and analyse rock samples for signs of life, past or present. Pillinger's characteristically enthusiastic and dishevelled appearance became the public face of the mission, and he was instrumental in gaining funding, sponsorship and celebrity endorsement for the venture. It ended in disappointment for although *Beagle 2* was released close to the planet for a landing scheduled for 25 December 2003, no signal was ever received to suggest that it had successfully reached the Martian surface and the craft was formally declared lost in February 2004. A commission of inquiry into the failure attributed some blame to Pillinger's management of the project, although the scientist himself remained phlegmatic, arguing that scientific successes were achieved only by being prepared to accept failures. He received a number of honours in his career including being elected Fellow of the Royal Society (1993), made a CBE (2003), and receiving the Royal Society's Faraday medal (2012). In 2010 he published a well-received book about the failed project with which his name would be forever linked: *My Life on Mars—The Beagle 2 Diaries*. Died 7 May.

Pincher, Chapman (b. 1914), English journalist and author renowned for his work on matters of espionage. Pincher was born to a military family stationed in India and later educated at Darlington grammar school before studying botany and zoology at King's College London. Afterwards he taught at the Liverpool Institute high school for boys until 1940. During the war he served as a tank gunner in the Royal Armoured Corps and then worked as technical officer in the Rocket Division of the Ministry of Supply in 1943-45. It was in this role that he began feeding stories to a friend at the *Daily Express*. After being demobilised, he joined the newspaper in 1946 as a science and defence correspondent and, in addition to producing regular articles, he began to write the first of more than 30 books. He was a natural reactionary and a passionate patriot, with a taste for fine dining, field sports and country living. He used his extensive contacts within the British establishment to uncover stories, particularly in the field of intelligence, and also cooperated with the authorities on occasion in writing deliberately misleading articles. Amongst his major scoops was the revelation in 1964 that the defence manufacturer Ferranti had been overcharging on its contract for *Bloodhound* missiles, a story which provoked a major political scandal. Similarly, the British government in 1971 expelled more than 100 diplomats after Pincher highlighted espionage activities at the Soviet embassy. He left the *Daily Express* in 1979 and in 1981 published his best known book, *Their Trade is Treachery*, which alleged that MI5's former director general, Roger Hollis, had been a Soviet agent. Died 5 August.

Reynolds, Albert (b. 1932), Irish taoiseach who played a key role in the Northern Irish peace process. Born in Rooskey, County Roscommon, Reynolds was educated at Summerhill College, in County Sligo. He gave up a secure post at Córas Iompair Éireann, the state transport company, in order to pursue a career as an entrepreneur. After achieving success in the leisure and food industries he entered politics, winning election to the Dáil in 1977 as the Fianna Fáil party's representative for the constituency of Longford-Westmeath. It was a seat that he was to hold until his retirement in 2002. After two years as a backbencher, his career lurched forward when he supported Charles Haughey's successful bid for the party leadership. He was rewarded in 1979 with the posts and telegraphs portfolio and won plaudits for his campaign to replace Ireland's antiquated manually operated telephone system with a automatic network. In 1980 he added the portfolio of transport to his responsibilities and in 1981, after a brief period in opposition, he became minister of industry and energy. The government fell in 1982 but returned to office in 1987 and Reynolds became minister for industry and commerce and then, in 1988, minister of finance. With the party forced into a coalition government at the election of 1989, Reynolds capitalised on the growing discontent with Haughey's leadership and eventually succeeded in 1992 in ousting him. Reynolds became Fianna Fáil leader and taoiseach, posts that he was to hold until late 1994. His tenure was notable for his close relationship with British Prime Minister John Major and his energetic participation in negotiations with those involved in the conflict in Northern Ireland. His efforts were rewarded when he and Major in December 1993 presented an agreed roadmap for formal peace talks. A ceasefire followed in 1994 and in 1998 the Good Friday agreement secured peace in the province.

Reynolds also contributed to Ireland's "Celtic Tiger" economic boom, although the later economic disaster that befell the country illustrated the shoddy foundations of this gaudy success. Indeed, Reynolds's time in office coincided with a period of deep and endemic political corruption, and he was widely accused of profiting from the powers and patronage of office. It seemed to many that he was keen to retain office for reasons of venality rather than as a means of achieving any wider public ambition—a view that fatally undermined his political integrity. He was toppled in November 1994 after his coalition partner, the Labour Party, withdrew its support over a scandal which involved the failure to extradite to Northern Ireland a paedophile priest. Although the record of Reynolds was later criticised by the Mahon Tribunal—the long-running judicial inquiry into corruption—the former taoiseach escaped formal questioning in 2008 because of his ill health. Died 21 August.

Sharon, Ariel (b. 1928), controversial general and politician who served as prime minister of Israel. He was born as Ariel Scheinermann in Kfar Malal, a secular Jewish settlement in British-administered Palestine, to parents who had emigrated from Russia. As a youth he participated in various Jewish paramilitary organisations, including Haganah, the forerunner of the Israel Defence Forces (IDF). He fought in Israel's 1948 war of independence and thereafter led in an elite army group, Unit 101, which conducted aggressive guerrilla attacks inside neighbouring Arab states. Amongst the most controversial of the group's activities was the Qibya massacre in October 1953 when around 70 Palestinian civilians (half of whom were women and children) were killed. He fought in the wars of 1956 and 1967, displaying a blend of ruthlessness and impetuosity that was often militarily effective, although costly in terms of the lives of Arab civilians and, on occasion, his own troops. In the Yom Kippur war of 1973 he turned the tide in Israel's favour by crossing the Suez Canal and threatening to encircle Egypt's forces. After the war his status as a national hero saw him elected to the Knesset in December 1973 but he later resigned in order to serve as security adviser to the Labour

prime minister, Yitzhak Rabin. Sharon returned to the legislature at the election of 1977 and became agriculture minister in the right-wing Likud government. He encouraged the building of Jewish settlements in the occupied territories, urging settlers to "grab as many hilltops as they can", in order to ensure the retention of the land by Israel. As defence minister in 1982 he launched an invasion of Lebanon to drive out the Palestine Liberation Organisation, and in so doing mired Israel in a long and costly conflict which gave rise to Hezbullah, a new and formidable enemy among the formerly friendly Shia population of southern Lebanon. The early stages of the war also saw the greatest controversy of his career when, in September 1982, IDF forces allowed Phalangist militiamen to massacre up to several thousand Palestinian civilians in the refugee camps of Sabra and Shatila. An Israeli commission of inquiry held Sharon personally responsible for an atrocity that caused international outrage and he was eventually forced to resign the defence portfolio in February 1983, although he remained in government. Thereafter he held numerous other Cabinet posts and remained a popular figure on the Right, encouraging Jewish settlements in the occupied territories and opposing the 1993 Oslo peace process. When Likud was ejected from office in 1999 Sharon assumed the leadership of the party. In September 2000 he helped spark the second Palestinian Intifada by making a high-profile visit to the Temple Mount complex in Jerusalem, and within months had won the general election of 2001 on a platform of crushing the uprising. Although he was re-elected in 2003, Sharon's premiership was characterised by scandal, economic austerity and continuing violence with the Palestinians. Israel cracked down harshly, with a policy that included assassinating Palestinian leaders, and in turn suffered from Palestinian terrorist attacks and suicide bombings. In an unexpected move in February 2004, Sharon infuriated his right-wing supporters by announcing that Israeli troops would dismantle Jewish settlements and withdraw from Gaza. The withdrawal was effected in August 2005 and in November Sharon broke free from Likud and announced the creation of a new centrist party, Kadima. He was expected to win the forthcoming general election although opinion remained divided over whether these were the manoeuvres of a wily political operator or whether the old general had genuinely decided to use his huge prestige to force through a sacrifice of land for peace. As such it offered a tantalising glimpse of the possibility of a lasting peace settlement with the Palestinians and a resolution of one of the world's most intractable conflicts. His true intentions were never revealed for he suffered a massive stroke in January 2006 that left him in a persistent vegetative state for the remainder of his life. Died 11 January.

Shevardnadze, Eduard (b. 1928), reformist Soviet foreign minister and later president of his native Georgia. Shevardnadze was born in Mamati, near the Black Sea, and joined the Communist Party in 1948 at the age of 20. By the mid-1960s he had risen to become first secretary of the party in Georgia and minister of the interior, pursuing a successful anti-corruption campaign which was supported by the leadership in Moscow. His administration was also characterised by economic growth and a willingness to undertake agrarian and political reforms. In 1985 the rise of the reformist young Soviet leader Mikhail Gorbachev saw Shevardnadze appointed as foreign minister in place of the veteran Andrei Gromyko. He rapidly became a key figure in the new Soviet regime, working towards Gorbachev's goals of openness, restructuring and democratisation. Nicknamed the "Silver Fox", Shevardnadze used his abundance of intellect, warmth and easy charm to pursue détente with the West. He negotiated nuclear arms deals with the USA, was instrumental in ending the unwinnable Soviet war in Afghanistan, withdrew forces from Eastern Europe, and facilitated the reunification of Germany. Like Gorbachev he was a pragmatist, but both men were increasingly despised by Communist Party hardliners who held them responsible for accelerating the Soviet Union's decline. In the face of this antagonism he unexpectedly resigned in December 1990 and later became the first Soviet leader to leave the Communist Party. He returned briefly as foreign minister in November 1991 but stepped down once again in the following month—along with Gorbachev—upon the dissolution of the Soviet

Union. In 1992 he returned to Georgia as speaker of parliament, struggling as de facto president to preserve the country's territorial integrity over the next four years as the newly independent state tore itself apart in civil war. In November 1995 the Georgian presidency was restored and Shevardnadze was elected to the post, and subsequently re-elected (amid allegations of vote-rigging) in 2000. However, Shevardnadze's administration was undermined by his close association with the West and by allegations of corruption involving family members. He resigned in November 2003, after a disputed legislative election sparked the "Rose Revolution" in Georgia, and lived out the remainder of his life in retirement in his home in Tbilisi. Died 7 July.

Seeger, Pete (b. 1919), radical US folk singer and songwriter. Born in New York city to musical parents—his mother was a concert violinist and his father a musicologist with a particular interest in the American folk tradition—Seeger was privately educated. He began playing the ukulele at the age of eight and then graduated to the five-string banjo for which he would become best known. A political radical from an early age, he joined the Young Communist League in 1936 and from 1942 to 1949 was a member of the Communist Party of USA (CPUSA), and remained an unashamed communist throughout his life. He entered Harvard University in 1937 to study journalism and sociology, but dropped out in 1939 after being persuaded by the legendary radical folk singer Woody Guthrie that he could "learn more from hitting the road". In the following years he travelled widely across the USA participating in local political causes and learning musical techniques from idols such as Guthrie and Lead Belly. He made his first recordings in 1940 with the Almanac Singers, a radical group of musicians who initially opposed, but after the Nazi invasion of the Soviet Union in 1941, supported US entry to the war. After military service he was a founder of the Weavers, a group that was instrumental in reviving the popularity of traditional folk music but which was blacklisted during the McCarthyite repression of the 1950s. In 1955 Seeger was hauled before the House Committee on Un-American Activities, where his courageous refusal to answer questions concerning his political beliefs or contacts led to his indictment—and eventual conviction—for Contempt of Congress. He remained true to his ideals and eventually re-emerged to public prominence in the vanguard of the folk revival and radicalism of the early 1960s. Covers of songs he had written or recorded became global hits, most notably his anti-war song *Where Have All the Flowers Gone?*, whilst his rendition of *We Shall Overcome* was adopted as the unofficial anthem of the civil rights movement in which he was an active participant. He also influenced a generation of rising music stars, including Joan Baez, Judy Collins, Joni Mitchell, Arlo Guthrie and, the most able and feted of them all, Bob Dylan. The latter's renunciation of traditional folk music by appearing as the headline act at the 1965 Newport Folk Festival with an electric guitar and band caused audience consternation and upset Seeger so much that he unsuccessfully called for an axe to cut the power cables. Throughout the remainder of his long career Seeger continued to record and to play music in support of radical causes, believing passionately in the power of song to effect political change. He opposed the war in Vietnam, supported the environmental movement, and remained a tireless participant in civil rights and labour causes, including actively supporting the Occupy Wall Street movement even though he was by then in his 90s. Died 27 January.

Temple Black, Shirley (b. 1928), prodigious child film star and later US diplomat. She was born in Santa Monica, California, and enrolled by her parents in a dance school in 1931 where she was spotted by a studio agent. The saccharine cuteness of her infancy was complimented by her blonde ringlets, styled in imitation of the silent film star Mary Pickford. She was signed by Educational Pictures to appear in a series of short films but, propelled by her ambitious mother, before she had turned six she had secured a contract with 20th Century-Fox. Her first feature film, *Stand Up and Cheer!* (1934), saw her perform "Baby Take A Bow", a song-and-dance number that proved hugely popular. She appeared in another seven movies that year, including *Bright Eyes*, where she sang her trademark ditty,

"On the Good Ship Lollipop", a banal confection that rapidly sold 500,000 sheet music copies Temple rapidly became an international brand, spawning dolls, toys, clothes and cosmetics, and exuding a cloying charm that seemed able to span continents, genders, generations and classes. After only a year in the movie business, her astonishing impact was recognised by the award of a Special Oscar "in grateful recognition of her outstanding contribution to screen entertainment". In the years that followed she was an unstoppable force, starring in a succession of movies, including *Curly Top* (1935), in which she played a cute orphan; *Stowaway* (1936), in which she impersonated Al Jolson and Ginger Rogers amongst others; *Wee Willie Winkie* (1937); and *Little Miss Broadway* (1938). The conventional view of her phenomenal success was that the chirpy little cherub was an antidote to the Depression and the uncertainty of the 1930s. Graham Greene, however, saw the explanation as darker, citing the "dubious coquetry" and "dimpled depravity" which lurked beneath a mask of infancy and enticed "middle-aged men and clergymen". Greene's opinions landed him with a libel suit from the studio which was resolved in Temple's favour. But time was running out for the child star who, by the end of the decade, was teetering on the brink of adolescence. The *Blue Bird* (1940)—Fox's answer to MGM's *The Wizard of Oz*—failed, and though she continued to make films until 1949, some of which were successful, the magic with which she held the world in thrall had been broken. She married in 1945, had a daughter, but then divorced in 1949. She married again in 1950, this time to Charles Black, and disappeared into relative obscurity, interspersing motherhood and homemaking with occasional forays into television. She returned to the public eye in the 1970s as a right-wing Republican activist. She served as US ambassador to Ghana (1974-76); White House chief of protocol (1976-77); and ambassador to Czechoslovakia (1989-92). Died 10 February.

Thorpe, Jeremy (b. 1929), British politician who led the Liberal party before being disgraced by allegations of involvement in a homosexual murder conspiracy. Thorpe was born in Surrey

into an illustrious political family. He was educated at Eton and Trinity College, Oxford, where
he read law, and served as president of the Oxford
Union in 1951. He was called to the bar in 1954
but by that time was already active as an aspiring
Liberal party candidate and at the election of
1955 made deep inroads into the Conservative
majority in his chosen seat of North Devon. His
lively and effectively campaigning style brought
him victory, albeit by the slimmest of margins, in
the seat at the 1959 election. As a young MP he
managed to combine a foppish personal style,
complete with a biting wit and coterie of rich and
famous friends, with a genuine radicalism and
contempt for ill-deserved privilege. When Liberal
leader Jo Grimond retired in 1967, Thorpe was
the clear choice as his successor. Although the
Liberals lost half of their MPs at the 1970 general
election, being reduced to a mere six seats in the
House of Commons, Thorpe retained the leadership and received widespread public sympathy
for the death of his wife, Caroline, in a car crash
a few days after polling. In the early 1970s
Thorpe presided over a rebuilding of his party
and at the general election of February 1974 it
polled 6 million votes (19 per cent of the total)
and won 14 seats. However, Thorpe's willingness
to discuss the possibility of keeping the defeated
Conservative government of Edward Heath in
office proved unpopular and in the October 1974
election the party lost support. Despite Thorpe's
marriage (and remarriage in 1973) there were
persistent rumours of homosexuality going back
to 1961, a period when such conduct was illegal
in the UK. Norman Scott, a former stable boy,
made repeated claims that he and Thorpe had had
a sexual relationship but he was kept publicly
silent on the matter with regular payoffs. The
media also withheld the story as a mark of respect
for Thorpe's position. However, the matter
exploded into the public domain in 1975 when
Scott's dog was shot dead on Exmoor in what
was said to have been a botched attempt to
murder the blackmailer in a convoluted plot
organised by Thorpe whereby a hit man had been
paid with Liberal party donations. Although
Thorpe denied any impropriety, the legal and
political fallout forced his resignation as party
leader in May 1976. He was subsequently

indicted for conspiracy and incitement to murder
and was roundly defeated at the May 1979 general election. At his subsequent trial at the Old
Bailey he chose not to give evidence and was
acquitted in June 1979 after the judge gave a
summing-up that was lampooned for its bias in
his favour. Although technically innocent,
Thorpe's career was ruined and he lived out the
remainder of his life in relative seclusion,
shunned by his former colleagues. Died 4
December.

Van Kirk, Theodore (b. 1921), navigator and last
surviving member of the crew of the *Enola Gay*,
the US aircraft that dropped the atomic bomb on
Hiroshima. Van Kirk, whose nickname was
"Dutch", was born and raised in Northumber-
land, Pennsylvania, and went to Susquehanna
College for a year before joining the US Army
Air Corps's aviation cadet programme in October
1941. Two months later the Japanese bombed the
US naval base at Pearl Harbour and in April 1942
Van Kirk entered combat as a qualified navigator,
having trained at Kelly Field, Texas. In July he
joined a B-17 Flying Fortress squadron based in
England and served with Paul Tibbets, the highly
regarded aviator who would later pilot the *Enola
Gay*. They participated in strategic bombing
operations over Europe and North Africa, and in
mid-1943 Van Kirk returned to the USA having
flown 58 combat missions. He then served a
period as an instructor before being transferred in
late 1944 to a specially created unit which—a
mission known only to its commander, Tibbets—
was to drop the world's first atomic bomb. After
more than six months of training, their heavily
laden B-29 Superfortress (renamed in honour of
Tibbets's mother), took off from the Pacific
island of Tinian at 2.45am (local time) on 6
August 1945. Through Van Kirk's faultless navigation they arrived over central Hiroshima—a
city that had hitherto escaped the incendiary air
raids which had burnt so many Japanese urban
centres—precisely on schedule at 8.15am. Their
4.5 tonne uranium bomb, nicknamed "Little
Boy", exploded 580m above the ground, some
240m from their target point, the Aioi bridge. It
produced a fireball with a temperature in excess
of 3,000C and resulted in a firestorm which laid

waste to the ancient city and killed some 80,000 of the city's 340,000 inhabitants. By the end of the year the death toll had risen to around 140,000, and even today the radiation released by the bomb continues to claim lives. Van Kirk, who described the broiling scene below him as like "a pot of boiling black oil", was sanguine over his role in the mass killing of civilians, believing it to have been necessary in precipitating Japan's unconditional surrender. With the war over, he left the air force in 1946 with the rank of Major, and took a degree (followed by a Master's) in chemical engineering at Bucknell University, Lewisburg. For 35 years thereafter he worked for the DuPont chemical corporation. In later life he gave lectures and interviews about his role in the Hiroshima bombing and in October 2007 auctioned off the flight log of the *Enola Gay*'s mission for $358,500. Died 28 July.

Whiteman, Kaye (b. 1936), journalist who was an internationally recognised authority on West Africa and, in particular, Nigeria. Born in London to Quaker parents, Whiteman was educated at religious schools in Saffron Walden and York, showing a talent for geography and music. His religious beliefs meant that he registered as a conscientious objector and thereby avoided national service, instead serving in the Friends' Ambulance Unit (1954-55). He read history at Queen's College, Oxford, in 1956-59, developing a deep fascination for Africa and the process of decolonisation. After gaining his degree he worked in journalism and in 1963 joined *West Africa* magazine where he served as deputy editor until 1973. He left to work as a senior information officer for the European Commission dealing with development issues relating to Africa, a post which he gave up in 1982 when he returned to *West Africa* to take on the editorship. In 1993 he published a commemorative volume of the magazine entitled *West Africa Over 75 Years: Selections from the Raw Material of History*. He stepped down from the editorship in 1999 but later served as editor-in-chief and general manager before the magazine ceased publication in 2005. He also worked as a director of information at the Commonwealth Secretariat in London (1999-2000), and in Lagos as a media adviser (2001-02), particularly with regard to the

newspaper *Business Day*, to which he also contributed a regular column. Whiteman was a contributing editor of *Africa Today* from 2002 onwards, and was a research associate at the Centre of African Studies at the School of Oriental and African Studies (SOAS), and a trustee of the Africa Centre in London. He contributed widely to a range of newspapers as well as writing a number of books. Throughout his career he was a regular visitor to West Africa meeting many of the region's leaders and reporting on a huge range of political and cultural topics. These included the human suffering in Biafra, which he witnessed firsthand at the time of its surrender to the Nigerian government in 1970. Whiteman believed in the power of informed discourse to change the world but in his later years often found himself depressed by the mismanagement, corruption and military despotism within the region that he so loved. He was also a longtime contributor to *The Annual Register*, bringing his expertise and compassion to bear upon Francophone Africa; in this capacity he will be deeply missed by the book's current editors. Died 17 May.

Whitlam, Gough (b. 1916), reforming Australian prime minister who was controversially dismissed in 1975 in a constitutional coup d'état. Born in Melbourne, Whitlam enrolled at the University of Sydney in 1935 before volunteering for wartime service in the Royal Australian Air Force. After the war he completed his studies, qualifying as a lawyer in 1947. By then he was active within the Australian Labour Party (ALP) and secured election to the federal House of Representatives in 1952. An able debater, Whitlam became leader of the bitterly divided party in 1967 and drove through a series of reforms designed to make it once again electable. The ALP performed well at the election of 1969, achieving its best result since losing office in 1949, but narrowly failed to unseat the Liberal-Country Party government. At the subsequent election in 1972, the party rode to power on a public mood for change and Whitlam became prime minister. His administration undertook a flurry of reforms—including ending conscription, freeing jailed draft resisters, fostering ties with Asia, improving access to healthcare, abolishing university tuition fees, advancing the status of women, and expanding justice for Aborigines—which transformed the country's political, economic and cultural landscape. The government was criticised, however, for its alleged economic mismanagement and it faced entrenched obstruction in the Senate where the opposition used its majority to reject legislation passed in the House. The government was narrowly re-elected in 1974 but failed to gain control of the upper house and remained vulnerable to continuing Opposition obstruction. In October 1975 a full-blown political crisis was provoked by the Opposition's attempt to force an election by using the Senate to block the government's budget requests. Whitlam refused to dissolve the House and planned instead to hold a Senate election. In November, however, the matter was resolved in an unprecedented manner when the county's governor general, Sir John Kerr, used the powers of the monarchy to dismiss Whitlam and appoint Opposition Leader Malcolm Fraser as prime minister. An immediate election was called and the ALP was defeated. Although Whitlam remained as party leader until December 1977, his political career was over and he retired from Parliament in 1978, doomed to be forever remembered not for his reforming credentials but for the manner of his dismissal. Died 21 October.

Williams, Robin (b. 1951), US actor and comedian. Born into a wealthy family in Chicago, Williams initially studied political science at college before switching to drama. From an early stage he displayed the high-energy, improvisational skills and bewildering vocal range that would be hallmarks of his acting career. Initially, he worked as a stand-up comedian and later confessed to have used alcohol and drugs to ease the stress of live performances. After a number of small parts in film and television, Williams achieved fame with a starring role in the successful television sitcom *Mork & Mindy* which ran from 1978 to 1982. His first major film role was in Robert Altman's *Popeye* (1980), and he went on to make more than two dozen further movies. Some were critically acclaimed, including *The World According to Garp* (1982), *Good Morning, Vietnam* (1987), *Dead Poets Society* (1989),

Awakenings (1990), *The Fisher King* (1991), *Aladdin* (1992), *Mrs Doubtfire* (1993), *Good Will Hunting* (1997), for which he won an Oscar, and *One Hour Photo* (2002). For at his best, when managing to restrain his natural tendency towards over-exuberance, Williams could achieve dramatic depth and vulnerability for his characters, wherein comedy evoked genuine pathos. Too many of his films, however, were "family entertainment" stalwarts which saw him reprise stereotypically manic comedy roles. Having overcome his addiction to alcohol and cocaine in the 1980s, Williams substituted physical exercise (particularly cycling) as a means of combating his recurring bouts of depression. However, he began to drink once more in 2003 and on several occasions sought treatment for alcoholism. He also underwent heart surgery in 2009 and, prior to his death, was diagnosed with the early stages of Parkinson's disease. He ended his life by hanging himself at his home in California. Died 11 August.

Ziolkowski, Ruth (b. 1926), driving force behind the ongoing project to carve a giant monument to Crazy Horse in the Black Hills of Dakota. Born in West Hartford, Connecticut, as Ruth Ross, she met the Polish-American sculptor Korczak Ziolkowski when she was 13 years old. He had worked on the giant monument at Mount Rushmore in the 1930s and later Ross helped him as a student volunteer on a project to create a sculpture of Noah Webster in West Hartford. In 1947 Korczak Ziolkowski acquired Thunderhead Mountain, located 30 km from Mount Rushmore, from the federal government as a site for the construction of a monument to Crazy Horse. A leader of the Oglala Lakota tribe, Crazy Horse was renowned for his courage and tactical acumen and played a leading role in the 1876 defeat of General Custer at the Battle of Little Bighorn (known to American Indians as the Battle of Greasy Grass Creek). Korczak Ziolkowski began work on his giant sculpture in 1948 and was once again assisted by Ruth Ross. Though 18 years his junior, she married him in 1950 and subsequently bore 10 children. The family lived in a cabin and whilst Korczak worked on the sculpture, Ruth raised their children and handled the logistics of the project. She dealt with the finances, fielded media inquiries, staffed the visitor centre, and ordered the materials needed by her husband. With Korczak having declined financial assistance from the federal government, she also earned much needed income from running a lumber mill and dairy farm. Her key role in the project was later formalised when she became chairman and chief executive officer of the board of directors of the Crazy Horse Memorial Foundation. It was Ruth's decision to concentrate on carving the face of Crazy Horse first rather than his horse, as Korczak had planned. Korczak Ziolkowski died in 1982 and was buried at the base of the mountain. Ruth, assisted by her children, continued to drive the project forward and in 1998 the face of Crazy Horse was finally completed. Although the sculpture was far from finished at the time of her own death, the single-minded dedication of Ruth Ziolkowski secured the future of a work which, at 195 metres wide and 172 metres high, was set to become the world's largest sculpture. Furthermore, her stewardship of the project was crucial in ensuring that it remained faithful to her husband's original vision—the central point of a site dedicated to the celebration of American Indian culture—rather than a mere tourist attraction. Died 21 May.

D.S. Lewis

XIX DOCUMENTS AND REFERENCE

SPEECH BY PRESIDENT OBAMA ANNOUNING AIRSTRIKES AGAINST
ISIS INSURGENTS IN IRAQ

Transcript of televised address from the White House by President Barack Obama on 7 August, in which he formally announced that he had authorised US air strikes against the insurgents of the Islamic State of Iraq and Syria (ISIS or ISIL) who had overrun large areas of Iraq. He justified his action on the grounds that ISIS was threatening genocide against the Yazidis religious minority and advancing upon Irbil (Erbil), the capital of the Kurdish Autonomous republic. He reassured the public that the USA would not "be dragged into fighting another war in Iraq". Following the speech, US aircraft began attacking targets in Iraq which succeeded in breaking the ISIS siege of the Yazidis (Yezidis) on Mount Sinjar and provided air support to Kurdish forces who drove ISIS fighters back from the strategically important Mosul Dam.

Good evening. Today I authorised two operations in Iraq—targeted airstrikes to protect our American personnel, and a humanitarian effort to help save thousands of Iraqi civilians who are trapped on a mountain without food and water and facing almost certain death. Let me explain the actions we're taking and why.

First, I said in June—as the terrorist group ISIL began an advance across Iraq—that the United States would be prepared to take targeted military action in Iraq if and when we determined that the situation required it. In recent days, these terrorists have continued to move across Iraq, and have neared the city of Erbil, where American diplomats and civilians serve at our consulate and American military personnel advise Iraqi forces.

To stop the advance on Erbil, I've directed our military to take targeted strikes against ISIL terrorist convoys should they move toward the city. We intend to stay vigilant, and take action if these terrorist forces threaten our personnel or facilities anywhere in Iraq, including our consulate in Erbil and our embassy in Baghdad. We're also providing urgent assistance to Iraqi government and Kurdish forces so they can more effectively wage the fight against ISIL.

Second, at the request of the Iraqi government—we've begun operations to help save Iraqi civilians stranded on the mountain. As ISIL has marched across Iraq, it has waged a ruthless campaign against innocent Iraqis. And these terrorists have been especially barbaric towards religious minorities, including Christian and Yezidis, a small and ancient religious sect. Countless Iraqis have been displaced. And chilling reports describe ISIL militants rounding up families, conducting mass executions, and enslaving Yezidi women.

In recent days, Yezidi women, men and children from the area of Sinjar have fled for their lives. And thousands—perhaps tens of thousands—are now hiding high up on the mountain, with little but the clothes on their backs. They're without food, they're without water. People are starving. And children are dying of thirst. Meanwhile, ISIL forces below have called for the systematic destruction of the entire Yezidi people, which would constitute genocide. So these innocent families are faced with a horrible choice: descend the mountain and be slaughtered, or stay and slowly die of thirst and hunger.

I've said before, the United States cannot and should not intervene every time there's a crisis in the world. So let me be clear about why we must act, and act now. When we face a situation like we do on that mountain—with innocent people facing the prospect of violence on a horrific scale, when we have a mandate to help—in this case, a request from the Iraqi government—and when we have the unique capabilities to help avert a massacre, then I believe the United States of America cannot turn a blind eye. We can act, carefully and responsibly, to prevent a potential act of genocide. That's what we're doing on that mountain.

I've, therefore, authorised targeted airstrikes, if necessary, to help forces in Iraq as they fight to break the siege of Mount Sinjar and protect the civilians trapped there. Already, American aircraft have begun conducting humanitarian airdrops of food and water to help these desperate men, women and children survive. Earlier this week, one Iraqi in the area cried to the world, "There is no one coming to help." Well today, America is coming to help. We're also consulting with other countries—and the United Nations—who have called for action to address this humanitarian crisis.

I know that many of you are rightly concerned about any American military action in Iraq, even limited strikes like these. I understand that. I ran for this office in part to end our war in Iraq and welcome our troops home, and that's what we've done. As Commander-in-Chief, I will not allow the United States to be dragged into fighting another war in Iraq. And so even as we support Iraqis as they take the fight to these terrorists, American combat troops will not be returning to fight in Iraq, because there's no American military solution to the larger crisis in Iraq. The only lasting solution is reconciliation among Iraqi communities and stronger Iraqi security forces.

However, we can and should support moderate forces who can bring stability to Iraq. So even as we carry out these two missions, we will continue to pursue a broader strategy that empowers Iraqis to confront this crisis. Iraqi leaders need to come together and forge a new government that represents the legitimate interests of all Iraqis, and that can fight back against the threats like ISIL. Iraqis have named a new President, a new Speaker of Parliament, and are seeking consensus on a new Prime Minister. This is the progress that needs to continue in order to reverse the momentum of the terrorists who prey on Iraq's divisions.

Once Iraq has a new government, the United States will work with it and other countries in the region to provide increased support to deal with this humanitarian crisis and counterterrorism challenge. None of Iraq's neighbours have an interest in this terrible suffering or instability.

And so we'll continue to work with our friends and allies to help refugees get the shelter and food and water they so desperately need, and to help Iraqis push back against ISIL. The several hundred American advisors that I ordered to Iraq will continue to assess what more we can do to help train, advise and support Iraqi forces going forward. And just as I consulted Congress on the decisions I made today, we will continue to do so going forward.

My fellow Americans, the world is confronted by many challenges. And while America has never been able to right every wrong, America has made the world a more secure and prosperous place. And our leadership is necessary to underwrite the global security and prosperity that our children and our grandchildren will depend upon. We do so by adhering to a set of core principles. We do whatever is necessary to protect our people. We support our allies when they're in danger. We lead coalitions of countries to uphold international norms. And we strive to stay true to the fundamental values—the desire to live with basic freedom and dignity—that is common to human beings wherever they are. That's why people all over the world look to the United States of America to lead. And that's why we do it.

So let me close by assuring you that there is no decision that I take more seriously than the use of military force. Over the last several years, we have brought the vast majority of our troops home from Iraq and Afghanistan. And I've been careful to resist calls to turn time and again to our military, because America has other tools in our arsenal than our military. We can also lead with the power of our diplomacy, our economy, and our ideals.

But when the lives of American citizens are at risk, we will take action. That's my responsibility as Commander-in-Chief. And when many thousands of innocent civilians are faced with the danger of being wiped out, and we have the capacity to do something about it, we will take action. That is our responsibility as Americans. That's a hallmark of American leadership. That's who we are.

So tonight, we give thanks to our men and women in uniform—especially our brave pilots and crews over Iraq who are protecting our fellow Americans and saving the lives of so many men, women and children that they will never meet. They represent American leadership at its best. As a nation, we should be proud of them, and of our country's enduring commitment to uphold our own security and the dignity of our fellow human beings.

God bless our Armed Forces, and God bless the United States of America.

(Source: White House press office.)

SPEECH BY PRESIDENT OBAMA ANNOUNING AIRSTRIKES AGAINST ISIS INSURGENTS IN SYRIA

Transcript of televised national address by President Barack Obama on 10 September in which he announced an escalation of the US air campaign against ISIS (ISIL) insurgents by extending it into Syria. Obama also announced plans to train and arm Syrian rebels engaged in fighting ISIS. Although he ruled out sending US forces to Syria, he announced almost 500 additional troops for Iraq to assist Iraqi and Kurdish forces in their campaign against ISIS. The president's speech reflected growing public demands for a more aggressive response to ISIS in the aftermath of the release by the insurgents of videos which showed the decapitation of two US hostages.

My fellow Americans, tonight I want to speak to you about what the United States will do with our friends and allies to degrade and ultimately destroy the terrorist group known as ISIL.

As Commander-in-Chief, my highest priority is the security of the American people. Over the last several years, we have consistently taken the fight to terrorists who threaten our country. We took out Osama bin Laden and much of al Qaeda's leadership in Afghanistan and Pakistan. We've targeted al Qaeda's affiliate in Yemen, and recently eliminated the top commander of its affiliate in Somalia. We've done so while bringing more than 140,000 American troops home from Iraq, and drawing down our forces in Afghanistan, where our combat mission will end later this year. Thanks to our military and counterterrorism professionals, America is safer.

Still, we continue to face a terrorist threat. We can't erase every trace of evil from the world, and small groups of killers have the capacity to do great harm. That was the case before 9/11, and that remains true today. And that's why we must remain vigilant as threats emerge. At this moment, the greatest threats come from the Middle East and North Africa, where radical groups exploit grievances for their own gain. And one of those groups is ISIL—which calls itself the "Islamic State."

Now let's make two things clear: ISIL is not "Islamic." No religion condones the killing of innocents. And the vast majority of ISIL's victims have been Muslim. And ISIL is certainly not a state. It was formerly al Qaeda's affiliate in Iraq, and has taken advantage of sectarian strife and Syria's civil war to gain territory on both sides of the Iraq-Syrian border. It is recognised by no government, nor by the people it subjugates. ISIL is a terrorist organisation, pure and simple. And it has no vision other than the slaughter of all who stand in its way.

In a region that has known so much bloodshed, these terrorists are unique in their brutality. They execute captured prisoners. They kill children. They enslave, rape, and force women into marriage. They threatened a religious minority with genocide. And in acts of barbarism, they took the lives of two American journalists—Jim Foley and Steven Sotloff.

So ISIL poses a threat to the people of Iraq and Syria, and the broader Middle East—including American citizens, personnel and facilities. If left unchecked, these terrorists could pose a growing threat beyond that region, including to the United States. While we have not yet detected specific plotting against our homeland, ISIL leaders have threatened America and our allies. Our Intelligence Community believes that thousands of foreigners—including Europeans and some Americans—have joined them in Syria and Iraq. Trained and battle-hardened, these fighters could try to return to their home countries and carry out deadly attacks.

I know many Americans are concerned about these threats. Tonight, I want you to know that the United States of America is meeting them with strength and resolve. Last month, I ordered our military to take targeted action against ISIL to stop its advances. Since then, we've conducted more than 150 successful airstrikes in Iraq. These strikes have protected American personnel and facilities, killed ISIL fighters, destroyed weapons, and given space for Iraqi and Kurdish forces to reclaim key territory. These strikes have also helped save the lives of thousands of innocent men, women and children.

But this is not our fight alone. American power can make a decisive difference, but we cannot do for Iraqis what they must do for themselves, nor can we take the place of Arab partners in securing their region. And that's why I've insisted that additional U.S. action depended upon Iraqis forming an inclusive government, which they have now done in recent days. So tonight, with a new Iraqi government in place, and following consultations with allies abroad and Congress at home, I can announce that America will lead a broad coalition to roll back this terrorist threat.

Our objective is clear: We will degrade, and ultimately destroy, ISIL through a comprehensive and sustained counterterrorism strategy.

First, we will conduct a systematic campaign of airstrikes against these terrorists. Working with the Iraqi government, we will expand our efforts beyond protecting our own people and humanitarian missions, so that we're hitting ISIL targets as Iraqi forces go on offense. Moreover, I have made it clear that we will hunt down terrorists who threaten our country, wherever they are. That means I will not hesitate to take action against ISIL in Syria, as well as Iraq. This is a core principle of my presidency: If you threaten America, you will find no safe haven.

Second, we will increase our support to forces fighting these terrorists on the ground. In June, I deployed several hundred American service members to Iraq to assess how we can best support Iraqi security forces. Now that those teams have completed their work—and Iraq has formed a government—we will send an additional 475 service members to Iraq. As I have said before, these American forces will not have a combat mission—we will not get dragged into another ground war in Iraq. But they are needed to support Iraqi and Kurdish forces with training, intelligence and equipment. We'll also support Iraq's efforts to stand up National Guard Units to help Sunni communities secure their own freedom from ISIL's control.

Across the border, in Syria, we have ramped up our military assistance to the Syrian opposition. Tonight, I call on Congress again to give us additional authorities and resources to train and equip these fighters. In the fight against ISIL, we cannot rely on an Assad regime that terrorises its own people— a regime that will never regain the legitimacy it has lost. Instead, we must strengthen the opposition as the best counterweight to extremists like ISIL, while pursuing the political solution necessary to solve Syria's crisis once and for all.

Third, we will continue to draw on our substantial counterterrorism capabilities to prevent ISIL attacks. Working with our partners, we will redouble our efforts to cut off its funding; improve our intelligence; strengthen our defences; counter its warped ideology; and stem the flow of foreign fighters into and out of the Middle East. And in two weeks, I will chair a meeting of the UN Security Council to further mobilise the international community around this effort.

Fourth, we will continue to provide humanitarian assistance to innocent civilians who have been displaced by this terrorist organisation. This includes Sunni and Shia Muslims who are at grave risk, as well as tens of thousands of Christians and other religious minorities. We cannot allow these communities to be driven from their ancient homelands.

So this is our strategy. And in each of these four parts of our strategy, America will be joined by a broad coalition of partners. Already, allies are flying planes with us over Iraq; sending arms and assistance to Iraqi security forces and the Syrian opposition; sharing intelligence; and providing billions of dollars in humanitarian aid. Secretary Kerry was in Iraq today meeting with the new government and supporting their efforts to promote unity. And in the coming days he will travel across the Middle East and Europe to enlist more partners in this fight, especially Arab nations who can help mobilise Sunni communities in Iraq and Syria, to drive these terrorists from their lands. This is American leadership at its best: We stand with people who fight for their own freedom, and we rally other nations on behalf of our common security and common humanity.

My administration has also secured bipartisan support for this approach here at home. I have the authority to address the threat from ISIL, but I believe we are strongest as a nation when the President and Congress work together. So I welcome congressional support for this effort in order to show the world that Americans are united in confronting this danger.

Now, it will take time to eradicate a cancer like ISIL. And any time we take military action, there are risks involved—especially to the servicemen and women who carry out these missions. But I want the American people to understand how this effort will be different from the wars in Iraq and Afghanistan. It will not involve American combat troops fighting on foreign soil. This counterterrorism campaign will be waged through a steady, relentless effort to take out ISIL wherever they exist, using our air power and our support for partner forces on the ground. This strategy of taking out terrorists who threaten us, while supporting partners on the front lines, is one that we have successfully pursued in Yemen and Somalia for years. And it is consistent with the approach I outlined earlier this year: to use force against anyone who threatens America's core interests, but to mobilise partners wherever possible to address broader challenges to international order.

My fellow Americans, we live in a time of great change. Tomorrow marks 13 years since our country was attacked. Next week marks six years since our economy suffered its worst setback since the Great Depression. Yet despite these shocks, through the pain we have felt and the gruelling work required to bounce back, America is better positioned today to seize the future than any other nation on Earth.

Our technology companies and universities are unmatched. Our manufacturing and auto industries are thriving. Energy independence is closer than it's been in decades. For all the work that remains, our businesses are in the longest uninterrupted stretch of job creation in our history. Despite all the divisions and discord within our democracy, I see the grit and determination and common goodness of the American people every single day—and that makes me more confident than ever about our country's future.

Abroad, American leadership is the one constant in an uncertain world. It is America that has the capacity and the will to mobilise the world against terrorists. It is America that has rallied the world against Russian aggression, and in support of the Ukrainian peoples' right to determine their own destiny. It is America—our scientists, our doctors, our know-how—that can help contain and cure the outbreak of Ebola. It is America that helped remove and destroy Syria's declared chemical weapons so that they can't pose a threat to the Syrian people or the world again. And it is America that is helping Muslim communities around the world not just in the fight against terrorism, but in the fight for opportunity, and tolerance, and a more hopeful future.

America, our endless blessings bestow an enduring burden. But as Americans, we welcome our responsibility to lead. From Europe to Asia, from the far reaches of Africa to war-torn capitals of the Middle East, we stand for freedom, for justice, for dignity. These are values that have guided our nation since its founding.

Tonight, I ask for your support in carrying that leadership forward. I do so as a Commander-in-Chief who could not be prouder of our men and women in uniform—pilots who bravely fly in the face of danger above the Middle East, and service members who support our partners on the ground.

When we helped prevent the massacre of civilians trapped on a distant mountain, here's what one of them said: "We owe our American friends our lives. Our children will always remember that there was someone who felt our struggle and made a long journey to protect innocent people."

That is the difference we make in the world. And our own safety, our own security, depends upon our willingness to do what it takes to defend this nation and uphold the values that we stand for—timeless ideals that will endure long after those who offer only hate and destruction have been vanquished from the Earth.

May God bless our troops, and may God bless the United States of America.

(Source: White House press office.)

EXTRACTS FROM AMNESTY INTERNATIONAL REPORT INTO ISIS CRIMES AGAINST YAZIDI MINORITY

Extracts from a report titled Escape from Hell - Torture and Sexual Slavery in Islamic State captivity in Iraq, *issued by the human rights organisation Amnesty International in December 2014. The report cited evidence of war crimes committed by ISIS fighters, particularly in regard to their treatment of the Yazidi (Yezidi) minority in Iraq. The UN estimated that some 5,000 Yazidi men had been massacred by ISIS and up to 7,000 women and children abducted and forced into slavery.*

SUMMARY

As they swept through large parts of northern Iraq, fighters with the armed group calling itself "Islamic State" (IS) systematically targeted members of non-Arab and non-Sunni Muslim communities, as well as Sunni Muslims who oppose them. But even within the context of its persecution of minority groups and Shi'a Muslims, the IS has singled out the Yezidi minority, notably its women and children, for particularly brutal treatment.

In August 2014, IS fighters abducted hundreds, possibly thousands, of Yezidi men, women and children who were fleeing the IS takeover from the Sinjar region, in the north-west of the country. Hundreds of the men were killed and others were forced to convert to Islam under threat of death. Younger women and girls, some as young as 12, were separated from their parents and older relatives and sold, given as gifts or forced to marry IS fighters and supporters. Many have been subjected to torture and ill-treatment, including rape and other forms of sexual violence, and have likewise been pressured into converting to Islam.

Up to 300 of those abducted, mostly women and children, have managed to escape IS captivity, while the majority continue to be held in various locations in Iraq and in parts of Syria controlled by the IS. They are moved frequently from place to place. Some are able to communicate with their displaced relatives in areas outside IS control but the fate and whereabouts of others are not known.

Some of the women and girls who have escaped IS captivity, as well as some of those who remain captive, have given harrowing accounts to Amnesty International of the torture and abuses they have suffered.

Rape and other forms of torture and sexual violence, hostage taking, arbitrary deprivation of liberty and forcing persons to act against their religious beliefs constitute war crimes. Some of the violations and abuses documented in this report also constitute crimes against humanity, including torture, rape and sexual slavery. The IS continues to hold hundreds of captives, including children....

THE CONDUCT OF THE ISLAMIC STATE: WAR CRIMES AND CRIMES AGAINST HUMANITY

International humanitarian law (IHL, the laws of war) applies in situations of armed conflict. In Iraq, there is currently a non-international armed conflict involving forces aligned with the central government and the KRG, including international coalition members, and the armed group the Islamic State and other armed groups opposed to the government. The rules of IHL therefore apply and are binding on all parties to the conflict, including the IS. These rules and principles seek to protect anyone who is not actively participating in hostilities, notably civilians, and anyone, including those who were previously participating in hostilities, who is wounded or surrenders or is otherwise captured or incapacitated.

Torture and cruel treatment, rape and other forms of sexual violence, hostage taking, arbitrary deprivation of liberty and forcing persons to act against their religious beliefs are prohibited and constitute war crimes.

Under IHL, individuals, whether civilians or military, can be held criminally responsible for war crimes. Leaders and commanders of armed groups must be particularly diligent in seeking to prevent and repress such crimes. Military commanders and civilian superiors can be held responsible for crimes committed by their subordinates if they ordered such acts or if they knew, or had reason to know, such crimes were about to be committed and did not take necessary measures to prevent their commission, or to punish crimes that have already been committed. Individuals are also criminally responsible for assisting in, facilitating, aiding or abetting the commission of a war crime.

Crimes against humanity are prohibited acts committed as part of a widespread or systematic attack directed against a civilian population as part of a government or organizational policy. The violations and abuses documented in this report also constitute crimes against humanity. The IS have deliberately targeted the civilian population, and their crimes have been widespread, as well as systematic in nature, and have been part of the group's organizational policy. The crimes against humanity committed by IS include murder, enslavement, imprisonment, torture, rape and sexual slavery, and persecution.

The UN Security Council, in Resolution 1820 (2008), condemned sexual violence in armed conflict. It noted that "women and girls are particularly targeted by the use of sexual violence, including as a tactic of war to humiliate, dominate, instil fear in, disperse and/or forcibly relocate civilian members of a community or ethnic group". And it stated that "rape and other forms of sexual violence can constitute a war crime, a crime against humanity, or a constitutive act with respect to genocide".

The Security Council affirmed its intention "when establishing and renewing state-specific sanctions regimes, to take into consideration the appropriateness of targeted and graduated measures against parties to situations of armed conflict who commit rape and other forms of sexual violence against women and girls in situations of armed conflict".

CONCLUSION AND RECOMMENDATIONS

Despite worldwide condemnation, the IS has shown no intention of putting an end to the war crimes and crimes against humanity which its fighters have been committing on a large scale, including against the Iraqi women and girls they have abducted and continue to hold captive. Any party, in Iraq or outside, with any influence over the IS should use that influence to secure the release of these captives.

A small proportion of those abducted have managed to escape IS captivity, many after having been subjected to acts of unspeakable brutality. But the survivors interviewed by Amnesty International are not receiving the help and support they desperately need. Survivors of sexual violence should be proactively sought out and provided with adequate and timely medical care and support services. The KRG and the UN agencies and humanitarian organizations who are providing or putting in place such services should ensure that they are physically, geographically and financially accessible, and that survivors are provided with adequate and timely information on the available support services and how to access them. Information and materials about medical and psycho-social services, and must be made available in the appropriate languages so survivors are able to access them.

Such services should include prompt medical and forensic examination in accordance with survivors' wishes, including trauma support and counselling; sexual and reproductive health care including emergency contraception, HIV counselling, testing and post-exposure prophylaxis, testing and treatment for sexually transmitted infections, the option for safe and legal abortion services and maternal health support; legal and financial assistance; access to shelters or housing, education and training; and assistance in finding employment.

It is crucial that the privacy and confidentiality of those who have escaped IS captivity is respected at all times, whether or not they say that they have not been subjected to rape or other sexual violence. Notably, journalists should not attempt to interview escapees without ensuring they have given their informed consent, and relatives, activists and community leaders should not put any pressure on escapees to speak to media or others if they do not feel comfortable doing so.

(Source: Amnesty International.)

SPEECH BY PRESIDENT PUTIN ON THE "REUNIFICATION" OF CRIMEA WITH RUSSIA

Speech by Russia's President Vladimir Putin before both houses of the Russian legislature, the Federal Assembly, on 18 March, justifying the incorporation into the Russian Federation of the Republic of Crimea and the city of Sevastopol (formerly parts of Ukraine), and accusing the West of double standards for opposing it.

Federation Council members, State Duma deputies, good afternoon. Representatives of the Republic of Crimea and Sevastopol are here among us, citizens of Russia, residents of Crimea and Sevastopol!

Dear friends, we have gathered here today in connection with an issue that is of vital, historic significance to all of us. A referendum was held in Crimea on March 16 in full compliance with democratic procedures and international norms.

More than 82 per cent of the electorate took part in the vote. Over 96 per cent of them spoke out in favour of reuniting with Russia. These numbers speak for themselves.

To understand the reason behind such a choice it is enough to know the history of Crimea and what Russia and Crimea have always meant for each other.

Everything in Crimea speaks of our shared history and pride. This is the location of ancient Khersones, where Prince Vladimir was baptised. His spiritual feat of adopting Orthodoxy predetermined the overall basis of the culture, civilisation and human values that unite the peoples of Russia, Ukraine and Belarus. The graves of Russian soldiers whose bravery brought Crimea into the Russian empire are also in Crimea. This is also Sevastopol - a legendary city with an outstanding history, a fortress that serves as the birthplace of Russia's Black Sea Fleet. Crimea is Balaklava and Kerch, Malakhov Kurgan and Sapun Ridge. Each one of these places is dear to our hearts, symbolising Russian military glory and outstanding valour.

Crimea is a unique blend of different peoples' cultures and traditions. This makes it similar to Russia as a whole, where not a single ethnic group has been lost over the centuries. Russians and Ukrainians, Crimean Tatars and people of other ethnic groups have lived side by side in Crimea, retaining their own identity, traditions, languages and faith.

Incidentally, the total population of the Crimean Peninsula today is 2.2 million people, of whom almost 1.5 million are Russians, 350,000 are Ukrainians who predominantly consider Russian their native language, and about 290,000-300,000 are Crimean Tatars, who, as the referendum has shown, also lean towards Russia.

True, there was a time when Crimean Tatars were treated unfairly, just as a number of other peoples in the USSR. There is only one thing I can say here: millions of people of various ethnicities suffered during those repressions, and primarily Russians.

Crimean Tatars returned to their homeland. I believe we should make all the necessary political and legislative decisions to finalise the rehabilitation of Crimean Tatars, restore them in their rights and clear their good name.

We have great respect for people of all the ethnic groups living in Crimea. This is their common home, their motherland, and it would be right - I know the local population supports this - for Crimea to have three equal national languages: Russian, Ukrainian and Tatar.

Colleagues, in people's hearts and minds, Crimea has always been an inseparable part of Russia. This firm conviction is based on truth and justice and was passed from generation to generation, over time, under any circumstances, despite all the dramatic changes our country went through during the entire 20th century.

After the revolution, the Bolsheviks, for a number of reasons - may God judge them - added large sections of the historical South of Russia to the Republic of Ukraine. This was done with no consideration for the ethnic make-up of the population, and today these areas form the southeast of Ukraine. Then, in 1954, a decision was made to transfer Crimean Region to Ukraine, along with Sevastopol, despite the fact that it was a federal city. This was the personal initiative of the Communist Party head Nikita Khrushchev. What stood behind this decision of his - a desire to win the support of the Ukrainian political establishment or to atone for the mass repressions of the 1930's in Ukraine - is for historians to figure out.

What matters now is that this decision was made in clear violation of the constitutional norms that were in place even then. The decision was made behind the scenes. Naturally, in a totalitarian state nobody bothered to ask the citizens of Crimea and Sevastopol. They were faced with the fact. People, of course, wondered why all of a sudden Crimea became part of Ukraine. But on the whole - and we must state this clearly, we all know it - this decision was treated as a formality of sorts because the territory was transferred within the boundaries of a single state. Back then, it was impossible to imagine that Ukraine and Russia may split up and become two separate states. However, this has happened.

Unfortunately, what seemed impossible became a reality. The USSR fell apart. Things developed so swiftly that few people realised how truly dramatic those events and their consequences would be. Many people both in Russia and in Ukraine, as well as in other republics hoped that the Commonwealth of Independent States that was created at the time would become the new common form of statehood. They were told that there would be a single currency, a single economic space, joint armed forces; however, all this remained empty promises, while the big country was gone. It was only when Crimea ended up as part of a different country that Russia realised that it was not simply robbed, it was plundered.

At the same time, we have to admit that by launching the sovereignty parade Russia itself aided in the collapse of the Soviet Union. And as this collapse was legalised, everyone forgot about Crimea and Sevastopol - the main base of the Black Sea Fleet. Millions of people went to bed in one country and awoke in different ones, overnight becoming ethnic minorities in former Union republics, while the Russian nation became one of the biggest, if not the biggest ethnic group in the world to be divided by borders.

Now, many years later, I heard residents of Crimea say that back in 1991 they were handed over like a sack of potatoes. This is hard to disagree with. And what about the Russian state? What about Russia? It humbly accepted the situation. This country was going through such hard times then that realistically it was incapable of protecting its interests. However, the people could not reconcile themselves to this outrageous historical injustice. All these years, citizens and many public figures came back to this issue, saying that Crimea is historically Russian land and Sevastopol is a Russian city. Yes, we all knew this in our hearts and minds, but we had to proceed from the existing reality and build our good-neighbourly relations with independent Ukraine on a new basis. Meanwhile, our relations with Ukraine, with the fraternal Ukrainian people have always been and will remain of foremost importance for us.

Today we can speak about it openly, and I would like to share with you some details of the negotiations that took place in the early 2000s. The then President of Ukraine Mr Kuchma asked me to expedite the process of delimiting the Russian-Ukrainian border. At that time, the process was practically at a standstill. Russia seemed to have recognised Crimea as part of Ukraine, but there were no negotiations on delimiting the borders. Despite the complexity of the situation, I immediately issued instructions to Russian government agencies to speed up their work to document the borders, so that everyone had a clear understanding that by agreeing to delimit the border we admitted de facto and de jure that Crimea was Ukrainian territory, thereby closing the issue.

We accommodated Ukraine not only regarding Crimea, but also on such a complicated matter as the maritime boundary in the Sea of Azov and the Kerch Strait. What we proceeded from back then was that good relations with Ukraine matter most for us and they should not fall hostage to deadlock territorial disputes. However, we expected Ukraine to remain our good neighbour, we hoped that Russian citizens and Russian speakers in Ukraine, especially its southeast and Crimea, would live in a friendly, democratic and civilised state that would protect their rights in line with the norms of international law.

However, this is not how the situation developed. Time and time again attempts were made to deprive Russians of their historical memory, even of their language and to subject them to forced assimilation. Moreover, Russians, just as other citizens of Ukraine are suffering from the constant political and state crisis that has been rocking the country for over 20 years.

I understand why Ukrainian people wanted change. They have had enough of the authorities in power during the years of Ukraine's independence. Presidents, prime ministers and parliamentarians changed, but their attitude to the country and its people remained the same. They milked the country, fought among themselves for power, assets and cash flows and did not care much about the ordinary people. They did not wonder why it was that millions of Ukrainian citizens saw no prospects at home and went to other countries to work as day labourers. I would like to stress this: it was not some Silicon Valley they fled to, but to become day labourers. Last year alone almost 3 million people found such jobs in Russia. According to some sources, in 2013 their earnings in Russia totalled over $20 billion, which is about 12 per cent of Ukraine's GDP.

I would like to reiterate that I understand those who came out on Maidan with peaceful slogans against corruption, inefficient state management and poverty. The right to peaceful protest, democratic procedures and elections exist for the sole purpose of replacing the authorities that do not satisfy the people. However, those who stood behind the latest events in Ukraine had a different agenda: they were preparing yet another government takeover; they wanted to seize power and would stop short of nothing. They resorted to terror, murder and riots. Nationalists, neo-Nazis, Russophobes and anti-Semites executed this coup. They continue to set the tone in Ukraine this day.

The new so-called authorities began by introducing a draft law to revise the language policy, which was a direct infringement on the rights of ethnic minorities. However, they were immediately 'disciplined' by the foreign sponsors of these so-called politicians. One has to admit that the mentors of these current authorities are smart and know well what such attempts to build a purely Ukrainian state may lead to. The draft law was set aside, but clearly reserved for the future. Hardly any mention is made of this attempt now, probably on the presumption that people have a short memory. Nevertheless, we can all clearly see the intentions of these ideological heirs of Bandera, Hitler's accomplice during World War II.

It is also obvious that there is no legitimate executive authority in Ukraine now, nobody to talk to. Many government agencies have been taken over by the impostors, but they do not have any control in the country, while they themselves - and I would like to stress this - are often controlled by radicals. In some cases, you need a special permit from the militants on Maidan to meet with certain ministers of the current government. This is not a joke - this is reality.

Those who opposed the coup were immediately threatened with repression. Naturally, the first in line here was Crimea, the Russian-speaking Crimea. In view of this, the residents of Crimea and Sevastopol turned to Russia for help in defending their rights and lives, in preventing the events that were unfolding and are still underway in Kiev, Donetsk, Kharkov and other Ukrainian cities.

Naturally, we could not leave this plea unheeded; we could not abandon Crimea and its residents in distress. This would have been betrayal on our part.

First, we had to help create conditions so that the residents of Crimea for the first time in history were able to peacefully express their free will regarding their own future. However, what do we hear from our colleagues in Western Europe and North America? They say we are violating norms of international law. Firstly, it's a good thing that they at least remember that there exists such a thing as international law - better late than never.

Secondly, and most importantly - what exactly are we violating? True, the President of the Russian Federation received permission from the Upper House of Parliament to use the Armed Forces in Ukraine. However, strictly speaking, nobody has acted on this permission yet. Russia's Armed Forces never entered Crimea; they were there already in line with an international agreement. True, we did enhance our forces there; however - this is something I would like everyone to hear and know - we did not exceed the personnel limit of our Armed Forces in Crimea, which is set at 25,000, because there was no need to do so.

Next. As it declared independence and decided to hold a referendum, the Supreme Council of Crimea referred to the United Nations Charter, which speaks of the right of nations to self-determination. Incidentally, I would like to remind you that when Ukraine seceded from the USSR it did exactly the same thing, almost word for word. Ukraine used this right, yet the residents of Crimea are denied it. Why is that?

Moreover, the Crimean authorities referred to the well-known Kosovo precedent - a precedent our western colleagues created with their own hands in a very similar situation, when they agreed that the unilateral separation of Kosovo from Serbia, exactly what Crimea is doing now, was legitimate and did not require any permission from the country's central authorities. Pursuant to Article 2, Chapter 1 of the United Nations Charter, the UN International Court agreed with this approach and made the following comment in its ruling of July 22, 2010, and I quote: "No general prohibition may be inferred from the practice of the Security Council with regard to declarations of independence," and "General international law contains no prohibition on declarations of independence." Crystal clear, as they say.

I do not like to resort to quotes, but in this case, I cannot help it. Here is a quote from another official document: the Written Statement of the United States America of April 17, 2009, submitted to the same UN International Court in connection with the hearings on Kosovo. Again, I quote: "Declarations of independence may, and often do, violate domestic legislation. However, this does not make them violations of international law." End of quote. They wrote this, disseminated it all over the world, had everyone agree and now they are outraged. Over what? The actions of Crimean people completely fit in with these instructions, as it were. For some reason, things that Kosovo Albanians (and we have full respect for them) were permitted to do, Russians, Ukrainians and Crimean Tatars in Crimea are not allowed. Again, one wonders why.

We keep hearing from the United States and Western Europe that Kosovo is some special case. What makes it so special in the eyes of our colleagues? It turns out that it is the fact that the conflict in Kosovo resulted in so many human casualties. Is this a legal argument? The ruling of the International Court says nothing about this. This is not even double standards; this is amazing, primitive, blunt cynicism. One should not try so crudely to make everything suit their interests, calling the same thing white today and black tomorrow. According to this logic, we have to make sure every conflict leads to human losses.

I will state clearly - if the Crimean local self-defence units had not taken the situation under control, there could have been casualties as well. Fortunately this did not happen. There was not a single armed confrontation in Crimea and no casualties. Why do you think this was so? The answer is simple: because it is very difficult, practically impossible to fight against the will of the people. Here I would like to thank the Ukrainian military - and this is 22,000 fully armed servicemen. I would like to thank those Ukrainian service members who refrained from bloodshed and did not smear their uniforms in blood.

Other thoughts come to mind in this connection. They keep talking of some Russian intervention in Crimea, some sort of aggression. This is strange to hear. I cannot recall a single case in history of an intervention without a single shot being fired and with no human casualties.

Colleagues, like a mirror, the situation in Ukraine reflects what is going on and what has been happening in the world over the past several decades. After the dissolution of bipolarity on the planet, we no longer have stability. Key international institutions are not getting any stronger; on the contrary, in many cases, they are sadly degrading. Our western partners, led by the United States of America, prefer not to be guided by international law in their practical policies, but by the rule of the gun. They have come to believe in their exclusivity and exceptionalism, that they can decide the destinies of the world, that only they can ever be right. They act as they please: here and there, they use force against sovereign states, building coalitions based on the principle "If you are not with us, you are against us." To make this aggression look legitimate, they force the necessary resolutions from international organisations, and if for some reason this does not work, they simply ignore the UN Security Council and the UN overall.

This happened in Yugoslavia; we remember 1999 very well. It was hard to believe, even seeing it with my own eyes, that at the end of the 20th century, one of Europe's capitals, Belgrade, was under missile attack for several weeks, and then came the real intervention. Was there a UN Security Council resolution on this matter, allowing for these actions? Nothing of the sort. And then, they hit Afghanistan, Iraq, and frankly violated the UN Security Council resolution on Libya, when instead of imposing the so-called no-fly zone over it they started bombing it too.

There was a whole series of controlled "colour" revolutions. Clearly, the people in those nations, where these events took place, were sick of tyranny and poverty, of their lack of prospects; but these feelings were taken advantage of cynically. Standards were imposed on these nations that did not in any way correspond to their way of life, traditions, or these peoples' cultures. As a result, instead of democracy and freedom, there was chaos, outbreaks in violence and a series of upheavals. The Arab Spring turned into the Arab Winter.

A similar situation unfolded in Ukraine. In 2004, to push the necessary candidate through at the presidential elections, they thought up some sort of third round that was not stipulated by the law. It was absurd and a mockery of the constitution. And now, they have thrown in an organised and well-equipped army of militants.

We understand what is happening; we understand that these actions were aimed against Ukraine and Russia and against Eurasian integration. And all this while Russia strived to engage in dialogue with our colleagues in the West. We are constantly proposing cooperation on all key issues; we want to strengthen our level of trust and for our relations to be equal, open and fair. But we saw no reciprocal steps.

On the contrary, they have lied to us many times, made decisions behind our backs, placed us before an accomplished fact. This happened with NATO's expansion to the East, as well as the deployment of military infrastructure at our borders. They kept telling us the same thing: "Well, this does not concern you." That's easy to say.

It happened with the deployment of a missile defence system. In spite of all our apprehensions, the project is working and moving forward. It happened with the endless foot-dragging in the talks on visa issues, promises of fair competition and free access to global markets.

Today, we are being threatened with sanctions, but we already experience many limitations, ones that are quite significant for us, our economy and our nation. For example, still during the times of the Cold War, the US and subsequently other nations restricted a large list of technologies and equipment from being sold to the USSR, creating the Coordinating Committee for Multilateral Export Controls list. Today, they have formally been eliminated, but only formally; and in reality, many limitations are still in effect.

In short, we have every reason to assume that the infamous policy of containment, led in the 18th, 19th and 20th centuries, continues today. They are constantly trying to sweep us into a corner because we have an independent position, because we maintain it and because we call things like they are and do not engage in hypocrisy. But there is a limit to everything. And with Ukraine, our western partners have crossed the line, playing the bear and acting irresponsibly and unprofessionally.

After all, they were fully aware that there are millions of Russians living in Ukraine and in Crimea. They must have really lacked political instinct and common sense not to foresee all the consequences of their actions. Russia found itself in a position it could not retreat from. If you compress the spring all the way to its limit, it will snap back hard. You must always remember this.

Today, it is imperative to end this hysteria, to refute the rhetoric of the cold war and to accept the obvious fact: Russia is an independent, active participant in international affairs; like other countries, it has its own national interests that need to be taken into account and respected.

At the same time, we are grateful to all those who understood our actions in Crimea; we are grateful to the people of China, whose leaders have always considered the situation in Ukraine and Crimea taking into account the full historical and political context, and greatly appreciate India's reserve and objectivity.

Today, I would like to address the people of the United States of America, the people who, since the foundation of their nation and adoption of the Declaration of Independence, have been proud to hold freedom above all else. Isn't the desire of Crimea's residents to freely choose their fate such a value? Please understand us.

I believe that the Europeans, first and foremost, the Germans, will also understand me. Let me remind you that in the course of political consultations on the unification of East and West Germany, at the expert, though very high level, some nations that were then and are now Germany's allies did not support the idea of unification. Our nation, however, unequivocally supported the sincere, unstoppable desire of the Germans for national unity. I am confident that you have not forgotten this, and I expect that the citizens of Germany will also support the aspiration of the Russians, of historical Russia, to restore unity.

I also want to address the people of Ukraine. I sincerely want you to understand us: we do not want to harm you in any way, or to hurt your national feelings. We have always respected the territorial integrity of the Ukrainian state, incidentally, unlike those who sacrificed Ukraine's unity for their political ambitions. They flaunt slogans about Ukraine's greatness, but they are the ones who did everything to divide the nation. Today's civil standoff is entirely on their conscience. I want you to hear me, my dear friends. Do not believe those who want you to fear Russia, shouting that other regions will follow Crimea. We do not want to divide Ukraine; we do not need that. As for Crimea, it was and remains a Russian, Ukrainian, and Crimean-Tatar land.

I repeat, just as it has been for centuries, it will be a home to all the peoples living there. What it will never be and do is follow in Bandera's footsteps!

Crimea is our common historical legacy and a very important factor in regional stability. And this strategic territory should be part of a strong and stable sovereignty, which today can only be Russian. Otherwise, dear friends (I am addressing both Ukraine and Russia), you and we - the Russians and the Ukrainians - could lose Crimea completely, and that could happen in the near historical perspective. Please think about it.

Let me note too that we have already heard declarations from Kiev about Ukraine soon joining NATO. What would this have meant for Crimea and Sevastopol in the future? It would have meant that NATO's navy would be right there in this city of Russia's military glory, and this would create not an illusory but a perfectly real threat to the whole of southern Russia. These are things that could have become reality were it not for the choice the Crimean people made, and I want to say thank you to them for this.

But let me say too that we are not opposed to cooperation with NATO, for this is certainly not the case. For all the internal processes within the organisation, NATO remains a military alliance, and we are against having a military alliance making itself at home right in our backyard or in our historic territory. I simply cannot imagine that we would travel to Sevastopol to visit NATO sailors. Of course, most of them are wonderful guys, but it would be better to have them come and visit us, be our guests, rather than the other way round.

Let me say quite frankly that it pains our hearts to see what is happening in Ukraine at the moment, see the people's suffering and their uncertainty about how to get through today and what awaits them tomorrow. Our concerns are understandable because we are not simply close neighbours but, as I have said many times already, we are one people. Kiev is the mother of Russian cities. Ancient Rus is our common source and we cannot live without each other.

Let me say one other thing too. Millions of Russians and Russian-speaking people live in Ukraine and will continue to do so. Russia will always defend their interests using political, diplomatic and legal means. But it should be above all in Ukraine's own interest to ensure that these people's rights and interests are fully protected. This is the guarantee of Ukraine's state stability and territorial integrity.

We want to be friends with Ukraine and we want Ukraine to be a strong, sovereign and self-sufficient country. Ukraine is one of our biggest partners after all. We have many joint projects and I believe in their success no matter what the current difficulties. Most importantly, we want peace and harmony to reign in Ukraine, and we are ready to work together with other countries to do everything possible to facilitate and support this. But as I said, only Ukraine's own people can put their own house in order.

Residents of Crimea and the city of Sevastopol, the whole of Russia admired your courage, dignity and bravery. It was you who decided Crimea's future. We were closer than ever over these days, supporting each other. These were sincere feelings of solidarity. It is at historic turning points such as these that a nation demonstrates its maturity and strength of spirit. The Russian people showed this maturity and strength through their united support for their compatriots.

Russia's foreign policy position on this matter drew its firmness from the will of millions of our people, our national unity and the support of our country's main political and public forces. I want to thank everyone for this patriotic spirit, everyone without exception. Now, we need to continue and maintain this kind of consolidation so as to resolve the tasks our country faces on its road ahead.

Obviously, we will encounter external opposition, but this is a decision that we need to make for ourselves. Are we ready to consistently defend our national interests, or will we forever give in, retreat to who knows where? Some Western politicians are already threatening us with not just sanctions but also the prospect of increasingly serious problems on the domestic front. I would like to know what it is they have in mind exactly: action by a fifth column, this disparate bunch of 'national traitors', or are they hoping to put us in a worsening social and economic situation so as to provoke public discontent? We consider such statements irresponsible and clearly aggressive in tone, and we will respond to them accordingly. At the same time, we will never seek confrontation with our partners, whether in the East or the West, but on the contrary, will do everything we can to build civilised and good-neighbourly relations as one is supposed to in the modern world.

Colleagues, I understand the people of Crimea, who put the question in the clearest possible terms in the referendum: should Crimea be with Ukraine or with Russia? We can be sure in saying that the authorities in Crimea and Sevastopol, the legislative authorities, when they formulated the question, set aside group and political interests and made the people's fundamental interests alone the cornerstone of their work. The particular historic, population, political and economic circumstances of Crimea would have made any other proposed option - however tempting it could be at the first glance - only temporary and fragile and would have inevitably led to further worsening of the situation there, which would have had disastrous effects on people's lives. The people of Crimea thus decided to put the question in firm and uncompromising form, with no grey areas. The referendum was fair and transparent, and the people of Crimea clearly and convincingly expressed their will and stated that they want to be with Russia.

Russia will also have to make a difficult decision now, taking into account the various domestic and external considerations. What do people here in Russia think? Here, like in any democratic country, people have different points of view, but I want to make the point that the absolute majority of our people clearly do support what is happening.

The most recent public opinion surveys conducted here in Russia show that 95 percent of people think that Russia should protect the interests of Russians and members of other ethnic groups living in Crimea - 95 percent of our citizens. More than 83 percent think that Russia should do this even if it will complicate our relations with some other countries. A total of 86 percent of our people see Crimea as still being Russian territory and part of our country's lands. And one particularly important figure, which corresponds exactly with the result in Crimea's referendum: almost 92 percent of our people support Crimea's reunification with Russia.

Thus we see that the overwhelming majority of people in Crimea and the absolute majority of the Russian Federation's people support the reunification of the Republic of Crimea and the city of Sevastopol with Russia.

Now this is a matter for Russia's own political decision, and any decision here can be based only on the people's will, because the people is the ultimate source of all authority.

Members of the Federation Council, deputies of the State Duma, citizens of Russia, residents of Crimea and Sevastopol, today, in accordance with the people's will, I submit to the Federal Assembly a request to consider a Constitutional Law on the creation of two new constituent entities within the Russian Federation: the Republic of Crimea and the city of Sevastopol, and to ratify the treaty on admitting to the Russian Federation Crimea and Sevastopol, which is already ready for signing. I stand assured of your support.

(Source: Russian Presidential website, Kremlin.ru)

MINSK PROTOCOL AND MEMORANDUM IN UKRAINIAN CONFLICT

Text of the Minsk Protocol, signed on 5 September, to bring about a ceasefire in the conflict in eastern Ukraine between Ukrainian military forces and pro-Russian rebels, followed by the text of the Memorandum, signed on 19 September, clarifying measures to implement the provisions of the Minsk Protocol. Parties to the Minsk negotiations were the Trilateral Contact Group on Ukraine, established in June 2014 (which consisted of representatives from Ukraine, Russia and the OSCE), and representatives of the self-proclaimed Donetsk and Lugansk People's Republics.

Minsk Protocol of 5 September 2014

1. Ensure an immediate bilateral ceasefire.

2. Ensure the monitoring and verification by the OSCE of the ceasefire.

3. A decentralisation of power, including through the adoption of the law of Ukraine "about local government provisional arrangements in some areas of Donetsk and Lugansk Oblasts" (the law on special status).

4. Ensure the permanent monitoring of the Ukrainian-Russian border and verification by the OSCE with the creation of security zones in the border regions of Ukraine and the Russian Federation.

5. To immediately release all hostages and illegally detained persons.

6. A law on preventing the prosecution and punishment of persons in connection with the events that have taken place in some areas of Donetsk and Lugansk Oblasts.

7. Continue the inclusive national dialogue.

8. To take measures to improve the humanitarian situation in Donbas.

9. Ensure early local elections in accordance with the law of Ukraine "about local government provisional arrangements in some areas of Donetsk and Lugansk Oblasts" (the law on special status).

10. Withdraw the illegal armed groups, military equipment, as well as fighters and mercenaries from Ukraine.

11. To adopt the programme of economic recovery and reconstruction of Donbas region.

12. To provide personal security for the participants in the consultations.

Memorandum of 19 September 2014 outlining the parameters for the implementation of commitments of the Minsk Protocol of 5 September 2014

1. The ceasefire is considered universal.

2. Units and military formations of both sides stop at the line of contact as of 19 September.

3. Use of all types of weapons and offensive operations is banned.

4. Within 24 hours of adoption of this memorandum, weapons of more than 100 mm in calibre are to be pulled back at least 15 km from the line of contact by both sides, including from population centres, which makes it possible to create a ceasefire zone at least 30 km wide, a security zone. Artillery systems of more than 100 mm calibre at the line of contact are to be pulled back out of range.

5. Heavy weapons and military hardware are banned from an area within the boundaries of specific population centres.

6. It is banned to set up new mined obstacles at the boundaries of the security zone. All mined obstacles set up in the security zone previously are to be cleared.

7. From the moment this memorandum is adopted, military aircraft and foreign aircraft, with the exception of OSCE aircraft, are banned from flying above the security zone.

8. An OSCE monitoring mission, consisting of OSCE observers, is to be deployed in the ceasefire zone within 24 hours after this memorandum is adopted. The above zone should be divided into sectors, with the number of their borders to be agreed during preparations for the work of the OSCE observation mission monitoring group.

9. All foreign armed groups, military hardware as well as militants and mercenaries are to be withdrawn from Ukrainian territory under OSCE monitoring.

Participants of the Trilateral Contact Group:
OSCE Ambassador Heidi Tagliavini
Second President of Ukraine Leonid D. Kuchma
Ambassador of Russian Federation to Ukraine Mikhail Y. Zurabov
Aleksander V. Zakharchenko, chairman of the Donetsk People's Republic
Igor.V. Plotnitskiy

(Source: OSCE, Euromaidan Press)

SPEECH BY PRESIDENT OBAMA ON US SURVEILLANCE AND INTELLIGENCE-GATHERING

Transcript of speech by President Barack Obama, delivered at the justice department on 17 January, in which he addressed the public furore created by the disclosures by former National Security Agency (NSA) worker Edward Snowden concerning the USA's huge surveillance and intelligence-gathering programmes. The speech constituted a formal response to the report, submitted in December 2013, by the Review Group on Intelligence and Communications Technology. Although Obama promised reforms to the existing protocols, these were for the most part left vague, with their precise nature to be determined in Congress.

At the dawn of our Republic, a small, secret surveillance committee borne out of the "The Sons of Liberty" was established in Boston. And the group's members included Paul Revere. At night, they would patrol the streets, reporting back any signs that the British were preparing raids against America's early patriots.

Throughout American history, intelligence has helped secure our country and our freedoms. In the Civil War, Union balloon reconnaissance tracked the size of Confederate armies by counting the number of campfires. In World War II, code-breakers gave us insights into Japanese war plans, and when Patton marched across Europe, intercepted communications helped save the lives of his troops. After the war, the rise of the Iron Curtain and nuclear weapons only increased the need for sustained intelligence gathering. And so, in the early days of the Cold War, President Truman created the National Security Agency, or NSA, to give us insights into the Soviet bloc, and provide our leaders with information they needed to confront aggression and avert catastrophe.

Throughout this evolution, we benefited from both our Constitution and our traditions of limited government. US intelligence agencies were anchored in a system of checks and balances—with oversight from elected leaders, and protections for ordinary citizens. Meanwhile, totalitarian states like East Germany offered a cautionary tale of what could happen when vast, unchecked surveillance turned citizens into informers, and persecuted people for what they said in the privacy of their own homes.

In fact, even the United States proved not to be immune to the abuse of surveillance. And in the 1960s, government spied on civil rights leaders and critics of the Vietnam War. And partly in response to these revelations, additional laws were established in the 1970s to ensure that our intelligence capabilities could not be misused against our citizens. In the long, twilight struggle against Communism, we had been reminded that the very liberties that we sought to preserve could not be sacrificed at the altar of national security.

If the fall of the Soviet Union left America without a competing superpower, emerging threats from terrorist groups, and the proliferation of weapons of mass destruction placed new and in some ways more complicated demands on our intelligence agencies. Globalisation and the Internet made these threats more acute, as technology erased borders and empowered individuals to project great violence, as well as great good. Moreover, these new threats raised new legal and new policy questions. For while few doubted the legitimacy of spying on hostile states, our framework of laws was not fully adapted to prevent terrorist attacks by individuals acting on their own, or acting in small, ideologically driven groups on behalf of a foreign power.

The horror of September 11th brought all these issues to the fore. Across the political spectrum, Americans recognised that we had to adapt to a world in which a bomb could be built in a basement, and our electric grid could be shut down by operators an ocean away. We were shaken by the signs we had missed leading up to the attacks—how the hijackers had made phone calls to known extremists and traveled to suspicious places. So we demanded that our intelligence community improve its capabilities, and that law enforcement change practices to focus more on preventing attacks before they happen than prosecuting terrorists after an attack.

It is hard to overstate the transformation America's intelligence community had to go through after 9/11. Our agencies suddenly needed to do far more than the traditional mission of monitoring hostile powers and gathering information for policymakers. Instead, they were now asked to identify and target plotters in some of the most remote parts of the world, and to anticipate the actions of networks that, by their very nature, cannot be easily penetrated with spies or informants.

And it is a testimony to the hard work and dedication of the men and women of our intelligence community that over the past decade we've made enormous strides in fulfilling this mission. Today, new capabilities allow intelligence agencies to track who a terrorist is in contact with, and follow the trail of his travel or his funding. New laws allow information to be collected and shared more quickly and effectively between federal agencies, and state and local law enforcement. Relationships with foreign intelligence services have expanded, and our capacity to repel cyber-attacks have been strengthened. And taken together, these efforts have prevented multiple attacks and saved innocent live—not just here in the United States, but around the globe.

And yet, in our rush to respond to a very real and novel set of threats, the risk of government overreach—the possibility that we lose some of our core liberties in pursuit of security—also became more pronounced. We saw, in the immediate aftermath of 9/11, our government engaged in enhanced interrogation techniques that contradicted our values. As a Senator, I was critical of several practices, such as warrantless wiretaps. And all too often new authorities were instituted without adequate public debate.

Through a combination of action by the courts, increased congressional oversight, and adjustments by the previous administration, some of the worst excesses that emerged after 9/11 were curbed by the time I took office. But a variety of factors have continued to complicate America's efforts to both defend our nation and uphold our civil liberties.

First, the same technological advances that allow US intelligence agencies to pinpoint an al Qaeda cell in Yemen or an email between two terrorists in the Sahel also mean that many routine communications around the world are within our reach. And at a time when more and more of our lives are digital, that prospect is disquieting for all of us.

Second, the combination of increased digital information and powerful supercomputers offers intelligence agencies the possibility of sifting through massive amounts of bulk data to identify patterns or pursue leads that may thwart impending threats. It's a powerful tool. But the government collection and storage of such bulk data also creates a potential for abuse.

Third, the legal safeguards that restrict surveillance against U.S. persons without a warrant do not apply to foreign persons overseas. This is not unique to America; few, if any, spy agencies around the world constrain their activities beyond their own borders. And the whole point of intelligence is to obtain information that is not publicly available. But America's capabilities are unique, and the power of new technologies means that there are fewer and fewer technical constraints on what we can do. That places a special obligation on us to ask tough questions about what we should do.

And finally, intelligence agencies cannot function without secrecy, which makes their work less subject to public debate. Yet there is an inevitable bias not only within the intelligence community, but among all of us who are responsible for national security, to collect more information about the world, not less. So in the absence of institutional requirements for regular debate—and oversight that is public, as well as private or classified—the danger of government overreach becomes more acute. And this is particularly true when surveillance technology and our reliance on digital information is evolving much faster than our laws.

For all these reasons, I maintained a healthy scepticism toward our surveillance programs after I became President. I ordered that our programs be reviewed by my national security team and our lawyers, and in some cases I ordered changes in how we did business. We increased oversight and auditing, including new structures aimed at compliance. Improved rules were proposed by the government and approved by the Foreign Intelligence Surveillance Court. And we sought to keep Congress continually updated on these activities.

What I did not do is stop these programs wholesale—not only because I felt that they made us more secure, but also because nothing in that initial review, and nothing that I have learned since, indicated that our intelligence community has sought to violate the law or is cavalier about the civil liberties of their fellow citizens.

To the contrary, in an extraordinarily difficult job—one in which actions are second-guessed, success is unreported, and failure can be catastrophic—the men and women of the intelligence community, including the NSA, consistently follow protocols designed to protect the privacy of ordinary people. They're not abusing authorities in order to listen to your private phone calls or read your emails. When mistakes are made—which is inevitable in any large and complicated human enterprise—they correct those mistakes. Labouring in obscurity, often unable to discuss their work even with family and friends, the men and women at the NSA know that if another 9/11 or massive cyber-attack occurs, they will be asked, by Congress and the media, why they failed to connect the dots. What sustains those who work at NSA and our other intelligence agencies through all these pressures is the knowledge that their professionalism and dedication play a central role in the defence of our nation.

Now, to say that our intelligence community follows the law, and is staffed by patriots, is not to suggest that I or others in my administration felt complacent about the potential impact of these programs. Those of us who hold office in America have a responsibility to our Constitution, and while I was confident in the integrity of those who lead our intelligence community, it was clear to me in observing our intelligence operations on a regular basis that changes in our technological capabilities were raising new questions about the privacy safeguards currently in place.

Moreover, after an extended review of our use of drones in the fight against terrorist networks, I believed a fresh examination of our surveillance programs was a necessary next step in our effort to get off the open-ended war footing that we've maintained since 9/11. And for these reasons, I indicated in a speech at the National Defence University last May that we needed a more robust public discussion about the balance between security and liberty. Of course, what I did not know at the time is that within weeks of my speech, an avalanche of unauthorised disclosures would spark controversies at home and abroad that have continued to this day.

And given the fact of an open investigation, I'm not going to dwell on Mr. Snowden's actions or his motivations; I will say that our nation's defence depends in part on the fidelity of those entrusted with our nation's secrets. If any individual who objects to government policy can take it into their own hands to publicly disclose classified information, then we will not be able to keep our people safe, or conduct foreign policy. Moreover, the sensational way in which these disclosures have come out has often shed more heat than light, while revealing methods to our adversaries that could impact our operations in ways that we may not fully understand for years to come.

Regardless of how we got here, though, the task before us now is greater than simply repairing the damage done to our operations or preventing more disclosures from taking place in the future. Instead, we have to make some important decisions about how to protect ourselves and sustain our leadership in the world, while upholding the civil liberties and privacy protections that our ideals and our Constitution require. We need to do so not only because it is right, but because the challenges posed by threats like terrorism and proliferation and cyber-attacks are not going away any time soon. They are going to continue to be a major problem. And for our intelligence community to be effective over the long haul, we must maintain the trust of the American people, and people around the world.

This effort will not be completed overnight, and given the pace of technological change, we shouldn't expect this to be the last time America has this debate. But I want the American people to know that the work has begun. Over the last six months, I created an outside Review Group on Intelligence and Communications Technologies to make recommendations for reform. I consulted with the Privacy and Civil Liberties Oversight Board, created by Congress. I've listened to foreign partners, privacy advocates, and industry leaders. My administration has spent countless hours considering how to approach intelligence in this era of diffuse threats and technological revolution. So before outlining specific changes that I've ordered, let me make a few broad observations that have emerged from this process.

First, everyone who has looked at these problems, including sceptics of existing programs, recognises that we have real enemies and threats, and that intelligence serves a vital role in confronting them. We cannot prevent terrorist attacks or cyber threats without some capability to penetrate digital communications—whether it's to unravel a terrorist plot; to intercept malware that targets a stock exchange; to make sure air traffic control systems are not compromised; or to ensure that hackers do not empty your bank accounts. We are expected to protect the American people; that requires us to have capabilities in this field.

Moreover, we cannot unilaterally disarm our intelligence agencies. There is a reason why Black-Berrys and iPhones are not allowed in the White House Situation Room. We know that the intelligence services of other countries—including some who feign surprise over the Snowden disclosures—are constantly probing our government and private sector networks, and accelerating programmes to listen to our conversations, and intercept our emails, and compromise our systems. We know that.

Meanwhile, a number of countries, including some who have loudly criticised the NSA, privately acknowledge that America has special responsibilities as the world's only superpower; that our intelligence capabilities are critical to meeting these responsibilities, and that they themselves have relied on the information we obtain to protect their own people.

Second, just as ardent civil libertarians recognise the need for robust intelligence capabilities, those with responsibilities for our national security readily acknowledge the potential for abuse as intelligence capabilities advance and more and more private information is digitised. After all, the folks at NSA and other intelligence agencies are our neighbours. They're our friends and family. They've got electronic bank and medical records like everybody else. They have kids on Facebook and Instagram, and they know, more than most of us, the vulnerabilities to privacy that exist in a world where transactions are recorded, and emails and text and messages are stored, and even our movements can increasingly be tracked through the GPS on our phones.

Third, there was a recognition by all who participated in these reviews that the challenges to our privacy do not come from government alone. Corporations of all shapes and sizes track what you buy, store and analyse our data, and use it for commercial purposes; that's how those targeted ads pop up on your computer and your smartphone periodically. But all of us understand that the standards for government surveillance must be higher. Given the unique power of the state, it is not enough for leaders to say: Trust us, we won't abuse the data we collect. For history has too many examples when that trust has been breached. Our system of government is built on the premise that our liberty cannot depend on the good intentions of those in power; it depends on the law to constrain those in power.

I make these observations to underscore that the basic values of most Americans when it comes to questions of surveillance and privacy converge a lot more than the crude characterisations that have emerged over the last several months. Those who are troubled by our existing programs are not interested in repeating the tragedy of 9/11, and those who defend these programs are not dismissive of civil liberties.

The challenge is getting the details right, and that is not simple. In fact, during the course of our review, I have often reminded myself I would not be where I am today were it not for the courage of dissidents like Dr. King, who were spied upon by their own government. And as President, a President who looks at intelligence every morning, I also can't help but be reminded that America must be vigilant in the face of threats.

Fortunately, by focusing on facts and specifics rather than speculation and hypotheticals, this review process has given me—and hopefully the American people—some clear direction for change. And today, I can announce a series of concrete and substantial reforms that my administration intends to adopt administratively or will seek to codify with Congress.

First, I have approved a new presidential directive for our signals intelligence activities both at home and abroad. This guidance will strengthen executive branch oversight of our intelligence activities. It will ensure that we take into account our security requirements, but also our alliances; our trade and investment relationships, including the concerns of American companies; and our commitment to privacy and basic liberties. And we will review decisions about intelligence priorities and sensitive targets on an annual basis so that our actions are regularly scrutinised by my senior national security team.

Second, we will reform programs and procedures in place to provide greater transparency to our surveillance activities, and fortify the safeguards that protect the privacy of US persons. Since we began this review, including information being released today, we have declassified over 40 opinions and orders of the Foreign Intelligence Surveillance Court, which provides judicial review of some of our most sensitive intelligence activities—including the Section 702 program targeting foreign individuals overseas, and the Section 215 telephone metadata program.

And going forward, I'm directing the Director of National Intelligence, in consultation with the Attorney General, to annually review for the purposes of declassification any future opinions of the court with broad privacy implications, and to report to me and to Congress on these efforts. To ensure that the court hears a broader range of privacy perspectives, I am also calling on Congress to authorise the establishment of a panel of advocates from outside government to provide an independent voice in significant cases before the Foreign Intelligence Surveillance Court.

Third, we will provide additional protections for activities conducted under Section 702, which allows the government to intercept the communications of foreign targets overseas who have information that's important for our national security. Specifically, I am asking the Attorney General and DNI to institute reforms that place additional restrictions on government's ability to retain, search, and use in criminal cases communications between Americans and foreign citizens incidentally collected under Section 702.

Fourth, in investigating threats, the FBI also relies on what's called national security letters, which can require companies to provide specific and limited information to the government without disclosing the orders to the subject of the investigation. These are cases in which it's important that the subject of the investigation, such as a possible terrorist or spy, isn't tipped off. But we can and should be more transparent in how government uses this authority.

I have therefore directed the Attorney General to amend how we use national security letters so that this secrecy will not be indefinite, so that it will terminate within a fixed time unless the government demonstrates a real need for further secrecy. We will also enable communications providers to make public more information than ever before about the orders that they have received to provide data to the government.

This brings me to the program that has generated the most controversy these past few months—the bulk collection of telephone records under Section 215. Let me repeat what I said when this story first broke: This program does not involve the content of phone calls, or the names of people making calls. Instead, it provides a record of phone numbers and the times and lengths of calls—metadata that can be queried if and when we have a reasonable suspicion that a particular number is linked to a terrorist organisation.

Why is this necessary? The program grew out of a desire to address a gap identified after 9/11. One of the 9/11 hijackers—Khalid al-Mihdhar—made a phone call from San Diego to a known al Qaeda safe-house in Yemen. NSA saw that call, but it could not see that the call was coming from an individual already in the United States. The telephone metadata program under Section 215 was designed to map the communications of terrorists so we can see who they may be in contact with as quickly as possible. And this capability could also prove valuable in a crisis. For example, if a bomb goes off in one of our cities and law enforcement is racing to determine whether a network is poised to conduct additional attacks, time is of the essence. Being able to quickly review phone connections to assess whether a network exists is critical to that effort.

In sum, the program does not involve the NSA examining the phone records of ordinary Americans. Rather, it consolidates these records into a database that the government can query if it has a specific lead—a consolidation of phone records that the companies already retained for business purposes. The review group turned up no indication that this database has been intentionally abused. And I believe it is important that the capability that this programme is designed to meet is preserved.

Having said that, I believe critics are right to point out that without proper safeguards, this type of program could be used to yield more information about our private lives, and open the door to more intrusive bulk collection programs in the future. They're also right to point out that although the telephone bulk collection program was subject to oversight by the Foreign Intelligence Surveillance Court and has been reauthorised repeatedly by Congress, it has never been subject to vigorous public debate.

For all these reasons, I believe we need a new approach. I am therefore ordering a transition that will end the Section 215 bulk metadata program as it currently exists, and establish a mechanism that preserves the capabilities we need without the government holding this bulk metadata.

This will not be simple. The review group recommended that our current approach be replaced by one in which the providers or a third party retain the bulk records, with government accessing information as needed. Both of these options pose difficult problems. Relying solely on the records of multiple providers, for example, could require companies to alter their procedures in ways that raise new privacy concerns. On the other hand, any third party maintaining a single, consolidated database would be carrying out what is essentially a government function but with more expense, more legal ambiguity, potentially less accountability—all of which would have a doubtful impact on increasing public confidence that their privacy is being protected.

During the review process, some suggested that we may also be able to preserve the capabilities we need through a combination of existing authorities, better information sharing, and recent technological advances. But more work needs to be done to determine exactly how this system might work.

Because of the challenges involved, I've ordered that the transition away from the existing program will proceed in two steps. Effective immediately, we will only pursue phone calls that are two steps removed from a number associated with a terrorist organisation instead of the current three. And I have directed the Attorney General to work with the Foreign Intelligence Surveillance Court so that during this transition period, the database can be queried only after a judicial finding or in the case of a true emergency.

Next, step two, I have instructed the intelligence community and the Attorney General to use this transition period to develop options for a new approach that can match the capabilities and fill the gaps that the Section 215 program was designed to address without the government holding this metadata itself. They will report back to me with options for alternative approaches before the programme comes up for reauthorisation on March 28th. And during this period, I will consult with the relevant committees in Congress to seek their views, and then seek congressional authorisation for the new program as needed.

Now, the reforms I'm proposing today should give the American people greater confidence that their rights are being protected, even as our intelligence and law enforcement agencies maintain the tools they need to keep us safe. And I recognise that there are additional issues that require further debate. For example, some who participated in our review, as well as some members of Congress, would like to see more sweeping reforms to the use of national security letters so that we have to go to a judge each time before issuing these requests. Here, I have concerns that we should not set a standard for terrorism investigations that is higher than those involved in investigating an ordinary crime. But I agree that greater oversight on the use of these letters may be appropriate, and I'm prepared to work with Congress on this issue.

There are also those who would like to see different changes to the FISA Court than the ones I've proposed. On all these issues, I am open to working with Congress to ensure that we build a broad consensus for how to move forward, and I'm confident that we can shape an approach that meets our security needs while upholding the civil liberties of every American.

Let me now turn to the separate set of concerns that have been raised overseas, and focus on America's approach to intelligence collection abroad. As I've indicated, the United States has unique responsibilities when it comes to intelligence collection. Our capabilities help protect not only our nation, but our friends and our allies, as well. But our efforts will only be effective if ordinary citizens in other countries have confidence that the United States respects their privacy, too. And the leaders of our close friends and allies deserve to know that if I want to know what they think about an issue, I'll pick up the phone and call them, rather than turning to surveillance. In other words, just as we balance security and privacy at home, our global leadership demands that we balance our security requirements against our need to maintain the trust and cooperation among people and leaders around the world.

For that reason, the new presidential directive that I've issued today will clearly prescribe what we do, and do not do, when it comes to our overseas surveillance. To begin with, the directive makes clear that the United States only uses signals intelligence for legitimate national security purposes, and not for the purpose of indiscriminately reviewing the emails or phone calls of ordinary folks. I've also made it clear that the United States does not collect intelligence to suppress criticism or dissent, nor do we collect intelligence to disadvantage people on the basis of their ethnicity, or race, or gender, or sexual orientation, or religious beliefs. We do not collect intelligence to provide a competitive advantage to U.S. companies or U.S. commercial sectors.

And in terms of our bulk collection of signals intelligence, US intelligence agencies will only use such data to meet specific security requirements: counterintelligence, counterterrorism, counter-proliferation, cybersecurity, force protection for our troops and our allies, and combating transnational crime, including sanctions evasion.

In this directive, I have taken the unprecedented step of extending certain protections that we have for the American people to people overseas. I've directed the DNI, in consultation with the Attorney General, to develop these safeguards, which will limit the duration that we can hold personal information, while also restricting the use of this information.

The bottom line is that people around the world, regardless of their nationality, should know that the United States is not spying on ordinary people who don't threaten our national security, and that we take their privacy concerns into account in our policies and procedures. This applies to foreign leaders as well. Given the understandable attention that this issue has received, I have made clear to the intelligence community that unless there is a compelling national security purpose, we will not monitor the communications of heads of state and government of our close friends and allies. And I've instructed my national security team, as well as the intelligence community, to work with foreign counterparts to deepen our coordination and cooperation in ways that rebuild trust going forward.

Now let me be clear: Our intelligence agencies will continue to gather information about the intentions of governments—as opposed to ordinary citizens—around the world, in the same way that the intelligence services of every other nation does. We will not apologise simply because our services may be more effective. But heads of state and government with whom we work closely, and on whose cooperation we depend, should feel confident that we are treating them as real partners. And the changes I've ordered do just that.

Finally, to make sure that we follow through on all these reforms, I am making some important changes to how our government is organised The State Department will designate a senior officer to coordinate our diplomacy on issues related to technology and signals intelligence. We will appoint a senior official at the White House to implement the new privacy safeguards that I have announced today. I will devote the resources to centralise and improve the process we use to handle foreign requests for legal assistance, keeping our high standards for privacy while helping foreign partners fight crime and terrorism.

I have also asked my counsellor, John Podesta, to lead a comprehensive review of big data and privacy. And this group will consist of government officials who, along with the President's Council of Advisors on Science and Technology, will reach out to privacy experts, technologists and business leaders, and look how the challenges inherent in big data are being confronted by both the public and private sectors; whether we can forge international norms on how to manage this data; and how we can continue to promote the free flow of information in ways that are consistent with both privacy and security.

For ultimately, what's at stake in this debate goes far beyond a few months of headlines, or passing tensions in our foreign policy. When you cut through the noise, what's really at stake is how we remain true to who we are in a world that is remaking itself at dizzying speed. Whether it's the ability of individuals to communicate ideas; to access information that would have once filled every great library in every country in the world; or to forge bonds with people on other sides of the globe, technology is remaking what is possible for individuals, and for institutions, and for the international order. So while the reforms that I have announced will point us in a new direction, I am mindful that more work will be needed in the future.

One thing I'm certain of: This debate will make us stronger. And I also know that in this time of change, the United States of America will have to lead. It may seem sometimes that America is being held to a different standard. And I'll admit the readiness of some to assume the worst motives by our government can be frustrating. No one expects China to have an open debate about their surveillance programs, or Russia to take privacy concerns of citizens in other places into account. But let's remember: We are held to a different standard precisely because we have been at the forefront of defending personal privacy and human dignity.

As the nation that developed the Internet, the world expects us to ensure that the digital revolution works as a tool for individual empowerment, not government control. Having faced down the dangers of totalitarianism and fascism and communism, the world expects us to stand up for the principle that every person has the right to think and write and form relationships freely—because individual freedom is the wellspring of human progress.

Those values make us who we are. And because of the strength of our own democracy, we should not shy away from high expectations. For more than two centuries, our Constitution has weathered every type of change because we have been willing to defend it, and because we have been willing to question the actions that have been taken in its defence. Today is no different. I believe we can meet high expectations. Together, let us chart a way forward that secures the life of our nation while preserving the liberties that make our nation worth fighting for.

Thank you. God bless you. May God bless the United States of America.

(Source: White House press office.)

EXTRACTS FROM SENATE INTELLIGENCE COMMITTEE'S REPORT INTO CIA TORTURE

Extracts from a report by the intelligence committee of the US Senate, compiled from early 2009 to late 2012 from an examination of more than 6 million pages of CIA material, on the agency's detention and interrogation programme. The full report, which ran to more than 6,700 pages, had been submitted to the president and a number of other executive departments and agencies in 2013 but remained classified. In April 2014, however, the committee had voted to release portions of the report, a move supported by President Obama who ordered the CIA to redact information within it that might endanger national security prior to its release. Accordingly, the report's executive summary and findings and conclusions were made public on 9 December. Its revelation of the details of the brutal and degrading treatment routinely used against suspects provoked widespread criticism, a reaction exacerbated by the report's findings that such practices were ineffective in obtaining useful information and that the CIA had routinely misled politicians over the nature and effectiveness of its torture programme.

Senate Select Committee on Intelligence
Committee Study of the Central Intelligence Agency's Detention and Interrogation Program
Approved December 13,2012
Updated for Release April 3, 2014
Declassification Revisions December 3, 2014

Foreword

On April 3, 2014, the Senate Select Committee on Intelligence voted to send the Findings and Conclusions and the Executive Summary of its final Study on the CIA's Detention and Interrogation Program to the President for declassification and subsequent public release.

This action marked the culmination of a monumental effort that officially began with the Committee's decision to initiate the Study in March 2009, but which had its roots in an investigation into the CIA's destruction of videotapes of CIA detainee interrogations that began in December 2007.

The full Committee Study, which totals more than 6,700 pages, remains classified but is now an official Senate report. The full report has been provided to the White House, the CIA, the Department of Justice, the Department of Defence, the Department of State, and the Office of the Director of National Intelligence in the hopes that it will prevent future coercive interrogation practices and inform the management of other covert action programs.....

I have attempted throughout to remember the impact on the nation and to the CIA workforce from the attacks of September 11, 2001. I can understand the CIA's impulse to consider the use of every possible tool to gather intelligence and remove terrorists from the battlefield, and CIA was encouraged by political leaders and the public to do whatever it could to prevent another attack.

The Intelligence Committee as well often pushes intelligence agencies to act quickly in response to threats and world events.

Nevertheless, such pressure, fear, and expectation of further terrorist plots do not justify, temper, or excuse improper actions taken by individuals or organizations in the name of national security. The major lesson of this report is that regardless of the pressures and the need to act, the Intelligence Community's actions must always reflect who we are as a nation, and adhere to our laws and standards. It is precisely at these times of national crisis that our government must be guided by the lessons of our history and subject decisions to internal and external review.

Instead, CIA personnel, aided by two outside contractors, decided to initiate a program of indefinite secret detention and the use of brutal interrogation techniques in violation of U.S. law, treaty obligations, and our values.

This Committee Study documents the abuses and countless mistakes made between late 2001 and early 2009. The Executive Summary of the Study provides a significant amount of new information, based on CIA and other documents, to what has already been made public by the Bush and Obama Administrations, as well as non-governmental organizations and the press.

The Committee's full Study is more than ten times the length of the Executive Summary and includes comprehensive and excruciating detail. The Study describes the history of the CIA's Detention and Interrogation Program from its inception to its termination, including a review of each of the 119 known individuals who were held in CIA custody.

The full Committee Study also provides substantially more detail than what is included in the Executive Summary on the CIA's justification and defence of its interrogation program on the basis that it was necessary and critical to the disruption of specific terrorist plots and the capture of specific terrorists. While the Executive Summary provides sufficient detail to demonstrate the inaccuracies of each of these claims, the information in the full Committee Study is far more extensive....

Dianne Feinstein
Chairman
Senate Select Committee on Intelligence

Findings and Conclusions
The Committee makes the following findings and conclusions:

#1: The CIA's use of its enhanced interrogation techniques was not an effective means of acquiring intelligence or gaining cooperation from detainees.

The Committee finds, based on a review of CIA interrogation records, that the use of the CIA's enhanced interrogation techniques was not an effective means of obtaining accurate information or gaining detainee cooperation.

For example, according to CIA records, seven of the 39 CIA detainees known to have been subjected to the CIA's enhanced interrogation techniques produced no intelligence while in CIA custody. CIA detainees who were subjected to the CIA's enhanced interrogation techniques were usually subjected to the techniques immediately after being rendered to CIA custody. Other detainees provided significant accurate intelligence prior to, or without having been subjected to these techniques.

While being subjected to the CIA's enhanced interrogation techniques and afterwards, multiple CIA detainees fabricated information, resulting in faulty intelligence. Detainees provided fabricated information on critical intelligence issues, including the terrorist threats which the CIA identified as its highest priorities.

At numerous times throughout the CIA's Detention and Interrogation Program, CIA personnel assessed that the most effective method for acquiring intelligence from detainees, including from detainees the CIA considered to be the most "high-value," was to confront the detainees with information already acquired by the Intelligence Community. CIA officers regularly called into question whether the CIA's enhanced interrogation techniques were effective, assessing that the use of the techniques failed to elicit detainee cooperation or produce accurate intelligence.

#2: The CIA's justification for the use of its enhanced interrogation techniques rested on inaccurate claims of their effectiveness.

The CIA represented to the White House, the National Security Council, the Department of Justice, the CIA Office of Inspector General, the Congress, and the public that the best measure of effectiveness of the CIA's enhanced interrogation techniques was examples of specific terrorist plots "thwarted" and specific terrorists captured as a result of the use of the techniques. The CIA used these examples to claim that its enhanced interrogation techniques were not only effective, but also necessary to acquire "otherwise unavailable" actionable intelligence that "saved lives."

The Committee reviewed 20 of the most frequent and prominent examples of purported counterterrorism successes that the CIA has attributed to the use of its enhanced interrogation techniques, and found them to be wrong in fundamental respects. In some cases, there was no relationship between the cited counterterrorism success and any information provided by detainees during or after the use of the CIA's enhanced interrogation techniques. In the remaining cases, the CIA inaccurately claimed that specific, otherwise unavailable information was acquired from a CIA detainee "as a result" of the CIA's enhanced interrogation techniques, when in fact the information was either: (1) corroborative of information already available to the CIA or other elements of the U.S. Intelligence Community from sources other than the CIA detainee, and was therefore not "otherwise unavailable"; or (2) acquired from the CIA detainee prior to the use of the CIA's enhanced interrogation techniques. The examples provided by the CIA included numerous factual inaccuracies.

In providing the "effectiveness" examples to policymakers, the Department of Justice, and others, the CIA consistently omitted the significant amount of relevant intelligence obtained from sources other than CIA detainees who had been subjected to the CIA's enhanced interrogation techniques— leaving the false impression the CIA was acquiring unique information from the use of the techniques.

Some of the plots that the CIA claimed to have "disrupted" as a result of the CIA's enhanced interrogation techniques were assessed by intelligence and law enforcement officials as being infeasible or ideas that were never operationalised.

#3: The interrogations of CIA detainees were brutal and far worse than the CIA represented to policymakers and others.

Beginning with the CIA's first detainee, Abu Zubaydah, and continuing with numerous others, the CIA applied its enhanced interrogation techniques with significant repetition for days or weeks at a time. Interrogation techniques such as slaps and "wallings" (slamming detainees against a wall) were used in combination, frequently concurrent with sleep deprivation and nudity. Records do not support CIA representations that the CIA initially used an "an open, nonthreatening approach," or that interrogations began with the "least coercive technique possible" and escalated to more coercive techniques only as necessary.

The waterboarding technique was physically harmful, inducing convulsions and vomiting. Abu Zubaydah, for example, became "completely unresponsive, with bubbles rising through his open, full mouth". Internal CIA records describe the waterboarding of Khalid Shaykh Mohammad as evolving into a "series of near drownings."

Sleep deprivation involved keeping detainees awake for up to 180 hours, usually standing or in stress positions, at times with their hands shackled above their heads. At least five detainees experienced disturbing hallucinations during prolonged sleep deprivation and, in at least two of those cases, the CIA nonetheless continued the sleep deprivation.

Contrary to CIA representations to the Department of Justice, the CIA instructed personnel that the interrogation of Abu Zubaydah would take "precedence" over his medical care, resulting in the deterioration of a bullet wound Abu Zubaydah incurred during his capture. In at least two other cases, the CIA used its enhanced interrogation techniques despite warnings from CIA medical personnel that the techniques could exacerbate physical injuries. CIA medical personnel treated at least one detainee for swelling in order to allow the continued use of standing sleep deprivation.

At least five CIA detainees were subjected to "rectal rehydration" or rectal feeding without documented medical necessity. The CIA placed detainees in ice water "baths." The CIA led several detainees to believe they would never be allowed to leave CIA custody alive, suggesting to one detainee that he would only leave in a coffin-shaped box. One interrogator told another detainee that he would never go to court, because "we can never let the world know what I have done to you." CIA officers also threatened at least three detainees with harm to their families— to include threats to harm the children of a detainee, threats to sexually abuse the mother of a detainee, and a threat to "cut [a detainee's] mother's throat."

#4: The conditions of confinement for CIA detainees were harsher than the CIA had represented to policymakers and others.

Conditions at CIA detention sites were poor, and were especially bleak early in the program. CIA detainees at the COBALT detention facility were kept in complete darkness and constantly shackled in isolated cells with loud noise or music and only a bucket to use for human waste. Lack of heat at the facility likely contributed to the death of a detainee. The chief of interrogations described COBALT as a "dungeon." Another senior CIA officer stated that COBALT was itself an enhanced interrogation technique.

At times, the detainees at COBALT were walked around naked or were shackled with their hands above their heads for extended periods of time. Other times, the detainees at COBALT were subjected to what was described as a "rough takedown," in which approximately five CIA officers would scream at a detainee, drag him outside of his cell, cut his clothes off, and secure him with Mylar tape. The detainee would then be hooded and dragged up and down a long corridor while being slapped and punched.

Even after the conditions of confinement improved with the construction of new detention facilities, detainees were held in total isolation except when being interrogated or debriefed by CIA personnel.

Throughout the program, multiple CIA detainees who were subjected to the CIA's enhanced interrogation techniques and extended isolation exhibited psychological and behavioural issues, including hallucinations, paranoia, insomnia, and attempts at self-harm and self-mutilation. Multiple psychologists identified the lack of human contact experienced by detainees as a cause of psychiatric problems.

#5: The CIA repeatedly provided inaccurate information to the Department of Justice, impeding a proper legal analysis of the CIA's Detention and Interrogation Program.

From 2002 to 2007, the Office of Legal Counsel (OLC) within the Department of Justice relied on CIA representations regarding: (1) the conditions of confinement for detainees, (2) the application of the CIA's enhanced interrogation techniques, (3) the physical effects of the techniques on detainees, and (4) the effectiveness of the techniques. Those representations were inaccurate in material respects.

The Department of Justice did not conduct independent analysis or verification of the information it received from the CIA. The department warned, however, that if the facts provided by the CIA were to change, its legal conclusions might not apply. When the CIA determined that information it had provided to the Department of Justice was incorrect, the CIA rarely informed the department.

Prior to the initiation of the CIA's Detention and Interrogation Program and throughout the life of the program, the legal justifications for the CIA's enhanced interrogation techniques relied on the CIA's claim that the techniques were necessary to save lives. In late 2001 and early 2002, senior attorneys at the CIA Office of General Counsel first examined the legal implications of using coercive interrogation techniques. CIA attorneys stated that "a novel application of the necessity defense" could be used "to avoid prosecution of U.S. officials who tortured to obtain information that saved many lives."

Having reviewed information provided by the CIA, the OLC included the "necessity defense" in its August 1, 2002, memorandum to the White House counsel on Standards of Conduct for Interrogation. The OLC determined that "under the current circumstances, necessity or self defence may justify interrogation methods that might violate" the criminal prohibition against torture.

On the same day, a second OLC opinion approved, for the first time, the use of 10 specific coercive interrogation techniques against Abu Zubaydah—subsequently referred to as the CIA's "enhanced interrogation techniques." The OLC relied on inaccurate CIA representations about Abu Zubaydah's status in al-Qa'ida and the interrogation team's "certain[ty]" that Abu Zubaydah was withholding information about planned terrorist attacks. The CIA's representations to the OLC about the techniques were also inconsistent with how the techniques would later be applied.

In March 2005, the CIA submitted to the Department of Justice various examples of the "effectiveness" of the CIA's enhanced interrogation techniques that were inaccurate. OLC memoranda signed on May 30, 2005, and July 20, 2007, relied on these representations, determining that the techniques were legal in part because they produced "specific, actionable intelligence" and "substantial quantities of otherwise unavailable intelligence" that saved lives.

#6: The CIA has actively avoided or impeded congressional oversight of the program.

The CIA did not brief the leadership of the Senate Select Committee on Intelligence on the CIA's enhanced interrogation techniques until September 2002, after the techniques had been approved and used. The CIA did not respond to Chairman Bob Graham's requests for additional information in 2002, noting in its own internal communications that he would be leaving the Committee in January 2003. The CIA subsequently resisted efforts by Vice Chairman John D. Rockefeller IV, to investigate the program, including by refusing in 2006 to provide requested documents to the full Committee.

The CIA restricted access to information about the program from members of the Committee beyond the chairman and vice chairman until September 6, 2006, the day the president publicly acknowledged the program, by which time 117 of the 119 known detainees had already entered CIA custody. Until then, the CIA had declined to answer questions from other Committee members that related to CIA interrogation activities.

Prior to September 6, 2006, the CIA provided inaccurate information to the leadership of the Committee. Briefings to the full Committee beginning on September 6, 2006, also contained numerous inaccuracies, including inaccurate descriptions of how interrogation techniques were applied and what information was obtained from CIA detainees. The CIA misrepresented the views of members of Congress on a number of occasions. After multiple senators had been critical of the program and written letters expressing concerns to CIA Director Michael Hayden, Director Hayden nonetheless told a meeting of foreign ambassadors to the United States that every Committee member was "fully briefed," and that "[t]his is not CIA's program. This is not the President's program. This is America's program." The CIA also provided inaccurate information describing the views of U.S. senators about the program to the Department of Justice.

A year after being briefed on the program, the House and Senate Conference Committee considering the Fiscal Year 2008 Intelligence Authorization bill voted to limit the CIA to using only interrogation techniques authorized by the Army Field Manual. That legislation was approved by the Senate and the House of Representatives in February 2008, and was vetoed by President Bush on March 8, 2008.

#7: The CIA impeded effective White House oversight and decision-making.

The CIA provided extensive amounts of inaccurate and incomplete information related to the operation and effectiveness of the CIA's Detention and Interrogation Program to the White House, the National Security Council principals, and their staffs. This prevented an accurate and complete understanding of the program by Executive Branch officials, thereby impeding oversight and decision-making.

According to CIA records, no CIA officer, up to and including CIA Directors George Tenet and Porter Goss, briefed the president on the specific CIA enhanced interrogation techniques before April 2006. By that time, 38 of the 39 detainees identified as having been subjected to the CIA's enhanced interrogation techniques had already been subjected to the techniques. The CIA did not inform the president or vice president of the location of CIA detention facilities other than Country [redacted].

At the direction of the White House, the secretaries of state and defense - both principals on the National Security Council - were not briefed on program specifics until September 2003. An internal CIA email from July 2003 noted that "... the WH [White House] is extremely concerned [Secretary] Powell would blow his stack if he were to be briefed on what's been going on." Deputy Secretary of State Armitage complained that he and Secretary Powell were "cut out" of the National Security Council coordination process.

The CIA repeatedly provided incomplete and inaccurate information to White House personnel regarding the operation and effectiveness of the CIA's Detention and Interrogation Program. This includes the provision of inaccurate statements similar to those provided to other elements of the U.S. Government and later to the public, as well as instances in which specific questions from White House officials were not answered truthfully or fully. In briefings for the National Security Council principals and White House officials, the CIA advocated for the continued use of the CIA's enhanced interrogation techniques, warning that "[t]ermination of this program will result in loss of life, possibly extensive."

#8: The CIA's operation and management of the program complicated, and in some cases impeded, the national security missions of other Executive Branch agencies.

The CIA, in the conduct of its Detention and Interrogation Program, complicated, and in some cases impeded, the national security missions of other Executive Branch agencies, including the Federal Bureau of Investigation (FBI), the State Department, and the Office of the Director of National Intelligence (ODNI). The CIA withheld or restricted information relevant to these agencies' missions and responsibilities, denied access to detainees, and provided inaccurate information on the CIA's Detention and Interrogation Program to these agencies.

The use of coercive interrogation techniques and covert detention facilities that did not meet traditional U.S. standards resulted in the FBI and the Department of Defense limiting their involvement in CIA interrogation and detention activities. This reduced the ability of the U.S. Government to deploy available resources and expert personnel to interrogate detainees and operate detention facilities. The CIA denied specific requests from FBI Director Robert Mueller III for FBI access to CIA detainees that the FBI believed was necessary to understand CIA detainee reporting on threats to the U.S. Homeland. Information obtained from CIA detainees was restricted within the Intelligence Community, leading to concerns among senior CIA officers that limitations on sharing information undermined government-wide counterterrorism analysis.

The CIA blocked State Department leadership from access to information crucial to foreign policy decision-making and diplomatic activities. The CIA did not inform two secretaries of state of locations of CIA detention facilities, despite the significant foreign policy implications related to the hosting of clandestine CIA detention sites and the fact that the political leaders of host countries were generally informed of their existence. Moreover, CIA officers told U.S. ambassadors not to discuss the CIA program with State Department officials, preventing the ambassadors from seeking guidance on the policy implications of establishing CIA detention facilities in the countries in which they served.

In two countries, U.S. ambassadors were informed of plans to establish a CIA detention site in the countries where they were serving after the CIA had already entered into agreements with the countries to host the detention sites. In two other countries where negotiations on hosting new CIA detention facilities were taking place, the CIA told local government officials not to inform the U.S. ambassadors.

The ODNI was provided with inaccurate and incomplete information about the program, preventing the director of national intelligence from effectively carrying out the director's statutory responsibility to serve as the principal advisor to the president on intelligence matters. The inaccurate information provided to the ODNI by the CIA resulted in the ODNI releasing inaccurate information to the public in September 2006.

#9: The CIA impeded oversight by the CIA's Office of Inspector General.

The CIA avoided, resisted, and otherwise impeded oversight of the CIA's Detention and Interrogation Program by the CIA's Office of Inspector General (OIG). The CIA did not brief the OIG on the program until after the death of a detainee, by which time the CIA had held at least 22 detainees at two different CIA detention sites. Once notified, the OIG reviewed the CIA's Detention and Interrogation

Program and issued several reports, including an important May 2004 "Special Review" of the program that identified significant concerns and deficiencies.

During the OIG reviews, CIA personnel provided OIG with inaccurate information on the operation and management of the CIA's Detention and Interrogation Program, as well as on the effectiveness of the CIA's enhanced interrogation techniques. The inaccurate information was included in the final May 2004 Special Review, which was later declassified and released publicly, and remains uncorrected.

In 2005, CIA Director Goss requested in writing that the inspector general not initiate further reviews of the CIA's Detention and Interrogation Program until reviews already underway were completed. In 2007, Director Hayden ordered an unprecedented review of the OIG itself in response to the OIG's inquiries into the CIA's Detention and Interrogation Program.

#10: The CIA coordinated the release of classified information to the media, including inaccurate information concerning the effectiveness of the CIA's enhanced interrogation techniques.

The CIA's Office of Public Affairs and senior CIA officials coordinated to share classified information on the CIA's Detention and Interrogation Program to select members of the media to counter public criticism, shape public opinion, and avoid potential congressional action to restrict the CIA's detention and interrogation authorities and budget. These disclosures occurred when the program was a classified covert action program, and before the CIA had briefed the full Committee membership on the program.

The deputy director of the CIA's Counterterrorism Center wrote to a colleague in 2005, shortly before being interviewed by a media outlet, that "we either get out and sell, or we get hammered, which has implications beyond the media. [C]ongress reads it, cuts our authorities, messes up our budget... we either put out our story or we get eaten. [T]here is no middle ground." The same CIA officer explained to a colleague that "when the [Washington Post]/[New York Times] quotes 'senior intelligence official,' it's us... authorized and directed by opa [CIA's Office of Public Affairs].

Much of the information the CIA provided to the media on the operation of the CIA's Detention and Interrogation Program and the effectiveness of its enhanced interrogation techniques was inaccurate and was similar to the inaccurate information provided by the CIA to the Congress, the Department of Justice, and the White House.

#11: The CIA was unprepared as it began operating its Detention and Interrogation Program more than six months after being granted detention authorities.

On September 17, 2001, the President signed a covert action Memorandum of Notification (MON) granting the CIA unprecedented counterterrorism authorities, including the authority to covertly capture and detain individuals "posing a continuing, serious threat of violence or death to U.S. persons and interests or planning terrorist activities." The MON made no reference to interrogations or coercive interrogation techniques.

The CIA was not prepared to take custody of its first detainee. In the fall of 2001, the CIA explored the possibility of establishing clandestine detention facilities in several countries. The CIA's review identified risks associated with clandestine detention that led it to conclude that U.S. military bases were the best option for the CIA to detain individuals under the MON authorities. In late March 2002, the imminent capture of Abu Zubaydah prompted the CIA to again consider various detention options. In part to avoid declaring Abu Zubaydah to the International Committee of the Red Cross, which would be required if he were detained at a U.S. military base, the CIA decided to seek authorization to clandestinely detain Abu Zubaydah at a facility in Country [redacted]—a country that had not previously been considered as a potential host for a CIA detention site. A senior CIA officer indicated that the CIA "will have to acknowledge certain gaps in our planning/preparations," but stated that this plan would be presented to the president. At a Presidential Daily Briefing session that day, the president approved CIA's proposal to detain Abu Zubaydah in Country [redacted].

The CIA lacked a plan for the eventual disposition of its detainees. After taking custody of Abu Zubaydah, CIA officers concluded that he "should remain incommunicado for the remainder of his life," which "may preclude [Abu Zubaydah] from being turned over to another country."

The CIA did not review its past experience with coercive interrogations, or its previous statement to Congress that "inhumane physical or psychological techniques are counterproductive because they do not produce intelligence and will probably result in false answers." The CIA also did not contact other elements of the U.S. Government with interrogation expertise.

In July 2002, on the basis of consultations with contract psychologists, and with very limited internal deliberation, the CIA requested approval from the Department of Justice to use a set of coercive interrogation techniques. The techniques were adapted from the training of U.S. military personnel at the U.S. Air Force Survival, Evasion, Resistance and Escape (SERE) school, which was designed to prepare U.S. military personnel for the conditions and treatment to which they might be subjected if taken prisoner by countries that do not adhere to the Geneva Conventions.

As it began detention and interrogation operations, the CIA deployed personnel who lacked relevant training and experience. The CIA began interrogation training more than seven months after taking custody of Abu Zubaydah, and more than three months after the CIA began using its "enhanced interrogation techniques." CIA Director George Tenet issued formal guidelinesfor interrogations and conditions of confinement at detention sites in January 2003, by which time 40 of the 119 known detainees had been detained by the CIA.

#12: The CIA's management and operation of its Detention and Interrogation Program was deeply flawed throughout the program's duration, particularly so in 2002 and early 2003.

The CIA's COBALT detention facility in Country [redacted] began operations in September 2002 and ultimately housed more than half of the 119 CIA detainees identified in this Study. The CIA kept few formal records of the detainees in its custody at COBALT. Untrained CIA officers at the facility conducted frequent, unauthorized, and unsupervised interrogations of detainees using harsh physical interrogation techniques that were not—and never became—part of the CIA's formal "enhanced" interrogation program. The CIA placed a junior officer with no relevant experience in charge of COBALT. On November [redacted], 2002, a detainee who had been held partially nude and chained to a concrete floor died from suspected hypothermia at the facility. At the time, no single unit at CIA Headquarters had clear responsibility for CIA detention and interrogation operations. In interviews conducted in 2003 with the Office of Inspector General, CIA's leadership and senior attorneys acknowledged that they had little or no awareness of operations at COBALT, and some believed that enhanced interrogation techniques were not used there.

Although CIA Director Tenet in January 2003 issued guidance for detention and interrogation activities, serious management problems persisted. For example, in December 2003, CIA personnel reported that they had made the "unsettling discovery" that the CIA had been "holding a number of detainees about whom" the CIA knew "very little" at multiple detention sites in Country [redacted].

Divergent lines of authority for interrogation activities persisted through at least 2003. Tensions among interrogators extended to complaints about the safety and effectiveness of each other's interrogation practices.

The CIA placed individuals with no applicable experience or training in senior detention and interrogation roles, and provided inadequate linguistic and analytical support to conduct effective questioning of CIA detainees, resulting in diminished intelligence. The lack of CIA personnel available to question detainees, which the CIA inspector general referred to as "an ongoing problem, persisted throughout the program.

In 2005, the chief of the CIA's BLACK detention site, where many of the detainees the CIA assessed as "high-value" were held, complained that CIA Headquarters "managers seem to be selecting either problem, underperforming officers, new, totally inexperienced officers or whomever seems to be willing and able to deploy at any given time," resulting in "the production of mediocre or, I dare say, use-less intelligence...."

Numerous CIA officers had serious documented personal and professional problems—including histories of violence and records of abusive treatment of others—that should have called into question their suitability to participate in the CIA's Detention and Interrogation Program, their employment with the CIA, and their continued access to classified information. In nearly all cases, these problems were known to the CIA prior to the assignment of these officers to detention and interrogation positions.

#13: Two contract psychologists devised the CIA's enhanced interrogation techniques and played a central role in the operation, assessments, and management of the CIA's Detention and Interrogation Program. By 2005, the CIA had overwhelmingly outsourced operations related to the program.

The CIA contracted with two psychologists to develop, operate, and assess its interrogation opera-tions. The psychologists' prior experience was at the U.S. Air Force Survival, Evasion, Resistance and Escape (SERE) school. Neither psychologist had any experience as an interrogator, nor did either have specialized knowledge of al-Qa'ida, a background in counterterrorism, or any relevant cultural or lin-guistic expertise.

On the CIA's behalf, the contract psychologists developed theories of interrogation based on "learned helplessness," and developed the list of enhanced interrogation techniques that was approved for use against Abu Zubaydah and subsequent CIA detainees. The psychologists personally conducted interrogations of some of the CIA's most significant detainees using these techniques. They also eval-uated whether detainees' psychological state allowed for the continued use of the CIA's enhanced inter-rogation techniques, including some detainees whom they were themselves interrogating or had inter-rogated. The psychologists carried out inherently governmental functions, such as acting as liaison between the CIA and foreign intelligence services, assessing the effectiveness of the interrogation pro-gram, and participating in the interrogation of detainees in held in foreign government custody.

In 2005, the psychologists formed a company specifically for the purpose of conducting their work with the CIA. Shortly thereafter, the CIA outsourced virtually all aspects of the program.

In 2006, the value of the CIA's base contract with the company formed by the psychologists with all options exercised was in excess of $180 million; the contractors received $81 million prior to the con-tract's termination in 2009. In 2007, the CIA provided a multi-year indemnification agreement to pro-tect the company and its employees from legal liability arising out of the program. The CIA has since paid out more than $1 million pursuant to the agreement.

In 2008, the CIA's Rendition, Detention, and Interrogation Group, the lead unit for the detention and interrogation operations at the CIA, had a total of [redacted] positions, which were filled with [redacted] CIA staff officers and [redacted] contractors, meaning that contractors made up 85% of the workforce for detention and interrogation operations.

#14: CIA detainees were subjected to coercive interrogation techniques that had not been approved by the Department of Justice or had not been authorized by CIA Headquarters.

Prior to mid-2004, the CIA routinely subjected detainees to nudity and dietary manipulation. The CIA also used abdominal slaps and cold water dousing on several detainees during that period. None of these techniques had been approved by the Department of Justice.

At least 17 detainees were subjected to CIA enhanced interrogation techniques without authori-zation from CIA Headquarters. Additionally, multiple detainees were subjected to techniques that were applied in ways that diverged from the specific authorization, or were subjected to enhanced interrogation techniques by interrogators who had not been authorized to use them. Although these incidents were recorded in CIA cables and, in at least some cases were identified at the time by supervisors at CIA Headquarters as being inappropriate, corrective action was rarely taken against the interrogators involved.

#15: The CIA did not conduct a comprehensive or accurate accounting of the number of individuals it detained, and held individuals who did not meet the legal standard for detention. The CIA's claims about the number of detainees held and subjected to its enhanced Interrogation techniques were inaccurate.

The CIA never conducted a comprehensive audit or developed a complete and accurate list of the individuals it had detained or subjected to its enhanced interrogation techniques. CIA statements to the Committee and later to the public that the CIA detained fewer than 100 individuals, and that less than a third of those 100 detainees were subjected to the CIA's enhanced interrogation techniques, were inaccurate. The Committee's review of CIA records determined that the CIA detained at least 119 individuals, of whom at least 39 were subjected to the CIA's enhanced interrogation techniques.

Of the 119 known detainees, at least 26 were wrongfully held and did not meet the detention standard in the September 2001 Memorandum of Notification (MON). These included an "intellectually challenged" man whose CIA detention was used solely as leverage to get a family member to provide information, two individuals who were intelligence sources for foreign liaison services and were former CIA sources, and two individuals whom the CIA assessed to be connected to al-Qa'ida based solely on information fabricated by a CIA detainee subjected to the CIA's enhanced interrogation techniques. Detainees often remained in custody for months after the CIA determined that they did not meet the MON standard. CIA records provide insufficient information to justify the detention of many other detainees.

CIA Headquarters instructed that at least four CIA detainees be placed in host country detention facilities because the individuals did not meet the MON standard for CIA detention. The host country had no independent reason to hold the detainees.

A full accounting of CIA detentions and interrogations may be impossible, as records in some cases are non-existent, and, in many other cases, are sparse and insufficient. There were almost no detailed records of the detentions and interrogations at the CIA's COBALT detention facility in 2002, and almost no such records for the CIA's GRAY detention site, also in Country [redacted]. At CIA detention facilities outside of Country [redacted], the CIA kept increasingly less-detailed records of its interrogation activities over the course of the CIA's Detention and Interrogation Program.

#16: The CIA failed to adequately evaluate the effectiveness of its enhanced interrogation techniques.

The CIA never conducted a credible, comprehensive analysis of the effectiveness of its enhanced interrogation techniques, despite a recommendation by the CIA inspector general and similar requests by the national security advisor and the leadership of the Senate Select Committee on Intelligence.

Internal assessments of the CIA's Detention and Interrogation Program were conducted by CIA personnel who participated in the development and management of the program, as well as by CIA contractors who had a financial interest in its continuation and expansion. An "informal operational assessment" of the program, led by two senior CIA officers who were not part of the CIA's Counterterrorism Center, determined that it would not be possible to assess the effectiveness of the CIA's enhanced interrogation techniques without violating "Federal Policy for the Protection of Human Subjects" regarding human experimentation. The CIA officers, whose review relied on briefings with CIA officers and contractors running the program, concluded only that the "CIA Detainee Program" was a "success" without addressing the effectiveness of the CIA's enhanced interrogation techniques.

In 2005, in response to the recommendation by the inspector general for a review of the effectiveness of each of the CIA's enhanced interrogation techniques, the CIA asked two individuals not employed by the CIA to conduct a broader review of "the entirety of the "rendition, detention and interrogation program." According to one individual, the review was "heavily reliant on the willingness of [CIA Counterterrorism Center] staff to provide us with the factual material that forms the basis of our conclusions." That individual acknowledged lacking the requisite expertise to review the effectiveness of the CIA's enhanced interrogation techniques, and concluded only that "the program," meaning all CIA detainee reporting regardless of whether it was connected to the use of the CIA's enhanced interrogation techniques, was a "great success." The second reviewer concluded that "there is no objective way to answer the question of efficacy" of the techniques.

There are no CIA records to indicate that any of the reviews independently validated the "effectiveness" claims presented by the CIA, to include basic confirmation that the intelligence cited by the CIA was acquired from CIA detainees during or after the use of the CIA's enhanced interrogation techniques. Nor did the reviews seek to confirm whether the intelligence cited by the CIA as being obtained "as a result" of the CIA's enhanced interrogation techniques was unique and "otherwise unavailable," as claimed by the CIA, and not previously obtained from other sources.

#17: The CIA rarely reprimanded or held personnel accountable for serious and significant violations, inappropriate activities, and systemic and individual management failures.

CIA officers and CIA contractors who were found to have violated CIA policies or performed poorly were rarely held accountable or removed from positions of responsibility.

Significant events, to include the death and injury of CIA detainees, the detention of individuals who did not meet the legal standard to be held, the use of unauthorized interrogation techniques against CIA detainees, and the provision of inaccurate information on the CIA program did not result in appropriate, effective, or in many cases, any corrective actions. CIA managers who were aware of failings and shortcomings in the program but did not intervene, or who failed to provide proper leadership and management, were also not held to account.

On two occasions in which the CIA inspector general identified wrongdoing, accountability recommendations were overruled by senior CIA leadership. In one instance, involving the death of a CIA detainee at COBALT, CIA Headquarters decided not to take disciplinary action against an officer involved because, at the time, CIA Headquarters had been "motivated to extract any and all operational information" from the detainee. In another instance related to a wrongful detention, no action was taken against a CIA officer because, "[t]he Director strongly believes that mistakes should be expected in a business filled with uncertainty," and "the Director believes the scale tips decisively in favor of accepting mistakes that over connect the dots against those that under connect them." In neither case was administrative action taken against CIA management personnel.

#18: The CIA marginalized and ignored numerous internal critiques, criticisms, and objections concerning the operation and management of the CIA's Detention and Interrogation Program.

Critiques, criticisms, and objections were expressed by numerous CIA officers, including senior personnel overseeing and managing the program, as well as analysts, interrogators, and medical officers involved in or supporting CIA detention and interrogation operations.

Examples of these concerns include CIA officers questioning the effectiveness of the CIA's enhanced interrogation techniques, interrogators disagreeing with the use of such techniques against detainees whom they determined were not withholding information, psychologists recommending less isolated conditions, and Office of Medical Services personnel questioning both the effectiveness and safety of the techniques. These concerns were regularly overridden by CIA management, and the CIA made few corrective changes to its policies governing the program. At times, CIA officers were instructed by supervisors not to put their concerns or observations in written communications.

In several instances, CIA officers identified inaccuracies in CIA representations about the program and its effectiveness to the Office of Inspector General, the White House, the Department of Justice, the Congress, and the American public. The CIA nonetheless failed to take action to correct these representations, and allowed inaccurate information to remain as the CIA's official position.

The CIA was also resistant to, and highly critical of more formal critiques. The deputy director for operations stated that the CIA inspector general's draft Special Review should have come to the "conclusion that our efforts have thwarted attacks and saved lives," while the CIA general counsel accused the inspector general of presenting "an imbalanced and inaccurate picture" of the program. A February 2007 report from the International Committee of the Red Cross (ICRC), which the CIA acting general counsel initially stated "actually does not sound that far removed from the reality was also criticized. CIA officers prepared documents indicating that "critical portions of the Report are patently false or misleading, especially certain key factual claims..CIA Director Hayden testified to the Committee that "numerous false allegations of physical and threatened abuse and faulty legal assumptions and analysis in the [ICRC] report undermine its overall credibility.

#19: The CIA's Detention and Interrogation Program was inherently unsustainable and had effectively ended by 2006 due to unauthorized press disclosures, reduced cooperation from other nations, and legal and oversight concerns.

The CIA required secrecy and cooperation from other nations in order to operate clandestine detention facilities, and both had eroded significantly before President Bush publicly disclosed the program on September 6, 2006. From the beginning of the program, the CIA faced significant challenges in finding nations willing to host CIA clandestine detention sites. These challenges became increasingly difficult over time. With the exception of Country [redacted], the CIA was forced to relocate detainees out of every country in which it established a detention facility because of pressure from the host government or public revelations about the program. Beginning in early 2005, the CIA sought unsuccessfully to convince the U.S. Department of Defense to allow the transfer of numerous CIA detainees to U.S. military custody. By 2006, the CIA admitted in its own talking points for CIA Director Porter Goss that, absent an Administration decision on an "endgame" for detainees, the CIA was "stymied" and "the program could collapse of its own weight."

Lack of access to adequate medical care for detainees in countries hosting the CIA's detention facilities caused recurring problems. The refusal of one host country to admit a severely ill detainee into a local hospital due to security concerns contributed to the closing of the CIA's detention facility in that country. The U.S. Department of Defense also declined to provide medical care to detainees upon CIA request.

In mid-2003, a statement by the president for the United Nations International Day in Support of Victims of Torture and a public statement by the White House that prisoners in U.S. custody are treated "humanely" caused the CIA to question whether there was continued policy support for the program and seek reauthorization from the White House. In mid-2004, the CIA temporarily suspended the use of its enhanced interrogation techniques after the CIA inspector general recommended that the CIA seek an updated legal opinion from the Office of Legal Counsel. In early 2004, the U.S. Supreme Court decision to grant certiorari in the case of *Rasul v. Bush* prompted the CIA to move detainees out of a CIA detention facility at Guantanamo Bay, Cuba. In late 2005 and in 2006, the Detainee Treatment Act and then the U.S. Supreme Court decision in *Hamdan v. Rumsfeld* caused the CIA to again temporarily suspend the use of its enhanced interrogation techniques.

By 2006, press disclosures, the unwillingness of other countries to host existing or new detention sites, and legal and oversight concerns had largely ended the CIA's ability to operate clandestine detention facilities.

After detaining at least 113 individuals through 2004, the CIA brought only six additional detainees into its custody: four in 2005, one in 2006, and one in 2007. By March 2006, the program was operating in only one country. The CIA last used its enhanced interrogation techniques on November 8, 2007. The CIA did not hold any detainees after April 2008.

#20: The CIA's Detention and Interrogation Program damaged the United States' standing in the world, and resulted in other significant monetary and non-monetary costs.

The CIA's Detention and Interrogation Program created tensions with U.S. partners and allies, leading to formal demarches to the United States, and damaging and complicating bilateral Intelligence relationships.

In one example, in June 2004, the secretary of state ordered the U.S. ambassador in Country [redacted] to deliver a d*emarche* to Country [redacted], "in essence demanding [Country [redacted] Government] provide full access to all [Country [redacted]] detainees" to the International Committee of the Red Cross. At the time, however, the detainees Country [redacted] was holding included detainees being held in secret at the CIA's behest.

More broadly, the program caused immeasurable damage to the United States' public standing, as well as to the United States' longstanding global leadership on human rights in general and the prevention of torture in particular.

CIA records indicate that the CIA's Detention and Interrogation Program cost well over $300 million in non-personnel costs. This included funding for the CIA to construct and maintain detention facilities, including two facilities costing nearly $[redacted] million that were never used, in part due to host country political concerns.

To encourage governments to clandestinely host CIA detention sites, or to increase support for existing sites, the CIA provided millions of dollars in cash payments to foreign government officials. CIA Headquarters encouraged CIA Stations construct "wish lists" of proposed financial assistance to [redacted] [entities of foreign governments], and to "think big" in terms of that assistance.

(Source: Office of Dianne Feinstein.)

SPEECH BY PRESIDENT OBAMA ANNOUNING BEGINNING OF PROCESS OF NORMALISING DIPLOMATIC RELATIONS WITH CUBA

Transcript of speech by President Barack Obama, in which he announced the beginning of the normalisation of diplomatic relations with Cuba. The announcement, which was also made simultaneously by Cuban president Raul Castro, had been secretly negotiated in the preceding months with the assistance of Pope Francis. The agreement, which also involved a prisoner exchange, opened the prospect of an end to the US trade embargo against Cuba which had been in place for more than 50 years.

Good afternoon. Today, the United States of America is changing its relationship with the people of Cuba.

In the most significant changes in our policy in more than fifty years, we will end an outdated approach that, for decades, has failed to advance our interests, and instead we will begin to normalise relations between our two countries. Through these changes, we intend to create more opportunities for the American and Cuban people, and begin a new chapter among the nations of the Americas.

There's a complicated history between the United States and Cuba. I was born in 1961—just over two years after Fidel Castro took power in Cuba, and just a few months after the Bay of Pigs invasion, which tried to overthrow his regime. Over the next several decades, the relationship between our countries played out against the backdrop of the Cold War, and America's steadfast opposition to communism. We are separated by just over 90 miles. But year after year, an ideological and economic barrier hardened between our two countries.

Meanwhile, the Cuban exile community in the United States made enormous contributions to our country—in politics and business, culture and sports. Like immigrants before, Cubans helped remake America, even as they felt a painful yearning for the land and families they left behind. All of this bound America and Cuba in a unique relationship, at once family and foe.

Proudly, the United States has supported democracy and human rights in Cuba through these five decades. We have done so primarily through policies that aimed to isolate the island, preventing the most basic travel and commerce that Americans can enjoy anyplace else. And though this policy has been rooted in the best of intentions, no other nation joins us in imposing these sanctions, and it has had little effect beyond providing the Cuban government with a rationale for restrictions on its people. Today, Cuba is still governed by the Castros and the Communist Party that came to power half a century ago.

Neither the American, nor Cuban people are well served by a rigid policy that is rooted in events that took place before most of us were born. Consider that for more than 35 years, we've had relations with China—a far larger country also governed by a Communist Party. Nearly two decades ago, we re-established relations with Vietnam, where we fought a war that claimed more Americans than any Cold War confrontation.

That's why—when I came into office—I promised to re-examine our Cuba policy. As a start, we lifted restrictions for Cuban Americans to travel and send remittances to their families in Cuba. These changes, once controversial, now seem obvious. Cuban Americans have been reunited with their families, and are the best possible ambassadors for our values. And through these exchanges, a younger generation of Cuban Americans has increasingly questioned an approach that does more to keep Cuba closed off from an interconnected world.

While I have been prepared to take additional steps for some time, a major obstacle stood in our way—the wrongful imprisonment, in Cuba, of a US citizen and USAID sub-contractor Alan Gross for five years. Over many months, my administration has held discussions with the Cuban government about Alan's case, and other aspects of our relationship. His Holiness Pope Francis issued a personal appeal to me, and to Cuba's President Raul Castro, urging us to resolve Alan's case, and to address Cuba's interest in the release of three Cuban agents who have been jailed in the United States for over 15 years.

Today, Alan returned home—reunited with his family at long last. Alan was released by the Cuban government on humanitarian grounds. Separately, in exchange for the three Cuban agents, Cuba today released one of the most important intelligence agents that the United States has ever had in Cuba, and who has been imprisoned for nearly two decades. This man, whose sacrifice has been known to only a few, provided America with the information that allowed us to arrest the network of Cuban agents that included the men transferred to Cuba today, as well as other spies in the United States. This man is now safely on our shores.

Having recovered these two men who sacrificed for our country, I'm now taking steps to place the interests of the people of both countries at the heart of our policy.

First, I've instructed Secretary Kerry to immediately begin discussions with Cuba to re-establish diplomatic relations that have been severed since January of 1961. Going forward, the United States will re-establish an embassy in Havana, and high-ranking officials will visit Cuba.

Where we can advance shared interests, we will—on issues like health, migration, counterterrorism, drug trafficking and disaster response. Indeed, we've seen the benefits of cooperation between our countries before. It was a Cuban, Carlos Finlay, who discovered that mosquitoes carry yellow fever; his work helped Walter Reed fight it. Cuba has sent hundreds of health care workers to Africa to fight Ebola, and I believe American and Cuban health care workers should work side by side to stop the spread of this deadly disease.

Now, where we disagree, we will raise those differences directly—as we will continue to do on issues related to democracy and human rights in Cuba. But I believe that we can do more to support the Cuban people and promote our values through engagement. After all, these 50 years have shown that isolation has not worked. It's time for a new approach.

Second, I've instructed Secretary Kerry to review Cuba's designation as a State Sponsor of Terrorism. This review will be guided by the facts and the law. Terrorism has changed in the last several decades. At a time when we are focused on threats from al Qaeda to ISIL, a nation that meets our conditions and renounces the use of terrorism should not face this sanction.

Third, we are taking steps to increase travel, commerce, and the flow of information to and from Cuba. This is fundamentally about freedom and openness, and also expresses my belief in the power of people-to-people engagement. With the changes I'm announcing today, it will be easier for Americans to travel to Cuba, and Americans will be able to use American credit and debit cards on the island. Nobody represents America's values better than the American people, and I believe this contact will ultimately do more to empower the Cuban people.

I also believe that more resources should be able to reach the Cuban people. So we're significantly increasing the amount of money that can be sent to Cuba, and removing limits on remittances that support humanitarian projects, the Cuban people, and the emerging Cuban private sector.

I believe that American businesses should not be put at a disadvantage, and that increased commerce is good for Americans and for Cubans. So we will facilitate authorised transactions between the United States and Cuba. US financial institutions will be allowed to open accounts at Cuban financial institutions. And it will be easier for U.S. exporters to sell goods in Cuba.

I believe in the free flow of information. Unfortunately, our sanctions on Cuba have denied Cubans access to technology that has empowered individuals around the globe. So I've authorised increased telecommunications connections between the United States and Cuba. Businesses will be able to sell goods that enable Cubans to communicate with the United States and other countries.

These are the steps that I can take as President to change this policy. The embargo that's been imposed for decades is now codified in legislation. As these changes unfold, I look forward to engaging Congress in an honest and serious debate about lifting the embargo.

Yesterday, I spoke with Raul Castro to finalise Alan Gross's release and the exchange of prisoners, and to describe how we will move forward. I made clear my strong belief that Cuban society is constrained by restrictions on its citizens. In addition to the return of Alan Gross and the release of our intelligence agent, we welcome Cuba's decision to release a substantial number of prisoners whose cases were directly raised with the Cuban government by my team. We welcome Cuba's decision to provide more access to the Internet for its citizens, and to continue increasing engagement with international institutions like the United Nations and the International Committee of the Red Cross that promote universal values.

But I'm under no illusion about the continued barriers to freedom that remain for ordinary Cubans. The United States believes that no Cubans should face harassment or arrest or beatings simply because they're exercising a universal right to have their voices heard, and we will continue to support civil society there. While Cuba has made reforms to gradually open up its economy, we continue to believe that Cuban workers should be free to form unions, just as their citizens should be free to participate in the political process.

Moreover, given Cuba's history, I expect it will continue to pursue foreign policies that will at times be sharply at odds with American interests. I do not expect the changes I am announcing today to bring about a transformation of Cuban society overnight. But I am convinced that through a policy of engagement, we can more effectively stand up for our values and help the Cuban people help themselves as they move into the 21st century.

To those who oppose the steps I'm announcing today, let me say that I respect your passion and share your commitment to liberty and democracy. The question is how we uphold that commitment. I do not believe we can keep doing the same thing for over five decades and expect a different result. Moreover, it does not serve America's interests, or the Cuban people, to try to push Cuba toward collapse. Even if that worked—and it hasn't for 50 years—we know from hard-earned experience that countries are more likely to enjoy lasting transformation if their people are not subjected to chaos. We are calling on Cuba to unleash the potential of 11 million Cubans by ending unnecessary restrictions on their political, social, and economic activities. In that spirit, we should not allow US sanctions to add to the burden of Cuban citizens that we seek to help.

To the Cuban people, America extends a hand of friendship. Some of you have looked to us as a source of hope, and we will continue to shine a light of freedom. Others have seen us as a former coloniser intent on controlling your future. José Martí once said, "Liberty is the right of every man to be honest." Today, I am being honest with you. We can never erase the history between us, but we believe that you should be empowered to live with dignity and self-determination. Cubans have a saying about daily life: "No es facil" — it's not easy. Today, the United States wants to be a partner in making the lives of ordinary Cubans a little bit easier, more free, more prosperous.

To those who have supported these measures, I thank you for being partners in our efforts. In particular, I want to thank His Holiness Pope Francis, whose moral example shows us the importance of pursuing the world as it should be, rather than simply settling for the world as it is; the government of Canada, which hosted our discussions with the Cuban government; and a bipartisan group of congressmen who have worked tirelessly for Alan Gross's release, and for a new approach to advancing our interests and values in Cuba.

Finally, our shift in policy towards Cuba comes at a moment of renewed leadership in the Americas. This April, we are prepared to have Cuba join the other nations of the hemisphere at the Summit of the Americas. But we will insist that civil society join us so that citizens, not just leaders, are shaping our future. And I call on all of my fellow leaders to give meaning to the commitment to democracy and human rights at the heart of the Inter-American Charter. Let us leave behind the legacy of both colonisation and communism, the tyranny of drug cartels, dictators and sham elections. A future of greater peace, security and democratic development is possible if we work together—not to maintain power, not to secure vested interest, but instead to advance the dreams of our citizens.

My fellow Americans, the city of Miami is only 200 miles or so from Havana. Countless thousands of Cubans have come to Miami—on planes and makeshift rafts; some with little but the shirt on their back and hope in their hearts. Today, Miami is often referred to as the capital of Latin America. But it is also a profoundly American city—a place that reminds us that ideals matter more than the colour of our skin, or the circumstances of our birth; a demonstration of what the Cuban people can achieve, and the openness of the United States to our family to the South. Todos somos Americanos.

Change is hard—in our own lives, and in the lives of nations. And change is even harder when we carry the heavy weight of history on our shoulders. But today we are making these changes because it is the right thing to do. Today, America chooses to cut loose the shackles of the past so as to reach for a better future—for the Cuban people, for the American people, for our entire hemisphere, and for the world.

Thank you. God bless you and God bless the United States of America.

(Source: White House press office.)

GLOBAL OVERVIEW 2014 BY INTERNAL DISPLACEMENT MONITORING CENTRE

The Internal Displacement Monitoring Centre (IDMC), part of the Norwegian Refugee Council, launched its Global Overview 2014 *on 14 May, 2014, at the UN in Geneva. The report highlighted a record 33.3 million internally displaced people worldwide in 2013, of whom 8.2 million were newly displaced—an increase of 1.6 million on 2012—and also noted that 43 per cent of the newly displaced were in Syria. The text below is the IDMC's "at a glance" summary of its report.*

Global Overview 2014: people internally displaced by conflict and violence

Record internal displacement for the second year running
At the end of 2013, there were at least 33.3 million people internally displaced by armed conflict, generalised violence and human rights violations in the world. This figure represents a 16% increase compared with 2012, and is a record high for the second year running.

In 2013, IDMC marked its 15th year of monitoring internal displacement across the globe. While there were 19.3 million internally displaced people (IDPs) worldwide in 1998, this past decade has shown a longer-term upward trend from around 25 million in 2001.

Internal displacement per region

As of the end of 2013, sub-Saharan Africa had the largest total number of IDPs (12.5 million) followed by the Middle East and north Africa (9.1 million).

63% of all IDPs globally come from just five countries affected by conflict: Syria, Colombia, Nigeria, the Democratic Republic of Congo (DRC) and Sudan.

Around 8.2 million people were newly displaced in 2013, an increase by 24% compared with 2012.

78% of all those newly displaced in 2013 came from just five countries affected by conflict: Syria, DRC, the Central African Republic (CAR), Nigeria and Sudan.

Middle East and north Africa

- There were over 9.1 million IDPs in the Middle East and north Africa region at the end of 2013.
- Syria surpassed Colombia this year as the country with the highest total number of IDPs, with a total 6.5 million people internally displaced as of the end of 2013.
- In terms of new displacement, Syria accounted for 43% of new displacements worldwide in the year. Just over 3.5 million people were forced to flee their homes in the region in 2013, a 39% increase compared with 2012.
- Syrian citizens continue to bear the brunt of the escalating hostilities, and faced indiscriminate attacks by all parties to the conflict that included government airstrikes on displacement camps in the north
- In Iraq, ongoing sectarian violence newly displaced nearly 11,800 people in the year, and new displacements were also reported in Palestine and Yemen.
- With more than 12.5 million IDPs in 21 countries at the end of 2013, sub-Saharan Africa remained the region with the largest number of IDPs.
- As in previous years, DRC's total displaced population remained at nearly 3 million.
- Nigerian authorities published official figures for the first time this year, and put the number of IDPs in the country at 3.3 million.
- Just over 3.7 million people were newly displaced in sub-Saharan Africa in 2013, which represents a 55 % increase from 2012.
- As many as 1 million people fled inter-communal violence, land disputes and violence by state and non-state armed groups in DRC.
- The crisis in CAR escalated from March to December following a coup by the predominantly Muslim armed coalition Séléka, displacing around 935,000 people during the year.
- An increase in attacks by the Islamist armed group Boko Haram, heavy handed counter insurgency operations and ongoing inter-communal violence triggered the displacement of at least 470,500 people in Nigeria in 2013, while in Sudan 470,000 were newly displaced

South and south-east Asia

- The number of IDPs in south and south-east Asia fell for the third year running, leaving at least 3.2 million people displaced as of the end of 2013.
- The region's IDPs were concentrated in seven countries - Pakistan, Myanmar, Afghanistan, India, the Philippines, Indonesia and Sri Lanka.
- The number of new displacements in south and south-east Asia fell by almost half, from 1.4 million in 2012 to 712,000 in 2013.
- Fewer people fled their homes in India and large-scale returns took place in north-west Pakistan,

where the number of newly registered IDPs fell by two-thirds.
- Armed conflict and generalised violence displaced people in the Philippines, Pakistan and Afghanistan, which together accounted for more than 80% of new displacement in the region.

The Americas
- By the end of 2013, at least 6.3 million people were internally displaced in the Americas.
- The vast majority were in Colombia, where the figure has increased consistently over a ten-year period and now stands at 5.7 million. The country's protracted conflict is the main cause of displacement, but spreading criminal violence has also forced tens of thousands of people to flee their homes across the region including in Mexico and Honduras.
- The number of people newly displaced fell by around 23% in the region, from 230,000 in 2012 to 176,900 in 2013.
- Most new displacement took place in Colombia. The government has been in peace talks with the FARC since 2012, but in the absence of a ceasefire civilians in rural areas continue to suffer the ravages of the conflict.
- In Mexico, the activities of criminal groups, and large-scale military operations against them, also forced people from their homes.

Europe, the Caucasus and central Asia
- There were still at least 2.2 million IDPs in Europe, the Caucasus and central Asia.
- The figure is the lowest of the five regions IDMC covers for the seventh consecutive year, but with many people having fled their homes more than 20 years ago, the protracted nature of displacement there remains a major challenge.
- No new displacement was reported in Europe, the Caucasus or central Asia in 2013.

Key concerns

Challenges of collecting data on IDPs
Challenges to data collection on IDPs remain, as access to displaced people in remote areas is difficult and information is lacking on unregistered IDPs or on those who have returned, integrated locally or settled elsewhere.

Also, the definition of an IDP varies from country to country. For example, in Azerbaijan, Cyprus, Georgia and Palestine, children born in displacement are counted as IDPs. As this is not the case in other countries, such differences can paint an unbalanced picture.

The best available data often comes from outdated sources, with little or no reliable information to indicate the number of people who may have achieved long-term solutions. This was the case in many countries monitored by IDMC, including: Bangladesh, Burundi, India, Indonesia, Guatemala, Senegal and Thailand.

The combined impact of conflict and natural hazards
A natural hazard often forces IDPs to flee again, either from places where they had taken refuge from conflict, or from places to which they had returned or relocated.

In the Philippines for example, those living in poorly equipped camps and makeshift shelters in central Mindanao were more exposed to flooding than their counterparts in the general population.

Natural hazards and environmental degradation can also create tensions over scarce resources.

In Nigeria, for example, deforestation, desertification and recurrent floods reduced sustainable access to land and other natural resources and forced many to head south in search of pastures and arable land. This put them in direct competition with local communities, leading to increased insecurity and violence.

IDPs outside camps

In a large proportion of countries monitored by IDMC, IDPs were living outside camps, mostly in towns and cities.

This reality complicates protection and assistance due to significant information gaps concerning the number of IDPs, their specific vulnerabilities, needs, and living conditions.

Key challenges for IDPs outside of camps include security of tenure, substandard housing and living conditions, and the risk of increased vulnerability and marginalisation, especially in towns and cities where they can be exposed to forced evictions.

For example, Iraqi IDPs living in and around informal settlements in Baghdad are under constant threat of eviction, and similar concerns are faced by urban IDPs in countries such as Afghanistan, Somalia and Colombia.

Protracted displacement

After an initial crisis passes, less visible challenges remain for displaced populations that are often harder to overcome.

Without sustained leadership and commitment from a broad range of organisations and institutions, IDPs are often unable to resolve their displacement and have no prospect of rebuilding their lives or achieving a durable solution.

In Bangladesh and Cyprus, for example, IDPs have been living in protracted displacement since the 1970s, and IDPs in Myanmar, Palestine and Colombia for even longer, with displacement dating back to the 1960s.

The assessment of IDPs' progress towards achieving a durable solution requires gauging whether they have become more or less vulnerable over time, which in turn requires a significant long-term investment in data gathering.

Response to displacement 15 years on

Calls for a more nuanced understanding of the causes and effects of displacement, alongside the year-on-year increases in the numbers of IDPs around the world, re-emphasise the need for fundamental changes in efforts to prevent and respond to internal displacement.

Despite a strong consensus at the global level on the need to develop coordinated and longterm strategies to respond to displacement, the challenge ahead lies in overcoming the perception of internal displacement as a solely humanitarian issue and positioning it as a matter for development agencies, private companies and others to address in order to move towards long-term solutions to displacement.

2013 served as a stark reminder that emergency response systems still need a lot of improvement. With 8.2 million people forced to flee their homes, the concurrent crises in 2013 went beyond what anyone could have prepared for. They put enormous strain on the humanitarian system and tested its ability to respond to unparalleled needs.

(Source: IDMC, Norwegian Refugee Council)

WORLD HEALTH ORGANISATION 2014: ANTIMICROBIAL RESISTANCE: GLOBAL REPORT ON SURVEILLANCE

The World Health Organisation issued its first Report on Antimicrobial Resistance, *in April 2014, which highlighted the dangers of antibiotic-resistance, particularly in seven different bacteria responsible for common serious diseases.*

Summary

Antimicrobial resistance (AMR) threatens the effective prevention and treatment of an ever-increasing range of infections caused by bacteria, parasites, viruses and fungi. This report examines, for the first time, the current status of surveillance and information on AMR, in particular antibacterial resistance (ABR), at country level worldwide.

Key findings and public health implications of ABR are:
- Very high rates of resistance have been observed in bacteria that cause common health-care associated and community-acquired infections (e.g. urinary tract infection, pneumonia) in all WHO regions.
- There are significant gaps in surveillance, and a lack of standards for methodology, data sharing and coordination.

Key findings from AMR surveillance in disease-specific programmes are as follows:

- Although multidrug-resistant TB is a growing concern, it is largely under-reported, compromising control efforts.
- Foci of artemisinin resistance in malaria have been identified in a few countries. Further spread, or emergence in other regions, of artemisinin resistant strains could jeopardize important recent gains in malaria control.
- Increasing levels of transmitted anti-HIV drug resistance have been detected among patients starting antiretroviral treatment.

Surveillance of ABR and sources of data

There is at present no global consensus on methodology and data collection for ABR surveillance. Routine surveillance in most countries is often based on samples taken from patients with severe infections - particularly infections associated with health care, and those in which first-line treatment has failed. Community-acquired infections are almost certainly underrepresented among samples, leading to gaps in coverage of important patient groups.

Nevertheless, it is critical to obtain a broad picture of the international scope of the problem of ABR. To accomplish this, WHO obtained, from 129 Member States, the most recent information on resistance surveillance and data for a selected set of nine bacteria-antibacterial drug combinations of public health importance. Of these, 114 provided data for at least one of the nine combinations (22 countries provided data on all nine combinations).

Some data sets came from individual surveillance sites, or data from several sources rather than national reports. Many data sets were based on a small number of tested isolates of each bacterium (<30), adding to uncertainty about the precision of the data; this reflects a lack of national structures to provide an overview of the situation and limited capacity for timely information sharing. Most data sets, individual sites or aggregated data, were based on hospital data. Non-representativeness of surveillance data is a limitation for the interpretation and comparison of results.

The data compiled from countries indicate where there may be gaps in knowledge and lack of capacity to collect national data. Among WHO regions, the greatest country-level data were obtained from the European Region and the Region of the Americas, where longstanding regional surveillance and collaboration exist.

Current status of resistance in selected bacteria

In the survey forming the basis for this part of the report, information was requested on resistance to antibacterial drugs commonly used to treat infections caused by seven bacteria of international concern. The chosen bacteria are causing some of the most common infections in different settings; in the community, in hospitals or transmitted through the food chain. [...]

The high proportions of resistance to 3rd generation cephalosporins reported for *E. coli* and *K. Pneumoniae* means that treatment of severe infections likely to be caused by these bacteria in many settings must rely on carbapenems, the last-resort to treat severe community and hospital acquired infections. These antibacterials are more expensive, may not be available in resource-constrained settings, and are also likely to further accelerate development of resistance. Of great concern is the fact that *K. pneumoniae* resistant also to carbapenems has been identified in most of the countries that provided data, with proportions of resistance up to 54% reported. The large gaps in knowledge of the situation in many parts of the world further add to this concern. For *E. coli*, the high reported resistance to fluoroquinolones means limitations to available oral treatment for conditions which are common in the community, such as urinary tract infections.

High rates of methicillin-resistant *Staphylococcus aureus* (MRSA) imply that treatment for suspected or verified severe *S. aureus* infections, such as common skin and wound infections, must rely on second-line drugs in many countries, and that standard prophylaxis with first-line drugs for orthopaedic and other surgical procedures will have limited effect in many settings. Second-line drugs for *S. aureus* are more expensive; also, they have severe side-effects for which monitoring during treatment is advisable, increasing costs even further.

Reduced susceptibility to penicillin was detected in *S. pneumoniae* in all WHO regions, and exceeded 50% in some reports. The extent of the problem and its impact on patients is not completely clear because of variation in how the reduced susceptibility or resistance to penicillin is reported, and limited comparability of laboratory standards. Because invasive pneumococcal disease (e.g. pneumonia and meningitis) is a common and serious disease in children and elderly people, better monitoring of this resistance is urgently needed.

The resistance to fluoroquinolones among two of the major causes for bacterial diarrhoea, nontyphoidal *Salmonella* (NTS) and *Shigella species* were comparatively lower than in *E. coli*. However, there were considerable gaps in information on these two bacteria, particularly from areas where they are of major public health importance. Some reports of high resistance in NTS are of great concern because resistant strains have been associated with worse patient outcomes.

In *N. gonorrhoeae*, finally, decreased susceptibility to third-generation cephalosporins, the treatment of last resort for gonorrhoea, has been verified in 36 countries and is a growing problem. Surveillance is of poor quality in countries with high disease rates, where there is also a lack of reliable resistance data for gonorrhoea, and where the extent of spread of resistant gonococci may be high.

Health and economic burden due to ABR

Evidence related to the health and economic burden due to ABR in infections caused by *E. coli*, *K. pneumoniae* and MRSA was examined through systematic reviews of the scientific literature. Patients with infections caused by bacteria resistant to a specific antibacterial drug generally have an increased risk of worse clinical outcomes and death, and consume more healthcare resources, than patients infected with the same bacteria not demonstrating the resistance pattern in question.

Available data are insufficient to estimate the wider societal impact and economic implications when effective treatment for an infection is completely lost as a result of resistance to all available drugs.

AMR in disease-specific programmes

Tuberculosis
Globally, 3.6% of new TB cases and 20.2% of previously treated cases are estimated to have multidrug-resistant TB (MDR-TB), with much higher rates in Eastern Europe and central Asia. Despite recent progress in the detection and treatment of MDR-TB, the 84 000 cases of MDR-TB notified to WHO in 2012 represented only about 21% of the MDR-TB cases estimated to have emerged in the world that year. Among MDR-TB patients who started treatment in 2010, only 48% (range 46%-56% across WHO regions) were cured after completion of treatment (with 25% lost to follow-up). The treatment success rate was lower among extensively drug-resistant (XDR-TB) cases.

Malaria
Surveillance of antimalarial drug efficacy is critical for the early detection of antimalarial drug resistance, because resistance cannot be detected with routine laboratory procedures. Foci of either suspected or confirmed artemisinin resistance have been identified in Cambodia, Myanmar, Thailand and Viet Nam. Further spread of artemisinin-resistant strains, or the independent emergence of artemisinin resistance in other regions, could jeopardize important recent gains in malaria control.

HIV
HIV drug resistance is strongly associated with failure to achieve suppression of viral replication and thus with increased risk for disease progression. Data collected between 2004 and 2010 in low- and middle-income countries showed increasing levels of transmitted anti-HIV drug resistance among those starting antiretroviral treatment (ART). Available data suggest that 10%-17% of patients without prior ART in Australia, Europe, Japan and the United States of America (USA) are infected with virus resistant to at least one antiretroviral drug.

Influenza
Over the past 10 years, antiviral drugs have become important tools for treatment of epidemic and pandemic influenza, and several countries have developed national guidance on their use and have stockpiled the drugs for pandemic preparedness. However, widespread resistance to adamantanes in currently circulating A(H1N1) and A(H3N2) viruses have left neuraminidase inhibitors as the antiviral agents recommended for influenza prevention and treatment. Although the frequency of oseltamivir resistance in currently circulating A(H1N1)pdm09 viruses is low (1%-2%), the emergence and rapid global spread in 2007/2008 of oseltamivir resistance in the former seasonal A(H1N1) viruses has increased the need for global antiviral resistance surveillance.

AMR in other related areas

Antibacterial resistance in food-producing animals and the food chain
Major gaps exist in surveillance and data sharing related to the emergence of ABR in foodborne bacteria and its potential impact on both animal and human health. Surveillance is hampered by insufficient implementation of harmonized global standards. The multisectoral approach needed to contain ABR includes improved integrated surveillance of ABR in bacteria carried by food-producing animals and in the food chain, and prompt sharing of data. Integrated surveillance systems would enable comparison of data from food-producing animals, food products and humans.

Resistance in systemic candidiasis
Systemic candidiasis is a common fungal infection worldwide and associated with high rates of morbidity and mortality in certain groups of patients. Although it is known that antifungal resistance

imposes a substantial burden on health-care systems in industrialized countries, the global burden of antifungal-resistant *Candida* is unknown. Resistance to fluconazole, a common antifungal drug, varies widely by country and species. Resistance to the newest class of antifungal agents, the echinocandins, is already emerging in some countries.

NEXT STEPS

This report shows major gaps in ABR surveillance, and the urgent need to strengthen collaboration on global AMR surveillance. WHO will therefore facilitate:

• development of tools and standards for harmonized surveillance of ABR in humans, and for integrating that surveillance with surveillance of ABR in food-producing animals and the food chain;
• elaboration of strategies for population-based surveillance of AMR and its health and economic impact; and
• collaboration between AMR surveillance networks and centres to create or strengthen coordinated regional and global surveillance.

AMR is a global health security threat that requires concerted cross-sectional action by governments and society as a whole. Surveillance that generates reliable data is the essential basis of sound global strategies and public health actions to contain AMR, and is urgently needed around the world.

(Source: World Health Organization)

LIVING PLANET REPORT 2014: SPECIES AND SPACES, PEOPLE AND PLACES

The conservation agency, WWF (World Wide Fund for Nature), issued the 10th edition of its flagship Living Planet Report *in September 2014. It highlighted a sharp fall—more than half—in the total number of vertebrates since 1970. The text below is the "at a glance" summary of the WWF's* Living Planet Report 2014: Species and Spaces, People and Places

Chapter 1: The state of the planet
BIODIVERSITY IS DECLINING SHARPLY

• The global *Living Planet Index* (LPI)* shows an overall decline of 52 per cent between 1970 and 2010. Due to changes in methodology to better reflect the relative sizes of species groups across biomes, this percentage has decreased considerably in comparison with previous publications.
• Falling by 76 per cent, populations of freshwater species declined more rapidly than marine (39 per cent) and terrestrial (39 per cent) populations.
• The most dramatic regional LPI decrease occurred in South America, followed closely by the Asia-Pacific region.
• In land-based protected areas, the LPI declined by 18 per cent, less than half the rate of decline of the overall terrestrial LPI. Our demands on nature are unsustainable and increasing

OUR DEMANDS ON NATURE ARE UNSUSTAINABLE AND INCREASING

• We need 1.5 Earths to meet the demands we currently make on nature. This means we are eating into our natural capital, making it more difficult to sustain the needs of future generations.

- The carbon Footprint accounts for over half of the total Ecological Footprint, and is the largest single component for approximately half of the countries tracked.
- Agriculture accounts for 92 per cent of the global water footprint. Humanity's growing water needs and climate change are exacerbating challenges of water scarcity.
- The dual effect of a growing human population and high per capita Footprint will multiply the pressure we place on our ecological resources.
- The Ecological Footprint per capita of high-income countries remains about five times more than that of low-income countries.
- By importing resources, high-income countries in particular, may effectively be outsourcing biodiversity loss. While high-income countries appear to show an increase (10 per cent) in biodiversity, middle-income countries show declines (18 per cent), and low-income countries show dramatic and marked declines (58 per cent).
- Countries with a high level of human development tend to have higher Ecological Footprints. The challenge is for countries to increase their human development while keeping their Footprint down to globally sustainable levels.

Chapter 2: Developing the picture
ADDITIONAL INDICATORS AND WAYS OF THINKING GIVE NEW PERSPECTIVES ON THE STATE OF THE PLANET.

- The planetary boundaries concept defines nine regulating processes that keep the Earth in a stable state where life can thrive.
- Transgressing any of the nine boundaries could generate abrupt or irreversible environmental changes. Three appear to have been crossed already: biodiversity loss, climate change and nitrogen.
- Urgent and sustained global efforts could still keep temperature rises below 2°C - the level defined as "safe" - but our window of opportunity is fast closing.
- Nitrogen is essential to global food security, but nitrogen pollution has severe impacts on aquatic ecosystems, air quality, climate and human health.
- Local and thematic analysis helps identify the causes and effects of global challenges, and provides insights for devising practical solutions.

Chapter 3: Why we should care
ENVIRONMENTAL CHANGES AFFECT US ALL

- Human well-being depends on natural resources such as water, arable land, fish and wood; and ecosystem services such as pollination, nutrient cycling and erosion control.
- Putting ecosystems at the centre of planning, and managing activities that depend on natural resources, brings economic and social benefits.
- While the world's poorest continue to be most vulnerable, the interconnected issues of food, water and energy security affect us all.
- For the first time in history, the majority of the world's population lives in cities, with urbanization growing fastest in the developing world.

Chapter 4: One planet solutions
LIVING WITHIN THE PLANET'S MEANS IS POSSIBLE

- Individuals, communities, businesses, cities and governments are making better choices to protect natural capital and reduce their footprint, with environmental, social and economic benefits - as demonstrated in real-world case studies.

• Changing our course and finding alternative pathways will not be easy. But it can be done.

*The LPI is calculated using trends in 10,380 populations of over 3,038 vertebrate species (fishes, amphibians, reptiles, birds and mammals). These species groups have been comprehensively researched and monitored by scientists and the general public for many years, meaning that a lot of data is available to assess the state of specific populations and their trends over time.

(Source: The WWF Living Planet Report 2014.)

SYNTHESIS REPORT OF THE IPCC'S FIFTH ASSESSMENT REPORT

Headline Statements* from the Summary for Policymakers of the Synthesis Report. Contribution of Working Groups I, II and III to the Fifth Assessment Report of the Intergovernmental Panel on Climate Change *released on 2 November. The IPCC is the international scientific body established by the World Meteorological Organisation and the UN Environment Programme to assess information regarding climate change.*

* *Headline statements are the overarching highlighted conclusions of the approved Summary for Policymakers which, taken together, provide a concise narrative.*

Climate Change 2014: Synthesis Report

Observed Changes and their Causes

Human influence on the climate system is clear, and recent anthropogenic emissions of greenhouse gases are the highest in history. Recent climate changes have had widespread impacts on human and natural systems.

Warming of the climate system is unequivocal, and since the 1950s, many of the observed changes are unprecedented over decades to millennia. The atmosphere and ocean have warmed, the amounts of snow and ice have diminished, and sea level has risen.

Anthropogenic greenhouse gas emissions have increased since the pre-industrial era, driven largely by economic and population growth, and are now higher than ever. This has led to atmospheric concentrations of carbon dioxide, methane and nitrous oxide that are unprecedented in at least the last 800,000 years. Their effects, together with those of other anthropogenic drivers, have been detected throughout the climate system and are extremely likely to have been the dominant cause of the observed warming since the mid-20th century.

In recent decades, changes in climate have caused impacts on natural and human systems on all continents and across the oceans. Impacts are due to observed climate change, irrespective of its cause, indicating the sensitivity of natural and human systems to changing climate.

Changes in many extreme weather and climate events have been observed since about 1950. Some of these changes have been linked to human influences, including a decrease in cold temperature extremes, an increase in warm temperature extremes, an increase in extreme high sea levels and an increase in the number of heavy precipitation events in a number of regions.

Future Climate Changes, Risks and Impacts

Continued emission of greenhouse gases will cause further warming and long-lasting changes in all components of the climate system, increasing the likelihood of severe, pervasive and irre-

versible impacts for people and ecosystems. Limiting climate change would require substantial and sustained reductions in greenhouse gas emissions which, together with adaptation, can limit climate change risks.

Cumulative emissions of carbon dioxide largely determine global mean surface warming by the late 21st century and beyond. Projections of greenhouse gas emissions vary over a wide range, depending on both socio-economic development and climate policy.

Surface temperature is projected to rise over the 21st century under all assessed emission scenarios. It is very likely that heat waves will occur more often and last longer, and that extreme precipitation events will become more intense and frequent in many regions. The ocean will continue to warm and acidify, and global mean sea level to rise.

Climate change will amplify existing risks and create new risks for natural and human systems. Risks are unevenly distributed and are generally greater for disadvantaged people and communities in countries at all levels of development.

Many aspects of climate change and associated impacts will continue for centuries, even if anthropogenic emissions of greenhouse gases are stopped. The risks of abrupt or irreversible changes increase as the magnitude of the warming increases.

Future Pathways for Adaptation, Mitigation and Sustainable Development

Adaptation and mitigation are complementary strategies for reducing and managing the risks of climate change. Substantial emissions reductions over the next few decades can reduce climate risks in the 21st century and beyond, increase prospects for effective adaptation, reduce the costs and challenges of mitigation in the longer term, and contribute to climate-resilient pathways for sustainable development.

Effective decision making to limit climate change and its effects can be informed by a wide range of analytical approaches for evaluating expected risks and benefits, recognizing the importance of governance, ethical dimensions, equity, value judgments, economic assessments and diverse perceptions and responses to risk and uncertainty.

Without additional mitigation efforts beyond those in place today, and even with adaptation, warming by the end of the 21st century will lead to high to very high risk of severe, widespread, and irreversible impacts globally (high confidence). Mitigation involves some level of co-benefits and of risks due to adverse side-effects, but these risks do not involve the same possibility of severe, widespread, and irreversible impacts as risks from climate change, increasing the benefits from near-term mitigation efforts.

Adaptation can reduce the risks of climate change impacts, but there are limits to its effectiveness, especially with greater magnitudes and rates of climate change. Taking a longer-term perspective, in the context of sustainable development, increases the likelihood that more immediate adaptation actions will also enhance future options and preparedness.

There are multiple mitigation pathways that are likely to limit warming to below 2°C relative to pre-industrial levels. These pathways would require substantial emissions reductions over the next few decades and near zero emissions of carbon dioxide and other long-lived greenhouse gases by the end of the century. Implementing such reductions poses substantial technological, economic, social, and institutional challenges, which increase with delays in additional mitigation and if key technologies are not available. Limiting warming to lower or higher levels involves similar challenges, but on different timescales.

Adaptation and Mitigation

Many adaptation and mitigation options can help address climate change, but no single option is sufficient by itself. Effective implementation depends on policies and cooperation at all scales,

and can be enhanced through integrated responses that link adaptation and mitigation with other societal objectives.

Adaptation and mitigation responses are underpinned by common enabling factors. These include effective institutions and governance, innovation and investments in environmentally sound technologies and infrastructure, sustainable livelihoods, and behavioural and lifestyle choices.

Adaptation options exist in all sectors, but their context for implementation and potential to reduce climate-related risks differs across sectors and regions. Some adaptation responses involve significant co-benefits, synergies and trade-offs. Increasing climate change will increase challenges for many adaptation options.

Mitigation options are available in every major sector. Mitigation can be more cost-effective if using an integrated approach that combines measures to reduce energy use and the greenhouse gas intensity of end-use sectors, decarbonize energy supply, reduce net emissions and enhance carbon sinks in land-based sectors.

Effective adaptation and mitigation responses will depend on policies and measures across multiple scales: international, regional, national and sub-national. Policies across all scales supporting technology development, diffusion and transfer, as well as finance for responses to climate change, can complement and enhance the effectiveness of policies that directly promote adaptation and mitigation.

Climate change is a threat to sustainable development. Nonetheless, there are many opportunities to link mitigation, adaptation and the pursuit of other societal objectives through integrated responses (*high confidence*). Successful implementation relies on relevant tools, suitable governance structures and enhanced capacity to respond (*medium confidence*).

(Source: IPCC Secretariat Geneva IPCC, 2014: Climate Change 2014)

UNITED KINGDOM COALITION GOVERNMENT

(as at 31 December 2014)

Members of the Cabinet

Prime Minister, First Lord of the Treasury and Minister for the Civil Service	Rt Hon David Cameron MP (Con)
Deputy Prime Minister, Lord President of the Council (Cabinet Office) (with special responsibility for political and constitutional reform)	Rt Hon Nick Clegg MP (LibDem)
First Secretary of State and Leader of the House of Commons	Rt Hon William Hague MP (Con)
Chancellor of the Exchequer	Rt Hon George Osborne MP (Con)
Home Secretary	Rt Hon Theresa May MP (Con)
Secretary of State for Foreign and Commonwealth Affairs	Rt Hon Phillip Hammond MP (Con)
Secretary of State for Justice and Lord Chancellor	Rt Hon Chris Grayling MP (Con)
Secretary of State for Defence	Rt Hon Michael Fallon MP (Con)
Secretary of State for Business, Innovation and Skills	Rt Hon Vince Cable MP (LibDem)
Secretary of State for Work and Pensions	Rt Hon Iain Duncan Smith MP (Con)
Secretary of State for Health	Rt Hon Jeremy Hunt MP (Con)
Secretary of State for Communities and Local Government	Rt Hon Eric Pickles MP (Con)
Secretary of State for Education	Rt Hon Nicky Morgan MP (Con)
Secretary of State for International Development	Rt Hon Justine Greening MP (Con)
Secretary of State for Energy and Climate Change	Rt Hon Edward Davey MP (LibDem)
Secretary of State for Transport	Rt Hon Patrick McLoughlin MP (Con)
Secretary of State for Scotland	Rt Hon Alistair Carmichael MP (LibDem)
Secretary of State for Northern Ireland	Rt Hon Theresa Villiers MP (Con)
Secretary of State for Wales	Rt Hon Stephen Crabb MP (Con)
Secretary of State for Culture, Media and Sport	Rt Hon Sajid Javid MP (Con)
Secretary of State for Environment, Food and Rural Affairs	Rt Hon Elizabeth Truss MP (Con)
Chief Secretary to the Treasury	Rt Hon Danny Alexander MP (Lib Dem)

Also attend Cabinet meetings

Leader of the House of Lords and Lord Privy Seal	Rt Hon the Baroness Stowell of Beeston MBE (Con)
Parliamentary Secretary to the Treasury and Chief Whip	Rt Hon Michael Gove MP (Con)
Minister for the Cabinet Office and Paymaster General (Cabinet Office)	Rt Hon Francis Maude MP (Con)
Minister for Government Policy and Chancellor of the Duchy of Lancaster	Rt Hon Oliver Letwin MP (Con)
Minister of State (Cabinet Office) (Jointly with the Department for Education)	Rt Hon David Laws MP (LibDem)
Minister of State (Department for Business, Innovation and Skills) (Universities and Science)	Rt Hon Greg Clark MP (Con)
Attorney General	Rt Hon Jeremy Wright QC MP (Con)
Minister without Portfolio (Cabinet Office)	Rt Hon Grant Shapps MP
Minister of State (Department for Business, Innovation and Skills)	Rt Hon Matthew Hancock MP (Con)
Minister of State (Department for Work and Pensions) (Cabinet)	Rt Hon Esther McVey MP (Con)
Minister of State (Foreign and Commonwealth Office)	The Rt Hon the Baroness Anelay of St Johns DBE (Con)

UNITED STATES DEMOCRATIC ADMINISTRATION

(as at 31 December 2014)

President of the United States   Barack Obama

Members of the Cabinet

Vice President of the United States	Joseph R. Biden
Secretary of State	John Kerry
Secretary of the Treasury	Jack Lew
Secretary of Defence	Chuck Hagel*
Attorney General and Head of Department of Justice	Eric H. Holder, Jr
Secretary of the Interior	Sally Jewell
Secretary of Agriculture	Thomas J. Vilsack
Secretary of Commerce	Penny Pritzker
Secretary of Labour	Thomas E. Perez
Secretary of Health and Human Services	Sylvia Mathews Burwell
Secretary of Housing and Urban Development	Julián Castro
Secretary of Transportation	Anthony Foxx
Secretary of Energy	Ernest Moniz
Secretary of Education	Arne Duncan
Secretary of Veterans' Affairs	Robert McDonald
Secretary of Homeland Security	Jeh Johnson

Positions with status of Cabinet-rank

White House Chief of Staff	Denis McDonough
Administrator of Environmental Protection Agency	Gina McCarthy
Director of Office of Management and Budget	Shaun L.S. Donovan
United States Trade Representative	Michael Froman
Ambassador to the United Nations	Samantha Power
Chairman of Council of Economic Advisers	Jason Furman
Administrator of Small Business Administration	Maria Contreras-Sweet

*Resignation announced 24 November 2014

NOBEL LAUREATES 2014

THE NOBEL PRIZE IN PHYSICS 2014

Isamu Akasaki, Hiroshi Amano and **Shuji Nakamura**
"for the invention of efficient blue light-emitting diodes which has enabled bright and energy-saving white light sources"

THE NOBEL PRIZE IN CHEMISTRY 2014

Eric Betzig, Stefan W. Hell and **William E. Moerner**
"for the development of super-resolved fluorescence microscopy"

THE NOBEL PRIZE IN PHYSIOLOGY OR MEDICINE 2014

John O'Keefe, May-Britt Moser and **Edvard I. Moser**
"for their discoveries of cells that constitute a positioning system in the brain"

THE NOBEL PRIZE IN LITERATURE 2014

Patrick Modiano
"for the art of memory with which he has evoked the most ungraspable human destinies and uncovered the life-world of the occupation"

THE NOBEL PEACE PRIZE 2014

Kailash Satyarthi and **Malala Yousafzai**
"for their struggle against the suppression of children and young people and for the right of all children to education"

THE SVERIGES RIKSBANK PRIZE IN ECONOMIC SCIENCES IN MEMORY OF ALFRED NOBEL 2014

Jean Tirole
"for his analysis of market power and regulation"

(Source: Nobelprize.org.)

INTERNATIONAL COMPARISONS

The following table gives population and economic data for selected countries.

	Population millions 2012	Average annual population growth % 2000-13	Gross domestic product ($ billions) 2012	GDP average annual growth % 2000-12
Algeria	39.2	2	204.3	3.7
Australia	23.1	1	1,534.4	3.1
Austria	8.5	0	407.6	1.7
Bangladesh	156.6	1	133.4	6.0
Belgium	11.2	1	498.9	1.5
Brazil	200.4	1	2,248.8	3.7
Canada	35.2	1	1,821.4	1.9
Chile	17.0	1	266.3	4.1
China (excl Hong Kong)	1,357.4	1	8,229.5	10.6
Colombia	48.3	1	370.3	4.5
Denmark	5.6	0	322.3	0.7
Egypt	82.1	2	262.8	4.9
Finland	5.4	0	255.8	1.7
France	66.0	1	2,686.7	1.2
Germany	80.6	0	3,533.2	1.1
Greece	11.0	0	249.5	0.7
Hungary	9.9	0	126.8	1.7
India	1,252.1	1	1,858.7	7.7
Indonesia	249.9	1	876.7	5.5
Irish Republic	4.6	1	222.0	2.2
Italy	59.8	0	2,091.8	0.2
Japan	127.3	0	5,954.5	0.7
Kenya	44.4	3	50.3	4.6
South Korea	50.2	1	1,222.8	4.2
Malaysia	29.7	2	305.3	4.9
Mexico	122.3	1	1,186.5	2.3
Netherlands	16.8	0	823.1	1.4
New Zealand	4.5	1	171.5	2.4
Nigeria	173.6	3	463.0	8.8
Norway	5.1	1	500.0	1.5
Pakistan	182.1	2	224.4	4.4
Philippines	98.4	2	250.2	4.9
Poland	38.5	0	496.2	4.2
Portugal	10.5	0	218.0	0.4
Russia	143.5	0	2,017.5	4.8
South Africa	53.0	1	382.3	3.7
Spain	46.6	1	1,355.7	1.8
Sweden	9.6	1	543.9	2.1
Switzerland	8.2	1	666.1	2.0
Thailand	67.0	1	366.0	4.2
Turkey	74.9	1	788.9	4.6
United Kingdom	64.1	1	2,614.9	1.6
USA	316.1	1	16,163.2	1.7
Venezuela	30.4	2	381.3	4.3
Vietnam	89.7	1	155.8	6.6

(Source: World Bank, Washington, DC)

XX CHRONICLE OF 2014

JANUARY

1	Latvia became the 18th EU Member State to adopt the euro as its currency
5	The general election in Bangladesh, boycotted by the main opposition Bangladesh Nationalist Party, was won by the ruling Awami League.
6	The city of Fallujah, in Iraq, was reported to have fallen to fighters from ISIS.
10	China released figures showing that in 2013 it became the world's largest trading nation in goods, overtaking the USA.
13	In Nigeria, President Goodluck Jonathan signed legislation criminalising same-sex relationships.
	India marked three years since its last reported case of polio—the period necessary to declare the country polio free.
15	In a referendum, Egyptian voters approved a new draft "non-Islamist" constitution.
19	In Ukraine, the anti-government demonstrations in Kiev swelled to 100,000 people.
20	The Central African Republic transitional legislative body elected Catherine Samba-Panza as president, amidst ongoing sectarian violence
	Iran began implementing a six-month "Joint Plan of Action" agreed with the P5+1 group of world powers, to curtail its nuclear energy programme.
	Laimdota Straujuma became Latvia's first female prime minister.
22	In Somalia a Cabinet was named under newly appointed Prime Minister Abdiweli Sheikh Ahmed.
	UN-brokered negotiations in the Syrian conflict began in Geneva.
24	Formal negotiations opened on Serbia's accession to the EU.
25	President François Hollande of France announced that his companion, Valérie Trierweiler, had ceased to be "first lady".
	In Madagascar, Hery Rajaonarimampianina was inaugurated president, following December's elections.
26	Tunisia received a new constitution and a new government under Mehdi Jomaa.
27	Juan Hernández was inaugurated for a four-year term as president of Honduras.
28	Prime Minister Mykola Azarov of Ukraine resigned; anti-government street protests continued.
29	In Czech Republic, the president formally appointed a new three-party coalition government.

FEBRUARY

2	Police stormed a mosque in the Kenyan port of Mombasa and arrested 129 alleged members of the al-Shabaab Islamist militant group.
	Legislative elections in Thailand failed to produce a result because of opposition protests on polling day.
3	Janet Yellen was sworn in as the first female head of the US Federal Reserve.
6	In Pakistan, a first formal meeting was held between government and Pakistani Taliban (TTP) negotiators in Islamabad, though militant attacks continued.
7	The Winter Olympic Games opened in southern Russia amid tight security.
9	In Japan, Yoichi Masuzoe, an independent and a supporter of nuclear power, won Tokyo's gubernatorial election.

10	Nepal's Constituent Assembly elected Sushil Koirala of the Nepali Congress Party prime minister.
11	The Republican-controlled House of Representatives voted to raise the US debt ceiling—without preconditions—for the first time since 2011.
12	US scientists researching nuclear fusion reactions announced that they had generated more energy than they had put into the nuclear fuel.
	A demonstration in Venezuela against insecurity and inflation turned violent, leading to further opposition protests.
15	After 10 months of negotiations, Lebanon received a new "consensus government" under Prime Minister Tammam Salam.
	A second session of the "Geneva II" peace talks in the Syrian conflict ended without progress.
17	A UN report detailed "unspeakable atrocities" committed by North Korea against its citizens.
18	In South Sudan a short-lived ceasefire between government and rebel forces collapsed.
20	Prosecutors in China filed charges, including murder, against billionaire Liu Han, who had allegedly been under CCP protection.
	Voters in Libya elected a new Constituent Assembly.
	The governor of Nigeria's Central Bank was suspended; he had revealed a $20 billion shortfall in the national accounts.
	In Ukraine, snipers opened fire on demonstrators in Kiev after two days of street violence; over 100 people died.
21	Al-Shabaab fighters attacked the presidential palace in the Somali capital, Mogadishu; all nine were killed.
22	Matteo Renzi of the Democratic Party (PD) became Italy's youngest prime minister, having deposed PD premier Enrico Letta.
	Ukraine's legislature voted to remove President Viktor Yanukovych.
24	The Ugandan president, Yoweri Museveni, signed into law a bill imposing severe penalties against homosexual acts.
25	A UN report alleged the Sri Lankan government may have committed war crimes during its 2009 defeat of the Tamil Tigers.
	In Turkey, protesters in 11 cities called for the resignation of Prime Minister Recep Tayyip Erdogan over corruption allegations revealed via YouTube.
28	In Ukraine's Crimea region, armed men in unmarked uniform seized control of strategic sites.

MARCH

1	In China, a group of Uighur separatists attacked passengers at Kunming railway station with knives.
2	In Egypt, a new Cabinet was formed, partly of technocrats, under Ibrahim Mehleb.
8	Malaysian Airlines flight MH370, a Boeing 777, flying from Kuala Lumpur to Beijing, disappeared over the South China Sea.
9	The second round of presidential elections in El Salvador were narrowly won by ruling party candidate, Salvador Sánchez Cerén.
11	Michelle Bachelet, the left-wing former president (2006-10) of Chile, was inaugurated for a second term.
	Ceremonies in Japan commemorated the third anniversary of the earthquake and tsunami that had triggered the Fukushima nuclear disaster; they drew attention to continuing problems with the cleanup operation.

12	In Estonia, Taavi Roivas became prime minister and formed a centre-left coalition government.
14	The UN Security Council was warned that because of sectarian violence in Central African Republic "the risk of genocide remains high".
15	Government forces in Syria recaptured the rebel-held town of Yabrud, north of Damascus, with support of Hezbullah fighters from Lebanon.
16	US navy seals seized control of the *Morning Glory*, an oil tanker captured by rebels, and handed it back to Libyan government control.
	A referendum in Crimea—which had been part of Ukraine since 1954—endorsed the region's union with Russia by near-unanimous approval.
	In Serbia, the right-wing nationalist Serbian Progressive Party (SNS) and its allies won legislative elections.
17	The EU and the USA began imposing sanctions on Russian officials.
18	In a speech to the Russian Federal Assembly, President Vladimir Putin celebrated Crimea's "return" to Russia.
19	South Africa's public prosecutor's office found that President Jacob Zuma had "benefited unduly" from state financed improvements to his residence.
21	Thailand's Constitutional Court ruled that the 2 February elections were invalid.
	Ukraine and the EU signed their Association Agreement, which had been rejected by deposed Ukrainian President Viktor Yanukovych.
23	Guinea notified the WHO of "a rapidly evolving outbreak" of the Ebola virus.
	Local council elections in France, with a second round on 30 March, saw heavy defeats for the ruling Socialist Party (PS) and gains for the National Front (FN).
24	The G-7 suspended co-operation with Russia as the G-8.
27	The government of the Philippines and the MILF rebel group signed a comprehensive peace agreement, creating an autonomous region.
	US President Barack Obama announced a plan to end the bulk collection of US phone data by the National Security Agency.
29	Andrej Kiska, a businessman, was elected president of Slovakia.
30	The ruling Justice and Development Party (AKP) of Prime Minister Recep Tayyip Erdogan won Turkey's local elections.
31	The Greek legislature narrowly approved a package of reforms demanded by the IMF and EU, in return for continued international financial assistance.

APRIL

1	Japan introduced a new policy allowing it to export weapons.
	NATO announced the suspension of "all practical and military cooperation" with Russia.
2	In Kazakhstan, former prime minister Karim Masimov (2007-12) resumed that post; Serik Akhmetov stepped down.
3	A new Cabinet under Djoomart Otorbayev was named in Kyrgyzstan.
5	Presidential elections were held in Afghanistan to choose the successor to Hamid Karzai.
	In France, Manuel Valls, the Socialist Party prime minister, formed a new government.
6	In Costa Rica, left-wing opposition candidate, Luis Guillermo Solís, won the second round of presidential elections.
	The ruling Fidesz-led coalition won legislative elections in Hungary.
7	Voting commenced in India's elections.
	World leaders attended a ceremony in Kigali to mark the 20th anniversary of the 1994 Rwandan genocide.

8	The anti-corruption department of the Chinese Communist Party launched a new webpage, on which members of the public were invited to report corruption by officials.
9	Indonesia held national and regional legislative elections.
10	The UN Security Council approved the establishment of MINUSCA, a new 10,000-strong peacekeeping mission for Central African Republic.
11	Kathleen Sibelius was replaced as US health secretary by Sylvia Mathews Burwell, as President Obama's heathcare reforms took effect.
12	Pro-Russian demonstrators, some armed, began occupying government buildings in towns of eastern Ukraine.
13	A new government was formed in Armenia under Hovik Abrahamian.
	Guinea-Bissau held presidential and legislative elections
	Abdallah al-Theni resigned as Libya's interim prime minister after one month in office.
14	Boko Haram Islamist militants abducted more than 240 girls from a school in north-eastern Nigeria.
15	Rebel forces in South Sudan's Unity State massacred at least 400 civilians.
16	A South Korean passenger ferry, the *Sewol*, sank; over 100 schoolchildren were drowned.
17	In Algeria, President Abdelaziz Bouteflika was re-elected for a fourth term.
18	An avalanche on Mount Everest killed 16 Sherpa guides; it was the worst such accident since 1921.
19	The US continued its drone attacks on fighters from Al-Qaida in the Arabian Peninsula (AQAP) active in Yemen.
23	In Palestine, Fatah and Hamas announced their agreement on a unity government of technocrats; Israel suspended peace talks.
27	In elections in Macedonia, President Gjorgje Ivanov and his party were returned to power.
28	The EU and the USA tightened sanctions against Russia.
29	In the USA, a botched judicial execution at Oklahoma state penitentiary prompted a national debate over the death penalty.
30	Brunei began the phased introduction of Sharia law.
	Iraq held legislative elections amidst sectarian violence.

MAY

4	Juan Carlos Varela, the vice president and opposition candidate, won presidential elections in Panama.
7	South Africa held general and provincial elections, which the ANC won, though with its smallest majority since 1994.
8	In Syria, the last rebel fighters left Homs, ending the two-year government siege of the city.
9	A new ceasefire in the ethnic and political conflict in South Sudan was signed; it swiftly collapsed.
11	Referendums on independence were held in the eastern Ukrainian regions of Donetsk and Lugansk.
13	ISIS claimed responsibility for detonating nine car bombs in Shia areas of Baghdad, in revenge for Western "aggression" against Fallujah.
	Demonstrations in Vietnam against Chinese interests turned violent over disputed Chinese oil exploration in disputed waters.
15	The prime minister of Vanuatu was replaced by parliamentary vote.
	The opposition Hindu nationalist BJP under Narendra Modi won a landslide victory in India's elections.

In Libya anti-Islamist forces commanded by a former general, Khalifa Hiftar, attacked militia bases in Benghazi.

A visit to northern Mali by newly appointed Prime Minister Moussa Mara provoked renewed attacks from Touareg separatists.

17	Portugal exited its EU-IMF bailout programme, having emerged from recession.
18	In Guinea-Bissau, José Mário Vaz of the ruling PAIGC won presidential elections.
19	The US justice department indicted five Chinese military officers over alleged cyber espionage against US companies.
20	In Malawi, Peter Mutharika won presidential elections, amidst accusations of vote-rigging.
	Flooding in Serbia and Bosnia-Herzegovina caused over 70 deaths.
22	In China, 43 people died in an attack on a market in Urumqi, Xinjiang region, which was attributed to Uighur separatists.
	In Thailand, the military announced that it had taken control of the country.
24	A French national of Algerian origin killed four people in a gun attack at the Jewish Museum in Brussels.
25	Elections to the European Parliament ended in significant gains for eurosceptic parties throughout the EU.
	In Ukraine, confectionary magnate Petro Poroshenko won presidential elections.
26	Ukrainian government forces attacked Donetsk airport, which had been captured by separatists.
28	Egypt's former army commander, Abdel-Fattah Sisi, won presidential elections.
	President Obama set out key US foreign policy principles in a speech at West Point military academy.
29	Paris Club creditors agreed a repayment schedule for Argentina's debt, marking the country's return to international capital markets.
31	In a prisoner exchange, Sergeant Bowe Bergdahl, a US soldier captured in Afghanistan in 2009, was released in exchange for five senior Taliban figures held at Guantanamo.

JUNE

1	In northern Cameroon, heavy fighting was reported between government troops and Boko Haram militants from Nigeria.
	Russia banned smoking in public places.
2	Telangana—India's 29th state—was officially born; it was formed from the northern districts of Andhra Pradesh.
	President Barack Obama announced an ambitious plan to reduce greenhouse gas emissions arising from US power plants.
3	In Syria, President Bashar Assad was elected for a third consecutive seven-year term, amidst an opposition boycott.
4	Germany's chief prosecutor opened a formal investigation into allegations that the US National Security Agency had bugged the mobile telephone of Chancellor Angela Merkel.
5	The G-7 ended their summit in Brussels; prior to Russia's annexation of Crimea, they had been due to convene as the G-8 in Sochi, Russia.
8	The ruling Democratic Party was returned in early legislative elections in Kosovo.
	The Pakistani Taliban attacked Karachi airport.
10	ISIS captured the Iraqi city of Mosul.
12	The opposition Antigua Labour Party, under Gaston Browne, won Antigua & Barbuda's general election by a landslide.

	The FIFA World Cup football tournament opened in Brazil, where protests continued against poverty and social deprivation.
13	Ukraine claimed to have destroyed two of three Russian tanks said to have crossed the border the previous day.
14	Pro-Russian rebels shot down a Ukrainian Il-76 transport plane attempting to land in Lugansk.
14	Abdullah Abdullah and Ashraf Ghani contested the second round of Afghanistan's presidential elections.
15	In Colombia, President Juan Manuel Santos won the run-off presidential elections, giving him a second consecutive term.
	In Pakistan, the army launched an offensive against militant strongholds in North Waziristan; negotiations with the Pakistani Taliban had collapsed.
	Al-Shabaab fighters from Somalia targeted coastal towns in Kenya over two days, killing over 60 Christians.
17	The first Cabinet of Egypt's President Abdel-Fattah Sisi was sworn in.
18	King Juan Carlos of Spain abdicated in favour of his son, who became King Felipe VI.
20	Ukraine's government announced a temporary ceasefire in its conflict with pro-Russian rebels.
21	In Mauritania, incumbent President Mohamed Ould Abdelaziz won presidential elections.
23	Alexander Stubb became Finland's new prime minister.
24	The EU decided to grant candidate status to Albania.
	Prime Minister Shinzo Abe of Japan unveiled the "third arrow" of his radical reform— economic restructuring.
25	In Libya, there were elections—with a very low turnout—to the new legislature, replacing the GNC elected in June 2012.
26	Yemen joined the WTO, its 160th member.
27	Jean-Claude Juncker was formally nominated as president of the European Commission: the UK and Hungary alone of 28 EU Member States opposed his nomination.
29	ISIS proclaimed a "caliphate"—an Islamic state—across areas of Iraq and Syria.
30	The bodies of three young Jewish settlers were discovered in the West Bank; the men had been abducted on 12 June.

JULY

1	A large pro-democracy demonstration was held in Hong Kong.
	Japan's Cabinet approved a constitutional change that would allow the military to assist allied countries.
	President Poroshenko of Ukraine announced the end to a widely-ignored 10-day ceasefire in the campaign against pro-Russian rebels in the east of the country.
2	Islamic State (ISIS) leader and self-proclaimed "caliph", Abu Bakr al-Baghdadi called on Muslims worldwide to unite under him to "capture Rome".
3	Saudi Arabia deployed 30,000 troops on its border with Iraq in light of the advance of ISIS forces.
5	The Ukrainian military recaptured the rebel-held town of Slavyansk, among other objectives.
6	Mohammed Dionne was appointed prime minister in Senegal following the dismissal of Aminata Touré.
9	Public sector workers in Greece held a 24-hour strike to protest against international lenders' austerity programme.
	Pope Francis replaced the chairman and board of the Vatican Bank.

10	India's new government presented a budget that aimed for "sustained annual GDP growth of 7-8 per cent" by 2016-17.
13	Germany defeated Argentina in the football World Cup final; in the semi-finals Germany had knocked out the hosts, Brazil, 7-1.
	Slovenia held legislative elections in which traditional parties lost badly.
15	In the UK, Prime Minister David Cameron reshuffled his Cabinet.
16	China announced the withdrawal of its oil drilling platform from waters disputed by Vietnam.
17	Australia repealed its 2012 "carbon tax".
	Malaysian Airlines flight MH17 was brought down over Ukraine, presumably by a missile fired by pro-Russian separatists; all 298 people on board died.
19	France's President François Hollande announced a new Franco-African military force, "Operation Barkhane", for the Sahel.
	The "Joint Plan of Action" agreed with international powers over Iran's nuclear programme was prolonged.
21	Russia banned fruit and vegetable imports from Moldova.
22	In Cambodia, the main opposition party announced the end of its boycott of the National Assembly.
	In Indonesia, Jakarta's governor, Joko Widodo, was declared to have won the 9 July presidential election.
	A new constitution was promulgated in Thailand, replacing that suspended during the military coup in May.
23	Muslim Seleka rebels and Christian anti-Balaka militia of Central African Republic signed a peace agreement in Brazzaville, Congo.
	In north-western Nigeria, a suicide bomb attack was carried out against opposition leader General Muhammadu Buhari; he survived.
24	Kurdish politician Fouad Masoum was elected as president of Iraq by the new legislature.
	In Rwanda, Anastase Murkezi was appointed prime minister and reshuffled the Cabinet.
	UNICEF warned that 50,000 children were at risk of famine in South Sudan.
28	Russia was ordered by the Permanent Court of Arbitration in The Hague, to pay $50 billion in damages to former shareholders in the expropriated Yukos oil company.
29	The EU and the USA announced punitive sectoral sanctions against Russia.
30	Argentina formally defaulted on its sovereign debt because of a US court order in a suit brought by "holdout" creditors.
31	The CIA admitted spying on staff from the US Senate intelligence committee, who were investigating torture claims against the CIA.

AUGUST

1	The WHO director general and the presidents of Guinea, Liberia and Sierra Leone announced a $100 million "response plan" to the Ebola virus outbreak.
3	Portugal had to bail out a failing bank, BES.
4	Libya's new legislature, the Council of Representatives, convened in Tobruk, since the security situation in Tripoli or Benghazi was too precarious.
6	President Nursultan Nazarbayev of Kazakhstan announced a major government reorganisation, focusing on the energy sector.
	Russia banned for one year the import of foodstuffs from the USA, the EU and a number of other Western countries.
7	US President Barack Obama authorised US air strikes against ISIS in Iraq, highlighting the threat to the Yazidi minority.

In Cambodia, the UN-backed court trying the two senior surviving Khmer Rouge leaders convicted them of crimes against humanity.

8 Israel launched "Operation Protective Edge" in Gaza in response to Hamas rocket attacks.

9 Police in Ferguson, Missouri, USA, shot dead an unarmed black teenager, Michael Brown; days of rioting and looting ensued.

10 In Turkey, Recep Tayyip Erdogan—prime minister since 2003—became the country's first directly elected president.

11 Haider Abadi became Iraq's prime minister in succession to Nouri Maliki.

12 In Guatemala, the president unveiled an ambitious 18-year development plan, focusing on social justice and sustainability.

13 In Brazil, the opposition Socialist Party's presidential candidate, Eduardo Campos, was killed in a plane crash.

15 In Pakistan, twin protest marches from Lahore reached Islamabad; with demands for the resignation of Prime Minister Nawaz Sharif.

16 As rioting continued in Ferguson, USA, the governor of Missouri imposed a night-time curfew and declared a state of emergency.

19 ISIS released a video showing the beheading by an ISIS militant of US journalist James Foley, kidnapped in Syria in 2012.

21 In Thailand, the leader of the recent military coup, General Prayuth Chan-ocha was elected prime minister by the newly-appointed National Legislative Assembly.

22 The UN human rights body said that the recorded death toll since the start of Syria's civil war in March 2011 was 191,369.

24 In Yemen, Prime Minister Mohammed Salem Basindwa resigned as Houthi militia advanced into the capital Sana'a.

In Nigeria, the leader of Boko Haram claimed to have control of the town of Gwoza, which he said was now "part of the Islamic caliphate".

In Syria, ISIS forces captured the last government stronghold in northern Raqqa.

25 Libya's Islamist-dominated rump former legislature (GNC) convened in Tripoli and declared the new Council of Representatives (meeting in Tobruk) illegitimate.

26 Israel signed a ceasefire with Hamas; the latest war in Gaza had cost 2,100 Palestinian lives, and those of 70 Israelis, and destroyed much of Gaza's infrastructure.

28 The town of Novoazovsk on Ukraine's Black Sea coast fell to Russian-backed forces.

30 Ukrainian troops abandoned the city of Ilovaisk to Russian-backed rebels, with numerous casualties.

31 The state election in Saxony, Germany, saw the new anti-EU Alternative for Germany (AfD) win its first seats in a Land parliament.

Protesters encamped in Islamabad, the Pakistan capital, unsuccessfully attempted to break through to the government quarter.

SEPTEMBER

1 The main leader of Al-Shabaab, Ahmed Abdi Godane, was killed in a US air strike in central Somalia.

2 ISIS posted a video showing the beheading of another US citizen, journalist Steven Sotloff.

5 The NATO summit in Wales ended.

A ceasefire in the Ukraine conflict, underpinned by some measure of autonomy for rebel regions, was agreed following talks in Minsk.

8	Iraq's new prime minister, Haider Abadi, formed a new Cabinet, more inclusive than the previous one.
9	Prime Minister Donald Tusk of Poland resigned to take up a senior EU post; Ewa Kopacz replaced him.
10	US President Obama announced the escalation of action against ISIS, including air action in Syria and additional US troops in Iraq.
14	Local elections were held across Russia; all 30 regional governors contesting their posts were re-elected.
15	In Central African Republic, a new UN peacekeeping force, MINUSCA, took over from the African Union-led MISCA.
17	Fiji held its first legislative elections since the military coup of December 2006.
18	Scotland held a referendum on whether it should become independent; the answer was "No".
	Miro Cerar of the Party of Miro Cerar formed a new coalition government in Slovenia.
	Uganda's President Yoweri Museveni dismissed Prime Minister Amama Mbabazi, appointing in his place Ruhakana Rugunda.
19	A court in Hunan province, China, found UK pharmaceutical company GlaxoSmithKline guilty of bribery, and imposed a record fine of 3 billion yuan.
20	The National Party in New Zealand was elected to a third consecutive term in government.
21	Albania hosted Pope Francis's first visit to a European country since he took office.
	A three-day "lockdown" aiming to halt the spread of Ebola ended in Sierra Leone; citizens had not been allowed to leave their homes.
	Some 130,000 Syrian Kurdish refugees fled into Turkey to escape an ISIS attack on the Syrian city of Kobane.
	In Yemen, President Mansour Hadi was forced to agree a ceasefire with Houthi rebels who had captured the capital, Sana'a.
23	The USA began bombing raids against ISIS targets in Syria, with assistance from a coalition of Arab countries.
26	More than 40 student teachers were abducted from a college in south-western Mexico.
27	Pro-democracy campaigners of the "Occupy Central" movement in Hong Kong mobilised 80,000 people in a peaceful demonstration.
28	Russia-backed rebels in Ukraine launched an offensive against Donetsk international airport.
29	In Afghanistan, Ashraf Ghani was sworn in as president, the disputed election result having been resolved in his favour; he appointed his rival Abdullah Abdullah as "chief executive".
30	The first UK bombing raids were carried out against ISIS positions in Iraq; this followed French action on 19 September.

OCTOBER

1	President Ashraf Ghani of Afghanistan ordered a fresh judicial investigation into the $900 million Kabul Bank scandal.
2	Prime Minister Narendra Modi launched a "Clean India" campaign and promised 110 million new toilets by 2019.
	Turkey's legislature, the GNA, authorised military action against ISIS.
	ISIS made advances in Iraq's north-western Anbar province, including capturing the town of Hit.
3	A minority "red-green" coalition government was formed in Sweden, following the 14 September elections, under Prime Minister Stefan Lofven.

	ISIS posted a video of the beheading of UK aid worker, Alan Henning.
4	There were legislative elections in Latvia.
5	Early legislative elections took place in Bulgaria
6	A Spanish nurse became the first person in Europe to be confirmed as having contracted the Ebola virus.
7	A coalition government was formed in Belgium under Charles Michel; elections had been held in May.
	In Turkey's majority Kurdish regions, there were riots over the perceived inaction of the government over ISIS attacks on Kobane.
8	Kenya's President Uhuru Kenyatta became the first sitting head of state to appear before the International Criminal Court (ICC).
	A Liberian man died in a Texas hospital from Ebola, triggering the imposition of quarantine and travel restrictions within the USA.
9	French military operating in Niger attacked a convoy of Al-Qaida in the Islamic Maghreb (AQIM) transporting weapons from Libya to Mali.
	The anti-EU UK Independence Party (UKIP) won its first House of Commons seat in a by-election triggered by the defection in August from the Conservative Party of Douglas Carswell.
12	President Evo Morales of Bolivia won a third term in office.
	There were legislative elections in São Tomé and Príncipe.
	Ukraine's defence minister resigned following heavy criticism for the defeat of Ukrainian forces at Ilovaisk.
	Presidential and legislative elections took place in Bosnia-Herzegovina at various levels of government.
13	A Chinese delegation in Moscow, led by Premier Li Keqiang, signed 38 deals with Russia.
14	North Korea's leader Kim Jong Un made his first public appearance since 3 September.
15	Presidential elections in Mozambique were won by Filipe Nyusi of Frelimo; the party also won legislative elections.
22	In Canada, a lone gunman shot dead a soldier at the National War Memorial and entered the Parliament buildings in Ottawa.
23	In the most serious violation of NATO airspace by Russia since the end of the Cold War, a Russian maritime spy plane entered Estonian airspace.
24	Elections in Botswana returned the governing Botswana Democratic Party to power.
	Egypt declared a three-month state of emergency in Sinai, fearing the influx of Islamist militants from Gaza.
25	In Italy, a million demonstrators protested in Rome against the government's labour reforms.
26	The incumbent, Dilma Rousseff was re-elected in the second round of presidential elections in Brazil.
	In Ukraine, two pro-EU coalitions won elections to a new national legislature.
	In Tunisia, the secular NT (Tunisia's Call) won elections to the Assembly of People's Representatives.
28	President Michael Sata of Zambia died; the vice-president Guy Scott took office.
29	The US Federal Reserve announced it was to end QE3—its current, third, round of quantitative easing.
31	President Blaise Compaoré of Burkina Faso stepped down amidst popular protest.
	Russia and Ukraine signed an EU-brokered "winter package" gas supply deal.

NOVEMBER

2	At the only border crossing between Pakistan and India, a Pakistani Taliban suicide bomber killed more than 60 people.
	Israel announced the indefinite closure of its border crossings with the Gaza Strip.
	Donetsk and Lugansk regions in Ukraine went ahead with elections, in defiance of the 5 September Minsk agreement.
3	France's interior minister visited Calais amidst troubles caused by 2,500 African and Middle-Eastern immigrants seeking to reach the UK.
4	Mid-term elections in the USA resulted in the Republican Party winning control of Congress.
5	In Latvia, a new centre-right coalition government took office, under Prime Minister Laimdota Straujuma.
	Mongolia's Great Hural dismissed Prime Minister Norov Altankhuyag, replacing him on 21 November by Chimed Saikhanbileg.
7	Boiko Borisov formed a minority coalition government in Bulgaria.
	In Syria, al-Nusra Front—an al-Qaida affiliate—was reported to have gained control of much of Idlib province.
9	An unofficial referendum in Catalonia saw more than 80 per cent of the one-third of voters who participated vote for the region's independence from Spain.
	A new government of technocrats took office in Yemen under Khaled Bahah.
10	Japanese Prime Minister Shinzo Abe and Chinese President Xi Jinping held their first—frosty—meeting.
	Russia's Central Bank abandoned the euro-dollar exchange rate band for the rapidly weakening Russian rouble.
	In Iraq, Shia militia, US, Iraqi government and Peshmerga forces successfully concluded an operation to secure part of Babil province from ISIS control.
12	At the APEC summit, the hosts, China, and the USA announced an unexpected agreement to limit greenhouse gas emissions.
	The European Space Agency's *Philae* lander from the *Rosetta* mission became the first spacecraft to land on the surface of a comet.
14	Greece's economy had the fastest growth rate in the eurozone in the third quarter 2014.
16	Pakistan said the army had killed 1,198 militants in North Waziristan since starting an operation against the Pakistani Taliban in June.
	Presidential elections in Romania were won by Klaus Iohannis, who defeated Prime Minister Victor Ponta.
17	Michel Kafando became interim president of Burkina Faso.
18	Amidst rising tension in Israel, four rabbis were murdered in a Jerusalem synagogue by two Palestinian men.
	Japan's Prime Minister Shinzo Abe called an early election, and postponed a scheduled consumption tax rise.
	The authorities in Hong Kong began action to clear pro-democracy demonstrators' protest camps.
19	Solomon Islands held a general election.
	Nicola Sturgeon, leader of the Scottish Nationalist Party, became first minister of Scotland.
20	A series of massacres took place in North Kivu province of DRC, apparently perpetrated by DRC armed forces.
	The UN said almost 1,000 people had been killed in Ukraine since the 5 September ceasefire agreement.

US President Barack Obama announced an executive order that would give 5 million undocumented immigrants the right to work legally.

After a by-election, the UK Independence Party increased its tally of seats in the House of Commons to two.

22	In Istanbul, US Vice President Joe Biden failed to persuade Turkey to do more in support of US efforts to combat ISIS.
24	Russia and the separatist Abkhazia region of Georgia signed an alliance.

Fresh rioting broke out in Ferguson, Missouri, USA, after a grand jury decided not to indict the police officer who had shot Michael Brown.

27   A five-party governing coalition named "European Ukraine", was formed in Ukraine, following October's elections.

28   Legislative elections in Namibia were won by the ruling SWAPO; Prime Minister Hage Geingob won the presidential election.

In a suspected Boko Haram attack, bombs at a mosque in Kano in northern Nigeria killed more than 100 people.

29   Elections in Bahrain boycotted by the opposition were won by pro-government independents.

30   Legislative elections in Moldova saw the vote split between pro-EU and pro-Russian forces.

In Uruguay, former president Tabaré Vázquez of the ruling Broad Front won the presidential elections.

DECEMBER

1   Russia cancelled the "South Stream" gas pipeline project.

2   The Iraqi government agreed a deal with the Kurdish Regional Government over oil revenues.

Israel's Prime Minister Binyamin Netanyahu called early elections.

NATO foreign ministers denounced Russia's "destabilisation" of eastern Ukraine.

The Ukrainian legislature endorsed a Cabinet led by Arseny Yatsenyuk.

3   A grand jury in New York decided not to indict a white police officer over the death in July of Eric Garner, a black man held in a choke hold; protests ensued.

5   Prosecutors at the ICC dropped charges against Kenya's President Uhuru Kenyatta.

In China, the former internal security apparatus chief, Zhou Yongkang was expelled from the CCP over charges of bribery and corruption.

7   President Joseph Kabila of DRC unveiled a new government of national unity.

8   The ruling Dominica Labour Party under Roosevelt Skerrit won a general election.

President Robert Mugabe of Zimbabwe dismissed Vice President Joice Mujuru in an internal struggle in the ruling ZANU-PF.

9   A new coalition government was endorsed in Kosovo after a lengthy political dispute.

The report of the US Senate intelligence committee into the CIA's use of torture against detainees was released in part.

10   The opposition Alliance Lepep won legislative elections in Mauritius; Anerood Jugnauth formed a new government on 16 December.

13   In the USA, a complex $1,100 billion omnibus spending bill was passed by the Senate, having been approved by the House of Representatives on 11 December, to finance government spending for the remainder of the fiscal year.

14   Elections in Japan returned Prime Minister Shinzo Abe's government in an endorsement of his economic reform policies.

15   Police dismantled the last protest camp in Hong Kong's pro-democracy "Occupy Central"
          movement.
          In Sydney, Australia, a self-proclaimed Muslim cleric took people hostage in a café in a
          siege lasting 17 hours.
16   Islamist militants in Pakistan attacked the Army school in Peshawar; they killed 132
          pupils and three teachers.
          A steep rise in interest rates by the Russian Central Bank did not prevent the rouble
          falling to 80 to the US dollar on "black Tuesday".
17   Umar Abdirashid Ali Shermarke was nominated prime minister in Somalia after the
          previous government led by Abdiweli Sheikh Ahmed fell on 6 December.
18   Kurdish Peshmerga fighters, backed by US air strikes, claimed to have broken the ISIS
          siege of Sinjar in northern Iraq, from which the Yazidi minority had been driven
          in August.
19   A Turkish prosecutor issued an arrest warrant for President Recep Tayyip Erdogan's rival,
          US-based Fethullah Gulen, following raids across Turkey directed against Gulenists.
20   In Colombia, the FARC began to observe an indefinite ceasefire.
21   In Tunisia, presidential elections were won by Beji Caid Essebsi.
23   As part of continued efforts against Islamists, Algeria's defence ministry claimed to have
          killed the leader of Jund al-Khalifa.
          Ukraine's legislature voted to endorse a decision to repeal neutrality and seek NATO
          membership.
24   ISIS captured a Jordanian pilot, Muaz Kasasbeh, near Raqqa in Syria.
27   Belarus's President Alyaksandr Lukashenka replaced his prime minister and other senior
          members of the economic team.
28   The Western combat mission in Afghanistan formally ended.
29   Prime Minister Antonis Samaras of Greece called an early election for January, 2015,
          which the anti-austerity SYRIZA was expected to win.
31   Germany's Chancellor Angela Merkel reiterated her condemnation of the expanding anti-
          immigrant PEGIDA demonstrations in Dresden.
          WHO released the figure of over 20,200 confirmed and suspected cases of Ebola since
          the beginning of the outbreak of the disease a year previously.

Wendy Slater

INDEX

Page references in bold indicate location of main coverage.